# HOW WE LIVED THEN

A History of Everyday Life
During the Second World War

NORMAN LONGMATE

PIMLICO

Published by Pimlico 2002

2 4 6 8 10 9 7 5 3

Copyright © Norman Longmate 1971

First published in Great Britain by Hutchinson & Co Ltd 1971
Pimlico edition 2002

Pimlico
Random House, 20 Vauxhall Bridge Road,
London SW1V 2SA

Random House Australia (Pty) Limited
20 Alfred Street, Milsons Point, Sydney,
New South Wales 2061, Australia

Random House New Zealand Limited
18 Poland Road, Glenfield,
Auckland 10, New Zealand

Random House (Pty) Limited
Endulini, 5A Jubilee Road, Parktown 2193, South Africa

The Random House Group Limited Reg. No. 954009
www.randomhouse.co.uk

A CIP catalogue record for this book
is available from the British Library

ISBN 0-7126-6832-2

Papers used by Random House are natural,
recyclable products made from wood grown in sustainable forests.
The manufacturing processes conform to the environmental
regulations of the country of origin

Printed and bound in Great Britain by
Mackays of Chatham Ltd

# Contents

# Illustrations

*The Phoney War and its ending*

The start, September 1939

Defeat in Norway, April 1940

(Note the copies of *Picture Post*, price 3d, and *Woman*, price 2d)

Defeat in France, June 1940

Attack on England, July 1940

(To save paper, news-bills were now forbidden and vendors wrote their own—complete, as here, with misspelling of Messerschmitt)

SECTION TWO

*Awaiting Attack*

Painting out L.M.S. station name in Hertfordshire, June 1940

Uprooted signposts in Kent

The first route march. Local Defence Volunteers in Berkshire, June 1940. (As yet their only uniform is an armband and many have no weapons)

Weapon-training. Members of the London County Council Home Guard under instruction, August 1940.
(By now they have denim uniforms and rifles. Machine guns were as yet few and far between)

Anti-landing obstructions, July 1940

(Sewer pipes, wooden posts and old cars were all used as obstacles to prevent enemy troop carriers or gliders landing)

Building a strongpoint at Admiralty Arch, May 1940

(This emplacement would have commanded Trafalgar Square and, at the rear, the Mall, leading to Buckingham Palace)

*Shelter*

*Piccadilly Circus underground station during the Blitz*

The un-moving staircase

The platform where no-one 'hurries along'

Rescue men removing a body after an 'incident'

Visiting a shot-down Messerschmitt

(The usual charge for a close inspection was 6d for the local
Spitfire Fund)

*Victory*

V.E. Day procession in Whitehall

(The young men in civilian clothes, an unusual sight, were
university students)

The end of the civilians' war. A bonfire in a Croydon street,
V.E. night.

# Acknowledgements

Acknowledgements for the use of illustrations are due as follows: Messrs. Hitchcock Williams, 1; 'Radio Times' Hulton Picture Library, 2, 3, 4, 8, 10, 11, 12, 13, 14, 15, 17, 19, 20, 21, 22, 23, 24, 25, 26, 29, 30, 36, 43, 44, 46, 48, 51, 55, 59, 64, 69, 70, 72, 73; The Imperial War Museum, 5, 42, 49, 50, 54; the late Mr Walter Lee and Grantham Public Library, 6, 7, 40, 41; the Women's Royal Voluntary Services, 9, 47; Mr Reece Winstone, Bristol, 16, 18, 67, 68; the Controller of Her Majesty's Stationery Office, to whom acknowledgement is also due for the use of quotations from official documents and advertisements in the text, 63, 65, 66; the Corporation of Kingston upon Hull, 31; Syndication International, 37; Keystone Press Agency, 45, 56.

It has not proved possible to trace the original copyright-owners of the remaining photographs and apologies are offered for any inadvertent breach of copyright in these cases.

# Foreword

Although nearly nine-tenths of the population of Great Britain remained civilians throughout the war or—like myself—for a large part of it, their story has so far largely gone untold. In contrast with the thousands of books on military operations only one history of the Home Front designed for the general reader has appeared, and that is concerned rather with social trends than with individual experience. In Churchill's vast history of the war, the problems of the ordinary family are barely mentioned; food rationing, for example, receives less space than the pursuit of a solitary enemy warship; clothes rationing, travel, the black-out hardly appear; even the air raids get little space and the shortage of essentials like saucepans and razor blades almost none at all.

This book is an attempt to redress the balance; to tell the civilian's story largely through his own—or more commonly her own—recollections and often in his or her own words. I have throughout concentrated on the ordinary and the typical in preference to the unusual and the striking and I have deliberately avoided the dramatic experiences of a few people in favour of the more mundane recollections of the vast majority. As the Blitz and V.1 and V.2 attacks, like the activities of the Home Guard and the anti-invasion measures of 1940, are essentially aspects of the military side of the war I have devoted very little space to them, especially as they have all been the subject of previous books by other authors. It is the ordinary family's trials with water in the Anderson shelter which have interested me, rather than such famous incidents as the saving of St. Paul's. Similarly, I have been concerned to show the enormous variety of little ways in which the war affected everyday life as well as the great and obvious ones. Compared with the sufferings of millions during the war, the fact that a teenage boy had to forgo the turn-ups on his first suit, that a young woman could not buy the cosmetics she wanted are, of course, of trifling significance, but to the people concerned they often seemed of overwhelming importance at the time.

Clearly, despite all the efforts of Lord Woolton and other ministers to ensure fair shares, there was not—could not be—complete equality of sacrifice during the war. The sufferings of those who lost lives, or limbs, or loved ones, or homes, clearly outweigh many of the innumerable less spectacular acts of unselfishness and endurance chronicled in this book. Yet the people who performed them deserve their place, too, in any civilians' history of the war; the more so, perhaps, because at the time their work was so often taken for granted.

The book is based on the personal recollections of many individual women, and of a smaller number of men, which make up most of the text of this book. I have also, however, included a good deal of factual information, since I believe that those who were affected by wartime conditions will wish to know, as they often did not know at the time, just why there was a shortage of coal or cups or cutlery, or why they were urged to eat potatoes or 'go easy on the tea'. I have also, since no rationing scheme, however ingenious, could by itself have won the war, given at various points a brief history of the main military events that were taking place. These were occurring, however, it should be remembered, 'off-stage', as far as the civilian was concerned. While the great battles were being fought in Egypt or Normandy, the civilian was necessarily preoccupied with such less exciting matters as crowded trains, worn-out clothes and the availability of dried egg. To obtain this civilian's eye view of the war, I have drawn on the personal recollections of about a thousand people who answered my appeals in the press. As I was anxious that the picture should be as complete as possible and should cover every section of society, every main occupational group and every part of the country, and not merely the small, untypical, articulate group who have published autobiographies and diaries, I wrote initially to nearly three hundred newspapers and magazines asking interested readers to contact me. To those who responded I sent a long list of headings, designed to jog their memory rather than serve as a questionnaire. Interestingly enough, the 'quality' newspapers and literary magazines, which regularly print appeals from authors writing on obscure subjects which can only affect a tiny handful of their readers, all failed to print my letter, with the valuable exceptions of *The Times*, which made it the basis of an interview, and *New Society*, which, not unexpectedly, yielded some highly literate contributions. I also received most fruitful co-operation from the local press and from the women's magazines, so often sneered at by those who never read them, and these together produced the bulk of the response. In addition, I received a considerable number of, often highly informative, replies from the numerous religious, professional, recreational and trade papers I contacted. Many busy doctors and clergymen's wives found time to let me have their recollections and I was also particularly grateful for the response from the readers of such papers as *The Fish Friers Review*, *The Grocer* and *Footwear Weekly*—in none of which, I suspect, had an appeal for literary assistance ever appeared before. This enabled me, as I was anxious to do, to look at rationing not merely from the customer's side of the counter, but from the point of view of the often unjustly criticised shopkeeper. I am grateful to the editors of all those publications, from *Astronomy* to *The Walthamstow Guardian*, which printed my appeal, as without their help this book could not have been written, and to the producer of the radio programme *Home This Afternoon*, whose interview with me brought in a hundred helpful letters from listeners. But my main debt is clearly to those who, from no motive except that famous wartime spirit of helpfulness, and usually with no previous experience of writing, set down their private recollections of the war, often at length and frequently with considerable journalistic skill. Some contributors sent me several sets of reminiscences and all answered most patiently my supplementary questions. Many correspondents also entrusted me with their wartime diaries, and with such invaluable items as notebooks kept by teachers escorting evacuees, letters sent home by evacuated children, the unofficial log books of wardens' posts, and—outstandingly valuable—in one case, a set of correspondence written almost daily from London throughout the war. Few contemporary historians can have been fortunate enough to have had such a wealth of primary source material at their disposal, or have been so generously helped by so many people. To all these co-authors, whose names are recorded later in this book, I acknowledge my warmest thanks. My thanks are also due to those who have helped me personally, particularly Mrs. Sue Sabbagh, Mrs. Sheila Bailey and Mrs. Angela Taylor, who assisted me at various stages of the book, and to Miss Sarah Barham and Miss Maureen Hewitt. Occasionally, as some correspondents themselves suggested, I have slightly altered the original text to make the meaning clear. In quoting bad language, I have done what I believe most of my correspondents would have wished, only rendering it in full where it seemed essential. Except where otherwise indicated, descriptions like 'a City secretary' or 'a Newcastle Civil Servant' refer to the informant's status at the time, not today.

The title of the book is borrowed from that of a similar, but less comprehensive, book about the first world war and, although I have used so much original material, this is a history, not an anthology. Solely for reasons of space, a great deal of excellent material, both published and unpublished, has had to be omitted. Much of this will appear in *The Home Front*, an anthology which I have edited for publication by the Woburn Press.

## Note to the Arrow Books edition

For this paperback edition, I have corrected one or two very minor errors in the original text and have brought up to date one reference which had become incorrect due to events occurring after publication. I have also, sadly, had to record the death of some of the original contributors. The several hundred letters I have received since *How We Lived*

*Then* first appeared, both from contributors and from other readers, make me feel hopeful that they would have regarded what some correspondents described as 'our book' as in some measure a memorial to their wartime service.

N.R.L.

# JOIN THE A.R.P.

'Under the spreading chestnut tree,
Neville Chamberlain said to me:
"If you want to get your gas mask free,
Join the blinking A.R.P." '

Playground song, 1938

When the national anthem was played on the radio we all stood up. That was how the war began for my family and for millions of other families throughout Great Britain. Few can have foreseen on that sunny September morning the six years of disillusionment, danger, drudgery and discomfort which lay ahead. Certainly, as a schoolboy of thirteen, enjoying the excitement, I did not anticipate that before the war was over I should be in the Army on the Continent, my twin sister in the 'Wrens' in Plymouth, soon to go to the Far East, my elder brother in the R.A.F. in Italy, and my elder sister working on the night shift in a munitions factory. Many other families listening that September morning were to undergo far greater transformations.

Yet though no one foresaw what lay ahead, for himself or the nation, the war which began on that sunny autumn morning, the 3rd September, 1939, was the least unexpected war in history. My own childhood had coincided with the steady drift towards war. I can recall the newspaper posters in 1933, bearing the single word '*Ja!*', announcing that the Germans had accepted Hitler as Chancellor; a fellow schoolboy coming into the classroom in 1935 and saying 'Heard the news? Italy has invaded Abyssinia'; the newsreels of German and Italian bombers in Spain which were part of almost every cinema programme from 1936 onwards.

Although the inter-war governments were later to be criticised for leaving the country unprepared, a Sub-Committee of the Committee of Imperial Defence had been set up to consider Air Raid Precautions as early as 1924 under a young and highly-respected Civil Servant, John Anderson. The letters A.R.P. began to become familiar to local authorities from the 9th July 1935 when a circular was issued urging them to prepare plans on the subject and by the Air Raid Precautions Act, two years later, they were formally required to submit their plans for government approval. But in many places the desire to keep the rates down still took precedence over all else. From the first, many A.R.P. workers, both paid and part-time, were treated with shabby meanness, and in one Central London borough the wardens were even expected to pay the full price when using the municipal baths to wash off the blood and grime acquired on duty.

Many private citizens refused to take A.R.P. seriously at all. An auxiliary fireman, who attended the very first A.F.S. class in his town in March 1938, recalled how on 'the exercise call to the "fire" at the Wanstead Golf Club . . . some club officials took umbrage at our arrival and told us to "go somewhere else and play"'. In East London, the Mayor of Stepney later recalled, 'A.R.P. had been looked upon as a joke'.

Some people indeed regarded patriotism itself as suspect. As a Harrow woman noted in her diary with a certain grim satisfaction in 1940, 'Several friends rated me very severely for taking anti-gas lectures in 1936 and 1938 and said it was people like myself who made wars.' Systematic national recruiting really began with a broadcast by the Home Secretary, Sir Samuel Hoare, on 14th March 1938, just after Hitler had overrun Austria. Hoare appealed for 'At least a million men and women . . . for work that in an emergency would be exciting and dangerous' but less than half this number responded and during the spring and summer of 1938 there were many similar appeals. The most effective was probably that of Lady Reading, chairman of the newly-formed Women's Voluntary Services for Civil Defence in June, calling upon 'every kind of woman in every kind of sphere of life . . . to prepare patiently and thoroughly . . . a protection . . . for our loved ones and our homes.'

Such broadcasts were reinforced by local efforts, with the few wardens who had already enrolled canvassing house to house in search of further recruits, but in Chesterfield at this period it was still possible for one of the questions in a general knowledge quiz at a company dance to be 'What is the meaning of the letters A.R.P. ?'. By summer the government was seriously alarmed at the poor response to its campaign and was planning a major recruiting drive for the autumn. At this point Hitler came to its rescue. Out of a clear sky, as it seemed, came his threat to Czechoslovakia. War, from being a remote possibility, became almost overnight an immediate danger. I can remember at my boarding school, where the wireless was banned and interest in politics discouraged, how suddenly one evening, soon after the start of the Christmas term, the lights began to dim in a trial black-out, and how, when they were raised again, the staff hurried in with armfuls of small cardboard boxes and one by one we were fitted with a gas mask.

This was what brought home to most people the real meaning of the crisis. The speed and efficiency with which 38 million masks were assembled and distributed—though there were as yet no special masks for babies or small children—was remarkable and encouraging. In Woodford 800 voluntary workers laboured day and night to complete the job in five days. In Luton hundreds of hat-workers were called in to help; in Dorchester the prisoners in the jail lent a hand. Boy Scouts, W.V.S. members, and Red Cross workers were all called in, but everywhere the chief burden of fitting the newly assembled respirators fell on the handful of air raid wardens, and the arrival of a warden to fit his mask at home caused many a citizen to realise for the first time that such a person existed. The crime-novelist Margery Allingham described how the Munich crisis broke over her remote village in Essex, where on a miserably wet night 450 inhabitants, of a possible 600, turned out to receive their masks at the village hall. While her husband lectured on gas in the main room, against an incongruous blackcloth showing a peaceful forest glade, batches of fifteen people at a time filed in to the adjoining room where heaps of large and medium gas masks—there was a general shortage of small ones—were stacked on the billiard table. Once fitted, the villagers disappeared into the rain with them 'clasped to their bosoms like puppies, under their coats'.*

In Bethnal Green, which was later to suffer more than 1,000 air raid casualties, one local official noted, surrounding the filling of sandbags to protect key points, 'such an air of gaiety and so many sightseers that the atmosphere was . . . more akin to children playing with their spades and buckets on one of the popular seaside beaches, than to the potential horrors of total war'. One Burton-on-Trent mother remembers collecting gas masks for her family from the crowded parish hall. Her two daughters were still awake when she arrived home and had a joyous game galloping round the bedroom in their new masks while an elderly relation staying with the family sat down and wept at the sight.

Everywhere the crisis called forth a spontaneous desire to help and a heartening readiness to improvise. Where sirens were not yet ready—the BBC even broadcast one so that people could recognise the warning when they heard it—arrangements were made to use factory hooters instead. In Wanstead when the First Aid Commandant found himself short of equipment he designed for himself a prototype stretcher of match boarding and within forty-eight hours the local boys' club had produced thirty copies of it, while local chemists had promised to make up the other missing supplies.

The Chamberlain government has often been accused of wasting the year gained by the abandonment of Czechoslovakia at Munich, but during those twelve months an immense amount was in fact done to prepare for war. In particular the Munich crisis transformed the A.R.P. situation. Before it recruits had been few and their training something

* This story is told by Margery Allingham in her book *The Oaken Heart*.

of a joke to those outside. Now, suddenly, there were more volunteers than instructors.

A typical new recruit was a local photographer at Grantham in Lincolnshire. He first became aware of A.R.P. on his way back to his studio from the local hospital carnival one Saturday evening in September 1938, when he saw on every tree an appeal for people to enrol as air raid wardens. For him the resulting sacrifices began the evening he called at the local Art Club, to which he had belonged for years, to say that he would be attending no more, as he was on his way to his first A.R.P. lecture.

The government wisely went ahead after Munich with the plans already made for a great A.R.P. recruiting drive. Cabinet ministers stumped the country exhorting their fellow citizens to come forward, conscientious mayors climbed on to cinema stages to make the same appeal, clergy repeated it from the pulpit, posters on every hoarding and leaflets thrust through every letter box underlined it. Recruiting for the Auxiliary Fire Service was particularly vigorous, especially in London where the aptly-named Chief Officer of the London Fire Brigade, Commander Firebrace, was loyally supported by Herbert Morrison, leader of the Labour majority at County Hall. The London Fire Brigade was at this time a *corps d'élite*, immensely jealous of its reputation, and drawn almost exclusively, like its head, from ex-sailors. The A.F.S. were at first not popular, partly perhaps because it was feared they would take over the regular firemen's jobs. The recruitment of women aroused even greater opposition. 'My God! Have we come to this?', one officer asked Firebrace. Most women recruits worked as telephonists and as canteen staff but some drove taxis which, at the suggestion of the cab-drivers' union, had been bought to tow trailer pumps. Like other women volunteers for transport work they often came from well-off families—many had been 'Bright Young Things' in peacetime. The trailer pump was soon automatically associated with the A.F.S., a grey, practical, utilitarian-looking object compared to the dashingly romantic red fire-engines of peacetime.

By now no one in Great Britain had any excuse to plead ignorance of what war was likely to mean. Directly after the Munich crisis the government had begun to deliver to every home in the country a buff-covered, thirty-six-page booklet, *The Protection of Your Home Against Air Raids*, which urged 'the head of the house' to 'consider himself as the captain of the ship', and compared the taking of precautions to the life-boat drill, essential, even if unlikely ever to be needed. It was followed in July and August 1939 by a stream of other Public Information Leaflets on such subjects as *Your Gas Mask* and *Masking Your Windows*.

A key step in the government's recruiting drive was the distribution of a solid forty-eight-page booklet, *The National Service Handbook,* described by the Prime Minister in a broadcast on 23rd January 1939 as 'A scheme to make us ready for war' and which listed the qualifications and age limits for service in the regular and reserve Forces, in nursing and the Women's Land Army, in the Observer Corps, which kept watch for enemy planes, and, above all, in Civil Defence.* The patriotic citizen could, if he were male and over twenty, become a special constable, or an auxiliary fireman, who would be called up for full-time service if war broke out. There were openings for fit men up to fifty, particularly from the building and similar trades, in the Rescue and Demolition Parties and Decontamination Squads, for a few men, from thirty to fifty, and more women, from eighteen to fifty, as ambulance drivers and attendants, and for men over forty-five and women over eighteen in the Report Centres, which would also need switchboard operators, stenographers, clerks and doorkeepers. Even youths under eighteen could find a job, in the Communications Service—later known as the Messenger Service— to run messages on foot, on cycle or motor cycle. The W.V.S., it was explained, had a dual role, in passing women on to the service most suited to them and in itself undertaking such jobs as escorting evacuees and manning canteens. The greatest need of all, however, was for air raid wardens, the backbone of the A.R.P. The warden was expected to be a mature and responsible person, the women over twenty-five, the men over thirty, or twenty-five 'if not available for more active service'. The government hoped, it explained, to have one Wardens' Post, manned by five or six wardens, to every four or five hundred people in urban areas. They were the Civil Defence's maids of all work, who would be trained to identify poison gas, administer first aid, call out the appropriate rescue or medical services, direct people to shelter or rest centres, and, above all, stop panic.

During the winter of 1938–9 the new recruits got down to serious training. A Warwickshire woman whose husband, a local government employee, became A.R.P. officer for the surrounding rural area, remembers this as the period when the threat of war first began to disrupt their peaceful family life. Her husband was out every night organising meetings and gas-mask fitting, and putting up posters calling people to meetings, her thirteen-year-old son busy with a loudspeaker van for the same purpose, and she herself attending St. John Ambulance Brigade classes in first aid. Margery Allingham was highly impressed by the ex-colonel, now an A.R.P. officer, who visited her Essex village to demonstrate the use of a dustbin and scoop to scrape up an incendiary bomb and who pointed out that a hay-fork, or other long-handled implement, could be

* I reluctantly decided that, as part of the air defence system, the Observer Corps was outside the scope of this book, particularly as its story has already been told elsewhere.

used instead. If anti-gas helmets for babies were still not available when war came a truss of hay stuffed down the chimney would make any room gas-proof. She was even more struck by the ex-Army instructor who for twelve weeks came to conduct two-hour sessions in the village school. While the new wardens squeezed into infants' desks too small for them, he hung up on the blackboard coloured charts showing the effects of mustard gas blisters on the limbs. They contrasted strangely, she felt, with the paintings of *The Light of the World* and of a child lying down with a lion and a lamb, which hung above them.

The Grantham photographer, Walter Lee, recalled how 'We were shown charts with blood gushing out of a cut artery and the ends of broken bones protruding through the skin . . . We often said to each other laughingly, "Oh, happy days to come." ' In Grantham the wardens began their practical training by noting how long it took them to get to their posts in the dark and the time required to reach an 'incident', the official name for a fire or damage caused by a bomb, in any part of their district. They soon learned that anti-gas precautions, which dominated the training syllabus, could be overdone, discovering, Walter Lee recorded, that it was almost impossible to use a pencil with oilskin gloves on and that by the time they were taken off and put away 'our report forms had become soaked and were impossible to write upon. . . . Two of us then went in search of a phone.' This too produced useful experience, for they discovered that few houses in the locality were on the telephone, and that most of these were already shut up for the night. A survey showed that none of the wardens' homes had a telephone and future exercises, and the first real bombs, were reported with the help of a friendly family, which left their telephone in the porch after going to bed.*

One of the largest sources of A.R.P. recruits was that large pool of middle-class women who had either never worked for their living or had been forced to resign their jobs on marriage, then an inflexible rule in most white-collar occupations. For the better off the Ambulance Service had a particular appeal, for driving was at this time a relatively rare skill, and car-ownership, particularly by women, a luxury.† The wife of a college official in Oxford recalls being one of thirty recruits taught by the owner of a local taxi service to drive taxis towing trailers containing racks for stretcher cases, the first A.R.P. ambulances. She has vivid

*In 1938 there were 3,300,000 telephones installed in the United Kingdom, of which 1,200,000 were in private homes. In 1970 the comparable figures were 14,250,000 instruments installed, 6,900,000 of them in private homes.
† In 1938 there were 3,085,000 vehicles on the roads, of which 1,900,000 were private cars and 460,000 were motor cycles. In 1969 the totals were 15,100,000 vehicles, 11,500,000 private cars and 1,140,000 motor cycles.

memories of practising driving in the dark, in a gas mask, by the light of dimmed side-lights during the long, dark winter after Munich. On some exercises two drivers started out from opposite ends of Wytham Woods, without lights, and with instructions to approach each other through the odd mile or so of winding road and to pass safely when they met. Anxious to avoid a head-on collision, more than one driver wandered completely off the road and was later found somewhere in the middle of the woods, totally lost.

In London the W.V.S. also organised a special course of driving without lights, in pitch darkness, in Croydon, but was rebuffed by the Regent's Park authorities when it asked for the lamp standards to be turned out for similar exercises in the West End. Even so, many women learned to drive in the dark, avoiding palliasses stuffed with straw, scattered on the road to represent casualties, and to carry out running repairs on their vehicles. Not everyone had yet realised, however, the basic toughness of the female sex. In one London borough where exercises for wardens were accompanied by a gramophone record of exploding bombs, the volume was turned down when 'lady wardens' were involved so that the bombs exploded with gentle pops.

In Woodford one first aid class collapsed with laughter at the sight of two of its members trying to undress a supposedly injured fat man who was also feigning hysteria. In an old-established textile firm, in the shadow of St. Paul's, where forty of the 800 staff had enrolled for the first aid course, one employee during a lecture on knots enthusiastically gagged another into total silence with a bandage round his mouth. Rescue work, the firm's historian recorded, was 'extremely popular, perhaps due to the reason that the mock "victims" were sometimes lady members of the staff'. A woman office worker in Wimbledon remembers a first aid practice in which the unit duly rescued a mother who had supposedly just given birth, but her 'baby', a piece of rolled-up blanket, was mislaid and forgotten. A Birmingham first aid worker enjoyed a gas cleaning exercise, in which a number of small boys agreed to act as victims and be scrubbed on all exposed parts of their body. 'I can see them now', she remembers, 'with rosy, shining faces all bright and fresh in their clean pyjamas'. A Hertfordshire teacher remembers the hilarity which greeted her when with great presence of mind she extinguished a flaring primus stove, intended for sterilising hot water at incidents, with an enamel bed-pan. The lecture on emergency child-birth had the same class shaking with suppressed laughter when both legs fell off the ancient doll which a woman doctor was using for her demonstration. In a London store one enthusiastic girl fire-fighter caused equal amusement by repeatedly falling down while hurrying to an imaginary fire in her brand new dungarees and rubber boots. She had forgotten to cut the string tying her wellingtons together.

It is difficult to identify the precise moment in 1939 when people ceased to say 'if war comes' and began instead to say 'when', but it was probably in mid-March 1939, after Hitler had marched into the remaining part of Czechoslovakia, thus finally repudiating the Munich agreement. Two weeks after Hitler had entered Prague the British government formally guaranteed the independence of Poland, and in April, against Labour opposition, carried the National Service Act, calling up for a year's military training in the Militia all young men of twenty. This, a nineteen-year-old Coventry girl noticed, for the first time brought the coming war home to her circle as men in her age-group disappeared reluctantly into the Army. Discussion about the rival merits of Ibsen and Chekhov, she remembers, gave place to heated arguments about Hitler, Chamberlain and, above all, conscription. The young men, she admits, were concerned more about their threatened careers than about Hitler, and patriotism was singularly lacking.

In July, not before time, a new Civil Defence Act strengthened the powers of the local authorities to build shelters, requisition premises and prepare for evacuation and fire-fighting. It also, for the first time, directly affected many thousands of private firms. Any employer with more than thirty workers was now required to organise A.R.P. training and services among them; while anyone employing more than fifty people, in a large city or other danger area, had to provide shelter for them. Sir John Anderson, now, as Lord Privy Seal, in charge of Air Raid Precautions, described the Act as 'putting the yoke to a willing horse', and the chief criticism of it by Herbert Morrison, the Labour spokesman on Civil Defence and later Anderson's successor, was that the government's plans did not go far enough.

Behind many of the government's preparations lay the fear of a 'knock-out blow' from the air that would paralyse the country, shatter morale and perhaps lose the war before it had properly begun. Shortly before Munich the government had, in deep secrecy, designated a number of individuals as Regional Commissioners, and in April 1939 the duties and names of the twelve areas and thirteen men concerned (London had two Commissioners) were made public. The Regional Commissioner had two duties—to co-ordinate the work of the Civil Defence and other authorities, such as those concerned with health and food supplies, in his region, and in a real emergency, such as invasion, to take over, if necessary, the civil government, becoming a virtual dictator over all its inhabitants, with almost life and death powers.

Although the government now spoke of Civil Defence, the general public continued to prefer the now-familiar initials of A.R.P. and in school playgrounds the children who a year or two earlier had sung ribald rhymes about Mussolini now had a new rhyme to the tune of the currently popular song *Under the spreading chestnut tree.*

> Under the spreading chestnut tree,
> Neville Chamberlain said to me:
> 'If you want to get your gas mask free,
> Join the blinking A.R.P.'*

About this time a shrewd cigarette manufacturer issued, in place of the traditional pictures of footballers and film stars, a set of fifty cigarette cards, with album to match, entitled *Air Raid Precautions.* In April 1939 appeared Nevil Shute's *What Happened to the Corbetts*, an imaginary account of the sufferings of a Southampton family under air attack, the publishers patriotically distributing a thousand copies free to A.R.P. workers. In the following month Richmal Crompton published the latest of her collections of short stories about a lovable but mischievous school-boy, William Brown, *William and A.R.P.* William, having complained that 'grown-ups got all the fun . . . Smellin' gases and bandaging each other and tryin' on their gas masks', assembles the local children at his headquarters, the Old Barn, and lectures to them from his sister Ethel's A.R.P. notes. 'I *dunno* why they smell of pear-drops', the lecturer tells his class, in answer to questions about gases, and the meeting ends in a free fight over the possession of a bandage, previously obtained by William's fellow outlaw, Henry, by the simple expedient of cutting himself.

In the much-loved radio comedy series, *Band Waggon*, one episode in 1939 revolved round the delivery to the flat of 'Big-hearted' Arthur Askey and Dicky 'Stinker' Murdoch, in Broadcasting House, of a large package described as 'an arp', as it is labelled A.R.P., which turns out to be an air raid shelter. After quarrelling over its erection 'Big and Stinker' compose their differences with the rhyme:

> Big and Stinker must agree
> Now they've joined the A.R.P.

Many people were by now making their private preparations for war. An Ipswich girl remembers her father warning her not to dispose of any out-of-date clothing, so that when peace came she still possessed a long 1937-style coat, fit for remodelling for further duty as a skirt and coat. The parish clerk of a Middlesex church ordered an extra supply of

* The song was misleading. You got your gas mask free whether you joined the A.R.P. or not, although A.R.P. workers did receive a superior form of mask.

coke, and began to build up a small reserve of wafers and communion wine and to prepare a safe hiding place for the parish papers in an oak chest made from an old piano, and a repository for the church valuables in the clock case in the tower. A Lancashire cotton worker managed out of her £2 a week earnings to buy extra food for her store cupboard, despite relations telling her, with North Country bluntness, that she was 'daft'. The deteriorating international situation was reflected in the shopping list of a Tolworth, Surrey, woman. In July she began accumulating a few extra tins of soup, meat, milk and vegetables, later adding to these such standby 'fillers' as rice, oats and lentils and finally buying dried yeast and extra flour so that in a real emergency she could bake her own bread. The real meaning of events was brought home to a girl working for a Jewish tailor as he was called on to help more and more Jewish refugees from Europe. It became a joke among her workmates that if their employer gave away any more of his stock the firm would go bankrupt.

The headmaster of Malvern College, opening some belated Christmas cards on Boxing Day 1938, discovered among them a heavy grey envelope labelled 'Secret', which contained the news that his school buildings would be requisitioned in the event of war. Eventually, after a long search by the headmaster, the Duke of Marlborough, who had offered Blenheim Palace to the nation 'for the duration', agreed to accept Malvern in place of the government offices he had expected and a coming-out ball for the Duke's daughter in June confirmed that the Palace's ancient kitchens could probably cater for 450 boys and staff. At a girl's boarding school at Bexhill the hymns that summer became progressively more patriotic as the traditional titles were replaced by *Land of Hope and Glory* and *I vow to thee, my country*. 'It seemed', one pupil recalls, 'as if our headmistress thought we could sing away the war and certainly if sheer lung power could have helped our efforts would have brought peace.'

During these months of waiting, the signs of preparation for war were everywhere. In my Berkshire home town I can recall the walls of sandbags appearing outside the back-street building which had become the A.R.P. Control Centre, the derelict pub which suddenly reopened its doors as an A.F.S. sub-station, the long-disused school on which notices blossomed proclaiming it a First Aid Centre, with separate entrances for gas-contaminated casualties.* Brick-built shelters were now appearing in streets and parks all over the country and in danger areas back gardens were changing their shape with the appearance of hump-backed Anderson shelters, of which by September 1939 the government had distributed nearly two million.

Less obvious were the preparations to disperse the population. The

* The building was never used, being wrecked by the first bomb to fall on the town.

government had published in the month after Munich Sir John Anderson's report on evacuation and in May 1939 it announced the division of the country into 'danger' areas, where evacuation was recommended, 'neutral' areas with no movement and 'safe' or 'reception' areas. Each contained roughly a third of the population. Throughout the 'danger' areas in the spring of 1939 lists were being compiled of children wishing to be evacuated and there were several large-scale rehearsals, while in the 'safe' areas Billeting Officers were equally busy compiling tables of potential hosts. Thousands of organisations and firms in the big cities were, like the government itself, making similar plans to move, and there was a boom in the sale of large country houses which could house whole offices and their staffs and in block bookings in country hotels.

In its protection of the population from the dreaded 'knock-out blow', the government relied as much on the proposed black-out as on evacuation. From the autumn of 1938 onwards increasingly large-scale tests of the black-out were held, conducted, however, with that half-heartedness so characteristic of the Chamberlain government. The first test, in Yorkshire, was actually held between 1 a.m. and 3 a.m. to reduce the inconvenience to the public and in London it was seriously argued that no black-out could begin before midnight because this would embarrass theatre-goers. To avoid alarming the public, tests of the newly-installed sirens were only held during the day. What *The Times* described as their 'fluctuating, high pitched moan' was first heard over most of Greater London simultaneously in December 1938. The sirens were heard again in Chelsea in mid-June in 1939, when they ushered in the biggest Civil Defence exercise held before the outbreak of war. Four hundred wardens were on duty, 'all wearing a distinctive and serviceable outfit of brown overalls and steel helmets', the Control Centre at the Town Hall was manned, the A.F.S. and the first aid parties stood by, and, partly no doubt to keep the streets clear, 5,000 children were removed to stations from twenty schools in the borough to test arrangements for evacuation. Prompt at 12.30 the sirens sounded over Sloane Square, the traffic stopped, the public obligingly moved into roped-off enclosures, to represent the as-yet-unbuilt shelters, and loudspeakers warned that bombers would arrive in eight minutes. 'Bells clanged and fire brigade units dashed off to deal with imaginary fires', *The Times* reported. 'Mobile First Aid Units and ambulances went off on their various duties. High Explosive bombs were supposed to have burst at nine separate places, wrecking buildings, severing gas and water mains and causing casualties.'

Two hundred A.R.P. observers from all over England watched from the roof of Peter Jones's store. An employee of the firm described in its house magazine how 'When the sirens were sounded at 12.30 customers and partners [i.e. staff] in all departments seemed to melt away and in a minute or two they were all in their refuge stations. Only three customers in the whole shop did not wish to take part . . . One was what is technically known in the trade as "difficult". Rumour had it that she cancelled her order; said she'd go to——'s, walked out of the shop and was immediately thrust into a refuge pen by an air raid warden in Sloane Square.'

Frances Faviell, a Chelsea artist and first aid worker, had a pavement's eye view of the affair as she lay on the ground posing as a casualty, listening to the onlookers jeering at the wardens. (Some, she admitted, did look strange, for the uniforms were often a bad fit and the seats of the women wardens' trousers reached almost to their knees.) From her prone position she found herself gazing at an A.R.P. recruiting poster signed by the chairmen of the local Conservative, Labour and Communist parties. 'Although we differ in many aspects of policy', it ran, 'we unite in urging you to volunteer for training to protect yourselves and your neighbours'—an impression of unity somewhat spoiled by the swastika scrawled on it by a dissenting Fascist.

# REPORT FOR DUTY

'A state of emergency has been declared and you are asked to report at once for duty in accordance with your undertaking.'
—Letter from Town Clerk of Wandsworth to volunteer warden, 1st September 1939

The holiday season of 1939 was not a happy one. Some resorts, like Scarborough, tried to tempt reluctant visitors by a promise in their official guide-books that bookings cancelled because of a national emergency need not be paid for, but the government's announcement on 1st August that petrol would be rationed immediately if war broke out hardly encouraged people to leave home, any more than the railways' warnings that normal services would be disrupted once evacuation began. Many people wisely decided, however, to make the most of what might be their last chance of a break for years, and compromised by taking their gas masks with them. The memories of those who went abroad during these sunlit months, and August was one of the warmest and driest on record, have still a particular nostalgia. A Northampton family remember, for example, a cruise in the fiords of Norway, for within a year the places they visited were to be overrun by the Germans and the ship they sailed in was sunk. A future landgirl, cycling amid the Burgundy vineyards in mid-August, still remembers being astonished when a French boy pointed out to her the blacked-out glass roof of Dijon station and warned her that the Germans in the youth hostel were probably spies.

For the days of peace were almost over. On Tuesday 21st August an astonished world learned that Russia was entering into a non-aggression pact with Germany. It was formally signed two days later and the BBC announcer Stuart Hibberd, who read the news to the nation with his usual impassive calm, described it privately in his diary as 'a bombshell'. A typical listener, the Grantham photographer and warden, Walter Lee, noted in his journal that he was 'dumbfounded' by it. All over Europe people hearing the news realised that it meant war. The telegrams began to flow out recalling the reservists and everywhere tourists and holiday-makers set out for home. A young London woman, just beginning a travel and study scholarship at a small seaside resort in southern France, sadly saw the call-up posters appearing and the hotels beginning to empty and, at station after station on the journey home, the heartbreaking sight of women waving goodbye to their men. Another Englishwoman, staying with a French family, remembers sitting in the pavement cafés and hearing one alarmist radio news bulletin after another, until the family cook arrived with the news that her two sons had been called up. After a nightmare journey from Boulogne, jammed shoulder to shoulder on the boat, she arrived at a blacked-out Waterloo, to be struck by the contrast between the hysterical excitement prevailing in France and the resigned composure of her countrymen. A woman on holiday in Middle-burg, Holland, remembers the crowds anxiously reading the call-up notices on the walls of the town hall and her journey back to Dover in a boat crammed with foreign-speaking British citizens and their luggage, returning to a country they had almost forgotten. 'The Cliffs', she remembers, 'looked wonderful from the sea with gunners at their posts silhouetted against the night sky.' The headmaster of Malvern College, on holiday in France, heard the news of the Russo-German pact—and that of the call-up of his landlady's son—on the following day, and instantly began packing. The headmaster of Dulwich College Preparatory School, peacefully fishing on a loch in the Western Highlands, looked up to see his wife running down the hillside waving the morning paper. Within minutes he was on the telephone to set the long-perfected evacuation plans for his school in motion. A Yorkshire family, enter-taining a French schoolboy, found themselves deeply involved in trying to get him home safely before the war began, at last managing to find him a place on a ship travelling from Glasgow instead of London. At an international scout camp further south the tents began to empty as one by one the boys from the Continent were summoned home.

For many people on holiday in Great Britain the problem was whether to enjoy the last few days of peace or to get home before the skies became dark with enemy bombers. Frequently, telegrams of recall from their employers, now packing up for evacuation, solved the problem. In the nine o'clock news on 22nd August it was announced that Parliament had been recalled, the first time this had been done by radio, and when the two houses met on 24th August they immediately passed the Emergency Powers (Defence) Act, 1939, the basis of the Defence Regulations which were to affect every aspect of the citizen's daily life in the next six years.* On the 25th August the BBC, which had in the past broadcast its first news of the day at 6 p.m., began to provide 'special news' at 10.30 a.m. and 1 p.m. with interruptions in other programmes for particularly urgent announcements. Now bulletin remorselessly followed bulletin and all the news they contained was bad. On Thursday 24th August the holidays came to an abrupt end for tens of thousands of schoolteachers affected by evacuation when they were recalled by radio to their posts.

* For example, the black-out was imposed under Defence Regulation No. 24.

The headmistress of the Mary Datchelor School in Camberwell, which had almost been evacuated in 1938, had enjoyed just one day's break in Dorset when she heard the news and began travelling home through the night.

That same day Stuart Hibberd noted that 'the entrance hall of Broadcasting House looked like King's Cross on Christmas Eve. The advance party [for the BBC's wartime studios in the country] was preparing to leave. On 25th August all leave was cancelled and everyone was busy taking black-out precautions. All possible precautions were taken in Broadcasting House, even to fixing gas-doors in position on the lower floors. That evening 10.30 p.m. Phillips [his announcer colleague, Frank Phillips] rang up to tell me that the first warning had come in and that I was to report at 9.30 a.m.' Other parts of the BBC were also on the move. A secretary in the Variety Department remembers drawing on 25th August £10 emergency pay, to cover the approaching evacuation, in addition to her customary £3 19s. 6d., and moving to a colleague's flat at Hounslow as the staff had been told to wait as far west as possible for the expected order to set out for their wartime home. An official of the BBC Publications Department had unluckily chosen Saturday 26th August for his wedding, but got only as far as Weymouth en route to his planned honeymoon in the Channel Islands, for the boat service had been cancelled. On the following Wednesday the unhappy bridegroom was himself summoned back to London to help with the evacuation of his department. It proved a bad omen; the marriage ended in divorce.

The government recall of teachers had served as a lead to many firms and the great dispersal was by Saturday 26th August well under way. Already two special trains had carried 800 bank clerks and typists from the Central Clearing House in London to their new offices on a former ducal estate near Stoke-on-Trent, and that day the first 450 headquarters staff of the Prudential Assurance Company set off for previously hired hotels in Torquay.

Besides the official movement and that of private businesses, there was, too, much 'self-evacuation' by those who, sensibly enough, wanted to be out of the cities when the sirens sounded. The artist Frances Faviell noted that Sunday how, while the Chelsea pavements were full of men and women in uniform, the roads were crowded with streams of cars leaving London, piled high with toys, prams and luggage and the family pets. Already the war was affecting her professional work; she was having to hurry to complete the portraits of two South African clients who were anxious to leave for home.

Throughout the succeeding week the tension tightened. The Daily Service with which broadcasting began on Monday 28th August reflected the nation's uncertainty. While the introit was *Blessed be the Peacemakers*, the hymn was *A Safe Stronghold our God is Still*. Later that day there was county cricket on the radio, Middlesex *v*. Surrey and Hampshire *v*. Yorkshire, but by now even cricket enthusiasts had more important preoccupations than the current score.

Step by step the country was moving towards war and each new stage directly affected some section of the population. A shorthand typist working for a film company in Tottenham Court Road remembers seeing the growing preparations on her daily bus journey from Fulham, with trenches being dug in the parks, builders busy reinforcing basements, Anderson shelters being sunk in back gardens and brick surface shelters going up on the pavements. The secretary of a plastics firm on the North Circular Road found herself involved in ordering A.R.P. equipment for its basement shelter. For her the war came suddenly closer when, on Wednesday 23rd August, she received a telephone message from the local police that the factory hooter was not to be sounded again except as an air raid warning. The following Sunday, she remembers, she managed to stay dry-eyed through prayers for peace at church, only to weep right through the sailors' hymn, *Eternal Father, Strong to Save*, which reminded her of her brother at sea somewhere in the Persian Gulf. The government's announcement, on Tuesday 29th August, that all place names visible from the air must be obliterated immediately affected the appearance of many railway stations, as all but the smallest name boards were taken down. A Barnsley woman remembers that her husband, a ganger with a local electricity supply company, was soon working sixteen hours a day painting out the firm's name, which it had proudly inscribed in large letters on many of its power stations.

Even those less personally involved in the nation's preparations found it impossible to escape the prevailing mood. A woman office worker remembers enjoying the lunchtime sunshine in the City streets that August until, in Finsbury Circus, she saw piles of dark green metal stretchers being unloaded from a lorry and carried into one of the buildings. The scene reminded her of an illustration to a Victorian allegory, with a grim ogre lurking in the background of an otherwise gay picture. An assistant in a Liverpool department store was equally distressed by the gaiety of the children brought to her counter to choose a gaily-coloured gas mask case as a pre-evacuation 'treat'. An Essex mother noticed a similar incongruity. While her fifteen-month-old boy and girl twins were competing in a Baby Show at the Southend Kursaal, in the town's last pre-war Carnival, workmen were busily blacking out the vast roof above them.

Throughout August recall notices had been going out individually to hundreds of thousands of Army, Navy and R.A.F. reservists, but it was not till Thursday 31st August at 11.7 a.m. that the decisive step was taken which affected millions of civilian homes: the government issued orders for evacuation to begin the following morning. The 1 p.m. news that day warned that 'no one should conclude that this decision means that war is now regarded as inevitable', but four hours later it was announced that the fleet had been mobilised, the classic sign that Britain was in earnest, and all remaining R.A.F. and naval reservists were now ordered to report for duty. That night, as tearful mothers in cities all over the country finished packing their children's clothes for an early start next day, the BBC broadcast a special service of intercession, though few can have had any illusions that prayer alone was likely to stop Hitler.

The announcement of the calling out of the Territorial Army made a deep impression. An Ipswich Civil Servant remembers hearing it at her tennis club. Without a word, three men in the group shook hands with their friends and amid shouts of 'Good luck!' walked out of their lives. The wife of a Scottish Territorial on holiday on a farm with her year-old son recalls receiving a message from her husband that he had been mobilised and she must make the arrangements to return herself. Her host, with wartime helpfulness, obligingly loaded cot, playpen, luggage and family on to his milk truck and drove them back to Glasgow. The daughter of an Oldham headmaster remembers how for days the guests at the hotel in Petworth, Sussex, where her family was on holiday, had gathered round a wireless set on the reception desk at news-time. Now the receptionist predicted disaster so convincingly that she emptied the hotel, the headmaster observing, 'If we don't go now, we shall find the road blocked with tanks!', a remark which later became a family joke. As they filed out, the first evacuees were already moving in.

But the only tanks on the move that day were Hitler's. When millions of listeners eagerly tuned in at 10.30 a.m. on Friday 1st September to the first news of the day they heard a solemn-voiced announcer reporting the invasion of Poland. This, for most civilians, was the day the war really began. Walter Lee in Grantham learned what had happened from a dialogue between two workmen building a garage. ''Ave yer 'eard the news, Bill?' called the man at the foot of the ladder. ''Itler's gone into Poland!', to which his mate called down the heartfelt response, 'The b——!' A twenty-one-year-old Edinburgh University student, getting up late that morning, was brought up short by hearing as he dressed that 'Warsaw and Lowicz' had been bombed, for he had visited both places with Polish student friends earlier that year. A nineteen-year-old girl in Denbigh, North Wales, remembers going out that day to buy a roll of wallpaper for redecorating her bedroom and seeing the placards outside newsagents' shops, 'Poland Invaded'. A woman living in a village in central Scotland and leading a very sheltered life caring for her invalid mother felt an urgent need to do something energetic. She finally collected all the family's laundry and began furiously washing it. 'No German', she resolved, 'was going to catch us with our linen unwashed.' With the washing safely on the line she had another urgent thought, to buy sugar from the travelling shop which visited the village on Fridays—her mother had told her how scarce this had been in World War One. The wife of a Plymouth shopkeeper remembers customers buying extra sugar, flour and candles. A draper's assistant in Andover recalls that her employers had prudently bought up so much stock that it was difficult for the staff to move. Many housewives found it difficult to decide when prudent stocking-up degenerated into unpatriotic hoarding. The mother of one Blackburn girl felt it was permissible to buy extra food but only in instalments. Her daughter, then aged thirteen, was sent eight times that day to the shops, to obtain a quarter of a pound of tea and two pounds of sugar on each trip.

To many people what was now happening seemed like a nightmare; a London woman remembers going to the cinema that day and seeing many of the audience in tears as the already out-of-date newsreels of Poland were shown. A Fleet Street journalist noticed the crowds round the newspaper sellers—and the teams of men already stacking sandbags in front of windows. That evening, a wet one in London and the first night of the black-out, he visited a doctor friend who had offered his services for A.R.P. work and found him grimly reading a textbook entitled *Emergency Surgery*. In Bolton by four o'clock that day male workers had already received their calling-up papers, by five they were back at the mills in uniform to say goodbye.

Friday 1st September was the day that your children were evacuated—or other people's arrived—the day that the black-out began, the day that the A.R.P. was mobilised. Travel to work that morning was disrupted, as buses and trains were busy with evacuation, and everywhere, on hoardings and walls and telegraph poles, the white posters were appearing, some headed 'Lighting Restrictions', warning that the black-out was to come into force at sunset, others more dramatically beginning 'By the King, a Proclamation', formally announcing the declaration of a state of emergency. Of all these events it was the black-out which affected most people and which did most to lower their spirits. From 7.47 p.m., British Summer Time, that night no one could any longer ignore the approach of war. A woman on holiday with her husband at Torquay remembers how that week as they had looked from the windows of their lodgings at the newsagent's opposite the placards outside had daily grown grimmer and grimmer. They had tacitly agreed to ignore the news, but on Friday 1st September went in to dinner to find the lights dimmed for the first night of black-out—and the dining room crammed with newly-arrived Jewish evacuees, in a state of obvious terror. Next day she travelled back with her husband, who had been recalled to his office, in an unlighted train, crowded with troops trying to sleep in the corridors—a fitting introduction to wartime travel.

This was the day that one unlucky architect in Surrey had chosen to move house. He and his wife spent their first night feeling their way about in a strange building, with no curtains up, afraid to put on a light. Their first contact with their neighbours was a desperate appeal to borrow a newspaper to black out one window, and with the paper pinned over the frame they settled miserably down beside a single candle. The first call the husband made in his new neighbourhood next morning was to Putney Police Station to collect his tin hat, cape and truncheon as a War Reserve Policeman.

In many places the black-out was that first night enforced with ridiculous stringency. A Bath schoolgirl, summoned home from a holiday in London, found that the coach she was travelling on was stopped by soldiers who ordered that even the sidelights—permitted by the regulations—should be turned off. A Lincoln woman, who had heard the news that reservists had been recalled while she and her husband, on holiday in London, were preparing to go to the theatre, remembers the nightmare drive homewards to enable him to report, for they were stopped by the police and told to drive entirely without lights.

In Ramsgate a hostile crowd gathered outside a house with unscreened upstairs windows and prepared to pelt them with stones from the garden rockery. The owner, who claimed never to have heard of the black-out, was later fined £15.

Wars had always begun with partings, but never had there been so many as in 1939. The reservists were the first to go. The manager of a stage company appearing at the old Grand Theatre, Croydon, had begun the last week of peace with the company rehearsing an Edgar Wallace thriller, but before long one of the leading actors was 'called for' by an army lorry. By the end of the week the company included so many replacements that there were six prompt scripts on stools round the stage to help the newcomers, and the unfortunate producer was also doubling as scene shifter, props man and front-of-the-house manager. That night Sir Henry Wood spoke to the Promenade Concert audience from the platform at Queen's Hall, the first time he had ever done so. The 'Proms', he announced, were closing that night as the Symphony Orchestra would no longer be available. It was, in fact, destined for Bristol—and before it returned to London Queen's Hall was a ruin. A Bath housewife, having sent her husband to collect the weekend joint, learned when he returned hours later that he had volunteered instead to deliver other orders in his car, the butcher's delivery man having been called up. A Middlesbrough woman remembers how her husband, reluctant to leave her alone with two small babies, ignored the first O.H.M.S. letter recalling him to the Army. Only when a second arrived, warning him to report that day or be arrested, did the family set off, the husband for Richmond barracks, the wife for her father's home at Darlington. 'I did not know that my father would want me and two babies thrust upon him', she admits. 'I was very relieved to receive a warm welcome.'

For days past many local authorities had also been quietly mobilising their reserves. A Birmingham woman, who had been attending A.R.P. classes at the local school, and her next-door neighbour, found themselves summoned, a week before war broke out, to man a first aid post at the local swimming baths. The helpers soon organised themselves into shifts, the housewives covering the 8 a.m. period, with office- and shop-workers and men filling in the night hours. The baths were, she remembers, in a filthy condition, due to their hasty conversion, and the housewives spent their shifts in the essential, but unmartial, activities of scrubbing and cleaning. Many buildings were quietly taken over as emergency mortuaries and a W.V.S. worker remembers seeing in a requisitioned East End school stacks of prefabricated dark brown, cardboard coffins, stored flat like collapsible cake-boxes, with large bolts of material intended for making into shrouds. The government, with typical Chamberlain economy, had prudently bought up unwanted oddments, so that some were, rather incongruously, bright red, and others white with patterns of pink roses and blue forget-me-nots.

The formal mobilisation of Civil Defence personnel was announced by telegram to local authorities and in the six o'clock news on Friday 1st September. For members of the A.F.S. it had a particular significance, for from being part-time volunteers they now became full-time professionals. An Essex woman remembers that as her husband left for duty at London Fire Brigade headquarters next morning she felt she would never see him again. 'The bottom had dropped out of my little world.' A Richmond A.F.S. man heard the call to duty after a hard day's cycling, for after evacuating his wife and baby to Burghfield in Berkshire, he had set out by bicycle to spend his summer holiday with them. That night, after a few hours with his family, he mounted his bicycle again for the long ride back. At 10.30 on Saturday morning he was at his post as Liaison Officer at a Report Centre.

A part-time warden in South West London received her call to duty by a note delivered by messenger and at 9.30 p.m. that evening she assembled with others who had lightheartedly volunteered months before and, she noted in her diary, 'excited, fearful, expectant, we waited . . . nothing happened'. The expected equipment failed to arrive and at 1 a.m. they dispersed, 'tired, grumbling, disappointed'. It was not, perhaps, a bad introduction to the frustrations and waiting of war and at 10 a.m. next day they reassembled to learn another lesson from the District Warden, a forthright old soldier. 'You wanted to be air raid wardens?' he asked them. 'Well now you blooming-well are air raid wardens. It won't be long now, I don't suppose, before we get our share and it wouldn't surprise me if we didn't get a whiff of gas as well . . . If any of you think you'd like to pack up before the fun starts, now's the time to do it. Well, good luck.' Gathering up their gumboots and oilskins, which had at last arrived, his pupils departed, much chastened, the sickly smell of the hot rubber in their nostrils.

On the evening of Friday 1st September there occurred another event that affected almost every home in the country. In the six o'clock news that evening, and every few minutes thereafter until 8.15, the BBC announced that it was merging its National and Regional services and would in future broadcast only one programme—available continuously from 7 a.m. till a quarter past midnight. Listeners were asked to tune in in future to either 391 or 449 metres, the wavelengths in happier times of the Scottish and North Regional programmes.

With everyone in the country dependent upon the BBC these changes made a great impression, making everyone realise both the scale of the emergency and the thoroughness of the preparations made to meet it. Another BBC event that day attracted far less attention. That morning the BBC Head of Drama had been rehearsing his first full-length play for television, Somerset Maugham's *The Circle*, when, simultaneously, a messenger arrived with the tennis rackets and balls needed as props, and a telephone call informed him that the 'emergency period' had begun. At noon that 'Black Friday', as it was nicknamed by television enthusiasts, as a Mickey Mouse cartoon ended with the words, in Garbo-like accents, 'Ah tink ah go home', the 20,000 television sets in Britain went blank. They were not to carry a picture again till 1946.

The first programme heard on the new wireless wavelength on Saturday 2nd September was a news bulletin and many more followed that day, alternating with records and a sound that recalls for many the beginning of the war, Sandy Macpherson at the theatre organ. 'Sandy', summoned back from holiday at Looe, now found himself the sole survivor of the Variety Department left in London. 'St. George's Hall', he noticed that morning, 'seemed very empty after they had all gone . . . There was a silence almost death-like in its intensity.'

A sombre sense of expectancy hung over the whole nation that day. The black-out had come, the evacuees had gone, the A.R.P. were ready— all that was lacking was the war. An Edinburgh University student noticed that the Saturday morning crowds, instead of strolling in the sunshine in Princes Street, were standing in groups with 'a curious, half-frozen look'. That evening the family gloomily celebrated his sister's birthday in a blacked-out drawing room drinking her health in Cointreau. What followed, her brother recalled, was 'pure Mrs. Miniver'. His sister corked the bottle decisively after that first glass and announced, 'We shall drink the rest when victory is won.'

As the black-out shutters went up that evening in the fishing village of Ardglass in Northern Ireland a London woman then living there was cheered to hear the patriotic tunes being played by an old fiddler in the corner of the local pub. The locals, Irish-born, took more comfort in the record catch of herrings that day and the further shoals of fish said to be coming in—an excellent omen, they felt, for Britain's prospects in the coming war.

That Saturday only a few people sought entertainment outside their own homes. At the Theatre Royal in London the audiences for *The Dancing Years* had been growing thinner and thinner throughout the week and by Saturday the stalls were so sparsely occupied that Ivor Novello invited people from the gallery to come down and fill the empty seats, the evening developing into an impromptu concert. An Ipswich Civil Servant faced that day a difficult decision. Should she obey the orders given the staff at work that morning not to leave the city in case they could not return, or pay her usual weekend visit to her mother at Colchester, as it might be their last chance to meet for a long time? Greatly daring, she decided to go, enduring a memorable journey in unlighted trains and a nightmare walk across a blacked-out station, in which she repeatedly bumped into shadowy figures in Army uniforms or tripped over their kit-bags.

A few people stoutly refused to be deterred from their holiday plans, like the couple who caused astonishment by asking at Hull station for tickets to Hornsea, a coastal resort thought likely to be an early target. The first afternoon in their holiday bungalow was spent pinning brown paper over the windows and that night, as some were still uncovered, they sat romantically by candlelight.

But most movement that day was homewards. A Welwyn Garden City shop assistant spent the day travelling home from his holiday at Herne Bay in Kent, which was already almost empty, though 7,000 mothers and children from the Medway towns were expected at any moment. 'Lovely day, but London very depressing', he recorded in his 'war diary'. 'Men working feverishly sand-bagging important buildings. Arrived home 7 p.m. and started work blacking out windows. Tired and hot.'

One film technician who had been told on Friday that the film he was working on was to be restarted with a 'war angle' learned that Saturday morning that it was to be scrapped altogether. After seeing Euston jammed with travellers, and narrowly escaping being run down by a bus in the black-out, he answered the call of a poster in a café, 'Join the A.F.S.', and walked straight to the nearest fire station. Within minutes he had been signed on and was on his way to war, in a taxi towing a trailer pump to an emergency fire station, a requisitioned school.

The editor of *The Sunday Chronicle*, emerging from his London office for an evening stroll, was struck by the unfamiliar sight of the special constables on duty in civilian clothes and steel helmets, by the vast array of barrage balloons in the sky, and by the ever-present soldiers, laden down with kitbags, on their way to join their units. Returning to his office, around 8 p.m., he found his staff gathered round the tape machine, reading the text of the Prime Minister's speech in the House of Commons as it clattered off the keys. As the realisation spread among the little group that Chamberlain was still not going to announce the declaration of war, though it was now nearly two days since Hitler had invaded Poland, you could, the editor recalled, 'see on everybody's face the contempt and sense of disillusion'.

The day had been hot and sunny but, as darkness fell, a series of violent thunderstorms swept the country. A mile or so further east the daughter of an East London policeman, on duty that night, felt it seemed like a warning of impending doom. The wife of a Chesterfield factory-owner, alone in the house as her husband was absent on A.R.P. duties, noted in her diary: 'Dreadful thunderstorm. All lights out. Busy with blinds.' A woman travelling back to London from a curtailed holiday in the West Country watched the lightning flashes light up the faces of the passengers jammed in the darkened coaches, which were in total blackness, except for the occasional gleam from the guard's lantern as he struggled down the crowded corridors. At Portsmouth the rumour spread that the war had already begun, as four barrage balloons, struck by lightning, caught fire and lit up the night sky. And so, tumultuously, died the last day of peace.

# THE DAY WAR BROKE OUT

'The day war broke out, my missus said to me: "It's up to you . . .
You've got to stop it." I said, "Stop what?" She said, "The war." '

—catchphrase of wartime comedian Robb Wilton

Sunday the 3rd of September, 1939, began with a bright and sunny morning. The storm during the night had cleared the air and those who were up early—sunrise was at 6.16 a.m. British Summer Time—were conscious of the invigorating freshness of the atmosphere, as though the decision to fight had dispelled the oppressive sultriness of the previous evening. A Worcestershire telephone engineer noticed it as he started work at 7.30 that morning wiring up the stately home of Croome Court, intended as a wartime retreat for the royal family. A London woman noticed it as she went to early mass that morning in a Franciscan chapel. There were no prayers for peace. Those unworldly men, the friars, appeared to be unaware of the crisis.

Millions of people that Sunday morning were busy in their gardens, preparing the ground for Autumn crops or struggling to erect home-made or Anderson shelters. In Colchester, Essex, a woman watched her husband and male neighbours, stripped to the waist, digging a trench linking their garden to the adjoining house. The cutting down of the fence was, he felt, symbolic of the way barriers between neighbours were now being removed. For one newly-enrolled special constable in Shropshire the war had already begun. In the early hours of 3rd September he had had to tour the local farms knocking up the German farm workers and warning them they must not travel further than three miles without police permission. A young woman working on a Sussex farm self-consciously took her gas mask with her that morning as she went to feed the chickens and to fetch the cows in for milking. A Leeds University student, spending the weekend at home in Bingley, decided that war was inevitable and went up on the moors that morning with a girl friend. They lay silently in the heather, smoking and enjoying the sunshine, as the last minutes of peace ebbed away. Although even the most extreme sabbatarians had always permitted 'works of necessity' on the Sabbath, there was some doubt as to whether erecting a shelter for one's own protection qualified under this heading. A Southampton girl, evacuated to Jersey, was deeply shocked to see her hosts and other islanders busily working on their dug-outs that morning.

For women the first job that morning, once the breakfast was washed up, was the same as for days past, sewing permanent black-out curtains. Everywhere the wireless was on. The first news bulletin at 7 a.m. had reported that no reply had been received from Hitler to the British demand made two days before that he would withdraw from Poland. At eight there were optimistic Polish reports about German aircraft and tanks destroyed.

The announcement for which everyone was waiting came at ten: the Prime Minister would speak to the nation at 11.15. Housewives with a wireless in the kitchen—a rare amenity in 1939—were able, as they began to peel the potatoes and mix the batter for the Yorkshire pudding, to listen to a selection from *Princess Ida* and to Parry Jones singing *The Passionate Shepherd*, followed by a recorded talk, *Making the Most of Tinned Foods*.

There were still that morning a million families where the breadwinner was unemployed and many people could not afford a wireless set, but already traditional British reserve was breaking down and set-owners invited their neighbours in. This was the first time the family next door had ever been inside our house, though we had lived side by side for nine years.

Neville Chamberlain was now a man of seventy and his voice was old, tired and sad.

I am speaking to you from the Cabinet Room at No. 10 Downing Street. This morning, the British Ambassador in Berlin handed the German government a final note, stating that unless the British government heard from them by 11 o'clock that they were prepared at once to withdraw their troops from Poland, a state of war would exist between us. I have to tell you now that no such undertaking has been received, and that consequently this country is at war with Germany. . . . The situation in which no word given by Germany's ruler could be trusted and no people or country could feel itself safe, has become intolerable. Now we have resolved to finish it. . . . May God bless you all. May he defend the right, for it is evil things that we shall be fighting against—brute force, bad faith, injustice, oppression and persecution; and against them I am certain that the right will prevail.

The national anthem followed Chamberlain's speech. In private houses and A.R.P. centres many people stood up for it. In hotels they were more self-conscious. A young law student at an expensive country hotel near Guildford remembers the residents sitting tight: they had come there for safety, not to make patriotic gestures. One Essex woman claimed that her dog climbed loyally out of his basket at the sound and stood firmly to attention, until she took him on her lap for mutual comfort. A South Benfleet woman, alone in her bungalow with her small son—her husband was in the A.F.S.—took her baby from his pram and hugged him to her, praying that they might survive the war. She then wrote a long letter to her mother begging her to care for her grandson if she should be killed, packed her jewellery and family papers in a small case and stowed them in the bottom of the pram, along with food and a spare set of clothes and nappies. A Hereford teenager, due to start her first job the following day, was still in bed when war was declared. Her immediate reaction was to get up and dress in her Sunday best. She then set off for the High Street, and stood on the pavement waiting to see the soldiers march off to war, led by brass bands, as in the films of 1914. She was very disappointed that the streets seemed deserted apart from a few worried-looking churchgoers on their way home, and even the station, instead of being packed with troop trains and weeping relations, was silent and empty. A fourteen-year-old Kidderminster girl, however, found events unfolding just as she had expected. On going round to the Drill Hall to see her 'Terrier' boy friend who had been summoned there the previous Friday, she found his unit marching off to entrain for a destination 'somewhere in England'.

A Newcastle boy, camping with a friend in a Northumberland village, listened with half a dozen others in the village shop, specially opened for the occasion, looking out at the river and fields beyond. Then they packed up and cycled home, where he found his brother and father hard at work glueing adhesive tape to the windows.

The news of the declaration of war spread rapidly that morning, even to those a long way from a radio. One young boy, on a neighbour's boat on the Thames, remembers that even they could not escape it, for a policeman, pushing his bicycle along the bank, called to them, 'It's happened!' A district midwife in Horsham, Sussex, heard the news as she left a small house where she had been up all night delivering a baby boy, and the milkman called to her, 'Nurse, we are at war with the Germans.' She was, she acknowledged, unmoved; her thoughts were of her recent patient and the hard day's work still ahead. A Sheffield girl, on holiday with her fiancé at Scarborough, remembers they learned the news while walking along the deserted front from firemen dashing wildly about. One London mother who had evacuated her family to relations in Dorset remembers she was taking them for a country walk when she heard through the open windows of the cottages that war had been declared. One W.V.S. member, seeking homes for evacuees in Walton-on-the-Naze, was surprised to be asked inside and given a glass of sherry while listening to the Prime Minister. This was perhaps the last time that, as a Billeting Officer, she found herself actually welcome.

The immediate reaction to the news varied between a stunned silence and an urgent desire to discuss it. One London mother, staying with her in-laws, remembers hastily taking her small son down to the bottom of the garden to watch the trains go by, to get away from the depressing talk indoors. A Norfolk woman, married in May after an argument with her husband—who had wanted to wait a few months as 'it would soon be all over'—remembers that the declaration provoked a new discussion: as he might well be killed, should they have a baby? As before, his wife won the argument and her fears proved groundless. By the end of the war the family numbered four.

Tears were common that morning. A twenty-year-old Yorkshire girl was horrified to see her father, 'a hard man' in his sixties, weeping. A South Norwood woman watched the tears rolling down her mother's cheeks, while she herself, aged twenty-five, wondered, 'Shall I ever be twenty-six?' One eighteen-year-old Liverpool girl at work as a Lyons waitress, or 'nippie', sobbed so bitterly that the cashier deserted her desk to console her, while a fellow waitress brought a cup of tea and pressed upon her the first cigarette she had ever smoked in her life.

For families with evacuees the declaration of war seemed the justification of all their inconvenience. A woman in Cheadle, Cheshire, caring for two small girls from Moss Side, Manchester, found their company a real consolation. They had sat soberly on the terrace, with the dog and the kitten at their feet, while Chamberlain spoke, then one eight-year-old, reacting like millions of older women that day, said, 'Come on, Auntie, let's go and make a cup of tea.' Soon they were watching fascinated as 'Auntie' made cakes and put them in the oven; they had only seen shop-made pastry before.

Even those following their normal routine that morning felt moved to mark the day by some departure from their usual way of life. At Lichfield Theological College the war had not been allowed to interrupt the usual morning service, but on learning the news on their return to their rooms the students did something unprecedented on a Sunday and began to play cards.

The most enterprising clergy that day had made arrangements to inform their congregation if war were declared. The ten-year-old daughter of the vicar of a village near Canterbury experienced feelings of mingled pride and shyness as she opened the church door and walked up the aisle in mid-service to break the news to her father. The wife of a Cambridgeshire vicar remembers how, as the news was announced to the congregation, there was an audible gasp and matins was abandoned and a short improvised service of prayers and hymns substituted so the congregation could get home early. A Devon woman remembers the deep sadness which gathered over the congregation in her church as they listened to the speech on a battery set resting on one of the pews. One Church of Scotland service, in Lanarkshire, began with a young divinity student describing his experiences in the preceding two days in helping in the reception of children evacuated from Glasgow, and having broken the news of the declaration he led his congregation in singing *O God, Our Help in Ages Past.*

Some people that day stalwartly refused to let a mere war interfere with their plans. In Coventry the local Art Group met as usual in the old weaving shed which was its headquarters, but one member felt 'it was not a happy meeting and art was very far from our thoughts. We did not know how long we would have any young men left.' A Liverpool rambling club had chosen this day for their annual outing by coach. As their bus carried them through the lovely countryside of North Wales they paid less and less attention to the scenery and more and more to the grim news coming over the coach radio. Lunch was a somewhat tense meal for the proprietress of the guest house was expecting an evacuated school to arrive at any moment. That night the returning ramblers discovered with a shock that theirs was the only vehicle heading for Liverpool. All the other traffic was flowing in the opposite direction as evacuees poured from Merseyside into Wales.

Some people that morning heard the news of the declaration with relief. A thirteen-year-old schoolboy in Cheltenham was delighted, for his friends had got hold of the notion that all schools would be closed indefinitely if war broke out. Great was their disappointment when they discovered that as the town was a reception area school would be open as usual, but with evacuees from Birmingham sharing the premises. A Worcestershire farmer also welcomed the news, since for years he had seen his neighbours going bankrupt one by one. Now, he felt, 'at last we are going to be wanted'.

Eight minutes after the Prime Minister had finished speaking, at 11.28 a.m., the sirens sounded over Greater London, and a few minutes later, over many other parts of the country, including much of East Anglia and the Midlands. In Central London the warning system worked admirably. There was little traffic about and as some policemen cycled through the streets bearing large 'Take cover' notices on the fronts and backs of their uniforms, like cycling sandwich-board men, the few people in the streets filed into the trenches in the parks. In many residential areas, however, the picture was a good deal less orderly. A few A.R.P. workers, in the excitement of the moment, forgot their months of training and began frantically to twirl their heavy rattles, intended only to warn of the presence of gas. At Carshalton, one mother, seeing a warden running along the street sounding a rattle, remembers that 'I clasped my baby, sent aloft a prayer and waited for the worst'. At a village near Gains-borough in Lincolnshire, another young mother remembers seeing her neighbours, too scared to go out, peering from their windows with their gas masks on and gesturing to her to put hers on. Deeply apprehensive lest she were suffocating the child, she settled her baby inside its anti-gas helmet and began to operate the pump. One London woman remembers a neighbour remarking as they entered the shelter that Chamberlain had spoken of having received no reply from Hitler, and that here *was* his reply. An eleven-year-old Battersea girl was moved to tears at the prevailing gloom, until a few moments later, when the siren sounded, she was diverted by the sight of an eccentric woman in the road running up and down in hysterics. A Dulwich woman remembers seeing a young girl rush from a nearby house wearing only one shoe, carrying her baby, and screaming hysterically. A North London woman, alone and expecting a baby, felt she must take shelter with someone in the same situation, and hurried to a pregnant friend in the next road, only to rush back again when she realised she had forgotten her gas mask. Then she discovered she had broken the heel off her shoe; by the time she was calm again the 'All Clear' had sounded. One seven-year-old girl, terrified by the wailing siren, soon recovered her spirits and promptly went into the garden in the hope of seeing the invading German planes. A Nottingham woman remembers how, after the declaration of war, people stood about in small groups, seeking comfort in company, until they rushed into their houses when the siren went. She was, she admits, 'quite literally terrified', huddled with her children under the oak dining table, praying for their lives and 'fully expecting to see hordes of German bombers over our houses dropping loads of bombs'. A Stepney woman, having made a mad rush for the shelter, faced an agonising decision: should they risk their lives from high explosive by going back for their gas masks, or stay where they were and be gassed?

The ten-year-old daughter of a Palmers Green family delightedly put on her gas mask and firmly refused to take if off, while watching the milkman dutifully unfastening his horse, reversing it, and tying it up with a special halter with its head between the shafts.* In a Fulham street one local shopkeeper watched another hurrying his wife and two small girls along to shelter at his mother-in-law's home with shouts of 'I'm not going to stay there and be bloody well killed'. It was a classic case of death being in wait elsewhere. The shop survived the war; the whole family were, in 1940, wiped out in the same cellar to which they had hurried that first morning. The first casualty of the war in the home of a newly-married couple in Kingston-on-Thames was a prized wedding present, a beautiful crystal bowl. As they swung a heavy sideboard across

* This was the recommended procedure, as described in Chapter 22.

an alcove and crouched behind it, waiting for the bombs to drop, it fell and smashed into fragments. Not far away, the owners of houses on the Kingston by-pass dashed into the road to offer shelter to passing motorists. 'We bagged a dear old lady who doddered into the lounge with her chauffeur,' one woman remembers. 'My two dogs, an alsatian and a cocker spaniel, loved visitors and kept running round the room in excitement. Suddenly the spaniel disappeared and then reappeared with a burnt offering for our new guest . . . an old pair of cotton pants . . . I used as a floor cloth.' It is doubtful whether guests or host were more relieved at the 'All Clear', but no sooner had they left than the neighbours arrived demanding that the alsatian be destroyed in case in the next raid he ran amok and bit them. His devoted owner admits that she sat down and howled, until, her husband having persuaded the visitors to leave, they began to work out plans to remove the animals to safety.

That first siren of the war caught one London family half-way across Waterloo Bridge on their way to a wedding. Turning down the driver's suggestion of taking shelter, they hurried on, only to find they had the church to themselves, with no guests, no clergyman and no bride and groom. Eventually the wedding started half an hour late, but without the bride's parents, who had failed to hear the 'All Clear'. A nurse from St. George's Hospital, hastily married the day before because of the war, was walking in the Surrey countryside with her new husband, enjoying their one day honeymoon, when the sirens sounded in the distance. But nothing could depress them that morning. She remembers they laughed immoderately as an air raid warden drove down the road in his Baby Austin while his wife leaned out of the window shouting, 'Take cover!', to a landscape containing only a few bushes and a tumbledown pig-sty.

A Hounslow woman, who had hurried her children off to a friend's shelter, remembers they sat discussing the situation with such interest that they failed to hear the 'All Clear'. The first they knew of it was when her husband arrived home from his milk round to find the house empty, the joint ruined and the kettle boiled dry. In a Civil Service office in Newcastle the staff had been on duty since ten, having assembled to learn the contents of the sealed envelope labelled 'To be opened only on the outbreak of hostilities'. The oldest member of the female staff found herself suddenly in demand in the shelter as the younger clerks and typists pleaded with her to tell them, from her first world war experience, what shortages to prepare for. Her reply, 'Buy up hairpins, kirby grips and elastic for knickers!'—sound advice as it turned out—led next morning to the counters of the local Woolworths being stripped bare of these items as the Civil Service women of Newcastle descended *en masse* in search of them.

The cinema industry had already been warned that places of entertainment would be closed on the outbreak of war and on the 3rd September the manager of the *Granada*, North Cheam, in accordance with Head Office Memorandum No. 7, Section 18 (Staff Morale), assembled his staff in the restaurant to break the news to them. He had just announced, 'Above all, we must at all times keep calm', when he was interrupted by the siren, at which his audience abruptly dispersed. Most rushed into the street but two or three cleaners clung to the hand rail at the top of the circle steps, screaming at the tops of their voices.

For those on A.R.P. duty the warning had a special significance. One Putney warden found herself that morning in a post in the kitchen of a private house, where the A.R.P. equipment was heaped on the table beside the Sunday joint and the telephone did duty for both private and official calls. When it rang she seized it eagerly, only to hear a voice asking, 'Is that Mum?' Chamberlain's speech reduced her to tears and another warden helpfully handed her a wad of gauze bandage to dry her eyes, the first use of the borough's first aid stores in war. The siren pulled her together more rapidly even than her colleagues' sympathy and she found herself taking messages with complete composure. At Eltham, South East London, where a large house was being converted into an A.R.P. Control Room, the waiting telephonists and other staff had felt rather in the way of the electricians and carpenters who were hard at work. When the siren went the position changed dramatically, the A.R.P. personnel scattering carpenters, wires and toolbags out of their way as they manned their telephones and map-boards. With the 'All Clear' the situation was again reversed as the builders once more took over.

Not all A.R.P. workers reacted heroically to this first call to action. A City secretary, on duty that Sunday at an A.F.S. station near Potters Bar, remembers with self-conscious composure and due regard for the correct procedure taking the 'Air Raid Warning Red' message to the operational crew. Not one was to be seen: at the first sound of the siren all had felt an urgent need to visit the lavatory.

After the 'All Clear' there was a distinct sense of anticlimax. The one o'clock news carried a whole series of official announcements, including the news that a War Agricultural Executive Committee had been appointed for each county, an appeal for more midwives in emergency hospitals and an offer of free sand for sandbags to any firm in London which cared to collect it. None of this was very exciting, though it all added up to a picture of a well-prepared nation steadily moving into war, an impression reinforced by the sight of the barrage balloons rising remorselessly into the autumn sky, their silver fabric glittering in the sunshine. To people approaching London from the country these strangely shaped objects, like swollen oval fish with outsize tails, were the first reminder of the capital's vulnerability. By those whom they protected they were often regarded with humorous affection. In Chelsea two local balloons were known as 'Flossie' and 'Blossom', while M.P.s nicknamed the balloons moored behind County Hall on the other side of the river from the Palace of Westminster 'The Bishop of London' and 'Herbert Morrison'. There was some amusement when, after the declaration of war, 'Herbert Morrison' proved reluctant to leave the ground. A balloon based in the recreation ground at Walthamstow was known as 'Bertha' and a local messenger noticed how the 'curious, soft, almost melodic whine' emitted by Bertha's cable in a light breeze, combined with similar sounds from other balloons on a windy night to produce a 'symphonic' result. A London woman writing to an American friend was positively lyrical about the thirty balloons she could see from her window. 'When the sun is low and strikes below them early in the morning and at sunset they gleam like quicksilver, their fins shadowy—fish in a deep-blue sea.'

Some shopkeepers were already involved in the government regulations which were soon to order their business lives. A radio announcement at noon had stated that the 'government's scheme for the distribution of fish comes into operation as from today' and ordered all fishmongers and fish friers (better known outside the trade as the proprietors of fish and chip shops) to report with the permits already issued to previously selected centres. The secretary of one local trade association later described in *The Fish Friers Review* how at Chorley, Lancashire, 'The meeting room was crowded as the clock moved to 2.30, when I realised I was the only official present'—the other officers and committee members being all absent on Civil Defence duties. Eventually he was given a blank cheque to go and purchase fish on behalf of all the members from the distribution depot at St. Helens, but none of the members owned a car. Eventually a wholesaler hired them a van and driver and at 4.30 next morning the secretary set off, after a slight delay when the driver told him 'Go and get thy gas mask', to face their first experience of driving twenty-four miles in the black-out. Rather disappointingly, after all this effort, the government scheme proved a failure. With real news scarce, the shortage of fish and chips in Lancashire due to the government's alleged bungling was the first big story of the war, and the whole elaborate system was scrapped within a fortnight.

Already, after only a few hours of war, a new friendliness was apparent. Suddenly, a Kent woman found, 'we were going into neighbours' houses, speaking to strangers on buses and in the shops'. An artist in Chelsea remarked how 'I saw neighbours who never spoke to each other chatting excitedly. . . . Everyone . . . gathering in small groups to discuss the events of the morning.' In Oldham a headmaster's daughter discovered that, for the first Sunday in memory, the children were allowed to play in the back alleys between the houses and that the adults were so busy chatting that, even more remarkable, no one called them in as darkness fell.

The BBC news at 4.30, as families everywhere were settling down to tea, announced the setting up of a War Cabinet and revealed that the morning's warning had been a false alarm. It reported, too, that 'All places of entertainment will be closed until further notice', including 'indoor and outdoor sports gatherings', that all schools in the evacuation and neutral areas were to be shut for at least a week and that banks and the stock exchange would not re-open until Tuesday. 'Keep off the streets as much as possible', listeners were told. 'Carry your gas masks with you always. Make sure that every member of your household has on them their names and addresses clearly written on an envelope or luggage label.' Most important of all—the announcer's copy of the script still bears his marginal note, 'Slowly and emphatically'—was a warning that 'The amount of lighting on the roads after sunset is still so great as to constitute a grave danger to public security'.

The King's broadcast at 6 p.m., with a recorded repeat later, was universally praised. It marked a new peak in the affection in which the British public held this simple and honourable man, to whom every speech was an ordeal:

> In this grave hour, perhaps the most fateful in our history, I send to every household of my peoples, both at home and overseas, this message. . . . For the sake of all that we ourselves hold dear and of the world's order and peace it is unthinkable that we should refuse to meet the challenge. . . . To this high purpose, I now call my people at home and my peoples across the seas. I ask them to stand firm and united in this time of trial.

Many who missed church that morning felt a sudden need to attend it that night and congregations were good. A seventeen-year-old Birmingham girl was impressed by the rows of gas mask boxes lining the pews at evensong. A Brixton Methodist congregation met for the first time in a downstairs room, as the chapel could not be blacked out. After communion the congregation discussed plans for the future and decided to change the time of the evening service to 4 p.m. The officers of one Congregational church in Hull, who had cancelled evening service for fear of the expected raids, were embarrassed when an exceptionally large number of church members turned up and had to be directed to the rival Methodist establishment across the road, which was packed out.

By now the weather had deteriorated, especially in the North. A woman in Central Scotland was struck by the way in which 'The sky darkened and soon rain was falling in a continual drizzle, as if Nature was joining in our mood of apprehension and uncertainty'. A nurse in a

Clydeside hospital remembers the thunderstorm which hurled rain angrily against the windows that afternoon and the blinding flashes of lightning as the off-duty staff assembled to paste black paper on the panes.

For those at home that evening the highlight of the BBC's programmes was the first instalment of J. B. Priestley's *Let the People Sing*, read by the author, the first novel specially written for radio. The rest of the evening was largely taken up with a service, records and, inevitably, Sandy Macpherson at the theatre organ. In that first week of the war he was to broadcast twenty-three programmes; in the next twenty-two, but his unique contribution to the war effort as one of the few live performers left on the air was not universally appreciated and one listener even wrote unkindly to the BBC: 'I could be reconciled to an air raid, if in the course of it a bomb would fall on Sandy Macpherson and his ever-lasting organ, preferably while he was playing his signature tune.'*

The BBC had planned its programmes to fill in between frequent and, it was expected, dramatic news bulletins, but at six o'clock it had nothing more inspiring to report than 'There is little fresh news from the war zone'. At 7.30 p.m. it was stated that 'it is the official view that since five o'clock France has been at war with Germany', the French government, even more reluctant warriors than the British, having failed to commit themselves unequivocally. At 9 p.m. the nation learned that Australia was at war—'Where Britain stands stand the people of the Empire', her Prime Minister had said—and at 10.30 that Lord Gort had been appointed commander of the British Field Force. Of more interest to most civilians was the news that from the following day 'one grade only of motor spirit will be supplied to the public . . . called "Pool" . . . and on sale . . . at one and six a gallon', with rationing beginning in a fortnight. Broadcasting ended at midnight with *The Londonderry Air*, and one new item of somewhat unmartial information: from the following morning pigs could not be sold for slaughter over a price of thirteen shillings a score, dead weight.

By now the black-out covered the British Isles. Hitler had not after all, come that day, but many went apprehensively to bed, dreading a night attack. To Stuart Hibberd, whose calm, polished voice had brought reassurance into millions of homes, 'London after dark' seemed 'strange and eerie, yet with an unsuspected beauty, the buildings on either side of Portland Place rising like the steep sides of a Norwegian fiord'. As darkness fell the sharp beams of the searchlights, scattered all over the country, began to sweep the night sky, seeking the still expected raiders. In a Cheshire village a café proprietor took her two small boy evacuees from Manchester outside to see the pretty patterns the searchlights formed in the night sky. And so, peacefully, ended the first day of war.

* The organ was in fact destroyed a year later, but Sandy, happily, survived.

# PUT THAT LIGHT OUT!

'In war, one of our great protections against the dangers of air attack after nightfall would be the "black-out".'

*Public Information Leaflet No. 2,* July 1939

The black-out was the first of those shared experiences of wartime which were to unite the nation in a bond of common misfortune. Although practice black-outs had not on the whole been taken very seriously, for months the government had been issuing warnings about the masking of lights when war came. *Public Information Leaflet No. 2,* distributed in July 1939, gave detailed advice to every householder. 'The most convenient way of shutting in the light is to use close fitting blinds', it recommended. 'These can be of any thick, dark coloured material such as dark blue or black or dark green glazed Holland, Lancaster or Italian cloth. If you cannot manage this, you could obscure your windows by fixing up sheets of black paper or thick dark brown paper mounted on battens.' The leaflet also included a helpful recipe for a dye guaranteed to make any material opaque and in the light evenings of that hot summer, particularly after a government warning on 23rd August, millions of men were busy carrying out the directions to take '1 lb of concentrated size, 3 lbs lamp black in powder form, $\frac{1}{2}$ gill of gold size. The size and lamp black should be thoroughly mixed and $2\frac{1}{2}$ gallons of boiling water added. This quantity will cover about 80 square yards of material.'

I can remember painting this repellent-looking mixture on to an old screen, cut down into separate panels to fit the sitting room window, in the small back yard of our tiny council house in Berkshire. The housekeeper of a large castle near Ashford in Kent, part of which went back to medieval times (the Norman cellars later came in useful as a shelter), was meanwhile doing the same in its vast grounds. With an Austrian cook, a refugee from the Nazis, she had rescued from the attic a stock of old bleached linen blinds, edged with attractive crochet lace, to cover the countless windows of the vast house, and watched as the cook stirred the large bowl of black mixture with a walking stick. 'No witches' brew', the housekeeper remembers, 'could ever had had more evil spells cast with every stir in the deep cauldron—venom, hate and misery were mixed into the evil-looking stew.' For months afterwards the formerly immaculate green lawns bore the black marks where the blinds had been laid out to dry in the sunshine.

At the beginning, some optimists insisted, despite official talk of a three-year war, that it would be 'all over by Christmas' and that to take trouble over a permanent black-out was a waste of time and money. But within a few weeks all but the most incorrigibly optimistic had learned that paper tended to tear when put up and taken down daily and window frames ceased to grip drawing pins which were driven into the same corners night after night. Other methods, popular at first, which soon fell into disfavour were removing the bulbs altogether from some rooms, or painting them blue and placing cardboard shades, often made from hatboxes, round the bulbs, but these created such a gloomy impression that most people finally settled for heavy curtains or shutters and adequate light indoors.

The government, with admirable if little-acknowledged foresight, had arranged for the shops to have large stocks of black-out material, usually of heavy sateen, costing about two shillings a yard, but many under-ordered and during the first rush stocks in many places ran out. This provided an early challenge to the ingenuity of wartime housewives. A Darlington woman remembers feeling proud of her thrift when she tacked up an old bed quilt, unfit for further use, over the living room window. Soon, however, the wardens were complaining that they could see light through the threadbare patches and in desperation she was reduced to dyeing a pair of perfectly sound sheets black to replace it. In Stonehaven, Scotland, a young woman remembers that her family were forced to use blankets for the same purpose. A Hertfordshire woman persuaded a local tailor to let her have black lining material, intended for men's dress suits. A Lancashire woman obtained navy blue material used for industrial overalls from a local mill, at fourpence a yard, fastened it across the top of the window with tacks, fixed a towel rail in the hem at the bottom and rolled it up to the top of the window during the day, tying it with tape. When in position it was fastened down the sides to the window frame with snap fasteners—effective but producing a highly claustrophobic feeling. But unless curtains fastened like this or were very generously made they often left a crack of light showing at the sides or bottom and a Birmingham woman remembers her husband spending his first, brief wartime leave pasting three-inch-wide strips of black material round the windows while she, like millions of other wives, was busily sewing new curtains.

The other popular method of blacking-out private houses was by shutters, usually indoors, for it was troublesome to go outside on cold, dark nights to fit external ones, and unless strongly made they tended to warp after the first shower or flap infuriatingly in every gust of wind. Indoors, too, the first flimsy arrangements of paper pinned to light wooden laths were before long replaced by tougher fabrics like calico, nailed to heavy frames. Once properly tailored to fit the window, however— no easy matter with curved bay windows, fanlights and other trouble-spots—such shutters were usually sturdy enough to last right through the war. In my home the single living room was blacked out by four or five shutters held in place by a coiled curtain wire stretched between hooks. As I grew older and taller I found the shutters progressively easier to lift. We made no attempt to black out the bedrooms, going to bed by candle placed well away from the window.

A girl in a Cheshire village remembers how when her father proudly prised their ancient dining room and drawing room shutters apart he discovered that they caught on the central heating radiators, installed since the house was built. It proved easier to lower the radiator legs than to alter the shutters: a really good black-out was too precious to be en-dangered. Constructing a reliable black-out, like making a shelter, provided an eagerly seized chance for home handymen to show their skill—the day of the home handywoman was to come a few years later. A Civil Servant living in a large old house near Ipswich Docks remembers her tennis partner generously offering to make a plywood screen for her large windows. The work was immaculate in conception and execution— except that when the carpenter and his mate knelt to lift the masterpiece into position they found they had nailed it securely to the solid oak floor. It took several hours of effort to free it.

Some women lined their black-out curtains with more cheerful, patterned material. A Birmingham youth club held a competition to see who could produce the brightest black-out curtains, the most popular design consisting of cut-out silver stars, sewn on to the black material. A Sunbury housewife is still proud of the moonlight scene which she created in silver paint on the blind covering her lounge window, while a Cambridge teacher remembers signing her name in white pencil on a friend's black-out, which she used as a form of combined decoration and visitors' book, the signatures later being embroidered on to the cloth.

The backs of plywood and plaster-board shutters often provided an irresistible temptation for wartime humorists and innumerable other graffiti-writers, but they also made useful notice-boards. A boy living in a mining village near Swansea remembers using the cardboard screen in his bedroom for his childish messages.

Blacking out large houses could be a nightmare. The wife of one Cambridgeshire clergyman still remembers realising with horror that their rambling Victorian rectory contained fifty-three windows. Each evening it took her husband a full twenty minutes to tour the house to ensure that the black-out was secure in every room and passage. He was relatively lucky. To black out the tall church-like windows of one Somerset rectory took a full hour. But the house was, his wife remembers, noticeably warmer with all the usual draughts shut out by blinds and shutters.

The daughter of a Sussex farmer remembers making up sateen curtains on her ancient sewing machine and fixing them with rings and hooks to all the windows except the kitchen, which merited an outside shutter, of roofing felt on a wooden frame. 'At first', she remembers, ' "doing the black-outs" was an exciting ritual every evening, but when the novelty wore off it became merely another chore.' An Oxfordshire farmer's wife considered that blacking out their large farmhouse was a work of art, especially in the sitting room, her husband periodically reporting, when he went out to see a sick or calving cow, that a chink of light was showing above the shutters. One night, finding a superintendent of police outside, she fully expected to end up in court and suffer a heavy fine. Instead he had come with the innocent, bucolic enquiry: 'Would you mind asking your husband to let us know when he starts sheep dipping?'

Fear of the police was soon, at least in rural districts, far more effective in producing observance of the black-out than fear of the Germans. A Northamptonshire woman remembers cottages which were only blacked out at the front as they backed on to fields. The daughter of one Sussex farmer admits that when the searchlight station between her home and her parents, house was in action she put on her headlights, reasoning that with 'all the light they were making, my little bit wouldn't be noticed'.

Even in business and industrial premises, thanks to the ample warning given by the government, the black-out was imposed with surprisingly little difficulty. For large firms it was a costly business. The great H.M.V. company estimated that to black-out their factory at Hayes would cost £12,000, while a large City textile firm, with fifty skylights, discovered that it needed altogether 8,000 square yards of material. In many businesses during the early days of the war work was almost suspended while the black-out was being perfected. In cinemas, closed by government order, the staff's work on putting up curtains led to the first demand of the war—a request for trousers instead of their traditional short skirts, for usherettes required to climb ladders. At the Granada, Woolwich, the staff were also entertained as they laboured by tunes on the theatre organ. In danger areas shopkeepers had often already obscured a large part of their windows by sandbags and boards, and everywhere screens were now put up to prevent light from inside the shop escaping through the window. Doorways proved troublesome. The proprietor of a shop in Staines High Street found that large customers often became trapped in the 'air-lock' entrance and needed to be dislodged by a smart push, while others, stuck halfway, would become immovable with laughter.

Even people punctilious about the black-out in their own homes were often careless about it elsewhere. Public houses were the worst sufferers, as cheerful revellers tended to push the black-out aside on leaving. The West End store, Peter Jones, was plagued by thoughtless members of its staff who, failing to find the keys to the cycle-shed in the darkness, tore down the black-out to climb in through the window. Some women customers, too, deposited their handbags on window ledges in the restaurant, thereby disturbing the curtains. The owner of a café in a Cheshire village, a wooden building seventy-two feet long, had a nightly struggle to black-out fourteen large windows, which meant clipping on to the outside of each a wooden frame covered with a tarpaulin. A Scarborough boarding house proprietor discovered she needed fifty-four yards of twill sheeting dyed black and cut into three-yard lengths. She spent the first evening of the war, as her guests had all fled home after Chamberlain's speech that morning, making the material up into curtains on her sewing machine.

At my school in Sussex no attempt was made to black-out the dormitories, which were lit by very faint blue bulbs, while in the centre of the room a 'box' of blankets was constructed round a table, lit by a normal bulb, where the monitor in charge could work at his 'prep'. The school timetable was rearranged, since not all classrooms could be blacked out, with a complicated 'eight day week' to ensure that different lessons were affected every week, and some classes were held in the dayrooms of the houses, which were blacked out, like the favoured classrooms, with heavy plaster board shutters. A rota of boys was responsible for black-out duty and between 'junior' and 'senior' prep on winter evenings the shutters were taken down for a ten-minute ventilation period and fifty boys were expected to sit or stand still in total blackness. This hope often proved illusory and sounds of scuffles and noisy insults echoed through the darkness. A government leaflet, *Ventilation in the Black-out*, recommended a right-angled shelf below the bottom curtain to form a light trap, while a top window was open, and 'a "scuttle" of cloth, rather like a tent ventilator' in the curtains themselves, but most families did not bother with such devices.

When the black-out began, on 1st September 1939, reactions to it varied. One Coulsdon woman remembers thinking that it was sufficient in itself to make life intolerable, 'even without a war to go with it'. An Andover woman, who had entered a cinema in broad daylight that afternoon with her daughter, was astounded to come out into total blackness. 'I felt like rushing back and saying "Oh please let me stop until morning"', she recalls, reliving the unforgettable walk home, colliding with one unseen stranger after another. To some people, especially the young, however, those first blacked-out nights often seemed to possess a holiday atmosphere. A Blackburn woman going home from the cinema on aptly-named 'black Friday', 1st September, joined in an informal sing-song as a crowd of her friends formed up behind a young man who was walking along playing on his mouth-organ a hit tune of the moment, *Aye, Aye, Aye, I like you very much*. A Sheffield housewife shared in the hilarity with which her fellow players greeted the black-out as they emerged into it for the first time that night from a whist-drive—and walked past her own front door three times before recognising it.

The black-out was the first of the great sources of wartime jokes, one of those disagreeable but universal experiences which might as well be laughed at as it could not be remedied. One newspaper started a popular *Heard in the Black-out* feature. A typical anecdote concerned the girl overheard saying in a blacked-out train, 'Take your hand off my knee! Not you, you!' 'I can see a chink in your window', began another comic exchange, to which the reply was 'Can't you recognise the Japanese ambassador when you see him?' An enterprising publisher brought out *The Black-Out Book*, containing 200 pages of puzzles and topical jokes, like the story of the pilot who dropped his parcels of propaganda leaflets on Berlin unopened and was reproved by his superior: 'Good lord, man, you might have killed somebody!' Another current joke concerned the policeman who shone his torch on a couple in a darkened shop doorway and asked 'What do you think you're doing in there?' On a nervous male voice answering, 'Er, nothing, constable', the policeman was said to have replied, 'Then come out here and hold my torch, while I take over!' There were innumerable jokes about wardens and police who stooped to detect cracks of light under windows, and many people claim to have made the classic retort, 'You expecting the Germans to come by submarine?' Relatively daring for the time were jokes about the probable rise in the birth rate due to the black-out and its popularity with lovers which tended to get coarser as the war progressed. A typical black-out sketch in one amateur pantomime about 1943 ended with one character asserting that nothing had happened in an encounter in the black-out, and another declaring 'Oh yes it did!' and producing a pair of panties.

Although for most adults adjustment to the black-out took months, children often became at home in the darkness far more quickly. In one Cambridgeshire village the children played 'ghosts' in the churchyard, emerging silently from behind the gravestones to frighten passengers alighting at a nearby bus-stop. In Peckham two youths caused near panic by drawing skeletons in luminous paint on their dark clothing. In

West Hampstead the favourite evening amusement of one girl and her friend was 'Your black-out is showing'. They would tour the district after dark in search of the faintest streak of light, then gleefully rouse the occupants of the offending house. Most were grateful, but they were occasionally met with slammed doors and abuse. Full compensation came one day when they discovered a huge coal fire blazing in the empty house of a neighbour, who had gone out and forgotten it. 'This we pounced upon with great excitement', she remembers, and the fire brigade had to be called to force an entry and put the fire out.

Many people discovered during the war, for the first time in their lives, the beauty of the night sky. An Essex woman remembers on such nights dismissing the warnings of the pessimists that ' "They'll be able to see where they're dropping 'em!" When', she remembers, 'the town was bathed in moonlight and one could see the clouds and midnight blue of the sky everything took on an aura of mystic beauty. I even enjoyed the long walk home after a tiring late shift at the factory . . . I would drink in the sudden beauty which the moon could give to the unlovely buildings and bomb-scarred streets. We were . . . starved of beauty. Everything was hard, unreal, boarded up and shut off.'

The only group, apart from lovers and criminals, to welcome the black-out were those who developed an interest in astronomy, for the new darkness revealed many stars hitherto concealed by the urban glow. A fourteen-year-old Walthamstow schoolboy, who had managed to enrol as an A.R.P. messenger by producing a forged letter of consent from his father, discovered that 'an amateur astronomer was looked upon as a crank in those days, but . . . all the leg pulling of my comrades was more than compensated for by a couple of hours observing on the top of the Wardens' Post or an exciting glimpse of a planet or constellation I'd not hitherto seen, rising just before dawn'. He spent many fine nights observing the craters and mountains of the moon—and eventually obtained, 'for the then enormous sum of £4 10s. 0d. an old brass push-pull three tube telescope' from a shady shop which, he suspected, obtained its goods from looted bombed premises.

If the first great wartime shortage was of black-out material, the second was the disappearance from the shops of electric torches and even more of torch batteries. The greatest demand was for the small round torch to fit in handbag or pocket and throughout the war the No. 8 battery, which fitted it, remained scarce. At first the use of torches was, in theory, banned in the open but from 13th September it became legal to shine a torch provided it was pointed downwards and the glass was masked by two thicknesses of tissue paper, reducing the beam to a diffused glow. This added immeasurably to the ease of getting about on foot and the battery shortage, especially of the popular No. 8 size, was a gift to comedians. 'Heard about the prizes in the raffle?', ran a typical story. 'The third prize was a radio, the second a bicycle, and the first was a torch battery.'

The battery shortage affected cyclists worst, for rear lamps as well as front ones had, for the first time, become compulsory on the outbreak of war; previously a reflector on the rear mudguard had been sufficient. The police still prosecuted offenders, but the magistrates often took a lenient view. A Suffolk girl summonsed for cycling without a light, who explained to the court that she had been unable to obtain a battery for her lamp and had to get home from Ipswich at night or her parents would deduce the worst, was fined eightpence. She paid the fine with a shilling, cheekily telling the clerk to 'Keep the change!'

At first, too, smokers had a hard time. Anyone smoking in the street was liable to be assailed by shouts of 'Put that cigarette out!' and some smokers were actually prosecuted. Here, too, commonsense later prevailed and for most of the war a smoker who did not actually strike a succession of matches in the street during a warning was unlikely to get into trouble.

But despite the increasing tolerance shown over lights in the street, the black-out was still rigorously enforced on householders and both police and wardens soon became thoroughly unpopular for their excessive zeal in hunting down trifling breaches of the law. There was, of course, little as yet to keep the A.R.P. services occupied, while their paid idleness was bitterly resented by a large part of the population. More important still, in the opinion of a Nottingham woman, on whose door the wardens knocked angrily three nights in succession at the start of the war, wartime camaraderie between officials and public had yet to be born. At the start of the war the courts were choked with black-out cases. In Oxford alone there were forty in one week in October, a city where, as it happened, not a single bomb was to fall. A girl in Bournemouth, a town crammed with evacuated businesses and wealthy refugees, absentmindedly switched on the light before pulling her bedroom curtains. Instantly the doorbell rang and a policeman pushed past her, taking the stairs two at a time, and switching off the light without a word. Later she was fined five shillings for the offence and, seeing it recorded in the local newspaper, felt, she admits, 'like a fifth columnist'. Rotherham was another place where many inhabitants thought the wardens over-zealous. One girl remembers the irate exchanges in the darkness of the road outside, the wardens bellowing 'Get that b—— light out!', while the culprits made an equally vigorous reply. Even the clergy found it hard to maintain a charitable demeanour on such occasions. *The Times* reported that one rector near Bletchley, when challenged for showing a light visible twenty yards away, had shouted at a special constable, 'Go away, you brute, you scoundrel!'—an outburst which cost him a £3 fine. Everywhere the cry of 'Put that light out!' echoed down the darkened streets and lanes. A Walthamstow engineer returned home from A.R.P. duty to find two special constables on hands and knees outside his front door, so engrossed in agreeing that 'That ruddy light is too bright', that they failed even to notice when he joined them on the ground.

A Yorkshire farmer remembers the police calling about a light said to appear every night over his buildings, which turned out to be the evening star. An Islington teacher remembers a warden calling at her wartime billet near Hitchin, to complain of the bright light shining in her window which was, she discovered, the reflection of the full moon in the glass. A Hull woman rejoiced in the discomfiture of a warden who was unable to find the light he alleged she was showing, as, he explained, 'I haven't got my torch with me.'

Even when the public were co-operative—and some were for ever denouncing their neighbours—police and wardens had a thankless job. A Shropshire special constable, who was also the village grocer, found that the first five people he had to report for black-out offences were all his customers, the fifth being an obstreperous motorist who had driven down the main street of Oswestry with his head-lamps full on and who threatened: 'If you book me my wife will never come into your shop again!' He soon found he had mistaken his man and was promptly charged, not merely with the original offence but with obstruction and using foul language as well.

A sizeable minority, whether from stupidity, obstinacy or a love of being awkward, seemed determined not to accept the black-out without a struggle. One Sussex preparatory school matron insisted that she had no time to do the black-out until the boys were in bed, and she had had her supper, and fixed her private black-out at 10.30 p.m. irrespective of when darkness fell. As the dormitory wing was on high ground and had rows of picture windows, so that the light from it dominated the countryside, the school was fined several times. But the matron was too valuable to lose; she remained. A Leytonstone girl was deeply embarrassed by her ninety-six-year-old grandmother who simply ignored the black-out, cheerfully lighting a candle with the curtains drawn back. To her daughter's remonstrances about the warden she would simply retort, 'I'd like to know what he thinks he will do with me', until the warden himself abandoned the struggle. Some elderly people even managed to remain blithely unaware of the black-out. An L.M.S. booking clerk remembers an old lady asking at the booking office, at the height of the war, for a through ticket from Derby to Blackpool to see the illuminations.

Many wardens and police, during their long night vigils, were probably in search of company and conversation rather than, as some disgruntled citizens darkly suggested, promotion. The night sister in a Nottingham hospital was puzzled when night after night a policeman called around 4 a.m. to complain about a non-existent chink of light until he asked pointedly, 'You do have your tea about now, don't you?', and she took the hint. The wife of a Surrey dentist, who often worked with him into the early hours of the morning in their garage workshop, found that a warden or policeman would regularly call around 1 a.m., nominally to check the black-out but in fact for a hot drink and a warm. The hour bred confidences; one police sergeant revealed that he had a hundredweight of sugar and other goods, illicitly obtained, stored at his house, as he was determined that his daughter, a student nurse, should have enough to eat.

At first there was no street lighting, no lights in trains and very little light on motor vehicles, but in mid-September the rules for both road and rail travel were slightly relaxed. Just before Christmas the government authorised 'diffused' street lighting, more expressively known as 'glimmer' or 'pin-prick' lighting, which gave a pale glow round the base of the few lamp-posts on which it was installed. In most streets the only light came from the small, shielded crosses of colour of the traffic lights and, during business hours only, the 'Open' signs, often consisting of letters cut out in the side of a biscuit tin, in the doorways of shops and pubs. In December 1939 some modest concessions for shop window lighting were also allowed.

Opinion as to whether the black-out was worse in the town or the country was divided. In the town there were innumerable hazards, like kerbs, lamp-posts, pillar boxes, sandbags, the corners of buildings and, most dangerous of all, carelessly parked bicycles. Most permanent obstructions were, however, given lavish bands of white paint, which was also compulsory on the bumpers and running boards of motor vehicles. In the country these dangers were lacking, but there was no footpath to follow, and other perils unknown in town, such as straying cattle. The shortage of torch batteries caused special problems too. A Suffolk woman dreaded having to fetch coal from an outhouse or visit the ancient lavatory at the end of the garden without a torch for guidance. A torchless West Country landgirl recalls finding her way home by the faint glimmer of a handful of glow-worms, placed on the mirror from her handbag—a device reminiscent of a Hardy novel.

Most people were probably at some time lost in the black-out. A young Aberdeen wife remembers that, though nothing stronger than tea was served, several people walked straight out of a dance held in a hall in the middle of a park and into the adjoining pond. An Essex woman, after crossing a wide road and missing the other side completely, ended up 'paddling' in a stream some distance away down a side road. A Hertfordshire teacher, recovering from the birth of her baby in a temporary hutted hospital, remembers her husband losing his way in the extensive grounds in the black-out after a visit and only escaping by climbing an eight-foot-high gate. A South Norwood housewife was horrified to discover in Woolworths one Saturday afternoon that it had grown dark and she could not remember how many steps there were from the door to the pavement, so she asked a soldier, ' "Please would you let me take your arm going down the steps?" He was', she recalls, 'only too happy to oblige, soldiers being what they are.' The warden of a rest home for war workers in an eighteenth-century mansion in Shropshire once found himself hopelessly lost in the grounds. The trees and shrubs which had earlier looked so friendly now seemed sinister and the screechings and rustlings in the foliage and undergrowth were far more unnerving than the air raid noises to which he had grown accustomed in London. After tripping over a root and breaking his most precious purchase, an egg, he was finally put on the right path by a G.I. and his girl, a courting couple trespassing in search of privacy. A Red Cross worker in Hertfordshire remembers losing all sense of direction between the doors of an evacuated hospital and the gates, and her sense of bewilderment as she felt grass instead of gravel underfoot. I once became totally lost within seconds of leaving the school library and did not even know in which direction to walk back to my own house, a journey I had made twice daily for years, and having located the avenue of residential houses by the noise of boys talking, I was forced to wait in the darkness until one came within touching distance to identify the house concerned. It was in fact my own, but even after six years I could not recognise it in the dark.

It is hard for anyone who did not experience the total darkness of those wartime nights to comprehend the sense of isolation, verging on panic, that could so easily descend if one missed one's way. One could often hear solitary male figures swearing aloud in the darkness as they groped for some clue to their whereabouts, while many women admit to being reduced to tears. A Darlington woman found herself circling round and round a green after leaving a shop, unable to get across it and back to her house. She was sobbing from frustration when she finally identified it. A Dulwich man remembers following an elderly woman along a cemetery wall with buttresses protruding from it and hearing her, as she just missed bumping into each one, politely apologising, 'I am sorry, I do beg your pardon.'

But however cautiously one moved it was almost impossible to avoid an occasional accident. In towns, trolley buses, long known as 'the silent peril', were particularly dangerous; the old-fashioned tram, with its noisy approach, was far less troublesome. In the country it was reckless to walk several abreast. The black-out led to an upsurge in deaths from drowning, especially as, after the great fire raids of 1940 and 1941, the number of deep water tanks multiplied. At Leith in Scotland, so many foreign seamen fell into the docks when returning to their ships at the curfew hour of 10 p.m., that it was extended until midnight, to give them time to sober up after the pubs closed, and finally to 5 a.m.

A Cardiff woman who stumbled over a low wall in pitch darkness found herself crunching through apparently endless bushes of chrysanthemums supported by sticks. She realised later how furious the owners of the garden must have been at the ruin she left behind, but was angry enough herself at having torn her clothes, and ruined a precious pair of rationed stockings. A Nottinghamshire housewife's technique of carefully following the kerb edge led her at different times into the drive of a large mansion, into a public house, and into various back gardens. She still blushes at the memory of the unladylike things she said to some other pedestrians and remembers, during a lapse into politeness, apologising to a pillar box.

The black-out became the classic excuse for any minor injury. A Darlington bus conductress, who ran full face into a pillar box when hurrying to her voluntary work as an auxiliary nurse, turned up for work next day with broken glasses and a black eye. 'I was kidded terribly', she remembers. A woman warden in Putney who fell down a public staircase in the black-out and fractured her right shoulder blade escaped with far slighter injuries when she was bombed out and debris and glass were scattered all over her.

Alone, and perhaps lost, in the darkness, it was often difficult not to feel frightened, not merely of human but of supernatural adversaries. A Battersea bus driver, going on early turn, had a shock on seeing a white figure walking through a churchyard towards him. It proved to be a baker, covered in flour after his night's work, taking a short cut home. A Greenock postwoman was terrified on her way to work in the small hours of a dark and windy morning by someone apparently following her, who stopped whenever she did. At last she plucked up courage and turned to face him, only to be confronted by a large sheet of brown paper blowing along the pavement.

Taking the dog for a bedtime walk was a custom endangered by the dark nights, for in the darkness a cunning animal could prove remarkably elusive while a lead might trip up passers-by. One Dunfermline family solved the problem of retrieving their small black Scots terrier by fixing a bell to her collar.

The black-out also aided those carrying on an illicit affair. A Sevenoaks woman remembers so hastily turning away to avoid running into her boss, in the company of his secretary, that she walked head-on into a lamp post and ended up in hospital. She bears the scars she suffered for discretion to this day. Other beneficiaries were the makers of luminous buttons, luminous arm-bands, luminous artificial flowers, and luminous discs for electric torches, supposed to give a phosphorescent glow even when the precious battery was switched off, and all in my experience totally useless.

The government tried to mitigate the effects of the black-out by shortening the hours it was in force rather than by relaxing the regulations. From 3rd November 1939, each night's black-out was cut by an hour, so that it now ran from half-an-hour after sunset until half-an-hour before sunrise and later, during the summer months, these periods were extended by a further fifteen minutes. Summer time, due to end on 8th October 1939, was first extended to 19th November and then reintroduced on 25th February 1940 for the rest of the war. The hours of daylight at the end of the day were lengthened still further by Double Summer Time, which put the clocks forward for a second hour from May to August in 1941, and from the beginning of April to mid-August from 1942 to 1944. Double Summer Time ended for the last time on 15th July 1945, and the clocks finally went back, for the first time in five years, on 7th October that year.

Double Summer Time had some curious results. A Newbury munitions worker remembers the strange feeling of walking off the tennis court in the light at a quarter to eleven in the evening. A Stafford scoutmaster remembers struggling to get boys to bed in camp at 10 p.m. when it was still broad daylight. Often camps solved the problem by instituting their own Camp Time, normal Greenwich Time, which ignored the government's manipulation of the clocks, for in high summer it was not really dark until after midnight.

Some farmers simply ignored the change in the clocks. One housewife with three grown-up sons was for ever cooking meals, for one worked for a farmer who kept 'God's time', the second for another farmer, who preferred 'Single Summer Time', and the third was the village postman who had to conform to the official government time. A Poole warden has not forgotten the cry from the heart of one puzzled G.I., seeking privacy for himself and the girl on his arm: 'Say, warden, doesn't it ever get dark in this goddam country?'

# REGISTER FOR EVACUATION NOW!

'Some children may try your patience by wetting their beds, but do not scold or punish; as this will only make matters worse.'

W.V.S. leaflet, *Information for Householders Taking Evacuees.*

July 1944

For hundreds of thousands of families the war began, not with the black-out at sunset on Friday 1st September, but before sunrise. The start of evacuation had been announced on the radio the day before and in the residential streets of the great cities soon after dawn mothers were packing into small cases the garments lovingly cleaned and pressed over the last few days. A Jewish mother in Clapton, East London, remembers the 'terrible task' of waking her two small daughters at 5.30 in the morning and the tears of the eight-year-old; her sister, a year older, took it well. An hour or two later, as the children marched off with their school their parents watched, stunned, wondering if they would ever see them again. That Friday morning, in an equal number of other homes in quieter parts of the country, other women, almost as deeply moved, were beginning their very different preparations, dusting out the spare room or looking out their own children's discarded toys.

The government had decided that evacuation should be voluntary but that billeting should, if necessary, be compulsory. Although few people wanted to accommodate adults, there was, in 1939, little difficulty in finding foster-homes for children. The woman M.P. who told of women in moorland villages in Durham 'who went home weeping because they had not had a child allocated to them', the male M.P. who des-cribed seeing 'a regular fight' on the platform of a North Wales station as two would-be hosts competed for the privilege of taking in two small boys from Liverpool, were not exaggerating. The arrival of the evacuees at Luton was typical. The first arrivals, from Walthamstow, that Friday found the Mayor, the Town Clerk and the Chief Constable waiting at the L.M.S. station to welcome them, while as the first party of four hundred mothers and children from the East End walked down the streets the Luton housewives poured out of their front doors to carry the mothers' luggage and to press cups of milk upon the children.

Many schools had been assembling the children every morning for the past week to keep them together, and one helper at a North London infant and junior school believes she will never get out of her ears the chorus of *Ten Green Bottles*, sung by hundreds of five- to twelve-year-olds as they sat on the floor of the school hall during these days of waiting. The departure when it actually came was, by universal agreement, a model of efficiency. Usually the children were mustered in the playground, parents being asked to stay outside, then each school set off for the station led by a 'marked man', often the caretaker, carrying a placard giving its name and reference number. The effort involved was prodigious. Seventy-two London transport stations were involved, and in four days the main-line railway companies carried more than 1,300,000 official evacuees, in nearly 4,000 special trains. The famous red London buses were also busy, transporting nearly 230,000 passengers to London stations or to their wartime homes. Some bus-drivers went for thirty-six hours without sleep, while a teacher visiting an L.C.C. education office in North London was shocked to find the usually immaculate staff 'absolutely exhausted, working round the clock in shirt sleeves and unshaved'.

The hardest burden of all that day fell on the parents and many comforted themselves with small details, like the fact that their daughter looked proud of her new gas mask case, or their son seemed thrilled to have secured his favourite front seat upstairs on the bus. A teacher who escorted an Islington school to Northampton remembers one six-year-old girl innocently asking, 'Why are some mummies crying?', and being satisfied with the explanation, 'Because they can't come on holiday with us too.' The escorting teachers were more apprehensive, for none, apart from schools which had made their own arrangements in advance, knew where they were going until they arrived. The teachers at a Muswell Hill boys' grammar school passed the journey in speculation on this subject, Cambridge being the popular choice. They found themselves instead at St. Neots, which none of them had ever heard of, and were then hurried further into the country to the village of Buckden, five miles from Huntingdon, 'to the increasing horror of 250 boys and staff'. The billeting officers and hosts awaiting them at the local rifle range were almost equally appalled; *they* were expecting two hundred junior girls. Meanwhile the old, empty grammar school at Huntingdon, for which they had been destined, was occupied by a girls' school from Highbury. In villages round Charing, Kent, the authorities were equally nonplussed when six hundred girls and staff of the Mary Datchelor School descended upon them; they had expected seven elementary schools. The headmistress saw her pupils disperse 'in drizzling rain and gathering gloom to their unknown villages'; it was not for a fortnight that they were reunited in Ashford, and not for some time after that that the last four girls were finally located.

The railways were during these days crowded with military traffic and most journeys, as well as being mysterious, were extremely slow. A Liverpool teacher, travelling with ninety children who had assembled at 10 a.m., found that they did not reach their destination, Cleobury Mortimer in Shropshire, until 7.30 p.m. A London woman felt hours after joining a train at Vauxhall that they must be at least in Devon, and was highly disappointed to realise that they were being unloaded in Reading, only forty miles away. But the slow journey did provide an opportunity for many teachers, travelling with strange schools, to get to know their new pupils. One woman escorting an Islington Roman Catholic school was astounded at their poverty; most lacked suitcases and had brought their scanty spare clothing with them in pillow slips and cushion covers. A master travelling with a Liverpool school was equally shocked by his boys' ignorance of the countryside. They enlivened the journey by arguing whether the animals to be seen from the train were pigs or sheep.

Many unfortunate children and escorts travelled in non-corridor coaches and arrived damp, soiled or, at best, uncomfortable. In at least one case the lack of a lavatory decided the destination of the train. Part of a West Ham school, travelling to Somerset, rebelled halfway and were instead unloaded at Wantage.

The protracted journey had another unforeseen result; some of the children, more from boredom than unhappiness, passed the time writing pathetic messages on the printed, franked postcards issued to them to notify their new address. 'Dear Mam, I want to come home. Pleas come and tack us home', reads one surviving card, duly delivered next morning to a Liverpool mother. Only the postmark enlightened Mam as to her children's whereabouts. The writer had forgotten to include his address. 'Dear Mum, I hope you are well', ran another card. 'I don't like the man's face. I don't like the lady's face much. Perhaps it will look better in daylight. I like the dog's face best.'

Bus journeys, though shorter, presented a different problem. An eleven-year-old Gravesend girl travelling to Sudbury in Suffolk remembers that the whole bus load were sick. A fourteen-year-old Bradford girl remembers a similar journey by 'sharra'—charabanc—to Nelson, with the party singing *Run Rabbit Run* and *Umbrella Man*. They reached the reception centre, a chapel hall, at two o'clock and, she remembers, 'chaos reigned. Four hundred boys and girls of all ages were assembled . . . tots of five, pimply adolescents of sixteen . . . No one seemed to know what to do . . . Well-meaning women rushed about . . . A few hosts turned up and hovered around the edges of the unruly assembly . . .

"Oh, let us have him", pointing to a curly-haired cherub, or "We really want an eight-year-old girl to play with our Madge." . . . Adolescents, perhaps understandably, were not in great demand.'

Few people who witnessed it have forgotten the arrival of the evacuees. I can vividly remember the crocodile of small children, laden with cases and gas masks, filing out of Newbury station and walking two by two up the road to the reception centre at the nearby council school. Some carried buckets and spades, for, to ease the pain of parting, their mothers had assured them that they were going to the seaside.

Many people still have bitter memories of the 'slave market', at which they were allocated to foster-parents—in one Lincolnshire town the cattle market was actually used as a distribution centre. A couple who took eighty children from Wembley to a village near Chard in Somerset noticed how the largest were immediately chosen by farmers needing unpaid help, the smallest being left to last. A thirteen-year-old Girl Guide in the village of High Broome, near Tunbridge Wells, noticed that smartly dressed little girls were soon 'spoken for', but 'a small tousled-haired boy, trousers too big, socks round his ankles, threadbare shirt and jacket and a small paper parcel of his belongings tied to his gas mask case', remained unclaimed for a long time.

The 'slave market' method at least avoided the sad trudge from door to door in search of a welcoming home. An Islington teacher was moved by the sight of a five-year-old girl, who had kept cheerful all day, finally sinking down on the kerb of a Northampton street in tears, and not even being consoled by the bar of chocolate in her bag. Before long, however, 'that lost feeling was cuddled away by the warm-hearted "aunt"'. Visiting her charges later that evening, the same teacher found them all happily tucked up in bed.

This was the general experience. The nation's mothers revealed on the 1st September 1939, and the days immediately following it, a warmth and good nature towards other people's children that many of their guests still recall with affection nearly thirty years later. The inevitable childish accidents were accepted with exemplary patience. The daughter-in-law of a Yorkshire country vicar, then aged sixteen, recalls the arrival of two small girls, aged eleven and seven, from Sunderland. They were very clean and well-behaved—'especially selected for the Vicarage', she suspects—but the excitement, or the contrast between the vicarage food and their usual diet of pie and chips and bread and jam, proved too much for the younger one, who was immediately sick on the dining-room carpet. Both soon improved enormously in health and became much-loved members of the family, keeping in touch until they married.

Placings with unmarried women were often surprisingly successful. At Combe Raleigh, Devon, one billeting officer placed, with some misgivings, a three-year-old toddler with three elderly maiden ladies. On arrival he stood solemnly gazing round at his new home with tears pouring down his cheeks and announced: 'My name is Robert; I am a big boy and I don't cry—well, not often.' Within a few months he was idolised by the whole household and when his mother eventually came to see him she was horrified when at bedtime he knelt down and prayed: 'O God, don't let this woman take me away; she says she's my mother, but I want to stay here with my aunties.'

Since the poorest families were least able to make private arrangements for their families, the evacuees included an exceptionally large number of ragged and neglected children. A Dorset woman, then aged seventeen, remembers going with her mother to collect two evacuees from the railway waiting room at Sherborne at ten o'clock on a wet, cold, dark night. The two little sisters, aged five and seven, whom they took home were cold, frightened and crying and, once in the light, proved also to be filthy and in rags. When they took the children to the bathroom, they were greeted with hysterics, the girls imagining that they were about to be drowned. Next morning, their hostess, by no means well-off, bought them both a completely new outfit and the children became contented members of the family, particularly delighting in frequent baths. When, a year later, they were finally removed after the government had begun to press the parents for a contribution to their support, 'I do not know who cried most, us or the children', their hostess recalls.

There were many such successes, but, understandably, it was the failures which made the headlines. The commonest complaint was of bed-wetting. A leading article in *The Lancet* remarked that, 'Somewhat unexpectedly enuresis has proved to be one of the major menaces to the comfortable disposition of evacuated urban children. . . . Every morning every window is filled with bedding, hung out to air in the sunshine.' Official estimates of the number of children afflicted varied from 4 to 33 per cent and the constant washing of bedding soon represented a serious burden on many a housewife. Ministers drawn from a world where laundry was left to the servants were slow to act. It was not for months that hostels were opened for incurable bed-wetters and not until June 1940 that a modest allowance, of around three-and-sixpence a week, was approved for householders with enuretic evacuees.

Even more widespread than wet beds were vermin-infested heads. In parts of Wales, half the evacuees from Merseyside had heads crawling with lice, and rural Scotland, suffering an invasion from Glasgow, had a similar experience. In part of Wigtown, in Scotland, the medical officer, aided by three detachments of V.A.D.s, resourcefully bought up all the hair clippers in sight and cut the hair of every mother and child in a particularly verminous detachment of Glaswegians. One aristocratic hostess was said to have driven her evacuees through the sheep dip. 'The only subject of conversation on market day was the best method of delousing', a woman doctor wrote to *The Lancet* from Northallerton, suffering an invasion of evacuees from Gateshead and Leeds. A Saxmundham, Suffolk, woman found herself going out to dinner with her husband when both smelt of some 'particularly strong-smelling liquid' with which the household had been drenched by 'some official female' as part of the great battle against nits. 'We wondered whether to say merrily we had just been drenched or pretend we always smelt like that', she remembers.

Many evacuees, too, came from homes where no sentence was complete without a swear word. One teacher remembers a two-year-old boy scandalising a Cambridgeshire village by leaning from a front window shouting words never heard there from such tender lips before. 'He said F', an outraged woman reported to her. A W.V.S. Billeting Officer in Cornwall had to cope with an angel-faced five-year-old from an Irish docker's family in the East End of London who electrified a respectable farmer's family by casually remarking when she dropped a fork, 'Blast the f—ing b——!' When reproved she retorted, 'I'll tell my dad about you and he'll come and knock your bleeding block off.'

Another common complaint was of the inadequate and unsuitable clothes in which many children had been sent away. Some had been sewn into their clothes for the winter or encased in a layer of brown paper near the skin as a substitute for warm underclothes. A nurse living in the Rhondda was surprised on preparing to give her five-year-old evacuee a bath to be told by his mother, 'Bill don't want a bath, as I've plastered him up for the winter.'

The most widespread problem of all was providing the evacuees with proper footwear. 'Boot funds' for poor children were still a commonplace in 1939 and innumerable evacuees arrived with cracked and broken shoes quite inadequate for country roads—Liverpool, the subject of so many critical stories, earning the nickname of 'the plimsoll city'. Eventually the Ministry of Health began, in great secrecy, to disgorge funds to local authorities to make good the worst deficiencies but often it was the foster-parents who paid.

Parents' weekend visits provided another source of expense. Even in towns in 1939 it was often not easy to find somewhere to eat on a Sunday and in many villages disconsolate groups of temporarily reunited parents and children could be seen standing miserably about, unfed, on the village green until the invaluable W.V.S. and public-spirited organisations like Rotary equipped village halls as meeting places.

As with the children, it was the unsatisfactory minority of parents who attracted attention. A woman in a village near Skipton had to welcome no fewer than seven relatives of one of her evacuees from Bradford, and two of the other, the first weekend. A Mansfield woman, caring for a ten-year-old girl, was surprised to find her evacuee's mother taking sixteen other women on a conducted tour of the house. They had visited other houses where their daughters were billeted but had graciously decided, they informed her, that hers was the best.

To some unlucky foster-parents it began to seem in those first, disillusioning weeks that life in the back streets of London and other large towns could hardly have changed since Dickensian times. It was, perhaps, the beginning of that great movement of opinion towards social reform that was to gather momentum throughout the war. At the time, however, the predominant emotion was horror. Soon everyone in the reception areas had an evacuee story, just as later everyone in the blitzed cities had a bomb story. At Warminster, Wiltshire, one boy who refused to eat his food at one meal and had it set before him a second time soundly abused his hosts, ending, 'Now hit me and I'll fetch a copper.' In Blaenavon in Monmouthshire two small girl evacuees caused great amusement by asking their hosts as they prepared to go out for a walk on the first evening if, like mum and dad, they were going out to get drunk. The sober Welsh couple caring for them there were less amused on their return home; the girls had stripped the wallpaper from the wall, explaining that their mother always did this in a new house to see if there were bugs behind it. A small boy in Oxford astonished the two respectable elderly ladies who had taken him in by helpfully remarking after supper that he would put himself to bed, 'so you two old geezers can get off to the boozer'.

More serious was the dishonesty in which some parents had deliberately trained their children. A Mansfield hostess was shattered, when taking her ten-year-old evacuee shopping for embroidery silks in Woolworths, to have a handful dropped into her basket, with the explanation, 'That's the way you do shopping, buy one or two, drop them when the assistant gets your change, then grab a handful.' Another evacuee, sent shopping in Eastbourne, returned proudly with both goods and money; he had stolen everything on his list. A third fried his hosts' tropical goldfish, worth £25, to eat.

The restricted diet of many children from the cities was also a revelation to their hosts. In Eastbourne many children firmly refused chicken, demanding their usual fish and chips instead. A Dorchester woman's chief memory of evacuees is of their sitting on the well-scrubbed doorsteps of this respectable town eating fish and chips from newspaper. A farmer's wife in Perthshire who provided a chicken for her evacuees from Glasgow was astonished when, after asking suspiciously what it was, they pushed their plates away, announcing, 'We dinna like a hen wi''

parritch in it. Tak' it awa an" gi'e us a richt denner, sausages or somethin'.'
A Liverpool teacher accommodated two brothers who, never having seen
an egg before, attempted to eat one shell and all.

The evidence is unanimous that Roman Catholic evacuees were by
far the dirtiest, the most ragged and, since they tended to come in large
family groups, the hardest to place. The contingents of ill-disciplined
and neglected Catholics from over-large families in the slums of Liverpool,
Glasgow and London's dockland who descended upon various Protestant areas might have been designed to confirm the inhabitants in their
distrust of Rome, and to discredit its teachings on birth-control. For a
Billeting Officer in a village near Thame in Oxfordshire the neglect that
forty Roman Catholic children from Tower Hill in the charge of two
nuns had suffered was symbolised by the uncut toe-nails of the seven-
year-old boy she took in, which were 'turned up . . . like little horns'.
The school moved on before long as the village could not cope with
'their Catholic requirements', for even teachers indifferent to their
pupils' physical well-being were punctilious about the observance of
their religious duties.

Jewish evacuees, by contrast, caused little trouble. One East London
mother remembers appreciatively that in Biggleswade at least there were
Hebrew classes for Jewish children and the usual Sabbath services, while
Jewish festivals such as the Passover were observed as usual. In Chertsey,
Surrey, the foster-mother of a ten-year-old Jewish boy from the East
End discovered that he kept a huge, razor-sharp knife under his pillow.
Having read of the German atrocities against his race, he was afraid
his turn might come next. A Devon woman found her two German boys,
aged eleven and twelve, 'a very odd mixture—arrogant and yet pitifully
humble'. The older, when offered pocket money, retorted rudely,
'We don't want charity from you', and would accept it only as a loan
to be repaid when he was grown up. The younger asked her privately,
'Does anyone listen at the door or look in at the window?', and she had
to take him all round the house to reassure him. At the end of the tour he
picked up a copy of *Punch* and asked, 'So, please may I laugh at this
picture of Hitler?'

Coloured children in 1939 were welcomed as an intriguing novelty.
Two small coloured brothers were the first non-whites one Welsh
mining village had ever seen but they were accepted without hesitation
and became general favourites. A Nottingham woman found their few
coloured evacuees seemed far less foreign than the white children
from Hackney, whose speech was almost unintelligible.

The coming of the evacuees widened horizons in other ways also. A
sixteen-year-old Hereford girl remembers admiring the newcomers,
because they were independent of their parents and had come from the

sophisticated big city. The children in a Northamptonshire village were, one then aged ten remembers, very impressed by a senior girl's school from Clapton. 'They knew about film-stars, shops and clothes . . . They taught us rhymes . . . and to yodel in a peculiar way that the adults called cat-calling and annoyed them intensely.' A nine-year-old child 'privately' evacuated to Mansfield in Nottinghamshire to stay with an older cousin was made much of as the only London child attending one local school. The headmistress detailed other children to carry her books, and she was also allowed to miss lessons to gather lettuce leaves from the kitchen garden for the school pet, because 'I don't suppose our little evacuee from London has ever *seen* a rabbit before'.

Only occasionally did jealousy blossom between hosts and guests. One six-year-old girl in Sussex caused great embarrassment to her parents by remarking of their twelve-year-old evacuees: 'You like that one better, but I prefer this one!' She consolidated her unpopularity with the two girls by 'splitting' on them to her mother, a strict sabbatarian, for playing tennis in the garden one Sunday evening. A small boy in a Welsh mining village, the idolised baby of the family, did his best to make life unpleasant for the fourteen-year-old evacuee from Chatham who joined the family, his offence in being there at all being heightened by his having the unusual name of Bramwell. In one Lancashire household there were bitter quarrels between the ten-year-old daughter of the house and a girl evacuee of the same age. When the evacuee spilled her tea her hostess's daughter sneered, 'You ought to live with pigs', to which the evacuee smartly riposted, 'Oh, but I do now'.

Although many evacuated children took jobs locally on leaving school the majority never adjusted very enthusiastically to rural life. The then headmistress of the Mary Datchelor Girl's Grammar School, evacuated from Camberwell to Kent and then, in 1940, to South Wales, was amused that as the coach loads of girls drove through the streets of the industrial town of Llanelly they greeted with cheers such signs of civilisation as cinemas and Woolworths. A woman living in the Dorset village of Piddletrenthide noted that the 'vacs' from a Southampton school asked immediately where these essential amenities were, and on finding them missing, went home again in six weeks. Even those who had spent nights on end in shelters, neglected by working mothers, pleaded to return, preferring raid-smitten Southampton to the quiet of village life.

With some obvious exceptions, children were in general welcome, at least in 1939, but few hosts wanted adults to share their homes. A Suffolk head teacher remembers that it was a great deal easier to find homes for the fifty children who flooded into her village school in 1939 than for their four teachers. Much of this reluctance to accept teachers as lodgers was unjustified but, as with children, a few unreasonable teachers could give a whole school a bad name. A woman at Saxmundham, Suffolk, did her best to be welcoming to the guardian of one contingent of ten evacuees from Birmingham, aged from four to fourteen, 'a short, aggressive elderly Yorkshire female, who was so outspoken and demanding that we reckoned anyone so unpleasant must be dead honest and conceal a heart of gold. We were', she acknowledges, 'no judge of human nature, as she started by eating all the evacuees' bacon ration to keep up her strength, and ended by stealing blankets from our Austrian refugees.'

Expectant mothers were even less welcome than teachers. The government's plan, sound enough on paper, was that temporary maternity hospitals should be opened as soon as war broke out in requisitioned nursing homes and large houses, with expectant mothers being billeted in the district until they needed residential care. Few escorts had a more nerve-racking job than those travelling with such women. One male escort still remembers the journey from London on Saturday 2nd September, as he apprehensively watched three very pregnant women, wondering what to do if any baby showed signs of arriving prematurely, while nursing a five-month-old infant on his lap. It was 10.30 p.m. before the last mothers, some in tears, were settled in an East Anglian village, and he was himself reluctantly taken in by most unwilling hosts who only allowed him a bed and a cup of weak cocoa on his promising to see the Billeting Officer about other accommodation in the morning.

Only about 13,000 expectant mothers were involved in the first evacuation, but to many bemused residents in coastal towns it seemed that every street had suddenly been taken over by mothers-to-be. A woman visiting Bridlington remembers feeling that its whole population had suddenly become pregnant, while on the south coast these evacuees were known as the Brighton Balloon Barrage. A nurse at an emergency hospital for London expectant mothers in Bexhill remembers that the town was dismayed by the sudden invasion, but the mothers drifted back to London so rapidly that in December all the nurses were paid off. A nurse at a Rustington convalescent home remembers the arrival of a hundred expectant mothers in this then quiet coastal village, which largely consisted of a private, fenced-off estate, and how 'The sight of the London "mums" wheeling babies down the exclusive avenues horrified the inhabitants'.* A professor of forestry living in a large country house near Ashford in Kent found himself confronted, his wife being out, with a difficult choice: did he prefer to have his peace disturbed by verminous East End children, of whom alarming reports were already circulating, or a bus-load of expectant mothers, larger, but presumably

---

* The estate survived the experience. It is still there, with the same admonitory notices and locked gates.

cleaner. He chose the mothers, greeting them as they stepped hot and weary from the coach with the immortal remark, 'I want you to understand that I will not have any baby born in my house.' None ever was. The women soon moved on to be replaced by a safely non-pregnant group, the 17/21st Lancers.

Even less welcome than expectant mothers were women with small children. About 524,000 mothers with infants under five were evacuated in 1939, but so decisively did the scheme fail—by January 1940 only 65,000 remained away—that it was never attempted on any large scale again. As with the children of school age, a few slovenly or dishonest mothers were enough to give them all a bad name and, since many such parties arrived at places which were not expecting them, relations were often strained from the start. The government recognised that not even the Defence Regulations could force two women to share the same kitchen if they simply did not get on, so the householder's only legal obligation to a mother with her own children was to provide a bed and access to washing and sanitation. He was also expected, but not compelled, to provide cooking facilities.

While many wartime children still have happy memories of their foster parents, very few evacuated mothers recall their hosts with anything except distaste. A woman from South East London remembers how the first two households to whom she and her small son were offered in Reading firmly said no and, though accepted grudgingly at a third they were forced to spend all day out of the house, like many others. 'All London seemed to assemble in the Park', she recalls. 'As our hosts never liked us, we returned to London.' A Hull woman, then aged seven, remembers how, with her mother acting as an escort, and another child, she was billeted on an old woman in the village of Melbourne near York. Their hostess was very different in character from the 'old ladies' of so many cosy wartime anecdotes, for she placed all three in a bedroom furnished only with an old iron bedstead dragged from a shed for the purpose. Her mother, she remembers, wept all night long, but next day, after a complaint to the Billeting Officer, they were moved to a more friendly home. Here, too, however, the diet left a lot to be desired; tea, every night without exception, consisted of tomato soup and chips, with not one green vegetable during their whole stay. It was hardly surprising that by Christmas the family were back home, where her father, waiting to join the Navy, was also delighted to be freed from returning to a cold house and the need to cook his own evening meal. A young Walthamstow mother with a small son reluctantly allowed herself to be persuaded to accept evacuation to St. Albans. Here, after a long wait in a school, she was selected by a local 'lady of the manor', who looked her over, brought a friend to inspect her and finally removed her in a large car to her spacious house. Having publicly 'done her duty', she ignored her guests, who were given a former servant's room, a tiny attic with a high, old-fashioned bed to sleep in, with a large drawer for the baby. The maid was instructed to point out which part of the garden the family could use to remain invisible to their hosts. Despite the kindness of the housekeeper, who finally removed the family to her own home, within a few months they were back in London.

This evacuees' eye-view differs little from the recollections of hosts. The wife of a Hannington, Hampshire, poultry farmer remembers how the mother and two children from Croydon who came to live there were at first thrilled by the details of daily life—drawing the water from the well, getting milk from the cows on the next farm, filling the oil lamps hanging from the ceiling and collecting their eggs from the poultry shed. The first blizzards of the winter, however, were enough to send them back to the bombs. The headmistress of a village school in Dorset found that child evacuees from Walworth settled in with her pupils, and were soon splashing happily in the district's famous salmon river, much to the disgust of the local anglers. But the mothers complained succinctly of 'No chip shop, no pictures, no pawnshops', and within six months only one family was left.

Few stayed as long. Some women, after one horrified look at the empty fields around them, simply crossed over on to the departure platform. A Billeting Officer in a Somerset village remembers one such mother being appalled to learn that the single train that day had already gone. But the prize for the shortest stay on record must surely go to a Southampton mother who, on reaching the Dorset village of Netherbury, refused even to get out of the bus and returned with it.

Many hard-up women in reception areas were shocked at the apparent inability of so many evacuee mothers to cope with the simplest domestic crisis and their evident lack of occupation without Woolworths and the cinema to visit. Their habit of throwing away worn clothes, instead of repairing them, seemed particularly shocking to thrifty country wives. But if evacuation opened the eyes of many country dwellers to life in the urban slums, it equally revealed to the city-dweller the primitive conditions which generations of housewives had tolerated in the villages. Fresh vegetables and free rabbits were in many evacuated mothers' eyes a poor recompense for well water, oil-lamps and an earth closet at the end of the garden.* It was not surprising that some, already suffering all the discomfort of sharing someone else's home, simply loaded their babies into their prams and started to push them homewards.

* A survey carried out by the Women's Institute in 3,500 villages in 1944 showed that 1,000 had no piped water supply of any kind, and in some counties only 23 per cent of the houses had normal sanitation.

Some evacuated mothers were natural spongers, who tried the delights of one district after another, leaving a trail of indignant householders and unfairly discredited Billeting Officers behind them. A few were what would now be called 'problem families' whose misdeeds, as in the case of school-children, tended to be quoted as typical and to be exaggerated in the telling. A sergeant in the 'specials', responsible for billeting over a large area of West Cumberland, had two such mothers to deal with. Within two days of placing them with farmers' families, the farmers' wives were pleading with him to remove them and their large brood of un-house-trained children. The sergeant enterprisingly took an empty cottage, with a beautiful view of Wasdale and the mountains, borrowed furniture and saucepans, and moved his two problem families in together, the local farmers generously contributing coal, vegetables, and even a shoulder of bacon. Ten days later they asked, to general relief, to be sent home, one woman explaining, 'Them bloody 'ills drive me crackers every time I look at them.' It was then discovered that all the bedding was filthy and had to be burned and that not a potato of the ten stone provided had been cooked, only the tinned food having been used.

Long before Christmas 1939 the great drift homewards was well under way. The death blow to the largest and most successful scheme, that for unaccompanied children, was inflicted by the government itself, which, as it had all along intended, began from the end of October to demand a contribution from parents to help support their evacuated children. The amounts involved were less than the official billeting allowance of 10s. 6d. for one child, 8s. 6d. each for more than one, for six shillings a child would, it was announced, be accepted in full settlement, but the scheme proved literally more trouble than it was worth, burdening hard-pressed officials with an enormous amount of extra work and yielding only a trivial financial return.* In innumerable cases it tipped the scale in deciding parents to bring their children home, the government's poster campaign to 'Leave the children where they are', which showed a sinister Hitler-figure whispering in a mother's ear, 'Take them back', being contradicted by the increasingly pressing demands for payment which fell through the family letter box. The natural desire to spend Christmas at home, though many W.V.S. branches nobly organised parties for evacuees and many foster parents, even more nobly, welcomed their evacuees' parents into their homes, accelerated an already well-pronounced trend. By the 8th January 1940 900,000 of the nearly

---

* Billeting allowances were later raised by various stages until July 1944 when the rates were fixed on a sliding scale from 10s. 6d. for a child under five to 17s. 6d. for a young person aged seventeen or over. The allowance for an adult, i.e. a mother, helper or teacher, expected to provide their own food, was 5s. plus 3s. for each accompanying child.

one-and-a-half million adults and children evacuated in September 1939 had gone home. In London and Liverpool only a third of all children were still away, in Glasgow and Birmingham only a tenth, in Sheffield, Derby and Coventry even fewer. By May 1940, when the whole war situation changed, an evacuee in many country towns and villages had again become a rare sight. In the danger areas, despite a new publicity campaign, only one family in five registered their children for evacuation if heavy raids began. In the reception areas, only one householder in fifty now volunteered to take in evacuees, despite such improvements as medical inspection of children before they left and a far more generous provision of all the items suggested by experience, from hostels for difficult children to mackintosh sheets.

Such arrangements help to explain why later evacuations, though affecting overall far more people than the first great flight of 1939, caused much less disturbance and are less remembered. From May 1940, with the growing threat of invasion, the government began to clear school-children from a belt ten miles inland from Norfolk to Sussex, and in the next few months there was a similar movement of children from supposedly dangerous towns, from Hull to Portsmouth, and from London and the Thames-side towns. Although owing to pressure on the railways schools were sometimes split up, there was less confusion than in 1939, though altogether some 213,000 children were moved. After the previous failure no attempt was made compulsorily to billet mothers with young children, the government relying largely on 'assisted private evacuation', described in the next chapter. By autumn 1940 about 56,000 mothers and children from the coastal areas had been officially billeted in reception areas, while another 328,000 people, of both sexes and all ages, had moved under their own arrangements.

After the start of the London blitz in September 1940, the government operated a 'trickle' scheme under which small parties, mainly of mothers and small children, and homeless people, left London each week. By now the early goodwill had evaporated and evacuees were unfashionable, so that few jobs needed a tougher skin than that of Billeting Officer. A woman who took on this 'most hated job' in Chertsey still regards the district with real bitterness. 'There was a terrible lot of "old pals association", where voluntary billeting had first been accomplished,' she remembers, 'so that small slum houses were overcrowded but big wealthy houses left untouched. The average "life" of a Billeting Officer was six months ... One had no support from the locals and very little from the Ministry. Laws were ambiguous and impossible to enforce. I could have papered my walls with the doctors' certificates I received immediately I sent out a compulsory billeting notice.'

But it was not always selfishness that made placing children difficult.

A woman responsible for billeting under-fives in a village near Honiton remembers that, with every house crowded with relations from Plymouth or other bombed cities, the regulations had to be stretched as it was a case 'of pushing a little one in where I felt they could be looked after'. She often received a telegram, 'Meet three from train', and collected 'tearful, dirty, frightened infants', just sent down from London, often having to care for them herself until she could find room elsewhere.

By 1944 most people in the reception areas were war-weary and unwillingness to accept evacuees had become even more pronounced, when in June there occurred the fourth and last great wave of evacuation as the flying bombs clattered over southern England and on to London. In the next few weeks nearly a million adults and children left the capital, 552,000 of them under officially-assisted private arrangements, the rest in organised parties. This included many small children whose mothers could not go with them, but even these poor, frightened infants could not rekindle the old enthusiasms of 1939. A woman shop-owner remembers that though the first children to arrive in Morecambe from the V.1 raids were 'complete nervous wrecks with pale faces and blinking eyes', the local Billeting Officers had considerable difficulty in finding them homes.

The government rather rashly announced the end of official evacuation on 7th September 1944, the day before the first V.2 rocket fell on London, but even these new attacks failed to halt the steady return to the cities, which reached its peak during the autumn of 1944. One after another from September onwards the former danger districts were proclaimed 'go home' areas, until by the end of the year only Hull and London were not yet considered safe. Their turn finally came on 2nd May 1945, six days before the European war ended, but it was to be nearly another year before the evacuation scheme was officially wound up. Few, it must be acknowledged, mourned its end.

# FROM A SAFE HOTEL

'Charming country residence in "Real Safety Zone"—Yorkshire West Riding.'

advertisement in *The Times*, 4th September 1939

The war years were a restless time. Between September 1939 and August 1945 at least two million people were evacuated under official arrangements, but many more moved themselves out of danger areas, often after being made homeless by bombs, or to follow a husband in the Forces or working for an evacuated business. To have seven or eight homes, none of them permanent, during those six years was not at all uncommon, and altogether during this period sixty million changes of addresses were recorded in England and Wales in a civilian population of thirty-eight million. Among the first to go were the great hospitals. On the 26th August they were told to cease admitting patients, except for urgent cases, many patients were sent home to clear 140,000 beds for air raid casualties, and out-patients departments and special clinics closed down. Staff and patients soon afterwards began to move to previously prepared bases in the country, largely in Green Line coaches which, with the seats removed, made excellent ambulances. Car-sick nurses found regular road travel between their London base and their wartime home one of the great personal trials of the war years. One still remembers with gratitude the sympathetic driver who tactfully pretended that it was the patient, not the nurse, who was responsible for the overflowing vomit bowl which invariably needed to be emptied on arrival.

The West London Hospital, Hammersmith, like many others, moved to a country mental hospital, in this case at Park Prewett, near Basingstoke, to await the expected flood of bomb victims. One first year nurse found herself, with fifteen colleagues, sleeping in a corridor, for every dormitory was full, while the dining hall seemed thronged with queues of hungry women waiting to be fed. 'The poor sisters in charge', she remembers, 'had no idea which nurses belonged to their ward as we were all from different hospitals.' There was, too, the unfamiliar problem of 'hundreds and hundreds of nurses and not a single patient'. In intervals of making dressings and learning to use primus stoves for sterilisation in case the power supply was cut off, the nurses made 'stacks of dripping toast' and explored their new home. As the building had been designed for the mentally ill they soon found that there were no bolts on the lavatory doors and baths had to be taken in company, two to each bathroom, but they managed to force open the hospital windows, supposed to open only two inches, to climb in after late night excursions to relieve the tedium of waiting. The medical students, equally bored, caused much trouble locally by changing round the signposts at local crossroads, and were only forgiven after attending at the local police station to help fill sandbags.

A second year student nurse from another London hospital, who was evacuated to a large mental hospital in Hertfordshire, also found time heavy on her hands. 'We smoked like chimneys', she remembers, 'because we were bored and hungry . . . We raided the orchard and ate all the apples . . . We played table tennis, we took the workers' train to London for our days off, but mostly we were bored.' When the familiar Green Line coaches arrived with hundreds of casualties from the evacuated British Expeditionary Force, the nurses were so delighted to have something to do that they *ran* to meet them.

The Fall of France sent institutions all along the south and east coasts hurrying inland. A nurse at a Convalescent Home from Felixstowe found herself living, after July 1940, in a large country house, owned by a millionaire, in rural Suffolk. The nurses enjoyed the country life and dances in the village hall, but the chief disadvantage was that 'it was a creepy place for night duty, as there was a minstrels' gallery and long narrow corridors with creaky boards'.

The wartime surroundings of a Liverpool Eye Hospital were even more inappropriate, a former theological college. A nurse who worked there remembers 'the long narrow corridors with small rooms leading off them, and punctuated with lighting wells, surrounded by wrought ironwork', while beds had even been placed in the chapel. A story told to every newcomer was that one patient, awaking from an anaesthetic and finding himself looking up at a stained-glass window showing a holy scene of angels in haloes, had imagined himself already in heaven.

Innumerable other moves were taking place at the same time. A Worcestershire Post Office engineering inspector found himself preparing one stately home, Hindlip, to receive the Prime Minister and his staff, Wood Norton, near Evesham, for the BBC, Malvern College for Boys for the Admiralty, the Malvern Girls' College for the Board of Trade and premises at Droitwich for the War Office. The Air Ministry, meanwhile, had installed itself in the former workhouse at Worcester, while part of the Ministry of Information had opted for the more luxurious quarters of the Abbey Hotel, Malvern.

A Civil Service scientist, evacuated from Aldwych to Bristol with another department of the Air Ministry, remembers how, when the staff were assembled the night before, the women were confined to certain offices and locked in, to protect them from their male colleagues, who were assumed to become inflamed with lust once darkness fell. The entrainment and journey went without a hitch but he found it 'an odd experience' ringing the bell at a large house in a wealthy suburb near Clifton and announcing to the manservant that he had been billeted there. Conditions in the office were, by comparison, primitive, with no furniture, no files, and only one telephone, but in any case work was impossible owing to the security rule that all correspondence had to be sent via London, to prevent any section of the department knowing the location of any other. When 'Lord Haw-Haw' helpfully announced a full list of addresses of evacuated government departments, there was a collective sigh of relief from the Civil Servants concerned, as the previous restrictions were lifted. Another Air Ministry Civil Servant, evacuated to Harrogate, discovered that billets were allocated solely in alphabetical order so that many people found themselves sharing a double bed with a colleague they had never met before.

During the early months of the war, before accommodation had been found for wives to join evacuated husbands, there were many no doubt exaggerated stories of the 'goings on' in evacuated government offices. One current joke quoted the reply made by the wife of an evacuated Civil Servant to the wife of a Serviceman, who had pointed out that her husband was also away from home: 'Yes, but yours hasn't got his typist with him.' A shorthand-typist in the Ministry of Labour in Newcastle, which received an influx of Civil Servants from London, remembers how one case became so flagrant that the woman concerned was posted back to London and the man found a house locally and sent to fetch his family. The trains of the departing mistress and the errant husband returning to Newcastle were bound to pass midway, and the male staff of the office relieved the day's routine by poring over maps, trying to pinpoint the exact spot.

Being an evacuated Civil Servant rarely had such consolations and they suffered far more restrictions than other evacuated workers, being, for example, forbidden to travel home for Christmas 1939 'to set a good example'. Many, too, felt unwelcome. In Bath, housing much of the Admiralty, one indignant Civil Servant denounced his hosts in the local press as 'despicable, money-grabbing billetors', complaining that a colleague and himself had to 'eat, sleep and live in a dimly-lit room where dust accumulates undisturbed. We must buy our own coal and light our own fire. A fruit basket is our coal-scuttle, a stair rod our poker . . . Two wafer-like slices of a sausage, hostile in nationality if not in odour, with bread and margarine and a pot of tea is our usual repast. We grow thin while our billetor and his family grow fat on our butter, tea, sugar and meat rations. What . . . is the mentality of these vile things who would help the enemy by starving the workers?' But most 'guinea-pigs', as they were known—the billeting allowance was 21*s*. 0*d*.—seem to have been more fortunate, and Bath was clearly no worse than anywhere else.

Despite the secrecy surrounding it, one of the most widely known moves was that of the BBC. The BBC Catering Department, which had run six establishments pre-war, now found itself responsible for seventy-four.

The largest contingents from London went to Bristol and Evesham. A BBC production secretary remembers how during August all the members of the Variety Department had been allotted to various cars and then waited at home for the signal to move. Most of her colleagues were doleful at leaving London but her spirits rose all the way to Bristol on Saturday 2nd September, for she left behind an unhappy love affair and 60,000 accumulated letters for the *Listeners' Choice* section of her programme, which had been on her conscience for weeks. (The whole pile vanished a year later in the same fire that destroyed Sandy Macpherson's organ.)

The BBC's peaceful West Region swelled overnight from seventy staff to nine hundred and 'BBC close-carpeted bureaucracy vanished overnight', she noted. 'Christian names everywhere (often unheard of in Town), slacks, kindness and comradeship. Bristol was horrified but gradually they came to like us.' The local children acquired a new interest, waiting outside the Clifton Parish Hall and other temporary studios in search of autographs from Arthur Askey and similar celebrities. The craze died away after a few months, helped by the habit of members of the Variety Orchestra of signing themselves 'Toscanini'. The same secretary found herself making tea for thirty-seven in one house during the first carefree days, when 'we hadn't even our typewriters, just empty rooms and bare boards and trestle tables . . . Our helpful radio engineers set us girls up with corners for ironing and clothes-lines, etc.'

In the spring of 1941, with Bristol under attack, many of the BBC evacuees moved on again. The Variety Department went to Bangor in non-conformist North Wales, where *ITMA* was produced from a church hall, and outraged local residents could be heard indignantly exchanging gossip in their native tongue, with only the name 'BBC' intelligible. Bedford was more fortunate, receiving Religious Broadcasting and Music, the most decorous of BBC departments—a local newspaper announced: 'Religion leaving Bristol'. Many BBC concerts were staged in the Bedford Corn Exchange, while religious services were broadcast from the parish church and the Bunyan Chapel.

Another large BBC party went in September 1939 to the quiet Worcestershire town of Evesham, where the BBC had converted a large mansion, Wood Norton, into offices and emergency studios. It was at first known by the code-name 'Hogsnorton', the imaginary town created by the comedian Gillie Potter.

To Bruce Belfrage, later one of the best known announcers, 'that lovely sunny autumn spent with most congenial companions in such surroundings was more like a continuous picnic than a war'. He enjoyed, too, the freedom from official memos which the staff enjoyed for the first few days. The first instructions which did arrive were characteristic of the time: that women employees need no longer resign on marriage but that secretaries, even when evacuated, must continue to wear stockings in the office. The standing instruction at Evesham, that on the siren sounding staff must take to the surrounding woods in pairs, also led to much jocularity, and the solitary rehearsal was not repeated; many employees happily left their desks and disappeared into the countryside and were not seen again that day.

The BBC's Drama Department, along with its repertory company of actors, also appeared in Evesham. Its head later described these first unhappy weeks, dealing with 'the harassed programme official, deafened by typewriters operated upon parquet floors . . . the wild-eyed producer trying to cope with the peculiar acoustic qualities of metamorphosed stables and billiard-rooms'. The house itself might almost have been a stage set for 'Originally the property of a former Pretender to the throne of France, its walls were hung with deep blue, liberally sown with *fleurs-de-lis* . . . The royal device was everywhere—even on the bath-plugs and the weather-vane.' Conditions elsewhere in the town were less imposing. One visitor was surprised to find part of the mighty Corporation housed in 'a dreadful little workman's hut at/the station, marked BBC in chalk letters not even of a uniform character. The town hall was a positive shambles of prone young men in truckle beds.' A local family she spoke to described the newcomers as 'very foony people, very foony indeed', and her heart went out to 'unfortunates . . . billeted with aspidistras and china swans, with cheap ornaments and overmantels, and landladies who thought of them as naughty boys and girls believed that all actors and actresses must be immoral'. The Drama Department moved on, without regret, in 1940 to more sophisticated Manchester, relieving Evesham of the sight which to many symbolised the BBC invasion, that of men in beards riding bicycles.

Another, very different, national institution which was dispersed on the outbreak of war was Billingsgate fish market. One part of it moved into old brewery buildings in Reigate, Surrey, where the respectable inhabitants of a quiet residential area were soon swamped by 'porters in white jackets and wearing their leather hats', while signs reading

'Fish Transport Only' appeared in the car parks and empty shops suddenly blossomed out as workmen's cafés, with traditional London menus painted on the windows. Another section moved to a garage in Maidstone, where the proprietor of a Rochester fish and chip shop observed 'a pretty hopeless conglomeration of anxious traders swarming around . . . reminiscent of the Klondyke gold rush . . . The "wide boys" got what they wanted by devious methods. One was to pass the salesman a newspaper which had the odd pound note inside and the message that "Fred" would take all those plaice . . . The Battle of Britain mercifully put an end to all this.' Soon Billingsgate, like many other evacuated institutions, was back in London.

Almost every organisation of any size sent at least some departments to the country. The Royal College of Art appeared in Ambleside, the Central Clearing House of the London banks at a ducal mansion near Stoke-on-Trent, the National Union of Teachers at Toddington Manor in Gloucestershire. The headquarters staff of the National Association of Local Government Officers moved in to the holiday camp run for its members at Croyde Bay. 'Today the work is going on at full pressure', the union's magazine reported in October 1939. 'Accounting machinery clatters in half the dining room . . . What was once the sun lounge is the headquarters of . . . the Approved Society. The Building Society is established in the billiard room, using one of the tables as a gargantuan desk. . . . All over the centre, chalets have become offices or are housing typewriters, dictating and addressing machines and duplicators.'

Other office workers found themselves in even stranger surroundings. The headquarters staff of the Great Western Railway moved from Paddington to huts at Aldermaston in Berkshire, waiting rooms at Reading and to restaurant cars parked at Newbury Racecourse. The fortunate employees of the Prudential Assurance Company evacuated to Torquay, at first, 'lounged on the beaches or enjoyed sea and sunbathing', a peaceful existence enlivened by a spy-scare when a man trying to attract the attention of 'a girl from the Pru' working in the Victoria and Albert Hotel was suspected of heliographing to the Germans.

In the Prudential, as elsewhere, formal City dress and office etiquette were left behind in London, with male clerks appearing at the office in gumboots in wet weather and the women wearing hoods. 'The Centre became a club as well as an office', the company's historian noted, with a laundry for the use of women staff, billiard tables for the men, and nearby allotments on which both 'dug for victory' after office hours. At Wakefield there was croquet on the lawn in the lunch hour, at Darlington 'the beauty of rural surroundings contrasted favourably with the drabness of Holborn', at Wigan the chief problem was a revolt against the local tradition of high tea, which might be missed altogether by staff working late.

These experiences were paralleled in innumerable smaller concerns.

Those of a woman supervising the machine room of an office machine company in Central London were not untypical. She found that she and her husband were going different ways—he with the Milk Marketing Board to Thames Ditton (still its home), she with her firm's headquarters to its factory at Letchworth. (Rather than move to this notoriously 'stuffy' spot, which lacked a single public house, many of the staff resigned on the spot.) As the office manager drove her towards Hertfordshire, she expected never to see her husband or her home again, but in fact life in Letchworth during the bitter winter of 1939–40 revolved round begging coal from a coal cart to try and keep warm. In March 1940 the firm, like many more, moved back to London. She gladly joined her husband in Thames Ditton, travelling to work each day.

A shorthand typist in a company selling vending machines found herself on Friday 1st September, arriving in the late evening in the Oxfordshire village of Bodicote, where the firm had leased a manor house. Conditions could hardly have offered a greater contrast to office life in City Road, E.C.1. Four girls found themselves working in a greenhouse, with tomatoes growing around them, which was intolerably hot in sunny weather and the sleeping quarters, too, were congested with two single beds in one bedroom and a double bed into which three girls were squeezed. Later in the year, in the most severe winter of the century, uncomfortable heat was replaced by agonising cold. The draughts rose incessantly between the bare boards of the floor, and there was no heating in bathroom or bedrooms. Morning after morning the staff found their towels frozen solid and the girls wore woollen mittens when not actually working to try to keep their hands warm enough for typing and built barricades of corrugated cardboard under and round their desks to keep out the draughts. The only fire was in the office but when they hung their stockings and underclothes to dry round it their boss complained. One new duty was added to the usual office routine during those chill months—the clerical staff took it in turns to tour the house in pairs pulling the lavatory chains and running the taps to prevent the pipes freezing up. During the night each team in turn set an alarm clock and placed it by the bedside of those next on the rota. This novel form of guard duty was not unpopular for, the same informant recalls, 'we got quite a lot of fun out of going round the house with a candle or torch in the middle of the night'.

A woman working in an insurance brokers' office in the City remembers her firm moving to two large houses at Chalfont and Chalfont St. Giles in Buckinghamshire. Some of the staff slept and worked in one of the buildings but took all their meals in the other, two miles away. She remembers the girls cheerfully piling into a large lorry driven by the assistant manager, until the firm provided bicycles for the journey. For her, the worst feature was the lack of privacy, with everyone sleeping in dormitories and sharing a common room, so that, like many people in institutions, she used to read her private letters in the lavatory.

Many wives faced the difficult decision as to whether or not to accompany an evacuated husband. The wife of an office worker in a London engineering firm, evacuated to the Midlands, witnessed the incongruous sight of her husband and his colleagues going off to their work in black jackets and striped trousers in a cold and dirty hut in the middle of a field, and being 'ribbed by the locals, who were mostly coal miners, steel workers or workers in the brickfields—a tough lot'. A woman whose husband's firm had been evacuated to Bristol remembers the miserable and lonely months which followed, 'home alone to a freezing house . . . plus endless burst pipes'. No sooner had she joined him in Bristol than the raids on the Bristol aircraft factories drove the firm back to London, but after a fortnight in their own home the blitz caused another move to Bristol and the firm finally set up its headquarters in a country house in Gloucestershire, until it came home for good in March 1941.

Unlike state schools, private schools had to make their own arrangements for evacuation and in 1939 requisitioning displaced many far from the danger areas. Few schools were as unlucky as Malvern which, having been forced to give up its premises to the Admiralty in 1939, had been back in them only five terms, after a year in Blenheim Palace, when it was forced to move again, by the Ministry of Aircraft Production, to provide a new home for the Telecommunications Research Establishment, which was developing radar.* Malvern now found shelter with Harrow, and many other schools 'doubled up' in the same way, Marlborough, for example, accommodating the City of London School, and Shrewsbury making room for Cheltenham, another victim of requisitioning. Few preparatory schools were affected by evacuation until 1940, when the coastal areas of Kent and Sussex favoured by headmasters earned a new reputation as 'bomb alley'. By 1941 eighty-eight of the 104 boys' preparatory schools formerly in these counties were listed in *The Public and Preparatory Schools Yearbook* under new addresses; from Broadstairs alone seven private schools had scattered to as many counties inland. Some of the schools' entries blithely ignored these moves and still described their pre-war buildings, but others now stressed new amenities. Bromsgrove, in a village in Breconshire, could offer 'its own golf course

* The T.R.E. had been at Swanage. This was felt to be vulnerable to a possible reprisal raid by German parachutists following the British commando attack on the Bruneval radar station in February 1942.

and four miles of trout fishing'; Lancing, at Ludlow, boasted of 'facilities for valuable service and experience in wartime work such as forestry', while Wycliffe College, now with St. David College, Lampeter, claimed that 'there is no . . . military objective within twenty miles and . . . the local siren has only once been sounded during the first fourteen months of the war'.

One particularly unlucky school was Dulwich College Preparatory which, by June 1940, was comfortably established in a hutted camp near Charing in Kent—and in daily increasing danger of being bombed or machine-gunned. The headmaster's wife devotedly set off in search of safer quarters but, 'as she went further west', her husband recorded, 'she found that each hotel was full of lean and hungry schoolmasters with harassed expressions on their faces. As soon as the news went round that there was a suitable house in the district everybody leapt into their cars and a mad rush followed.' Eventually, thanks to a tip-off from a sympathetic officer, Dulwich Prep was re-established in a converted hotel and various other premises in the North Wales village of Bettws-y-Coed, where it only escaped losing some vital classrooms through requisitioning by the happy chance that the officer concerned was an old boy.

The proprietors of a Bexhill boarding school, with 150 girls aged from nine to seventeen, decided to move when the first tennis match of the summer term 1940 was played to the accompaniment of the noise of gunfire from across the Channel. While the British Army was being rescued from Dunkirk, mistresses, maids and children were struggling to transform a country house near Horsham into a wartime home, with classes being held in the summer house, the gunroom, a drawing room and the corner of a huge indoor tennis court. The girls revelled in the break from routine and in the unexpected treasures their new home revealed, from the deer in the park to the bath-chair in the indoor tennis court, which was in demand for rides in 'break'. A few months later, as the war followed the school inland it had to move further west until in 1941 it was finally merged with another in Wiltshire, ending an independent existence which had lasted 120 years.

Another Bexhill boarding school moved to Topsham near Exeter and again, a year later, to a country house on the Thames at Buscot in Berkshire. Here the girls delighted in their new surroundings though bewildered over the purpose of the bidet in the well-equipped bathroom, only resolved by the triumphant guess of one girl, 'It's a bottom bath!'

Although the government in 1939 had encouraged everyone to leave the cities if they could, within a few weeks criticism was being voiced of 'rich refugees'. At a time when men were being called up there was certainly something distasteful about announcements in *The Times* headed 'A.R.P.', which offered a farmhouse in Suffolk or a furnished cottage in the Chilterns. As late as September 1940 the same paper still listed 'Sanctuary Hotels recommended by Ashley Courtenay ... Torquay. You can sleep at the Grand Hotel, for the drone of an aero engine is rare and sirens even more infrequent ... Queen's Hotel, Penzance ... for a sense of security cannot be beaten'. In its editorial columns *The Times* took a sterner line. 'The hotels are filled with well-to-do refugees', it complained in January 1941, 'who too often have fled from nothing. They sit and read and knit and eat and drink and get no nearer the war than the news they read in the newspapers.'

Understandably, none of these much-abused individuals seems to have answered back, but the romantic novelist Ursula Bloom, who had, very sensibly, sought a quiet place to carry on her trade as a writer, later described the extreme tedium of her months as a voluntary evacuee. In her guest house in Warwickshire one resident firmly switched off the wireless whenever any popular programme such as *Bandwagon* was broadcast, and in the village the only entertainment was provided by the local doctor's amateur films of hospital life in the nineteen-twenties. Life with an aunt at Hurst in Kent, where she moved in desperation, proved little more stimulating. Here the long evenings were filled with ludo and halma, though Miss Bloom did win four and nine-pence on snakes and ladders. 'To go by bus to Ashford was the wildest dissipation I could hope for', she noted, and she returned to London just before Christmas, holding a home-coming party to celebrate her return.

Evacuees without private means had more to contend with than boredom. The wife of an Admiralty chart corrector, evacuated to Exeter, found that the prim spinster on whom the family was billeted objected to any noise, so night after night they desperately played 'Happy Families' to keep their daughter silently amused. A mother who had evacuated herself to Sutton on Sea in Lincolnshire lived under the constant strain of incessant complaints from her landlady because her baby son woke her early every morning. She was determined, however, to send her husband, serving overseas, a cheerful photograph, and had one taken of herself smilingly holding the baby aloft on the seafront, against a background of barbed wire.* Relations could be as trying as strangers. A Manchester woman's worst fourteen months of the war were spent with her mother in Morecambe, as she turned out to detest small children, not excluding her three grandsons. Her daughter had only one night out during her whole stay, for, having gone to see George Formby at a local theatre, she came home to find all four blind drunk. Her mother had, most effectively, kept the children quiet by sharing a bottle of whisky with them.

* This picture survived and can be seen on page 13 of the illustrations.

A Birmingham mother spent an even more miserable few weeks in the home of a village policeman in Warwickshire, for the tiny cottage was already overcrowded with another mother and baby, and the policeman's wife, an atrocious cook, refused to let either mother use the kitchen or to hang up washing to dry in the house. This woman remembers miserable nights sleeping with still-damp nappies and baby clothes in her bed, as she tried to air them, and miserable days wandering about the countryside with her children, waiting for darkness when she could take them home and go to bed. When the family were reunited in two furnished rooms ten miles from Birmingham they suffered from a rude and inquisitive hostess. 'One day,' her evacuee recalls, 'we had a humble meal of sausages with tinned tomatoes and as usual she came into our room. . . . When she spotted the almost forgotten tomato she excitedly called to her husband, "Billy, come and see what they are eating!" ' The final insult came when, after the Birmingham family had received a food parcel from relations in America and had hidden it under their bed, they found their landlady serving her family with identical meals, made from food pilfered from it. For this family, as for many more, the return 'to Birmingham and bombing' could not come soon enough.

At first, people who found their own homes in safe areas received no official help, but in June 1940 'assisted private evacuation' began entitling mothers with children under five who found themselves somewhere to stay to a free travel voucher and a 'billeting certificate' which entitled them to a lodging allowance. Older children who were still at school could also go with the family. From October the scheme was extended to expectant mothers and invalids and to homeless people of both sexes in heavily bombed districts. Like official evacuation, private evacuation died away after the great blitzes of 1940 and 1941, but was revived by the menace of the flying bombs in July and August 1944, when more than half a million people left London and the South East armed with 'billeting certificates'.

One of the half million was the wife of an Essex Probation Officer who sought shelter with old friends in Somerset. After a crowded journey she and her children were met at the other end by a farm cart. 'The peace and quiet was unbelievable. It was heaven', she remembers, while after a few days of home-grown vegetables, fruit, rabbits and duck, her son remarked, 'There's no war on here.' After a three-months' respite in autumn 1944 they went back to Woodford for the elder daughter to attend her High School. The V.1s were not yet over and the first time they saw one, from the garden, her son remarked, 'Look, there's a funny plane', while his sister, more worldly-wise, took one look and said, 'Run!'

The great cities, though battered by bombs and partly emptied by evacuation, remained cities still, but many resorts on the coast, following the exodus of June 1940, became ghost towns. Except in a few areas required for training grounds or defence works, no one was compelled to leave, but official notices urged everyone who could to go while there was still time and warned that compulsory evacuation might become necessary at a few hours' notice. With memories of the hordes of refugees being herded like sheep down the roads of France by machine-gunning German fighters, this was enough for most people, and within a few months 330,000 inhabitants voluntarily left the coastal belt from Great Yarmouth to Littlehampton, in addition to more than 100,000 mothers and children officially evacuated. A Southend woman remembers the Saturday morning when the milkman brought her the news of the government advice to leave. With a seventy-year-old mother to care for she decided to set off at once for Buckinghamshire. The compartment was crowded and included one humorist who displayed an alarm clock, 'to be on time when we go back'. On subsequent visits she found the High Street deserted except by six or seven people, and strangers such a rarity that people would cross the road solely to speak to them. The population of Folkestone shrank in a few weeks from 46,000 to 6,000; one grocer had to be given special permission by the Ministry to carry on with only eight registered customers, eighteen less than the qualifying minimum under the rationing regulations. In the shopping centre of Margate grass grew in the streets.

Shortest-lived of all the evacuation schemes was that for sending children overseas, reluctantly introduced by the government in June 1940, in answer to well-meaning offers from the Dominions and the United States, and because better-off parents, with relations and friends in these countries, were already sending their children to safety there. Many parents suffered agonies of indecision as they weighed the risk of impending invasion against the dangers of a long sea voyage but eventually 200,000 applications for passages were received, provoking from Winston Churchill a scathing reference to the 'stampede from this country'. By September only 2,700 'official' evacuees and 11,000 private ones had left, when the scheme came to a tragic end after the torpedoing of the *City of Benares* with the loss of seventy-three children. A memorial service for the dead children was broadcast on *Children's Hour*. Hearing one speaker, deeply moved, read the text: 'And God shall wipe away all tears from their eyes', was for many mothers, their own children safe at home or in reception areas, the saddest moment of the war.

# 7

# ALWAYS CARRY YOUR GAS MASK

'Hitler will give no warning—So always carry your gas mask.'

Official poster 1939

Monday 4th September 1939 was the first working day of the war and that morning everyone was carrying a gas mask. In the country, farm labourers trudged to work with the buff, cardboard boxes slung incongruously over their working clothes; in industrial towns they bounced on the backs of factory workers cycling through the factory gates; on suburban trains they crowded the luggage racks, alongside the customary umbrellas and bowler hats; whenever schools were open children swung the boxes by their string, or discussed in awed tones the meaning of this new toy. To remember one's gas mask seemed at this stage of the war an elementary civic duty. It was only later that in a wartime Will Hay film, *The Goose Steps Out*, a German spy training to be landed in Britain was told that if he wished to be accepted as a true Englishman he must be sure *not* to carry his gas mask. Lost gas mask cases were soon cluttering up the shelves of lost property offices everywhere. A *Punch* cartoon showed a worried mother explaining to a resigned-looking official, behind whom stretched rows of identical boxes, 'It's got "Mum" written on the top.' A Burgess Hill woman was surprised that when she left her gas mask in a London taxi the driver posted it back to her and would not accept any reward for doing what, he insisted, was so plainly his duty. The gas mask was at this stage of war regarded as a talisman, a concrete sign of the government's preparedness. This faith was not wholly undeserved. Great Britain was far better protected against gas than any other country—infinitely more so than Germany where many civilians had still not received a mask by the end of the war. At the entrance to most large shelters were heavy blankets on rollers, to be let down if the rattles sounded; many private citizens had painstakingly stopped up cracks around the windows of their refuge rooms with putty or pulped newspaper; the tops of city pillar boxes had been painted green or yellow to reveal the first droplets of the dreaded Lewisite or mustard gas. For several months the more rigorous employers sent their workpeople home again, often with loss of pay, to fetch masks they had left behind. The management of John Lewis's addressed a stern, if not very happily worded, reprimand to such delinquents on their staff at the end of September: 'We may think that there is no risk but we have got to make the best of the government we have elected. They tell us that for the present we must carry gas masks and we must do it. Partners who come without theirs must not be surprised if they are dismissed as unsuitable for employment in time of war.'

In May 1940 there were rumours of a deadly new weapon, 'arsine', said to penetrate the existing mask with deadly arsenic smoke. Within two months, to counter this danger, every mask in the country had been fitted with an additional 'contex' filter, a cylinder like a small tobacco tin, fastened with adhesive tape. This unforeseen addition had the effect of making it difficult to close some 'unofficial' gas mask containers, like my own black metal box, though I was less concerned about the mask than the chocolate which I kept hidden in the case.

By now the shops were full of fancy cases in American cloth, circular tins and 'bucket' shaped plastic bags, the favoured colours, according to Mass Observation, being brown, white, cream and green. Later, as the housewife had to carry more and more possessions with her, large hand-bags went on sale, with special compartments for gas mask, ration book and identity card. As early as Christmas 1939 so many varieties were available that John Lewis's introduced a nice social distinction between the different types, the cheaper versions being sold from the A.R.P. counter, the better-class models in the Handbag Department.

The gas mask carrying habit, however, declined rapidly, despite a poster campaign by the government on the theme 'Hitler will give no warning, so always carry your gas mask'. Advertisements showed one good citizen, just roused from sleep, carefully closing the windows in his gas mask and pyjamas, while his wife, sitting up in her single bed in her nightdress, duly held her breath before putting on her mask. A Mass Observation survey on the fourth day of the war showed nearly 70 per cent of the population carrying their masks in London, with another 30 per cent carrying containers that might have held masks. In Bolton, presumed a safe area, the number was already only 14 per cent. As early as October a keeper in a London park was being jeered at by boys for carrying his mask and that month the government admitted that it was no longer necessary to carry a mask everywhere in reception areas, though it was not until 1942, when the need to save rubber became paramount, that a similar concession was announced for danger areas. Many establishments held periodic tests throughout the war, requiring staff to work in their masks for fifteen minutes or more on one day each month. The wife of an army officer vividly recalls their horror when the rattles sounded early one morning during a weekend at a London hotel when they had decided to 'chance it' and leave their masks at home. 'Fortunately it was an exercise, but we never left them at home again.'

There was no legal obligation to carry a gas mask, but at first many places of entertainment refused admission to patrons without them. After a few months the only one still insisting on the practice was the Shakespeare Memorial Theatre, Stratford on Avon, in the safest of safe areas. One land girl, after cycling there for a Saturday afternoon performance, and being scrutinised by a commissionaire as she 'filed past the entrance gates', managed to pass muster with a friend's box camera, half hidden beneath her jacket. A Quaker father, turned back with his wife and two children at the same spot while on a cycling holiday in August 1940, was unable to stoop to such deception. They simply missed the play. He had already, like a few other citizens, refused to accept masks for his family and when his evacuated ten-year-old daughter was issued with one at school, had removed it and hidden it in the loft of his home. He ultimately burned it, his principles intact and his daughter, fortunately, still ungassed.

By the outbreak of war, everyone except the very young had received a civilian-type respirator, to give the gas mask its official name. Those likely to be exposed to a heavy concentration of gas, like the decontamination squads, were issued with the military-type mask, with its heavy twin goggles and rubber tube leading to a metal container carried in a haversack. Other Civil Defence workers proudly carried the 'Civilian Duty' mask, with separate eye pieces, a large can-shaped filter at the front, and a rubber earpiece at the side, to enable the wearer to telephone. The ordinary citizen's mask, said to cost the country a modest half-crown to manufacture, was a simpler version of this, with a smaller filter and a single transparent panel over the eyes. To put it on one held the mask in front of the face, thrust the chin well into it, and pulled the three straps, which were held together by a buckle, over the head. This operation took only a few seconds and fitting a mask was a simple job, a card or small book being held in front of the filter while the wearer breathed in to check that the seal round the face was airtight. Thick-sided spectacles had to be taken off, though for essential users there were government-issue 'gas mask glasses', with small lenses and flat-sided frames. Less fortunate were women with elaborate hair-styles and men with beards. A Birkenhead woman warden still remembers her struggle to protect the few bearded residents of her district, though a correspondent in *The Times* claimed to have saved her husband's 'magnificent beard' from being shaved off by rolling it tightly under the chin and fastening it with curling pins. Bearded Cistercian monks, however, found the problem insoluble. With no curling pins or helpful wives handy they were forced to become cleanshaven for the duration.

Some people felt about to choke as soon as they put their mask on and would remark that they would rather be gassed than suffocated. One such sufferer, aged eleven at the time of Munich, admits that she still feels grateful to Chamberlain for the prolonging of peace. 'He gave me a year to get used to a gas mask . . . time to come to terms with it, ready to blow "raspberries" as good as the next child by 3rd September 1939.'

Personally I never found the slightest difficulty in wearing my gas mask and welcomed the frequent gas mask tests as a break from routine. After a few minutes the mica 'window' steamed up, preventing reading, but it could easily be kept clear by applying a thin film of soap to the inside just before putting the mask on, and the shops also sold special preparations which claimed, misleadingly, to give indefinite protection of this kind. A twelve-year-old Birmingham girl at her school during daylight raids remembers that 'we used to wear our gas masks and see how long we could go on with our reading before the visor became too steamed up'. A Sussex woman remembers the daily gas mask practice at her school. 'Every class had to stop work and don masks as fast as possible. The teacher timed us with a stop watch and the fastest class earned a silver star for the "gas chart" on the wall.' Even infants took gas masks in their stride. A teacher evacuated to Tring in Hertfordshire found that her class of six-year-olds were fascinated by her demonstration of how to put on a gas mask and continue reading. When one child remarked 'we look like the three little pigs', characters in a current cinema cartoon, it brought the house down. It was the teacher, not the pupils, who glanced apprehensively at the stack of cardboard boxes piled up each day on top of a cupboard, the children 'carrying them as casually as if they were a school satchel'. Anti-gas preparations, like other aspects of the war, were for the ordinary child a source of new and interesting experiences, not a cause of fear. A Cardiff woman remembers the warden who fitted her family's masks saying encouragingly to her three children, 'We'll try one on Mam first and see how brave she is.' They soon saw only too well. Unable to breathe and feeling about to faint, 'Mam' promptly tore her mask off. ' "Oh well," ' he said philosophically, ' "give them plenty of time. They'll get used to it." They did.' Soon the children were chasing each other happily in their gas masks and, as an additional joke, pretending to be afraid, while their mother had privately resolved never to wear hers again, as 'If gas attacks came I would suffocate either way'.

For toddlers below school age, only the ordinary adult type masks were available at first and an Essex woman still recalls admiringly the patience with which local A.R.P. workers persuaded young children to try them on. A Civil Defence worker in the Isle of Wight has a similar picture in her mind, 'of a roomful of babies being coaxed into masks that made them look like "baby monsters" '. With unexpected imagination the government had, however, arranged for supplies of a special 'Mickey Mouse' mask for children aged from about two to four-and-a-half.

It was painted cheerfully in red and blue, had large ears and did indeed resemble the famous Walt Disney cartoon character. By January 1940 two million of these had been issued. A nurse running an L.C.C. day nursery in the Old Kent Road shrewdly organised the popular musical game of 'Mickey Mouse Drill' whenever the siren sounded. 'When a certain tune was played on the piano, they left whatever they were doing, ran to the cloakrooms and put on Mickey Mouse. They knew their own pegs from the picture of an animal over each. Then they were marched to the shelter to play noisy games until the All Clear.' The arrival of a health visitor with a toddler's first mask was an indication that babyhood was over, just as the replacement of his 'Mickey Mouse' by a 'grown up' one three years later meant that schooldays were approaching.

The realisation that their baby was growing up was far more welcome to mothers than in normal times, for it meant the end of their dependence on the hated gas helmet. The issue of these appliances, designed to protect a baby from birth until he graduated to a 'Mickey Mouse' mask, had begun just before the outbreak of war, but at first there was none to spare for the reception areas. A Cambridgeshire vicar's wife remembers her horror at this news. 'We were told that in the event of a gas attack', she recalls, that 'we must wrap our babies up tightly in a blanket. I knew that my child would fight furiously to get out, and I should not be able to hold her, also I should have to get my own gas mask on first, otherwise I should become gassed myself.' By January 1940 nearly one-and-a-half million helmets were ready for use and thereafter it was often the disagreeable job of the district nurse or maternity home midwife to teach a mother how to keep her baby alive in a gas attack, along with the usual instructions on how to feed, change and bath him.

The gas helmet was built round a metal framework, like that of a haversack, with at the base a lattice work of webbing and above a 'cocoon' of rubber, with a large mica window at one end. The baby was laid on his back, on a nappy, inside and strapped in, air being supplied through a rubber tube, connected to a small bellows, which the mother had to pump up and down. It was a well-planned, well-made appliance, but most babies protested vigorously when placed inside it and a woman from Macclesfield, Cheshire, can still hear in her memory the screaming of the babies she saw as they emerged, red as beetroots, from their helmets. A Worcestershire woman was, like many others, worried as to how she could cope with protecting both her children simultaneously, for her small son was frightened of his mask 'and I knew the baby's helmet had to have air pumped by hand to keep her alive'. A South London woman was relieved when told that the baby she was expecting would not be twins, being appalled at 'the thought of two gas masks, each requiring hard pumping in use'.

A few babies, however, contentedly accepted this unusual form of bed. A Coventry soldier's wife who put her infant son into his helmet at least once a week to accustom him to it found that 'without fail, he always expressed his appreciation by instantly going to sleep'. Her experience was that 'very young babies accepted the mask in the same way they accepted a cradle, bed or pram and familiarity made them positively enjoy the mask as they grew older'. But nothing could overcome the drawback that if the mother stopped pumping her baby would suffocate and this same woman made vigorous efforts to obtain a Mickey Mouse mask for her older son, one year old when his brother was born, since she knew she could never pump two helmets simultaneously. To his mother's immense relief he 'loved the new toy and wore it with delight and afterwards our weekly gas drill was greeted with delight by my toddler and he would play most happily with his Mickey Mouse over his face'. Her other son, however, a delicate and ailing child, 'reacted to going into his helmet in the same way as he reacted to everything else, by crying weakly and persistently, until he dropped into the sleep of exhaustion'.

Almost worse, in some mothers' eyes, than the helmet was the box in which it was carried, a bulky cardboard container resembling a tea chest and big enough to project on either side of an ordinary pram when laid across one end. An Ilford woman used to dread taking out her baby son for fear that in a gas attack she would not be able to cope with getting his large helmet out of the box, getting him into it and starting to pump, while putting on her own mask. 'Of course I used to practise at home', she recalls, 'but it was the thought of it happening outside that was a nightmare.' Travelling with a gas helmet, let alone two, added immeasurably to the difficulties of going anywhere with a child. One London woman, evacuated to Woking, still remembers her nightmare weekend journeys to see her mother, which involved not merely a train journey but pushing the pram, with baby and helmet, four miles to the station and back.

Gradually, as thousands of civilians were killed by bombs and bullets and not one by gas, fear of this weapon dwindled, though in 1944 there was a brief resurgence of old terrors when it was rumoured that Hitler planned massive gas attacks as a desperate last throw to frustrate the preparations for D Day. Happily they proved unfounded. The millions of pounds spent by the Chamberlain government and its successors on anti-gas precautions proved to have been money well spent, for the Germans clearly realised that a gas attack was bound to fail against a nation so well prepared for it. The humble gas mask, the subject of endless jokes and criticism and never used, proved after all to have justified its existence, though most ended their lives ingloriously as salvage, or were packed with earth and transformed into hanging plant pots.

# 8

# CALLED UP

'Before the war, even in the last weeks of August, the only response to shots of soldiers was laughter. On not one occasion since the war has any soldier been laughed at.'

Mass Observation report, *The Content of Newsreels*, 28th January 1940

The war was only a few hours old when Parliament passed, almost without debate, the National Service (Armed Forces) Act, which made all fit men aged from eighteen to forty-one liable to military service, and a further Act in 1941, which also made women liable to call-up, extended the age limit for men to fifty-one, though only a few men over forty-one were conscripted and none over forty-five. In the closing months of 1939, 727,000 men were registered; in 1940, 4,100,000; in 1941, 2,222,000. Thereafter the numbers fell off sharply, for the only sources of recruits left were men previously in reserved occupations and each fresh generation reaching the minimum age.

Unlike 1914, there was no rush of volunteers to the colours. The prevailing attitude, among both sexes and all ages was 'When they need us, they'll tell us so'.* Even in 1940, one thirty-five-year-old Sheffield clerk noted that the reaction of his fellow conscripts to being passed medically fit for service was 'Oh my God: I've had it', and to those like himself, who had been rejected, 'You lucky devil, you're out of it', or 'How did you manage to swing it?' An Edinburgh University student was delighted when told by the examining doctor 'Ye'r in *tairrible* condition' and when he was turned down for the second time he got drunk to celebrate his escape. But reluctance to serve very rarely led to actual evasion of the call-up; nor, though a few employers dismissed them, was there any of the brutal persecution of concientious objectors, who numbered only 60,000 of the 8,400,000 men registered, that had disgraced the first world war. The worst that happened to the small contingent of 'conchies' in a Welwyn Garden City department store was to be known collectively as 'the rats'.

* This was one reason why the Chamberlain government, with its emphasis on 'what a free people can do', was such a failure. The free people were eager to surrender their freedom in return for positive leadership.

The Armed Forces, which in 1938 had numbered only 381,000, had risen after a year of war to two and a quarter million, and by 1945 to a peak of 4,680,000, of whom 437,000 were women. By D Day, in mid-1944, nearly a third of the whole male population of working age were in the Services, and as over half the men in the Forces were married at least two and a half million housewives lost their husbands' help and companionship, just when the difficulties of daily life often seemed insuperable. But even more serious than loneliness was poverty. The nation treated the families of the men who defended it with scandalous meanness.

At the start of the war the ordinary soldier was paid only two shillings a day, by the end of the war only three shillings, and from this miserable sum a married man was compelled to allot part to his family. The tiny official allowance which was added was utterly inadequate. Some employers made up their serving employees' pay to its earlier level, though one council actually dismissed them rather than do so, and many families received no such subsidy.*

As the official historians admit, 'The wives of the lowest ranks of the Services (privates and their Naval and Air Force equivalents) who had small children and no other income but their allowances and their husband's compulsory allotments, must have lived until the last year of the war in conditions that certainly were near to hardship even if they did not topple over the borderline.' Until there was a public outcry, the wife of a private with two small children received twenty-five shillings a week, plus seven shillings stopped from his pay, leaving him with one shilling a day for leaving his home and risking his life. Only in 1944 was the same mother's income raised to a reasonable figure, sixty shillings, half or a third of what many men safe in munitions works and shipyards were earning.

Many wives were driven to undertake sweated 'out-work'. One Bethnal Green woman, struggling to live on her army allowance—a pound a week after paying her rent—has bitter memories of embroidering luxury gloves, at a shilling a pair, in the long lonely evenings. By incessant stitching after her daughter had gone to bed, she could complete six pairs a week. A Manchester woman, whose husband was a prisoner of the Japanese, supported her mentally handicapped son by, ironically, sewing Union Jacks. The wife of an R.A.F. volunteer, with three children, and on exactly 17s. 6d. a week left, after paying her rent, was reduced to picking potatoes and scrubbing cinema steps. Soldiers' wives seeking a supplementary allowance were subjected to an inquisition by a Public Assistance official, the hated 'means test man' of pre-war days. One Coventry woman, expecting her second child, had to produce an empty

* It was taken to court by the men's union and forced to reinstate them and make up their pay.

baby-food tin in support of her claim and give details of the soap she used in washing her son's nappies. Finally, when asked if the expected baby was her husband's, she exploded with fury, and was given an extra fifteen shillings a week, on condition her husband sacrificed a further five shillings of his meagre pay. Thus generously did the nation reward its defenders and their dependants.

Most men in the Forces regarded those who had managed to escape the call-up with envy rather than indignation. At first, under the Schedule of Reserved Occupations issued in September 1939, men in a vast range of trades and professions, from boiler-makers to teachers, were exempt from military service, but gradually one calling after another was removed from the list or the age of reservation raised, and the block reservation of whole groups was replaced by individual deferment of key individuals. It was true that those who remained usually had to work far harder than most men in the Forces, on a far worse diet, but they were still widely regarded as the lucky ones. A film which showed a factory-worker remarking to a sailor, 'We're both doing our bit for the war effort, you in your submarine and me in my reserved occupation', made the point neatly. A Leytonstone woman whose husband was reserved still remembers the 'dirty looks from the people whose sons were at war'. But a soldier's wife in Leicester is equally indignant that her evacuees, who had their husbands with them, complained constantly because 'they had to be ready to firewatch, if necessary, on Thursday evenings. This was their only bit of war effort.'

The bitterness of family separation was softened, except for those whose husbands were stationed far away, by what, characteristically, the Forces called 'privilege leave' and there were also various short-term passes—'forty-eights', 'thirty-sixes', and even 'twenty-fours', with compassionate leave, often jocularly known as 'passionate' leave, for family emergencies. Leaves were, for wives even more perhaps than husbands, treasured oases in a desert of loneliness. A Hertfordshire woman, married to a fellow teacher, felt that 'the whole of our lives was geared to the times when Daddy might be coming home on leave'. For a Romford woman every leave 'was like a second honeymoon. I saved all my clothing coupons to buy myself new clothes to greet him.'

With so many families split up, the postman or, increasingly, the postwoman, assumed unprecedented importance. 'If he went past our day was ruined', a Northern Ireland girl remembers. 'We all went through the stage of being in the clouds, because a letter had arrived, and then down in spirit again as we worried about what might have happened since the letter was written.' The wife of a naval officer remembers 'the joy of watching the post-girl pushing an envelope with a foreign stamp through the letter box'. A Devon naval wife could never decide whether it was better to go out before or after the postman had been. 'If I went before there was always the hope that there would be mail on my return.'

A young woman living near Ipswich watched every morning for a local post-woman, easily distinguished at a distance, for she hurried along like a racing walker, with arms moving in a 'scrubbing' motion across her chest. Several times a week she brought a letter from an absent boy friend. 'Often she came into view waving one wildly, just as the bus passed to pick me up. The conductor would say "Well, run then!" and I'd tear up the road to grab the letter with a hasty "Thank you" and rush back, to grins from the other occupants and a blissful journey into town.' Such friendliness was typical of wartime. Many women have recollections of complete strangers, happy at receiving a letter from a serving husband, or perhaps worried at not hearing from him, relating their life stories on a bus or train journey.

With large numbers of men in the Middle East, and sea transport scarce and slow, the government introduced one of the happiest inventions of the war, the airgraph, a single-sheet, photographic copy of a larger original letter, written on a special form. These smudged, grey prints, five inches by four, are still treasured in many homes, the general opinion being that, in the words of one woman, 'they were better than nothing, but not as good as the real thing'.

Although the second world war is often spoken of as the civilian's war, it was still far more dangerous to be a soldier. Of nearly 5,900,000 men and women who served in the Forces at some stage of the war, 265,000 were killed, 277,000 wounded and 172,000 taken prisoner; the comparable figures for the 40,000,000 civilians were 61,000 killed and 86,000 badly injured. For millions of women, worry was therefore a constant companion and, if letters were longed for, telegrams were dreaded. A former hairdresser at Barking, Essex, working in a factory making assault barges, remembers how 'Sometimes a girl's name would be called over the inter-com to report to the main gate. This would be to give her a telegram telling her that her husband or son had been killed in action or that he was a prisoner. A silence would fall and one could sense it above the noise of the machinery. It was a type of unanimous commiseration.' The same woman remembers a man who worked close to her receiving the news that his only son had gone down with the *Hood*. He spoke little about it, but one day, hearing *God send you back to me* sung on the radio, followed by *When you come home dear*, she saw tears streaming down his face, which he tried to brush away while carrying on with his work. An East Ham woman who had evacuated herself and her three small children to a relation's farm in Wiltshire recalls with affection the contents of the parcel her husband sent her for her fifth wedding anniversary: two packets of baby food, a torch to enable her to read in bed, a tiny iced cake—and five roses. In 1944 he was killed in action near Caen.

A similar poignancy often overshadows the recollections of those whose own loved ones came home safely, but who came in close contact with other servicemen who did not. Many people had soldiers or airmen billeted on them and on the whole they were popular guests, partly because of their generous scale of rations. One Godalming woman still remembers some of the men billeted at her home—the 'homesick boy from an Andover chicken farm' and the soldiers who, unknown to her parents, taught her the art of making her shoes shine by spitting on them. But the one who stands out in her memory is the young man to whom she wrote when he was posted away, 'although', she admits, 'I knew it was my elder sister he was interested in. I grew up quickly when the letters were returned by his mother, who thanked me for writing to her son, now buried in the desert.' A Liverpool woman, married to a Merchant Navy officer, still remembers the young officers, all working for their masters 'tickets', who filled her mother's parlour. 'I can still hear them saying *The Articles*, especially *Article 6*, "In fog, mist, falling snow, heavy rain storms: all vessels must proceed at a moderate speed."' The old family tobacco cutter was used to rap out practice messages in Morse code for them to 'read'. For her, Christmas 1942 was a sad time for, though her husband was with her, she thought of all these visitors who would never come back. Such reflections were even more common among those who lived near bomber airfields. The Army did its fighting far from home; the airmen whom one met one evening in the local pub might lie dead in Germany by the next. In 1940 it had been possible to reach the front line, in the shape of the Essex fighter stations like Debden, by London Transport trains. During 1942 and 1943 the R.A.F.'s front line ran through East Anglia, as described in one of the most successful wartime plays, *Flare Path*.* One woman who spent childhood holidays with relations at Brigg in Lincolnshire remembers her aunt running out into the lane each night as the bombers from nearby Scampton airfield roared off into the dusk, shouting, with tears trickling down her cheeks, 'Safe return, lads.' A teacher living in the Huntingdon village of Buckden endured a night when no one could sleep after the heavy raids on Peenemunde, where the Germans were developing their V weapons, as 'the surviving bomber crews from Gravely yelled themselves hoarse as they tried all night to drown the memory of their dead comrades'. A Godalming man used to watch the planes going out in the early morning. 'It was the coming back that was terrible. My pals and I used to sit in my garden and count the planes back.'

* See Chapter 38.

Before the war the Army had been regarded by the general public as something of a joke. A report by Mass Observation, in January 1940, on the reaction of cinema audiences to newsreels noted that 'Even in the last weeks of August, the only response to shots of soldiers was laughter. On not one occasion since the war has any soldier been laughed at.' From 1940 onwards there seemed to be military uniforms everywhere, and many women generously gave up their time to helping in the canteens which were opened at railway stations and in church halls and scout huts.* The cheerfulness of these helpers who, after a hard day cooking for their own families or doing a wartime job, served behind the counter or worked in the kitchen, was remarkable, and they often undertook a myriad other jobs, like sewing on buttons or listening patiently to long anecdotes about absent families. In the village of Blyth, near Doncaster, an old building on the main road, which had once served as a leper hospital and more recently as the village school, had a new lease of life as a canteen serving army convoys. 'Those of us living round the green got to recognise the grinding of gears and brakes as they slowed down and we all poured out of the houses and produced anything up to a hundred cups of tea, etc., in a twinkling', the then vicar's wife remembers. An officer's wife who served in W.V.S. canteens elsewhere in Scotland remembers the aggrieved reply of soldiers whom she accused of queueing twice to get extra chocolate: 'Oh no, miss, that was my twin brother.' She was puzzled why the biggest queue always formed at her position on the counter until one customer revealed that she was more generous with the sugar than the other helpers. A Nottinghamshire guide captain and her fellow rangers helped at an all-night canteen in Nottingham, where they could manage only two hours' uncomfortable sleep a night 'in a cold and lonely room on a camp bed under hairy blankets'. But, she insists, 'we liked the work, the men were very courteous and grateful'. A Scots teenager who helped as a waitress at her church in Angus remembers the great favourite was 'stovies', made of potatoes, onions and dripping. A New Cross woman, working as a wages clerk at Shell Mex House, used to spend every Sunday evening from ten o'clock to eight next morning working in the Y.M.C.A. at Waterloo Station, until she came to 'hate the sight of sausages, thirty-six across and thirty-six down on huge trays in the oven'. She remembers struggling to sleep on a camp bed, wearing a tin hat, with the station rocking as the trains ran in and out. One night, having been told the price of cigarettes, she sold two large cartons of packets at record speed. Having declined the cigarette which one customer offered her, explaining that she was a non-smoker, he told her cheerfully, 'I can see that. You've

* I must record here a special debt of gratitude to the Central London Y.M.C.A., in whose 'quiet room' I wrote my first book, alas still unpublished, in 1944.

been selling Players at Weights prices.' 'That,' she admits wryly, 'was the end of my popularity.' A helper in another canteen which, like many others, took customers' hats as a deposit for magazines, ping-pong balls and other items, was astonished one evening to be left with a huge pile of Army caps and none of the precious games. Only then did she discover that the regiment concerned was being issued with new berets on the following day.

Many people also opened their own homes to servicemen, darning their socks, sewing on their stripes and offering the chance of a hot bath. On the whole it was the less well off, who understood what it was like to be far from home with little money, who were the most welcoming. I experienced personally as a soldier the striking contrast between the warm-hearted hospitality of working class Lanark and the chill indifference of suburban Woking, where the local people, with a few honourable exceptions, could hardly have made us less welcome had we belonged to the German Army rather than the British.*

In one Bath family Sunday dinner was always shared with some soldiers or airmen and there was often a stranger sleeping on a camp bed in the drawing room. In one equally hospitable home in Hull twenty-two airmen slept on chairs and on the floor of one six-roomed house after missing their connection. A woman living near Chatham who invited a couple of soldiers for tea on Sunday felt well rewarded when one Cockney remarked, 'Lor, Mum, isn't it lovely to put your feet under a table like this.' A Scarborough boarding house keeper felt she could 'never do enough for all these people who were helping to win the war for us'. Even washing up every day for six hundred airmen billeted at a local hotel did not dampen her patriotism and in the evenings she would invite small groups home to tea and cards. And there were other compensations for being in the Forces. The son of a Lincolnshire farmer and his five brothers 'found that when we went to a dance the girls were not interested in us at all. They were all crazy for the boys in uniform.' To rub salt in the wound 'our wheatfields suffered badly from the courting couples who used to hide in them'. The wife of a submariner remembers how in Dundee open market, where she and her husband were killing time before his next trip, one stallholder called out, 'Look the Navy's come to protect us!', and insisted on handing over, with 'no questions asked', and no mention of ration books, a huge portion of meat for his dinner, with the words, 'There's a pound of the best rump steak, we're that pleased to see you.'

* In 1940, after a party of child evacuees had been sent back to London as no one would take them in, the Ministry of Health had threatened to take over from the local authority to enforce compulsory billeting. Many other places had a record that was little better.

# CARELESS TALK COSTS LIVES

'Your Courage, Your Cheerfulness, Your Resolution, Will Bring Us
Victory'.

Ministry of Information poster, 1939

When the war failed to begin as expected with mass air attacks there
was a general feeling of having been let down, encouraged by a series of
false alarms. The first siren on the 3rd September was followed by another
early next morning, with nerves even more on edge. At Allenton, on
the outskirts of Derby, some families fled to the moors, while others
took refuge in the tunnels of the railway serving the local quarries. In
a Nottingham hospital the night sister hurried into the corridor and
collided with a young nurse wearing her gas mask and in the resulting
laughter tension was dispelled. In Burton-on-Trent later that morning
one housewife felt very brave as she ventured into the garden, glancing
apprehensively at the sky as she pegged out Monday morning washing on
the line.

Gradually such fears declined and when at last, in mid-October, the
Germans did raid the Forth Bridge and naval vessels in the vicinity, no
warning was sounded and one Edinburgh resident remembers, 'We
stood about in the streets . . . and watched the aircraft swooping about the
sky and said, like one man near me, "My! Yon's a rer [rare] practice!" '

The Navy was already bearing the brunt of such fighting as there was.
On the 4th September the liner *Athenia* was torpedoed, and on the 17th
the aircraft carrier *Courageous* was sunk by a submarine in the Bristol
Channel. More than one woman wept at this first reminder that men's
lives were being lost, but the country thrilled to the story that, as the fatal
torpedo struck, the captain on the bridge 'put out his hand to steady
himself against the rail and said to the Yeoman of Signals, "That was a
damned good shot!" ' The sinking of the *Royal Oak* (often since
confused with the *Ark Royal*) in Scapa Flow a month later caused anger
and alarm as well as grief. In London people swarmed round the news-
vendors—the queueing habit was not yet established—and discussed the
event with strangers, the general reaction being that the government
was to blame. In December it was the Navy which produced the first
good news of the war when, after the Battle of the River Plate, the pocket

battleship *Graf Spee* was scuttled off the coast of Uruguay. Three months later the crews of the victorious warships marched through London to a heroes' welcome. 'The crowds were such as there had not been since . . . King George's Jubilee', one Londoner wrote to a friend. 'People kept on running forward and touching the men as they passed. One white-haired old man . . . kept on clapping them on the shoulder or shaking them by the hand and saying "Well done, boy!" ' On land, despite optimistic stories about French troops advancing into Germany, there was stalemate on the Western Front and Poland, for whose defence Britain had gone to war, was already lost. In the air the R.A.F. had so far dropped little except eighteen million leaflets which optimistically assured the Germans that their government had begun a war 'they cannot even hope to win'. This somewhat unmartial operation was not popular. The fact that our planes were dropping paper and not bombs seemed already all too characteristic of the government's method of waging war.

When, in these first months of the war, the government did have good news to tell it was invariably mishandled. When the British Expeditionary Force landed, promptly and efficiently, in France, the police on the censor's orders invaded newspaper offices to prevent the news being printed and dragged bundles of newspapers from the newspaper trains. When an R.A.F. pilot was awarded a medal the official statement refused to confirm that he had led the raid on Kiel on 4th September, though 'any newspaper which assumes that he was would not be inaccurate'—a communiqué received in the Ministry of Information press room in incredulous silence, followed by derisive laughter. The Ministry, on security grounds, 'killed' or held up such morale-boosting stories as the visit of the young Princesses to evacuees in Scotland or of the King's inspection of the Fleet: it even refused, to universal amusement, to release the text of the leaflet dropped on Germany. It was no wonder that the Ministry of Information, with its 999 employees, became the first great national joke of the war. *The Times* commented on it as early as 14th September that 'the confidence both of the press and of the public . . . has been badly shaken', while the *Daily Mirror* said bluntly: 'Fred Karno's Army has nothing on the Ministry of Information.' Comedians told the story of a woman who, misled by its name, had called there to ask the way to Clapham and had been told they didn't know, and if they did they couldn't tell her. M.P.s and journalists gleefully invented new nicknames for it—the Ministry of Muddle, the Ministry of Malformation, the Mystery of Information. Civilians passed on the rumour that running it was what the Crazy Gang did during the day. A two-hundred-page book appeared recounting the Ministry's misdeeds in detail, including the story that the Civil Servants who ran it—it employed only sixteen journalists—seeing 'P.A.' on press releases had interpreted this as 'Put away', instead of sending them to the Press Association. When reporters telephoned the Ministry for news during a warning in October they could get no reply—all the gallant 999 had taken refuge in the shelters. In four months the unfortunate Ministry had three ministers, and it remained the graveyard of ministerial reputations. Though it later produced much excellent publicity material, it never did find its Beaverbrook or its Woolton, its Morrison or its Bevin, and after the war it somehow succeeded in being the only major department whose work was not recorded by the official historians.

The first signs of the government's concern with morale were a series of bright red posters carrying the message 'Your Courage, Your Cheerfulness, Your Resolution, Will Bring Us Victory', though they might more usefully have been displayed in Downing Street and Whitehall, where these qualities were most obviously lacking, rather than in such places as Woolworths. The posters made little impression, apart from producing some caustic comments on the implication that 'you' were fighting for 'us', though a woman teaching an evacuated class in a dingy classroom in a Cambridgeshire village found that one provided a cheerful splash of colour on the wall, behind 'a great black kettle full of spindle berry which lit up the whole room'.* A second poster, 'Freedom is in Peril. Defend it with all your Might', made equally little impact. The bombardment of the citizen by such propaganda continued throughout the war, on hoardings, in trains and Food Offices, and before long on the walls and boarded-up doorways of bombed buildings. As the war went on the wordy exhortations of the early months grew shorter and crisper, reaching the ultimate in brevity in a quotation from Herbert Morrison, soon seen in vivid letters everywhere: 'Go to it!'

More effective in raising spirits were the modest increases in street and vehicle lighting in mid-September, and the gradual reopening of places of entertainment.

Cinemas in the reception and neutral areas were allowed to open again until 10 p.m. from 9th September: then half the West End cinemas and theatres at a time, provided they closed at six, and finally from December all were allowed to open simultaneously, closing between 10 and 11 p.m. In the cinema the successes of these months were *Jamaica Inn*, with Charles Laughton, *Goodbye, Mr. Chips*, with Robert Donat, *Where's that Fire*, with Will Hay, *Come on George*, starring George Formby, *The Stars Look Down*, with Michael Redgrave, and the propaganda film, *The Lion Has Wings*. There were long queues for this when I was taken to see it, and the audience seemed to swallow enthusiastically the absurdly complacent story, which showed cowardly

* So unmemorable was this poster, however, that even she did not remember the text correctly.

German pilots turning back at the mere sight of the balloon barrage. In the London theatre the great successes were the cheerful musical *Me and My Girl*, a sophisticated review *Black Velvet* and an Agatha Christie mystery *Ten Little Niggers*, while in the provinces one could see *Gaslight*, *Lilac Time* and *The Corn is Green*, all performed that winter at the King's Theatre, Southsea.

By the end of October 1939 professional football had been resumed, horse-racing began again in mid-October and grey-hound racing, now held in the afternoons. After the initial drop, both book loans and book sales rose, though many libraries closed at black-out. The war was hardest to forget in the dance-halls, where nearly half the tunes soon had a wartime flavour, including the smash-hit *There'll Always Be An England*, which became almost a second national anthem. Of less happy memory are *We're Going to Hang Out the Washing on the Siegfried Line* and *God Bless You, Mr. Chamberlain*,

> For deeds we can't forget . . .
> You look swell holding your umbrella
> All the world loves a wonderful feller.

The most important influence on morale at this time was the BBC, which had, as its head of drama remarked, prepared most efficiently for the wrong war. It had been assumed that for the first seven weeks the public would want nothing but news bulletins with record and theatre organ fill-ins. Instead there was a clamour for entertainment. By a remarkable feat of adaptability, programmes were almost back to normal by 6th September on the Home Service and from 7th January 1940 the Forces Programme provided an alternative of popular music and variety and magazine programmes. It also gave a new lease of life to Sandy Macpherson, who was soon attracting 5,000 requests a week from the Forces and their families for tunes to be played in *Sandy's Half Hour*. On the Home Service the outstanding serious series that winter was a history of Nazism, *The Shadow of the Swastika*, but the programme no one liked to miss was *Band Waggon*, on Saturday evening. Its return was even announced in the House of Commons and characteristically commented on by Arthur Askey in the first of the new series, on 16th September 1939:

Well, playmates . . . I think it's a stroke of genius putting *Band Waggon* on the air. It'll make old Nasty realise what the British Public will put up with. Anyway, they had to do something to give the gramophone a rest . . . Old Stuart Hibberd's nearly worn out winding it up—and, of course, you probably notice how muffled it sounded for a few days. Well, they investigated and found there was a pair of Freddie Grisewood's socks pushed down the horn. They'd been there since the Savoy Hill days when the neighbours used to complain about the noise.

In the same edition was a letter from 'Big' and 'Stinker's' old charwoman, Mrs. Bagwash, now 'somewhere in Essex . . . on work of international impotence', with a P.S. about her daughter Nausea, who having been 'attached to the balloon-barrage in Hyde Park as a blower-upper' had 'changed her job, because she got so out of breath', becom ng instead 'a puncture detector . . . When the balloons are blown up, she dips them in the Serpentine to see if any bubbles come up'. Lewis the goat, Arthur reported, had wanted to do his bit, but 'as soon as he got in the streets, all the A.R.P. wardens rushed out with their hand rattles . . . and he was carted off by the Decontamination Squad'. Later editions, however, contained noticeably fewer references to the war and in December 1939, to general regret, *Band Waggon* was broadcast for the last time.

Apart from *Monday Night at Eight*, established before the war, and *ITMA*, which achieved its greatest fame later, the most typical programme of these months was *Garrison Theatre*, which moved into the *Bandwagon* spot and ran for a year. Many people have happy memories of Jack Warner's regular exchanges with his 'little girl', Joan, who constantly rebuffed his advances, merely repeating her refrain of 'Programmes, Chocolates, Cigarettes', and of the 'Letters from my brother Syd', supposedly stationed in France, which had always been heavily censored. 'Yesterday the colonel caught his thumb in a tank. His only remark was twenty-four blue-pencils.' Jack Warner's catchphrases, 'Mind my bike!', 'blue-pencil' and 'di-da-di-da' (meaning 'etc'), soon passed into everyday use and office wits vied with each other inventing curious occupations, like his 'straightener out of corkscrews for teetotallers', 'tearer off of buttons in a laundry' and, most famous of all, 'bunger up of ratholes'.

Above all, however, the nation looked to the BBC for news. At first many people listened to every one of the frequent bulletins, until it became clear there was no news; indeed, except by those suffering from evacuation or the call-up, it began to be questioned whether there was really any war. It was almost possible to sympathise with the news-vendors who loudly called out 'Germans in . . .' and then added, softly, 'Berlin', though one in Portsmouth was sent to jail for two months for displaying the prophetic poster, 'Germany attacks Holland', despite his explanation that 'not being much of a scholar' he had omitted the 'if'. The dance hall which advertised a *Victory Ball* for 31st October 1939 was agreed to have been a little premature, but the ninety-year-old woman at Worthing, fined for a black-out offence, who explained 'I thought it was all over' had perhaps more excuse. Even now, just how the Chamberlain government did plan to win the war is a mystery. A typical official pamphlet, which 'proved' the German position to be hopeless, explained that 'We do not have to defeat the Nazis on land, but only to prevent them from defeating us'. The Prime Minister's constant insistence that Great Britain had no quarrel with the German nation encouraged those who argued that the war was bound to be over soon. A Mass Observation poll revealed that 21 per cent of the population expected the war to be over in six months, though 19 per cent thought it would last at least three years, and a doleful 1 per cent predicted it would go on for ever. One man polled had gloomily commented, after complaining of the road deaths caused by the black-out, that 'We're sure to win the war . . . when Hitler dies of old age and the German people take pity on us'.

One alarming symptom of low morale was the growing number of British citizens who listened to Lord Haw-Haw, the chief German broadcaster in English. Haw-Haw's real name was William Joyce and he was a Fascist, of Irish-American birth, who at the age of twenty-three fled to Germany in 1939 with his second wife. (The reports that he had run off with a chorus girl or embezzled the funds of the National Socialist League he had founded were propagandist lies.) He was given his nickname by a Fleet Street journalist because of his supposedly aristocratic drawl, heard at its best in his widely-imitated opening announcement, 'Jairmany calling.'

If Haw-Haw himself sounded like a stage Englishman, the characters he created were even more obviously stock figures: Orpington and Orpington, two old men grousing about the war in the smoking room of their club; the Jewish tax evader, Sir Izzy Ungeheimer; the fatuous Foreign Office diplomat, Sir Jasper Murgatroyd and 'good old Bumbly Mannering', a clergyman with shares in armament firms. These were precisely the sections of society which many ordinary British people distrusted, and though few people ever admitted to deliberately tuning in to Haw-Haw, a surprising number, estimated at a million, appeared to stumble on him regularly while idly twiddling the knob. A facetious mock-biography of him was a best-seller and the revue *Haw-Haw* at the Holborn Empire did good business, but the *Public Opinion Quarterly* reported that 'Haw-Haw's propaganda is listened to with enjoyment. It is common to hear people say that "there is a great deal of truth in it".' His success is reflected in the results of a Mass Observation survey; 17 per cent of those asked why the war was being fought replied 'for the Jews' or 'to save the capitalists' money'.

By July 1940 the government had become sufficiently alarmed at Haw-Haw's success to issue a press warning against listening to him in its 'What do I do . . .?' series:

What do I do ... if I come across German or Italian broadcasts when tuning my wireless? I say to myself: 'Now this blighter wants me to listen to him. Am I going to do what he wants?' ... I remember nobody can trust a word the Haw-Haws say, so just to make them waste their time, I switch 'em off or tune 'em out!

But by now the blighter's greatest days were over. His audience had shrunk and attacks on 'that liar, braggart and cheat, Churchill' only provoked anger. A Cheltenham shorthand typist, whose family still listened, observed that 'my father was ready to bash the set in'. Newcastle people still listened to such threats as 'You people in Jesmond Dene will not have your Dene much longer', but one housewife, goaded beyond endurance by Haw-Haw's statements that no one in Britain had seen bacon for months, held up her frying pan full of sizzling rashers to the wireless, remarking, 'You lying so and so. Take a good sniff!' Increasingly it was Haw-Haw's blunders which were quoted. An Eastbourne woman remembers the delight of local residents at his boast that Eastbourne harbour had been completely destroyed; the town has no harbour.* Sometimes Haw-Haw was proved right. A Bath woman remembers hearing him say, 'We are coming to the Queen of the West. We know the Admiralty is there.' A Manchester woman recalls him saying, 'Are you listening in Hulme? We'll soon get rid of all the vermin there: when all those old houses are bombed away.' 'They had a good try, as well,' she acknowledges. A land-girl in billets in Evesham in 1941 observed how, 'our landlord, a very morose, taciturn character, glued himself to the set, scowled darkly and at intervals muttered "Liar ... Bloody liar!" It was his sole patriotic gesture ... and it sent us into shrieks of laughter.'†

Reassuring public morale was one of the functions of the unpopular Ministry of Information and throughout the war selected observers sent in regular reports on the conversations they overheard in public houses, shops and trains. The Ministry also kept in touch with public opinion through local Information Committees, which organised public meetings and film shows and arranged for speakers for bodies like Women's Institutes. The standard was high. The wife of a Nottingham headmaster found that the regular Friday meetings she helped to organise were always crowded, none more so than the one addressed by the leader of the 'dam-busters', Guy Gibson, v.c.—later killed—whom she

---

* Another famous German error was their claim to have attacked the town of Random, following a British communiqué that 'bombs were dropped at random'. It provided the title for the best-selling wartime novel, *Random Harvest*.

† After the war Joyce was executed as a traitor, unjustly, in my view, as he had repeatedly tried to give up his British citizenship.

introduced with a memorable spoonerism, as 'the famous bomb-duster'. He played up beautifully by pretending to polish an imaginary bomb.

In 1940 it became an offence punishable by a £50 fine to pass on any rumour likely to cause 'alarm and despondency', but like the attacks on listening to Haw-Haw, which was never illegal, the campaign really came too late. It was the first few months of the war, and especially the first few days, which were the rumour-mongers' golden age. Two girl evacuees from Bradford, evacuated to Nelson, were not cheered by being told by their hostess's daughter, even before the war had started, that their home-town had been 'totally demolished' by a secret weapon. Nor were spirits raised in the Gloucestershire village where, on 6th September, the milkman, a popular bearer of rumours in many places, carried with him on his rounds the 'news', hushed-up by the authorities of course, that Romford had been heavily bombed and Chatham lay in ruins. In rural Essex the usual rumour about a shortage of wood due to the demand for civilian coffins was greatly improved on: the wood, it appeared, had all gone, not on the coffins themselves but merely on the racks to store them. Another popular story was of hosts who had caught V.D. from their evacuees. When raids really began the rumours redoubled. Mass Observation recorded, after the heavy attacks on Liverpool in May 1941, that one lorry driver had reported, with a nice mixture of detail and vagueness, that 'There's 50,917 dead and God knows how many wounded' (The actual number of deaths was 1,400).

Although ministers, in speeches and press advertisements, denounced the 'chatter-bugs' and urged citizens to 'Join the Silent Column', many rumours were harmless. One widespread report was that Goering himself had flown over London during the Battle of Britain and in Plymouth two years later some people even claimed to be able to identify his plane by the distinctive note of its engine. One man actually asserted that he had encountered Goering, in a dark corner of a shelter and helped to unlace his flying boots, only realising his identity after he had commented on the devastation wrought by the bombers and remarked in a foreign accent that all would now be peaceful 'as their work is done'. There were, too, many versions current of the story heard in the small Lancashire town of Leyland, that one enemy pilot had flown low enough to be recognised as a former apprentice at the Leyland Motor Works.

Urging others not to spread rumours became a popular occupation. Newspapers harangued their readers, clergy their congregations, headmasters their pupils. Special anti-rumour rallies were even held in some places. But far more successful than the anti-rumour drive was the government's campaign against giving information to the enemy. This began with a pompous pronouncement, typical of the Ministry of Information at that time:

WARNING

DO NOT DISCUSS ANYTHING WHICH MIGHT BE OF
NATIONAL IMPORTANCE

THE CONSEQUENCE OF ANY SUCH INDISCRETION
MAY BE THE LOSS OF MANY LIVES

Little better were the laboured rhyming slogans which followed:

> If you've news of our munitions,
> Keep it Dark!
> Ships and guns and troop positions,
> Keep it Dark . . .*

The best and most enduring of wartime slogans on this theme was 'Careless Talk Costs Lives', which easily outlived 'Walls have ears', 'Keep it under your hat' and 'Be like Dad, keep mum'. Like many successful slogans it was taken over by the humorists. 'What did Father say when mother told him she was expecting?', ran a typical witticism. 'Oh, that careless stork'. Most effective of the 'careless talk' posters were those drawn by the *Punch* artist, Fougasse, which, over the caption 'You never know who's listening', showed women gossiping on a bus, while Hitler and Goering filled the seat behind, men exchanging secret information in a club beneath an oil painting which concealed Hitler, and similar pictures of Nazi leaders stretched out, ears agog, on luggage racks in trains and beneath tables in restaurants. A full-length feature film, *Next of Kin*, showing the defeat of a commando raid due to careless talk, was a commercial as well as a propaganda success.

In fact if there were any undetected German spies in Britain they remained undiscovered even after the war, and those who were caught were invariably ill-trained, being given away by elementary blunders like writing the figure 7 with a stroke through it, or answering '*Ja*' to sudden questions. No allied operations seem to have been endangered by loss of surprise, not even the Dieppe Raid, though the Canadians taking part in it announced their destination almost openly to anyone in earshot.

There were many stories of apparent German omniscience, encouraged by Lord Haw-Haw's habit of welcoming R.A.F. and United States Air Force squadrons and government departments to new locations, but such information could often be deduced from the interrogation of captured airmen and the scrutiny of local newspapers. The popular

---

* Advertising men may like to know that the only rhyming slogan still widely remembered is one of the London Transport 'Billy Brown' series, and that only because of the parodies of it.

story of Haw-Haw's having correctly referred to a certain church clock being ten minutes slow seems to have been wholly unfounded.

Although a few people were still suspicious of some individuals they met, the country as a whole escaped the spy-mania of 1914. Usually it was those furthest from danger who gave themselves the illusion of helping the war effort by being excessively zealous. A Newcastle Civil Servant on holiday in a village in a remote part of Northumberland, where 'they didn't know there was a war on', still laughs at the memory of being interviewed by an apologetic inspector, after the locals, who had previously refused to answer her questions about beauty spots in the neighbourhood, had finally reported her for 'drawing plans of the village', the least military of targets, when she had sat on a wall outside the village pub writing picture postcards.

On 29th September 1939 a National Registration census recording particulars of every citizen was compiled and this was followed by the issue of the Identity Card, a small document containing one's name, address and National Registration number, supposed to be carried at all times. Also issued in October was another document which became even more familiar, the ration book, though, owing it was said to a *Stop Rationing!* campaign by the *Daily Express*, the start of rationing was postponed from November to January, when bacon, ham and butter went on coupons, followed in March by meat.*

One Labour leader accused the Cabinet of having 'had cold feet' over rationing and it also succumbed to an even more irresponsible campaign for a drastic reduction on A.R.P. expenditure. Many of the full-time, paid wardens and rescue workers recruited on the outbreak of war were dismissed, some returning to unemployment after their first job for years. Even more serious, A.R.P. workers were within a few weeks being widely criticised as parasites. Volunteer ambulance drivers found themselves jeered at as they cleaned their vehicles, wardens were mocked as '£3 a week wallahs' as they did their rounds. The firemen who asked in a six-year-old girl who had peeped round the door of their station in Chelsea were a little taken aback when she confided in them, 'My daddy says you're a waste of public money!' The men from one London A.F.S. station never wore uniform in the street if they could help it because of loud remarks about '£3 a week men doing b——all', and some joined the Forces solely to escape such insults. Another volunteer, in East London, only narrowly escaped a fight with a soldier who shouted about 'windy Yids' through the railings at the firemen, many of whom were Jewish, as they drilled in the station yard. In May 1940

---

* The *Daily Express* also wanted the black-out to be lifted, Civil Defence to be cut, evacuated offices to be brought back, and the public to ignore government appeals to keep prices down by saving rather than spending.

the same fireman was actually asked to leave a Soho restaurant because he was in uniform, the manager only reluctantly agreeing that he could stay. Six months later during the blitz, still in uniform, he was given the best table, waited on by the manager personally and given his meal 'on the house' as 'Nothing can be too good for a London fireman!'.

In this fire station, many of the men believed that there had been no bombing because Hitler realised that 'the Chamberlain government never meant to fight the war and was only waiting to get a crack at the Soviet Union'. These suspicions, shared by many others, became sharper when, at the end of November, Russia invaded Finland and the government decided to send an expedition to help her, though, typically, its plans were so ineffective that Finland had surrendered before any troops set sail. In view of the hysterical pro-Russian feeling later in the war it is worth recalling that at this time Russia was, except on the far left, at least as unpopular as Germany, and the newspapers carried headlines like, 'The question the whole country is asking: War with Russia?' In retrospect the thought that Great Britain in 1939 could have taken on Germany and Russia simultaneously seems more laughable than frightening, though it shows how far both public and government had lost touch with reality and how desperate they were for action somewhere.* If opinion was divided about Russia, it was almost unanimous on the dismissal of the Secretary of State for War, Leslie Hore-Belisha, in January 1940. It was openly said that the Brass Hats had got rid of him for wishing to make the Army more democratic and for being a Jew. The keen ears and eyes of Mass Observation noted that in cinemas the former War Minister was clapped enthusiastically, while the Prime Minister 'was only applauded very feebly' and Lord Gort, commander of the B.E.F., not at all. 'When he gave a Christmas message ... the only response noted was from one woman who remarked, "Silly, isn't it?".'

Christmas trade in 1939 was 10 per cent up on 1938, despite higher taxes and the government's appeal to save. Apart from the black-out, the chief reminders of the war were the toy soldiers' uniforms and model Maginot Lines on sale in the toy shops, and some topical jokes in the Christmas pantomimes, like the explanation for an off-stage crash in *Cinderella*: 'That must be Goering changing his medals.' The outstanding event of the season was the King's Christmas broadcast, in which he quoted some then unknown lines which immediately became world famous: 'I said to the man who stood at the Gate of the Year, "Give me a light that I may tread safely into the unknown." And he

* The historian A. J. P. Taylor describes the proposal as 'the product of a madhouse. . . . The only charitable conclusion is to assume that the British and French governments had taken leave of their senses.'

replied, "Go out into the darkness and put your hand into the hand of God. That shall be to you better than light and safer than a known way." '*

For most civilians the chief memory of that depressing winter is of the weather, which the press was not allowed to mention. Birds froze on the trees. Roads were impassable. Trains arrived not hours but days late. Everywhere the mere struggle to keep going and to keep warm dominated daily life. Sir John Reith, who became Minister of Information in January, decided that there was now little real opposition to the war, but equally little enthusiasm for it. In January 1940, despite a desperate shortage of war material of every kind, from anti-tank guns to wardens' uniforms, there were still 1,600,000 unemployed. Meanwhile a suggestion that Krupps's arms factory should be bombed had been turned down by the government on the grounds that it was private property and a plan of Winston Churchill's to float mines down the Rhine had been postponed, in case it offended the French. The public did not know these things, but they suspected something of that kind. As one distinguished journalist later wrote, 'Nearly everywhere I went during those early months, I heard the same remark, "The British people will win this war in spite of their government." '

Only in February 1940 were spirits briefly raised by the freeing from the prison ship *Altmark*, in a Norwegian fiord, of nearly three hundred British seamen, captured by the *Graf Spee*. The cry of the boarding party from the rescuing destroyer, 'The Navy's here!', was proudly repeated in millions of homes and helped to raise still further the prestige of the Navy and the First Lord of the Admiralty. Throughout these dark months Churchill had emerged as the only member of the government with his heart in the war. After his first broadcast, in October, Mass Observation discovered that his talk of hunting down the U-Boats day and night had provided the first real boost to public morale and had led to widely-heard comment. 'He ought to be Prime Minister.' The Ministry of Information used an extract from another speech, in January 1940, for one of its most successful posters:

Come then let us to the task, to the battle and the toil, each to our part, each to our station. Fill the armies, rule the air, pour out the munitions, strangle the U-Boats, sweep the mines, plough the land, build the ships, guard the streets, succour the wounded, uplift the downcast, and honour the brave. Let us go forward together in all parts of the

* The poem had in fact been written in 1908 by Miss Minnie Haskins in aid of a missionary fund. By 1939 she was aged 64 and a retired university lecturer. She had not heard the King's speech. Reprinted, the poem sold 43,000 copies and its author was commissioned to contribute a weekly poem to a Sunday newspaper and inundated with offers to write texts for calendars and Christmas cards. It also earned her an entry in *Who's Who* and, later, an obituary in *The Times*.

Empire, in all parts of this island. There is not a week nor a day, nor an hour to be lost.

It had been the bitterest winter in living memory and it was followed by the finest spring. In April the grass, perhaps due to the long-lying winter snowfalls, had never looked greener, while everywhere the cherry trees were in bloom and the chestnuts in leaf. And with the spring the war at last began; on 9th April Hitler invaded Norway and Denmark. Soon it proved to be the old familiar story of retreat and defeat. Denmark was occupied in a few hours; Norway after a few weeks. The British force sent to help her was driven back almost into the sea. The few British aircraft were shot out of the sky or destroyed on the ground. Only the Navy emerged with enhanced credit, inflicting heavy losses on the German ships, particularly off Narvik where the British commander was awarded a posthumous V.C., after a famous signal from his shattered destroyer, 'Continue to engage the enemy.' The embittered servicemen returned to Britain to spread a tale of chaos and muddle. I can well recall a former master, back from Norway, standing in the house dayroom describing how the shells landed for his guns had all been of the wrong calibre.

Chamberlain had always had a weakness for the fatally inappropriate phrase, like his notorious boasts after Munich, about 'peace with honour' and 'peace for our time'. He was never to be forgiven for a speech on 4th April 1940, when he stated that Hitler had 'missed the bus'. It had been assumed that there were no signs of war factories being built only because the government had cleverly concealed them, and that British Forces had not so far attacked because they were secretly preparing a devastating spring offensive. In London, a BBC producer noted how the Norwegian campaign had banished the prevailing gloom, the general reaction being that 'Hitler has bitten off more than he can chew'. The disillusionment which swept the country as the truth dawned that Britain had suffered another humiliating defeat and that the government's sole plan was to wait till beaten on one battlefield after another, was correspondingly bitter. In private diaries, hitherto mild-mannered citizens to whom Chamberlain had up to now been a hero began to write of him in angry contempt. For the first time the ordinary civilian awoke to the possibility that the war would not drag on into a long stalemate ending with a German revolution against Hitler, but would end in a German victory. A shop assistant in Welwyn Garden City, 'which', he noted, 'looks its loveliest', pasted into his diary on April 30th one of the innumerable leading articles attacking the government as 'It seems to sum up the mess we are in'. On 3rd May he recorded that 'everyone was very disappointed. . . . There is plenty of criticism going on about it.' He ended the day by listening to Lord Haw-Haw, whose 'every sentence began, "The British defeat in Norway". Boy are they pleased!' On Wednesday 8th May he recorded, 'People are talking about us losing the war for the first time and saying our government are too old and slow to win.'

That day many were making the same comment more publicly in the great debate in the House of Commons on a motion of confidence in the government. Despite Chamberlain's appeal to his 'friends in the House' to rally round him, another maladroit phrase which helped to destroy him, late that night the Tory M.P., Sir Henry 'Chips' Channon, confided to his diary, 'There is no doubt that the government is seriously jarred and all confidence in it is gone.' This had not prevented him earlier that evening from voting for Chamberlain and in joining other Tory M.P.s in shouting 'Quislings' and 'Rats' at their fellow Conservatives who filed out of the 'Noes' lobby. No abuse could have been more misplaced. It was clear even then that Channon and the other 280 Conservative M.P.s who supported Chamberlain were, whatever their motives, voting for Hitler.* The true patriots were the thirty Conservatives who voted against their discredited leader, the sixty more who abstained, and the Labour and Liberal Opposition who voted solidly against him. When Chamberlain made some final, utterly discreditable efforts to hold on to office—'like a dirty old piece of chewing-gum clinging to a chair', as one of his disillusioned supporters put it—it was the Labour Party's flat refusal to serve under him which saved the nation, a belated atonement for its pre-war opposition to rearmament. On the morning of Friday 10th May 1940, another day of bright sunshine, the Germans attacked through Holland and Belgium towards France and the Channel. At six o'clock that evening Winston Churchill became Prime Minister. The country had found its leader at last. It had also, in one of his own famous phrases, 'found its soul'.

---

* The House of Commons, elected in 1935, was exceptionally unrepresentative in 1940. (A Gallup Poll in early May showed only 32 per cent of the population favoured Chamberlain as the Prime Minister.) The normal General Election was not held in 1940 due to the war. In 1945 136 Conservative M.P.s lost their seats, including many of Chamberlain's supporters. 'Chips' Channon's majority was impregnable but was cut from 25,000 to 3,000.

# BEATING THE INVADER

'Do not give any German anything. Do not tell him anything. Hide
your food and your bicycles. Hide your maps. See that the enemy gets
no petrol . . . Think always of your country before you think of
yourself.'

*If the Invader Comes,* June 1940

The change of atmosphere produced in the country by the new coalition
government was almost tangible. As one journalist wrote in his diary
that May: 'There is a speed-up all round. The atmosphere is electric,
bracing, instead of stagnant, as it was while Chamberlain pottered and
piffled.' In every aspect of his life the civilian began to feel the grip of
resolute and determined men upon the helm. Typical of the new men
was the massive, solid figure of Ernest Bevin, the trade union leader whom
Churchill considered to have 'the temperament of a born fighter' and
made Minister of Labour. Until Bevin's arrival little had been done to
mobilise manpower, except for the Forces, or to absorb the unemployed
or train new workers. Now all was changed. The Emergency Powers Act,
passed in a single day, 22nd May 1940, gave the government the legal
right to control all the resources, human and material, of the country,
and the first Defence Regulation passed under it empowered the Minister
of Labour to order any citizen to undertake, or remain in, any work he
required.

The second of the men on whom Churchill relied—he contemplated
forming, with them, a three-man 'Committee of Public Safety' if the
Germans landed—was Lord Beaverbrook, the millionaire proprietor
of the *Daily Express*. Later he became known in Whitehall as 'the great
disorganiser' but in 1940 one Civil Servant in his Ministry of Aircraft
Production, who found his new boss's 'politics and press activities
repulsive', found it 'a magnificent experience to be under Beaverbrook . . .
in those days; he cut through red tape and drove ahead with what really
mattered. Shocked civil servants did their utmost to keep to time-
honoured routines, but were brushed aside.' At my school the Old Boy
chosen to present the prizes at the end of the Summer Term was an
official from the Ministry of Aircraft Production, being introduced by
the headmaster as 'the man who dams the Beaverbrook'.

But it was the new Prime Minister who dominated the scene. Chamberlain had bowed himself out with a sad and dignified resignation broadcast, and when in November he died of cancer Churchill paid him a typically generous obituary tribute. More typical of public sentiment was a letter in *Picture Post* in June suggesting that the ministers responsible for the nation's present plight should be treated like sentries who had slept at their post and shot. For most people the outstanding memory of the summer of 1940 is of Churchill's speeches. That fine, confident voice, steadily rolling itself round the polished but solid phrases, the relish with which he warned of the fate awaiting 'the Narzee hordes' and 'that wicked man' who led them, breathed new heart into many a worried citizen.* Already by July a public opinion poll showed that 88 per cent of the population had complete confidence in him: the last figure for Chamberlain had been 32 per cent.

Churchill's first speech as Prime Minister was made to the House of Commons on the 18th May when he made his famous declaration: 'I would say to the House, as I have said to those who have joined this Government: "I have nothing to offer but blood, toil, tears and sweat." ' Six days later his first broadcast followed:

> I speak to you for the first time as Prime Minister in a solemn hour for the life of our country . . . One bond unites us all, to wage war until victory is won and never to surrender ourselves to servitude and shame, whatever the cost and the agony may be. . . . Upon all . . . the long night of barbarism will descend . . . unless we conquer, as conquer we must, as conquer we shall.

This was the moment when the ordinary, bewildered civilian became not merely willing but eager to take his part in the war. One evacuated Civil Servant listened to the speech sitting on the stairs leading to a crowded basement kitchen in Harrogate. 'The effect of that broadcast was magical', he remembers. 'A confused and frightened lot of people became courageous, hopeful, determined to see it through and no one that I came across ever slipped back into the defeatism that disgraced the country from Munich to that May.'

The upsurge in morale came only just in time for in the next few weeks there was bad news enough to make the bravest despair. One crushing blow followed another: the collapse of Holland, the surrender of King Leopold of the Belgians, thus endangering the British army which had gone to his aid—a betrayal still remembered with especial bitterness —the German break-through at Sedan. Only the return to Britain of its defeated army raised spirits.

* Some of the finest speeches, delivered in the House of Commons alone, are now lost for ever. The post-war recordings, made when Churchill was old and tired, lack the authentic feel of 1940.

By 4th June 338,000 troops had been rescued, 139,000 of them French, the rest British. The realisation that 'the boys were back', weary, lacking equipment and sometimes even boots, but safe, caused such a wave of relief to sweep through the nation that Churchill, referring to this 'miracle of deliverance' in the Commons that day, felt obliged to warn that 'wars are not won by evacuations'. He went on to deliver perhaps the most famous of all his declarations of defiance:

We shall defend our island home . . . and . . . outlive the menace of tyranny: if necessary for years, if necessary alone . . . We shall not flag or fail. We shall go on to the end. We shall fight in France, we shall fight on the seas and oceans: we shall fight . . . in the air. We shall defend our island, whatever the cost may be. We shall fight on the beaches, we shall fight on the landing grounds: we shall fight in the fields and in the streets, we shall fight in the hills; we shall never surrender.

Two hundred thousand British families whose menfolk had been saved had personal, as well as patriotic, grounds to rejoice at the news of Dunkirk. A woman awaiting the birth of her first son in a Manchester hospital learned at last where her husband was from a newspaper carrying the story of the evacuation. Soon afterwards he telephoned. 'To hear his voice was heaven', she felt. A Carshalton woman remembers a policeman arriving with her address scrawled on the back of a cigarette packet and the message 'Tell mum, I'm O.K., Jack'. He arrived later, wounded but safe.

A Dorchester woman witnessed the arrival of several trainloads sent to rest in the town. 'They were in a pitiful state. They tumbled out of the train so weary and tired that they hardly knew what they were doing. Their uniforms were torn and dirty . . . their boots cracked and worn out. A few were in stockinged feet. Buses had been sent to the station . . . but the men refused the conveyances, squared their shoulders and marched, or stumbled, up the road to the Barracks. They sat down at once to a meal but were so sleepy that they were asleep before the meal ended.'

Dutch, Belgian and French troops had been brought back with British soldiers. A Bournemouth girl witnessed the arrival of 'thousands of exhausted Frenchmen. I watched them coming along the road from the railway station, dragging their raw, blistered feet, trying to arrange themselves into something resembling military order . . . The crowds lining the road were handing out cigarettes and bars of precious chocolate. Cups of tea appeared from nearby houses and . . . I saw many in the crowd with tears streaming down their faces. At home I found a note from Mother' "Shall be a bit late. Down at the church hall washing French feet" '—her mother, a cripple, had at last found a way to help in the war.

Hardly had the nation absorbed the shock of Dunkirk than it learned of the fall of France, news which made so deep an impression that many people still remember the exact circumstances in which they heard it. The news that Marshal Pétain had asked for an armistice was given by Frank Phillips in the one o'clock bulletin on 'Black Monday', 17th June 1940. One of those who heard it was a woman teaching in a village school near Peterborough who that morning had welcomed her R.A.F. husband home on unexpected leave. He had written on the blackboard a list of countries in preparation for a lesson he planned to give that afternoon on 'Our Allies'. Without a word, on returning to school after lunch, he wiped the name of France from the list. In another school, in Guildford, a twelve-year-old girl heard the news as she walked into the geography room after school dinner. 'I had a sudden ball of ice in my stomach', she remembers. 'I felt "this is it, there is nothing between us and them now".'

At Llantrisant, Glamorganshire, miners waiting at the pit bottom realised that something was wrong from the glum faces of the afternoon shift coming to relieve them and called out, 'What's the matter, boys?'

A Cornish mother cycling on that 'beautiful Summer's evening' to listen with a woman friend to Churchill's speech, thought as she rode, 'Far worse than death would be for the children to grow up Nazis, so if they landed I must be prepared to shoot the children and myself.' She found a few minutes later that her 'gentle, conventional hosts had come to the same decision'. A North London woman, working seven days a week 'round the clock' in the office of a munitions factory, remembers one hysterical typist shrieking as the news came through, 'Whatever will we do now?' She was answered by 'a very bossy, bullying man, generally hated . . . "Do? Do?" screamed Old Bully: "We'll bloody well get on with it ourselves." ' In a bank at Accrington: Lancashire, one frightened local businessman arrived to draw his money out, asking in a panic, 'What shall we do when the Germans get here?' This time the bank's deputy-manager answered him: 'Do? I'll tell you what we'll do. We'll get a gun and we'll shoot the buggers!' Here surely spoke the authentic accents of Britain 1940.

Next day Churchill broadcast the famous speech which ended with the quotation:

Let us therefore brace ourselves to our duties: and so bear ourselves that, if the British Empire and its Commonwealth last for a thousand years, men will still say, 'This was their finest hour'.

Perhaps because of such leadership, this was not a gloomy time. George VI spoke for all his people when he wrote to his mother after he Fall of France, 'Personally, I feel happier now that we have no allies to be polite to.' A Low cartoon, published in the *Evening Standard* on 10th June 1940, perfectly reflected the nation's mood. It showed a British soldier: confronting a hostile sea and a horde of approaching bombers: crying 'Very well then, alone!'.

Everywhere now one began to see signs of the hourly-expected invasion —especially the roadblocks made of iron posts buried in holes in the road, barrel-like blocks of concrete, or home-made obstacles built up from wrecked cars, rusty ploughs and heaps of rubble. At my school in Sussex parties of boys turned out in football shorts and armed with spades to widen the River Arun as an anti-tank ditch. (One humorist suggested they should try painting themselves with woad, like the ancient Britons, to try to frighten the enemy away.) Across the school playing fields, as across parks, fields and other open spaces everywhere, sprouted obstacles to prevent enemy aircraft from landing, in this case wigwam-like tripods of poles. The road into the nearby town was protected by huge concrete cubes, reducing traffic to a slow-moving single line. My home in Newbury was further inland but the River Kennet which divided it was an inner defence line. Halfway down the hill leading into the town was a large tree trunk pinioned at one end to a concrete base and at the other attached to a wheel, ready to trundle it into position across the road. Commanding this obstacle was a sandbagged upper window in a house to the right and a summer house at the end of a garden on the left, with several bricks removed to provide a firing aperture.

Of all the anti-invasion preparations at this time, the one which inconvenienced the ordinary civilian most was the order, on 31st May, for the taking down of 'any sign which furnished any indication of the name of . . . or the direction of . . . or the distance to any place'. The removal of the signposts was followed by a wholesale uprooting of milestones, the defacing of the names of towns on war memorials and the painting over of shop and other signs identifying the town or village. Bus destination blinds were amended to read 'The Red Lion' or 'Top of the Hill'. The bus company's name now appeared on the side of its vehicles as '——— and District Ltd.', as though concealing some blacked-out obscenity, and local shopfronts displayed signs like ——— Village Stores or The ——— Cake Shop. Local newspaper editors often sent a reporter in search of items giving the name of the town which had been overlooked, telephone boxes, newsagents' advertisement boards, Mothers Union banners and parish magazines in churches and bus timetables being frequent culprits.

It was not until October 1942 that signposts could again be displayed in towns, not until May 1943 that villages became identifiable and not until October 1944 that all restrictions were removed.

At the same time as the signposts were being taken down, the ringing of church bells was banned, except to announce invasion, and there was a wholesale rounding-up of aliens, most German and Italian male adults being interned and all foreigners left at liberty being subject to restrictions on their movements. Four hundred British citizens of fascist sympathies were also rounded up—the release of their leader, Sir Oswald Mosley, three years later, on health grounds, causing a tremendous public outcry.* The government also distributed to every home a leaflet *If the Invader Comes*, which urged everyone 'to stay put' to avoid blocking the roads if the Germans did attack, following it up in March 1941 with more elaborate advice in *Beating the Invader*.

The pregnant wife of a London A.F.S. man with a three-year-old son, evacuated to a Surrey village, confided to her diary on 2nd June what must have been in many women's minds at this time. 'I pictured myself with my young baby in my arms and Michael beside me trying to fulfil what is asked of us in the leaflet about invasion, e.g., refusing water to the enemy, and the obvious result, and wondering how it would help my country to make my children motherless.' Two months later, still 'expecting', she was envisaging another frightening situation, not mentioned in the government's leaflet. 'In my fancy I saw myself stuck in a trench and unable to travel with fighting going on in the neighbourhood and my greatest anxiety was the nappy question . . . I visualised wet and soiled nappies with no means of washing them or getting fresh ones and tiny buttocks becoming very sore.' In fact, though few then realised it, the invasion was off. In June Hitler had attacked Russia and the men who might have stormed the beaches of Eastbourne or Lyme Bay were soon dying instead in front of Moscow and Stalingrad.†

But preparations for invasion continued to affect the lives of the civilian population until at least 1942. One little-published preparation was the distribution of reserve dumps of food in every town and village.

The two thousand people of the Bedfordshire village of Willington, for instance, would have been fed from three dumps, 'one being stored in the vicarage, one in Mr. A. Stokes's barn, and one at Mr. Golber's nurseries'. Each contained biscuits, corned beef, tinned soup, sugar, condensed milk, margarine and tea, and the Invasion Committee, consisting of representatives of the A.R.P., W.V.S. and other organisations, had also arranged an emergency slaughterhouse and bakery, and located enough wells to prevent the village going thirsty if the mains were broken. Country vicarages were favourite store-places and the daughter

* Mosley is still, in 1970, very much alive at the age of 72.
† The original German plan for the invasion, later modified, involved seaborne assaults between Ramsgate and the Isle of Wight, supported by parachute troops dropped behind Brighton and Folkestone and with follow-up landings between Weymouth and Lyme Regis.

of one clergyman living near Canterbury remembers hungrily eyeing the stacks of cartons and sacks piled in the empty bedrooms and loft of their house, which were not called in until almost the end of the war.

If the nation found an unofficial voice in these dangerous weeks, it was in the solid Yorkshire accents of J. B. Priestley. His *Postscripts*, delivered after the nine o'clock news from June until October, precisely caught the popular mood, from the very first one, which described how 'the pride of our ferry service to the Isle of Wight . . . the *Gracie Fields*', sunk at Dunkirk, would 'go on sailing proudly down the years'. In September, he delivered perhaps the most famous *Postscript* of the series, about 'a giant, almost superhuman, meat and potato pie, with a magnificently brown, crisp, artfully wrinkled, succulent looking crust' in his home-town of Bradford. He had found it, in its bomb-damaged home, 'as magnificent as ever . . . steaming away like mad. Every puff and jet of that steam defied Hitler, Goering and the whole gang of them. It was glorious.' When the first series of *Postscripts* ended on 20th October, it marked a milestone. As Priestley himself said, 'The high, generous mood is vanishing with the leaves.' The exhilaration produced by immediate danger was giving way to a grimmer resolve to see the business through to the finish.

On the 19th July Hitler had made his 'peace offer' speech in the Reichstag, apparently suggesting that Britain should allow him to keep his conquests. A few months earlier some people, at least, might have welcomed such an offer; now it was contemptuously dismissed. And when copies of the speech, entitled *A Last Appeal to Reason*, were dropped from German aircraft in August, copies were auctioned for local Red Cross and Spitfire Funds and a newsreel showed a grinning countryman tearing one into squares for what were euphemistically described as 'shaving papers'.

By now many civilians were actively involved in the war as part-time soldiers. On Tuesday 14th May 1940 the new Secretary of State for War, Anthony Eden, broadcast an appeal for men to join a new force of Local Defence Volunteers. The response was immediate. The daughter of a Guildford man can still remember him wearily 'reaching for his shoes after a long day at the factory', to set off for the police station to enrol. One Welsh boy was puzzled why his father's 'usually grave face' was now 'a picture of joviality'—he had returned from enlisting via the public house. In Kent, the most threatened area, men at Gillingham and Cranbrook were signing on while Eden was still speaking; at Folkestone eager volunteers were still queueing at midnight. Although the official age-limits were seventeen to sixty-five, there were gallant recruits in their eighties as well as fifteen- and sixteen-year-olds. Within twenty-four hours 250,000 men had enrolled; by mid-July the total had risen to more than a million.

One of the most urgent needs was for some kind of uniform to protect its wearer from being shot as a spy, and within a few days everyone had been issued with an armlet. A *Punch* cartoon showed a dignified butler carefully laying out on his employer's bed a strip of cloth labelled 'L.D.V.' with the announcement, 'Your uniform, my lord!' Within a few weeks denim overalls became available, usually far too large. A Hertfordshire woman still laughs at the memory of her husband and his greatest friend trying on their first, identical uniforms, for there was a difference of five stone in their weight. The friend's wife, when she could control her mirth, commented, 'Well, if only Hitler could see you two now, he would know that it was no good carrying on with the war.' A Plymouth woman discovered that the denim trousers issued to her husband were eight inches too long and ten inches too wide round the waist, though a large safety pin was thoughtfully supplied to make them fit, causing him always to refer to the garment as 'his rompers'. While boots were usually at least size ten, the earliest headgear was mainly size six-and-five-eighths, so that until steel helmets arrived men went on duty in absurdly capacious garments with tiny forage caps perched on their heads. By the time I joined, in January 1943, normal battle dress was being issued, indistinguishable from army uniform except for the shoulder flashes, 'Home Guard', the name officially adopted, at Churchill's suggestion, in August 1940.

One of the questions asked of all recruits was 'Are you familiar with firearms?' but in May 1940 the owner of an antique shop was more likely to have been acquainted with the weapons provided than an ex-soldier. Rifles of some kind were available for only about a third of the men who originally joined, many weapons in those days being literally museum pieces. The Imperial War Museum in London was raided for machine guns and rifles from the first world war; the humble borough museum at Newbury contributed for training purposes its solitary hand-grenade. The long-suffering wives of L.D.V.s lost the knobs from their brass bedsteads for use as dummy hand-grenades and often centuries-old blunderbusses and fowling pieces, for which—fortunately perhaps—no ammunition survived were carried in the hope they would frighten solitary parachutists into surrender. At least one man, at Banstead in Surrey, went on parade, his wife remembers, armed with a chair leg.

The first real step towards making the L.D.V. an armed force came with the arrival from the United States of half a million 0.300 rifles, and volunteers worked day and night to remove the thick coating of yellow grease in which the weapons had lain for twenty years. At the same time private citizens in America were sending their own shotguns and sporting rifles. A man then working at Rochester airport witnessed the arrival of two packing cases, each containing 150 fire-arms 'of all sorts and sizes . . . each of them had a luggage label tied on with sympathetic and encouraging messages from the sender, like "To help you in England in your hour of need from Mrs. and Mr. J. B. Harrison and family" and "For the defence of the old country from Mr. and Mrs. Jones" . . . We nearly cried when we read some of these messages.'

Curiously enough, just when the Home Guard was acquiring its first automatic weapons, one Sussex volunteer remembers, 'some armchair warrior had them withdrawn and replaced by a length of gas-piping with a bayonet welded to one end, graced by the title of "pikes" '. The issuing of pikes was a major blunder, and had a damaging effect upon morale. One Scottish Home Guard commander considered that 'a pike would be as innocuous . . . as a toothpick against . . . the . . . invading troops', and an unfortunate battalion in Essex which was photographed doing a street fighting exercise with them never lived it down after the picture was published with the caption 'Mind my pike!'.

Though allowing women to act as auxiliaries who manned telephones and field kitchens, the government refused to let them carry arms, but a number of private female armies were formed under names like 'The Women's Amazon Defence Corps' and many women learned to shoot. One Hampstead housewife took private lessons twice a week at an army barracks, keeping the reason for these regular outings dark for fear of ridicule from her family. To her own surprise she proved a crack shot and after scoring five bulls with five shots could no longer contain her pride and took the target home to show her family. 'Fortunately, my skill with a rifle was never needed,' she remembers, 'but I look back to those days with a glow of pleasure as an example of what one could do if one tried.'

In the 1940 atmosphere of strained nerves and high expectancy, false alarms were probably inevitable. A girl living in a Gloucestershire village near Cheltenham, after hearing the tremendous noise of heavy hurrying feet outside, called out 'Paratroopers, Dad!' Immediately 'he went out in his dressing gown and slippers, with his gun, while Mum and I sat trembling', only to return with the news that the 'paratroopers' were straying cart horses who had merely 'trampled all over his seed beds'. A district nurse remembers visiting one afternoon a street in the Rhondda where pandemonium reigned. 'A big, burly woman was carrying a pint bottle full of petrol and a box of matches, calling out, "This will settle the first b—— who dares to land!" Another woman shouted from her doorway, "I have lighted my copper fire and have the hose ready. Cuss the bloody Huns!" Small children were running about, one with a poker, another dangling a large table knife, everybody shouting and trying to out-do their neighbours'. At last the mystery was explained:

the sound of the wind on the tin roof of an adjoining factory had been mistaken for the church bells. One farmer living near Cardiff remembers his unit being called out early one morning to man the sea wall overlooking the Bristol Channel ready to repulse an expected landing from a submarine. Even to his inexperienced eye, this seemed unlikely, 'since any German soldier who could get through that mud, much less a German submarine, would be pretty amazing', and the operation ended, rapidly and ingloriously, when an enemy bomber flew over dropping a string of bombs. Nobody was hurt but our commanding officer came rushing along saying "Let's get to hell out of here as quick as we can!" ', and the brave defenders fled back to their homes.

The only false alarm on a national scale occurred on the evening of Saturday 7th September 1940, simultaneously with the first heavy German air attacks on London. At 8.7 p.m. the code-word *Cromwell* was signalled to army units all over the country, warning them that conditions were suitable for invasion, but widely interpreted to mean that the long-expected attack had actually begun. In East Anglia some enthusiastic enginers blew up bridges and laid mines, which killed several Guards officers, and in many places local commanders ordered the church bells to be rung and road-blocks to be set up. The excitement spread from one district to the next as the bells were heard in the distance. A Home Guard farming near Lewes, in Sussex, was manning a lonely coastal pill box with two regular soldiers that night. At 10 p.m. their commanding officer arrived to announce solemnly, 'There is to be no retirement.' His own men were suitably impressed but the Home Guard, whose home was nearby, broke the tension by asking involuntarily, 'What about my breakfast?' One farm worker at Piddletrenthide, Dorset, who could not see to dress because of the bedroom black-out, leapt into the garden and pulled on his uniform by moonlight. A City secretary, married to an ex-Grenadier Guardsman, remembers that as he left he handed her the garden fork, with a parting remark rarely heard in the respectable suburb of Potters Bar: 'Don't let anybody in, lovey, but if anybody gets in, don't hesitate to push this fork through his blasted guts.' It was a sad anticlimax when hours later he came back, remarking, 'What a bloody turn-out, looking for German invaders with nothing but the broom handle, which I took out of your broom.'

Perhaps because its services were never called upon in earnest, few people outside the Home Guard ever did take it very seriously. A journalist on *The Scotsman*, which formed an office platoon, sympathised with the member of staff who, surveying the newspaper's defenders, 'overwhelmingly middle-aged, pot-bellied, balding, grey-haired and generally inoffensive-looking', commented jocularly, 'Ah, the brutal and licentious soldiery.' This typified the popular attitude and before long, with the invasion apparently off, all but the keenest Home Guards felt less and less desire to give up their precious spare time, or lose vital sleep, to train for a non-existent battle, and commanding officers were soon discussing how to deal with the problem of absenteeism. In Shropshire one distinguished ex-regular told his men that anyone who failed to turn out when required would be stood against a wall, 'and a firing party will be detailed to shoot him'. He was puzzled when his subsequent appeal for more volunteers produced only smiles. A curate, who arrived at a working-class parish consisting largely of miners and railwaymen near Nottingham in late 1940, remembers that Home Guard duty, 'at first undertaken in a rather lighthearted and adventurous spirit... was becoming a very heavy burden to men who had already done a day's work. . . . They felt they had already done their bit for the nation.' A Norfolk girl remembers her father, who was expected to attend a parade on Sunday morning and do guard duty on the cliffs every Tuesday and Thursday night, finally rebelling after his heavy day's work on his farm, and being, to his great indignation, fined fifty shillings for persistent non-attendance.

In November 1941 the last traces of the old L.D.V. had vanished when the government introduced military ranks and discipline into the Home Guard and powers to make Home Guard service compulsory, all Home Guards now being liable to prosecution if they failed to attend for up to forty-eight hours of training a month. Existing Home Guards had the right to resign before the new law took effect, on 17th February 1942, and the influx of 'directed men'—the term 'conscripts' was avoided —helped to alter the character of the organisation still more. In its last two years, however, the Home Guard did its most useful work, when many of its members were trained to replace the soldiers manning static anti-aircraft units. By January 1943 Home Guards were on duty at gun and rocket sites in London. A Birmingham ex-serviceman, whose unit took over two of the eight guns in an Ack-Ack battery, found that the soldiers made them very welcome and invited them to 'join in the entertainments put on in the canteen. One night when an alert was sounded during a fancy dress dance . . . across the gun park flitted figures representing the Wild Man from Borneo, in grass skirt and armed with a gigantic club, the Angel with a Dirty Face, complete with halo and wings, and Salvage, covered with an assortment of bottles and tins which clanked at every step.'

On 14th November 1944 the Home Guard was at last stood down. If it never justified the high hopes of its founder members the real blame must lie with the government for building the organisation up from its planned strength of 150,000 to a peak of two million and of abandoning the original aim of recruiting men 'chiefly . . . in country parishes . . . small towns

... villages and ... less densely inhabited suburban areas'. Vast numbers of men were enrolled in city battalions and trained in street fighting, in which they would surely have been massacred by the professionals of the German Army. The early nickname for the L.D.V.—the Look, Duck and Vanish Brigade—admirably described its real role, to observe and report, but by 1942 it was actually proposed to combine individual units in large-scale formations to attack enemy task-forces head on. Contemplating my own battalion that year, with its companies of elderly estate workers, medically unfit schoolmasters and callow schoolboys, I can only feel profoundly thankful that we were never ordered into action.

# BUILD YOUR OWN SHELTER

'Everyone who has no form of shelter should busy himself at once with selecting and preparing a refuge room.'

Ministry of Home Security hand-out, 3rd September 1940

Before the Germans could invade the British Isles they had to obtain mastery of the air. On the 5th June 1940 the sirens were heard over a wide area for the first time since the previous September, ushering in a series of small-scale raids, and on 10th July began the succession of large-scale daylight raids now known as the Battle of Britain. On the 13th August, *Eagle Day*, the Germans began their all-out attack which continued almost daily until Sunday 15th September, when the R.A.F. brought down, it was thought, 185 German aircraft.* The Luftwaffe had already turned a week earlier to night attacks, and from mid-September the daylight raids grew smaller, dying out by the end of October. Small-scale daylight raids, frequently by a single intruder, continued until well into 1944, producing some appalling tragedies when, for example, a school was hit, while in the Dover and Folkestone area there was also frequent shelling.

To the civilian in the South East of England, the Battle of Britain meant vapour trails in the sky, the sound of aircraft engines, the frequent clatter of machine guns, followed by a hail of spent cartridge cases in the back garden, seven or even ten warnings a day, and the occasional crash as a bomb fell or an aircraft was shot out of the sky. To the rest of the country the battle meant listening to the communiqués read by Joseph Macleod, Frank Phillips, Alvar Lidell, Bruce Belfrage and other BBC announcers who, in June, had begun to identify themselves as an anti-invasion precaution. The practice made them seem family friends in many homes and more than one pet budgerigar was christened 'Alvar' or 'Frank', and produced innumerable jokes like one endured by Bruce Belfrage's schoolboy son: 'Here is an exam. paper and this is Julian Belfrage making a mess of it.'

The newsvendors scrawled in chalk or ink on their home-made placards '180 for 34', '185 for 26', as though the whole struggle was merely a

* The real German loss was 60.

form of cricket match, but for those living in South East England it was often a good deal more serious.

Not for the last time in the war the ordinary family in Essex, Kent and Sussex was now living a different life from that in the rest of the country, where even an isolated 50 lb. bomb would be the subject of excited comment for miles around. From his office window in Tunbridge Wells, a Ministry of Information Officer once counted 180 German planes simultaneously and on another occasion he saw five parachutes in the air at one time. Neither experience was exceptional. At Maidstone Grammar School the boys regularly cleared their playing fields of bomb splinters and cartridge cases before each game. At Tunbridge Wells the cricket pitch was ruined by a crater. At Canterbury, when the mayor opened a flower show with an air battle raging overhead, few people even bothered to look up. The photographs which appeared in the newspapers of local farmers harvesting with their steel helmets on while a battle raged in the skies above them were not exaggerated. In six months 70,000 bombs fell on the farmlands of Kent and it was not uncommon to find a machine gun bullet in one's milking pail or the apples stripped from the trees in one's orchard by blast or shell fragments, universally, though inaccurately, known as 'shrapnel'. In blown-out windows appeared the humorous notices soon to become tediously familiar: 'I have no pane, dear mother, now', 'Blast did this, blast it' and, most popular, 'More open than usual'. A *Punch* cartoon showed a BBC announcer breaking off reading a typical news bulletin of the period, 'And in a raid on a southeast coast resort several houses were destroyed', to interpolate, 'including, incidentally, my own. You never saw such a mess in your life. The wife and I were under the kitchen table at the time.'

In these months most people in the danger areas, like those in other much-bombed parts of the country later, became, if not courageous about air raids, resigned to them. A woman from Haslemere, Surrey, simply covered her two children with a tin bath, but as they always fought when they were together, 'there was more war under the bath', she remembers, 'than in the sky'. A Sussex woman remembers lying sunbathing on her lawn in Lewes, watching the 'slim silver pencils of the Dorniers going over to bomb London. A woman living on the main road between Ashford and Canterbury, where 'Sometimes the sirens would sound early in the morning and the All Clear didn't sound until it was nearly dark', accepted battles overhead and the crashing of shotdown aircraft as a regular part of daily life. One local family, picnicking in a normally peaceful meadow, were inconvenienced by more than the usual midges and wasps, for fleeing bombers jettisoned fifty bombs in the same field, showering the picnickers with stones and earth but leaving them unharmed. A then teenager was unimpressed when the bus taking her to school in Maidstone ran into a bomb crater; she simply finished her journey on foot. A teenage schoolboy travelling back to school by train from Woking was similarly not 'afraid at all but merely interested' when it was machine-gunned in a cutting near Micheldever. 'One could see the bullets hitting the bank and one or two ricocheted off the train . . . On arrival at school there was hell. My mother had been having hysterics on the phone.'*

For parents this was an appallingly worrying time. A Cambridgeshire clergyman's wife hated having to sew name tapes on her children's school tunics, 'so that they could be identified if they were picked up after being bombed out of doors. . . . We formed the habit of kissing each other goodbye whenever we went out for any purpose, even to do some shopping.' The wife of an Essex probation officer gave the eldest of her three children strict instructions to return home the same way each day and if necessary to ask for shelter in the nearest house, tying her hair ribbon on the gate to identify it for her mother.

The wreckage of German aircraft littering the fields of southern England convinced even the sceptical that the claims of staggering German losses were true. One 'graveyard' for wrecked aircraft lay close to the rectory in a village near Canterbury and the rector's daughter noticed with joy the layers of debris piling up until they were as high as a house. To her annoyance, she was sent away to boarding school in rural Derbyshire to enable her to continue her education in peace. Here even a solitary air raid warning produced hysterics in some girls, whom she promptly and unsympathetically 'told off'.

Crashed enemy aircraft became common landmarks, and *Punch* was only exaggerating slightly in a cartoon, published on 4th September 1940, which showed one countryman directing a visitor: 'Go down the lane past the Messerschmitt, bear left and keep on past the two Dorniers, then turn sharp right and it's just past the first Junkers.' 'Living in the Weald of Kent during the Battle of Britain was an exciting experience for a fourteen-year-old', a Cranbrook woman remembers. 'A gang of us toured the countryside on bicycles always hoping to be the first on the spot when a German parachuted down . . . We were not popular with the police as we were always trying to get souvenirs from crashed planes. . . . My most treasured relic, and I had boxes of them, was a piece of parachute which "an airman had burnt to death in and you can still smell the burnt flesh on it!" ' At a Guildford grammar school, one boy had a German pilot's helmet and another a whole instrument panel from a Messerschmitt 109. When the driver of a lorry carrying a single-

* I must confess to feeling grateful to the Germans, for the only time in the war, when my return to school in September 1940 was postponed for several weeks owing to the threat of invasion, and the heavy air raids of the period.

engined German fighter rashly left it near the school entrance, the boys
swarmed over it with such enthusiasm that later, puzzling over one
curiously shaped metal object, they realised they had stripped off part
of the lorry's tailboard. As the R.A.F. were always anxious to inspect
wrecked aircraft the headmaster appealed to his pupils to return their
prizes and soon his desk resembled a junkyard. Plane-spotting, a popular
hobby since the beginning of the war, now really came into its own. At
a village school in Hertfordshire 'during the Battle of Britain one of
the biggest boys at the school—an ardent and knowledgeable plane
spotter—would run out when an Alert sounded and stand on top of
the school shelter. . . . If he thought it looked as if one of "theirs"
might be coming down nearby he would shout "Miss—Quick!", whereupon the whole school would stream out and huddle in the shelter.'

The long lull from September 1939 to June 1940 had given both the
government and private citizens the chance to get their shelters ready,
and the Battle of Britain, accompanied late in August by the first scattered
night attacks on Birmingham, Plymouth and Liverpool, provided a
large-scale test for the A.R.P. services. One of the first changes was in
the warning system, once it was realised that a mere handful of aircraft
were causing millions of people to stop work or lose sleep, and in September 1940 the siren ceased to be sounded for every single raider and the
'Warning' became the 'Alert', with work stopping only when an enemy
plane was actually overheard. The new roof-spotters saved millions of
man-hours, though Churchill's suggested name for them of 'Jim Crow'
never caught on.

The year of waiting had also enabled the A.R.P. services to 'shake-
down' into a far more effective force than they had been a year before.
Gaps in equipment had been filled up, like that of the volunteer ambulance
driver in Stamford who 'had to warn the police officer on point duty . . .
that I was coming and he would always wave me on, as if stopped, the
vehicle might not start again'. A Birmingham A.R.P. worker spent hours
on duty making small, cotton bags with drawstrings for 'casualties
to put their valuables in', the sort of detail which later saved endless
trouble. The early volunteers had adjusted themselves, too, to the dis-
comforts of being on duty. In the same A.R.P. Centre the helpers, if
there was no Alert, slept on stretchers on the floor of the basement,
until one morning a cockroach crawled out of one of the beds; after that the
stretchers were mounted on chairs. A woman working for a large chemical
manufacturers in Manchester found that her weekly night on first aid
duty at the factory passed quickly enough 'playing darts and eating evil
cheese sandwiches and drinking cocoa made with water', but learning
to sleep on her camp bed in a hut took longer, for next door was a 'spooky'
machine that ran all night, with steam pipes thumping every five minutes.

A first aid team at Leamington Spa, manning an ambulance head-quarters in an old brewery, used to practise resuscitation and bandaging, and study local maps for rural Wardens' Posts where they might have to pick up casualties. A fireman at the Report Centre in Richmond filled his time in painting enamelled jewellery, or studying for the Cost Accountants' Intermediate Examination. 'We also used to give each other practice runs on the telephone,' he remembers, 'making up incidents which were often stigmatised as unduly horrific, but which could well have happened in later times.' One Bermondsey First Aid Post was on the ground floor of a school, where evening classes were held upstairs. 'One evening', a first-aider remembers, 'a teacher came down for volunteers to join a male voice choir to make up the numbers to keep the class open. As no men were willing, myself and three other women joined. One piece we learned was *O Peaceful England*.' A nurse from Chichester watched an artist warden filling idle hours on duty painting a picture of Hitler in the bottom of a china chamberpot. 'It was called "Hitler in Poland" ', she recalls. 'How we enjoyed "wetting his head"!' The early warnings also provided many A.R.P. workers with useful practice in turning out quickly. A warden on the Hampshire/Sussex border, like many more, became adept at 'falling out of bed at the first sound of alarm, siren, or telephone, dressing over pyjamas in the dark, and getting downstairs almost without waking up'.

Another useful lesson learned by many recruits was how to give the alarm when needed. In many places inexperienced wardens, blundering about in the black-out, sounded the siren instead of switching on the Post light, the procedure in such cases being to sound the All Clear immediately afterwards. A Leeds student discovered that she had failed to master the University switchboard only after waking up the Vice-President at four o'clock one morning instead of a fellow student. A part-time A.F.S. worker in Liverpool had an even more embarrassing experience. After taking her first fire call calmly and efficiently, 'checking address, pumps required, etc.', she pressed the alarm button and, to her great consternation, nothing happened. Uncertain what to do, she went into the duty room, whispering apologetically to the first man she met, 'Sorry to disturb you, but the bell won't work and there's a fire.' Immediately, she remembers, he shouted ' "Fire!", pushed me out of the way and made for the stairs, shouting and banging a tin helmet, the men pouring down in a clattering mass. It took me a long time to live down that episode.'

Gradually, during the waiting year, the living conditions of A.R.P. workers were improved. The first Wardens' Posts had often been in private houses and there, in rural districts, they usually remained, but in the cities many small sub-posts were now established in what were virtually sections of large sewer pipes, sunk in the ground on end and approached down a ladder. The equipment was far from lavish—a table, a couple of hard chairs, a telephone—the occupants themselves providing such comforts as an electric fire and a radio. In at least one London Wardens' Post the fittings finally included a carpet, deck chairs and even curtains over the ventilator, but Walter Lee in Grantham found that to shelter from the cold in his Post he had to huddle in a wooden chair padded with blankets, keeping the draughts off with a clothes-horse draped with more bedding. Few councils erred on the side of generosity. In Chelsea, the Council refused to strengthen one Post with steel supports but erected a notice offering a £7 10s. grant towards the funeral expenses of any warden killed on duty. In another London Borough, further east, no sanitation was provided for the wardens, both men and women being expected to use the adjoining churchyard as an open-air lavatory. The worst housed of all were usually the A.F.S., who also at first often had to provide their own food. A Stockport woman was shocked by the 'old church rooms, stables, rat-ridden cellars and old warehouses' which her husband's unit occupied, and she had to provide him with 'six lots of sandwiches'.

Eventually in most places conditions improved and everywhere during the long hours off watch or on during night patrols in the silent streets, A.R.P. workers from different backgrounds began to know and trust each other. The consequences of such mixing of the classes could be embarrassing. One former actress, who had become a warden in a poor district of London in May 1940, had learned to copy her comrades in simply throwing the dregs from her tea mug on the road. It became such a habit that 'On one of my Sundays off, in Cambridge, standing in front of the fireplace, cup and saucer in hand, I jerked the tea leaves on to the carpet, in a sudden and astonished silence'.

Of all Britain's defences perhaps the most unpleasant to those who lived in their shadow were the smoke-screens whose very existence was kept secret. One night sister at a Nottingham hospital spent hours looking for a fire, even rousing the duty engineer from his bed to search the boiler house, only to discover later that the smoke came from drums of oil-soaked waste lit on the outskirts of the city. Another Nottingham woman could easily identify the men working on this smoke-screen by their smell. A Birmingham woman remembers that 'The bedroom used to get so full of the stuff that even if the night was quiet it was difficult to sleep'. In Luton the residents were asked in the early days to make their own smoke-screen by burning sawdust and tar blocks from 11 p.m. to 1 a.m., but this experiment was abandoned just in time to prevent an epidemic of chimney fires, for the blocks produced an enormous amount of soot. Later 25,000 oil-burning canisters were planted along pavement edges and one motorist spectacularly breached the black-out regulation by knocking down a whole row, like so many ninepins, which turned the road into a sheet of flame. 'The smoke may have protected Luton from the Luftwaffe,' a local historian comments, 'but nothing could protect Luton houses against the smoke. A black oily deposit covering everything in the garden. Woe betide the housewife who had inadvertently left some laundry out at night.'

But by the beginning of September 1940 it was clear that more than smoke was going to be needed to protect the population from the coming bombs. 'It is most important that everyone who has no form of shelter should busy himself at once with selecting and preparing a refuge room', urged a Ministry of Home Security hand-out. Anyone who did lack such an essential should hurry round to the nearest Post Office and buy *Your Home as an Air Raid Shelter*, a threepenny pamphlet which was one of the best sellers of 1940. The writer addressed the citizen with admirable directness:

When a high explosive bomb falls and explodes a number of things happen. Anything very close to the explosion is likely to be destroyed and any house which suffers a direct hit is almost sure to collapse. Other dangers of a less spectacular kind can cause far more casualties. Blast can shatter unprotected windows at considerable distances and fragments of glass can be deadly, while bomb splinters can fly and kill at a distance of over half a mile if there is nothing to stop them. . . . There are three ways in which you can provide your household with shelter. First you can buy a ready-made shelter to bury or erect in the garden. Secondly, you can have a shelter of brick or concrete built into or attached to the house. Thirdly you can improve the natural protection given by your house, by forming a refuge room.

The booklet went on to offer practical advice like using the coal shute as an emergency exit from the cellar, and old doors and discarded paint-drums to protect doors and windows. 'Almost no shelter is proof against a direct hit from a heavy bomb,' it summed up comfortingly, 'but the chances of *your own* house getting a direct hit are very small indeed.'

Besides what the citizen could do for himself, the government had in fact already done a good deal for him. Dreading the effect on morale of direct hits on large communal shelters, it based its policy on small but numerous ones. Everywhere by the summer of 1940 one could see strangely shaped mounds of earth, brick or concrete, sandbagged walls and doorways, boarded up windows and signs reading 'Shelter this way', which might point to a strengthened railway arch, an excavated trench in a park, a strengthened basement or, most commonly, an oblong brick-built structure, with a flat, concrete roof, resembling a large garage. Inside there were usually long wooden slatted benches, lavatories and, in some cases, lighting. But surface shelters were never popular, due to the widespread feeling that real safety could only be found below ground level. A few places had natural shelters, like the caves in the cliffs at Dover, and the long tunnels in the chalk near Chislehurst. The largest shelters of all, the London underground, were, the government ruled, not to be used. The official reason was that they were needed to move vital supplies, but in fact the Chamberlain government had been afraid that many citizens would scuttle underground when the bombers came and refuse to come out. To protect their employees most large factories relied on covered trenches, while offices and large stores strengthened basements and cellars, and downstairs corridors with wooden supports for the roof and boards and netting over the windows. The usual day-school shelter was a tunnel-like brick construction, half sunk in the ground and covered with earth, though my own school was fortunate enough to have an underground tunnel linking the houses, which was divided by sandbag walls into blast-proof sections linked by telephone, and bucket latrines were provided in what were normally the drying rooms for wet games-clothes.

The most common type of domestic shelter was the 'Anderson', named after the then Home Secretary, Sir John Anderson, a reserved and retiring figure little known to the general public and nicknamed in the Civil Service 'pompous John' and 'Jehovah', though Churchill, looking deeper, considered him 'a man of singular capacity and firmness of character, sagacious and imperturbable amid gathering peril and confusion'. In November 1938, soon after becoming responsible for the country's Air Raid Precautions, Anderson had put the problem of providing a cheap and simple domestic shelter to his life-long friend William Patterson, a Scottish engineer, who produced the prototype within a fortnight. By September 1940, 2,300,000 Andersons had been produced, sufficient to protect 12,500,000 people, nearly a quarter of the population. The Anderson was supplied free to manual workers in danger areas and to others earning under £250 a year, a fair middle-class income in 1939, and families above this limit could buy them at around £7 plus the cost of erection. Where able-bodied men were lacking, local authority workmen, public-spirited wardens and, occasionally, stalwart Boy Scouts helped.

Erecting an Anderson was quite a formidable job. According to the official *Directions*, one began by digging 'a hole 7ft. 6in. long by 6 ft. wide . . . to a depth of 4ft.', into which were inserted six curved steel sheets, bolted together at the top to form an arch. At either end were flat steel plates, one containing a section which could be unbolted as an emergency exit, the other a hole at ground level through which one climbed down into the shelter. To be inside an Anderson felt rather like being entombed in a small, dark bicycle shed, smelling of earth and damp, but most people could comfortably stand up for it was 6 feet high in the centre and 4 feet 6 inches wide, and, if there were only two occupants, comfortably lie down, as the 'standard' Anderson was 6 feet 6 inches long. It was designed to shelter six people sitting or standing, but when bombing began this limit was often exceeded. Outside, an Anderson had to be covered with at least fifteen inches of earth, and to a Birmingham woman 'the whole effect was something like a brown igloo'. She covered hers with rock plants, a common choice, but in Chelsea, a horticulturally-minded borough, radishes, carrots and lettuces were all seen flourishing on the tops of Andersons and rambler roses round the entrances. Other popular Anderson-obscuring plants were nasturtiums and marigolds. Sir John Anderson, a notoriously humourless man, was not amused when complimented on the marrows growing on the familiar mounds in several back gardens seen from the train, replying, 'I had not intended the shelters for the cultivation of vegetables.'

Although the Anderson had only been designed to stand up to a 500 lb. bomb falling twenty feet away, or a 100 lb. one within six feet, it proved tough enough to withstand everything except a direct hit. It had, however, one outstanding defect: in wet weather, or even in dry weather in some districts, a layer of water rapidly collected in the bottom. A Croydon man who woke up in his after three hours' sleep, feeling very cold, found he 'was lying in three inches of ice-cold water. It had seeped up through cracks in the concrete floor.' In one York street, pumping out the Anderson became such a regular ritual that the neighbours arranged a distinctive tap on the wall to indicate that baling operations were about to begin. A family of toads moved into the shelter of one family living near Dudley, whose chief objection to these uninvited guests was that 'we were usually woken up in the night with loud splashes'. A Scottish A.R.P. worker found that despite a sump for drainage, their shelter filled up with water within a week. 'Without regret we wrote it off and thereafter, and for the rest of the war, we took our chance in the comfort of our own home.'

But under the strange conditions of wartime even a wet Anderson could prove a blessing in disguise. A Birmingham woman whose husband not merely built a sump, but 'rigged a very effective hand-pump from pieces of his old bicycle, using one of the pedals as a handle', found that 'after one or two raids when we woke in the mornings to find we had no tap water due to the bombing, the neighbours were glad to have this water—which was quite clean—for washing etc.' Even when dry, the Anderson needed some form of seating and most people soon installed plank benches, boxes, or old chairs, later replaced by improvised beds.

A Morden family used their bedroom doors for this purpose, while the baby slept happily in an orange box lined with corrugated cardboard. A Birmingham man stretched the coal-house door across his Anderson as a bed for his two-year-old daughter, making do himself with cushions and a ragged blanket in a deck-chair. An Ipswich woman learned that with two of the occupants sleeping in hammocks, four people could spend a comfortable night in an Anderson—indeed she even slept in hers during the day, when working on the night shift, to escape from noise.

A Ministry of Home Security leaflet suggested building simple full-length bunks from wood and wire netting, two resting on the ground and two more on the angle irons halfway up each end of the shelter, with shorter bunks, lying across the shelter, to accomodate the children. Whether any family ever settled down as neatly and cosily as in the Ministry's sketch is doubtful, but many people did succeed in making themselves surprisingly comfortable, particularly from the summer of 1941, when the government began to supply proper bunks.

In other back gardens in 1940 appeared small brick buildings officially known as 'domestic surface shelters', a smaller version of the familiar street shelters. Most were the same size as the Anderson, but some versions could house up to twelve people, and were often built in groups for mutual protection, with two entrances in different gardens—another blow to 'separateness'. Where there were no gardens, communal surface shelters of the same type, with space for forty-eight people, were often put in residential streets. Like others, these surface shelters were not popular. A South London woman thought one the Council erected in her garden 'so damp and . . . badly built it was not fit to keep hens in let alone to shelter humanity. After a week of misery, my mother, brother and myself refused to use it.' A Highbury woman's chief memory of her brick shelter is of 'backaches after dozing in the corner all night'.

In built-up areas of older houses without gardens, local authorities often strengthened basements. Pimlico, the 'poor end' of Westminster, could only provide gardens for 235 Andersons, but 8,000 coal cellars were cleared and strengthened, electric light installed and emergency exits provided by knocking gaps in the intervening walls. They proved excellent shelters, producing only one probelm, how to stop the occupants 'tapping' the mains to provide free power for electric fires.

Protecting people who lived in flats was more difficult. Where most of the people in a block earned less than £250 a year the government bore the cost of a communal shelter, where they earned more, the landlord had to provide one, if asked to do so by the majority of tenants, and to reclaim the cost through higher rents. Boiler rooms, basement store-rooms and downstairs corridors were all pressed into use, and one

Bournemouth flat-dweller remembers how her landlord had his cellar cleared and installed bunks so that she and her crippled mother did not have to use the public shelter. 'It was very comfortable, and all the tenants were extremely grateful,' she recalls, 'though nothing would make the landlord come down with us. I remember him saying that it would take more than ruddy Germans to separate him from his warm bed and his missis!'

People outside the danger areas, and those within them who earned too much to qualify for a free shelter, often built their own. I laboured away at the start of the war digging a deep trench in our allotment, which we covered with an old door and strengthened with sandbags left on the local common after army manœuvres. Friends nearby had a more elaborate version, with wooden supports along the sides, but both shelters, though they served as admirable meeting and hiding places during school holidays, collapsed with the first heavy rains. (The Council later provided a communal brick shelter, though I never used it, while my friends acquired a 'Morrison'.) Nor was water the only menace to comfort in home-made shelters. A Mansfield, Nottingham, woman encountered mice and large black beetles in theirs, while a man from a Welsh mining village found that the ten feet long ventilation pipe his father installed, for use if the entrance was blocked, became 'the favourite resort of numerous snails'.

Indoor shelters were usually more satisfactory. A Cheshire Red Cross worker slept in the former wine cellar of their house. A Sheffield family used an old, up-turned boiler as an emergency exit from their cellar. An Essex woman still admires the reinforced concrete shelter built by her uncle in Hull, complete with double doors, built-in bunks and an electric light which went out automatically when the door was opened. A London woman remembers that she 'took over the house where we still live, mainly because it had a good cellar . . . and the first thing I did after we moved in was to clean out the cellar and colour wash it. My husband shored it up with extra timber and we had rugs, pictures, Michael's cot, an electric fire and all that was needed to pass an evening and night.' A young Birmingham girl, who shared a reinforced cellar with two other families, 'slept on an improvised bed and one of the neighbours always lay with her legs across mine, giving a very trapped feeling, which was not relieved by looking at a towering load of coal which looked ready to crush us all in the event of a slight jolt, of which we had many. Another neighbour used to sleep in a deck chair and he snored so loudly that he eventually woke us and himself up.' A Rayleigh, Essex, woman still mourns the beautiful table-tennis table cut up to barricade the kitchen window. A woman who moved into a house in Essex recalls the satisfaction with which she found that the ceiling of the sitting room had already been reinforced with corrugated iron held up with posts.

One measure recommended by the government and enthusiastically followed in many families was to protect windows from splintering by sticking 'net fabric, like lace curtains, or transparent film' on them, either covering the whole surface or 'in strips . . . at intervals which leave not more than 6 square inches of glass clear'. The chief result was to darken many domestic interiors; the process gave little protection. The same publication warned that 'liquid preparations specially made to protect glass vary in effectiveness', but this was an understatement; everyone who used these fluids agrees that they were useless. Some proved, however, extraordinarily resilient and a twelve-year-old Sheffield girl remembers that the transparent substance painted over their windows was still there at the end of the war when it could only be removed by applying acid and then scraping hard. A woman from Berkhamstead, Hertfordshire, had an even more discouraging experience, after dutifully cutting up strips of newspaper and gluing them round the edges of the door and window of her larder to protect her stores from gas. It proved such an effective barrier that, she recalls, 'I couldn't get into the larder and for the rest of the war the paint bore the marks of knife and chisel from the hour I spent in getting the paper off again.'

# BRITAIN CAN TAKE IT

Dear Rescue men,
   Just a few lines thanking you for what you did for us on July 14th
. . . How you helped to get my mother out, and to get my two brothers
which was dead, how you help me to get to shelter when I hadn't any
shoes on my feet.

Letter from a Hull schoolgirl, 1943

During June and July and August 1940 the bombs had been creeping
closer to London. In mid-August, on a sunny Thursday evening, there
was a sharp attack on Croydon, where sixty-two people were killed in
less than half an hour, and at last, on Saturday 7th September, a year
after everyone had expected it, came the turn of the capital itself. It was,
one warden later remembered, 'one of those beautiful early autumn
days which feel like spring and can make even London streets seem
fresh and gay. There was hardly a wisp of cloud in the pale blue sky.'
When the sirens sounded that afternoon they marked, though no one
then realised it, the start of the blitz. London was to know barely a
single peaceful night until the All Clear on the morning of Sunday
11th May 1941 signalled the end of the last, and worst, major raid of the
war. During the same period, and after it, most of the country's major
ports and industrial cities were to undergo even more concentrated
attacks, though their ordeal usually lasted for only two or three nights at
a time.

Early on Sunday morning, while all over the country the first Home
Guards were going wearily home after the great invasion scare, the
people of East London emerged from their shelters to find the streets
thick with broken glass, and, in thousands of cases, a smoking heap of
rubble where their home had stood. Thousands more discovered a
shattered shell, with smashed windows, doors sagging from their frames,
tiles stripped from the roof and everywhere soot, plaster and broken
glass. Such experiences were to be the lot of millions of families, in London and other cities, during the next few months.

But one of the first results of the blitz was a widespread determination
among those who worked in London not to let 'that man' interfere with
their daily routine. On the Saturday night 430 people had been killed and
1,600 seriously injured and on Sunday 8th September the bombers came

again, in a raid which put out of action every railway line into London from the south. Yet nearly everyone got to work somehow. The experiences of a girl then living at Tooting and working for an insurance broker in King William Street in the City were typical of that Monday morning:

> The tube was closed at Balham. I hitch-hiked a lift from a lorry driver who took me to Elephant and Castle and from there I walked to the City. We walked over Southwark Bridge as we were not allowed to cross London Bridge, and when I got to the office I understood why. Rubble and glass were all over the place, and there was a gas main still belching flames at the end of the bridge. Firemen, who had been up all night, were standing round. They looked so tired, I remember I gave one of them my packed lunch. . . . Then I crunched up to the office and found various members of the staff wandering about in a daze. Finally we were told to go home again and await instructions.

During the blitz many hundreds of thousands of office workers shared experiences like that of a girl clerk with the Electricity Supply Department in a Lancashire town, who arrived at work one morning to discover 'a mixture of rubble, glass, inverted desks, stools and thousands of record cards from the cabinets, and ledgers, inches deep on the floor'. Temporary offices were set up in cafés and shops and a popular subject for discussion was whether it was worse sorting thousands of blast-scattered index cards back into order, or having the job of shaking out the glass and dust from between the pages of bombed files.

That winter absenteeism in most firms was actually less than normal, for one's job was something to cling to in an uncertain world. Post Offices were still open, though often with candles stuck in bottles on the counter, and no windows. In bombed streets postmen could be seen conscientiously attempting to deliver the mail at one heap of ruins after another and telegraph boys provided one of the strange new sights of the blitz, carrying notices 'Telegrams accepted' and turning round to provide a 'back' against which the customer could write his message.

Large stores at first shepherded all their customers into the basement when the sirens went. In John Lewis's, chocolate biscuits, Penguin books, knitting needles and wool were all on sale in the shelter, but by 21st September the firm had decided, like others, to give customers the chance to continue shopping. When a few days later its Oxford Street premises were badly bombed, the firm responded with a Churchillian blast of defiance in its house magazine: 'We shall defend our Partnership with the utmost energy. What matter if we are bombed out of John Lewis? We shall fight on at Peter Jones.' The spirit of 1940 is illustrated by the 'Special Instructions' on a delivery note for a parcel of china and glass ordered by one customer in West London: 'Ignore time-bomb, leave in hall if out.'

Before long most large stores, and many other firms, were closing at 4 p.m., for everyone's life was becoming geared to the nightly siren. At first nearly everyone sought shelter after dark, but by early November an official census showed that only 40 per cent of the population slept in a shelter, 9 per cent using a public shelter, 4 per cent the tubes, and 27 per cent a domestic shelter. The public outcry about conditions in the largest public shelters, often without sanitation or even lighting, and the appalling inadequacy of the over-loaded and ill-equipped rest centres for the bombed-out led to immediate improvements, but cost Sir John Anderson his job. He became, in Churchill's phrase, 'the Home Front prime minister', as Lord President of the Council. His successor as Home Secretary, Herbert Morrison, the son of a Lambeth policeman, was a far more accomplished Parliamentarian than Anderson and far better able to understand what life under bombing really meant to the poor. He transformed the rest-centres and shelters and restored confidence in the government's Civil Defence policy within a few weeks.

Once the night raids began, the public brushed aside the government ban on using the Underground to shelter, simply buying a 1½d. ticket to gain admission to the platforms and refusing to come up. By the 27th September 177,000 men, women and children were using the tubes every night, and though they were at least dry and warm, at first even the ordinary station lavatories were closed. 'The result was', one man who used Swiss Cottage station remembers, 'that every time anyone wanted "to spend a penny" it was necessary to board a train and travel to the next stop—Finchley Road.' Before long, however, temporary bucket lavatories were erected in the stations and 22,000 bunks had been installed on the platforms, usually in three tiers, the lowest one being usable as a seat during the evening. But many people still had to sleep on the ground and anyone arriving on a late train had to step over recumbent bodies to reach the exit. The L.C.C. and welfare organisations were soon providing drinking water, lending libraries and canteens and the tube became so popular that London Transport issued an appeal urging every male shelterer 'to be a man and leave' the available space 'to women, children and the infirm', though it produced little response.

That winter thousands of families, particularly in the East End, enjoyed the fullest social life of their lives, with sing-songs, concert parties, informal dances and even darts competitions between one shelter and the next. The usual BBC 'round the Empire' feature was this year called *Christmas under Fire* and described shelters in which paper chains hung from the bare brick walls, wardens wore paper hats instead of steel helmets and the faithful

W.V.S. distributed mince-pies in place of cheese rolls.

But most people recall life in a public shelter with a shudder and especially the misery of lying awake listening to other people's snoring, which became a serious national problem, never solved. If one could not lie down it was almost impossible to sleep in any case. A Liverpool woman endured 'sitting on a hard form in an unlighted, unheated street shelter . . . with my baby on my knee . . . cramped, cold and terribly frightened'. She told nursery stories to the children, but would stop suddenly and say, 'Oh no, not that story!' when she reached the phrase, 'I'll huff and I'll puff and I'll blow your house down'. One Ipswich Civil Servant remembers a woman who talked and knitted all night. 'We tried not answering or just grunting but it was no use. She was very hurt one night when one overwrought soul shouted, "Can't you shut up, and stop clicking those damn needles as well." '

Domestic shelters at least offered a little privacy, but many people rapidly found that one could pay too high a price for safety. A Northolt woman remembers that one night in a shelter, with her neighbours, two babies, a dog and a candle, was enough for her. An Ipswich household decided, after sitting up half the night in the cellar, to stay in bed, as 'if we were going to be blown up, we might as well be blown up in comfort'. A York woman would not use her Anderson because, she believed, 'there was more harm done by waking children up out of their sleep and taking them out into the bitter cold giving them a chill than there was from the bombs'. Many adults felt the same.

Yet it was possible, having once decided to shelter, to make oneself reasonably comfortable. A Highbury woman had a brick shelter in her garden, with electric light, a 'wicker chair, cushions, rugs, an oil stove in the centre and, of course, food and tea. A gate in the fence to the next door garden admitted neighbours who wanted to share with us', she remembers, and 'at 11 p.m., if all were quiet we had tea from the kettle boiling on the stove and usually biscuits, and then settled down and hoped for quiet the rest of the night'. In Hull, which had almost as many Alerts as London, one woman enjoyed 'happy times' in a neighbour's shelter, 'taking turns to dash into our respective houses to make tea and bring out our latest culinary effort'. A Birmingham woman remembers that their Anderson 'became our second home. I automatically put the children to sleep in there after tea, taking coffee and sandwiches for my husband to have when he arrived from work. . . . Before long . . . we found ourselves spending thirteen hours at a time in the shelter, though I preferred the pantry when my husband was fire-watching, ambulance driving or meeting troops from the station.'

A government leaflet offered advice on how to make oneself comfortable in the shelter. 'A home-made heater can be made with two large flower pots and a candle', it suggested. 'A Balaclava helmet, such as every soldier knows, will keep draughts off your head. Before you leave the house turn off all gas taps . . . switch off electricity at the main, leave buckets of water and earth on the front doorstep, put your stirrup pump . . . where it can easily be seen, draw back all your curtains and raise blinds . . . Dress yourself and your children warmly.' This routine now became familiar in millions of homes all over the country. A Lanarkshire woman 'would put out on a table a basket with a bottle of water, bottle of milk, biscuits, warm clothing for the children and ourselves. . . . My husband of course carried his pocket book with our money, etc. Each night, too, he filled the bath with water in case of fire. We had a box of sand in the garden, so we could deal with incendiary bombs.' One Surrey woman put a large notice on the back door, 'Don't forget, Handbag, Identity Card, Gas Mask, Ration Book'. In this family, as in many others, 'We dressed rather than undressed to go to bed.'

The growing reluctance of many people to go out of doors led the new Home Secretary to look again at the need for an indoor shelter. Herbert Morrison thought the risk from fire, which had hitherto prevented such a shelter being produced, worth taking. 'The . . . engineers and scientists would have argued for weeks', he later commented. 'I told them that I intended to lock them up in a room until they agreed . . . The experts had their designs . . . complete within twenty-four hours.' The result was the Morrison shelter, which resembled a large steel table, six feet six inches long, four feet wide and two feet nine inches high, with a steel mattress across the bottom and wire mesh at the sides. During the day it could be used as a table and at night it could, with a slight squeeze, accomodate two adults and two small children, lying down. The first were delivered in March 1941 and by the end of the war about 1,100,000 were in use, including a few two-tier models for larger families. Morrisons were supplied free to people earning up to £350 a year and were on sale at about £7 to people earning more. Though not as strong as the Anderson, the Morrison proved the most successful shelter of the war, particularly during the 'hit and run' and flying-bomb raids when a family had only a few seconds to get under cover. It was also a good deal easier to erect than an Anderson, and while most people remember their nights in the Anderson with horror, memories of the Morrison shelter are usually good-humoured. A Colchester woman, remembers it provided a 'lot of laughs', like the night 'a rather stout elderly lady was trying to crawl out of it and became stuck half in, and half out; she looked like a hippopotamus!' A Sussex child played happily in the Morrison in the kitchen at being a lion tamer in a cage, the family cat playing the part of the lion. A Wimbledon woman also welcomed the cat into hers, and he found it so comfortable that 'his purr sounded like a flying bomb sometimes'. A Teddington boy found the top 'particularly good for re-fighting sea and land battles with toy ships and soldiers', and a Staines girl, trained by her father on the top of the Morrison shelter, went on to become table-tennis champion of West Middlesex. A Battersea office worker was always amused to see 'very dignified executives . . . penned in like animals in the Morrison shelters during air raids'. Another London woman put hers to a use unforeseen by its designers. 'I stuck it for about two weeks' feeling like 'a bear getting into a cage . . . then, despite discomfort I made my bed up on top. It was solid, flat, ungivable metal. After two weeks I was comfortable, I slept like a baby through every raid, all the noise, the lot.' Most people would echo the verdict of a woman who after using a brick shelter in Brixton and an Anderson at New Cross, finally settled for her own Morrison at Catford, and found it the best of them all.

For those who had no Morrison the most popular place was under the stairs, which often survived even if the roof fell in, and the pantry was another popular choice. The lonely pantry evenings of a Ryde woman, whose husband was absent on Civil Defence duty, were cheered by the discovery of several long-forgotten bottles of blackberry wine. This once relatively innocuous brew had now turned into 'a lovely, heart-warming, brandy-type drink. A glass of that and let those damned Germans come!'

Strong, old-fashioned tables also returned, like cellars, to popularity in 1940. A government leaflet, *Shelter at Home*, pointed out that 'people have often been rescued from demolished houses because they had taken shelter under an ordinary table . . . strong enough to bear the weight of the falling bedroom floor'. I frequently worked beneath the solid oak tables in the school library during 'imminent danger periods' and, particularly before the arrival of the Morrison, families became accomplished at squeezing beneath the dining table during interrupted meals. Beds were also useful as shelters and in hospitals patients were regularly settled on the floor beneath theirs. One Cambridgeshire family, having brought the beds downstairs, then raised them on blocks to make it easier to get underneath them suddenly.

Some people had to go out however heavy the raid. 'Being the only doctor available for the hospital', a Morpeth, Northumberland, medical man remembers, 'I had to leap out of bed every time the alarm went. I got so proficient that I was up, dressed and in my car before the last diminuendo faded out. When it got to dressing three times a night I went up at the first siren and got into bed in one of the side wards.' A Southampton doctor actually welcomed night calls, since being out with a job to do was, he found, better than lying quaking in bed. Not everyone was as courageous. A Portsmouth woman remembers that, as she arrived with her mother at their front door one night during a heavy raid, 'a short, wide, little figure burst up the front path, pushed between Mother and me and demanded, "Quick, quick! Where do you go? Which door? Where?"' When her mother asked, 'Haven't you got the wrong house?', she received the unexpected answer, 'I don't care a b— *whose* house it is! Where's the bloody shelter?'

Many people had some private ritual which they persuaded themselves would keep them safe. One North London woman warden 'used to mutter "Oh my God!" as a sort of talisman' as she ran half a mile to her Post. She mentioned this to 'a friend who had a mile to go to her Report Centre and she said, in all seriousness, "I say The-Lord-is-my-Shepherd-I-shall-not-want, the-Lord-is-my-Shepherd-I-shall-not-want"'. A Bath woman, huddled under the stairs with her evacuees, read aloud to them the forty-sixth psalm, 'God is our hope and strength, a very present help in time of trouble'. Young Poles living in Paddington believed that they could only be hurt by bombs before midnight, while a Southampton woman discovered that her neighbours believed that so long as her greenhouse stood unharmed they would be all right and, miraculously, it survived with every pane intact. An African air raid warden, nicknamed 'Uncle Sam', reported that 'in the district where I work the people believe that because I am a man of colour I am a lucky omen'. He once calmed a panic in a shelter of 120 people, in the dark, by shining a torch on his face. Seldom had clergy been more welcome visitors than in the shelters that winter, and noisy hymns and songs which would drown the bombs were also popular. 'For the rest of my life,' one East London vicar wrote soon afterwards, 'whenever I hear the tune of *God Bless Charley, The Man who Invented Beer* I shall think of Haggerston at night in September 1940.' Many people admit to praying, as they heard the bombers passing over, 'God don't let them stop here!'. The same vicar, who pointed out to one of his parishioners, 'It's a bit rough on the other people if your prayer is granted', was put firmly in his place. 'I can't help that,' she told him, 'they must say *their* prayers and push it off further.'

Old people on the whole stood up surprisingly well to life in bombed cities. A Sanderstead woman remembers the eighty-four-year-old neighbour, who had tottered across the garden to share their shelter, saying perkily to her husband, 'Well, you never thought you would have me as a bed-mate!' A Haslemere woman remembers the seventy-seven-year old neighbour who grumbled that because of the raids he could make few plans for the future. A woman from Old Coulsdon, Surrey, was amused by her elderly aunt's precaution of always wearing her underclothes while bathing because she feared 'she might have to be rescued by someone before she finished'.

Most children were also remarkably unaffected by raids. One Scotswoman recalls that after the heavy blitz on Clydebank 'my son was thrilled to find bits of shrapnel in the garden and went round picking them up'. A Worcester Park, Surrey, woman found that when a stick of bombs fell on the nearby park, shattering their windows, her children's only reaction was to ask if they could go and see if the swings were still all right. A woman living near Croydon remembers 'distinctly counting the explosions and making a rhyme, "One two, button my shoe", of them to amuse Margaret [her fifteen-month-old daughter] who was watching me intently and would have been terror-stricken if I had shown the slightest sign of fear, but my voice was quivering'. A Kingston woman also remembers singing, 'in a very quavery voice', to her small son as they lay beneath her Morrison, until he complained, 'Mummy, stop singing, I can't hear the bombs!' The private dread of one woman in Hertfordshire was that 'the house might come down on us and that we might be buried alive in the debris. I felt I could not contemplate hearing the children's cries and not being able to get at them . . . I kept two spare pillows ready each night and prayed that I might have the courage and strength to smother them in time.' Yet while her children were out of the house no mother could feel secure. A York woman remembers standing by the ruins of her daughter's school, bombed during the night. 'I saw across the road on the grass verge one of her plimsolls and some of her books. . . . Had she been at school . . . she would have been blown to pieces and no trace of her left.' One London woman recalls how a local school was hit one dinnertime and it was 'my painful duty to help by picking up any article I saw unearthed as the men dug. I held aloft a small pink purse. No words were needed. The mother of the child to whom it belonged held out her hand, her face so anguished it was frightful to behold. She took it and was led wordlessly away.'

This dead child was one of 60,595 civilians killed by enemy action in Great Britain during the war. 86,182 were seriously injured and another 150,833 slightly injured. London, during the four months from 7th September to the end of 1940, accounted for the largest single group of these casualties: 13,339 dead, 17,937 seriously injured. Before the war it had been expected that each night's bombing would produce 3,000 killed and 12,000 wounded. The worst night's toll in London, on 10th/11th May 1941, was in fact 1,436 killed and 1,792 injured but over the blitz as a whole the pre-war estimate of fatal casualties per ton of bombs proved fourteen times too high. The government's cardboard coffins were never needed, though many victims were buried in mass graves. The youngest person killed was a baby eleven hours old; the oldest, a Chelsea Pensioner aged one hundred. 537 of the dead were never identified. The sole epitaph of one of them, a little girl found unconscious in the ruins of her home, is this entry in the register of Bath Infirmary;

Age about two years; hair, fair; eyes, blue grey; division between top row of teeth; no other distinguishing features.

Although the casualties were mercifully far fewer than expected, the damage to property was far greater. From September 1940 to May 1941 in London alone 1,150,000 houses were damaged and at least one person in six made homeless for a day or more, excluding those displaced by unexploded bombs. In Hull—a perpetual target, its sufferings concealed at the time under the description 'a North East Coast town'—only 6,000 out of 93,000 houses escaped some destruction; in Plymouth, nearly one house in four was put out of action and many more made temporarily unusable. Over the country as a whole, out of 13,000,000 houses in 1939, 200,000 were totally destroyed, and about 3,750,000 damaged, many of them several times. What bombs had left the looters often got. One A.F.S. man wrote bluntly: 'Everybody loots . . . The A.R.P. Wardens, Demolition Men . . . the Police.' A Liverpool schoolgirl, bombed out for the second time, found that her roller skates had been stolen. A bombed-out Birmingham family, returning for linen, cutlery and a few pieces of unbroken china, found most of it had vanished. A Coventry woman resisted tears when bombed out until she discovered that her small son's toys had been looted. 'I could hate the Germans, but I did not want to hate my own countrymen.'

Any heavy raid meant for the housewives of the affected city a massive clearing-up operation. A Plymouth woman remembers 'returning to a mere shell of a house. . . . No roof. No window panes. The door blasted open. . . . I'd have given my kingdom for a cuppa, but there was no electricity and no gas. I wasn't to know then that we would be without gas for almost six months.' Electricity, however, was usually restored in a few hours and piped water in three or four days. In the bombed cities millions of women adjusted themselves to the living conditions of their grandmothers' day, fetching water by the bucketful from standpipes and army lorries, doing their daily cooking over open fires, often made of wood from bombed houses, and taking the Sunday joint to be cooked in the baker's oven, if any local bakery survived unbombed. After their first experience of living without water, sensible housewives followed the official advice always to keep filled bottles in the house. One Bristol woman remembers making tea from the contents of her hot water bottle. Another Bristol housewife still feels proud of her ability, acquired in 1940, to wash and rinse her husband's shirt in a single quart. For many housewives the feel of those after-the-raid mornings is instantly brought back by the taste of burned food, for after an explosion soot from the chimney would settle insidiously on food and crockery. Sanitation was an even greater problem. People travelled long distances to find a usable lavatory or used buckets and buried the contents where they could; one conscientious East End doctor could be seen walking a mile every day, carrying a trowel, in search of a really hygienic and private spot.

Although it was high explosive, through blast, splinters or falling masonry which caused almost all the casualties in air raids, and interrupted public services, it was fire which did most of the damage, but the government were remarkably slow in taking effective measures either to prevent fire or to fight it. In raid after raid pumps sent to help some burning city had to stand idle as the connections would not fit the local hydrants, but it was not until August 1941, on Herbert Morrison's insistence, that the existing 1,666 fire authorities in England and Wales were merged into the National Fire Service. At the same time energetic steps were at last taken to provide a proper emergency water supply, with six-inch steel mains running along the gutters—they presented a new hazard in the black-out—and 'E.W.S.'—for 'Emergency Water Supply'—tanks appearing everywhere, on open spaces, on the roadsides, and in the basements of bombed buildings. Some resorts objected to static water tanks, as they were commonly known, as 'unsightly', but the sun sparkling on the surface often lent a new charm to the drab urban scene. The tanks also provided mothers with a new worry, for children were for ever floating home-made rafts of bomb-damaged timber on them, leading to at least one death from drowning every month.

Even more important, immediately after the City had been devastated by fire on the night of 29th December 1940, largely because whole office blocks had been left locked and unattended, the government launched the Fire Guard scheme, which made it compulsory in 'prescribed' areas, considered liable to attack, to have someone on duty in every building at all times, ready to extinguish any incendiaries that fell on it, or to summon help if the fire grew out of control.* Since not all firms had sufficient staff to protect them properly, fire-watching, either in one's own street or wherever else one was directed to serve, was made compulsory in any place considered to be at risk, which eventually included most urban areas. Under the first scheme, in January 1941, men aged sixteen to sixty were made liable to serve; in August 1942 the liability was extended to women aged from twenty to forty-five, and in September 1943 to men up to sixty-three. Men aged up to seventy and women from eighteen to sixty were encouraged to add to the numbers available by volunteering and in practice no one under eighteen was forced to serve. These measures produced in theory an army of six million fire-watchers, which only began to be stood down, area by area, from 13th September 1944, the last fire-watchers being disbanded on 2nd May 1945.

* Post-war research showed that, ton for ton, incendiary bombs were 4·8 times as effective at causing damage as high explosives.

On business premises the maximum anyone could be required to fire-watch was forty-eight hours a month, usually served a whole night at a time. In residential areas, people usually worked a rota, under which each person on duty in a street did two hours on duty and then knocked up the next watcher. Except during an Alert, no patrolling was necessary—to be up and awake was enough. In most places one's evening 'on' only came round every ten days or so, but even this could be a serious burden on someone already doing a full-time job. A then nineteen-year-old Somerset girl admits mildly, 'I never relished the two hours' fire-watching when they fell from 2 a.m. to 4 a.m.'—she had to be up at 4.30 a.m. for the 6 a.m. to 2 p.m. early shift at her war factory. It was not surprising that, as the years wore on, people grew more and more reluctant to turn out at night. Certainly on our council estate, where my father had prepared an elaborate duty rota, few of those listed ever appeared, even when the sirens sounded.

This seems to have been the almost universal experience, for, with some shining exceptions, fire-watchers were never a very enthusiastic body, and duty on business premises was particularly unpopular.

The position was made worse for the unlucky or conscientious minority because it was so easy to obtain exemption from fire-watching on grounds of 'exceptional hardship'. It was openly said among the officials trying to enforce the scheme that 'anyone not a congenital idiot could easily evade fire guard duty and in any case a congenital idiot was entitled to exemption'. Exemption on medical grounds was equally suspect. A Sheffield doctor found that those who applied to him for certificates usually explained that they were most anxious to do the job but 'felt they would be a danger to the rest of the party'. In some places the number claiming exemption reached 75 per cent. Although no one could legally refuse to join the Fire Guard a few fanatics pleaded that their 'conscience' required them to stand by while their neighbour's house burned down and their neighbour's family burned to death. Most, unhappily, escaped the punishment they deserved, for few local authorities had time to waste on pursuing this self-indulgent, lunatic minority.

The uniform of the Fire Guard, the name which replaced the former 'Street Fire Party' in August 1941, was an armlet and a steel helmet, shaped, for some unknown reason, like a high-crowned pudding basin, and without a chin strap, so it readily fell off. To one Cambridge Fire Guard it recalled 'a Victorian sun-bonnet'; others made cruder comparisons. The Fire Guard's weapon was the stirrup pump, an admirably simple piece of equipment, consisting of a small upright pump which went into a bucket, a metal bracket with a foot rest or 'stirrup', and a long hose with a nozzle readily converted from 'jet' to 'spray'. By 1943 there was at least one in every road, provided free or by a whip-round among the neighbours, and signs reading 'Stirrup Pump Here', 'Fire Guard Assembly Point' or 'Water' could be seen on gateposts everywhere. The new arrangements soon proved their value. In the Baedeker raid on Canterbury when 6,000 incendiaries were dropped, the fire-watchers saved the cathedral and in the Little Blitz on London in 1944 75 per cent of the fires started were put out without help from the N.F.S.* The truth was that, if tackled at once, incendiary bombs—unless of the rare, explosive kind—were not dangerous.

Usually they fell in a cluster, often from 'Molotov breadbaskets', which split open in the air, scattering a hundred or more bombs over a single street. Commander Firebrace described the noise of incendiaries hitting the ground as 'a curious plop-plopping sound'. Others compared them to leaves drifting along a road, and to one Liverpool housewife they resembled 'peas being dropped on a dish'.† This noise was enough in most roads to bring an eager crowd out of their houses ready to do battle with them. In the West End women in evening dresses on their way to a dance were seen contemptuously kicking spluttering bombs into the gutter. In Chelsea one group of indignant elderly people and children complained to the wardens because the residents of another road had moved in and put out 'their' bombs. The wife of an R.A.F. pilot remembers seeing 'little boys in Bristol running about with dustbin lids "bagging incendiaries"'. Also in Bristol one twelve-year-old girl modestly announced on arrival at a New Year's Eve party that she had put out nine fire bombs on the way. A woman living in Worcester Park, Surrey, remembers that after an incendiary raid the 'roads next morning looked like Kew Gardens', as her neighbours had dashed out with buckets of soil from their gardens. Even one solitary citizen could join in. In Lambeth, when incendiaries fell opposite a pub, the landlord's wife carried out a bucket of 'swipes'—beer-spillings—mistaking them for water, and plunged in her stirrup pump and doused the bomb in beer. One man, covered in beer foam, inevitably joked, 'What a glorious death.'

Hospitals, with their extensive buildings, were frequent targets for incendiaries. One male patient in Queen Elizabeth Hospital, Birmingham, was highly impressed that when 'hundreds of incendiary bombs showered down on the hospital, the nurses coolly kicked them off the balconies'. A nurse in training at Hither Green, in South East London, was in the bath when a Molotov breadbasket burst over her hospital but, determined

---

* The 1942 'Baedeker' raids were so called because they were designed to destroy historic towns singled out for praise in Baedeker's guide book—a reprisal for the British bombing of the beautiful old port of Lübeck. Besides Canterbury, Exeter, York, Norwich and Bath—where 400 people were killed—were also attacked.
† They were substantial 'peas'. The ordinary incendiary bomb was about one foot long by two inches diameter and weighed two pounds.

not to be left out, she pulled on a dressing-gown and joined her colleagues in a general onslaught on every incendiary in sight, finally reinforcing the party, led by sister tutor, who were climbing a ladder to deal with one obstinate bomb lodged in a gutter. More unnerving were incendiaries which crashed in sideways, through the windows, and a surprising number landed in chimneys, setting the roof on fire and sometimes falling right down into the grate.

But for every 'fire-bomb fighter', as Herbert Morrison had called them, who actually went into action there were scores who merely trained and waited.

Fire-watching in one's own street was not really disagreeable. One North London woman remembers her periods on duty as peaceful oases in the wartime round, spent working on her stamp collection, and a woman living in a Leytonstone block of flats enjoyed pleasant domestic reunions after fire-watching, when she and her husband would 'sit in bed, eating chocolate biscuits and drinking tea'. Duty in offices and shops was usually far less pleasant, despite the official subsistence allowance of three shillings a night. A then teenage girl from Huyton, Lancashire, like other fire-watchers in the Electricity Supply Department showroom in 'a rambling building', remembers that 'much more than bombs we feared the rats, which peered over the edge of a false ceiling at us, for all the world as though they wanted a sandwich'. A woman L.M.S. employee dreaded going on fire-watching duty at four-thirty in the morning, feeling terrified of the dark, and 'listening to loose windows or hoardings flapping'. One morning she was startled by a cat dashing out of a ruined building. 'I screamed,' she recalls, 'and was in a bad state of nerves when I reached the office.'

One woman Civil Servant whose office was in the Strand, recalls with distaste 'sleeping on the fifth floor of an old-fashioned building, covered by grey blankets which smelt peculiar'. A woman living near Tunbridge Wells found the worst feature of fire-watching in the solicitors' office where she worked was trying to sleep among the 'rows of gloomy legal books'. At a Tunbridge Wells girls' high school the person on the middle watch 1–4 a.m., was expected to chase the beetles from the school washroom. A male fire-watcher posted on the roof of a restaurant in Oxford had an even stranger duty: the two 'sweet old ladies' who owned it had given him strict instructions to use his stirrup pump to keep tom-cats away from their she-cat. But one tom was made of sterner stuff and refused to be discouraged, and eventually the old ladies' cat had her kittens. The fire-watcher and his wife were presented with one, which they named Peter Geekie, after a famous *ITMA* character, who never actually appeared.

The members of the six-man groups of fire-watchers on duty at the office of a Bristol evening newspaper would take it in turns every hour to 'put on a tin hat, arm ourselves with a thick stick, and tour the building to make sure there were no spies lurking behind the machinery'. Then on quiet nights they would settle down to a regular pattern of card games: cribbage from eight to ten, followed by supper, then pontoon till midnight, and from midnight poker 'until we were too tired to go on any longer'. At the Rugby telephone exchange one telephonist found her duty once in three weeks a splendid opportunity for beauty treatment, and she and a colleague would wash and set each other's hair and have a 'general tidy up of our complexions'. A Nottingham Civil Servant entertained his three colleagues with readings from Dickens—his favourite was *A Christmas Carol*. Perhaps the most unusual recreation was that of the fire-watchers at a newspaper warehouse in Angus, who spent the evenings scrutinising all visitors to the building since it shared an entrance with a reputed brothel, adding 'a little excitement to the boredom of fire-watching'.

# 13

# THE KITCHEN FRONT

'Carrot Flan . . . reminds you of Apricot Flan—but has a deliciousness all its own.'

Ministry of Food advertisement, 1941

One day in the middle of the war a Staines housewife baked a cake that contained so few of the usual ingredients that she christened it 'The Nothing Cake'. The name—and the fact that her family ate the cake with enjoyment, though it consisted mainly of flour, custard powder and dried egg—symbolised the difficulties which British housewives faced from 1939 to 1945 and the way in which they defeated them. Even those who never saw an incendiary bomb or heard an enemy bomber had to go into action several times a day against an enemy even older than Hitler, hunger.

Women who remembered the breakdown of food distribution in the first world war, with its perpetual queues, un-met ration coupons, and desperate shortage of every necessity from potatoes to edible margarine, dreaded similar experiences in the second. But this was one area where things turned out better than expected. The British system of wartime rationing and food control proved an immense success, due largely to the patriotic self-sacrifice and resourcefulness of the ordinary housewife. The Kitchen Front was the only one where Great Britain never lost a battle.

The housewife was introduced to rationing by easy stages. She first had to take her ration books when she went shopping on Monday 8th January 1940, though only for bacon or ham, four ounces a head a week, sugar, twelve ounces, and butter, four ounces. Meat rationing began in March with 1s. 10d. worth a week for everyone over six, and 11d. worth for smaller children, the adult ration later being reduced to 1s. 1d. and 1s. 2d. worth at various times, though offal was excluded. Fish remained unrationed, but was hard to find. A Ministry of Food advertisement optimistically predicted:

> The fishermen are saving lives
> By sweeping seas for mines,
> So you'll not grumble, 'What no fish?'
> When you have read these lines.

In July rationing really began, to use an appropriate word, to bite, when it was extended to tea, for the two ounces a week allowed were not enough for most families. Women now began to tear open their empty tea packets in search of a few hidden grains, or followed the Minister of Food's advice to use 'one spoonful for each person and none for the pot'. At the same time margarine and cooking fats went on coupons and before long the rations settled down at around two ounces of cooking fat, four ounces of margarine and four—later two—ounces of butter a week. Housewives began to scrape the last morsel of butter or cooking fat from its wrapper and finally to rub the greasy paper on dish or frying pan, while many people gave up sugar in their tea or coffee for the duration. The tea and sugar rations pressed hardest on old people. A Surrey girl, aged ten, used to feel sorry for her grandfather who was firmly upbraided by her mother for stealing an extra spoonful of sugar when her back was turned. Some people experimented with using honey or golden syrup in their tea, which turned it black and tasted strange, but in March 1941 jam, marmalade and syrup also went on coupons, followed by mincemeat, lemon curd and honey. The amount varied, according to the season, from eight ounces to two pounds a month. It was a heavy blow to most families when cheese was rationed in May 1941 at only an ounce a week, barely one decent mouthful, but the ration later went up and for most of the war was two ounces, with from August 1941 an extra eight ounces to a pound a week for agricultural workers, miners, and other heavy workers who carried their food with them. Every wartime housewife will remember, too, other highly-prized bonuses—the extra sugar during the jam-making season, the 'Ministry of Food' Christmas present of extra rations in December, the extra ounce of tea for the over-seventies introduced in December 1944.

By the end of 1940 most family store cupboards were almost empty. Nathaniel Gubbins's humorous column in the *Sunday Express* nicely reflected the universal experience in such melancholy news items as, in *Letter from an Aunt*, 'Your uncle George came to tea—last of the tinned salmon'. Tinned salmon, like tinned meat and fruit and many other items, was not on coupons but they had all disappeared almost everywhere until, on the 1st December 1941, the Ministry of Food unveiled its masterpiece, the points rationing scheme. Under the scheme every holder of a ration book received sixteen points a month, later raised to twenty, to spend as he wished, at any shop that had the items he wanted. At first only canned meat, fish and vegetables were 'on points', but in the next twelve months one item after another was added, including rice and canned fruit, condensed milk and breakfast cereals, biscuits and oatflakes. The points scheme brought back to the shops items which had not been seen for months, for the Ministry had built up stocks to get it off to a good start. It proved immediately popular for it made the housewife a discriminating shopper again, instead of a mere collector of rations. To the Ministry the scheme had the great advantage of being infinitely adjustable. If tinned sardines or baked beans proved too popular and stocks began to run low, they simply raised their points value; if cream crackers or tapioca were piling up unwanted, they had only to cut it to clear the shelves. Guessing, towards the end of a rationing period, which items were likely to go up or down, added a new interest to the weary routine of catering for a family, and housewives turned to the list of 'Changes in Points Value' in the newspaper with all the zeal of a gambler looking for the racing results. To discover some points 'bargain' was also a matter for deep satisfaction. The outstanding 'buy' was generally agreed to be the large tin of American sausage meat which cost a whole sixteen points, but besides providing enough meat for several main meals contained a thick layer of nearly half a pound of fat, invaluable for cooking. One Cambridgeshire woman thought it added 'a touch of pre-war luxury' to dull wartime diet and another, in Hertfordshire, served it so often to a Polish guest that he 'must have thought sausage meat was our national dish'. Another popular import was Spam, American canned spiced ham. It had soon become the great wartime standby, fried with bread as a main meal, eaten cold in sandwiches, serving as the meat in 'pork' pies, gracing wedding receptions as filling for the vol-au-vent.

The Ministry of Food constantly urged the public to try entirely new foods, especially in the case of fish, for which no satisfactory distribution system was ever found. The queues outside the fishmongers', the one unrationed item, apart from the even more elusive offal, which could provide a main course for a meal, were always the longest and the most frustrating. It will not surprise any wartime housewife that, as one remembers, the queue outside the fish shop was the only one not to disperse when the sirens went one morning in Paddington in 1944 and that even when a V.1 cut out overhead the queuers merely ducked. A Shenfield woman used to wait up to two hours in a fish queue for 'great slabs of salted cod that had the taste and texture of boiled flannelette'. A Nottingham woman queued for one and a half hours on a bitter February morning to obtain three herrings, and a Blackpool woman admits being moved to tears of disappointment on finding, after she had queued for an hour drawing nearer and nearer a splendid piece of hake, that only a wretched piece of tail was left when her turn came; the woman in front, who ran a billet for airmen, had bought twenty-six portions. To relieve the shortage the Ministry of Food scoured the world for obscure varieties, exhorting women to buy them with such verses as:

When fisher-folk are brave enough
To face mines and the foe for you
You surely can be bold enough
To try fish of a kind that's new.

But women who did try the new fish rarely did so twice. An East London woman still winces at the thought of 'great black slabs of . . . that awful tuna fish', and a Mansfield housewife simply threw away the evil-smelling and unnamed white fish pressed upon her. But it was whalemeat at which most palates rebelled. A Nottinghamshire woman never forgave the fishmonger's assistant who assured her that 'it was really nice. If I cooked it like stewing steak, no one would know'. The salesgirl had underrated her family, her husband 'demanding to know what he was eating. . . . The stunned silence, the expression on the face of the "victim" is something to remember.' A Falmouth hotel worker remembers a chef who grilled and served the whale as if it were steak but one guest promptly sent it back—a very brave thing to do with any dish in wartime—all the other diners also rejected their steaks and 'even the dog would not touch them'. A Bournemouth woman who tackled various 'fish of doubtful origin, like some sort of cat fish' and 'dried salted fish', admits, 'But the whalemeat beat me. I thought it was horrible.' 'Repulsive', 'revolting', 'ghastly', 'tough and fishy', 'like a lump of cod liver oil', 'like fishy liver', these are how other women describe it, and two sum up their reactions in the same brief monosyllable: 'Ugh!'

Offal was even scarcer than fish. What happened to the previously unwanted sections of cattle, now that everyone wanted them, was the cause of much indignant discussion in the butcher's queue—and of great rejoicing if one was in luck and actually offered some. 'If I got some liver I ran home as happy as if I had won a fortune', one woman remembers. Others acquired a taste for 'pigs' fry', pigs' trotters, brains, sweetbreads, cowheel and, according to a Deptford woman, 'best of all, ox-cheek'. In Lancashire tripe was praised as 'a good standby' though generally felt to need onions, and a Mansfield woman, who has never tasted one since, says 'we lived on beasts' hearts'. A few brave women even boiled down a sheep's head. One Ipswich woman will 'never forget the awful job of preparing it and getting the bones out. At any rate we had the tongue and some nourishing soup but I never attempted it again.'

Some offal found its way into sausages, which were unrationed. The sausage had always been considered comic, but during the war it became a target for two main jokes: that its ingredients were best not enquired into—one family nicknamed it 'sweet mystery of life' and another 'firewood sausages'—and that it contained little but bread. A Lincoln woman remembers a man remarking to her, as their bus passed a queue for sausages, 'Why queue?—you can get bread without queueing the other side of the road. One Essex housewife jokes, 'We didn't know whether to put mustard or marmalade on them'. One contemporary cartoon showed even the fish spurning the sausage which baited every hook. Yet sausages did provide a meat dish and, as one Ipswich woman who used to queue for an hour outside one shop before it even opened remembers, 'it seemed a matter of life and death . . . to get one pound'.

One of the first ways in which the war made itself felt to the ordinary housewife was in the sudden disappearance of onions, due to the loss of supplies from the Channel Islands and Britanny. This was, one Scottish journalist felt, 'the one real traumatic lack. Their absence was terribly noticeable.' The taste of this humble vegetable, so long taken for granted, seemed suddenly the peak of gastronomic pleasure, partly because with meat rationed by value, not weight, stews, which used the cheapest cuts, were in favour. At least two *Odes to an Onion* were written in 1941.

> O pungent root, so lately dear to me,
> Thou bulbous, aromatic rarity . . .
> Today thou are a treasure vainly sought . . .

began the lament of one frustrated cook at Tipton, Staffordshire, in January. By September the shortage was no better as, these verses in one London firm's house magazine testified:

> When I was quite a tiny child
> My temper was extremely mild;
> One thing alone could make me wild:
>     The evil-smelling onion.
>
> I grew adult, as children do;
> My tastes inclined to flavours new,
> And steadily upon me grew
>     A passion for the onion.
>
> Marmalade, butter, eggs and cheese,
> I bore it when they rationed these;
> But who could guess that they would seize
>     The sweet and lovely onion?
>
> My cupboard might as well be bare.
> Bereft, I wander everywhere
> And try, nose in the empty air,
>     To sniff a whiff of onion.

In February 1941 a one-and-a-half pound onion, raffled among the staff of *The Times*, raised £4 3s. 4d. and in March, when one woman remarked

A wartime wedding. The fire-fighting party of a City firm forming an archway for the bride and groom, April 1940.

Arrival of the Andersons in an Islington street, February 1939.

**Preparations**

Brick street shelter in Peckham, January 1940.

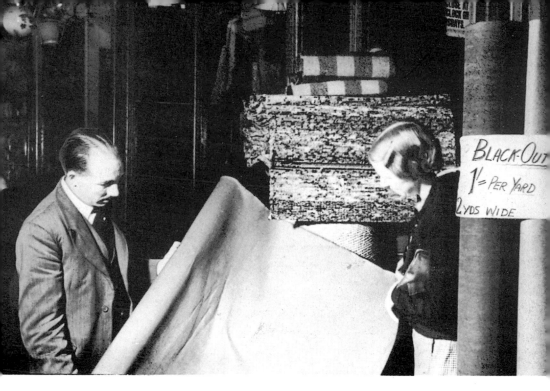

Black-out material on sale,
August 1939.

Fire-guard party preparing to
go to it. (The stirrup pump was
widely distributed in 1939; the
'sun-bonnet' type steel helmet,
especially designed for fire-
guards, did not come into use
until 1941.)

Infant's anti-gas helmet. A demonstration with a doll.

Toddler's 'Donald Duck' mask.

**Getting ready for gas**

The standard civilian gas mask. A fitting session at school.

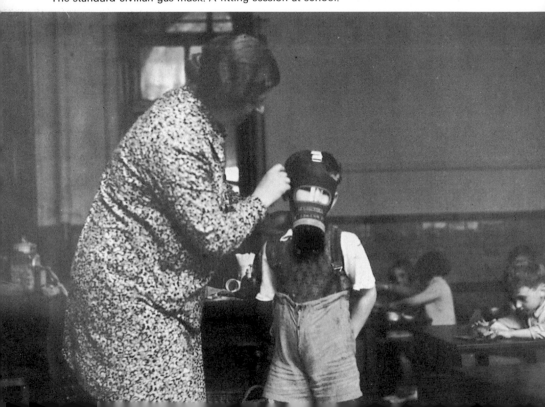

'Unaccompanied infants', escorted by W.V.S. helper.

**Evacuation**

School party leaving London for the West Country.

Evacuees filling in time on the South Coast, September 1939.

**Waiting**

Evacuees looking out for visiting parents, December 1939. (Special cheap excursions were arranged to discourage parents from taking their children home.)

**Waiting**

Hospital train at Streatham station, early 1940.

Animals A.R.P. Centre, Woodford Bridge, 1939.

## The Phoney War and its ending

The start, September 1939.

Defeat in Norway, April 1940. (Note the copies of
*Picture Post*, price 3d, and *Woman*, price 2d.)

Defeat in France, June 1940.

Attack on England, July 1940. (To save paper,
news-bills were now forbidden and vendors wrote
their own—complete, as here, with misspellin
of Messerschmitt.)

at a first aid lecture in Chelsea that she did not cry if she wore her gas mask when peeling onions, every woman present instantly shouted, 'Where did you get them?' Onions became popular prizes at socials and one wartime Girl Guide in Accrington can still recapture her pride at winning one in a treasure hunt, in honour of which her mother baked a special pie. A Cheshire doctor remembers 'taking home in triumph' the best gift he ever received from a grateful patient: a large Spanish onion. One 'aunt' on *Children's Hour*, wishing 'A Happy Birthday and lots of presents' to one small listener, added, 'I did hear of a lucky girl the other day who was given some onions, but we can't all expect a lovely present like that.' A Worcestershire woman used the same onion in cooking for a month before finally eating it, and in North Queensberry in Scotland one family 'tried putting an onion in a glass of water like a hyacinth bulb and, as the green shoots appeared . . . cut them off and used them for flavouring'. The Minister of Agriculture, announcing in February 1941 a fifteen-fold increase in the onion crop, expressed the hope that 'onions would then be eaten and not talked about', and by 1942 this expectation was being fulfilled.

Onions, like other vegetables, were never rationed, though the Ministry of Food operated for them a system of Controlled Distribution under which scarce items were allocated in turn to various parts of the country. The shopkeeper had to mark each customer's ration book, but if he had any surplus he was usually allowed to distribute it. From May 1941 there were occasional allocations of oranges in this way, though they were usually reserved for the under-fives and expectant mothers, or for those aged five to eighteen. A sympathetic greengrocer sometimes stretched the rules to a favoured customer and one woman who had benefited in this way still remembers her embarrassment when her landlady's small son, seeing her with some precious oranges, innocently asked, 'Have you got a green book [for expectant mothers] or are you under sixteen?' Her age was then forty-eight. To be caught trying to get a second share involved social disgrace and a Tunbridge Wells woman, a self-confessed rubber-out of pencil marks, still blushes at the memory of being finally 'shown up in a crowded Sainsburys'. When oranges were available the usual allowance was only a pound a book, and the peel was carefully hoarded for making marmalade. A woman doctor in Westmorland remembers being called in at midnight to see a small girl suspected of having appendicitis and finding there was a simpler explanation of her stomach pains—the patient had had for supper the first orange she had ever seen and, knowing no better, had eaten it peel and all.

Lemons simply vanished for the duration and one Tunbridge Wells woman, who had received a box of them from her nephew, in Sicily with the Eighth Army, proudly took them round to show her green-grocer who had not seen one for years. Bananas were the greatest rarity of all and there were many stories of children given one as a treat who tried to bite into the skin or howled at the unfamiliar sight. A Gloucester-shire teenager who won a banana in an office raffle in 1942—it had been given to one of the typists by a newly-arrived Australian airman—took it home, where, after it had been inspected by the neighbours, 'it was cut up into pieces with a taste for each member of the family. It seemed criminal just to throw the skin away, so we put it in the middle of the road outside the house and had a lot of fun watching the surprised looks of several passers by, a few of whom could contain curiosity no longer and picked it up to see if it were real.' Some other fruit were almost as scarce. One London resident remembers 'word going round that the greengrocer would have a few cooking apples, queue starting at 6 a.m. following morning. It was a mile long. One apple apiece until they had gone. I was first to be refused.' A Rotherhithe woman also turned out at 6 a.m. one Saturday to queue for three hours outside a greengrocer's. Her prize was 'three apples *or* a pound of rhubarb—then home for a warm drink and out again, this time to the offal shop'. For luxury fruit some ridiculous prices were paid, a melon in August 1941 fetching £2, for example, and grapes 17s. 6d. a pound.

A more serious shortage than fresh fruit was that of eggs, which became scarce during 1940 following cuts in imports and the slaughter of millions of hens to save feeding stuffs. Before the war everyone in Great Britain had eaten on average three eggs a week; during the war the total dropped to roughly one a fortnight, though there were long periods with none at all. Most people now realised for the first time the important role eggs had played in their diet. Anyone whose work took him into the country would now enquire, as a matter of course, at any likely-looking farm or cottage if there were eggs for sale. One Oxfordshire farmer remembers a driver, who was giving him a lift, gladly going eight miles out of his way—a serious offence during petrol rationing—to buy a dozen eggs from him. A woman who jokingly asked someone to be careful of her case on a railway journey as it was 'full of eggs', was embarrassed when one fellow passenger after another pleaded with her to sell them some. A wasted egg was a major disaster. A London woman remembers frying her husband their only egg that week for his breakfast, until 'it got more and more like lino as I kept it hot. In a fury I cast it into the kitchen boiler and gave him breakfast in bed after that.' But while the ordinary adult, 'the holder of R.B.1' in the jargon of the Food Office, went short, the 'priority classes' of expectant mothers and children under five actually received on average slightly more eggs during the war than the pre-war average. The sight of a small child reluctantly and messily toying with a precious egg, while other members of the family watched hungrily, was one to try the patience of even the most conscientious mother. A Lancashire curate's family compromised when their small daughter, born in December 1943, brought two welcome eggs a week into the household by letting her have what she wanted, but taking it in turns to eat any she refused.

To compensate for the shortage of shell eggs, from June 1942 onwards packets of another wartime novelty from America began to appear on the grocers' shelves. Few things more rapidly evoke the whole feel of wartime than the slightly biscuity (some said 'cardboard') taste of dried eggs. The Ministry of Food's publicity campaign stressed how much shipping space dried eggs saved—'Shell eggs are five-sixths water: Why import water?'—but to the housewife they possessed a simpler attraction: they were almost always available. Apart from a few months in 1942 and 1943 at least one drab, grey packet, its contents equivalent to a dozen fresh eggs, was available on every ration book every four weeks, and for long periods they could be sold without restriction to registered customers. Although one Southampton woman felt that 'everything tasted rubbery with dried egg and Yorkshire pudding came out of the oven as flat as it went in', personally I found a dried egg omelette perfectly palatable and scrambled dried eggs were the favourite bedtime snack among the monitors in my house at school. I found that a little cheese greatly improved the flavour, and the nurses at a Clydeside hospital favoured them spread with mustard. The small amount of dried egg powder required was deceptive. One Scotswoman, who proudly cooked the first breakfast of her married life in October 1944, 'mixed the egg as instructed on the tin. It didn't look very much so we doubled the amount. It still looked a bit on the small side so I added a bit more—by this time three-quarters of a tin had been used. What we didn't know was that it swelled in cooking and we had enough . . . to feed a family of twelve.' A little later in her marriage the mistake might have seemed less hilarious, as it did to the wife of a Middlesbrough cinema manager whose 'husband . . . decided to make an omelette from dried eggs and used up a whole precious packet, which nearly caused a divorce'. Dried egg became the universal resource for housewives puzzled what to give their family at the next meal. The wife of a miner living in Blaenavon, Monmouthshire, remembers that when she made her invariable reply, 'Wait and see', when he asked what was for supper, he would make the ritual, but only too truthful, retort: 'Oh, I know, dried egg!'

Almost as common a sight in wartime kitchens as the dried egg packet was the dried milk tin. Controlled Distribution of liquid milk began in November 1941, the usual amount allowed being from two to two-and-a half pints a head a week, and to supplement it from December tins of dried skimmed milk powder, known as Household Milk, went on sale. Each was said to equal four pints of liquid milk when water was added and, for most of the war, every family was allowed one tin a month. Household Milk, though barely drinkable by itself, was certainly better than nothing in coffee or cocoa and just better than nothing in tea, but really came into its own in cooking. Children under one, and later two, years old were also entitled to National Dried Milk, a full-cream product much nearer the real thing. To find a chemist with tins of this which had outlived the 'Not for consumption after . . .' date on the label, and could now be sold to ordinary customers, was a real triumph. One of the innumerable changes to which housewives had to become accustomed in those years was a new milkman, for even if their usual roundsman had not been called up, from the autumn of 1942 only one milkman, apart from the Co-op, visited each street, and deliveries were often cut to four days a week. The baker could call up to three times a week, but most other goods the housewife now had to carry home herself, usually unwrapped. This produced some strange sights. One could see dignified men in business suits carefully carrying kippers by their tails and fur coated women laden with string bags bulging with—a great treasure—ham bones. It became socially acceptable to stop a perfect stranger in the street and ask where she had found some scarce item and soon, as one woman remembers, the news would spread and housewives would be hurrying from all directions 'like flies round a jampot'.

Most familiar brands of goods simply vanished, as production was concentrated in a few factories to save labour. The 350 varieties of biscuits on sale pre-war were reduced to twenty, and soft drinks were sold under labels like 'Orange Squash, S.W. 153', the only clue to the manufacturer's name. Packages were standardised, labels grew smaller and less colourful, and if one saw a familiar name it was often on some old stock that the shopkeeper had been trying to get rid of for years. (One man remembers buying in 1943 a packet of porridge oats printed with an entry form for a competition that had closed in 1937.)

Although in most homes money was now more plentiful than before the war, the smallness of the rations made careful shopping more necessary than ever. One question much debated in the queues was whether it was better to spread one's ration books over several shops, to increase the chance of obtaining the vital extras, or to register the whole family with the same shopkeeper, in the hope of preferential treatment when some scarce but unrationed item like coffee, custard powder or pepper— known as 'white gold'—was available. People also argued about whether one did better at a large shop or a small one. Many women still praise the private rationing scheme run by the large firm of Sainsburys, but others have kindly memories of some 'small shop round the corner' which, perhaps, put a precious jelly aside when some child's birthday was approaching. Despite a few surly or bullying shopkeepers and assistants, who sent their customers out muttering darkly 'Just wait till after the war!', most shops, large or small, went to great trouble to be fair. The trouble taken in the village shop at Bourton in Dorset speaks for itself. The manager's wife, having received one Christmas seven pounds of dried fruit, actually counted out the various items to ensure that each registered customer got her fair share. One housewife's allocation was three prunes, four dates, twelve raisins and one ounce of sultanas. 'We made a Christmas cake,' she remembers, 'though it wasn't a very *big* cake.'

When, about once a year, new ration books were issued, it was possible to change one's retailer without explanation, but to do so in between was, in the words of a Coulsdon housewife, 'rather like getting a divorce'. It was obviously sensible to try to keep on good terms with your shopkeeper. In one Colchester shop it was a joke among the customers that when the owner put up the welcome notice 'Currents today' not one of them dared to correct his misspelling. To lose one's ration book was also a serious matter, though it was replaced on payment of a shilling, and on signature of a declaration witnessed by a responsible person. The most famous excuse was put forward by a travelling circus family who wrote to Blackpool Food Office, 'Please can we have new ration books as the others have been eaten by our elephant?'

An even greater disaster than a lost book was a waste of food. A woman living in Irvine, Ayrshire, who told off her son for drawing on her single egg for that week never did so again: full of contrition, he tried to rub out his picture, with disastrous results. An Ipswich woman who incautiously left a packet of tea—four people's ration for a week—in the baby's pram while choosing her books at the library, came out to find that the baby had emptied the whole half-pound on to the ground. A four-year-old girl in Paignton, mistaking the week's sugar ration for toilet cleaner, emptied it all down the lavatory. An Enfield woman put a precious gift of fresh eggs from a cousin in waterglass in a bucket kept in the bedroom, safely away from her small children, until 'One day the elder girl found she was tall enough to reach door handles, found the eggs and amused herself making a squishy mess'. One Northampton woman, who saw a dog dashing out of a butcher's shop with a large piece of suet in his mouth, followed him on her bicycle and watched him bury the suet. 'When the dog was safely away I went to the spot . . . and confiscated the hidden treasure . . . I took home that suet, cut out the mauled part and then made suet pudding.'

With food so scarce many women acted on the principle 'what the eye doesn't see . . .' or even, on occasion, 'what the eye *does* see . . .' One London woman, who dropped the family's entire butter ration on the kitchen floor, simply scraped it back on the dish for an important guest, though her small son made pointed remarks on the subject at table. A Birmingham woman, whose husband's dinner was knocked out of her hand, pushed it back on to the plate and 'tidied it up' with some more gravy so that 'the poor man never knew until long after the war'. A King's Lynn woman saw a neighbour who had dropped half a dozen eggs in the gutter when pushing her pram scraping them up; she scrambled them for supper. Even doctors relaxed their customary standards. A Westmorland doctor who found her weekly joint covered with maggots 'scraped them off and roasted the joint again'. She also salted down butter in a large bedroom jug. 'One morning I found a mouse drowned in the salty water,' she remembers, 'but I used the butter.'

Most women had some private 'wrinkle' to make the rations go further, like begging the grocer for the cheese rind for flavouring or the scraps of meat from the bacon slicer, mixing cornflour with the dried egg to stretch it out, shaking up the top of the milk in a bottle to make butter, melting the butter and spreading it with a brush, or putting saccharine in the teapot rather than the cup. Dripping on toast, baked potatoes served with bottled sauce, and bread soaked in Oxo were all useful for visitors, while the favourite snack taken to her munitions factory by my sister consisted of sandwiches filled with potato crisps. Keen cooks regarded each new shortage as a challenge to their ingenuity. Dried elderberries and chopped prunes were used in cakes as substitutes for currants, and one woman successfully tried wine gums, though they tended to sink to the bottom of the dish. Household Milk and melted chocolate was used for icing, and, until the vigilant Ministry of Food restricted sales to 'medicinal purposes only', glycerine and liquid paraffin in place of cooking fat. Little was thrown away. One Hertfordshire family ate to the last crumb a 'disinfectant cake' made by mistake with Dettol, which had been kept in a bottle labelled 'Almond Essence'. A Croydon housewife served her family 'M.I.5 Pudding', refusing to disclose the ingredients. They were, in fact, liver, sausage meat and onion, and her children 'thought it super'.

In wartime guests who did not do justice to the food set before them were rarely asked twice. A London woman remembers queueing for hours for some liver and cooking it with the week's bacon ration 'to make a delicious supper for a business guest and the wretched man let me give him the best helping and left it on the side of his plate'. Equally infuriating were husbands who did not appreciate their wives' sacrifices. One Melton Mowbray housewife can still barely forgive her husband for having secretly helped himself each morning to golden syrup to sweeten his tea from a two-pound tin she had hidden on a top shelf. Only when the time came to call on this vital reserve did she discover it was empty. And every wartime housewife will share the feeling of mingled exasperation and amusement of a Nottingham woman whose husband, having offered to do the shopping, returned home empty-handed. 'The queues,' he explained, 'were awfully long.'

To bridge the gap between rations and appetites the government expected every family to eat out, on average, about one day a month and for some members of the family to have their main meals at school or work. School dinners, which before the war had been available only to 250,000 children, were by its end almost universal, numbering nearly 1,850,000 a day. Factory canteens had numbered 1,500 in 1939. By 1945 there were 18,500 and any firm over a certain size was legally compelled to provide one. The most important innovation of all was the British Restaurant, a simply furnished cafeteria, providing a filling meal very cheaply. A typical dinner at one in London in 1942 consisted of roast beef and two vegetables, treacle pudding, bread and butter and coffee and cost only 11*d.* By the end of the war there were 2,000 British Restaurants serving more than half a million meals a day. Their nearest equivalent in the countryside was the Pie Scheme, launched in 1941, under which meat, and later fruit, pies were distributed to village centres for sale to workers in the fields. Sad to relate, not all the million pies sold each week were greatly appreciated. One young girl, living in a north Norfolk village, never forgot the local doctor's disgusted glance at the pie she had just taken up for her sick father's dinner, and his remark, 'Good God, man, if you can eat that, you can eat anything!'

After public criticism of the lavish meals being served in hotels and luxury restaurants, in July 1940 it became illegal to serve more than one main course at any restaurant meal, the restricted dishes being marked on the menu by a star. One unfortunate woman and her daughter, who arrived at Liverpool from India in September 1940, and as yet knew no better, confidently ordered whitebait, assuming it to be the fish course, only to learn later they were no longer entitled to a meat course, so they 'went to bed very hungry'. In June 1942, after complaints of profiteering, controls were tightened still further with the introduction of a 5*s.* maximum for all restaurant meals, though luxury establishments could demand an extra 7*s.* 6*d.* cover charge, and some luxuries, like oysters and caviare, were excluded. Certain 'patriotic' dishes, like lentil cutlets, were labelled with a V for Victory. One Scottish gourmet considered the V 'an indication of the victory of necessity over the palate'. 'It has been left to these later years,' he wrote sadly, 'the experience of potatoes and margarine as a main dish.'

Many famous West End resorts, like the Café Royal, would not accept bookings after 9.30 or had by then long since run out of food. Even the Savoy by 1942 served vegetables already on the plate. No coupons were surrendered for restaurant meals, though anyone staying in a hotel for more than three days had to hand in his ration book, or the emergency ration card one could obtain for journeys away from home. The only source of unrationed food to eat at home came in food parcels from the Dominions and United States, which went mainly to those with friends abroad. Like most people, I never saw one.

Charges were often made about the existence of a widespread Black Market but the opinion of one farmer that 'there was more talk than do about this' was also held by the then Minister of Food.* The Ministry was also remarkably successful in keeping down prices. In the first world war food prices had risen by 130 per cent; in the second, which was half as long again, they rose by only 20 per cent, and even without government subsidies the increase would have been only 50 per cent.

The most outstanding achievement of all was surely that at the end of six years of war the British people were far healthier than they had been at the beginning. In 1939 the average housewife hardly knew a calorie from a protein; by the end of the war, to the delight, if embarrassment, of the Minister of Food, she was angrily writing to complain if her corner shop was failing to provide her family's share of body-building, energy-giving and protective foods. This result reflected credit both on her and on the 15,000 employees of the Ministry of Food. But the greatest responsibility for the Ministry's success, which had ensured that Britain was not starved into surrender, rested upon one man: Frederick Marquis, 1st Baron Woolton.

When, in April 1940, Lord Woolton became Minister of Food he was aged fifty-eight and had had an exceptionally varied career. After leaving Manchester University he had become warden of a social-work settlement in the Liverpool slums, then, after the first world war, had risen to be managing director of the great Manchester store of John Lewis—not to be confused with the London firm of the same name. In 1939 he reluctantly agreed to become director-general of the Ministry of Supply and in 1940, even more reluctantly, Minister of Food. When Churchill came to power he told his cronies, 'We shall have to be ready with a rescue squad for Woolton', but instead, three years later, it was Woolton who was called in to rescue his Conservative colleagues, and forced, much against his will, to become Minister of Reconstruction, to show that the government was in earnest about post-war planning. As Woolton had foreseen, his abilities were totally wasted in his new

---

* Many Black Market rumours were really veiled anti-Semitism for it was constantly asserted that it was run by Jews. One author, who studied the press reports for three months of 1941–2, claimed that 80 per cent of those convicted had Jewish names.

post, while his successor as Minister of Food is now largely forgotten.*

From 4th April 1940 to 12th November 1943 Lord Woolton *was*, in the ordinary housewife's eyes, the Ministry of Food. 'I found the Ministry of Food suffering from a general depression', he wrote in his memoirs. 'The press was against them and they were dejected, and frankly puzzled, by their unpopularity.' His first step was to restore morale by visiting his staff in their offices and by inviting the King to tour his headquarters, which raised the Ministry's public standing. About its competence he had no fears; the detailed planning and administration which rationing involved was just the type of job at which the Civil Service excelled.

The next step was to gain public confidence. Although never an effective parliamentary speaker, Woolton became an excellent broadcaster. He would spend a day preparing a twelve-minute talk and sit in his shirt-sleeves in the studio, repolishing his script and working right through the lunch hour. Woolton's policy was simple: to ration nothing, however scarce, until there was enough to go round and then to ensure that the ration, however small, was always honoured. He had no sympathy with those who complained that others could get some luxury which they never saw. 'Food control,' he insisted, 'does not mean preventing the other fellow from getting something. It is a means of ensuring that we get all the things that are necessary.'

Lord Woolton's greatest success was in winning the ordinary housewife to his side with a brilliant publicity campaign. The phrase *The Kitchen Front* soon became universally familiar through a series of press advertisements carrying the message, 'Food is a munition of war. Don't waste it', supported by *Food Flashes* at the cinema, short talks every morning in *The Kitchen Front*, after the eight o'clock news, and comic dialogues between 'Gert and Daisy', Elsie and Doris Waters, who often appeared with Lord Woolton on the platform. Sometimes the Ministry offered recipes like 'Pigs in Clover—a novel way with baked potatoes and sausage', sometimes warnings like 'It's not clever to get more than your share', sometimes simple encouragement: 'Carry on Fighters on the Kitchen Front. You are doing a great job.' Its most sustained efforts were devoted to boosting the consumption of 'Carrots, bright treasures dug from good British earth' and 'Potatoes . . . a rich store of all-round nourishment'. The faces of Dr. Carrot and Potato Pete were soon looking out from the pages of every women's magazine, the one thin and alert, the other plump and reassuring. 'Call me often enough and you'll keep well', Dr. Carrot told mothers. The Ministry also constantly stressed that 'carrots contain sugar' but the public remained unconvinced. The claim that 'Carrot Flan . . . has a deliciousness all its own' proved only too true,

* He was in fact Colonel J. J. Llewellin.

and one wartime child has described how his father, after a single mouthful of carrot marmalade, simply picked up the pot, walked out and emptied it on the compost heap. The Ministry's master-stroke was spreading the belief that carrots enabled one to see better in the dark, thus explaining the sudden success of 'Cat's-eyes Cunningham', and other night-fighter aces, which was in fact due to the introduction of radar.

Potato Pete became so well known that one Battersea schoolgirl affectionately called a class-mate she 'had a crush on' by this name, and according to the Ministry there were few things he could not do, from saving fuel to combining with rhubarb and honey in "Sweet Potato Pudding'. The Ministry offered a weekly prize to the greengrocer with the best selling potato display, and organised 'Potato Pete's Fair' in Oxford Street, where visitors could buy 'Potato Stamps' to exchange for extra potatoes at their greengrocers'. Its efforts succeeded by the end of the war in raising the consumption of potatoes by 60 per cent, the largest increase in any commodity.

Woolton's other great 'filler' was bread and in April 1942 he launched the National Loaf made from grey, wholemeal flour. The public never really took to it and in his memoirs Woolton admitted that people blamed every minor ailment on 'this nasty, dirty, dark, coarse, indigestible bread', but by the end of the war 20 per cent more bread was being eaten than in 1939. Perhaps the rumour, passed on to Lord Woolton at a party, that it was an aphrodisiac, helped.

Over the staff entrance to the Ministry of Food was the inscription 'We not merely cope, we care' and complaints from the public were always carefully investigated, Lord Woolton personally signing many thousands of the replies. A woman living in a Sussex village, where the local shop refused to accept the Emergency Ration Cards issued by her children's boarding schools, who sent a protesting telegram to the Ministry at 8 a.m. one hot July day, was astounded when, at 6 p.m. that evening, while she was 'busy dismembering a revolting sheep's head . . . a departmental young man, with black coat, pin-striped trousers, umbrella and bowler hat, appeared on the terrace of our country cottage, perspiring in these unsuitable clothes after a country walk of five miles uphill. He had a local Food Office girl with him. "I'm the man from the Ministry", he said.' He explained that he had looked into her complaint, and had already put matters right. 'Next day I had urgent calls from the village stores, as the lorries began to arrive . . . asking if I could lend the services of the schoolboy sons to help unload.' Thus did Lord Woolton's Ministry cope and care.

Few wartime ministers can still be remembered with such admiration. One Dorchester housewife explains the reason. 'Lord Woolton was always so sympathetic and if he could not give us more butter he added an extra ounce to the margarine. We all trusted and loved him.' When this great public servant died in 1961 no one wrote his biography and no statue was raised in his memory and, ironically, his name is now linked with one of his Ministry's few failures, Woolton Pie, a combination of carrots, parsnips, turnips and potatoes, covered with white sauce and pastry. 'Dry and uneatable' was the general verdict, according to a Brighton war worker, and one London W.V.S. member recalls that when she placed 'about the hundredth of the war' before her five-year-old he took one look and burst into tears. An Ipswich British Restaurant manageress cautiously admits it was 'one dish which was not a favourite'. From Aberdeen a wartime dishwasher at a hotel, who saw what even the hungry British public would not eat, pays Lord Woolton's memory a sincere, if back-handed, compliment: 'I just can't believe that such a wonderful man could have given his name to such a dish'.

# 14

# THE CARDBOARD WEDDING CAKE

'I am issuing an Order prohibiting the use of sugar for the icing of cakes.'

Broadcast by Lord Woolton, 8th July 1940

Despite the war, love continued to flourish. Although at the beginning a few engaged couples decided to postpone getting married until times were normal, many more felt that they wanted to be united before the call-up, or evacuation, or bombing separated them. There was, too, a practical reason for speeding up the progress of courtship. The newest wife had a status which even the most long-standing fiancée lacked; evacuated employers would often help to find a home for her, and even the Forces paid a marriage allowance and—if the worst should happen—a widow's pension. Most women were, no doubt, moved by more romantic considerations. To have a husband, even if one's only contact with him was an occasional airgraph, was to occupy an island of permanence in an uncertain world.

In 1938 there had been 409,000 marriages in the United Kingdom, in 1939 there were 495,000 and in 1940, in which the call-up reached its peak, 534,000. From 1941, with 449,000, it began slowly to decline to 429,000 in 1942, 345,000 in 1943 and 349,000 in 1944, for millions of men were now overseas, surging up again in 1945 as the war ended and demobilisation began, to 457,000.

The typical wartime wedding was planned in a hurry, carried out under difficulties and followed by the briefest honeymoon. One 'outbreak of war' wedding was that of a nurse at St. George's Hospital, London, who had promised her fiancé to marry at once if war came. On Friday 1st September he telephoned the hospital to say that 'Hitler's bombing the Polish Corridor' and 'I switched my mind to my wedding', she remembers, 'from evacuating a ward full of mothers and new-born babies and turning it into a blood transfusion centre in case of air raids'. She was given time off till the following Monday to get married, while her future husband hurried round to the diocesan office in Westminster for a marriage licence. There was a long queue and by the time he and his bride met, as arranged, at a jeweller's shop, it had closed. But the proprietor let them in through the door in his shutters to choose the ring.

At home in Ealing the bride's mother was meanwhile baking a cake, ordering flowers, buying her daughter new underclothes and sending out the invitations. Next day—in splendid sunshine—they were married, although the best man never arrived, his car being held up on its way from Brighton by roads crammed with evacuees. The bride's cousin obligingly deputised and though the one-day honeymoon at Virginia Water next day was interrupted by the declaration of war and the first air raid warning, and the church where they had married was later destroyed by a bomb, these ill omens proved false. The happy couple are happy still, with grown-up children and memories of a happy, if more conventional, silver wedding.

The most worrying feature of many wartime weddings was whether both parties would actually manage to arrive at the church. A woman living in South East London remembers a message from her fiancé: 'Cancel the honeymoon, all leave stopped, massive postings. I'm having time for the ceremony and then have to report back . . . You must find another best man, ours has been posted to Scotland.' Later that day, already overwrought, she dropped her fiancé's photograph and broke the glass. 'I thought the worst,' she remembers, 'and dissolved into tears.' But 'the lad next door arrived home on leave and offered to be our best man', and as a result of 'a bigwig turning up at my husband's unit and being told of the impending wedding' he got his leave after all. The fiancé of a Warrington, Lancashire, woman 'couldn't put in writing anything that might disclose the ship's movements but in January 1943 she received a cable from America: 'A fortnight to change your mind'. He got back safely, complete with a 'fabulous pair of Fifth Avenue shoes' for her to wear at her wedding. A woman waiting to marry a major stationed at Crowborough, Sussex, received a telephone call in April 1941 saying 'come down tomorrow and bring a hat'—his battalion had been ordered overseas.

A Devon vicar's wife remembers a 'grand' wedding planned for 1.30 p.m., for which the bridegroom, an army officer, arrived four-and-a-half hours later. There was snow about and 'The guests all waited and froze'. At another wedding, one of the guests remembers, by the time the bridegroom arrived it was 6 p.m. and dark. The church could not be blacked out, so the ceremony was rather romantically performed by the light of four candles, two on the altar and two on the chancel steps.

Even where both parties were civilians getting time off to marry was not always easy. One Liverpool woman and her husband only managed to get to church simultaneously by 'going sick' in 1944 from the electrical factory where they worked.

The usual wedding preparations often had to be made at breakneck speed at the last minute. One woman was married in Salford in 1940 while her fiancé's ship was unexpectedly in port. He bought the wedding ring, guessing at its size, and she bought her wedding outfit, a hat, gloves and stockings, on her way to the church, putting them on in the shop. There was no time to notify relatives and friends, so there were 'just half a dozen of the ship's company as our guests'. A Liverpool woman, married to a naval chief officer in 1941, had a similar experience. Instead of more usual hymns like *O Perfect Love*, the one sung with most fervour at her wedding was *Eternal Father, Strong to Save*, and as she walked down the aisle her eye was caught by a seaman, 'white sweater under his uniform, dirty, and the crew all dirty, but they gave me a grin which seemed to say, "you are one of us now" '. A Newmarket woman was married at two hours' notice by special licence when her fiancé, who had refused to marry while a bomber pilot, was suddenly 'grounded' due to eye trouble. They had 'no best man or bridesmaids and a one-night honeymoon in a Cambridge hotel'. A Sheffield woman travelled on the first tram route to be reopened into the bombed centre of the city to buy her wedding ring. A telegram to her fiancé 'stating truthfully that we were "TIME BOMBED OUT" worked like a charm', for a sympathetic C.O. made sure he got his leave.

The arrival of the bridegroom was not the end of a bride's worries, however. An Ipswich woman began to fear she was marrying the wrong man, for her husband-to-be, previously dark-haired, arrived for the wedding, 'a brilliant and almost unrecognisable blond'. He had been the victim of a bizarre accident, his head having been covered in soot by a cookhouse smoke stack. To clean the soot off he had rashly soaked his hair in ammonia washing up powder, which turned it bright red, and, trying again, with peroxide, had turned his hair almost white.

Once both participants were duly 'gathered together in the face of this congregation' the chief hope, in the words of a Surrey woman, was 'that Jerry would not invite himself'. A North London woman, married two weeks after the Fall of France, was warned by the registrar at her wedding that if the sirens sounded he would have to leave immediately whether the ceremony had been completed or not. It was always felt to be a bad omen for the sirens to sound during a wedding. A Thames Ditton woman found that this tradition proved true in the case of her daughter's wedding in December 1941: seventeen years later the marriage ended in divorce.

In the early months of the war it was felt to be unpatriotic to have a 'showy, white wedding', but later, as rationing and other shortages began to make themselves felt, it became a matter of pride to have a wedding as near to peacetime standards as possible. This was rarely easy. The church itself might provide reminders of the war, in the shape of boarded up windows, and outside the usual photographer might be lacking, as photographic materials were scarce. Some couples had their wedding photographs taken months later, but usually some kind friend managed to record the occasion in amateur snapshots. As the couple drove away, they would not be pelted with ordinary confetti, as it was illegal to manufacture it, but many offices hoarded the small discs of paper from paper punches for this purpose. More romantic were real rose petals, and one Surrey woman remembers stripping her rosebeds to give her sister a suitable send-off. Less happy was the inspiration of the friends of a Norfolk couple to make their own confetti from chopped up 'window', the tinfoil strips dropped by aircraft to confuse the enemy radar. 'It was horrible,' the unlucky bride remembers. 'Like having chaff down your neck.' But the ban on confetti was popular with church officials who had for years fought a losing battle against it. One Parish Clerk, at Pinner, having warned the wedding guests that to throw rice was now illegal, suggested a practical alternative: Let the guests shake hands with the happy pair and *give* them a whole packet of rice instead.

After the ceremony, the reception. In July 1940 the long-hallowed tradition of the wedding cake was struck a heavy blow by a ban on making or selling iced cakes. The announcement followed public protests about the waste of sugar by confectioners when the sugar ration was only eight ounces a week. Although one M.P., a professional baker, offered to bake a 12 lb. wedding cake complete with icing from only 1 lb. 6 ozs. of sugar, 'The Sugar (Restriction of Use) Order, 1940' forbad from '5th August 1940 . . . the placing of sugar on the exterior of any cake after baking' and, after 2nd September, the sale or purchase of 'any cake so treated' or the manufacture of candied peel or crystallised cherries. Chocolate covering was still allowed, though a dark covering on a wedding cake struck a somewhat jarring note and had practical disadvantages. An Ipswich Civil Servant, married on a hot day in 1942, found that the chocolate-covered cake at her wedding reception started to melt and had to be put under the table. One Melton Mowbray mother, determined that her daughter should have a cake for *her* wedding in 1942 since she herself had had to manage without one in 1918, made her own castor sugar by putting a calico bag of ordinary sugar through a wooden mangle and used all her sweet coupons on bars of chocolate to spread over the top. With decorations on it, 'it was really quite smashing' she remembers, and for more solid fare the fortunate guests could enjoy a large tin of Spam, on which she had spent a whole month's points.

A few conventional white cakes were still made, as for one Yorkshire bride, though it was baked in deep secrecy as it broke the law, and 'the night before our wedding', she remembers, 'my fiancé and I were cutting the cake and wrapping it so our guests could have some to take home'. Home-made wedding cakes were not always a success. An East London woman felt that the cake she baked for her sister's wedding was 'more like a bread pudding' and, being short of eggs, 'the icing was rather runny and as it was sliding off the cake so I was smoothing it on again'. A Birmingham woman discovered that the custom of keeping the top tier of a wedding cake for the first anniversary was disastrous. Hers, made with dried eggs, crumbled away to dust when cut. But even dried egg cake was more than most brides managed. A Northolt woman offered the guests at her daughter's wedding in December 1941 'plain genoa', and the wife of a Leamington Spa Civil Servant remembers one 1940 wedding cake as a 'large sponge sandwich, covered in some synthetic cream'.

In many photographs of wartime weddings the cake appears every bit as impressive as in peacetime, a towering, decorated, three-tiered creation. The explanation is simple: that popular wartime device camouflage, for one could borrow from many bakers a splendid cardboard cover, looking like the most expensive type of traditional iced cake. A Saxmundham teacher, married in 1942, installed just such a case over their modest cherry cake with chocolate icing, and a woman married in the small cotton town of Great Harwood in the same year remembers their 'cake', slightly more elegant, being made of fitted white satin. No book of etiquette seems to have laid down just *how* the false cover was to be removed, whether with an open flourish amid cheering from the guests, or more discreetly while they looked the other way, but no doubt references to the wedding bond being, unlike the cake, 'the real thing' enlivened many a wartime speech. Sometimes the cake itself bore other signs of war. The cake of a Swanage woman, married in 1945, contained a centre-piece made from R.A.F. perspex, and a hairdresser from Goole in Yorkshire, married in January 1942, had a cake decorated with a V for victory.

One of the earliest visits paid by a woman preparing for her wedding was to the local Food Office, which issued permits for the extra food allowed for such occasions under the regulations, though as similar rules covered entertaining after funerals the official concerned had tactfully to adapt his demeanour to be festive or sympathetic. The limit to numbers—usually forty—was not wholly annoying, for it provided an excuse for not inviting unwelcome relations and saved the pocket of the bride's father. The allowances were far from lavish. One Sheffield woman, in October 1940, was allowed for each person ¼ oz. butter, ⅛ oz. sugar and one pint of milk for each twenty guests. A Plymouth woman was allowed 'small quantities of margarine, cooking fat, etc., and five points. We decided that the only way in which we could distribute five points-worth of food among forty guests was a pound of water biscuits and two pounds of dried peas! But our real problem was "five ounces of jam". On enquiring at our grocer's we were told, "Oh, that's all right. You just owe me eleven ounces and buy the pound." We still owe it.' Obtaining the permits was only the start of one's worries. The café where a Hull woman planned to hold her reception was bombed in April 1941, and it had to be transferred to her home. While the ceremony was taking place at a register office her family and guests stayed at home, frantically concocting fillings to put into the unbuttered and empty rolls which had been delivered.

A Sherborne woman married on Easter Saturday, 1942, arranged for relations among the fifty guests in various parts of the West Country to 'queue early in the morning at all the cake shops in their towns and collect as many and varied cakes as they could. The results were amazing. We could have fed another fifty.' A Birmingham woman remembers the typical refreshments served at her wedding reception in December 1941: sandwiches made from scrambled dried eggs, and soft drinks from children's welfare orange juice. An Ipswich woman remembers being given a large, tame rabbit which she killed and cooked for her daughter's wedding in 1942, flavouring it with herbs, removing the bones and leaving it in a bowl to get cold. 'When I turned it out it looked and tasted like chicken in aspic jelly . . . Not one of the twenty-five guests . . . realised their marvellous meal had been made possible by a lovely white rabbit.' A Woking woman helped to make sandwiches at a wedding in November 1941 from a 'black-market ham'. It was minced up, not merely to make it go further but to help hide the evidence. Drink was even harder to come by than food, but most people managed to produce a few bottles somehow. The drinks assembled for one Scotswoman's wedding in 1944 were probably more than most people achieved, but indicate how varied were sources of supply:

Six bottles of champagne, brought from France by my husband.
One bottle of gin and one of sherry, a present from the officers' mess.
A bottle of port and a barrel of beer from the local pub.
A bottle of whisky and one of gin which just appeared from somewhere.

'A right mixture,' the bride comments, 'but they certainly helped the proceedings along.' This was an occasion when even licensees unbent a little. A Sheffield woman remembers her future husband being refused a second whisky in one of the large hotels. 'Go on, he's getting married this afternoon', said the brother-in-law and, once the waitress had been convinced, they both got their whisky.

Although a wedding dress could often be hired, and girl friends rallied round with loans, many women preferred to be married in their own clothes. No extra coupons were allowed so the bride often faced an agonising choice: to lavish them on an impressive outfit for the day or husband them for her going-away wardrobe. A Leytonstone woman remembers abandoning her plans for a white wedding in 1941 when clothes rationing came in, and deciding to buy instead clothes for every-day wear. A woman in Harrogate borrowed her wedding dress in May 1945, so she could spend her clothes coupons on a 'going-away suit'. An Angus woman was left with exactly seven coupons for her wedding outfit, but 'A hat and handbag were coupon-free, I borrowed shoes and was lucky enough to be sent nylons from the United States'. Most brides managed to look exceedingly smart, like the Hull woman married in April 1944, who wore a 'just below the knee turquoise crêpe short-sleeved dress with matching jacket, light tan shoes, handbag and gloves and a . . . spray of orchids, a luxury indeed'. Her light tan felt hat, she thought, was her real extravagance: it cost 'the princely sum of £3 5s. 6d.'. One Yorkshire woman, married in 'a straight skirt' at a registrar's office in 1940, added a touch of luxury with a fur coat, and a Sheffield woman attended a wedding where the feathers on the bride's hat had been dyed in ink. A Swindon woman was married in 1941 in her dead grandmother's 'best black coat', with the addition of some strips of astrakhan, although 'one uncharitable relative was heard to remark that I looked more like a funeral than a wedding'. A Newcastle-upon-Tyne woman made a brides-maid's dress for her daughter from a curtain, and at a Liverpool wedding, when a borrowed dress of lilac taffeta would not fit its intended wearer, the groom's elder sister, his younger sister took her place. The guests, too, did their best to look smart, though often under difficulties. A V.A.D. from Wanstrow in Somerset found one of her brother's shirts too big to wear with her uniform to her sister's wedding, but did her best by putting on a clean collar. A Coventry woman bought from a bomb-damaged shop a new hat 'which the manageress kindly steamed into a smart shape', but ten minutes after getting it safely home there was a daylight raid and part of the ceiling fell on it. After a brushing it still looked good at the wedding she was attending. Hats, as in peacetime, were the great opportunity for display. A Hull woman was impressed by a cousin's at her own wedding in 1944: her father's 'Civil Defence beret at a forward angle, trimmed with a diamanté brooch'.

For a time it was illegal to send flowers by rail, but most brides man-aged to obtain enough for a bouquet, though they were expensive. At a Chingford, Essex, wedding in March 1945, the carnation buttonholes for the men cost 4s. 6d. each, the orchids worn by both mothers were 21s. each and the total flower bill was more than £16. Those unable to afford such prices often carried a prayer book, or wax flowers, though these were not popular, being heavy. Often friends came to the rescue. One Worcestershire countrywoman remembers with pleasure the white roses from the rectory garden which graced her wedding in 1943.

Although a few keen patriots recalled that Italian women had given up their wedding rings to help their country, most British brides felt this was still an essential item and even the government agreed, allowing the manufacture of 'utility' nine carat rings, though there were never enough to go round. (One retailer in December 1942 who needed three hundred had received only thirty.) Disappointed customers scoured the jewellers' and antique dealers' shops for secondhand rings or called on family heirlooms. The rings, like most utility articles, were excellent value. One woman, who spent 30s. 9d. on hers in 1943, reports that 'it has worn well as it has never been off my finger'. One Yorkshire woman wore for her wedding in 1943 her great-great-grandmother's wedding ring remodelled. The bridegroom of one Tooting woman, as no gold ring could be found when he married her in February 1941, placed a platinum ring on her finger. Twenty-five years later, on their Silver Wedding anniversary, he replaced it with the gold one she now wears.

Many other wartime shortages affected weddings in some way. A Gloucester shorthand-typist typed out her wedding invitations in 1940 as she could not find a printer to take on the job. A woman living in Sussex found that very few of her friends could attend her wedding at Christmas 1941, as she lived in a 'restricted' area. Petrol rationing also left its mark. One Kent farmer, who married a land-girl in 1943, remembers that his brother drove them nearly to the station to set off on their honeymoon—four days in Tunbridge Wells—in his car, on 'agricultural' petrol, but dropped them in a side street to avoid being caught by the police. A Tenterden, Kent, woman, married in 1940, remembers walking the three miles to her parents' home after having a wedding photograph taken, and then returning to work the next day. A Sheffield woman, married in October 1940, remembers that 'petrol was rationed and so we could only have one wedding car. It took my husband-to-be and his best man to church first, so they were waiting in church one hour before I arrived. On my way to church we saw a soldier thumbing a lift and my father told the driver to stop. . . . The young soldier told us he was on a forty-eight-hour pass and wanted to get home for it, so while the service was on our wedding car took the soldier ten miles further on his way. To make up for the petrol used, my parents and in-laws went on the bus to the reception and the bridesmaids came in the car with my husband and myself.'

The prospect of setting up house for the first time during the war was enough to make any woman hesitate to get married. One Chingford woman kept her 'precious bottom drawer chest' in the Anderson shelter, on which she would sit and knit for the Forces—a charming scene deserving to have been recorded by a war artist. A London office worker 'went to Woolworths and spent the few shilling a week I managed to save on kitchen cutlery'. Eventually she accumulated forty-seven articles which she kept in the cupboard under the stairs, as the safest place in the house. A Sheffield woman, engaged in 1940, succeeded in the next eighteen months in stockpiling seventy tins of soup. A Fife woman remembers her 'bottom drawer': numerous tiny 2 oz. packets of butter, margarine and lard, plus some tinned goods.

Never were wedding presents more welcome than during the war and the more mundane the gift the more useful it was likely to be. A *Punch* cartoon, which showed a policeman guarding the most valuable article in a splendid array of costly silver dishes and ornaments, a can of petrol, was barely exaggerating; one man can remember such a wedding present. A Roxburgh woman remembers that several war-brides benefited from her presents of soap and soap powders which she had begun accumulating even before the war. Most welcome of all was food. A woman who married a Dane in June 1943 particularly appreciated a carrier bag containing 1 lb. tea and 4 lb. of granulated sugar from two of her husband's bachelor friends, who preferred coffee. A York woman gave a neighbour's daughter a washing-up bowl, the one essential item she had failed to find anywhere, putting in it 'half a pound of margarine, a pound of sugar, a jar of jam, a small jar of Marmite, a quarter of a pound of tea and one or two more items. . . . She told me afterwards this was one of the best wedding presents she got.'

The war added some new elements of uncertainty to the honeymoon, even if 'Jerry' did not make an unwelcome third on the wedding night. A Sheffield woman spent the first night of her married life in the shelter. All the food and drink was taken there and the guests played cards intermittently and now and then climbed out to see what was happening. They emerged at 5 a.m. and 'at last my chief bridesmaid was able to return home, escorted by my husband'. Meanwhile her husband's parents, who had refused to stay in the City overnight, were having an adventurous journey home to Lincoln, for 'the Ack Ack batteries put the fear of God into the hired car driver', and they only got home after their youngest son had taken over the wheel. Another Sheffield woman had a more peaceful wedding night in the Hampstead Heath flat lent to them by her husband's sister. They arrived there at 10 p.m. and 'it was quite a job going round in the dark dealing with the black-out and trying to find the telephone, which we could hear ringing away. Our fervent hope was that the anti-aircraft guns would not have to go into action—we were only about a hundred yards away from them.' A Warrington woman and her sailor husband also spent their honeymoon in a friend's house but as 'her black-out arrangements were terribly difficult to cope with . . . after a long struggle, we decided they were best left put'. This led to 'ribald comments' from the neighbours, who were quick to notice that the bedroom black-outs were never taken down. An Essex woman, married in July 1940, discovered at the last minute before going to Eastbourne that access to the South Coast was now barred. Her honeymoon had to be postponed for a year. A London Civil Servant, who married an airman in November 1941, remembers an unusual 'entertainment' during their brief honeymoon at Bournemouth. 'On our walks along the cliffs we could watch the men at bayonet practice on stuffed dummies.' An East London woman's most vivid memory of her honeymoon, spent in an aunt's flat at Leigh-on-Sea, is of being hungry, for all the restaurants were closed due to mass evacuation, and the larder contained only 'a few potatoes, some bread and margarine and jam'. They had taken with them 'two tiny chops and a packet of vegetarian rissole meat' but 'we had gulps of fresh air along the Leas and were happy to snatch a honeymoon out of the war days'. A Dorset woman, married in 1942, remembers how 'two hours before the wedding was to take place a telephone call from Weymouth told us that relatives with whom we were to spend our three-day honeymoon had been bombed. . . . The house was so badly damaged we could not go.' The problem was solved by a cousin from Guildford, saying, 'Here take the key of my house and use that.' They arrived there at midnight, the train being two hours late owing to an air raid, and began their married life sitting up in bed 'eating fancy cakes and sandwiches that we had brought with us', the remains of their wedding feast.

It was on a honeymoon, whatever brave show might have been made at the wedding, that the real deficiencies of a wartime wardrobe were revealed. A Bexleyheath, Kent, woman married in 1944 has not forgotten that the first time her husband saw her in pyjamas they were in holes and 'beyond even patching'. A woman who married a fighter pilot at the height of the Battle of Britain found shrapnel holes in his clothes, for a bomb had demolished his hut at Manston R.A.F. station the day before the wedding. An army major's wife, married at a few hours' notice by special licence, discovered that her new husband had only his military kit with him on their one-night honeymoon before he went overseas and still recalls with affectionate amusement the sight of him going to the hotel bathroom in her frilly red taffeta dressing gown with 'yards of leg sticking out below'.

Two very different recollections sum up what it meant to get married during those strange wartime years. A Southwark woman, married in 1944, remembers that her wedding breakfast was spread out on the top of the family's Morrison shelter. The meal was in any case meagre 'but to crown it all, my little nephew of three crept in the dining room and while no one was looking bit a lump out of each bread roll on the plates'. The wedding night was spent on the floor of the sitting room 'with the piano pushed up against the side of our "bed" for protection, while the rest of the family slept in the Morrison with the wedding cake on top of them'. But the real essentials of a happy marriage still remained. A Swindon woman, married in 1941, spent her honeymoon at Torquay, 'blissfully happy despite a shortage of almost everything. . . . We sat on the front each night surrounded by rolls of barbed wire. The moon still looked good anyhow.'

# THE GREEN RATION BOOK

'Never buy more napkins than you really need. Remember, fair shares for others, too.'

Board of Trade leaflet, Getting Ready for Baby, c. 1943

'I took the risk of bringing a baby into the world while a war was on . . . as I wanted to have something if my husband did not come back.' This is how one Glasgow woman, married to a man then awaiting call-up to the Navy, remembers one of the great decisions of her war. The child was born four months after her father's ship had sailed; it was to be nearly three years before he saw his own child.*

Many women had similar experiences. One in Nottingham admits that 'previously we hadn't wanted children. . . . The sense of insecurity created an urge to immortalise one's marriage. . . . So we tried for a baby and I became pregnant.' Two years later there were sometimes other motives, for a surprising number of childless wives were suddenly overcome by maternal instincts when women without dependants began to be conscripted for war work, and pregnancy was nicknamed 'the prevalent disease'. At first, however, there was a sharp drop in the number of births, until by 1941 the birth-rate was the lowest ever recorded—thirteen per thousand population, compared with 17.6 in 1938. Thereafter the numbers began to climb sharply until in 1944 nearly 880,000 babies were born, compared with only 735,000 in 1938, and altogether between January 1940 and December 1945 about 4,600,000 children were born in the beleaguered British Isles.

Although bombing and rationing were still to come, probably the worst time of the whole war in which to have a baby was the very beginning, for maternity clinics and hospitals in the evacuated cities had been closed and the emergency hospitals in the country and on the coast were overcrowded. One mother, whose daughter was born at Brighton three weeks after the outbreak of war, remembers that 'the hospital was bursting at the seams. . . . As the days went by, we had to move from the large ward downstairs to little rooms at the top of the hospital to make room for the never-ceasing flow of mothers and babies.' By January 1940 the problem had solved itself, for nine out of ten expectant

* The reunion is described at the end of Chapter 40.

mothers had already gone home, most of them with babies still unborn. For the rest of the war the government relied mainly on 'unofficial' evacuation, providing emergency maternity homes in reception areas for mothers who had made their own arrangements to stay in the district, and sending down small parties of women who had stayed in the cities just before their babies were due. The wife of a London A.F.S. man, who had evacuated herself and her small son to the Sussex village of North Chapel, recorded in her diary how these arrangements had worked for her. Her first discovery was that ante-natal services in the country were not the same as those in the city. 'The nurse, under whose care I am supposed to be . . . has not given me an examination for at least six weeks', she noted in August 1941, 'and now I am well into the last month she has still not been to see me. What a contrast to the weekly examination I received in London during the last month of pregnancy.' She had been allocated a bed in a hospital at Hindhead and shortly before her confinement was moved to a residential home nearby, being 'comfortably settled in at the Woodlawns Hostel, which is a beautiful large house with lovely lawns and pine trees all round—a real beauty spot! I was received . . . with a cheery, welcome smile and later on I met the matron, who is a sweet woman. This place is most efficiently run. There is no complaining and it is all done like clockwork. The mothers make their own beds and wait on themselves at meal times . . . Three or four do the washing up. The food is good and I enjoyed a fish lunch today; the first fish I have tasted for six months.' As the local hospital proved to be overcrowded this mother agreed to move to another home at Woking, being driven there 'by a very sweet woman of the W.V.S. . . . We were met by a very jolly and friendly nurse who introduced us to the other waiting mothers . . . Soon after we arrived about nine new expectant mothers arrived from London after travelling all day and they were received in the same kindly manner . . . I feel tired but happy and content to leave my own and my baby's well-being in the hands of these kindly and efficient people.'

Three days later this woman became 'the mother of a dear little girl' and by 21st September she could record: 'The days are passing very quickly and baby is very contented—sleeping and feeding well.' But there were other worries. 'Last night we were giving our babies their last feeds at about 10 p.m. when an air raid siren sounded in the town. My whole body seemed to turn a dozen somersaults but I sat quiet and tried to continue feeding baby.... Then the night nurse came in and she was very good and when she came to take my baby I asked her to leave her with me until the All Clear, which she did, so we all had our babies in our arms until the All Clear, which was in about half an hour.' A week later the same mother 'went out . . . for the first time and rejoiced in my restored figure, thoroughly enjoying glances of a different kind from those I had received during the last few months, from the male population', and before long the W.V.S. had delivered her safely back to her former billet. Here her chief problem was comforting her three-year-old, who had stayed with relations in London while his mother was in hospital, and returned deeply distressed by the 'nasty bombed-out houses' and 'nasty old aeroplanes which bombed people'. To her assurance that 'They don't bomb people here', he replied with irrefutable logic that there was a big bomb crater in a wood 'and that he could walk to it'.

Other mothers were also impressed with their wartime maternity homes and for many women these few days in bed after the birth of their baby were the most tranquil period of the war, with someone else having the worry of coping with the rations and the rest of the family. Early in the war many such establishments had been in hastily-converted orphanages or poor law institutions, but those opened later were often in delightful surroundings, like the requisitioned hotel at Looe, where one young mother found herself after being bombed out in Plymouth. 'We could look out of the windows', she later wrote, 'and see sailing boats with blue and white and scarlet sails gliding past. We dared not think what we would have had to pay in such a hotel in peacetime. . . . The day my baby was born everyone was especially kind. One of the nurses was going sailing on the river with her boy friend that afternoon. "I'll wave as we go by," she promised, "if you're still in bed." I wasn't . . . I was in the labour ward', where matron's 'hand held mine tightly infusing courage into me' and, after a difficult delivery, her daughter was born and 'when she started to cry I wished they'd take her away and leave me in peace'.

A Kingston-upon-Thames woman had a more harrowing experience in June 1940. 'While I laboured to give birth a siren wailed, but I was too busy to care. When he was one day old and I lay drowsily meditating on my lovely child another warning shattered our peace. The maternity ward of the hospital was at the top of the building, which in its turn was on a hill.* All of us new mothers felt very vulnerable and were near panic. We were told not to worry, the babies would be taken to the basement, but we could still hear them crying in the nursery.' Although she realised that the babies would have been moved fast enough if the bombers had approached, the incident left its mark on this mother, for 'from that day on I had no milk for my baby and . . . I suffered the agonies of the electric pump, together with admonitions from the Ward Sister saying, "You must feed him. Suppose we can't get milk?" I felt like an outcast. There was nothing I wanted more than to be able to feed my child naturally.' Bottle feeding brought other worries, too, for when,

* It still is. Long after the war, my own daughter was born there.

later that summer, every night had to be spent in the public shelter and her son still needed to be fed at 10 p.m. and 6 a.m., 'it was worrying to know that people would be wakened by a baby yelling for his feed and not being able to cool it down quickly enough for him'. Eventually she stayed indoors at night and 'our son, now six months old, awoke to his first Christmas under a neighbour's dining room table'.

Inability to breast-feed one's baby was a common result of wartime anxieties. The daughter of a woman from Purley, Surrey, had arrived prematurely in 1940 after an unluckily-timed holiday at Ferring on Sea with 'soldiers digging trenches on the beaches' and 'explosions on the far side of the Channel'. Later the shock at hearing that her husband, a 'special', and then her mother had been badly injured in a raid on the City in March 1941 'prevented me from feeding her any more and I had to put her on to artificial food at once. She would not have a bottle so I had to feed her with a spoon and sometimes at four o'clock in the afternoon I was still giving her the two o'clock feed. It was a slow business . . . but in a week she was a different child. Obviously I had been in too strained a condition to feed her properly.' Three years later, the same woman's son was born to the sound of 'shrapnel falling through the trees outside' and though he proved 'a fine specimen of 9 lb. 3 oz. when he was born . . . I had to wean him at four months owing to exhaustion on my part'.

Wartime conditions were to blame, too, many women believed, for more tragic experiences. A Newcastle woman blames the loss of her child on 'the last siren of the war . . . I leapt out of bed to save my little daughter and brought on a miscarriage'. Other pregnant women suffered the even more bitter experience of bearing a stillborn child. A Staines woman remembers her stillborn son being delivered in an inadequately darkened nursing home by the light of torches held by nurses, after which the doctor had to insert eighteen stitches. It was, she felt, 'so horribly eerie, it seemed like a nightmare'. A thirty-four-year-old London woman, who had longed for a child since the age of eighteen, suffered a similar loss, though full of praise for 'the beautifully efficient Wandsworth Borough Maternity Home' where 'my first son was stillborn, an extended breech baby, after a seventy-eight-hour labour. Two of those three nights were spent in shelters at the Maternity Hospital with intense bombing and fire-raids, etc. The doctor who with two midwives finally managed a difficult delivery wore his M.O. helmet some of the time in addition to his red rubber apron—he had been outside helping with casualties. . . . We had a number of carryings out to the shelter . . . strapped to our mattresses like corpses ready for burial at sea . . . The straps always lay ready across the bedsprings under the mattresses so that we only had to fold our arms under the covers, get strapped up and away we went. . . .

During one very bad raid matron had all the babies brought to their mothers to keep them calm . . . I was the only one without a baby.'*

This mother, like many others, is full of praise for 'the nurses' bravery and efficiency . . . They were always full of cheerfulness and dashing back through raids by bike to come on duty.' Not all men were as heroic, as one nurse whose baby showed signs of arriving while she was staying with friends at a military camp in Hampshire remembers:

I made a twenty-two-mile dash through an air raid in the black-out to have my baby. The young army attendant was terrified I would produce on the spot, so pushed me into the dark, awful old ambulance and climbed in with the driver. I had a bunk to sit on—I was too uncomfortable to lie down—and a pile of pillows and blankets and a torch. My frightened little driver whizzed round the first corner like a Grand Prix winner. Away went case, pillows, blankets and torch into the darkness. I clutched the small ventilator and hung on for dear life (and twenty miles) with the rain pouring down my arm, and reviling everyone, especially Hitler. My daughter was born as the All Clear sounded.

To have one's baby at home during the war was even more difficult than to have it in hospital, for the black-out, or a raid, might delay the midwife and more than one husband delivered his own baby. This was the experience of one woman in Manchester:

My little son was born on the 19th March 1941 at 4.20 in the morning, with only a neighbour for company. After four days in labour he arrived as they dropped an unexploded bomb in the bottom of the garden. (Talk about fairies!) They evacuated all the other people out of the houses and flats but had to leave me there, as I was on blood transfusions by this time and too ill to be moved. A young doctor of twenty-four, my own age, stayed with me and suddenly . . . there was a terrific explosion and all the windows came in. I opened my eyes and saw a piece of flying glass had cut his cheek, but my new baby was quite safe in his arms and fast asleep.

Many midwives faced such conditions daily during the blitz. This was one night's work for a Birmingham midwife:

I was called to a case during a raid. We had orders not to go out in very fierce raids . . . but babies are quite clever at getting themselves born on their own in an emergency. . . . However I eventually got to my patient who was the proprietress of a little back street shop.

* Later in the war this mother had a 'Caesarean section resulting in Michael John, very tough and 8 lb. 10 oz.'

She had taken refuge under her little counter and there was nothing for it but to crawl in after her and deliver the baby, which was pressing to come into the world, air raid or not. The only light was a flickering candle . . . and afterwards I decided that I could do nothing but leave her there until daylight when I could get help to carry her to bed. . . . When I returned to my colleagues and told them I had delivered a baby 'under the counter' it was a riot.

Yet in one way the war actually made it easier to have a baby. 'In those days, before the National Health Service,' one Nottingham woman remembers, 'to have a baby, either at home or in a public hospital, was "not done" . . . We paid sixteen-and-a-half guineas for two weeks at a local private nursing home, plus, of course, fees to my own family doctor.'* To such women the quality of the attention and the food provided in state-run emergency maternity homes was a revelation. A London woman, whose experiences of the hostel at Woodlawns, Hindhead, and a maternity home at Woking have already been mentioned, noted while staying at the latter that 'There is a good deal more kindliness at this place and at Woodlawns than I met at the maternity home where I had Michael. The war has achieved one good thing in this case, it seems.' She had been asked for a contribution of £3 13s. 6d. for each week's stay, 'which is, of course, beyond me . . . but nurse seemed quite satisfied at the amount I suggested'.

This mother observed, too, another improvement brought about by the war. 'The babies in this home', she wrote in her diary in September 1941, 'are really lovely infants and compare favourably in size and appearance with the babies I remember in the maternity home in London where Michael was born [in 1938]. I asked one of the nurses if she found the wartime babies up to standard. "Every bit and better!" was the reply.' That this was true could be seen by everyone who used his eyes. Even in the poorest districts of the great cities the undersized, white-faced, half-starved-looking, ragged children of pre-war days had now almost totally vanished. The war, by curing unemployment, had for the first time in British history made it possible for millions of families to care for their children properly. The second reason was that many pregnant women and young children were better fed during the war than they had ever been in peacetime. The tighter rationing became for the rest of the population, the larger the share that went to 'the priority classes'. Lord Woolton, in his formative early years as a social worker in the Liverpool

---

* Working class women, whose husbands were covered by National Insurance—which excluded the better-off and the self-employed—were entitled to a small maternity grant, but for hospital treatment were dependent on having contributed to a hospital savings scheme or on finding a bed, financed from charitable funds or, less commonly, the rates, in a 'voluntary' or local authority hospital.

slums, had seen for himself the effects of malnutrition in pregnancy. His constant concern for his 'preggies' became something of a joke in the Ministry of Food, as did the photographs of bouncing infants regularly sent to him by proud and grateful parents with the ambiguous message, 'Another of Lord Woolton's babies'.

In the more progressive towns maternity clinics, and even cheap milk and vitamin tablets, had sometimes been available before the war, but the introduction of the welfare foods scheme in December 1941 extended these benefits to the whole community. As the Ministry of Food explained in its advertisement, *Welcome little stranger*:

> The very best welcome you can give your baby is a beautiful body, a contented disposition—and a healthy, happy mother. All these depend so much upon your having the right foods and *enough of them*. As the Radio Doctor says, you have to 'eat for one and a bit'; so in addition to your ordinary good mixed diet of *all* your rations, potatoes, plenty of green vegetables, and, within reason, anything else you fancy, you need a little extra of certain foods, for the sake of the little one . . .

The 'little extra' recommended by the Ministry covered a wide range: 'Orange juice, rich in Vitamin C, which gives vitality and general good health'; vitamin A and D tablets, 'which make for strong bones, good teeth and a sound constitution'; additional milk, 'the almost perfect food'; an extra half ration of meat, 'to help you rebuild tissue and to give baby a good firm body'; shell and dried eggs, ' "builders" like meat and help in the same ways'; and oranges, 'to give you and your unborn baby still more of the precious vitamin C'. The amounts provided—an extra pint of milk a day, an extra half ration of meat a week, an extra egg per allocation, sometimes adding up to three a week—were large enough to make a substantial difference to an expectant mother's meals.

The first person to know that a woman was 'expecting', apart from her doctor, was usually the milkman, for she was entitled to her extra daily pint at a reduced price of twopence, though really hard-up women obtained it free. Vigilant neighbours soon shared the same secret as they saw her arrive home laden with the familiar bottles of concentrated orange juice from the welfare clinic. This was an excellent substitute for lemon juice on pancakes and was invaluable as a soft drink at children's parties. It was also cheap: fivepence a bottle; the chocolate-covered vitamin tablets, a popular wartime sweet, cost tenpence, though both were free when necessary. One could, as an alternative, obtain cod-liver oil, though one woman admits to using it to liven up her cat's diet, not her own. So many mothers gave their extra meat to their families that the Ministry issued a special advertisement condemning 'meat pirates': 'Don't let Dad get all the meat.' Eggs were even more tempting. A Gloucestershire woman who had 'a shocking pregnancy, being sick before, during and after almost every meal . . . could see the family watching my egg and knowing darned well that I should swallow it and lose it in ten minutes'.

The key which unlocked the door to all these extras was the green ration book, issued to a pregnant woman in addition to her ordinary book on production of a medical certificate. This soon became the membership badge of a privileged fraternity. 'I never stirred without the precious document', a sister at St. George's Hospital remembers. A Kidderminster woman can still recapture 'the joy of walking straight to the front of any queue, bearing aloft the green book'. A Dagenham mother remembers 'the days when there would be a knock at the door and someone shouting, "Leave what you are doing, bring your green books, there are oranges over at the shops and there's a queue!" '. There was no legal obligation to give a pregnant woman priority but the convention rapidly became accepted. A Southampton woman, who showed her green book to a policeman at Waterloo, was immediately ushered to the front of a long taxi queue, even though with her husband. 'You can imagine the looks we got', she remembers.

Once a child was born, the mother's green book was replaced by one in her new baby's name, though she was still entitled to extra milk until he was a year old. Outings to the welfare clinic provided many women with their only social life of the week. 'Every Tuesday was welfare day and early closing', a Southport woman remembers, 'so I used to invite four or five young mums home with their babies for a cup of tea—my daughter's ration—and a good old chin-wag, swop hints and recipes and have a joke, then they would go home before black-out.' In 1942 the tea ration for under fives was withdrawn, and catering for a family became progressively more difficult as the youngest member of it grew older, until at five he was ready to be 'promoted to the Blue Book', which was held by children of school age. 'Thanks to the good start you've given him with the green ration book "extras" ', explained the Ministry of Food, 'he will have developed a set of strong little teeth and a healthy digestive system capable of dealing with the same kind of meals as the rest of the family.' Children in this age group received full adult rations, plus an extra half-pint of milk a day, and were now 'well in the running for the great prizes of lifelong health and fitness. "Green for go! Blue, the symbol of success, to win!" '

If anyone deserved to be awarded 'blue, the symbol of success', it was surely Lord Woolton and his staff. By 1944 expectant mothers and babies were actually consuming per head more milk and eggs than before the war and the maternal mortality rate, of mothers who died in childbirth, was little more than half the 1938 level. Infant mortality, of children who died under the age of twelve months, showed a sharp rise early in the war, but by 1942 had also fallen below the pre-war figure. Despite bombs and rationing and war-strain it had never been safer to have a baby, nor had a baby ever had a better chance of surviving into adult life.*

To have enough food for health was not the same thing as having as much as one wanted. Many pregnant women longed for sweet things and one who spent much of the war in North Wales found that 'local shopkeepers were helpful to ever-hungry pregnant mums, by saving the odd jam tart or doughnut, which were invariably eaten on the way home'. The staff of British Restaurants were equally helpful. A North London woman remembers extra meat being put on the plate of any customer who was obviously pregnant. Fruit was probably the most missed commodity, even though green books got priority for oranges or bananas. One woman living in Rothesay found that 'while I was expecting the baby I was craving for fruit—paid 7s. 6d. for one peach and it was worth every penny'. Another Scotswoman, in Fife, paid 5s. 6d. for her peach 'then had indigestion after I ate it when I thought about the price'. One West Country expectant mother, bombed out in Plymouth, who went to live in one room in an old gentleman's house in the country, admits creeping out at night to pick his raspberries, 'big and juicy and virtually pipless . . . when the craving grew too painful to bear'. When she entered an emergency maternity home at Looe food continued to dominate her thoughts. 'How very greedy we wartime mothers-to-be were. We brought with us all the little food luxuries we had managed to hoard, like squirrels, and the most popular, and sought after, member of our little clan was a grocer's wife, who brought with her a heavenly hoard of jam and sugar, biscuits . . . which she shared with everyone.'

When clothes rationing was introduced in June 1941 expectant mothers received no extra coupons, but it was hardly necessary for the Board of Trade to tell women to 'Try to avoid spending coupons on special maternity clothes. Almost all your existing clothes can be altered easily so that you can wear them comfortably until the baby is born, and you can wear them again afterwards. For instance, why not put an attractive matching or contrasting gathered or pleated panel in the front of the dress?' Many women had less glamorous ways of saving coupons. The maternity outfit of one South East London woman was a skirt made from an army blanket and for special occasions an old edge-to-edge coat worn over summer dresses, the side seams unpicked and held in

---

* Some of the credit was, of course, due to medical advances, particularly the use of new drugs. But it was probably diet which was the decisive factor. The figures were: Maternal mortality, 2·55 per 1,000 births in 1939, 1·53 in 1944; infant mortality, 51 per 1,000 live births in 1939, 45 in 1944.

place with tapes. An Essex woman used unrationed black-out sateen 'embroidered in bright colours', and a Bradford woman 'wore my husband's underpants and while in bed his old pyjama jackets'. A Stoke Newington woman, who borrowed a single maternity dress, felt she 'seemed to live in it for the last three months'. Never had women been more relieved to see the last of such clothes. One Gloucestershire wife who had only one maternity skirt, 'craftily made from my school gym-slip . . . burned it afterwards'.

Providing the baby's layette was even more difficult, for though there was a special allowance of fifty clothing coupons for the purpose, a single nappy required one coupon, so that the mother who provided three dozen, the normal minimum, would have barely enough left for a nightdress and romper suit. The women's magazines were full of helpful hints on how to spend the coupons most wisely and on unrationed substitutes, like white lint, coupon-free from the chemist. Many children's first coats were made from service blankets, smuggled home by helpful fathers. A Sheffield woman made her daughter a coat and bonnet from two pram rugs, trimmed with imitation fur, and the small daughter of a Liverpool Merchant Navy officer made her first public appearance in October 1942 in 'a christening gown made out of a bolster slip and covered . . . with net curtains'. A Board of Trade *Make Do and Mend* leaflet cheerfully advised mothers that 'Babies don't need nearly as many clothes as people used to think'. It suggested a modest layette: 'four or five gowns . . . to be used day and night, four vests, three matinée jackets, three pairs of bootees, and two medium sized shawls'. Shortages, it suggested, were even a blessing in disguise, for 'rubber knickers are not necessary and, quite apart from the fact that rubber is very scarce, they are very uncomfortable for the baby. . . . Pilches are not needed; napkins, put on properly, can look very neat and the external layer is inclined to overheat. . . . A laundry basket or even a deep drawer, suitably lined, can be adapted to make a very useful cot for the first few months.' Knitting was a great standby. A Nottingham woman, who had spent forty-eight of her fifty coupons on nappies, found that relatives and friends provided the rest of the layette by unravelling and reknitting worn-out woollen garments. 'Dresses, nighties, etc., . . . were made from the best parts of outgrown clothes. I remember great excitement when a friend gave me some very large bibs she had found in a drawer. . . . Granny also made some from the best parts of old towels.'

Although the Board of Trade never enjoyed the popularity of the Ministry of Food, it was not unresponsive to complaints. A woman whose daughter was born in Guildford in 1943 remembers that her nursing home, as well as ordinary nappies, asked for Harrington squares, which proved unobtainable, but a letter to her M.P. produced immediate action, for his daughter had had the same trouble—and 'in a very short time, Harrington squares appeared in the shops'. It was a lucky woman who managed to save any of her baby's coupons, but one Rochdale mother succeeded in doing so. She made her daughter's layette 'out of oddments of wool and material and used the coupons for my stepson who was just going into long trousers'. Of all the gifts sent to wartime Britain from Canada and the United States, none was more welcome than 'Bundles for Britain', at first distributed to bombed-out mothers, and then to other lucky recipients. 'What happiness these brought to young mothers . . . with a new baby to cope with', a Hastings W.V.S. worker recalls. 'I still remember the little clothes, vests, nighties and nappies, all carefully hand-stitched, and even a card of safety-pins. . . . It was one of my nicest jobs in the war to take these round my area.'

As the war dragged on every item of baby equipment became scarce. An Anglesey woman, whose daughter was born at the end of May 1945, had put her name down for a pram the previous January, 'but the day I had the letter to say it was in I also had an appointment at the hospital as they thought I had twins'. She was greatly relieved, since twins' prams were unobtainable, to be told after an X-ray 'One only'. A Birmingham woman remembers that her baby was six months old before *her* turn for a pram came round. To relieve the shortage of prams the government introduced a utility design, selling at £10, though most mothers felt it a sad come-down to be seen wheeling this 'box on wheels'. Its small wheels, hard tyres, lack of springs, and padding, were all much criticised, but its most alarming feature was the brake, which consisted of a 'dog lead' fastened to the frame which also clipped on to the wheel. 'I had to make sure the pram was on even ground and well wedged when leaving it', a Southport woman remembers. Even a utility pram, however, was a prize to be treasured. A Twickenham woman remembers that she had no difficulty in selling her first utility pram, when her first baby was stillborn, for the original £20 and the second for £8 10s. when, to her great joy, she had obtained a reconditioned pre-war Marmet. A Sussex mother, who was 'determined to get a pre-war coach-built one second hand . . . despite advertising, had had no luck until about three weeks before the baby was due. Then my mother played a golf match with the wife of the owner of the local furniture emporium and mentioned our difficulties. Two days later I had a phone call and a choice of two, at £10 each, the price they had cost when new four years ago.'

The best-looking prams and pushchairs were usually rebuilt. One Surrey woman who managed to find an old pram and have it reconditioned by a coachbuilder in 1942 remembers that as she brought it home by train 'everyone on the platform staring in amazement at what they thought was a new one'. Push-chairs were even harder to find than prams. A Southport woman remembers going into town every day for a week 'to try and get a folding push-chair and finally they got so fed up with seeing me every day, I got one'. A London woman still smiles at the memory of the push-chair, lent to her by a friend, which had been brought from Switzerland twenty years previously and was 'so high that it looked as if it belonged to one of Queen Victoria's children. When I took it to visit relatives a waggish uncle decided I had been robbing the Victoria and Albert Museum.'

Utility cots, price £7 complete with mattress, could be found if one were lucky, though the plain design was a disappointment to many mothers and more than one of Lord Woolton's healthy and high-spirited babies bounced its way through the base in a few months. A Liverpool woman made a cot from an old wash-stand 'draped with three-and-a-half yards of precious flannelette, which I later made into nightdresses for my babies'. A Nottingham woman, after walking three miles to look at a baby's crib, which proved to be not worth buying, solved the problem by having an osier basket specially made and recalls a 'pleasant evening in the osier marshes, watching the old man weaving the willows in and out'. Baby-sized cot linen had almost vanished from the market. One London woman remembers 'a kind man at the drapers' letting me have a large flannelette sheet without any coupons, which I cut into four to make cot sheets for my daughter'. Another mother, married to an architect, acquired some of his old architectural drawings, printed on linen, which she soaked to remove the plans then used them 'for cot sheets, pillow covers, etc.' Baby baths were another much sought after item. A Sutton woman remembers queueing in Woolworths for one for an hour after a consignment had come in. An Edinburgh woman remembers that 'a baby bath was impossible to get. I was even lucky to finish up with a dark green enamelled bath and that was only because the salesman was fed up with me calling. He told me later he was sure I was going to have the baby in his shop so thought giving me one was the easy way out.' Another essential was a baby's pot. One Sussex woman, who went shopping with a friend, managed to secure one in the same shop as a dozen nappies, for which the assistant forgot to ask for the coupons. 'This was a great thrill and we rushed out of the shop. . . . We carried nappies and "potty" unwrapped past a parade of grinning soldiers.' Many other items were also hard to find. A Nottingham baby played happily with a rattle made from a match-box filled with buttons and covered with crocheted scraps of silk and wool, with an old tooth-brush for the handle. A Glasgow woman, whose first baby was born in 1944, recalls that there were 'no rubber cot sheets, no bottle teats, and even new bottles were sold only after the chemist had proof that one had broken one. Baby powder was inferior and the maternity hospital advised you not to use it, but to rely on Vaseline.' An Uxbridge woman weaned her daughter straight on to milk from a spoon as it proved im possible to find a rubber teat anywhere. Olive oil, baby powder, tins of baby food—these were some of the other scarce items which chemists struggled to share out as best they could with a kindness still remembered by many mothers. A Newcastle mother also speaks for many when she praises her overworked doctor, called out of retirement to replace a younger man who had joined the Forces. 'He gave me constant attention and was as pleased as I was when my daughter, a tiny premature baby, began to improve.'

# 16

# A WHOLE ORANGE FOR CHRISTMAS

'I woke early . . . made sure the black-out curtains were over the windows and . . . had a little peep at my presents . . . I had a pair of slacks, Mummy made them out of a blanket . . . a bar of chocolate, a whole orange.'

Diary of a ten-year-old schoolgirl, Christmas Day 1941

'Mummy, what *is* a hoop?' This question, put to one mother by her six-year-old daughter in 1945, made her realise 'what little pleasures the children of this war have had to go without'. Another mother had a similar experience, when her 'younger son—he was nine-months-old when war was declared—came rushing home from school so excited. He said, "Mum, what do you think a boy told me today? . . . He said that after the war I shall be able to go into a shop and ask for a pennyworth of sweets without a ration book." ' A Sheffield woman remembers her small daughter, offered an ice-cream cornet for the first time, handing it back with the request 'Please peel it, Mummy'.

It was such incidents that many parents found particularly heart-rending. They were ready enough to make sacrifices themselves, but it was hard to see their children being deprived of the traditional pleasures of childhood. It was, many women now feel, children aged about four to thirteen who suffered most, for small children did not miss what they had never known and older ones could understand the reason for war-time shortages. To have to explain to a seven-year-old, however, why, when there were sweets in the shops and money in one's purse, it was not possible to buy them, or to disappoint a ten-year-old of some dearly-desired Christmas present, was enough to make the most mild-mannered mother curse the Germans and all their works. The first wartime shortage which really affected children was of sweets. From mid-1940, as sugar rationing made itself felt, the sweet-shop shelves grew steadily more bare, until the large glass bottles of sweets and toffees in which most brands were then stored stood empty and the only chocolate bars to be seen were wooden dummies, of which merely the wrapping was real. For chocolate, as for everything else, the Forces had priority. One Bradford girl still thinks with real gratitude of the R.A.F. officer who began to write to her after she had had two letters published in *Picture Post*. 'This correspondence . . . contributed largely towards my real education', she remembers. 'It also contributed towards satisfying my greed for sweets, for hardly a month went by without my receiving a parcel packed with "Mars" bars, Rowntrees Motoring Chocolate and Chocolate Logs.' A former W.A.A.F. married to an R.A.F. officer remembers that when their son was born he brought to the hospital 'his most precious gift', four ounces of chocolate.

Although sweets, unlike food and clothing, could hardly be considered a necessity, rationing of these essentials had by 1942 proved so successful that from July 1942 it was extended to sweets. The ration, irrespective of one's age, was usually eight ounces of sweets or chocolate every four weeks, though for various short periods it was raised to twelve or sixteen ounces. Two ounces a week, ample for the moderate sweet-eater, was appallingly little for the sweet-toothed, and children spent hours discussing the best way to spend their ration. 'Gob-stoppers', huge aniseed balls, costing a halfpenny, which could be sucked for half-an-hour or more, had their devotees, but most adults preferred chocolate, for nibbling in the shelter or on A.R.P. or Home Guard duty. One London woman spent her lunch-hour queueing for 'huge peardrops'. The substitute flavouring smelt 'terrible' but they 'took about thirty minutes to suck through'. Sweet coupons, known as 'personal points', could be spent anywhere, though some shops reserved chocolate for registered customers. Wartime chocolate tended to be darker, rougher, and more 'powdery' than the pre-war variety, and the greatest prize was 'blended' chocolate, a compromise between milk and plain. The wrapper, too, had an austerity look, being of waxed paper instead of silver foil. 'Mars' bars were a rare luxury and others combed the shops for 'Slam' bars and 'Eskimo' blocks, made of 'chocolate . . . cold to the taste, like cucumber', which have now vanished for ever. One Fulham shopkeeper remembers 'melting down a few bars of our precious chocolate supply and dipping dates into this and rolling some in desiccated coconut and some in chocolate vermicelli. . . . They went like hot cakes.'

The tiny sweet coupons, under an inch square, had to be cut out, not merely cancelled, and threading them together for return to the Food Office, to obtain a voucher to buy more supplies, was yet another job to be undertaken by the long-suffering shopkeeper and his wife in their scanty free time. Boarding schools, like mine, with their own tuck shop removed their pupils' coupons at the beginning of term and issued their own 'currency' instead, which could not, of course, be spent at shops outside. Real sweet-addicts found managing their ration a stern test of self-control, for it was all too easy to gorge the whole month's allowance in one glorious spree. A London shopkeeper remembers that 'the Sunday the new ration period started we were rushed off our feet', and one Birmingham woman nicknamed the following day each month 'Chew Monday', since so many people were eating sweets in the street. A Hull woman sums it up: 'The first week of the month was a bean feast and the last week was literally famine . . . but occasionally one could find a shop that would take next month's coupons.' A Coulsdon woman with a daughter aged nearly five when sweet rationing began recalls the methods they tried to make the precious rations last longer:

> Week One always began on a Sunday and sometimes, especially towards the end of the war when she was bigger, Sandra and I would make a red-letter day of it and walk to Banstead—a long walk up a tree-lined lane—and catch a bus to Epsom where there was a sweet shop which was open on Sundays. There we would spend an exquisite quarter-of-an-hour or so choosing our sweets. We tried all sorts of schemes: Dividing our rations into four and buying that amount each week . . . buying our whole ration in one go and only allowing ourselves a quarter of the amount each week. . . . Nothing ever did the trick and we were usually counting the days till the start of the next Week One from about the middle of the first week.

This mother remembers as one of the highlights of their war the Sunday when she and her daughter met 'a most unnatural person who NEVER ATE SWEETS!' Having been given this benefactor's coupons they each immediately bought and began to eat a small box of chocolates. 'Sandra finished hers first and threw her box into a litter bin which was fixed to the bus stop sign. After a while, I too, came to the end of mine, but upon examining the paper underneath . . . found there was another half a layer of chocolates in the bottom of the box, whereupon Sandra dashed to the litter bin and salvaged her discarded carton, raking through the papers like some old tramp. We were quite faint at the thought that the bus might have come before her error was discovered.'

Non-sweet eaters could never understand how vital it seemed that no one's coupons should be wasted. I can remember a mistress at my school admitting she had lost for ever the respect of one small boy after having failed one month to use her personal points, and probably few parents, or grandparents, ever ate their full ration themselves. One little girl in Newcastle felt grateful to the fairies who kindly left a sweet from their apparently unlimited ration in her coat pocket each morning. The 'fairy' was that benefactor of so many wartime households, 'Grandpa'. 'Grandma' made her donation more openly. When she arrived in the same house her shopping bag was thoroughly searched by her grandchildren and usually 'happened' to have some sweets in it. Others made even more heroic sacrifices. One family in Westcliff-on-Sea all went without sweets for a mouth to collect enough coupons for the son of the house to give a two-pound box of chocolates to his first girl friend for her birthday. The abstinence was wasted: he fell out with her the following week.

Many mothers welcomed the lack of sweets, and still attribute their children's excellent teeth to it, encouraging their children to eat instead such alternatives as baked potatoes, raw carrots, 'toffee carrots', in place of the varnished toffee apples, and even turnips. Hungry children also spent their pocket money on indigestion tablets, cough lozenges and, if desperate, dried peas. A junior nurse in a Northampton children's home satisfied her craving for sweets with a cocoa and milk mixture sent in gift parcels from America, while trying to prevent her charges creeping out of bed to eat the flavoured toothpaste included in the same parcels. The son of one grocery manager in Cheltenham, nearly fourteen when war broke out, made his private preparations for rationing by investing his total capital, eightpence, in a stock of two pounds of peanuts which, he calculated, should enable him to see the war out in comfort. 'Supplies did cease quite soon,' he remembers, 'and I was very disappointed when my supplies did not even last until Christmas.' The same boy, like many others, also searched eagerly for fish and chips. After Air Training Corps parade, he recalls, 'we used to hurry into town to see if we could find one of the two chip shops open. . . . If the one shop was closed we might meet another gang coming up the street munching away and we would be off—not always successful even after queueing.' These wartime chips were generally felt to fall below the peacetime quality, according to a Rotherham girl of the same age, because they 'were cooked in whale oil or some such substitute and looked rather pale. . . . They tasted all right if drowned in vinegar.'

Some successful home-made sweets, using substitute materials, were developed by ingenious mothers, with the help of recipes from the Ministry of Food and the women's magazines. The most successful and widely made were substitute peppermint lumps, said to be both 'tasty' and 'chewy', produced from dried milk, sugar, syrup, peppermint essence and a small nut of butter or margarine, melted together. To give them an authentic appearance one rolled the mixture on to a board 'floured' with dried milk and cut it into squares, or squeezed it into a long 'sausage' and cut it with scissors. 'Wartime toffee', made from golden syrup, sugar, cocoa and dried milk powder; 'wartime chocolates', of dried egg, cocoa, sugar and golden syrup; 'chocolate fudge' based on condensed milk and cocoa; toffee cracknel, using puffed rice dipped in golden syrup, and 'honeycomb', using golden syrup and bicarbonate of soda, were all made by various mothers. Substitute Easter eggs were rarely a success. One housewife produced something approximating to the real thing by melting chocolate in a saucepan and squeezing it into an egg shape with two large spoons. Another created some of marzipan 'made from soya flour set in two cups, then stuck together with egg white, from ducks' eggs' and 'sugar beaten with margarine and drinking chocolate powder or cocoa all sloshed together and made egg shaped in spoons'. She thought them 'revolting' but the children considered them 'marvellous'.

Normal ice-cream was unobtainable for most of the war, though some strange concoctions were produced from substitute materials. One London girl munched her way through 'an appalling mess, yellow and lumpy like scrambled eggs, with gritty little lumps of ice embedded in it'. A woman holidaying in Kendal in 1941 recorded in her diary eating some 'very odd-looking ice-cream, with bits of wood-shaving in it'. Next day another entry was needed: 'Feeling seedy, developed biliousness.' When ice-cream did reappear, shortly before the end of the war, I can remember the army office where I was working emptying as scores of young soldiers poured down the road in a body to taste this almost forgotten delicacy.

The lack of ice-cream made it even harder to give a festive look to the food at children's parties, but *The Kitchen Front* and the women's magazines were, as usual, invaluable. 'How well I recall dear Mabel Constanduros every morning with her tips', writes one Potters Bar mother. 'Nobody dared breathe aloud when she was on and I scribbled notes down. One day she gave a recipe for a cake made out of nothing more than flour, syrup and powdered ginger. . . . *Woman's Weekly* one week gave a chocolate cream bun mixture from rationed materials, even to the cream. I can see my friend next door now . . . large mixing bowl under her arm, standing out in the bright sunshine to help make . . . what looked like cart-grease soften. . . . Never has a chocolate cream bun tasted more beautiful.' A Somerset housewife remembers serving sponge containing 'milk chocolate spread' made from flour, cocoa and milk, and, in place of blancmange, arrowroot moulds 'flavoured with bottled fruit juice and coloured with cochineal'. Other favourites at children's parties were pilchard sandwiches, 'easy on the points', 'banana spread', made from parsnips mashed up with banana essence, and mock cream, produced from beaten-up dried milk. Iced birthday cakes could not be bought but many mothers did wonders with melted chocolate and dried milk instead, though a substitute icing made from dehydrated potato was, a Hendon girl remembers, so unsuccessful that 'we all gave up trying including the teacher'. 'Neither of my children had ever seen an iced birthday cake', a Hull mother remembers. 'For my son's fifth birthday I determined to give him a real party. I made a cake, mostly with chopped dates and dried bananas, but it looked all right. It was impossible to buy icing-sugar, but I spent some of my precious sweet coupons on two ounces of highly-coloured sweets called "torpedoes".' These she separated into different tumblers, soaked overnight, mixed the resulting liquids with sugar, water and gelatine, 'and iced my birthday cake pink and yellow and some small cakes and biscuits in blue, green, brown and orange. The children had never seen such a colourful display and the party was a huge success.' A Nottingham mother was grateful that her sons' birthdays were only two days apart: one cake did for both 'with a dividing line down the middle and their respective number of candles each side'.

The shortage of candles for a birthday cake was, in the opinion of one mother, 'one of the greatest disappointments', and one solution was a single large candle which each child blew out in turn. Other decorations were even scarcer but, in one mother's experience, the suggestion of a radio speaker of melting down ordinary candle wax, colouring it with cochineal and similar dyes and working it into shapes decorated with fragments of coloured wool, worked excellently. 'My, oh my,' the same mother remembers, 'never was such excitement seen as at the cake properly decorated. The tots were not as jubilant as the adults: we had given Adolf an extra cock in the snoot as our little ones were not missing a thing on their birthdays.'

Christmas provided the greatest challenge of all. Turkeys were scarce and expensive throughout the war and for an Oldham schoolgirl the privations of wartime were summed up in her family's Christmas dinner in 1944: mutton pie followed by 'wartime Christmas pudding', made with grated carrots. (The official recipes also suggested grated apples and chopped prunes and dried elderberries to replace the missing dried fruit. The results were rarely very palatable to those old enough to remember the real thing.) One Manchester woman had even more reason than most to remember the great blitz of December 1940, for 'my mother's house in Didsbury had had a direct hit *and* my mother-in-law's house in Chorlton and they all descended on me in my little flat. Our Christmas dinner consisted of corned beef hash and wartime Christmas pudding, but we listened to the wireless, sang, played cards and generally had a good time.' Alcohol of any kind was hard to find. The Radio Doctor, as usual, struck the right note when, broadcasting one wartime Christmas on the possible causes of a hangover, he remarked incredulously: 'It may even be due to too much drink, though if it was I'd like to know where you got it.'

Christmas cards were still sent during the war though most mantel-pieces contained more 'official' cards with coats of arms, from the Women's Land Army to the Home Guard, than stage-coaches and snow scenes. A few patriotic people made their own cards by stencilling designs on newspaper, but this was generally felt to be carrying austerity too far.

One might, if fortunate, find a Christmas tree, though one mother still remembers with regret that her child never had the joy of seeing a Christmas tree decorated with electric lights, but decorations of some kind could be improvised and one Essex woman's 'happiest memory' is of 'sitting for hours with my small son making flowers and stars from silver paper to put on an otherwise empty Christmas tree'. Painted egg-shells and fir-cones, and fragments of silver paper from processed cheese packets, were also used as decorations, 'angels' and 'fairy dolls' were made from stiff paper and the blue packets in which cotton wool was sold were opened out and cut into strips for paper chains. Crackers were usually missing, but one East Ham family even succeeded in producing a version of their own, from the cardboard centres of toilet rolls, wrapped in crêpe paper, with, inside each, a home-made paper hat and a fire-cracker left over from Home Guard exercises.

Few Christmas stockings were left unfilled despite the war. A Sheffield girl, two when the war began, eight when it finished, remembers asking in her letter to Santa Claus for ' "any little thing you can spare". This touched my mother—but at the time I couldn't see why. It just seemed logical.' A Surrey girl, six in 1939, remembers being put to bed one Christmas Eve in the shelter in the cellar and leaving detailed instructions on the dining room table to Santa Claus, lest he fail to locate this unconventional bedroom. A ten-year-old South London girl wrote in her 'war diary' this account of her Christmas in 1941.

> I woke early, my brother was asleep, so I made sure the black-out curtains were over the windows and with my torch on I had a little peep at my presents. I had a pair of slacks, Mummy made them out of a blanket, a paint book, a pencil box, a very nice handkerchief, a book of poetry from Mummy, a bar of chocolate, a whole orange. I have a very nice present for Mummy, I made it myself, a kettle holder, and a present for Daddy, I made it, it is a case with needles and cotton and buttons in, so when he goes away he can sew his buttons on. I also made him a shoe polisher. We had a lovely breakfast, fried bread and a nice egg, we're both very lucky, Richard and me, because Mummy and Daddy don't much care for eggs, or sweets.

A Liverpool woman remembers how another little girl was made happy that year despite the war:

> Christmas 1941. The men were away, except my elder brother who had served in the first world war and was in the Home Guard. My daughter had asked Father Christmas for a doll's house. We looked at each other in dismay. Then my brother found an old birdcage. During the raids he worked on it: found bits of cardboard for the walls. The

office wastepaper basket provided an old file which made the roof. He painted the floors. We hunted for all kinds of bits and pieces and a miracle was achieved. . . . A piece of hessian, dyed red, fringed, made an elegant carpet. Never will I forget her face that dark Christmas morning and her childish voice piping *There'll be Blue Birds over the White Cliffs of Dover* as she saw those tables and chairs, tiny pictures made out of cigarette cards, her cries of joy as she discovered each new thing.

During the early part of the war there was a flood of military toys—imitation steel helmets and rifles, clockwork tanks, and for the girls, V.A.D.s' and nurses' uniforms. Toy 'bombs' on a string holding a cap which exploded with a loud crack when dropped smartly on the pavement were popular. Perhaps even more likely to frighten passers-by were large whistles emitting a siren-like noise; fortunately one usually ran out of breath before producing a satisfactory 'warning', but, connected to a blown-up balloon, it produced a fair imitation of the All Clear. On the whole games and jigsaws were less affected by the war than might have been expected. The best-known manufacturers of board games, John Waddington Ltd., produced only a single military one throughout the war, *G.H.Q.*, an excellent game for two players in which 'armoured divisions', 'motorised divisions' and 'infantry divisions' confronted each other across a map of Western Europe. (The game's inventors had shown more wisdom than the strategists: it was possible under the rules to break through the Maginot Line and even to 'invade' England.) Another firm marketed *War Planes*, essentially *Happy Families*, but with groups of bombers and fighters replacing Mr. Bun the Baker and the rest. I also played *Flotilla*, in which two fleets attacked each other, and *Dover Patrol*, though this was of pre-war origin. Jigsaws now showed such gratifying scenes as a German tank-crew surrendering to British soldiers in the desert or a British torpedo-bomber taking off to attack the enemy, but as the war went on the rural views of peacetime tended to reappear. By 1941, as factories changed over to war production, most toys had in any case vanished from the shops. The John Lewis *Gazette* referred sadly in November 1941, with the Christmas rush just beginning, to 'the toy section—for department it cannot be called, consisting as it does of one small table'. The following month one employee was appealing on behalf of 'six-year-old twins who have set their heart on a doll's pram' and by March 1945 the firm was even inviting employees to sell it 'cuddly toys with interesting faces, well-made doll's house furniture and fun equipment, e.g. toy telephones', at up to ten shillings an item.

Most new toys on sale were rightly dismissed by parents as 'expensive rubbish' and the supply from reputable firms that did still reach the shops was soon snapped up. This meant, as one store acknowledged in its staff magazine in 1945, 'a few tears ... shed by disappointed youth when the supply was exhausted'; it also meant one more queue for weary mothers to join. A Hornchurch woman remembers queueing for 'Dinky toys'—miniature cars and lorries—at 7.30 one morning and a Manchester woman, whose son was born in 1940, queued up at 6 a.m. at a shop which did not open until nine to get him a train set for which he was still far too small, 'because I knew there would be nothing for him to play with for years to come'. The need to buy any item immediately it was seen made it hard to keep up the traditional secrecy over presents. A Porthcawl woman remembers buying her son's Christmas present, a Meccano set, in October 1942. As she carried it home unwrapped through the streets she was seen by the mother of one of his schoolfriends, and her son's first remark on arriving home was to enquire about the expected present. The main source of toys was those which other children had outgrown. On an Enfield estate 'one informed the baker or laundry man, etc., what one wanted and they would ask for that item at other houses where they called'. 'For Sale' and 'Wanted' columns of local newspapers were full of advertisements for second-hand toys and I had no difficulty at all in selling a toy typewriter and a microscope set which I had outgrown. Dolls' prams and, even more, tricycles, which were difficult to make at home, were particularly in demand. An Aberdeen mother remembers 'swopping an old, beloved gramophone for a tricycle' and a Swindon woman 'competed at a private sale for a 12s. 6d. tricycle. It finally went for £3 15s., which was nearly twice as much as I earned in a week'. Fortunately for her small son, for his father was in the R.A.F., 'my father was wonderful. He made a wheel-barrow, rocking horse, toy horse and innumerable small toys.'

Other grandparents proved equally resourceful and toy-making also became a favourite occupation in A.F.S. stations and Wardens' Posts during the long inactive hours. A Denton, Lancashire, youth club even obtained a professional handicraft instructor to teach them and was soon able to produce 'engines, ships, aeroplanes, black-boards and easels, dolls' beds and furniture, animal toys, trucks ... carts'. At one Nottingham girls' school there was a toymakers' club to help fill alternate afternoons, when the school was occupied with evacuees, which 'made lovely ducks and rabbits'. One Surrey girl, six in 1939, was delighted with 'Monty the Mouse' made from felt bought at a charity sale 'and unhappy was the day when I left him on a bus. . . . The vicar's kindly daughter heard of the loss and made a larger version with shoe-buttons (which didn't quite match) for eyes. This gave my mother ideas and she became an adept mouse-manufacturer, turning out a whole family of white mice from an old kid glove.' A West London woman greatly admired her husband's production of three-wheel scooters, mangles with little springs that really mangled, aeroplanes . . . rocking horses'. A Somerset woman, whose daughter was born in 1943, was equally impressed when her husband, 'who had never made a thing in his life, turned out wheel barrows, push carts and a wonderful "gee-gee" on wooden wheels which survives to this day and gives much pleasure to three small grandchildren'. Often the whole family joined in. A woman living near Dorchester recalls 'sitting up to the small hours making toys. . . . My husband made an engine out of a round log . . . I made a petrol tank from a cocoa tin . . . Our little five-year-old evacuee would not go to bed without a very funny golly my six-year-old daughter had made him.' 'At Christmas our house resembled Santa Claus's workshop,' remembers a Sunbury-on-Thames woman, 'with a brood of small nephews, nieces and friends to find presents for . . . every scrap of hoarded oddments came in useful. It was possible to get a coloured picture book now and then and the pictures were glued on to pieces of plywood and made into jigsaw puzzles. Building blocks were another favourite and one year we produced a large number of "rollers" made from National Dried Milk tins. With a few nuts and bolts inside to produce a pleasing rattle, and a wire handle fixed, we painted them with gay colours. . . . These were a great favourite with the toddlers.' One Yorkshire woman, whose 'only tools were a saw, rasp and several dinner knives', is proud of having made sledges, dolls' houses and forts, though less proud that 'one time I inadvertently sawed through the dining room table'.

On the whole, very small children probably came off best. Rag dolls, with button eyes, could fairly readily be made from old stockings, old coats could be converted into stuffed animals, seaboot stockings, unravelled, could be reknitted as teddy bears and, in one family in Somerset, an old pair of grey flannel trousers proved the basis for a pull-along elephant. Keen toy-makers hoarded every scrap of material, if not for sewing outside then for stuffing within; one family even saved the small plugs of cotton wool in the tops of aspirin bottles. Cardboard milk bottle tops and large buttons provided the mechanism of 'whizzers', which whirred round when their supporting strings were jerked tight, and in one Yorkshire factory toy-hungry fathers discovered that its basic product, round door-knobs, could serve a new use as yo-yos. A Birmingham builder, posted to London to help in repairs during the flying bomb raids, remembers that his workmates and himself 'made kaleidoscopes in our spare time, using bits of tinfoil, chips of coloured broken glass, etc.', and one mother, evacuated to Exeter with two small girls, brightened their Christmases with cardboard snowmen made from empty Vim canisters, covered with cotton wool and with a black circle of card for a hat, filled 'with little trinkets, sweets, etc., and perhaps an orange'. For slightly older children presents included toy scales, made from patty pans hung on string, cowboy outfits, like that which one ingenious mother made from 'brown curtain lining and a lampshade fringe', complete with 'a marshal's star from an old tin', and home-made games, with a sugar lump with numbers inked on it to serve as a dice.

Despite all their parents' efforts, many children did miss some of the customary pleasures during the war. One mother still feels sad that her daughter's only dolls were of the cardboard type, with cut-out clothes: the normal china type were simply beyond her means. Inevitably, too, the war deprived children of the pleasure of spending their pocket money as they wished. A Hawick, Roxburghshire, woman witnessed its effects on one small boy in 1944. He had called into the village Post Office to buy a comic, but was told 'They haven't come in this week'. He then asked for sweets, and was told 'No sweeties either' and, after a further question, 'Not even chewing gum'. At this, he asked for a penny stamp, walked out and stuck it on the pillar box outside, remarking 'That Hitler!'

# 17

# THE CROWDED CLASSROOM

'It should be remembered that these children have spent . . . nearly half of their school life . . . in improvised and often unsatisfactory conditions.'

Report of the Chief Inspector of Education, London County Council,
September 1943

For most children the war was an interesting time to be at school—or, all too frequently, to be away from it. The government, having evacuated their pupils, had intended to keep the schools in danger areas closed for the duration, and it was not until November 1939 that, very unwillingly, a few were reopened; many could not be as they were now Civil Defence depots or fire stations. By January 1940 nearly one school in ten in England and Wales was still requisitioned and, a month later, nearly a third of all children in the cities were receiving no education at all. Even as late as May, 10 per cent of children in elementary (i.e. primary) schools in England and Wales and about 4 per cent in Scotland were going wholly untaught, while another 30 per cent in England and 36 per cent in Scotland were only attending school part-time. More schools reopened in September 1940, just in time for the blitz. By July 1941 1,000 of the 23,000 state schools in England and Wales had been wholly or partly destroyed and 3,000 more damaged. Most schools were fortunately hit at night, but due to the strain of broken nights and interrupted travel school attendance again dropped sharply. In Manchester, for instance, in the Christmas term of 1941 a third of the children were away at least a quarter of the time and 10 per cent three-quarters. Family difficulties swelled the total, for where the mother had a war job, older children often had to stay at home to care for the babies or take her place in the queues. For the first time for a generation, too, lack of footwear—due now to the war, not to poverty—became a major cause of absence from school. Constantly the school attendance officers reported: 'Many children have one pair only and when repairs are needed . . . must stay at home.'

For most teachers, the outstanding feature of the war was not the empty desk, but the crowded classroom. Although 20,000 male teachers had been called up, 30,000 married women had returned to, or stayed in, teaching, but the transfer of teachers to other duties, like running rest centres, and the general disruption caused by the war, had made classes larger than ever. The ideal maximum was thirty pupils to a teacher, but by 1944 Sheffield alone had more than 400 classes with over fifty, and sixty with over sixty, while Birmingham had over 1,000. In village schools, crowded by private if not by official evacuation, children aged from five to eleven, or even to fourteen, were still to be found in the same classroom, supervised rather than taught by a single overworked elderly woman. With too many pupils, too few books, too little equipment—some classes even had to share pencils—teachers did heroic work, but, for the first time since education had become compulsory in 1870, education standards dropped. By 1943 the London County Council inspectors were finding that twice as many children aged thirteen to fourteen could not manage a simple reading book as twenty years before, that the number of misspellings in a simple composition had doubled, that performance in arithmetic, history and geography was 'appreciably lower', and the children's ability to express themselves in writing was 'extremely low'. Education, it was often said, was the first casualty of the war, and despite the 1944 Education Act, the basis of post-war educational reform, an unfortunate minority bear the scars of wartime conditions to this day.

In evacuated areas 'home schools' were common, with from eight to a dozen children meeting one or two mornings a week in a private house. An Enfield boy remembers his as involving mainly games with 'a bit of writing and reading', and when the local school did reopen all the lessons for all classes were given simultaneously in the hall, the smallest pupils sitting cross-legged on the floor. As this was his first experience of school he concluded it was the usual practice—like the fact that he 'had no idea what the teacher was saying'.

In the reception areas there was a great deal of 'doubling up', with two schools sharing the same premises, either on alternate days or with one school attending in the mornings and the other in the afternoons. The system usually worked well. The girls of King Edward's School, Birmingham, moving into the classrooms of Pate's School, Cheltenham, found a note of welcome, from its usual occupant, on each desk. A girl who attended a Technical School in Tonbridge, whose 'other half' was a boys' school, has pleasant memories of 'end of term parties' which often ended up 'practising dancing round the air raid shelters to an old "wind-up" gramophone'.

During the early days, schools were held in many unusual places, from nonconformist chapels to public houses. One teacher remembers her infant pupils gathered round her in a Cambridgeshire chapel perched on hassocks, and a Hull schoolgirl was taught from the pulpit of a village church near York. Church crypts and halls were also pressed into use. One West Ham teacher has described how, after enterprisingly taking over a 'semi-derelict church hall' in a Berkshire village, in the graphic phrase of one of his pupils 'the floor guv way' and 'the rows of children sank before my eyes like little ships going down'. One evacuated teacher taught a class in Hitchin with sixty children, one of them a mental defective who 'permanently sat alone', in a room designed for thirty, and sometimes the teacher 'would be given a section of the class to instruct in the cloakroom amidst dripping coats'. A Liverpool girl, thirteen when her school was bombed in 1940, enjoyed attending classes in a hotel. She and a friend would roller-skate to school and 'there were also R.A.F. men having lectures in the same hotel and I was beginning to get interested in the boys in uniform. . . . Smashing we thought it was.'

It was a difficult time to be a student teacher. One, evacuated to Kettering from London with her college, did her teaching practice in schools where two classes and two teachers shared a room and in an old church hall with no blackboard, books, paper or pencils, or desks— 'just benches and children'. In London in 1944, now qualified, she gave lessons in school shelters to 'boys lying in tiered bunks in semi-darkness' and one day, in a normal classroom, turned round from the blackboard to find her class had vanished; more experienced than her, they had heard a V.1 approaching and dived under their desks.

Some much-moved schools almost lost their identity during the war but most successfully survived a whole series of upheavals, especially grammar schools with a long tradition behind them. The adventures of St. Saviours and St. Olaves girls' grammar school from Southwark were typical. At first it was evacuated to Brighton, where it used the premises of a boys' grammar school every afternoon, and the girls settled down happily on a housing estate with foster parents of their own social class. In June 1940 the school moved again to a country house at Chertsey, a middle-class area with a reputation for being unwelcoming, though on this occasion it proved undeserved. None the less the customary drift home soon began and by mid-1941, despite the blitz, the school had reopened in its old premises, at first with only thirty girls, though before long there were more in London than in the country. In 1944, with the girls spending all night in the shelter, the staff at first organised quizzes and other 'soft' lessons during the day, until the girls themselves asked for the normal routine to be restored, even attempting to do 'gym' between rows of coats in the cloakroom, as the gymnasium had been bombed. The mistress in charge in London remembers that raids during school hours caused little alarm; the girls were far more anxious about the danger of spilling gravy on their neighbours' clothes, while trying to eat in the crowded shelter or hall.

Many wartime memories of school centre on long hours spent in the shelters. A Sussex girl, seven in 1939, observed 'no panic, just a feeling of excitement as each class marched quickly across the playground to the shelter ... There were wooden benches and caged lights on the walls which gave quite a good light. Each child had a tin or box in which we kept two or three comics, a book, some sweets and a favourite toy to keep us occupied during the raid.' At a Tunbridge Wells school 'on top of our headmistress's stock cupboard stood two large jars of sweets which we house captains were responsible for taking to the shelter in case we got stuck for hours'. A Hendon girl, aged eight in 1939, found that 'most of the time at school we spent trying to break the speed record to the shelters. The higher up the school we went the further away were the shelters, till seniors were dashing off to the local park.'

For most children, raids were a not unwelcome interruption to the day's routine. A man living at Hornsea, Yorkshire, where parents 'had the option of allowing their children to remain on the premises or at their own risk dash home', remembers that 'as nothing happened the number of those who wanted to be with their parents began to grow ... pressure, no doubt, being exercised by the youngsters on the mothers. ... It was interesting to note the difference between the dash for home and the time taken to cover the same distance back to school after the All Clear.' Those who did not run home were 'accommodated in the downstairs corridors or in the cloakrooms, where they were encouraged to sing their favourite songs ... *Ten Green Bottles* or *One Man went to Mow* suited both the adults and the children for both last for some time, but very often the last green bottle did not accidentally fall with the same resounding crash as the first and most of the singers began to tire when double figures of men and their dogs went to mow the meadow.' Alerts at night were equally popular, for if the siren sounded before midnight morning school was postponed for one hour, and invariably 'children reproved for arriving at the later hour were certain that it was before midnight by their clock that they were awakened'.

For children taking examinations, interruptions due to air raids were less welcome. One girl being prepared for an entrance scholarship to Oxford at St. Albans High School in 1940–41 had permission to stay at her desk and risk the bombs during warnings while the rest of her class took shelter. The fifth and sixth forms at Isleworth County School had special shelters in two internal corridors which permitted them to have normal lighting. Disturbed examinations were an even greater problem. While one boy at the school was sitting his own 'matric' in the summer of 1944 there were thirteen Alerts, but the candidates ignored them and simply carried on. A few schools were more cautious. A girl at a Swanage convent remembers being ushered into a cellar when the sirens sounded in the middle of her School Certificate examination and being kept in strict silence till the All Clear, when the candidates returned to their desks. The Examination Board sensibly made allowance for the unusual conditions of the time. The Oxford and Cambridge Schools Examination Board explained, in a circular in 1940, that 'to make allowance as far as possible for wartime difficulties, the Awarders of certificates will be instructed to maintain approximately the normal percentages of passes ... The Awarders will also have before them examination results of each School in previous years and ... the Board will be glad to receive from Schools, before the examination begins, reports of their special difficulties and of the conditions under which they have been working. ... Schools may also submit the opinions of the staff as to the subjects in which a candidate would have been expected to pass, or pass with credit, had the conditions been normal.' Many schools in fact achieved exceptionally good academic results during the war. The proud recollections of a Worcester Park, Surrey, mother are not untypical. Her elder daughter's education 'proceeded by fits and starts at odd hours, at different schools', and she 'did her matriculation examinations and Higher School Certificate examinations in the school shelters lying flat on her stomach', but none the less 'got a major scholarship to Bedford College, London'.

Even children not affected by evacuation and air raids suffered from the call-up of teachers. Schools at first tried to cope by redeploying their staff and chemistry specialists, for example, found themselves also teaching mathematics or even French. At one Palmers Green school the boys raised no objection to being taught P.T. by an attractive young woman, while another woman teacher in the Midlands found herself taking football. Many boys' schools, far worse hit than girls' by loss of staff, called in from outside elderly or medically unfit men, often with no experience of teaching. I recall with embarrassment the terrible ragging to which one temporary and obviously frail teacher of German was subjected at my school, until rescued by the head of the department, who, after one particularly rowdy lesson, descended to wreak terrible retribution on the offenders, and to deliver a highly impressive lecture on the class's lack of patriotism compared with that of the man it had persecuted.

Such appeals added at this time a powerful weapon to the teacher's armoury. One twenty-seven-year-old woman teacher, facing a class of forty-five tough eleven- and twelve-year-old Northamptonshire boys, remembers that 'When they engaged in the school sport of throwing pens as "darts" into the floor boards we used to tell them it was waste and so "helping Hitler" '. In this school, as in many others, paper-saving was also carried to great lengths. Margins were halved or abolished; every inch of space, to the very bottom and top of each sheet, had to be filled, and each pupil was rationed for painting to one six-inch square of paper a week. A Sutton Coldfield mother got 'lots of laughs' from the absence notes sent by parents which were handed out to her daughters to use as rough paper and which made her much more careful when writing such notes herself. In one Kent school the children were told to use the backs of their bus tickets for 'rough work', while one Bath private school was forced to go back a generation and distribute slates for arithmetic. As a Report by one Chief Inspector of Education in 1943 complained, the desire to save paper had 'degenerated into a parsimony' which was endangering some children's education.

Far more successful on the whole than the use of over-age or unfit men was the introduction of women teachers into boys' schools. At my school, hitherto a rigidly all-male society, attractive and intelligent women wrought a revolution. In my house the welfare of the younger boys was transformed by a female 'junior housemaster', and in school history classes were enriched by a young woman don from Cambridge. The friendships of the mistresses with the male staff and older boys provided, too, a fascinating subject of gossip and struck a useful blow at the prevailing homosexuality. Even in day schools women supplied a civilising influence. A Twickenham grammar school boy has 'always been grateful to these ladies as I think they added a lot of humanity and were mostly very fine teachers. The school, however, obviously regarded the war as a minor interruption in the ordained scheme of life and we had to address them as "Sir". The consequence was that for years I called every older woman I met "Sir".'

For those with no liking or aptitude for games the war was also a great liberator. Even at my games-mad school, which had compulsory games or military training every single day, except Sunday, it was at last possible to escape occasionally from the humiliation, boredom and time-wasting of the cricket or rugger pitch to work for a local farmer. (One was even paid for this, though I would gladly have worked for nothing.) Boys who were not hopelessly incompetent at games were still expected to devote themselves exclusively to them; even in wartime, there were *some* priorities to be observed at a British boarding-school.* Only the anti-aircraft obstructions across the playing-fields prevented even the games-infatuated, self-indulgent cricketers from wholly forgetting the war, though any ball which hit one was considered to have scored a boundary. At a Twickenham school the obstructions consisted of lines of pits. 'They were fun to play in for younger boys', one schoolboy considered, 'although annoying in winter if one had to retrieve a football from several inches of mud and water at the bottom.' A girl at a boarding school evacuated from the coast to a country house on the

---

* Curiously enough, to work on a farm instead of playing games was regarded as rather unpatriotic. What contribution boys idling their afternoons away on the cricket or rugger pitch were making to the war effort I never discovered.

Thames at Buscot near Reading also rejoiced at being set free from the futile misery of team games, for instead the local rector, a former rowing blue, coached the girls on the river. (The school showed its gratitude by going without its breakfast marmalade once a term to present him with a seven-pound jar.) Shortages of sports equipment, from hockey balls to gym shoes, also protected some children from the normal team-game tyranny. The girls of one Hull convent, which had lost its lacrosse fields, tennis courts and netball pitch to the Army, were reduced to playing table-tennis. In a Walthamstow school first aid classes 'replaced P.T., which we all detested', one boy remembers. 'On one occasion we had well bandaged and strapped to a stretcher a member of the class who was not particularly liked when the siren sounded and we all trooped to our shelter . . . We "overlooked" the casualty, who spent a worrying half-hour staring at the ceiling unable to move and hoping the school didn't get hit.'

On the whole, lessons were less affected than out-of-school activities. At a Middlesex school wartime chemistry lessons included instruction in water purification on which the sixth-formers would have been employed if bombs had breached the water mains, but due to the shortage of equipment 'most experiments had to be taken on trust'. Many schools welcomed speakers from organisations like the Free French and one woman who was at school in Hull can still sing the Czech National Anthem of that period, *Slovak Brother*, learned in honour of some visiting dignitary. At a Sheffield elementary school, one girl remembers, 'our singing was definitely war directed. Our morning assembly frequently included such hymns as *What Heroes hast thou Bred, O England my Country*. For a Birmingham schoolgirl 'Art lessons were mainly drawing pictures of Churchill and President Eisenhower . . . English lessons involved finding as many American phrases as possible and putting their equivalent in English'. The war led a Tunbridge Wells girls' grammar school to rewrite Oscar Wilde. Owing to the lack of men for a production of *The Importance of Being Earnest*, the butler became a maid. Even at my school, not the most progressive of establishments, the prevailing enthusiasm for post-war planning led to the setting up of study groups, at which the older boys discussed such subjects as post-war education and the future of India, though there were stern limits to freedom. When the school debating society voted, despite my eloquence on the other side, in favour of treating Germany leniently after the war, it was promptly suppressed for the duration.

In girls' schools the war made itself felt most in domestic science lessons, now more essential than ever, for many mothers were afraid to let their daughters experiment on scarce rations or clothing at home. Even laundry lessons were planned to avoid waste of soap and hot water.

One Swiss Cottage schoolgirl remembers that 'soap was provided . . . and each girl was allowed to bring home any small items she chose for laundry practice', while the teacher 'conquered the soap shortage a little by bringing along her personal underwear and getting a couple of girls to wash and iron it for her. The girls were not over-enthusiastic about this task and Miss C. would supervise the washing of her ample knickers with vigorous exhortations to "Rub the gussets, girls! Rub the gussets!" ' Some schools managed to provide material for sewing, though this was a temptation to coupon-hungry mothers. One head teacher near Peterborough was surprised to find that the cotton print material issued to one pupil for her exercises duly returned to school on her back, 'her mother having appropriated the fabric and made it up into a dress for a Sunday school party'.

Cookery lessons presented the biggest problem and a few schools simply gave up the struggle. In one Hull convent, when the school's domestic science rooms were requisitioned, cookery lessons were replaced by leatherwork, which was unlikely to satisfy a hungry husband. Many teachers, as the allowance of rations for teaching was inadequate, gave lessons on vitamins and nutrition and, corresponding to the Army's 'tactical exercise without troops', there were classroom sessions in which joints and cakes were cooked 'theoretically' without the oven being turned on. School recipes placed the emphasis on vegetables and items off the ration. In the memory of a Guildford schoolgirl, 'cookery seemed to consist of making oat cakes and potato pie and locking and unlocking the pantry door to safeguard rations from hungry girls'. At a senior girls' school near Nottingham the girls were taught to make eggless cake, boiled cake, potato soup, sardine and lentil rolls, with the help of a special wartime supplement to a standard text book, *The Battersea Polytechnic Cookery Book*, which also added carrot pudding and potato pastry to the normal list of dishes. Making lentil cutlets was a regular exercise at a school near Chislehurst. A Yeovil schoolgirl's chief memory is of endless recipes made with oatmeal and a Gravesend girl remembers that on a rare occasion when they cooked with apples she was reproved for peeling them too thick and was 'told to peel the peel'. A technical school at Tonbridge had a more ambitious syllabus, including 'corned beef . . . cut into squares . . . placed in batter and baked', or chocolate log cake, using dried egg, 'icing' made from dried milk and cocoa, and mock-cream, based on Household Milk. 'When meat dishes were concerned the classes were split into groups and a little meat from each girl went into the finished dishes . . . Fruit puddings or small cakes were also prepared on a sharing basis. "Community cooking", as we called it, saved food and fuel from being wasted.' This school provided a rigorous training for domestic life in wartime. If the girls drank their school milk in break, instead of saving it for cookery lessons, they had to use dried milk for cooking, while pea pods, as well as peas, went into pea soup. 'Young dandelion leaves could be washed and used as lettuce . . . Potato or rice water, thickened, made paste for the younger children's cut-outs.' The ultimate in economy was not merely to use stinging nettles but to do so twice over. 'When boiled you could drink the liquid and the cooked leaves were similar to spinach.'

One wartime change was destined to become permanent: the provision of a midday meal at school, free for the poorest children, 4½d. or later 5d. for the rest. 'Dinner duty' became yet another chore for the harassed teacher to crowd into the day and, at least in the beginning, the food was often poor. One Hull woman still vividly recalls her first school dinners. 'I recall the day the stew was bad. The smell was appalling and the head-master forbad us to eat it. We all shouted aloud when we found a cater-pillar and this was a regular occurrence. The so-called Cornish pasties were filled with something like sawdust. The taste of the watery, over-stewed cabbage was beyond words.' But at this school, as at others, the food later improved 'unbelievably'.

One unusual task placed upon head teachers was deciding which children were growing at more than the normal rate and thus entitled to additional clothing coupons. An Oldham girl, aged thirteen when clothes rationing came in in 1941, remembers the envy with which a classmate who began to develop an outsize bust was regarded, for this was both a desirable sign of growing up *and* entitled her to extra coupons. At another Oldham school the headmaster devised some simple tests to select the 'outsize' children, marking the heights appropriate to their various ages on his study wall and cutting out a number of cardboard patterns for the various sizes of foot. A headmistress in a remote Fenland village near Peterborough remembers her battles with indignant mothers seeking extra coupons. 'Some of the parents insisted that their children's feet were outsize—they measured round bunions, big toes, etc. . . . A mother of twins of twelve came and argued for a quarter of an hour to get my sanction to coupons, then, on my refusal, as a parting shot, said, "Anyway I got them at the Food Office yesterday." ' Another teacher, at a Kettering senior boys' school, had a pleasanter wartime duty, being driven round the countryside by a W.V.S. driver to visit pupils released from school for 'potato picking' weeks. It was, she thought, 'much preferable to teaching'.

Adaptability and resourcefulness had always been in demand in the teaching profession and the extent to which they were required during the war is illustrated by the experiences of one teacher, aged thirty-one in 1939. The approach of war had brought her hurrying back from France, where she was studying to perfect her French, and she was assigned to escorting a Roman Catholic senior girls' school from a poor area of North London, which was soon scattered over a large area of East Anglia. Here, after coping with the usual complaints about inadequate clothing, verminous hair, impetigo, bed-wetting and bad language, she finally assembled 'something less than twenty pupils of various ages, including boys of fourteen who were determined to be farmers for the rest of their lives', in an empty village school which 'consisted virtually of one large room . . . There were flimsy card tables which would serve as desks . . . and the earth closets were . . . emptied at regular intervals . . . I unearthed inkwells from a spidery backroom and in order to stop them falling over on rickety tables we used bits of cane and light wooden bases meant for basket work and made little cages to hold inkwells.' The books and other items she bought herself at Woolworths in Cambridge, but no sooner was the school running smoothly than it was decided to move it back, whereupon the parents all took their children back to London and their teacher 'packed up the spare books, pens, rulers, etc., borrowed a baby's pram' and pushed her load towards the nearest store. She then joined the staff of a Tottenham school sharing the premises of one in Cambridge, where even during the holidays 'to relieve the hosts of the evacuees . . . the London staff remained on duty'. By 1941 her billet had been damaged by bombs—'All our glass was out and some ceilings down'—and she was spending her evenings fire-watching, so that 'one felt fit for nothing when faced with a full day's work'. Beside the normal duties, she was now responsible for 'cataloguing and storing of babies', children's and women's clothes for use in an emergency', and distributing school milk, which was delivered in pint bottles so that 'form mistresses had to arrange for it to be poured into one-third pint beakers'.

By 1942 this teacher had moved to Bath, and a college of art, which, as its own premises had been requisitioned, was housed in two private houses. These were destroyed in the Baedeker raids and she found herself with a new duty: trying to salvage from a bombed-out shop 'every scrap of artist's materials to replace all that was lost in the demolished school'. Enterprisingly she borrowed a cart from a nearby builder's yard, and 'loaded all the paint, etc., that was easy to reach on to the truck and then pushed it through the city centre and up Lansdowne Hill to the headmaster's house'. When the college reopened she found herself facing a class with no blackboard or chalk. Her response was typical of wartime improvisation; she unearthed 'some unused rolls of old wallpaper in a cupboard', pinned them on the wall and wrote on them in lipstick.

But, from a child's point of view, the war was not a bad time in which to grow up. As one Sheffield woman, then a child, remembers: 'For me the war years were happy. We had more freedom than we would have done had the men been at home. We were allowed to roam in the woodlands and on the golf course without supervision. Parents didn't fear lurking prowlers in lonely places, as they assumed all the men who might do us harm were busily occupied.'

The war began to intrude into children's lives in the school playgrounds, where 'Spitfires' relentlessly roared down upon, and shot down, the 'enemy bombers'—a role for which the intruding evacuees were often cast—and little girls skipped to rhymes about Churchill and Hitler that can have meant little to them. As one grew older it played an ever larger role. For most boys, and for many girls, the great wartime amusement was aircraft recognition. The opportunity to add a genuine Junkers 87 or Messerschmitt 110 to one's list of sightings far overshadowed any feeling of danger and I can still recapture my own satisfaction at identifying my first Heinkel 111, as it hovered over Newbury, and of instantly recognising a Junkers 88 as it flew low over my school in Sussex. A sixpenny Penguin book of aircraft silhouettes was one of the outstanding bestsellers of the war. The yearly edition of *Aircraft of the Fighting Powers* and the weekly issue of the *Aircraft Spotter* were, one Loughton schoolboy remembers, 'eagerly awaited'. His club, of fourteen boys and a solitary girl, met each Saturday evening at his home and spent its annual holidays touring the country on cycle, each day's forty or fifty miles between youth hostels being carefully planned to include as many aerodromes as possible.

During the first two years of the war any boy or girl who really wanted to help the war effort could usually find a way to do so through an organisation like the Scouts or the Girls' Life Brigade, but there was no compulsion, except at schools like mine, which even in peacetime had compelled all its pupils to enrol in the Officers' Training Corps, now democratically renamed the Junior Training Corps. In December 1941, rather, one feels, because the registration of civilians had become a habit than for any practical reason, all young people of either sex had to register on reaching the age of sixteen so they could be given advice on joining a suitable youth organisation, though not legally forced to take it. In my experience, this made not the slightest difference to anyone; the patriotic were already 'doing their bit', the rest continued to enjoy their last years of freedom.

In February 1941 the Air Training Corps had been founded to provide preliminary training for those intending to join the R.A.F., and in 1942 the government launched the Sea Cadet Corps and the Army Cadet Force. For boys aged fourteen and upwards, these provided a harmless if not very valuable occupation for a few hours each week —the services gave no preference to former members of them—and, in many schools, like mine, the A.T.C. in particular became the refuge of those who were not militarily-minded. I can recall pleasant summer afternoons spent in sending and receiving morse signals across the school quadrangle, navigating a pram containing an aircraft compass around the playing fields, and plotting courses for imaginary aircraft on real maps of Germany. For girls, the Girls' Training Corps, launched nationally in 1941, and the Women's Junior Air Corps provided similar training in first aid, drill and signalling, though they also did more useful work in providing secretarial or catering help to the Civil Defence and W.V.S.

The oldest and largest of all the youth organisations were the Boy Scouts and Girl Guides, which together had a million members. A Hackney Guide remembers how her company, 'in August 1939 a thriving active group just returned from summer camp . . . by mid-September was non-existent', but by Christmas the company had been re-formed and when, a year later, the bombing began, the girls still met on Saturday afternoons, or had a day camp on an Essex camping ground.

In the reception areas the problem was never too few members but too many. A Kendal, Westmorland, Guide remembers that her company, which had shrunk to only six girls, doubled and then quadrupled in size. In Stafford, in the Midlands, an influx of new Scouts and Rovers from evacuated schools and war factories raised the number of local troops from six to ten, some with five or six patrols instead of three or four. In Swansea, the real problem was the lack of experienced leaders. Where a Scout troop was started in 1941 in an area that had never previously supported one, the only people available to run it were two fifteen-year-old boys who were patrol leaders in other troops.

A Nottingham teacher, twenty-three when the war began, gradually acquired new responsibilities until by the end of the war she 'had a Cub pack, a Ranger company, a Guide company, and when the Brown Owl was called up, I had to take on the church Brownies'. A Bristol teacher evacuated to near Yeovil, having started one Brownie pack and Guide company, was soon being called on to make 'a ten-mile journey to these Guides and Brownies once a week, staying overnight, and catching a workman's bus in the morning and walking the last three miles in order to be at school by 9 a.m.'. Soon afterwards she launched a new Guide company, in another village, and even became a lady Scoutmaster ('definitely *not* Scout-mistress') bravely taking the boys to camp. The Scouts showed their gratitude by presenting her with a 'spread' from saved-up rations and 'a pink nightie and case' from 'hoarded-up clothing coupons'.

Requisitioning of premises was almost as serious as lack of leaders. A Swansea troop, after the A.F.S. took over the church hall, had to squeeze into the tiny crypt. In Ealing, where another church hall was commandeered as a food store, the Guides were reduced to meeting in the grounds outside. A Guide company formed among evacuees in a rural district of South Somerset 'met in the vicarage loft, after turning out the junk. . . . We painted and scrubbed and hung curtains. We entered by a rickety ladder and saw by a hurricane lamp. No heating in the winter sent us to the servants' hall of the "Big House" for meetings.'

But in spite of all the difficulties, both Scouts and Guides flourished during the war. As one former thirteen-year-old Guide in the Kentish village of High Broome remembers: 'Our motto "Be Prepared" soon meant something. When we went to bed we learnt to lay out our clothes so that we could practically fall into them without a light. . . . We knew that in an emergency we would be wanted at the reception centre. . . . If nothing else, we could brew tea.'

The movement's most valuable contribution to the war effort was just such unspectacular drudgery cheerfully undertaken behind the scenes. The younger boys in one Croydon troop every Saturday morning 'checked and refilled the fire-buckets and tested the stirrup pumps' at a local hospital. One morning, one remembers, 'a nurse suddenly appeared from a maternity ward with a new-born baby in her arms. "Would you like to hold it?", she asked, and thrust it into my arms. What embarrassment and humiliation for a boy of eleven!' A Nottingham Guide captain still feels proud of the work her 'Guides did at the Nottingham general hospital twice a week. They helped to prepare the supper for the patients, they set the trolleys and washed up, they never grumbled though they had to travel home on the bus in the black-out.' They even endured bodies being wheeled past the kitchen on the way to the mortuary, which prompted one Guide to complain, 'The only patients *we* saw were dead ones.' One Sussex Girl Guide earned her War Service badge by working ninety-six hours at a local hospital, where she had to break endless eggs for the nurses' supper, then divide 'into tiny portions' the crumbly, brightly coloured wartime cake known as 'the yellow peril'.* A Hackney company supplied two Guides every night to help at the local hospital. One, on one occasion, 'helped head, tail and gut a hundred herrings. . . . The smell of fish stayed with me for days.' By such small, individual sacrifices, rarely noted, never honoured, the way to victory was paved.

The outstanding memory of the war for many Scouts and Guides is of making collections. There was always something that was needed: waste paper, silver paper, scrap iron, jam jars, rose-hips, acorns, conkers, even stinging nettles. A Nottingham Guider can still 'smell those dried nettles now—they gave me hay fever!' 'What ever did they use all those cotton reels for?', one wartime Guide still wonders. (Army signallers in fact wound thin wires on them.)

* The War Service badge was awarded for doing a certain number of hours of hospital work, gardening, running messages, etc. One could win a new badge each year.

Going away to camp had always been the highlight of the year for many town children but during the war trained helpers were few. 'I have been obliged to run annual camps single-handed with only sixteen to seventeen-year-olds for help', one assistant commissioner, then a Nottingham Scoutmaster, remembers. 'This nowadays I should consider dangerous to the point of folly, particularly with no car available.' The pre-war camping rules were also changed. Tents, instead of never being pitched beneath trees, could now not be placed in the open, unless camouflaged, for fear of air attack. A Bristol Guide captain found that this could lead to other dangers.

> Our camp was pitched in a wood. The first night was pretty terrifying, starting with yells, 'Captain, there's a man.' After sleepily telling them to go to sleep, I looked and saw a torch weaving in and out of the trees —very eerie. I gathered all the Guides into a hut in the middle of the wood and lay on the verandah, armed with a mallet. . . . In the loudest voice I could manage I yelled, 'Come out of that wood.' The man from the nearest cottage phoned the police, who arrived in the form of one young constable, the Guides immediately calling to him, 'Please, please, come and sleep with us!' Never was a poor young man so flustered. However, he said the whole British Army could hide in those woods and it was no place for girls. We got out and camped with the fowls in a nearby field. Wasps were the only nuisance for the rest of the week. No Guides went home—and I got my camper's licence.

A Sussex Scout who camped on a farm near Horley during the Battle of Britain found the two young heifers with whom the field was shared more trouble than the Germans, after camouflaging the 'tents with string netting over which was strewn handfuls of grass. During the night the heifers found delight in coming over to the tents to eat the grass off the nets, stumbled among the guy ropes and caused some alarm to the tent occupants.'

For most of the war catering was a far greater problem than air raids, especially when a camp lasted less than a week, for over that period the campers simply took their ration books and obtained a bulk supply permit from the local Food Office. 'When I helped to Q.M.' (act as quarter-master) one Guide remembers, 'it was a nightmare collecting all the little bits of marge, butter, bacon etc.', and one Hounslow Scout still has a detailed list of the items he had to bring: 'two tablespoons of sugar, one egg, one rasher of bacon, one ounce of butter, a piece of meat two inches by two inches, jam if available'. In this camp, on a permanent site at Chalfont St. Peter, 'all the bits and pieces of food would be collected together and a menu prepared around them. Unusual dishes developed a popular one being custard porridge.' One Scoutmaster enjoyed a camp where, due to their host's prowess as a shot, not merely did the dinner menu frequently include rabbit, but 'rabbit-skin belts, rabbit-skin hatbands and rabbit-skin on staffs' soon sprouted all over the camp. But even without such extras, as one Guide captain from Ealing remembers, 'we don't seem to have starved', as her menus for a weekend camp at Whitsun 1943 confirm:

| | |
|---|---|
| *Saturday Dinner* | Bacon roll, potatoes and greens, tinned apples and custard. |
| *High Tea* | Pilchard salad, bread and butter, cake, tea. |
| *Sunday Breakfast* | Porridge. |
| *Dinner* | Spam, sausage and vegetables, Summer Pudding made with tinned apples. |
| *High Tea* | Cheese Dreams. |
| *Monday Breakfast* | Scrambled eggs. |
| *Dinner* | Corned beef, boiled potatoes, salad, chocolate pudding. |
| *Tea* | All salad, bread and butter, etc., still left. |

The pleasure of sitting around the camp-fire at the end of the day had, however, to be abandoned for the duration, but this was less of a burden than it sounded for it was often light until 11 p.m.

Clothes rationing proved even more troublesome to the Scout and Guide movements than food rationing, for coupons were required for new uniforms. Many Guide companies collected the old uniforms of former members and loaned them to each new generation of girls, together with scarce items like belts and badges, while Brownies were often dressed in uniforms home-made from rolls of curtain material or old overalls. A Kendal Guide remembers that 'Hats were the problem. Because they were so hard to get, we were given permission to knit ourselves skull-caps of thick, double-knitting navy wool.' Harder to overcome was the loss of equipment through bombing. A single incendiary bomb on 'the old hut in the corner of a disused works in Swansea where our seventy-two-strong Scout troop met', recalls one Scoutmaster, destroyed 'all our equipment, enough to take us all fully kitted to camp', which had 'been raised by subscriptions of a maximum of threepence a week'. A Bristol Brown Owl remembers that her Brownie pack was twice bombed out, the second time from 'a "safe" room under the church' which 'went up in smoke, taking with it all the pack properties, including twelve new camp overalls and twelve new ties, camp equipment for pack holidays, plus toadstool'—the central feature of Brownie meetings. Here surely is one heroic achievement of the German Air Force that ought not to go unrecorded: they successfully bombed the Brownies' toadstool.

# STUDENTS WITH STIRRUP PUMPS

'Had you walked through the College on ... Sunday afternoon ... you
would have come upon a massed stirrup-pump practice with some forty
s.p.s attacking imaginary incendiaries from behind the pillars of
Nevile's Court—an impressive and unusual scene.'

Letter from A. S. M. Gow, Fellow of Trinity College, Cambridge,
12th December 1942

It was just as I had expected: the long, dark oak tables, dimly lit, the
ancient portraits looking down from the walls, the venerable college
servants discreetly serving beer in tankards—this was my first reaction
to my future college when, as a seventeen-year-old schoolboy sitting
for an entrance scholarship, I dined in hall for the first time in September
1943. Oxford, it seemed at first sight, had hardly been affected by the war.

This impression was, of course, misleading. The vast lecture rooms of
the Examination Schools had become, as in the first world war, a
military hospital; St. Hugh's, instead of echoing to the girlish chatter of
undergraduates, echoed to the girlish chatter of nurses and in many
colleges typewriters clattered and telephones rang in formerly peaceful
buildings where evacuated ministries had established their outposts.
In September 1940 refugees from the bombing had poured into Oxford
—the conditions under which several hundred were camping out in a
disused cinema became a national scandal—and nappies had been seen
hanging out to dry in Tom Quad, Christ Church, the most imposing
part of Oxford's most aristocratic college, for the first time in its four-
hundred-year history.

These changes were trifling compared with the upheaval undergone by
London University, whose headquarters building had been taken over
by the Ministry of Information and whose component colleges had been
scattered to the corners of the country. University College had moved
to Bangor and Aberystwyth, parts of King's College to Bristol, Glasgow,
Birmingham and Leeds, the Institute of Education to Nottingham,
Bedford College and Queen Mary College to Cambridge. Cambridge
was the great academic host of the war, welcoming every kind of invader
from the traditionally lively London medical students to the then more
sober pupils of the London School of Economics and the Chichester

Theological College. The city was soon intolerably crowded. One Trinity don, A. S. M. Gow, who sent a regular description of the Cambridge scene to his former pupils in the Forces throughout the war, recorded in December 1941 the long queue outside Marks and Spencers for acid drops and in 1943 the near impossibility of getting one's hair cut. Other signs that the times were not normal, were the prominently labelled Air Raid Shelters in the New Court of Trinity, the static water tank beside King's College chapel, and the onions and potatoes growing in the gardens of St. John's. Most shocking of all to the traditionalists, the feet of humble born, hungry citizens tramped through the premises of Cambridge's most exclusive and reactionary undergraduate society, the Pitt Club, now serving the common good as a British Restaurant.

In 1914 the rush into khaki had emptied the universities of men. In 1939, although the pre-war volunteers of the University Air Squadrons duly joined up—they included Richard Hillary of Trinity College, Oxford, who later became famous—other undergraduates settled down to wait their turn to be called. The Committee of Vice-Chancellors, representing all the universities in the United Kingdom, had assumed that all those reading Arts subjects would be called up as soon as war began. Instead the call-up at first applied only to men of twenty and above and those already in their final university year were able to complete it. But most male students had been only temporarily reprieved. Throughout the war medical, dentistry, science and engineering students, unless they failed their examinations, were able to finish their courses, though they then had to go into essential work or the Forces. For those reading Arts it was different. Ernest Bevin, who had himself left school at the age of eleven, was said to be much distressed at having to call up young men half way through their education, but this did not deter him from systematically stripping the Arts faculties of their male students.

Even in 1939 some colleges, like the London School of Economics, had already lost more than half their students and before long many universities were suggesting that young men should come up at seventeen, instead of eighteen or nineteen, or begin their courses in January instead of October to give them an extra two terms before being called up. University courses were also shortened. At Oxford a 'war degree' could be obtained in many subjects in two years, instead of the normal three; at Cambridge, anyone who had completed two years before being called up could have his first year in the Forces counted as 'time in residence' and could qualify for his B.A. without further examination. At Durham one could obtain an 'unclassed' degree, as an honours or pass degree student, after two years, but if one wished, come back after the war and do a further year's work to upgrade it into a 'classed' one. Women who showed promise could do the full three year course without interruption, and one professor of modern languages at King's College, Newcastle, then part of the same university, remembers that selecting those to be given the extra year caused 'some heart-burning'. Another change also meant problems, for 'The University became preponderantly female. One got unaccustomed to dealing with anyone but girls.' In his department only one solitary unfit male was able to pursue the usual three year course, pursued in turn, or at least surrounded, by scores of girls. At Newcastle, recognising that students were 'burdened with military training' and fire-watching, 'examiners had to lower their sights' but 'standards were by no means abandoned'. This was the general experience.

Until 1941 it was still possible for Arts students to complete two years at university provided they showed 'exceptional promise as potential officers, or intellectual ability above the average or evidence of a balanced combination of the two'. In March 1942 the Ministry of Labour announced that Arts students born in 1924, whom the call-up was now reaching, could still have one year at university provided they were 'of above average ability' and that boys 'of scholarship standard' could begin a three term course in January 1943 so long as they would not be more than nineteen-and-a-half when they finished it. In December 1942, however, the final blow fell when it was announced that all Arts students, irrespective of ability, would in future be conscripted at eighteen, with no deferment, either at school, to qualify for university entrance, or at university, beyond July 1943. Some M.P.s suggested that this meant the end of university life, but a government spokesman denied it. 'What would be closed down was Arts courses,' he insisted, 'and he was afraid that was necessary.... In the present strenuous and serious position of the war they could not possibly continue these courses.'

From October 1943 as the new regulations took effect the whole character of the older universities changed, as the humanities—English, history, politics, modern languages, classics—became represented among male students only by aliens exempt from service, the medically unfit, conscientious objectors and a few beardless youths of seventeen, uneasily waiting to be called up. A. S. M. Gow in Cambridge discovered that 'a good many members of this college, if not exactly sucklings, are at least entitled to an extra milk ration by reason of their tender years', and that in his subject, classics, he was 'lecturing to a class composed of thirteen ordinary undergraduates . . . young or unfit . . . eight R.N. cadets, seven R.A.F. cadets and two women'. The cadets, on 'university short courses' lasting six months, gave the impression to the casual visitor that times in the universities were more normal than they were. They were, in fact, awaiting commissions in the Forces and spent a good deal of each week on parades and military training, while Army cadets were

Painting out L.M.S. station name in Hertfordshire, June 1940.

**Awaiting Attack**

Uprooted signposts in Kent.

The first route march. Local Defence Volunteers in Berkshire, June 1940. (As yet their only uniform is an armband and many have no weapons.)

Weapon-training. Members of the London County Council Home Guard under instruction, August 1940. (By now they have denim uniforms and rifles. Machine guns were as yet few and far between.)

Anti-landing obstructions, July 1940. (Sewer pipes, wooden posts and old cars were all used as obstacles to prevent enemy troop carriers or gliders landing.)

Building a strongpoint at Admiralty Arch, May 1940. (This emplacement would have commanded Trafalgar Square and, at the rear, the Mall, leading to Buckingham Palace.)

## Shelter

*Piccadilly Circus underground
station during the Blitz.*

The un-moving staircase.

The platform where no-one
'hurries along'.

Rescue men removing a body
after an 'incident'.

Dover.

**Attack**

London.

## Duds

Royal Engineers removing a one ton bomb at an East London hospital.

Front garden in Hull, with land-mine.

Rescuing the files, Liverpool.

Rescuing the family treasures.

**Keeping going**

Collecting the mail.

Delivering the milk.

not allowed to attend lectures on any Arts subject. (The R.A.F. and Navy were more enlightened.)

Even the fortunate science students, who perhaps mixed a little uncomfortably with these transient military men, could not escape the war altogether. Early in the war University Joint Recruiting Boards were set up, including both military representatives and academic staff, to decide which students should be allowed to finish their academic courses or to re-take a failed examination. This rarely happened and anyone who 'ploughed' an examination was usually called up or, at best, directed to some menial scientific job in a war factory or government laboratory. As almost all male students, whatever their subject, were expected to do several hours a week National Service, either in the Senior Training Corps, successor to the pre-war Officers Training Corps, or in the Home Guard or Civil Defence, few had much time to spare. In 1943 one indignant club-man wrote to *The Times* from the comfortable seclusion of the Athenaeum alleging that many able-bodied men in this 'highly privileged class' were 'on various pretexts', doing nothing to help the war effort, but he was wrong. As one Cambridge tutor commented, 'Almost all the men concerned are engaged in squeezing three years' work into two. . . . My own worry for a long time past has been that they can hardly call their souls their own and are therefore missing a good deal of what in more spacious times the university has to offer them.'

Fire was a constant anxiety to the university authorities and fire-watching was taken very seriously. The defence of the famous buildings of Trinity College, Cambridge, rested on its senior tutor and among the classical texts on his desk, he remarked one day in March 1943, could now be seen *Simple Hydraulics for Firemen*, while the N.F.S. officer in charge of protecting the whole university was in normal times Professor of Hebrew. Dons now argued learnedly over such delightful trifles as whether the N.F.S. term 'static water', meaning a permanent supply, ought really to be applied to the River Cam, which was plainly in motion, while undergraduates enjoyed the opportunity to indulge legitimately in the popular Cambridge sport of roof-climbing. Foreign students, who could not be compelled to join the Forces and had no homes to go to in England, were often glad to stay on duty during vacations, when the colleges were most vulnerable. In August 1941 Gow at Trinity 'reinforced the Fire Party, which was already highly polyglot, with an Indian, a Lithuanian, a Rumanian and a brace of Turks for these . . . can stay behind and put the Library out', and at Christmas the colleges' safety rested on 'three Siamese, a German, a Russian and a Lithuanian'. 'Had you walked through the College on a Sunday afternoon', he wrote in December 1942, 'you would have come upon a massed stirrup-pump practice with some forty s.p.s attacking imaginary incendiaries from behind the pillars of Nevile's Court—an impressive and unusual scene. . . . I might have been found a fortnight later supervising in the greater privacy of the Lodge garden an s.p. practice for the Master, his wife and his domestic staff.'

Even without A.R.P. duties most university staff were hard worked, taking over the teaching of colleagues who had volunteered for government service. Some universities also squeezed an extra 'Long Vacation' term into the normal summer holiday, though at least one college decided that this merely deprived its students of time to absorb the past term's work and to relax before the next. 'In 1941 and later years', one academic remembers, 'Ernest Bevin . . . tried to "step up" production in degrees as in everything else. He considered one could compress not only the acquiring of information but that of . . . mental ripening into less time. . . . He would have liked everyone to have no more than two years at the university and for there to be four terms a year.' The general public, too, were unsympathetic to the universities' problems and there was frequently a good deal of hostility towards male students. A girl in Bangor witnessed an unpleasant scene 'one night in the chip shop when a little man came in half drunk and began to yell at the boys. He had had both sons killed that week at Tobruk and there were they, safe and protected and leading a lovely life. It ended in the little man fighting with tears streaming down his face.' When some cadets tried to revive the pre-war traditions of November 5th in Cambridge by starting bonfires in defiance of the black-out, there were angry demonstrations and shouts of 'You ought to be in the Army!', which, of course, most of the participants already were. A report in the *Daily Mirror* of one wartime Boat Race, rowed at Henley instead of in London, was derisively headlined: 'Oxford beat Cambridge by three lengths—as if you cared!' Other university sporting events were largely ignored, like the annual Varsity Rugger Match, now played alternately at Oxford or Cambridge instead of Twickenham. The Varsity Cricket Match was still held at Lord's, though it was noted in 1943 that the Oxford team contained no Old Etonians and few from other leading public schools; such boys, it was implied, knew where their duty lay. The traditional rivalry between the two ancient universities was kept up in other ways. It was said in 1940 that Oxford had attracted more freshmen than Cambridge because it had not been bombed—it never was—while when Cambridge beat Oxford at rugger in 1942 the *Oxford Magazine* suggested that many of the Cambridge side, being scientists, were able to escape military service while most Oxford stalwarts were doing their bit in the Army. Inter-college matches within the universities were also kept up, though on a reduced scale, the teams sometimes being reinforced by college servants.

On the surface, as I had discovered, apart from the sight of cadets drilling in the parks and notices about shelters and Fire Party Assembly Points littering the quadrangles and cloisters, Oxford and Cambridge looked remarkably unaffected by the war. Even gowns were still worn, though mostly secondhand, for when clothes rationing began in 1941 it was ruled that, though existing stocks were coupon-free, no more could be made. The same rules applied to the coloured silk and fur hoods worn by graduates on formal occasions, which were officially classed as hats. Mortar boards became scarce and wearing them ceased to be compulsory. Oxford, with its higher proportion of Arts students, was even more affected by the war than Cambridge. While it suspended most competitions for academic prizes for the duration, Cambridge continued to hold them but rewarded the winners of 'gold' medals with a substitute in bronze. Even 'rags' did not cease entirely. Some humorists in 1942 'improved' the appearance of the static water tank near King's College by floating on it punts and canoes painstakingly carried from the Cam. Other practical jokers, one don complained, still put 'inappropriate objects' on 'inaccessible pinnacles from which our decrepit and over-worked staff must risk their necks to retrieve them', stole 'notice-boards difficult or impossible to replace' and removed 'man-hole and coal-hole covers from the pavement so that those who walk the darkened streets . . . may break their legs'. In Oxford the hallowed peacetime tradition of taking a bath in a women's college was given an agreeable new twist by the war. One eighteen-year-old girl who, in October 1943, went up to St. Hilda's, always reputed to contain the most accommodating girls, was impressed by the ingenious reason advanced by some men visitors: with the amount of hot water for a bath strictly limited, one could have a deeper and more satisfying wallow in the smaller baths of the women's colleges than in the larger, older tubs in their own establishments.

If better off for hot water, however, women undergraduates in war, as in peace, probably came off worse for food. The same informant re-members seeing girls from another college nibbling loaves while working in a library, and invitations from men undergraduates to tea in their rooms were eagerly accepted, in the hope of getting a good meal—the men, she admits, often had other aims in mind. The girls returned hospitality by giving tea parties of their own, their personal rations of butter, tea and sugar, as in most institutions, being distributed in individual dishes.

Rationing soon took its toll, too, of the lavish catering for which before the war many men's colleges had been famous. By April 1940 even Trinity, Cambridge, had cut 'the undergraduate dinner by a course, limited private supply [for meals served in rooms] to dishes on the lunch and dinner menu and given notice to our more highly-paid chefs'. By Christmas 1941 the same writer was lamenting that 'the side-table, which should groan from Christmas to Epiphany with boar's head, game pies and the like', was bare, while by June 1942 even on High Table only three courses were being served for dinner, undergraduates were complaining that they got up still hungry and one fortnightly dining club, which had in the past provided 'seven courses and dessert', had been reduced after more than a century to 'a post-prandial party over some decanters'. In December 1944 the same author noted that 'rabbits and parsnips have again invaded the High Table in revolting force'. Oxford was little better off. One visitor to his old college, St. John's, in April 1942 unenthusiastically lunched in the Senior Common Room off such plebeian fare as sausage and mash.

Oxford and Cambridge colleges were slow to be affected by the wine shortage since they had usually laid in substantial cellars before the war. They suffered with the rest, however, from the lack of spirits and sherry which were rarely bought years ahead. By November 1942 at Trinity, Cambridge, sherry was being served to the dons only on Sundays, though 'claret still flows freely'. At Oxford, one 'short-course' naval cadet at Oriel in 1943 encountered no shortage of beer or cider, though every guest was expected to take a bottle with him to most parties. A St. Hilda's girl who went up in the same year discovered that the sole piece of advice given her beforehand by her father—'Don't drink whisky!'—was somewhat unnecessary as there was none to be had. 'Punch' of a not very potent kind continued to be served at college balls, Algerian wine could sometimes be bought, and some undergraduates, as at New College, could still buy sherry from the buttery, though rationed to one bottle a term. The brand was invariably the same and another girl, from a non-drinking home, admits she assumed that all sherry was called Dry Fly.

Although women M.P.s and other professional feminists complained throughout the war that women were not being given real equality with men, in the universities it was they who were the favoured sex. In October 1938 twice as many men as women were taking full-time university courses in Arts subjects in Great Britain; by 1943 male Arts students numbered only 3,500 against 8,100 women. Although women, like men, could obtain a degree in many subjects in two years, any who went up in 1943 or later were able to stay the normal three years if they wished, provided they passed their successive examinations. This was no mere formality. One girl reading history at Oxford found that it was essential not merely to pass her 'Part One' examination in the B.A. course, but to obtain 'first' or 'second' class honours, as anyone who only achieved a 'third' or a 'fourth' was promptly sent down. One student reading for her B.Sc. in dairying remembers 'a riotous year at Reading' before failing her Intermediate examination. 'Because of the war there were no second chances' and she had to leave and start work on a friend's farm. One seventeen-year-old girl discovered that at the University College of Southampton in 1942 to read for an Arts degree was 'considered unpatriotic', and that many girls found it impossible to cram a four year course into three years and were ruthlessly called up. Not surprisingly, with so much at stake, those who did survive did their best to forget about the war. It was, one girl at St. Hilda's, Oxford, remembers, never mentioned. Even volunteering was not encouraged. When this girl told her tutor she felt she ought to join the Forces she was sharply reminded that there was also a need in civilian life for the trained mind. She dutifully finished her course and went into the Board of Trade instead. A girl at Lady Margaret Hall who also felt guilty at not being in uniform was read an equally stern lecture and duly became on graduating an 'outdoor' inspector for the Ministry of Health, checking on pension claims and harrying farmers who objected to buying insurance stamps.

Unless called on to fire-watch, the only obligation on a girl student was to do at least two hours' national service a week during term, though war work during vacations was also encouraged. One girl at Southampton rolled bandages at a local hospital, and a woman undergraduate at Oxford cut sandwiches at a canteen for American servicemen and acted as a guide on their tours of the colleges. They were convinced that any girl at Oxford must come from a noble family and treated her with immense deference. A London university student experienced rather different reactions from British troops when doing her compulsory war work, 'carrying trays of egg and chips or fish and chips up three flights of stairs in an old house in Bangor to the sergeants' mess. . . . We usually went home rather bruised, as they pinched us and none of us quite knew how to cope with them.'

The war was clearly not the ideal time to be at university. A former professor at Durham feels that many students of that period 'look back without enthusiasm on their university life, not always realising that it was the war, not the university, that was to blame'. One London University student, who went up to a college dispersed by evacuation in 1939 and spent her whole three years under steadily worsening conditions, still feels 'cheated' when she compares her experiences with those of her sister, seventeen when the war finished, and those of her own three children, now enjoying student life in peacetime. In her day teaching was poor, for 'all the best people were in the ministries, all activities were curtailed and there were very few men about'. But another girl who went up to Southampton in 1942 found there was 'tremendous social life' due to the presence of R.A.F. air-crew cadets. 'Romances flourished, life hectic, very hard-up for money', she sums up her student life in phrases that would be equally characteristic of peacetime.

At Oxford, two St. Hilda's girls discovered, not merely were there too few men but even those were the wrong age. One girl arriving for her admission interview in 1942 was horrified, as her taxi crossed Magdalen Bridge, to see the succession of undersized male figures in caps and gowns on the pavement outside. She had been warned that the undergraduates might seem young, but these appeared mere children. They were; she was witnessing the arrival of the boys of Magdalen Choir School for Evensong in the college chapel.

The war produced, especially in Oxford, a dramatic change in the balance of the sexes. The normal surplus of men was replaced by an embarrassing shortage, made worse by competition from the most attractive evacuees in the country, the female students of the Slade School of Art. So scarce did boy friends become that even girls from Lady Margaret Hall, most socially exclusive of the women's colleges, used to go 'trawling', as they called it, in Blackwell's bookshop, pretending to take a close interest in the same display of books as some solitary male, until he took the hint and invited them to coffee. Hardly had one secured a man, however, than he was liable to go down, for cadets were up for only six months and ordinary undergraduates who came up at seventeen went off to the Forces after a year. Thus, while girls grew older, the men, apart from a few despised medical rejects or conscientious objectors, seemed to stay the same age. 'In one's first year it was not too bad, in one's second rather unsatisfactory and in one's third completely impossible', one girl, aged twenty-one when she went down, considers.

But, despite all the difficulties, a semblance of normal life was maintained, particularly at Oxford and Cambridge, where all through the war the innumerable literary and political clubs still met, and the Union still debated and elected its president, though from a narrow field of candidates. Women undergraduates, too, probably enjoyed more freedom than in peacetime, for their tutors had other preoccupations than their pupils' moral welfare. Elsewhere the war was often made the excuse for additional restrictions.

One University College student, evacuated from London to Bangor, found the atmosphere unsympathetic, with college dances finishing strictly at ten. The *Daily Express* (prompted by an Edinburgh University student, deprived of his usual partner) described how at the College of Domestic Science in Edinburgh in 1939 curfew now came down at black-out time. 'Some girls, who have not been able to see their boy friends for weeks, are threatening revolt against the curfew hour', ran the report. 'The authorities evidently want to make nuns out of us', one indignant girl was quoted as saying. If that was their intention they failed, for later the rules were relaxed.

Women teachers' training colleges had before the war been the most firmly disciplined and spartan of all further education establishments. One London student teacher, evacuated with the college which she had just joined, at the age of eighteen, in 1939 found herself attending lectures in the dining room of a country mansion, sleeping in a corridor and spending nights during warnings lying on a mat on the cold concrete floor of the laundry. A typical breakfast consisted of one apple and two slices of bread and margarine; the students saw one egg in two years. For her, college life was summed up in the black cocoa they drank night after night, almost milkless and with very little sugar. Another student of the same age was evacuated with the Froebel Educational Institute, from Roehampton to Knebworth House, Hertfordshire. Here the girls mainly occupied camp beds, but took it in turns to sleep in the imposing four-posters in the same bedrooms. In summer the butler would distribute bowls of beautiful chrysanthemums round the crowded rooms, and in the winter there was skating on the lake, to the music of a gramophone at the water's edge. To attend teaching practice the girls hitch-hiked. The principal worried about the dangers, but there was little alternative and the long-distance lorry drivers were, one student remembers, often most interesting company.

Most professional associations managed, by relaxing their regulations, to continue some form of entry during the war. It was, for example, still possible to qualify as a solicitor, though there were fewer examinations and no separate one for honours after November 1939. Time spent in the Forces counted towards qualifying, though—fortunately for future litigants—every would-be solicitor, war or not, still had to serve at least two years in a solicitor's office.

In 1939 part-time and evening study was still the most common method of obtaining most qualifications and, despite the black-out, before long many courses reopened. One woman who became secretary of the Technical (Evening) Institute at Richmond in 1941 remembers the unusual duties which the war imposed upon her. The Institute housed a party of North Country builders' workmen, sent to London to help in bomb-damage repair, 'who came in tired and dirty. Just as evening classes were about to start they were in the throes of undressing and washing themselves down. It was my duty to pilot the female students discreetly in through a side door. . . . All concerned thoroughly enjoyed it and were sorry when the men departed.' Her most unusual job, however, occurred when the siren sounded. She had then to go up to the Art class on the top floor, wrap the naked model in a blanket and escort her to the shelter protected, if not from enemy bombs, at least from prying eyes.

# A TIN HAT FOR THE BUDGIE

'Potatoes are plentiful and if you put in extra tubers when digging for victory you will not have it on your conscience that shipping space is being taken for food for your animals.'

R.S.P.C.A. leaflet, *Feeding Dogs and Cats in Wartime*, c. 1941

For pet animals the war must have been a bewildering, as well as a hungry, time and for many it proved fatal, not so much due to the malice of the enemy as to the over-solicitude of their owners. The British, a kindly, animal-loving people, were prepared to endure bombing themselves but were not ready to expose their pets to it. One duchess appealed for people to offer safe homes for unaccompanied animals in the country, and some enterprising firms offered to accommodate animal evacuees at rates from ten shillings a week for a normal-sized dog to a penny a day for a budgerigar. One Hampshire woman, living in the New Forest, whose main hobby was keeping animals and birds, found herself besieged with offers of horses and dogs to look after. One man, leaving London himself, turned up at the Rialto cinema, Enfield, with his six goldfish and asked if they could stay in the ornamental pool in the foyer for the duration. Others offered their animals to the Zoo. But the fate of an enormous number of much-loved pets was the lethal chamber. Of perhaps half a million dogs and one and a half million cats in Greater London, at least 400,000, mainly cats, were destroyed in the first four days of the war. 'The dust destructors', the R.S.P.C.A.'s war history recorded, 'could not . . . burn the bodies fast enough as they had to damp down furnaces at night owing to the black-out', and 80,000 dead pets were laid to rest in a secret, mass burial ground in the East End. Some veterinary surgeons were said to have moved to reception areas themselves, rather than continue this massacre of healthy animals. The tragedy was made worse by the fact that it was unnecessary and pet-owners drifted sheepishly back from evacuation to houses that must have seemed more empty because no dog wagged his tail in welcome and no purring cat climbed on to a familiar lap.

The R.S.P.C.A. had begun to make its plans for war as early as 1936 and its pamphlet *Air Raid Precautions for Animals* was soon the Bible on the subject. It included details of two devices for which thousands of animals and, their owners, were to have cause to be grateful in peace as well as in war, a 'cat and dog grasper', a running noose attached to a long handle which enabled frightened animals, or those wedged in inaccessible places, to be rescued and a 'quick release device', rather like that on a dog-lead or car safety belt, which made it possible rapidly to set free tethered animals in bombed or blazing buildings. Before the war began a National Air Raid Precautions Animals Committee, soon known as NARPAC, was set up which undertook such useful work as opening rescue centres for animals—there were seven hundred by 1945, often adjacent to rest centres for human beings. An appeal was broadcast for the public to lend garages and stables as air raid shelters for horses caught on the streets during a raid. The R.S.P.C.A. observed that 'a royal example was set by His Majesty the King who graciously allowed part of the Royal Mews to be set aside for the reception of bombed-out horses'. This later proved very useful and during the blitz brewery horses could be seen setting off on their rounds from these aristocratic surroundings.

For owners of pets, as for so many people in 1939, the great fear was gas. The People's Dispensary for Sick Animals produced a gas-proof kennel, a little like the Home Office gas helmet for babies but the animal himself operated the bellows supplying filtered air, costing £4, and there were many varieties of gas mask for dogs, the best of which, costing £9, was, ironically enough, made in Germany. The R.S.P.C.A. discouraged would-be purchasers of masks, however, since most pets would struggle fiercely against having a mask put on. Better, it advised, to give your pet a sedative tablet and swathe him in a wet blanket. A bee-keeper who, in all seriousness, wrote to enquire about gas masks for his bees was comforted with the reply that, 'although bees would no doubt be very sensitive to poison gas, it was unlikely that the enemy, with all his resources, could so saturate the air of the countryside as to harm the bees themselves'.

Pet-owners have always been inclined to claim exceptional intelligence for their pets but the evidence is overwhelmingly that both dogs and cats soon learned to recognise the sound of the siren, and even, it was claimed, to distinguish between the warning and the All Clear. Some animals began to stir even before the siren for dogs, with their well developed powers of hearing, sometimes picked up the noise of distant gunfire or aircraft before human ears could do so. Some dogs, in the early days at least, leapt happily to their feet at the sound of the siren, evidently believing it to be some super whistle summoning them to a gigantic walk; others dived hastily under the nearest bed or scuttled off under the stairs without bothering about their masters' safety. One Birmingham family conscientiously practised their air raid drill, which involved the mother carrying their son to the shelter while her husband clipped on the dog's lead. When the sirens really went he did not wait to be led, but 'as soon as the door was opened . . . was out and into the shelter before anyone. How pleased he looked with himself for being so clever!' Some dogs also remembered their obligations to their owners. One Banstead dog, when the siren went, would hurry upstairs to wake his master, who was in the Home Guard, and Dusty, the pet of a Birmingham A.R.P. worker, would, when the siren went, sit looking at her tin hat with a 'Do your duty' look on his face, wagging his tail in approval when she put it on then settling in to his own shelter under the stairs. Rex, a mongrel living near the Crystal Palace, had an even more elaborate routine. 'At the sound of the Alert Rex would rush to the hall-stand and knock the gas mask from its place there, then run back to his mistress . . . and . . . push her to the front door . . . Having installed his mistress in the garden shelter . . . he next proceeded to collect the next-door neighbour and, when both ladies were seated in deck-chairs in comparative safety, Rex would take up his post in the doorway to guard them from invaders. When the All Clear sounded, he shepherded his little party back to the house and shared their tea or cocoa with a complacent air.' Some families credit their dogs with saving their lives, like the man with a wife and six-year-old son whose Airedale bitch 'kept running to the cellar and back again pushing against my legs and whining . . . My wife said, "Look! The dog wants us to go to the cellar. Let's go." The three of us then rushed to the cellar with the dog following and we had only just reached it when the whole house collapsed. The table under which we had been sheltering was smashed to atoms.' Cats on the whole treated raids with their customary disdain. One London office cat regularly curled up on the papers in the 'In' tray when the sirens went, a perch normally denied him. A Crowborough family were puzzled because their cat failed to join them in the shelter during one lunch-time raid. They discovered the reason when the All Clear went; the cat, whose normal diet was threepenny 'pussy pieces' of fish, had discovered their four plaice dinners already on the table and stayed behind to eat the lot. 'I bought a bun on the way back to work', its owner remembers. An Isle of Wight cat, Megs, also had her priorities. She normally hated the raids but, even if 'all hell was let loose above', stayed out quite happily during the courting season. Mother cats with small kittens, as all cat-lovers would have expected, invariably put their families first. A Bristol woman remembers her cat carefully carrying her kittens one by one down to the cellar when the siren sounded, and many R.S.P.C.A. inspectors spent patient minutes trying to coax a bedraggled female cat out of a ruined building, so they could rescue her kittens. In one coastal town 'another heroic cat', shut up in the house, actually carried her fourteen-day-old kittens one by one 'from her warm basket in the kitchen to an open bedroom window and thence, by way of the telephone wires, to a potting shed in the gardens . . . Next day she was discovered . . . sound asleep with her babies in the new nursery she had found for them.'*

When pets and owners were reunited after a raid it was often difficult to say who was the more moved. A sixteen-year-old Bath girl remembers their cat staying all day in her arms in the rest centre, as though realising that she, or perhaps himself, needed company and reassurance. Some cats, which had refused to be nursed in normal times, now condescended with bombs falling to sit on any lap that was available. Sadly, however, not all pets could accompany their bombed-out owners to their new home. A Southwark housewife remembers how faithful Ginger had to be put to sleep when the family had to go to stay with relatives in Brixton. She made amends by burying him in the alien soil of their garden with an explanatory epitaph:

> Here lies Ginger from No. 1
> Who because of Hitler to death was done.

Small animals were often remarkably unperturbed by bombs. A Barking man noticed that his tame rabbit did not seem to be in the least put out when his hutch was spun round by blast or moved several feet. Birds, both chickens and domestic pets, rarely stood up to bombing so well. One Birmingham housewife still mourns 'an insignificant victim of war', her pet budgerigar, which, through excitement during a raid, flew violently against the top of its cage and broke its neck. Another Birmingham budgie was of a more heroic cast. 'Joey's cage', his owner remembers, 'was well equipped with playthings and at the top, with a handy perch just below, was a lovely bell, just the size of Joey's head. Now and again one of the family would cry excitedly, "Joey! The Germans are coming! Get under your tin hat!" Joey would hurriedly hop to his top perch, push hard until his little head was right inside the bell and exclaim in his croaky little voice: "Damn Hitler!" '

When the blitz did come, the A.R.P. arrangements for animals worked well. Horses, of which there were still 40,000 in Greater London at the start of the war, were the worst problem, for rescuers found it almost impossible to persuade them to leave burning stables or to walk past blazing houses. A traditional country trick was sometimes tried with, it was said, success, using a goat to lead the first horse, which seemed to calm its fears. Rescue workers and police, R.S.P.C.A. inspectors and veterinary surgeons, often spent hours trying to rescue trapped animals and in the East End people evacuating bombed houses often left their

* The R.S.P.C.A. points out that though this seems a tall story, cats had in the past been trained to do a 'tight-rope walk' as a music hall turn.

dogs tied to the gate posts of their houses, confident that someone would arrive to take care of them. One woman R.S.P.C.A. worker travelled round the City the morning after the great fire blitz collecting cats from the bombed office buildings, before they could add to the swarms of strays already roaming the bombed sites, often hungry and increasingly wild. Animals left behind when an area was evacuated, due to unexploded bombs, were a constant worry and in Hull an appeal was broadcast for the owners of temporarily empty houses to hand in keys so that the R.S.P.C.A. staff could get in, at their own risk, and feed the abandoned pets.

Rescuing animals was often a thankless job. A dog which the manager of the Dogs' Home in Hull patted reassuringly after 'the house had dropped on its kennel' promptly bit him, but he concluded philosophically that this was 'perhaps his way of thanking us'. Another night's work involved 'roaming in and out of burning warehouses, picking cats up' and, perhaps worst of all, rescuing the contents of a bombed pet shop, which included three pups and 'nine more dogs, very frightened'. In the two big raids of May 1941 he dealt with nearly 600 animals including, besides many dogs and cats, sixty-two birds, fifty-five pigs, forty-seven rabbits, ten chickens, two fish, two parrots and a monkey. Parrots were not uncommon in Hull, a seaport, and one showed its gratitude by singing 'true to tune, *Rule, Britannia.* . . . A very good and appropriate solo.'

The toughest caged birds were, this man found, canaries. 'Put seed and water in to them and nearly every time the canary would have a drink and a bath.' The frailest were budgerigars. 'Budgies just sat tucked up, never cleaned the dust from their throats and . . . died.' Fish were also vulnerable to shock and, of course, to their bowls being broken.

Owing to their decreased numbers, due to the mass slaughter at the start of the war and the difficulties of feeding them, cats and dogs proved less of a post-raid problem than had been expected, but chickens and rabbits were more numerous as many people were now rearing these for food and the normal restrictions by landlords and local authorities had been lifted. Bombs often demolished chicken runs and it was not at all unusual to find their occupants waddling along a city road the morning after a raid. One East End vicar was gratified to see a hen leaving his church after laying an egg in a pew. As petrol rationing drove lorries off the road the number of horses drawing delivery vans also increased.

These horses never went short of food. Hay was the 'filler' of the animal kingdom and, like bread for humans, remained unrationed throughout the war, though sometimes scarce and expensive. Work horses also received an official ration of food and, also like humans, were given a supplementary allowance where their work was especially hard. In one respect, however, they were luckier—outsize horses also got an extra ration. But horses kept for pleasure riding received no rations and some, the R.S.P.C.A. believes, 'had a very bad time'.

Of all domestic animals, dogs probably came off worst, for they needed something more substantial than scraps from the table, and in wartime even these were exceedingly few. Queues of dog-owners could regularly be seen outside pet-food shops, often with their pets standing patiently in line beside them. Some horse-meat intended for animals ended up on the black market and was probably the source of a good many of the steaks in restaurants, though meat not intended for human consumption was supposed to be sprayed with a bright green dye which both looked and smelt repellent. Though never officially rationed, it was strictly controlled in price, and R.S.P.C.A. inspectors were often in court to denounce those who were making illicit profits at the expense of some hungry terrier or spaniel. There was little public indignation against such opportunists, though one newspaper cartoon showed two long-tailed rodents arriving at the headquarters of the R.S.P.C.A. to complain that 'We can't have Black Marketeers described as rats!'

Tinned cat and dog food, though not on points, was even scarcer than fresh meat and the London journalist Charles Graves thought it worth recording in his published diary that he found in Harlech in September 1942 a tin of *Red Heart* for his dog. To buy dog biscuits also involved a long and often fruitless hunt. One Birmingham woman remembers her bull terrier had to manage on an inadequate ration of one pound of dog biscuits, but there were recipes for home-made ones, like that followed by a housewife from Rayleigh in Essex, which involved moistening wholemeal flour with Oxo in water, adding bacon rind and fragments of meat fat, shaping the mixture into balls and putting them in the bottom of the oven to bake slowly. One Ipswich dog thrived on whalemeat and a Bristol woman reared four healthy puppies on crusts, fish offal and horsemeat, eked out by goats' milk. A Wolverhampton dog lived to be fourteen on a diet of shredded wheat. One Scotswoman remembers that when her 'Scottish terrier, Sheila, presented us with a litter of puppies, after a love affair with a neighbour's Cairn, we had to give up our dried milk and dried egg ration for a month to let her fulfil her motherhood and to give her endearing litter a chance in life. It must . . . have been nourishing, for the brood were incredibly lively.' The puppies, 'three dogs and a bitch all showing characteristics of their Cairn sire in a slightly ginger hue, but otherwise miniatures of Sheila herself', caught the fancy of an army officer billeted on the household, who regularly brought them a parcel of kitchen scraps. If he forgot this he would turn round and cycle all the way back to barracks rather than disappoint the dogs. 'Tired as he was he could not face the eager committee of welcome without the parcel.'

Most cats managed to achieve their usual sleek, well-fed look even during the war, though a Durham nurse recalls how Felix, the handsome black cat who roamed the nurses' home and normally lived on lean chicken and cream, had gradually to adapt his aristocratic tastes to more humble fare. Great alarm was felt among cat-owners when it became illegal to give fresh milk to their pets, though some experts considered that fresh water was far better for them. 'Many cats', the R.S.P.C.A. admits, 'did not take kindly to the new regulations. . . . However, as a result of representations'—presumably from their owners—'the Ministry of Food were able to make a slight concession', releasing 'limited quantities of dried milk' for cats who were contributing to the war effort by keeping down mice and rats in warehouses and later making a similar allowance to sick cats.

The war produced, too, one unexpected benefit for cat-owners in cities. A nurse at the Middlesex Hospital who had found it difficult in peacetime to obtain earth in Central London for the cat she kept in her flat now filled his litter tray with sand from the balloon site in Regent's Park.

It became an offence to give bread to birds, and a Liverpool woman now confesses to 'skulking out like a thief in the night' to scatter crusts in the road for the sparrows. Caged birds suffered even more, and a Nottingham housewife's wartime misdemeanour was falsely declaring to a shopkeeper that she had two birds to get her budgie, Mickey, an extra ration. Such bird-seed as was available was sold often without millet, its most useful ingredient, and a Lancashire housewife remembers millet soaring to £1 per pound on the black market. A Rotherham woman remembers that even ordinary bird-seed reached this price, but was so unnutritious that the family budgie, like many more, simply went into a fatal decline when fed on it. Animals, like humans, did better if they lived in the country. One Worcestershire woman managed to keep an aviary full of canaries and budgerigars fed by gathering the fine seeds which fell from the local farmer's threshing machine, and the cats of a Tenderden family fed not merely themselves but their owners by hunting for rabbits. And some people still managed to feed large and unusual pets. A Blackpool housewife remembers tea with friends who owned a pet chimpanzee. 'I was hungry', she remembers, 'but couldn't eat—it tucked in to bits from my plate.' A Cambridgeshire housewife remembers visiting a stately home where a hungry peacock, usually an aloof creature, condescended to come down from the roof and eat cake-crumbs from her hand.

Feeding animals was not a responsibility of the Ministry of Food, but many NARPAC publications contained a strong echo of Lord Woolton's propaganda. One such booklet, *Wartime Aids for Animal Owners*, stressed the need for a balanced diet for cats and dogs, containing its proper quota of 'energy-giving', 'body building' and 'protective' foods. A large Pekinese weighing ten pounds needed, it warned, five to six ounces of carbohydrates, an ounce of protein and a quarter ounce of fat at each meal, while for a twenty-five-pound Scots terrier and a sixty-pound Airedale the amounts needed to be scaled up accordingly.

The R.S.P.C.A. also did its best to reassure harassed pet-owners. 'This country has not reached a stage when the wholesale destruction of household pets is necessary', one leaflet, *Feeding Dogs and Cats in Wartime*, comfortingly advised. 'Potatoes are plentiful and if you put in extra tubers when digging for victory you will not have it on your conscience that shipping space is being taken for food for your animals. . . . Potatoes boiled in their jackets . . . are not ordinarily recommended for dogs and cats but the harmful effect is avoided if they are mixed with gravies made from bones. The bones can then be used for waste collection . . . for war purposes. . . . Or you can purchase stewing meat with your coupons and give the gravy from such meat to your animal . . . a sacrifice that every owner would be prepared to make.' Other suggested diets for dogs consisted of stale bread and oatmeal, 'made into thick porridge' and mixed with meat scraps from the table, or stale bread mixed with 'chopped cabbage, cauliflower, brussels sprouts, turnip, carrot or other green leaves' moistened with 'soup or gravy made from bones or scraps'. Cats, the R.S.P.C.A. said hopefully, 'will usually eat the food recommended in the above diets, provided there is included some meat gravy, sardine oil, or oil liquids made from fish trimmings. . . . The Ministry of Food will not permit the use of cod liver oil for household pets.' About feeding birds, the R.S.P.C.A. was even more encouraging. 'Seeds from plantains, dandelions, groundsel and chickweed are all suitable for canaries and budgies and chopped raw root crops such as carrots, turnips and swedes will provide an alternative diet. For parrots, oats, rye, barley, wheat as well as sun-flower seeds may be used.' The R.S.P.C.A. urged bird-lovers to use every visit to the country to stock up their birds' larders and to dig for victory on their behalf and grow seeds for them, though—somewhat ironically—'It will be necessary to protect the plants from the depredation of birds'.

Animals did not on the whole take kindly to rationing and most owners suffered at some time from dishonest cats and dogs. The pig food bins, to an animal's eye clearly indistinguishable from normal dustbins, were one obvious target, and a Hull housewife remembers how they were often emptier in the mornings for, under cover of darkness, the local cats and dogs were getting there before the pigs. Shopkeepers, too, were the victims of raids by hungry animals and a housewife from Essex remembers seeing a couple of half-starved cats dragging the local fishmonger's only cod along the street whilst he was busy serving a customer. Even farm animals, usually well fed and well trained, sometimes forgot themselves. A Richmond cost clerk remembers the bacon ration being stolen by one of the cats on a farm in Bedford where he and his wife were staying, and a Birmingham Guide company lost all their bacon when the farmer's dog discovered it in the air raid shelter where it had been put to keep cool, though the farmer compensated them with duck's eggs. Relations between pets and their owners became strained when a cat or dog decided to supplement its rations at their expense. A Birmingham housewife recalls the shock of emerging from the shelter to discover that the cat had eaten the weekend joint, and a woman staying in Exeter remembers when her neighbour's Dachshund got hold of half a pound of butter and spent 'a glorious few minutes', together with her own Scottish terrier, 'licking up the butter from the flagstones in the sunshine outside their kitchen'. One Bristol family were starting on a supper of biscuits and the last of their week's cheese when the sirens went. 'We all dived under the large dining table as we heard the first bomb fall, and on emerging found our dog had polished off all our suppers. He was licking his lips, and looking not the least ashamed.'

If they reasoned the matter out at all, animals in wartime seem to have assumed that they were entitled to anything they could reach. The Scots dog-owner already mentioned insists that her terrier, Sheila, even with four puppies to support, 'would never have stolen anything from the house', but 'one day . . . the butcher, foolishly, left . . . our meat ration . . . on the step of the back door . . . and Sheila, always hungry, finding the meat on her own level, must have felt that the gods had been extra kind and it was legitimately hers. We were appalled when we came home and found her at the stage of licking the paper which had contained the treat. That evening it was *us* that had the dried eggs.' It was difficult, however, to make the same excuse for the Welsh puppy which, its owner remembers with a mixture of pride and exasperation, would pull the tablecloth off the dining room table to get at the food and lick the sugar basin and butter dish clean, nor for the Swindon dog which stole a whole cooked rabbit. 'Life wasn't the same for days', her owner remembers, 'and the dog slunk about like a criminal on short rations', and even though it was entirely her own fault, 'she objected loudly to a diet of Marmite and bread'. Even more infuriating were pets which stole from others. A London housewife remembers her cat creeping in one day with an enormous steak in her mouth, the source of which she never did discover, and one Sussex villager remembers the curious coincidence that whenever her Gordon setter killed a chicken it always turned out to be someone's best laying pullet, though she always insisted on keeping the dead bird after paying for it. Worst of all was a pet which stole from friends. A Crouch End housewife visiting a married friend with her dog, Judy, was deeply embarrassed to find that Judy had helped herself to the luncheon meat put out on the table for tea, which had cost an enormous number of points. 'I couldn't', she admits, 'wait to get out of the house.'

Racing pigeons were in a special position throughout the war, as the only pets also useful to the war effort. Many R.A.F. aircrews, shot down over the sea, owed their lives to birds trained and donated to the nation by one of the 20,000 pigeon fanciers who belonged to the National Pigeon Service.* A pigeon cannot, however, be trained overnight; it needs to be 'tossed'—released—over gradually increasing distances from the time it is ten weeks old until it can, perhaps after four seasons, fly from 700 to 1,000 miles, and for these reasons, although under strict controls due to fear of pigeons being used by spies, pigeon racing continued throughout the war. Special pigeons' ration books entitled every fancier to buy enough corn each week for twenty birds, but many had previously maintained far more and now had to harden their hearts and select for destruction those pigeons showing the least promise. In fact 'the food sold under the title of National Pigeon Corn was disgraceful', one authority remembers. 'In most instances pigeon fanciers were giving up eggs and other foodstuffs in order to feed their pigeons a protein diet on which robust young ones could be raised.'

Birds which survived the food shortage were always liable to fall victim to the bombs, for, unlike cats and dogs, pigeons in flight could not take shelter. One enthusiast, living at Weybridge during the V.1 period, remembers that 'Overhead were some thirty-six barrage balloons protecting the Vickers-Armstrong factory, so our birds had to thread their way through the balloon cables. . . . My wife and I will never forget dashing out to the pigeon loft to time-in racing pigeons as they dropped between exploding V bombs. . . . Altogether some 600 bombs fell round us but we and our pigeons possessed charmed lives because apart from some small damage to the house we all lived happily ever after.'

The biggest and best-known concentration of animals in the country was at the London Zoo in Regent's Park. For many of the animals, the war began with evacuation, to Whipsnade in Bedfordshire, the evacuees including, according to *The Times*, 'the giant pandas, the two mating elephants, two young yak calves, fallow red and Chinese water deer fawns, two baby brown bears, the little black lamb which was deposited by Princess Elizabeth and Princess Margaret, and several goats'. Some of the inmates left behind in London, including the poisonous snakes, had been destroyed at the start of the war and the aquarium was also

* The number of active fanciers pre-war was 70,000 and is now about 250,000.

drained for fear that a bomb might deluge the immediate vicinity with 200,000 gallons of water, plus some hundreds of rare, and no doubt surprised, species of fish. By mid-September 1939 the Zoo was able to reopen after its first period of closure for 110 years. Even the reptile houses could be visited again though they now contained only 'a small collection of lizards, crocodiles and harmless snakes', and visitors were reassured that 'On the All Clear being sounded the Zoo A.R.P. officers, before allowing anyone out of the shelters, will tour the gardens accompanied by riflemen, who in the event of any dangerous animals having been liberated by damage to their cages will round them up or shoot them'. Visitors were, however, slow to return and for some time it was a case of the animals watching the humans. 'Anybody who passes the sea-lions' pond', noted *The Times* reporter, 'invariably attracts its inhabitants out on to the verge of grass, where they follow him round like a string of waddling sausages, with the old male at the head.' The reason was, of course, that they missed their usual titbits of fish, but 'fish-eating animals are already being persuaded to accept a diet of meat instead'.

The Zoo's occupants suffered throughout the war more from food shortage than from bombs. By April 1944 its Director could report that though many buildings had been damaged not a single animal had been killed, though when 'The zebra house was demolished by a direct hit . . . the twenty-year-old "Johnson" . . . escaped from the Gardens and ran for half a mile before he was caught. On the same night the wall of the monkey hall was breached by a bomb and the colony of Indian rhesus monkeys ran wild for several days.' Later the camel house was also hit, but its two occupants proved equally contemptuous of the tiles clattering down on them. When I visited the Zoo early in 1944, I found it remarkably normal, and the number of visitors in 1943, 1,600,000, was not markedly down on the two million of 1938. The Director's claim that 'We feel we have helped materially in providing healthy recreation and instruction for members of our own and the allied forces and also for war workers who cannot go further afield' was obviously not unjustified, and by now the cages and enclosures offered almost the same range of animals as in peacetime, plus one new acquisition, Polly Anna, a young reindeer given to British sailors by a Russian warship and romantically brought to England by submarine.

Polly Anna was fed by a distant admirer who collected sackfuls of her normal food, Iceland moss, on the Welsh mountains and other 'kind friends from various parts of the country' provided evergreen oak for the okapi and bamboo shoots for the giant panda. Carnivorous animals survived on horse-meat, but it had, the Director admitted, 'been very difficult to find fish for our sea-lions, penguins and other fish-eating birds'. In despair the sea-lions had been reduced to two; two more had been sent to the United States, but, like human evacuees, had pined for home, one dying en route and the other on arrival. 'Fruit-eating mammals and birds . . . ' the Director reported, 'seem to thrive on vegetables, of which carrots are undoubtedly the most valuable'—a tribute which must have delighted the Ministry of Food. Nor had the dangerous snakes perished in vain, for their glass-fronted dens were 'now occupied by domesticated breeds of rabbit noted for their fur and food value'.

But if Zoo animals had not suffered real hunger, they had, like human beings, missed their traditional luxuries and instead of regarding with bored indifference the food offered to them by visitors, they now looked eagerly for it. A Shenfield woman remembers 'one perfect day in the summer of 1944' when her husband was on leave and they visited the Zoo together. 'It was almost deserted and as I'd managed to get a bag of peanuts . . . we received a great welcome from monkeys and parrots alike. The parrots shook the bars of their cages in their efforts to gain our attention, and recited their party pieces with wild abandon . . . to wheedle a peanut from me. I have never enjoyed a day at the Zoo so much.' A woman living near Bristol Zoo witnessed an even more significant scene which symbolised the deprivations of animals in wartime. One monkey she noticed, was busy parcelling up a banana-skin; it contained, not a banana, but a small potato.

# DIG FOR VICTORY

'We want not only the big man with the plough but the little man with the spade to get busy this autumn . . . Let "Dig for Victory" be the motto of everyone with a garden.'

Broadcast by the Minister of Agriculture, 4th October 1939

The Chamberlain government had always felt more at home with plough-shares than swords and the campaign for increased food production was the only one which it began to fight wholeheartedly and vigorously immediately the war began. The first appeal to farmers was made on 5th September 1939, and was followed a month later by a broadcast by the Minister of Agriculture, Sir Reginald Dorman Smith: 'Half a million more allotments properly worked will provide potatoes and vegetables that will feed another million adults and one and a half million children for eight months out of twelve. . . . So, let's get going. Let "Dig for Victory" be the motto of everyone with a garden and of every able-bodied man and woman capable of digging an allotment in their spare time.'

Besides cultivating allotments millions of men turned over their existing lawns and flower beds to vegetables. In those early days there was often more enthusiasm than skill. A Ryde woman, married to a professional gardener, felt that many first-class lawns and flower gardens were devastated to grow 'far from first-class cabbages and potatoes' and amateur efforts often began with a disillusioning disappointment, as at one Hertfordshire teacher training college, where the students having laboured to plant nine hundred cabbages found not one left next morning —rabbits had eaten the lot. A Birmingham man encountered a novel form of digging for victory by 'evacuees from London who encouraged their teenage children to dig in their own garden and tunnel under the fence into my friends'. Then they would steal the potatoes from underground leaving the foliage untouched.'

But most people took their new hobby very seriously and bean sticks and rows of cabbages were soon to be seen not merely in back gardens but in front. Keen local councils grew potatoes in their parks or on the grass verges of suburban streets. One woman remembers seeing in Tunbridge Wells 'the flower beds in the Calverley Grounds . . . planted with vegetables and very attractive they looked, with the feathery tops of carrots and slender spikes of onions'. An employee of a vegetable canning firm in Harrow recalls seeing 'beetroot and parsnips growing in borders where there should have been bedding plants' and helping to cultivate a former rubbish tip. 'We dug up everything', she remembers. 'Pails, baths, bicycle wheels, china, glass, old coins. . . . My best effort was a gold hatpin head set with turquoise. My worst was to find the soil moving about eight feet away when I was digging—it was a railway sleeper. But despite all that we grew wonderful crops. Shallots, leeks of enormous size and cabbages grew so fast they split and marrows that would not shame any harvest festival.' No manure was available but substitutes were found. 'Ashes and soot from the boiler-house, wool shoddy from the floors of mills . . . spent hops from a nearby brewery, dumped still warm from the vats. . . . What a time the birds had, sorting out the few grains left. They stumbled around and fell over, drunk.' Railway embankments, waste land and, before long, bombed sites in the hearts of the blitzed cities, all took on a new appearance as every square foot of land was eagerly made to yield its harvest. Even window boxes and the ornamental tubs outside West End clubs grew tomatoes. In some schools gardening replaced games as the chief outdoor exercise and it became the great spare-time occupation for all age-groups, with the number of allotments in England and Wales rising from 815,000 in 1939 to a peak of 1,450,000 in 1942.

A useful, little-publicised, contribution to the Grow More Food campaign was made by those who ran local allotment or gardening societies. One housewife on a new estate at Shirley, near Croydon, found that the war brought closer together the thirty-two families, most of them young married couples with small children, who lived in her road. Those who were not evacuated 'became closely knit as a band of neighbours, all out to help each other. We would exchange recipes and goods on coupons.' But it was digging for victory which cemented these new bonds, after the local council had 'let a large piece of waste ground at ten shillings per year for ten rods'. Her husband was a leading member of a local Horticultural Society who 'being over service age offered to do all he could to help the campaign. Our car was docked in a corner and the garage stocked with bags of lime and National Grow-more. It was a usual thing for us to be in and out during meal times, weighing up 7 lb. of Growmore for small boys who came in on Mum's behalf. Most of the young men had joined up and to help the wives to carry on we obtained seedlings of cabbage, leeks, Brussels, in fact anything that could be easily grown. . . . Over the years we . . . disposed of thousands of plants . . . especially tomato plants. . . . It was a work of art to pack thousands of small greens into packets of one dozen, which in some cases was all the garden would hold.'

The secretary of one Northumberland Allotment and Horticultural Society, founded in June 1940, discovered that his duties in this post took up what little spare time he had left from his job as a travelling Board of Trade Safety Inspector for docks and railways. On one August Saturday in 1942 he was up at 5 a.m. to open the hall for competitors in a fruit and vegetable show, held in aid of the Red Cross, and the same month found him busy at Percy Main, near North Shields. 'Disposal squad in the fields examining the craters and debris', he noted in his diary. 'I called a meeting in the playing field of people with damaged crops and greenhouses, gave out forms, told the meeting how to fill them in and arranged to send them on. . . . Had a series of small meetings on the plots and warned the people not to eat anything off the plots as they were riddled with glass splinters, tomatoes and cucumbers especially.' A few weeks later he was busily transporting 'six pullets, four cockerels and two fat hens' in an old tin trunk, with the lid wedged open, on a bus to Hull and 'the conductress had a fright when they started cackling'.

The transition from amateur horticulture to part-time · husbandry was one that many 'dig for victory' enthusiasts began to make from 1940 onwards. As *Fur and Feather*, the rabbit-fanciers' magazine, pointed out, courageously accepting that these animals could now serve their owners better as food than as pets, a single tame rabbit could yield two and a half pounds of meat for negligible cost. In 1940 the government lifted all legal restrictions on keeping poultry and rabbits in domestic gardens and many local councils, after years of banning back-yard poultry runs and rabbit hutches, began to encourage them. One West Country local government official had a new duty laid upon him: to turn the citizens of Weston-super-Mare into eager rabbit-breeders. He tackled the job energetically, with an article in the local press offering the mouth-watering prospect of 'Forty tons of coupon-free meat a year for Weston people . . . if every local allotment-holder will keep one doe rabbit for breeding purposes'. It seems unlikely that this optimistic target was ever achieved, but before long 'members of the Rabbit Club wore satisfied smiles and many more townspeople wore fur-backed gloves'.

Even the humble bunny was expected to earn his, or more especially her, keep in wartime and no official ration for rabbits was provided unless their owners undertook to sell half of every litter to an approved customer, such as a hospital. This regulation, one Hertfordshire rabbit-owner decided, was more trouble than it was worth, for the official ration was only four pounds of food a quarter for each breeding doe, and she soon had her hutches full of rabbits growing appetisingly plump on a diet of wallflowers and lupins. Other rabbits cheerfully gobbled up carrot tops and the tough outside leaves of cabbage and dandelion plants, happily unaware of the fate awaiting them, which weighed far more heavily on their owners. A young Birmingham housewife, who had lovingly boiled up potato peelings mixed with oats, and baked crusts of bread, for her rabbits, found that 'We couldn't bring ourselves to kill them'. Her scruples did one of the animals no good, for 'someone came one night and stole one, for a dinner no doubt'. A Liverpool factory worker whose cousin kept rabbits remembers that 'one day one was killed and prepared by the butcher. Dinner was duly served—but one by one the plates were pushed away untouched. Poor Daisy had died in vain and the other rabbits died of old age.' Phoebe, a large, fat, white rabbit nearly escaped eating, too, for a Dagenham schoolboy discovered that neither his mother nor sister could face consuming this old family friend. At last he was sent with her to an aunt in Southend where Phoebe was speedily converted into stew, though he tactfully concealed her background until the meal was over. A Hull woman who had 'never skinned a rabbit or plucked a hen in her life', or reared either, speedily learned all these arts with the aid of *The Smallholder*, which is still remembered with gratitude by many wartime readers. 'I never ate any of our own rabbits', she admits, 'but my husband enjoyed them.'

The most popular type of domestic livestock was poultry and the clucking of hens or the crowing of cocks became a familiar sound in many a suburban road during the war. The neighbours of a woman living in Laleham, Middlesex, were not at all pleased when she installed two dozen chickens—half of them cockerels given to loud crowing at dawn—in a home-made chicken run in her garden, but rapidly began to come round when the eggs began to arrive. They were wholly won over by being given three eggs a day in rotation and the promise of a chicken at Christmas, and were soon willingly contributing scraps to feed the birds.

The arrival of the first chicken in one's garden was often the beginning of a long and fascinating saga of adventures. This, for example, was the story of Dinah, one of two old hens whom a housewife living at Kesgrave, near Ipswich, attempted to rear.

Our egg ration was nil for weeks at a time . . . so it was frustrating that Dinah just would not be broody. Until, a very cold and early spring, Dinah decided she would do her bit, and became broody at last. Neighbours helped me with a sitting of eggs and because of the cold I put her coop in the warmest angle in a shed at the top of the garden. She sat well. I was thrilled, seeing already the cakes and puddings I would soon be making, with lashings of eggs. The last week of sitting was wild and blustery, I was glad when the final day arrived. Looking at the front eggs in the morning, and afternoon, I decided to leave operations until evening, which seemed very long in coming indeed.

However, at last I removed the front from the coop and oh! oh!, what a terrible shock! Eggs lay scattered everywhere, broken and stone cold of course. A rat had disturbed poor Dinah in those last few hours. Dejectedly I cleared away the mess and went indoors—to brood myself! After breakfast next day I went to move Dinah back with Daisy. She still sat and clucked to me. I said: 'Well, old girl, we've had it.' As I spoke a tiny black head, with yellow beak, shot out of her snow-white back feathers—gave me the once over, and shot back again. Delighted, I wondered if there were any more, but that was the only one. . . . I then decided to try her with day-old chicks, to make up the full brood. Everyone said she would not take them; she did, going mad with excitement. Strangely enough, she wouldn't have anything to do with her one natural chick, I had to feed him separately, but he always managed to slip into her feathers to sleep. . . . After the awful first disappointment, everything turned out well, Dinah and I not losing a single chick.

A Dorset housewife remembers how, after her family had decided to keep chickens, 'we converted an old shed and I will never forget the hours I spent cleaning out the place. The smell was awful. That and the smell of boiling potato peelings I will always remember.' A Burton-on-Trent housewife fed her chickens 'mostly . . . on dried bread crusts, which were baked and put through the mincer, along with cabbage, sprout or even dandelion leaves. We did get a ration of peculiar stuff called Balancer Meal, resembling sawdust, but it was never enough.'

To obtain this 'peculiar stuff' meant surrendering one's egg ration, though if you had fewer than twenty hens you could keep any eggs they laid. Above this number a permit from the Food Office was needed which entitled one to keep a specified number of eggs, though it was a conscientious citizen who did not smuggle an occasional extra egg into her own or her neighbour's kitchen. One might have to ask for the shell back later, less to conceal the evidence of crime than for pounding up to provide the chicken with grit to form new shells—an economical method which many women found distressingly suggestive of encouraging cannibalism.

Many wartime poultry-keepers gained their knowledge at a high price. One woman living at Tenterden, Kent, found that the three bantams for which she had surrendered her egg ration never laid an egg and also had the troublesome habit of getting out at night and perching in the apple tree, which she had to climb to retrieve them. A housewife from Kent with two hungry sons to feed who bought a dozen day old chicks at 1s. each still recalls her horror, after weeks of careful nurturing, at learning that they were all cockerels. She then exchanged them for four females which also failed to lay and had to be killed. Nothing daunted, she tried again, this time buying six 'gorgeous beauties' five months old. 'Soon, very soon,' she remembers, 'the first marvellous egg was in my hands, more precious to me than the crown jewels, and it had a double-yolk. It seemed as though the powers that be decided to take pity on the poor fool. Alas, how could I know my poor hen was slowly wearing herself out. After six double yolks she died. . . . In grief I dug a hole and gave her Christian burial. When my hungry fourteen-year-old came in from school he said, "You silly, we could have eaten her!" ' The remaining five, however, survived beyond the allotted span 'and did us proud'. Nor were all poultry-owners prepared for the difference in temperament between the two sexes. A Birmingham housewife decided to let out her chickens to scratch around as they seemed to be getting very fat. 'I did not realise that they were all cockerels. I was chased all round the field. . . . Never again.'

If an ordinary egg was a treasure, a duck's egg was a feast. The wife of a watchmaker in Kingston-on-Thames was proud of her two Khaki Campbell ducks, Alice and Maud. 'They knew what was expected of them . . . ate all the green stuff and were the ruination of the garden, but they laid and laid. Their eggs were much sought after as prizes for the street Victory celebrations.' Alice and Maud came to sad ends. 'One died in a thunder storm. The other a neighbour ate, we couldn't.'

Some people even kept goats. One Norfolk housewife 'learned to milk the hard way. My first effort netted me about as much as would fill a thimble, bruised legs and a very irritable Nanny.' Later, however, she became more expert and the local farmers' wives taught her to make goat's milk butter and cheese, though these are really an acquired taste. Goats were, however, even worse-tempered than cockerels. A young Surrey mother remembers the evening when her hosts' children's nanny 'shot past the window at a wonderful turn of speed followed by the nasty-tempered goat Daisy. Round and round she ran, while we stood helpless with laughter, then a flying leap and she was safe in among the chickens. The chickens went off lay and Nanny went off sick.' Goats were not at all difficult to feed, indeed their voracious appetites were notorious. Clothing, cigarettes, newspapers—anything left near them would vanish in a few minutes. Officially they ate greens and hedge-prunings and a Hertfordshire woman remembers that during a hard winter 'trees near us used to look very stripped, because our family had to bring in armfuls of ivy to feed the goats when they went for walks'. But they had one great drawback. Those that failed to provide milk were rarely welcome as food for goat's meat was repellent even to most wartime appetites, being tough and evil-smelling, with a taste like over-ripe game.

Cows, being more placid creatures, were even easier to care for than goats and a Burnham-on-Sea woman, needing milk for an invalid mother, joined with a friend, who owned a small paddock, to buy 'a beautiful Guernsey cow' for £14 14s. The investment proved a great success, providing 'beautiful creamy milk each day'. A Stamford housewife with a six-acre garden behind her house found keeping a Jersey cow little trouble, the whole family soon learning not merely to milk their new pet, but also to make butter.

Another rural skill which many amateurs now acquired was bee-keeping. The attraction was less the promise of honey than the certainty of extra sugar from the Ministry of Food. The cow-keeping family in Stamford found they could keep bees in their three hives perfectly content, and producing honey at the rate of a hundredweight a hive, by giving them back their own honey, while keeping their sugar for preserving fruit. Bees could, however, be dangerous charges even for the professionals. One Kent beekeeper who was transporting his hives to pollinate a fruit orchard one night found his lorry held up by 'a long queue of halted vehicles just as dawn was beginning to appear', due to an unexploded bomb on the road. 'The policeman was asked to inform the authorities that there was likely to be another incident any minute, with the arrival of something in the nature of an exploded bomb at the other end of the queue. . . . With the coming of early light, there would be several thousand inquisitive bees exploring the neighbourhood.' The police wisely decided the bomb was a lesser risk than angry bees; the lorry was allowed to jump the queue.

In Victorian England to acquire his own pig had been every poor man's ambition and now private pig-owning again became a popular activity. There were pig clubs on school playing fields, in open spaces like Battersea Park, and even in the swimming bath of the bombed-out Ladies Carlton Club in Pall Mall. The pigkeepers here, as in many places, were firemen and for the first time since the Middle Ages pigs could be heard snorting and snuffling in the heart of London.

Strict government regulations controlled pig clubs but it was difficult to enforce them all and one Kent farmer remembers how the Pig Club which he started among his employees was only 'allowed to kill a pig not weighing more than 100 lb., but somehow we kept putting it off and when we killed it it weighed 200, which suited everybody'. On an estate near Enfield twenty residents joined a pig club formed by a local smallholder, who 'provided the pig sty, a shed to hold a boiler and space for an outside run. One member obtained a large copper which was built by the others into a fireplace and chimney. . . . Two men at a time collected edible scraps from as many houses as possible, but this took so long that the Club put tin bins with lids, at intervals along the roads and people would put their scraps in themselves; the collectors emptied them each evening into a large bin on wheels. The scraps had to be boiled for two hours each evening, together with bran allocated and sold by the government. . . . Half was fed to the animals in the evening, half in the morning before the men went to work. This entailed quite hard work one day in ten', and 'the sties had to be scrubbed out each night'. As the members could keep only half the pork they produced, they began before long to wonder if the venture were really worthwhile, and it was finally killed by the growth of poultry-keeping, for local residents began to keep their kitchen waste for their own livestock, until it was taking six months instead of three or four to fatten up the club's four or six pigs for slaughter. Other pig clubs proved more enduring. A young Catford woman recalls how in 1943 a 'number of us had a 5s. od. stake in a pig which was being fed at the Fire Station. How we watched these pigs and gladly paid our money when it came round to Christmas and we were given permission to kill them. There were ten of us round the table for Christmas dinner. I don't think pork has ever tasted the same since.'

Despite the hard and patient hours which so many housewives spent in cleaning out the chicken run and boiling up the evil-smelling pig swill, the number of poultry in the country fell by a quarter during the war and the number of pigs by more than half, following the slaughter of farm stocks to save importing feeding stuffs. The sheep population also went down, by about a fifth, and a small increase in the number of cattle was not sufficient to make up for the loss of imported meat. The real burden of feeding the nation still rested upon its million farmers and farm-workers. The war was a good time to be a farmer. 'Farming previous to the outbreak of the war was a very depressed industry', a Surrey farmer remembers. 'The output from the farms was poor and was difficult to dispose of except at ruinous prices. . . . The war completely altered this picture. Farmers found themselves promoted from the rather despised poor relation to a much sought after and respected member of the family. These things completely changed their outlook and they put their hearts and souls into the job.' The change in East Anglia was equally striking. 'Farmers were as poor as church mice', one Norfolk woman remembers, 'but before the war was half over they had not one but two cars to their garage. It made most of them. The government were generosity itself.' An Oxfordshire smallholder remembers 'feeling that for the first time in my life the food we were producing really mattered and whatever we had for sale someone was waiting to buy it'.

On the outbreak of war, County War Agricultural Executive Committees were set up throughout the country, made up of farmers chosen jointly by the Ministry of Agriculture's expert advisory officers and the National Farmers Union. The country was split up into districts, each with its own committee, whose members received no reward for their work except extra petrol coupons. 'The members of the district committees were the men who actually did the work,' one of them from Surrey remembers, 'visiting the farms and arranging with the farmers which fields were to be ploughed.' They reported to the County Committee which fields had been earmarked—'scheduled' in the official jargon—and it then issued official ploughing orders which had the force of law. 'The whole essence of the scheme was that the schedulers were men who were well known and respected by the farmers of the district. The land required for ploughing was . . . obtained, except in very few cases, by persuasion, not orders. This was really a second revolution in farming. Whereas in the cut-throat pre-war conditions farmers were loath to disclose their knowledge to their neighbours, now these farmers gave away all the know-how they possessed to the farmers they visited and, before the advent of machinery pools, in many cases lent their own machinery to them.' This farmer remembers an incident which illustrates how this characteristically British system worked. 'I was scheduling a rather difficult farmer and after arguments in the fields we adjourned to the farmhouse for coffee. The arguments continued until at last I said, "Look here, Fred, I'm going to have ten acres off you and I shan't leave this kitchen until I get it." His wife burst in with, "Now listen, I'm not having you two in my kitchen any longer. Fred, tell Mr. C. you will plough Long Acre".' And Fred, like a wise man, did.

The secretary to a County Land Agent in East Anglia found that 'almost every letter my boss dictated started "Please find enclosed forms . . ." ', usually a 'ploughing up order' for 'All land that could be spared and some that couldn't was ordered to be ploughed up and cropped. . . . It was often pitiful for the farmers having to plough up their lovely grass paddocks, etc., and sometimes they came storming into the office to see if we could get an exemption. It was very rare that we could.'

Many farmers did not take kindly to either advice or direction though none seems to have refused the government grants and subsidies that accompanied them, and the figures speak for themselves. By 1944 the country had increased its area of arable land by 50 per cent, its pasture land by 66 per cent, had nearly doubled its output of wheat and barley and more than doubled its output of potatoes. In 1939 the average yield of wheat was thirty-three bushels; by 1943 it was fifty, though some districts reached eighty. It was such achievements that ensured that the country never starved and, by the end of the war, was importing only one-third of its food instead of two. The efforts of the 'War Ags' would have been in vain without the hard work of individual farmers. One fourteen-year-old schoolboy who had just left school when the war broke out to work on the 370 acre family farm, 'growing wheat, oats, barley, potatoes, sugar beet and flax', recalls how 'All the corn had to be cut with a binder and then stooked and carted to the threshing drum in the farmyard.... During the winter we were kept busy ploughing until midnight. There was very little machinery to help us.' Nor was life much easier for the women members of the family. This young man's future wife was then aged twelve and living on her father's farm in Cheshire. 'Every morning before school in the winter my father and I would go up to the field with a horse-drawn lorry to cut and cart a load of kale for the cows', she remembers. 'It was terribly cold and frosty sometimes and at other times the rain ran down my back. The milking was carried out in semi-darkness. Over each oil lantern we had an old trilby hat with a slit cut in the top for the handle, and while crossing the yard we had to pop it under our coats, at great risk of setting ourselves on fire.' Hard work was no novelty for any farmer's wife but the war often meant a larger number to cater for. This girl's future mother-in-law found herself having to 'look after, wash and cook for', with the arrival of two land girls and an evacuee couple, a household of thirteen. 'She had', her son remembers, 'to get up every Monday at 4 a.m. to do the washing in the old-fashioned wash boiler with a fire underneath and then dolly-peg the clothes in a dolly-tub and mangle them with a large wooden roller mangle.'

All this was rarely seen by the casual visitor and what impressed most townsfolk visiting the countryside was that for farmers rationing did not seem to exist. 'None of the one slice of bacon a week or two ounces of butter for them', comments a housewife from St. Leonards on Sea who spent her holidays on farms in Devon and Cornwall. A Hornsea man visiting a farm in the East Riding of Yorkshire with his father was amused by the grace offered before dinner:

> We bless the Lord, and make us able
> To eat all meat that's set on table.

Such a prayer would have seemed superfluous to most wartime families but proved very necessary here, for he was 'very surprised to see two large legs of roast mutton placed on the table ... and at once the farmer sprang into action ... cutting off thick pieces of the succulent mutton'. It came from an illicitly-killed sheep reported by the farmer as having been accidentally drowned in an irrigation ditch.

Many stories of similar breaches of the law circulated during the war. The commonest concerned two men who turned up at a farm claiming to be Ministry of Food enforcement officers, took away 'as evidence' the remains of a dead pig, which the farmer had boasted in the village pub the night before of having slaughtered illegally for his own use, and were never heard of again. Another story concerned sheep illicitly

slaughtered on the Welsh hills with—an essential detail in every version
—the fleece afterwards being buried. A third account described how men
engaged in the furtive slaughter of a pig after dark had been surprised by
the village policeman who, having observed their clumsy carving,
had said 'Give me the knife' and had then expertly finished the job,
keeping his mouth shut in exchange for the largest portion. Clearly
many such reports were exaggerated. What is indisputable is that eggs,
bacon, butter, cheese and meat—if only wild rabbit—appeared during
the war on farmers' tables in a profusion unknown elsewhere.

The call-up of some farm-workers meant that few farms ever had enough
labour and from 1942, which produced the heaviest harvest on record
until 1943's proved even better, there were frequent appeals to the public
to 'Lend a hand on the land'. In rural areas child labour became so popular
that M.P.s protested at the regulations being relaxed too far. Some schools,
like mine, virtually compelled boys to give up part of their holidays to
attending farm camps, though hundreds of thousands of boy-hours were
cheerfully wasted each term on the cricket or rugger field. Many people
made private arrangements with farmers, and one Midland newspaper
alone placed 6,000 volunteers through its 'Help the Farmer' scheme.
By 1943 about 70,000 schoolboys were helping on the land and that year,
the peak one, there were also more than 150 camps where 80,000 volunteers, two-thirds of them women, spent a week or more of their holiday.
The Ministry of Agriculture claimed that the camps contained a cross
section of British society, instancing one which included a dustman, two
typists and a bishop. The largest group of volunteers, however, were
students or Civil Servants. The former were often expected to undertake
some public service in their vacations and were glad of the money—
usually 24s. 6d. to 30s. a week, plus board and lodging. The attraction
for Civil Servants was an extra one or two weeks' leave. 10,000 helped
to bring in the 1943 harvest alone, though in 1944 the whole scheme
was less successful, due to travel restrictions and general war weariness.

Many work camps developed a character of their own. One in Surrey
was run by a retired admiral on naval lines, with early morning inspection
and meals at 'four bells'. A woman who superintended fifty undergraduates
at a Gloucestershire camp, where the girls slept on the floors of the local
church hall and the men in the Y.M.C.A. hut, recalls the only awkward
incident was when one young man nearly set the hut on fire after indulg-
ing unwisely in the local perry. At another camp she managed, on a
fruit farm in Herefordshire, the students slept in tents. 'The horse trough
was the dish-washing place and the horses' stable was the kitchen. . . .
The three cooks I had were excellent girls and used to get up at 5 a.m. to
get the awful stove going.' Few volunteers had realised beforehand what
hard work was involved. A G.P.O. telephonist from Coventry who

went potato picking in Worcestershire remembers that 'Our evenings were spent talking and singing. We were all too tired to do any dancing and ached all over.' Not infrequently a single day's work was enough, especially if the newcomers had gone out to the fields their first morning in thin sandals and shorts and come back with feet and legs scratched and bleeding. The wife of a Buckinghamshire farmer found that the twenty 'thin and pale' girls from Nottingham lace and cigarette factories who arrived to help with the potato picking simply did not turn up for work the second morning, leaving her with twenty large mugfuls of cocoa to dispose of.

Of all the volunteers who came to the help of the British farmer during the war the most numerous and the most useful were the members of the Women's Land Army. This had come into existence in June 1939 when a register began to be compiled of women willing to give up their ordinary jobs for farm work if war came. The aim was not to recruit country girls, but to attract girls from factories, offices and shops who had always longed for an open-air life, and probably the biggest single source of recruits was the textile mills of Lancashire and Yorkshire. Many military reservists were far from eager to go when the call came. Not so the land girls. One, asked by telephone on 1st September how soon she could be ready, replied, quite seriously, 'Can you give me twenty minutes?'

The Land Army was run solely by women and its honorary Director, Lady 'Trudie' Denman, handed over her own country home, Balcombe Place in Sussex, as its headquarters. Trestle tables and desks appeared in the baronial rooms, uniforms were piled in the stables and squash courts and Lady Denman's husband, not without relief, moved out to a hotel in Hove, from which he never returned.*

By 1943, when recruiting stopped due to the demands of industry, there were nearly 90,000 land girls, aged from eighteen to forty. The newspapers tended to romanticise the Land Army; a photograph in the *Daily Herald* showing an attractive ex-manicurist giving a pedicure to a Jersey cow called Buttercup was only too typical. The Land Army tried to correct this idealised picture by such publications as *Land Girl, A Manual for Volunteers* which advised potential recruits to test themselves by 'carrying buckets full of water for half-an-hour or more at a time', after which they should 'attempt to pitch earth on to a barrow ... for another hour or so'. Certainly there was little in a land girl's pay or conditions to attract anyone to the job. During her four weeks' training a girl received only 10s. a week and her keep and afterwards she might earn, in 1941, only 28s. a week. Even by 1944 the minimum was only 48s., leaving her with 22s. 6d. after paying for board and lodging. The land

* The couple did, however, remain on friendly terms.

girls were to the wartime female population what the ordinary airman and soldier were to the male: the most praised and the worst treated. In many respects a land girl was even worse off than a service-woman, with less leave, fewer free travel warrants and no prospect of promotion, since only one or two girls worked on a farm. She was in many places barred from Forces canteens and was at the end of the queue for uniforms. When gum boots became scarce it was the Land Army, who needed them most, who went without. An eighteen-year-old who joined the Land Army in Berkshire in 1941 obtained her first pair of Wellingtons only when she became a dairy worker. 'Only milkers got these and we were allowed one new pair in two years. . . . We patched our boots with cycle puncture outfits, but they always leaked. I spent the next four and a half years with wet feet, and chilblains in the winter.' Nor was the rest of the outfit much more satisfactory. 'Nothing seemed to fit and my breeches always slipped, so that the waist was resting on my hips.' This nearly had an embarrassing sequel when she was asked to take part in a parade through the streets of Reading to encourage women to volunteer for war work. 'I arrived at the starting point feeling very insecure, with my breeches slipping a bit and my felt hat too big and liable to blow away.' Fortunately she was 'immediately asked to be a member of a tractor crew . . . standing up beside the girl driving the thing . . . I was terrified of falling off, as I'd never had anything to do with tractors before'.

At first many land girls had to go without an overcoat, and though at last some were diverted from the A.T.S. these often proved too small for the land girls' sturdier frames. A twenty-two-year-old Birmingham girl, who began work in Worcestershire in 1941, recalls how poorly she and other land girls were equipped. She had no overcoat and wore 'breeches miles too large'. The 'boots and canvas gaiters' were 'inadequate in the water-logged fields where we were working. We had to borrow waders off the men which were much too large and generally reached to our armpits. . . . We "made-do", appearing in the winter in an odd assortment of garments. One of my friends sported a fur-lined "mac". She wore it with an air of "chic", perched on the back of an open lorry, probably on a pile of sprout nets—she looked like a queen wrapped in ermine. Once on a bitter day, when we were kicking parsnips out of frozen earth, a colleague appeared in a long A.R.P. coat, reaching from ears to ankles. Against the background of powdered snow, bare trees, frozen landscape, she reminded me of a figure from the picture of "Napoleon's Retreat from Moscow".' Another twenty-two-year-old, who joined the Land Army in 1942, and had to wait eight months for an overcoat, found life on a Hertfordshire farm in mid-winter could hardly have been more different from her previous job, as a dressmaker with the West End firm of Marshall and Snelgrove, for it consisted of 'dung spreading and in February snow was on the heaps. One girl used to turn purple with the cold.' Summer offered different afflictions. 'Threshing was a filthy job from stacks often a year old. The machine was driven by belts from traction engines, the boiler being fed with coal. If the wind was in the wrong direction we used to get black. Harvest time we worked from 7.30 a.m. to 9.30 p.m. just with packets of sandwiches and water to drink. Thermos flasks were impossible to get. If we were lucky some farmers' wives would make us tea or cocoa at lunch or tea-time! . . . Some farms we worked at were miles away from the house so we went without.' Many land girls failed even to eat well, despite living in the country. A woman who ran a hostel for land girls near Newark in the Midlands remembers having to add boiled rice to the scrambled egg to make it go further and one girl in Berkshire 'spent ten miserable months with a cowman's family where the wife was a poor cook and an erratic housewife. She did the weekly shopping on a Saturday; we had good meals for a day or so, then "starved" on bread and cheese for the rest of the week. I lost a lot of weight, and never felt well that first winter.' Her accommodation, too, left a lot to be desired, being 'a crowded, cold cottage, toilet down the garden, no hot water'. About a third of the girls lived in hostels, usually accommodating about thirty. These were far from lavish. One land girl living near Evesham remembers hers as being 'furnished with a narrow bed and a wooden chair per person, so we soon became adept at making bedside tables, cupboards, etc., out of old crates and boxes decorated with odd bits of cretonne scrounged from home, or made from dyeing the bean and pea "liners" '.

Probably the worst-off girls were those stationed in rural Wales. 'The Welsh farmer is usually more thrifty than the English and . . . his standard of living is consequently less high', warned one book about the Land Army, and what this meant in practice was often wretched accommodation, miserable diet and a chilling meanness. Some unfortunate girls found themselves living with a Welsh-speaking family in tiny communities where even the postman called only once or twice a week. One twenty-three-year-old girl wrote to W.L.A. headquarters from a lonely farm in Tregaron, Cardiganshire, that the only water was from a spring, that they had been without news for a week since the wireless battery had expired, and the only entertainment was the weekly sermon at the village chapel where a hell-fire preacher arrived by pony to denounce the evils of theatre-going and whist-drives, though as he spoke in Welsh she was still sunk in her sinful, urban ways.

But the Land Army had one great attraction denied to the Forces: freedom. The members could resign when they wished (though, of course, then liable to be directed into other work) or could be dismissed.

This did happen occasionally. Some farmers sacked their land girls every winter to save paying their wages and other girls clearly provoked their employers beyond endurance. The Land Army *Handbook* warned that 'A farmer is not made in a month and after training some girls are inclined to teach the farmer his business, often with unfortunate results'. Some such clash perhaps accounted for one question put to the Ministry of Agriculture: Was a farmer entitled to dismiss a land girl merely for calling him 'pigface'?

Those who particularly cherished their independence could always join the Timber Corps, whose members toured the country selecting growing trees as poles for telegraph posts and road blocks. The worst feature of such work was the lack of transport. One team who acquired bicycles, loading them with paint-pot, calipers, billhooks and other tools of their trade, discovered they were 'regarded as an advance part of the invasion' and one countryman refused them directions, as 'You be parachutists. Germans. I'll be fetching the police to thee.' Especially in Wales, Timber Corps workers also had to cope with grasping, inhospitable landladies and poor accommodation. One team was charged five shillings for a meal served on newspaper on an orange box; and in one hotel two dinner-jacketed guests walked out rather than dine in the same room as two land girls in uniform, an offence made worse because, unable to afford the set dinner, the girls were eating bread and cheese.

For some mysterious reason, 'from the start the land girls suffered from being considered rather comic—a suitable butt for press jokes and caricatures', one expert has admitted, and their large felt hat, resembling a Boy Scout's, became a familiar subject for cartoonists. 'Volunteers are asked to wear their hat correctly', pleaded the official handbook, but the Land Army's historian complained of the girl who 'builds hers up . . . adds a bootlace to her hat and uses it as a chin strap . . . not realising that to the casual observer she looks as though she were suffering either from toothache or from mumps.' Most girls in fact, once in the fields, went bareheaded and the cartoonists fortunately missed a far greater opportunity, that of land girls who peeled off their trousers. A Lymington, Hampshire, man farming 200 acres, remembers one 'hot August', after setting a dozen land girls to work setting up stocks of wheat, being amazed to 'find the entrance to the field . . . strewn with their very thick corduroy trousers. As a young man, I looked round expectantly but their smocks were just long enough to cover their panties.' Another Hampshire farmer also discovered that 'In hot weather they would strip off to a little round two places—very disturbing to susceptible young men.' Like other women in uniform, the land girls were the subject of many slanders on their morals, and the rumour that their motto was 'Backs to the land' was an early wartime witticism. All accounts, however, suggest they were particularly high-principled girls; and working almost exclusively among men many clearly felt they could not afford to give any male too much encouragement. One farmer remembers the 'local threshing proprietor getting his face well slapped in my barn, when he tried to snatch a dusty kiss off one extra-good-looker'.

A number of girls, including a former dancer, waitress and hair-dresser, volunteered to be trained as ratcatchers, and to the general public, with memories of Jack Warner's 'bunger-up of ratholes', this useful occupation seemed hilariously amusing, though it was in fact of great value, for a single rat could eat a hundredweight of food in a year. The lady ratcatchers, despite all the jokes, took their job very seriously, as one young man on a South Country farm discovered. 'A pretty land girl, known in my family as "Primrose Cream", did the job for us. Her name was Primrose and her skin of the peaches and cream variety. I used to look forward to her visits and suggested to her one day, slightly amorously, that we seemed to be getting on rather well. To which she replied, "Only with the rats, Mr R., only with the rats" '—a phrase which became a family saying when any male member let his eyes wander.

At first many farmers, conservative by nature, 'regarded land girls', one in Berkshire found, 'as a necessary evil . . . When they got used to having us around and had discovered that we were quite useful we were accepted as part of the wartime scene.' But this is too modest an assessment. 'Of all types of temporary labour we employed during the war, the land girls were the best', a Surrey farmer considers. 'They soon became accustomed to the work and did not mind what job it was, they would tackle it to the best of their ability. They were of course excellent with animals, especially with calves. They used to play with them, which was not only good for the girls, but good for the calves . . . they thrived under the treatment.' A Lymington, Hampshire, farmer 'greatly admired the guts' of the girls who worked for a threshing contractor and came to his farm at harvest time. 'Threshing stacks of corn [combines had hardly come in] is hard, dusty work for *men*—nobody liked it. But these girls, day after day, got their eyes and hair full of dirt and dust and stuck it splendidly . . . They certainly brightened the lives of the farmers and their workers.'

Farm labourers were not enthusiastic about having female help at first, largely because at most types of work it cut down their output to two-thirds the normal rate. There could be other reasons, too, as one eighteen-year-old discovered. 'When I first started working on the land I noticed that a sudden silence often fell when I approached a group of men either in a field or a cowshed. I imagined that they were just shy of having a girl around, until . . . I realised that every other word of their conversation was a swear word, and they were unable to converse at all without swearing, so it followed that they had to shut up altogether when I was around. . . . They were considerate and would carry a heavy bale of straw for me . . . . The men were also keen to protect me from dangerous tools. . . . When we were chopping the tops off mangolds, the men refused to allow me to use a really sharp knife in case I cut myself.' And there was one rural rite she was not allowed to witness. 'I don't think the men liked me to be present at the mating of cows to the bull, for they made elaborate excuses to send me on fictitious errands and if I arrived back too soon they were acutely embarrassed. For the same reason, I wasn't welcome at the birth of calves.'

The end of the Women's Land Army was not happy. From mid-1944 the number of recruits began to fall below the loss from resignations, and in February 1945, after the government had announced that land girls would not be eligible for the resettlement grants offered to Civil Defence workers, Lady Denman herself resigned in protest, though the Land Army was not finally wound up until 1950. In the following year King George VI, investing Lady Denman with a medal, told her: 'We always thought that the land girls were not well treated.'

Today few land girls seem to look back with bitterness on the muddy, dusty, windswept, sun-baked, icy-footed years of their hard and ill-rewarded war. The reasons were vividly expressed in a letter from one girl working in a remote part of Wales. 'Before joining the Woman's Land Army . . . I worked for five, long, dreary years in an office in Brixton. . . . Always I dreamt of hills and stars and green free spaces and sometimes, bending over a ledger in springtime, I could actually smell the primrose of my imagination.' The members of the Land Army were in fact moved by love, in every sense, of their native land. There were many worse reasons for choosing a wartime career.

# MAKE DO AND MEND

'I know all the women will look smart, but we men may look shabby. If we do we must not be ashamed. In war the term "battle-stained" is an honourable one.'

Broadcast by the President of the Board of Trade introducing clothes rationing, 1st June 1941

Whit Sunday 1941 should have been a peaceful day for the civilians of Great Britain. The blitz was over and the government had decided that the Bank Holiday, cancelled at the last moment in 1940, should take place as usual. Instead the day was spent in beginning to grapple with a new restriction: clothes rationing. To start this vast new scheme on this particular morning made sense, for it allowed the shops two full days to make their preparations and many shop assistants spent this long anticipated holiday making out window notices and pinning 'coupon value' tickets to coats and dresses. To many people, however, it seemed singularly ill-timed. One Birmingham woman voiced her indignation in a local newspaper:

> I sat in bed with morning tea
> And listened to the BBC. . . .
> On hearing the announcement made
> So calmly by the Board of Trade,
> It seemed to me a sorry way
> To start a Whitsun holiday.

The wife of a gown buyer for one West End store, also lying in bed, hurried upstairs to tell her husband cheerfully, 'Wake up, dear, you're in marg!', for to start with, it was explained, the unused margarine coupons in the ordinary ration book would be used to buy clothing.

That evening the President of the Board of Trade, Oliver Lyttelton, broadcast an appeal to the nation to show its patriotism by becoming ill-dressed. 'In war the term "battle-stained" is an honourable one', Lyttelton, an ex-Guards officer, told his audience. 'We must learn as civilians to be seen in clothes that are not so smart, because we are bearing . . . yet another share in the war. When you feel tired of your old clothes remember that by making them do you are contributing some part of an aeroplane, a gun or a tank.'

With experience of food rationing behind it, the public raised no objection to the coming of clothes rationing; throughout the war, public opinion was always in favour of extending rationing as the best guarantee of fair shares. Lyttelton's difficulties in pushing the scheme through all came from within the government, for Winston Churchill, who usually took very little interest in the civilian side of the war, had taken a violent dislike to the whole idea of rationing clothes. He accused the unfortunate Lyttelton, a successful businessman and old Etonian who had entered Parliament only on the Prime Minister's own insistence, of being willing to see the public 'in rags and tatters on the bureaucratic orders of a new minister'.* When Lyttelton insisted that the public were eager for sacrifice Churchill retorted robustly: 'Who are you to tell me what the public want? Why, I only picked you up out of some bucket shop in the City a few weeks ago!' The clothes rationing scheme after being turned down by the Prime Minister was only pushed through because Sir John Anderson next tackled Churchill on the subject when he was preoccupied with the hunt for the *Bismarck*. This time the Prime Minister retorted petulantly: 'Can't you see I'm busy? Do what you like, but please don't worry me now', and Anderson interpreted this as approval. By Tuesday 27th May, when the *Bismarck* was at the bottom of the sea, it was too late to stop the scheme. Churchill was at first furious but proved generous in defeat, greeting Lyttelton a week later, 'Here's Oliver, who rejects the Prime Minister's view on public opinion about clothes rationing and turns out to be right. . . . We will have an extra glass of champagne to celebrate.'

Clothes were put on coupons not because supplies were scarce, but because they were too plentiful. The chief aim of rationing was to save factory space, and by closing down small firms to release 450,000 workers for the munition industries. The Civil Service had done its usual skilful job in preparing the scheme, but the need for secrecy had made it hard for the Board of Trade to seek advice on its chief problem—what constituted a normal stock of clothes. According to Whitehall legend, one comfortably-off Civil Servant, after counting the items in his wardrobe, reported that he possessed forty suits. Fortunately others were also consulted, including Lady Reading. Her reaction was: 'It's splendid—and about time, too!', and she went on to ask embarrassed male officials searching questions about the coupon values of the various items of women's underclothes.

The clothes rationing scheme was based on the points principle later

---

* Churchill was guided in this, as in so many bad decisions, by his German-born adviser, Professor Lindemann, who had recently become Lord Cherwell. Cherwell, an almost universally detested figure, maintained throughout the war a remarkable record for being wrong.

also adopted by the Ministry of Food. For the twelve months from 1st June 1941 everyone in the country was to receive sixty-six coupons, twenty-six of them in the form of the unused margarine coupons in the current ration book. Every item of clothing was given a points value, varying according to how much labour and material were needed to produce it. For a man the heaviest items were a lined raincoat or overcoat, taking sixteen coupons, or a coat or blazer, needing thirteen, while trousers or a shirt needed eight, underpants four, and handkerchiefs were one coupon for two. For a raincoat or overcoat a woman had to surrender fourteen coupons, for a dress eleven, for a vest or pair of panties three, for a pair of stockings two. For children's clothes the points values were smaller, to allow for their rapid growth. Hats, braces, suspenders and, at first, most forms of household linen, excluding curtain material, were unrationed. People who wore uniform for their jobs had to part with coupons to their employers, a nurse, for example, surrendering ten coupons a year for her working dress and a policewoman having to give up six for her official-issue stockings.

The immediate response to clothes rationing was a sudden rush on the shops, many people apparently fearing that coupon values might soon be increased. A Liverpool store observed with astonishment the 'glorious burst of expenditure' of one man, who used up the whole coupon stock of himself and his wife in one go. At Peter Jones in Chelsea a correspondent admitted that 'Our first reactions to rationing were that women were mad!', and there was much speculation as to the offence of 'the gentleman who called in the Lingerie Department and purchased three nightdresses, using his own coupons. What a peace offering must have been needed!' Already, it was clear that it was fathers who were likely to come off worst. A child customer was heard to say confidently in a Winchester shop when all her coupons were gone: 'That's O.K., I'll go home for Daddy's book.' The use of margarine coupons caused some confusion and at John Lewis's one customer, having used up his margarine coupons, hopefully offered those for sugar, bacon and cheese as well.

Clothes rationing worked well and the system was steadily improved. From 1942 a system of 'bank accounts' for coupons saved shopkeepers a great deal of work, and from 1943 a detachable clothing coupon section inside the main ration book was introduced, which meant that each member of the family could look after his own, while leaving 'Mum' in charge of his food ration book. Clothes coupons could be used anywhere, and though officially it was illegal to offer loose coupons, except by post, this was one regulation that was frequently broken. Such transactions did not, after all, reduce the general stock of clothing, and it was clearly impossible for Board of Trade inspectors to pounce on every factory worker who sold a few coupons to a workmate. But rationing grew steadily more stringent. The first sixty-six coupons had covered only twelve months, but the second issue, of sixty, had to last fifteen months and by 1945 the allowance equalled only forty-one a year. Meanwhile the 'unofficial' cost of coupons soared, from as little as 2s. 6d. for a whole book in 1941 to £5 by 1944, while the rate for individual coupons rose from 3d. to 3s., the usual price being around 1s.

Most of such transactions were on a small scale between acquaintances. The British public, while welcoming a little 'fiddling', was firmly against anything more serious. One common practice was to exchange coupons for the good quality, cast-off clothes of wealthier friends or relations, and there were market stalls where it was understood that no awkward request for coupons would be made but the price would be adjusted accordingly. One woman remembers a shop assistant pointedly not removing her coupons, then waiting for a tip, which was not forthcoming. The customer had, as it happened, more coupons to spare than cash. When any member of a family died his relations were supposed to return his unused clothing coupons to the Registrar of Births and Deaths, but these sceptical officials soon discovered that apparently the last act of everyone who died between 1941 and 1945 had been to go on a final shopping spree. One Lancashire woman, who lived in her uncle's vicarage and was herself marrying a curate, admits that the curtain materials in her bottom drawer were obtained by coupons that were an unwitting legacy from her dead grandmother, and a Sheffield family, having pooled their coupons for one relative's wedding, had their reward when an uncle died, leaving behind him an untouched clothing book. 'What a beano we had!', one of the beneficiaries remembers.

In his broadcast introducing clothes rationing, Oliver Lyttelton had said that 'I know all the women will look smart but we men may look shabby. If we do we must not be ashamed.' Thrifty wives now darned socks until little of the original remained, unravelling the upper part to obtain wool to mend the foot. The tails of shirts were used to replace worn cuffs and collars, being replaced by oddments. Only on wash-day were these domestic secrets revealed when, a Dulwich woman remembers, shirts hanging on the washing line 'made a pretty picture with their odd tails'. Oddly enough, however, it was a regulation concerning men's wear which caused the greatest outcry. In February 1942 Hugh Dalton, a Labour economist lacking Lord Woolton's feel for what the public would accept, had taken over as President of the Board of Trade and in the following month he announced a series of measures designed to save work and cloth. From 1st May all men's jackets were to be single-breasted, with at most three pockets, and only three buttons on the front, while buttons on the cuffs, metal or leather and fancy belts were all banned. Waistcoats were rationed to two pockets, trousers to nineteen-inch-wide legs and elastic waistbands were forbidden. All this might have been accepted, but the total prohibition of turn-ups, announced at the same time, let loose a storm of protest. It would, said one spokesman for the trade, merely mean labour being 'expended in repairing frayed trouser bottoms', and bespoke tailors kept up the fight for years. In March 1943 a nation-wide deputation begged Dalton to restore men's trousers to their former glory and immaculately-turned-out M.P.s voiced in Parliament 'the serious dissatisfaction' the 'regulations were causing to business and professional men'. Dalton stood firm, insisting that 'the prohibition of turn-ups to men's trousers was saving millions of square feet of cloth a year', and he was equally emphatic at a hostile press conference. 'There can', he said, 'be no equality of sacrifice in this war. Some must lose lives and limbs; others only the turn-ups on their trousers.' But in October 1943 a Board of Trade inspector admitted, when prosecuting a tailor for making an illicit pair of turn-up trousers, that 'Utility trousers were very unpopular and . . . the general opinion of the trade was that they saved no cloth at all'. Still the rules remained, though if one searched hard enough one could sometimes find an obliging tailor willing, 'by mistake', to make your trousers several inches too long and then, quite legally, to make them fit by turning the legs up. One seventeen-year-old Dagenham schoolboy, proudly ordering his first ever grown-up suit, was bitterly disappointed that it lacked turn-ups and only ceased to feel disgraced in his own eyes when his mother put in a false turn-up by inserting a tuck in the material and pressing round it. Another of Dalton's decisions pressed hard, too, on growing boys eagerly awaiting that great landmark of going into long trousers. From May 1942 they had, by law, to wait longer. Henceforward, to save cloth, only shorts were to be made for boys up to the age of eleven or twelve.

In banks and offices pre-war standards had inevitably to be relaxed but at least one West End store, as late as March 1943, was still insisting on white shirts and collars. 'Coloured collars with business coats would look incongruous', ruled the Director of Personnel firmly. Many manual workers in heavy work had an easier time, for the Board of Trade made them a small extra allowance of coupons though his 'industrial ten' was often wheedled out of 'Dad' by clothes-hungry daughters. Even fewer of the 'industrial ten' issued to women went, as intended, on working clothes. A Shenfield, Essex, woman remembers seeing local factory-workers in tattered overalls: their supplementary coupons had all gone on stockings. The girls working in one Hereford factory office had a brainwave as to how to qualify for the 'industrial ten'. They decided, one of them remembers, to 'volunteer to work two or three hours for one or two days per week on the land, after a day's work', until they had completed the minimum number of hours necessary to count as agricultural workers. 'A local bus was laid on and off we went to the farm. Our job was to strip the bottom of the hop vines to six inches from the earth. . . . No one had told us to take gloves. Imagine stripping vines choked with thistles and nettles with bare hands. . . . My friend "got off" with the farmer, who gave her some gloves. The rest of us worked for one hour and went home, with no coupons and no trying again. My friend got her coupons—no comment.'

To those in a few particularly dirty occupations, like foundry work, mining and chemical manufacture, the Board of Trade also distributed an 'iron ration' of extra coupons, shared out through a works committee. This was a thankless job. The secretary of the 'Coupon Committee' in one South Wales steelworks, where some men 'worked in acid conditions which played havoc' with their clothes and others had holes burned in their garments by furnace sparks, remembers that the first year they took the easy way out and, after a mass meeting in their new canteen—another wartime innovation—shared out their 14,500 coupons on the basis of four per man. This was too few to be of use to anyone and in the second year a much better system was introduced, with employees producing 'burnt or damaged clothing' to an informal court of work-mates who allocated the coupons accordingly, the surplus being divided up among the whole works at the end of the year. Although 'you would occasionally get the smart chap who wanted more, most people played the game very well', this man found, and 'this scheme, like other wartime measures, gave people the idea that government . . . was just and trying to help them'.

For young women clothes rationing meant far greater deprivations than food rationing. The difficulties faced by girl students are typical of those of their age group. One eighteen-year-old started her course at Southampton in 1942 with a wardrobe of two dresses and a skirt, and 'Coupons were hoarded for weeks for one "big" garment, like a winter coat'. At Oxford one girl, who went up in 1943, remembers preparing for a college dance by making a long dress out of a hospital sheet given her by her sister, a nurse. She removed the edge, cut out a halter neckline and pinned the material together at the shoulder with a gilt, arrow-shaped brooch, studded with green stones, borrowed from a fellow student. The result was impressive; a heavy white dress, gathered in at the waist and falling in folds below it like a Roman toga. At the same dance another girl sparkled in a dress made from furnishing material, and a third created a stir in a black nightdress worn beneath a pink chiffon slip. This was a situation in which girls from hard-up homes, who were accustomed to 'making do', came off best. Richer girls, who simply sent for their mothers' evening dresses, ended up, to quote one student, looking like 'lamb dressed as mutton'.

It became for women everywhere a matter of pride to achieve startling results from unpromising materials. A South Norwood housewife remembers that 'One became a little sensitive about wearing new clothes and it was nice to be able to say, when someone asked in incredulous tones: "Is that a *new* skirt?" "Oh, no! I made it out of my old winter coat".' Black-out material was soon covering almost as many British women as windows; a black dirndl skirt, decorated with rows of brightly-coloured tape, could, one woman found, look very attractive. A Woking woman bleached black-out material to make a 'glamorous' evening top to wear with a long black skirt—'black-out material of course'— and a Hereford woman wore 'black-out' slacks and a blouse made from a net curtain. Black-out material was also used for petticoats and 'outsize' knickers, while curtain-net, cheese-cloth and butter-muslin, all unrationed, were employed in home-made bras. A young Yorkshire girl started her married life in a housecoat made from furnishing velvet, and one woman in Newmarket 'wore for many years, an evening dress made from brocade bought by my grandmother before the 1914 war to cover a sofa'. A London woman made herself 'a very nice pinafore dress from a heavy plain green door curtain', and a Paignton mother went to bed in nightdresses cut from a roll of cleaning rag, dyed pink. A shorthand-typist at a Cheltenham printing factory made a dress from two table-cloths and a Hoylake housewife one from book linen and linings. A young girl working in a government drawing office was given an old linen map, which she boiled to remove the starch and printer's ink. 'Then I washed it, dyed it with a fourpenny dye. Ironed it. Cut it out from a much-used blouse pattern. Made it up with a fivepenny reel of cotton and used the buttons from an old dress. Result—one new wearable garment. Total cost ninepence—no coupons. I was very proud of this blouse.' A Hendon family had an even odder windfall, when the father, for helping 'an old school friend who was the manager of a large under-takers' to salvage what was left from his bombed-out business, was rewarded with 'a large roll of the purple material . . . used to cover coffins that were going for cremation and another of . . . white muslin, used for lining coffins'. After soaking, the purple material 'came up a very pleasant shade of blue-grey' and was made into 'two long-sleeved winter dresses', while the white muslin now served the living as 'pillow cases, handkerchiefs and, most important, curtains'.

Surplus Service blankets occasionally appeared in the shops, and many thousands were converted into dressing gowns and winter coats. The new blanket coats which one London woman and her mother wore to a christening caused a sensation, one being dyed navy blue and the other dark brown, and they proved 'wonderfully warm and lasted till rationing ceased'. A Folkestone woman had an equal success with an Air Force blanket, costing five shillings, which was made up for her by a local dressmaker. 'We who had Air Force blanket coats', she recalls, 'felt we were "one up" on the women who had Army blanket coats.'

Never perhaps had underclothes been less glamorous than during the war. One woman remembers making winter petticoats and knickers from surgical lint and the wife of a London guardsman turned his long Army issue cotton underpants, which he refused to wear, into two pairs of warm briefs for herself. A Sheffield woman's panties had previously been exposed to view as her grandmother's bed valances. Women's underclothes had not been a subject publicly discussed before the war, but after the invasion of the Far East M.P.s rapidly learned from their postbags that the lack of rubber for elastic was, if not exactly a major threat to the war effort, a serious annoyance to the female half of the population. 'Elastic is scarce and still on war service', advised a government leaflet in 1945. 'When your suspenders wear out cut away the worn part and replace with an inch or two of strong tape or braid. Save spare parts. . . . Never throw away an old corset.' Many girl undergraduates at Oxford started to wear French knickers, wide-legged garments which had gone out of fashion but were fastened by buttons at the side instead of elastic. Older women, used to fuller-type directoire knickers, fastening round the leg, were, they complained, discriminated against, for these took three coupons instead of two. A forty-one-year-old Northolt housewife remembers that her daughters grew very cross at her extravagance in 'wasting' a coupon in this way.

A surprising number of people gave up wearing nightclothes for the duration and many women reverted to a nightdress, which needed only six coupons, from wearing pyjamas, which took eight. One wartime bride, married in 1944 on a stock of only twelve coupons, remembers her embarrassment on her wedding night at having to reveal her much-darned pyjamas to her husband. For women whose underclothes or night-clothes were becoming too shabby even for wartime the great blessing was coupon-free parachute silk. A landmine which fell on a village near Malvern, doing little damage, was, one resident remembers, regarded as 'manna from heaven' by the village girls. A fair-sized piece of parachute material cost only five shillings, but being cut 'on the cross' against the weave and heavily seamed, it was quite hard to handle on an ancient sewing machine. Some women complained that it had 'a cold slithery feel', and rustled, irritatingly, or excitingly, as one walked. In the later stages of the war parachutes were made of the then novel man-made fibre, nylon. One young London girl found that a single quarter of a nylon parachute was sufficient to make a sports shirt for her brother and a blouse, slip and panties for herself, the silk cord being used to hold up her pyjamas.

To most women 'nylon' meant stockings. Nylons arrived with the first G.I.s in 1942, and they could occasionally be found in the shops later in the war. A girl student at Southampton found that 'before dances the girls were crazy' to get nylons. A Lancashire shop assistant saw her first-ever pair when her mother brought them to her in hospital. 'I couldn't get up quickly enough to be able to wear them', she admits. To a generation growing weary of drab, wartime austerity, nylons gave promise of a more feminine, colourful life ahead and even women who rarely queued for food would queue for them for hours. One Golders Green woman admits to rising on Saturdays at five in the morning to queue at a shop which did not open till nine, in order to pay anything from fifteen shillings to a guinea for a single pair.

The stocking shortage was eased by the fact that slacks—eight coupons, against seven for a skirt—now came into general use. Leg make-up was also widely used. A popular substitute for the real-thing was sun-tan lotion, with a seam drawn in with eyebrow-pencil, but the nurses in one hospital produced an attractive tan shade with potassium permanganate crystals from the hospital dispensary, and a Blackpool woman stained her legs yellow with onion skins. Such expedients were not always successful: one Manchester teenager found that her tanned legs attracted more midges than men, and a Norfolk teenager's 'stockings' disintegrated halfway through the evening as the colouring became powdery and rubbed off. Even more embarrassing was the experience of a Lancashire girl who stained her skin with gravy browning, and was rudely greeted by the local boys with cries of 'Hello, Oxo legs!'

Bare legs were one thing, bare feet were another, and the search for shoes soon became a frustrating, time-consuming business. Output had been hit by the sinking of ships bringing hides, the demands of the Services, and the transfer to war work of too many footwear workers and repairers, who by 1944 were being encouraged to go back to their old jobs. Although the coupon value of shoes was raised in 1943, from seven to nine for men and from five to seven for women, the shortage grew steadily worse, especially of women's shoes, and often one had to queue for the right to join a shoe queue. A Liverpool woman remembers waiting for a ticket outside a large department store, which 'meant that at least you got into the shoe department', though this could be wasted effort, for 'they did not always have anything in your size'. In London, the shoe-shops were often sold out within twenty minutes of opening. A woman working in the ladies' department of a large shoe shop in Regent Street still vividly remembers those days. At the beginning of the week the shop might have fifty pairs of shoes for sale that day but by the end only ten so that they were sold out within half an hour. As orders by post were not accepted some people came from fifty miles away and stayed overnight at a hotel, to be first in the queue next morning.

The manufacture of crêpe rubber soles and heels was banned in 1942 and the height of heels limited to a maximum of two inches. The gap in supplies was filled largely with wooden-soled shoes, known as 'woodies', with a suède upper and a hinge in the sole, and in 1944 more than a million pairs were made for women alone. To save labour, little provision was made for anyone whose feet could not squeeze into a standard fitting. One Hampshire housewife found it impossible to buy a pair that fitted her and developed bunions which meant a long spell in hospital after the war. A woman working as a fitter's mate at an oil refinery wore boys' shoes to work: 'Less coupons, lasted longer and much more comfortable.' All-wooden clogs, which had been going out of favour, even in the industrial north, became so popular that one needed a certificate from a factory inspector to obtain a coupon-free pair, though one Lincoln housewife considered 'they were agony to wear'. Slippers could usually be found, though a Southsea teenager crocheted a pair in rug wool, reinforced with string, and an Uxbridge woman wore sandals made from a clothes-line which—typically of wartime—she had had trouble buying in the first place. Many felt hats were also demoted into slippers, instructions being given in magazines and 'Make do and mend' leaflets.

Many garments did duty, year after year, in various guises. A girl from Yorkshire, having made 'a woollen edge to edge coat . . . used it as such for a couple of seasons. Next I put buttons and buttonholes in and used a fur collar for another coat. Another season I took out the lining and made it into a button-through dress using a white lace bow at the neck. After that I made it into a skirt.' A Hayes housewife dyed her wedding dress first pink and then emerald green and finally sold it to buy clothing coupons. A South London husband found one evening that his treasured Harris tweed golfing trousers had been spotted by a sewing party meeting in his house and his wife, carried away by their enthusiasm, had turned them into an attractive skirt. He was, however, so furious at losing the trousers that his wife never dared to wear the skirt in front of him. Plus fours were much valued as raw material for skirts and boys' shorts, but even more in demand were discarded dinner jackets and trousers and to inherit one from a dead relative softened the blow of bereavement for any woman eager to make herself a smart dark suit or long evening skirt.

While the Ministry of Food was exhorting housewives to fight on the Kitchen Front, the Board of Trade constantly urged them to 'Make do and Mend'. 'Mrs. Sew and Sew', a fashionably thin puppet figure with a cotton reel body and clothes-peg legs, explained in the press and women's magazines 'How to patch a shirt', 'What Mother can do to save buying new' and how to 'Keep them tidy underneath'. ('Old shirts, too far gone for further repairs, will make inside yoke linings for night-dresses, cotton frocks, linings for small boys' trousers.') Fashion journalists showed in short films how to turn 'an old coat, that is on the long side . . . into a useful two-piece dress and jacket' and local 'Make do and mend' classes and advice centres reiterated the slogan:

> Mend and make do
> To save buying new.

Hugh Dalton's greatest success was the Utility Clothing scheme, which offered a restricted range of garments of simple, but sound, design, low price and guaranteed quality, made to detailed specifications.* The utility mark, two black circles with a segment cut out, became a guarantee of value for money and the scheme was later extended to cover furniture, while the public popularly labelled as 'utility' almost any unadorned, practical-looking item. The term became a source of numerous jokes. A drunk refused to be arrested by a 'special' because he was 'one of they utility coppers'. 'Heard about the utility woman?' ran another story, in more doubtful taste. 'She's single-breasted.' Utility tables were said to resemble chorus girls who had 'no drawers, not even a leaf', and in coarser circles one heard of the utility chamber-pot: 'Only the sides supplied. Put in your own bottom.'

Neither the Board of Trade nor Dalton himself ever achieved real popularity. 'I was regarded by many as a sort of universal provider for the civilian population', he complained in his memoirs. Yet this after all was just what Dalton's ministry was, but while Woolton welcomed critical letters, Dalton seemed to have resented them and he believed that public indignation on one issue—children's clothes—might have cost him votes in the 1945 General Election.†

The government was not unaware, as its critics suggested, that children were constantly growing, and kept the coupon values of children's clothes low and supplied extra coupons to those who were large for their age. But these measures never proved enough and it was, of course, not the children who suffered but 'Mum', a far more important 'universal provider' than any President of the Board of Trade. It was 'Mum' whose coupons enabled a teenage daughter to look smart for her first grown-up date, 'Mum' who kept the family in towels and curtains, 'Mum' who

* Utility clothes wore well. A Birmingham woman was still wearing one summer dress, bought about 1943, in 1967 when it began a new life as a cover for the cat's cushion.
† After the election Dalton became Chancellor of the Exchequer, until forced to resign in 1947 after a foolish Budget indiscretion. He died in 1962.

saved her children from the indignity of going to school dressed differently from everyone else. Many mothers with no pretensions to dressmaking skill bravely took up their needles or bought secondhand sewing machines, and children's clothes were made from an even wider variety of materials than adults'. A Shropshire mother dressed her children in cardigans made from dishcloths. A Glasgow housewife turned chamois leathers into children's coats, knitting on the sleeves and collars. Flourbags, costing 1s. to 2s. 6d. and providing a piece of material about one yard by two, printed in a cheerful floral pattern, were a great standby for small girls' dresses. The 'Exchange' columns in local newspapers were soon far longer than the 'For Sale' ones; a Leicestershire housewife remembers a typical transaction, trading a pair of curtains for a coat for her toddler. Some shopkeepers developed a sideline in secondhand children's clothing and one North London woman remembers clothing her children from goods bought from the greengrocer. Schools often arranged secondhand clothing sales, and the W.V.S. organised children's clothing exchange stalls, where no money changed hands, but each mother was given a number of 'points' for the clothes she handed in, to spend as she wished. Children's shoes were even harder to find than those for adults and even the most conscientious mothers were reduced to putting their children into secondhand shoes, 'said to be bad for their feet', as one mother recalls, 'but what could one do?' A South Benfleet mother remembers devoting a whole day to visiting thirty-five shoe shops in London in unsuccessful search for a 'DE' fitting for her son, and another Essex woman, from Shenfield, spent a day walking down the length of Oxford Street on one side, and back on the other, looking for a pair of 'Start-rite' shoes for her small son. The wife of a soldier stationed in Edinburgh could not send her daughter to school for part of one winter, as the snow lay deep outside and children's Wellingtons were one 'luxury' that had ceased to be made. Although more pairs of shoes per child were produced during the war than ever before, far more mothers could now afford to buy them, and with the disappearance of rubber and canvas plimsolls, the great standby of the poorer home, they now turned to leather shoes. Even when a pair of children's shoes had been found, it soon needed repairing and this could take another month, so some mothers, despite all their other preoccupations, now tried to teach themselves shoe-repairing, though even the materials for this were hard to find. One Cambridgeshire family's shoes were mended from old tyres, using 'the thin pieces for light soles and the thick pieces for the heels'.

One useful Order which the government did *not* make was to ban school uniform. One Staffordshire mother whose two daughters won scholarships to the local High School in 1943 and 1944 found that 'there was no relaxation in school uniform, the headmistress being of the stiff upper-lip variety. This meant that the whole family's clothes coupons had to be pooled to buy the necessary blazers, raincoats, material for blouses, games shorts and school dresses.' A Hull housewife had a similar experience when her children started at a boys' preparatory school and a girls' public school. 'Hereafter there were no coupons for anything excepting school uniforms. The children never had a change of clothes; all they had for best were new school uniforms and they got very tired of them.' Her daughter's school 'was a fussy one and she was not allowed to start school unless she had a red beret and I could not find one anywhere. After all, our big shops had all been bombed. I eventually got a pink one and dyed it red. It looked wonderful at first; but when it rained the red dye ran in streaks all down her face.'

Boys' schools could be equally unreasonable. The pleasure of a South Wales mother in her son's winning a place at a Grammar School was slightly marred by the fact that she needed fifty-two coupons for his uniform, and had only twelve. The Board of Trade, to whom she appealed for help, finally granted her an extra fourteen and apart from having to take his mother's dressing gown, her son went off to school well equipped, down to the regulation Eton collar, which cost her one much begrudged coupon.

Eton itself, it need hardly be said, also largely refused to lower its sartorial standards, but the prize for stupidity and selfish indifference to both the national need and common sense must surely go to my own school, which dressed its eight hundred boys in a ridiculous, uncomfortable and unhygienic Tudor ensemble of ankle-length gown, knee breeches, long, thick, yellow stockings and vast but shapeless shirt, without collar or cuffs. A less practical and more wasteful outfit it would have been hard to devise, but though the school did allow new boys to dress normally for their first year or two, the rest of us continued to look as if we were expecting the Spanish Armada rather than the German Army and almost all our coupons were simply appropriated to maintain this fatuous tradition.

Many women had promised themselves a great burst of spending on clothes 'after the war' and one soldier's wife in Glasgow began as the end approached to save coupons for a new dress in which to welcome her husband back from North Africa. But when the great day arrived she was still in her old, well-worn outfit. 'I rigged out the children instead', she admits, 'because I wanted him to see them looking as nice as possible.'

# DON'T YOU KNOW THERE'S A WAR ON?

'Cups and other drinking vessels are very scarce, largely because they
are the articles which the public wants to buy more than anything else.'

Board of Trade *Scheme for Ensuring Fair Shares for Small Retailers of
Pottery*, 1942

No one who lived through the war is likely to have forgotten Mr. Chad,
a plump-faced, long-nosed cartoon figure always seen peering over a
wall and uttering the same remark, 'Wot, no . . . !' Soon he was everywhere, for, as Tommy Handley might have said, there was a great deal
of nothing about. There was almost no article which did not at some
period of the war vanish from the shops, so that if 'You've had it!' was
the universal password in the services, the most often heard three
words in civilian life rapidly became 'In short supply'—which often
meant in no supply at all.

The government's efforts to cut down civilian consumption of goods
had begun early in the war, when the then President of the Board of
Trade had, to save metal, told the Coffin Manufacturing Association
that its members could in future only place two handles on their product
instead of six and had informed the Flushing Cisterns and Copper Balls
Association, to quote his own words: 'No more copper balls, I'm afraid.
. . . They will have to be made of plastic'. From 1940 onwards a series
of Limitation of Supplies Orders laid down the maximum amounts of
goods of specified types which manufacturers could supply to retailers.
The cuts were savage: in the first six months of 1941, for example, the
retailer could only receive a third of the suitcases or half the glassware
he had bought in the corresponding period of 1940, and only a quarter
of the saucepans, kettles, lawn mowers, and cameras. 'The object of the
Limitation of Supplies Order', explained the government, 'is to divert
raw materials, plant, capacity and labour from the production of goods
for the home trade. . . . Munitions must come first. This means . . . a
sacrifice of comforts, many of which are now regarded almost as necessities.'

By 1941 the housewife had discovered the truth of this warning for
herself. One of the first, and worst, shortages was of crockery. The
sixty-seven shapes of cup made pre-war were reduced to three and even

these were hard to find. From February 1942 it became illegal to decorate china for sale and, after a period with no cups at all, all that the shops could offer was thick, white crockery of the crudest design, often without handles. Oddments of chipped and cracked cups were now eagerly bought on market stalls and some families for a time had to use tin mugs and even jam jars. Pre-war 'best' china was now brought out for everyday use. 'When crockery suffered mishap', a Newcastle woman remembers, 'we had to resort to my grandfather's china and silver tea service. . . . It added a certain amount of dignity to our austerity.' Every possible drinking vessel was pressed into service. A Cornish farmer remembers seeing labourers building a new aerodrome enjoying their tea break with a 1937 Coronation mug gripped in each brawny hand. A girl working in an evacuated children's home in Sussex recalls the tiny hands of the children trying to clasp pint-size army mugs. My own family, all clean shaven, acquired a 'moustache cup', a large mug, with a ledge near the rim to prevent the drinker's moustache getting wet. A joke in *Punch* showed a duchess-like hostess politely offering her elegant friend a choice of mugs with the question, 'Will you have shaving or Coronation?' The breakage of any piece of crockery became a domestic tragedy. A Dumbarton mother was really upset when she smashed an irreplaceable lemon squeezer. In a Kent clergyman's home the rectory cat, a large 'marmalade' creature called Figaro, frightened by the noise of gunfire, knocked all the cooking glassware from the kitchen shelves to the stone floor, thus terrifying himself even more. For the rest of the war the household struggled along with the sole survivor of the disaster, an aluminium mixing bowl.

Supplies of cutlery had also been reduced to a quarter of the 1940 level, and spoons became particularly hard to find. At station buffets and in canteens a solitary teaspoon was often tied to the counter, and even in high-class teashops customers could be seen disdainfully stirring their tea with a fork-handle or a pencil. A Kettering schoolteacher remembers a relation and a Polish colonel who shared a table for breakfast at a first-class hotel being allowed only one spoon between them.

By 1942 millions of women were regretting the patriotic impulse which had led them two years earlier to give away their aluminium saucepans, for a new one of any kind was a rare sight. A Hayes factory worker had to use, irrespective of what she was cooking, a huge eight-pint saucepan; a land girl in Herefordshire was able, after queueing, to start her married life with exactly one saucepan, a severe challenge even to a skilled cook. Another housewife, finally, as a great concession, sold a saucepan to give to her daughter as a birthday present, was asked to hide it under her coat as she left the shop. A Sheffield nurse, given two hours off to spend with a friend who was on leave, sacrificed some of this precious time to queue for a saucepan, after seeing a girl carrying a new one, and asking her where she had obtained it. The aunts for whom she had bought it were not grateful; she was greeted 'with, "Well, we really wanted enamel!" They were a bit naive', she remarks indulgently. 'I don't think they realised how bad the shortages were.'

By early 1942 even the Board of Trade was admitting that 'shortages of commodities of a practical and non-luxury type were likely to be causing the public considerable inconvenience and difficulty'. This was an understatement. A survey carried out by the Board itself from 1943 onwards showed that fewer than half the women who had tried to buy a frying pan in the last month had managed to do so, and only one in four had obtained a saucepan. 37 per cent of women who needed a teapot had gone home empty-handed and 62 per cent of those who needed a small plate, most of them after trying in three shops or more. It all added up to a prodigious waste of time, effort and shoe-leather. Austerity in essential household supplies was, it is clear, overdone.

Mothers of families were also the worst sufferers from the shortage of household linen, for it was 'Mum's' coupons which were used to buy new curtain material or to keep the family in towels and tea-towels when, in October 1942, these too went on the ration. Most other items of household linen could not be bought, coupons or not. From June 1942 it became illegal to make bed-spreads or table-cloths, while sheets and blankets were virtually unobtainable except on 'dockets' issued only to the bombed-out and the newly wed. There was, too, very little choice. Towels were made only in three sizes and two colours, plain grey and plain white, and sheets only of coarse cotton, not linen. Most families simply ceased to buy such goods for the duration, 'making do and mending' instead. Flour sacks and sugar bags became curtains and a Leicestershire housewife remembers making cushion covers from the bags in which her chicken meal arrived. The same woman made a cot eiderdown from an old nightdress, filled with goose-down given to her by a farmer's wife. A Liverpool housewife describes flour bags as 'our great treasure', for bleached and dyed they became 'sheets, table-cloths, tea-towels and casement curtains . . . I used to walk down the streets amazed at the clean, smart windows of the small houses and a close look nearly always revealed flour bags plus ingenuity'. The curtain problem was also solved by the use of those invaluable stand-bys, chemist's gauze, balloon silk and butter muslin. A Coventry woman believes she must have been the only person in the country with strawberry-flavoured net curtains, for she had used strawberry essence to colour them when no dye was available. Black-out material, bleached and then dyed, could also be made to look reasonably attractive and another unrationed material was what a Brighton housewife describes as 'horrible hessian', used as cushion covers and loose chair covers, 'but the wretched stuff, being so loosely woven, soon wore through'. For houseproud women it was difficult to decide whether windows or furniture, living room or bedroom, needed brightening up most. A Kent housewife sacrificed a lace counterpane to make net curtains, while a Buckinghamshire house-wife turned some large white table-cloths she inherited into sheets. A Birmingham woman remembers an aunt solemnly dividing a large sheet one Christmas between three relations. A London nurse unpicked two silk pillow cases for conversion into short curtains and a midwife from Tooting who needed some curtains for a large bay window was told by one of her patients, 'Well, I will let you have a nice lace panel for a few quarters of tea but at the moment the dog has had her pups on it.' In due course, the family reared, she received the material and everyone admired her curtains.

Floor covering was considered by the government to be a luxury and second-hand carpeting of all kinds became extremely expensive. One London man moving house in 1943 was asked £120 for a small length of poor-quality stair carpet. Ordinary families could not afford such prices and rug-making became a minor domestic industry. Here, too, sugar sacks were invaluable, with strips of cloth or old stockings tied to the canvas. New wallpaper, too, disappeared but many 'people managed to redecorate their homes by buying ceiling whitening, and mixing it with different coloured dyes, or by distempering the walls and then applying another colour with a sponge, which produced an attractive 'stippled' effect mistaken by short-sighted or polite friends for real wall paper.

In July 1940 the supply of imported timber for furniture making had ceased and in 1942 the Board of Trade banned the manufacture of any furniture except twenty-two essential items. Strict price controls were introduced for both new and second-hand furniture, which could not be sold for more than its price when new. With the help of an advisory committee of the best designers in the country, the government intro-duced at the same time its utility furniture scheme, which offered soundly designed and well-made beds, sideboards, chairs, tables, kitchen cabinets and other necessities at reasonable prices. There was even an armchair, though no 'three-piece upholstered suite because of the considerable quantity of scarce materials . . . required in its manufacture'.

Utility furniture, although the choice was very restricted—there were two qualities and only three designs for each article—was one of the great successes of the war. A Board of Trade enquiry showed that 65 per cent of housewives questioned liked it and only 20 per cent positively disliked it, while nearly all, even had there been a choice—though from 1943 only utility furniture was made—would still have bought the utility kitchen cabinet. 'The furniture', its designers claimed with justice, 'is pleasant to look at and easy to keep in condition', but the materials were inevitably rather poor and the purchaser of one utility sideboard found that when 'the sun shone on the back under the thin oak veneer I could distinctly see the lettering "Apples" '. The chief complaint about utility furniture was that there was not enough of it to go round. Only people who had been bombed out, or had married since January 1941, could even apply for a purchasing 'docket', and they had to fill in a long questionnaire stating what furniture they already possessed. There was no fixed ration, and only enough furniture units were issued to give the applicants the barest minimum of furniture to set up house. The maximum was at first sixty units for a couple, plus another fifteen for each child, or expected child, but in July 1944 the allowance was cut to thirty units, too little even to furnish a single room. When you had received your permit you faced a long wait, for you could spend it only in a specified area and it had to be handed over before the shop concerned could order the goods. An engaged couple could apply for their docket two months before the wedding, but if the engagement was broken off the permit had to be returned. Working out how to spend their precious units provided many couples with an engrossing occupation. A twenty-five-year-old nurse from the Middlesex Hospital settled for a table at six units, four chairs at one each, a sideboard at eight and a wardrobe at twelve, which used up the whole allowance. Unfortunately, this left no units for a bed—five for a double or six for two singles—a fireside chair, a dressing table, or a bookcase. A Barnsley housewife filled an equally vital gap by borrowing a table from her office.

Bedding was even more essential than beds, for at a pinch one could always sleep on the floor, but supplies were too small even to ration and instead 'priority dockets' were issued to bombed-out and newly married people to give them first refusal of any sheets, blankets or pillows a retailer might have in stock. Only the most fortunate 'non-priority' shopper ever got a look in, though the wife of a West Country veterinary surgeon encountered an assistant in a famous London store who discovered that he had, after all, blankets to sell when she asked whether a dozen fresh Dorset eggs might improve the supply.

At first families who had set up house before 1941 had to manage as best they could, but eventually it became possible to apply—though not always with success—for a docket to buy some essential article where one's circumstances had changed. One South Benfleet housewife remembers having to explain to the Board of Trade that she needed two pairs of new single sheets as her children had outgrown their cots—one of the commonest reasons for an application. A Merchant Seaman's wife in Cheshire was less fortunate. She hopefully applied for dockets to buy new floor covering on moving house as, when they had moved in, someone had helpfully glued their carpets to the floor, but had her request turned down.

By the middle of the war there was barely any article which was not scarce or unobtainable and on all sides was heard the irritating response to almost any request, 'Don't you know there's a war on?' Undoubtedly, supplies to the civilian population were cut back too far. What was the use of the Board of Trade urging housewives to 'make do' when its own researchers found that three out of ten women were unable to buy a needle, and one in every four had not managed to obtain any darning wool? Was it really in the national interest, one wonders, that one house-proud Yorkshirewoman should have been forced to make her own floor polish from candles and beeswax, or a Gravesend house-wife should have had to crush down old batteries to black-lead her stove, or a third woman make her own brass-cleaning fluid out of salt and vinegar? Even less defensible was the shortage of toothbrushes; a Board of Trade enquiry showed nearly 40 per cent of people unable to obtain one. An Air Ministry secretary recalls the choice she faced when she had three hours to spare while changing trains at Inverness: should she go to a much-praised film or hunt for a toothbrush? 'The toothbrush won', she remembers, 'and I was lucky—in the seventh shop I tried.' There was no such happy ending, however, for the fire-watchers at her office who were 'quite upset when a shortage of ping-pong balls put an end to their nightly competitions'—yet the humble ping-pong ball, too, had its place as a guardian of morale. Another annoying shortage was of fountain pens. I can remember a typical wartime birthday present in 1944, the promise of a fountain pen when the shop received its next quota.

The Board of Trade did its best to ensure that all goods in demand were shared fairly throughout the country and to see that they reached those who needed them most: sports goods, for instance, being mainly supplied through recognised clubs and musical instruments being largely reserved for priority users, such as the BBC. The ordinary civilian inevitably came at the end of the queue, which was often jumped by someone flourishing a 'priority permit' issued by an employer or a doctor. This system was used for an enormous range of items, though in most cases the shopkeeper was merely asked—not legally compelled— to give preference to 'priority' customers. Thermos flasks were largely reserved in this way for shift workers and land girls, who could only obtain a replacement on producing the broken article. Requests for 'priority' certificates made a heavy demand on the scanty time of over-worked G.P.s. One woman doctor in Westmorland remembers a patient ringing her up at 11 p.m. to report an unusual medical emergency: 'Doctor, my hot water bottle has just burst. Will you please give me a certificate for a new one?' Another woman doctor in Cheshire even had to issue a medical certificate to enable an old, arthritic woman, who found bending down difficult, to obtain a bucket and mop. At one time it seemed almost as though a note from a doctor would be needed to buy a razor blade, a shortage which affected even hospitals. A nurse in County Durham found that 'shaving a patient ready for surgery was difficult with only a well-used, blunted blade', and even millionaires were not exempt, for in April 1942 'Chips' Channon thought it worth recording in his diary that a friend had brought six packets of razor blades for him from India. One young clergyman working near Nottingham is still grateful to a parishioner who enabled him to stay cleanshaven; he worked at the headquarters of Boots the chemist. Strops became almost as rare as new blades and one prison governor remembers as his most successful 'buy' of the war a strop, found in a shop in Lincoln, which enabled him to make two blades last for six months. Even more remarkable results were claimed for rubbing a razor blade in warm water against the inside of a tumbler. If this was done at least twenty times after use, it was said, and the blade kept in borax and water, it might last as long as eleven months. To let a visitor use one's razor became a mark of high friendship. A Civil Servant's wife at Blackpool can still not forgive the American soldier they befriended who, when they were out, used her husband's razor, and his one good blade, without permission—no doubt not realising the enormity of his offence.

Americans also found it hard to understand the difficulty of obtaining almost any kind of personal service. One frequently saw them standing in dry-cleaners' shops, bewildered that the assistant could not accept their uniforms because her quota for the day was full, or astounded to learn that cleaning might take several weeks. It was even more difficult to get one's watch or an electrical appliance mended. Laundries mainly ceased to accept new customers and newsagents were reluctant to add to their delivery rounds. One middle-class woman in Marylebone was surprised when ordering a newspaper in 1944 to be told 'I'll have to ask my boy as he's choosey as to whom he delivers to'.

All these inconveniences were merely troublesome, but the lack of another simple item, the alarm clock, must have cost the country thousands of man-hours of lost production. The alarm clock shortage was due to a failure of imagination on the part of both ministers and officials, who, with no experience of shift work and often accustomed to being wakened by servants, at first classed alarms, like other clocks, as luxury items. The results were serious. The public woke up—late—one morning to find that the alarm clocks it took for granted had been imported from

France, Switzerland and Italy, from which all supplies had been cut off, while imports from the United States had been reduced to save dollars. In 1940 one could still easily buy a good enamel alarm clock from Marks and Spencers for 3s. 11d., but by March 1941 an M.P. was warning the President of the Board of Trade of the 'very serious shortage of alarm clocks in the country', and by January 1943 a North Country M.P. was complaining that 'lack of alarm clocks is having a serious effect in the coalfields of the North, where large numbers of miners go to work at one and two o'clock in the morning', and was contributing to the prevailing absenteeism. Nor were miners the only sufferers. A wartime 'clippie' attended a union meeting in Sheffield where the union secretary 'quoted some pathetic letters from men and women who spent sleepless nights beset by the fear of oversleeping'. For a staff of 4,600 the transport department had received precisely twelve permits for alarm clocks. A journalist working on the 'dawn shift' from midnight to 8 a.m. at Bush House, headquarters of the BBC European Service, going to bed in the afternoon, more than once overslept and had an hour and a half's walk to work, with no transport running. Here the whole of the large Central News department received only three permits between them. An elderly postwoman in Sussex managed to get up in time only by having a long string dangling from her window tied to a handbell in her bedroom, the driver of the early morning mail van stopping to tug at it as he passed her cottage on his way to the sorting office at Petworth. The string proved too strong a temptation one night to some Canadian soldiers, but they were very repentant when she roundly told them off for waking her—and she in turn regretted her annoyance later: soon afterwards the men concerned went off to Dieppe and few came back.

To overcome the shortage an ugly, oblong clock in a black fibre case, known as a 'Waralarm', was put on the market and in February 1944 it was announced that future permits would only be issued, through employers and trade union branches, to those who regularly needed to get up between midnight and 5 a.m. Alarm clocks were said to be so few that it was impossible even to raise the qualifying time to 6 a.m. By June the Board claimed to have issued more than half a million permits but within a month M.P.s were complaining that many of the clocks distributed had already broken down and by October the shortage was so bad again that one M.P. was suggesting an alarm clock was needed to wake up the minister responsible. Rather oddly, having abolished permits, the Board of Trade tried to continue control by putting purchasers on their honour and retailers were expected to ask would-be customers to sign a declaration that they needed an alarm clock for their work, although there were no penalties for refusal—except presumably that you did not get your clock. This strange system survived till after the war when increased supplies finally made it unnecessary.

What was the most annoying shortage of the war? A schoolgirl living on a Nottinghamshire farm remembers one surprising one. 'There were a vast number of flies at the farm, and fly-papers were like gold-dust they were so rare', she recalls. 'We used to tour round the neighbouring villages, going from shop to shop asking for fly-papers. There was a great deal of jubilation if we had as many as half a dozen when we returned.' But most mothers, looking back, seem to regret most the absence of camera films which has left them without any record of the years when their children were growing up. At the time, the greatest vexation was probably caused by the periodic disappearance of matches. Some women carefully sliced matches in half to stave off the evil day of being without a light in the house and in July 1942, the very month in which the great fuel saving campaign began, others were having to keep a gas ring continuously alight solely for this purpose. In August the Board of Trade, with the consumption of matches down by half, declared that there was 'no question of rationing matches or putting them on points', but to overcome the snortage it had to divert metal and labour to manufacturing utility gas lighters, using a flint. The match shortage reappeared at intervals throughout the war, and smokers complained that whenever cigarettes were plentiful matches were scarce, not apparently appreciating that the two events were connected.

Although the war was a painful time for smokers, it is hard for a non-smoker, forced to endure the misery of smoke-filled trains, cinemas, canteens and barrack rooms, to feel much sympathy with their sufferings, or to find comprehensible the government's decision to waste on useless tobacco currency and shipping space that might have gone on real essentials, like alarm clocks. Well-known brands of cigarettes first became scarce early in 1941 and by May a definition of a millionaire was going the rounds: 'A man who smells like an onion and smokes the cigarettes he likes'. One BBC producer, meeting the Queen's brother at this time, was amused to hear him say ' "Look what I've got", in the proud tones of a man who had just bought a priceless piece of china', as he 'pulled out a packet of twenty Virginian cigarettes . . . almost the cheapest obtainable in the good old pre-war days'. By August the leading manu-facturers were optimistically appealing to smokers for 'A little restraint, please. Cigarette smokers have it in their own power to end the unhappy position now existing in the shops. If for the next few weeks they will cut down their consumption by smoking eight instead of ten, sixteen instead of twenty, then the shops will have time to acquire full stocks. . . . Be moderate, have patience and above all DO NOT HOARD.' But to be moderate and have patience was not in the nature of a frustrated smoker. One man who ran a tobacconists' shop in a Midland city found that 'Men and women fought for them more fiercely than for food. A very nice man of my acquaintance, when told we had no cigarettes, shouted at the innocent assistant "You're a flaming liar!" ', and his wife had to spend 'thirty minutes in the office drying the girl's tears'. Another customer shouted 'You've got them under the bloody counter!', and when finally convinced there were none to be had bellowed 'Then keep your papers', and threw down the newspapers he was buying. After being ordered out of the shop he held forth to the nearby bus queue on his maltreatment, until the owner had to threaten to call the police. In another shop an assistant grew so tired of being bullied that she hung a notice 'Sorry, no cigarettes' round her neck, and in Marylebone appeared a politer variant of the same message: 'We regret that only customers over ninety can be served and then only if accompanied by both parents'. Those who worked in tobacconists' shops were assiduously courted by desperate smokers. In Dorchester a customer would often look pointedly at the empty shelves as he put a tin of meat on the counter, and a Fulham tobacconist became used to receiving regular bunches of flowers, or offerings of new potatoes or peas from her male customers. (The casual customers contented themselves with giving her 'a dirty look' when she refused them.) A Sherborne hairdresser, whose shop also sold cigarettes, found it 'amazing to what lengths people would go to bribe you for more than we rationed each customer to'—ten for each non-regular. A Somerton woman remembers an immensely coveted first prize at a whist drive—a packet of twenty Players. Many women, with money to spare for the first time, took up smoking during the war, but not all shopkeepers approved and in Birkenhead some would sell cigarettes only to men.

An enormous amount of time was wasted in the search for cigarettes, for there was little enthusiasm for the obscure brands which now replaced the well-known ones. A Glasgow bus conductress remembers that whenever she went to the cinema there seemed to be someone nearby smoking Pashas, an unpopular Turkish brand with a distinctive smell, and many long waits in queues, she found, ended in one being allowed only five ordinary cigarettes and five Pashas. A Lincoln housewife used to spend her lunch hour touring the town with workmates and if they saw a queue they would automatically join it. 'Once for fun we started our own queue. Before you could say "Jack" the queue was fifty yards long. The shopkeeper came to the door and asked what we were queueing for and we mumbled "Cigarettes". To our amazement he had some and started to do a roaring trade. They were called "Walters" and tasted foul. We couldn't even give them away after the first puff.'

When a cigarette smoker did at last manage to satisfy his craving he made the most of his supplies, holding each cigarette on a pin, to smoke it to the bitter end, and then perhaps pounding the butts together to burn in a pipe. Pipe tobacco was rarely quite as scarce as cigarettes, though strange brands appeared, one of which was said to taste and smell like dried hay. An Aylesbury woman remembers her uncle mixing his tobacco with dried sorrel leaves and other herbs to make it go further, so that 'It smelt like a bonfire, but he seemed to enjoy it', and a Birmingham housewife and her neighbour went on expeditions to gather oak-leaves, coltsfoot leaves and dock seeds for the same purpose. Some people also experimented with home-grown tobacco, which was said to be particularly popular with country clergy.

While the war—and especially being hungry—caused some people to smoke it prevented some others acquiring the habit, like a then school-girl in Norfolk:

> One thing which I have never forgotten is the cigarette shortage. We children could always tell when the ration had been smoked. My step-father would wander round the house looking in vases, pockets and drawers. Our neighbour used to pace up and down the garden path, while another used to take his spite out on any cat, dog or child who happened to pass by. My uncle, who had red hair and was a bit snappy at the best of times, was a heavy smoker so I always kept well clear of him! Then the village shop received fresh supplies and all was serene again. I shall always remember seeing a group of adults standing in the village street passing a cigarette from mouth to mouth. Their hands were trembling and, although I was only fourteen years old, I thought how disgusting and degrading it was. I vowed then and there that I would never smoke and I never have.

Drinkers proved better able to endure the loss of their chief pleasure than smokers. During the first year of the war the supply of sugar and grain to breweries and distilleries had been sharply reduced and within a year beer production was down by a twentieth and the output of whisky by two-thirds. The Fall of France cut off supplies of most imported wines and in October 1941 all further imports of alcohol ceased for the duration, except for some Empire products, regarded by most drinkers as almost undrinkable. It was a black day when some long-hoarded item finally came to an end. The journalist Charles Graves noted in his diary in October 1942 drinking his last bottle of champagne and in July 1943 was present at another melancholy event, the last night of the Pimms No. 1 at the Royal Automobile Club. The Reform Club could still manage post-prandial port as late as March 1943, but by September no wine at all was available at the Athenaeum, most respected of London clubs.

Drink, due partly to successive Budgets, rose in price far more sharply than almost any other item. Beer was by 1944 1*s.* to 1*s.* 3*d.* a pint, compared with the pre-war 6*d.*, and spirits had also doubled to an official price—often exceeded—of 25*s.* 9*d.* a bottle, or about 1*s.* 6*d.* a nip. Far higher prices were often asked—and paid. Publicans everywhere told the story of the American soldier, who, offered a bottle of whisky at the correct price, had asked instead for the 'real stuff' at his usual price of £5. By 1943 £3 was being charged for a bottle of claret with a meal and £2 2*s.* for a bottle of vodka to take away—vodka had suddenly come into fashion along with all things Russian. By September 1944 Charles Graves was reduced to paying 32*s.* 6*d.* for a bottle of Australian port which he described as 'awful', and the Savoy, admittedly a luxury hotel, was asking ten shillings for a single glass of rum punch, though rum, being less popular, was never quite as scarce as gin.

Most sought after of all was whisky. Charles Graves recieved envious glances as he walked through the streets in 1942 carrying an unwrapped bottle of golden liquid— it was in fact Canadian maple syrup. A woman running a licensed grocers' in Morecambe in 1944 was offered a valuable set of gold coins in exchange for a bottle of Scotch and the son of a manager of an off-licence near Cheltenham was always being given a lift as soon as he stepped outside the door by customers who would ask when the whisky was due in, adding pointedly, 'Remember me to your father.' Many conscientious retailers reserved the few bottles of brandy they received for old people, who claimed to need them on medicinal grounds. A Blackpool aircraft worker paid £4 for a bottle of brandy for her invalid mother and a Hornsey housewife queued with a bottle at an off-licence to buy a single nip when the doctor prescribed it for hers.

From 1941 onwards the doleful sign 'No beer' was often to be seen displayed outside public houses and many pubs did not open until eight o'clock in the evening, or only on alternate nights, often rationing customers to a pint, or even half a pint, a head. The lack of glasses was almost as troublesome as the beer drought. Some licensees refused to serve anyone who did not bring a glass, while others would not refill a used one on the grounds that the customer must have had a drink already. Strangers in a pub were often met with surly suspicion. One elderly man evacuated from Birmingham to an Oxfordshire village found his visits to the pub marred by the villagers' resentment at his drinking 'their' beer. To save transport, beer was 'zoned' and every pub was supposed to get its supplies from within thirty miles but as different brands continued to be made a house 'tied' to one brewer might still have supplies while others in the same district were dry. Some keen drinkers developed a regular reconnaissance system. A publican from

Hook in Yorkshire remembers how people in Goole, a few miles away, would send a scout out on the bus to see if her pub had beer in stock. If he failed to return his friends followed him on the next bus.

Bottled beer was often scarcer than draught, and Guinness, though still to be found in some 'Irish houses', was most elusive of all. An Edinburgh man who joined the BBC Overseas Services in London in 1943 still recalls the off-licence in Belsize Park where he 'was presented with a vicious circle. I could get bottled beer if I presented an empty bottle. But having just moved in, I had no empties.' His problem was solved when, by producing his identity card, he convinced the retailer that he had recently changed his address—a use for this document not foreseen by its inventors.*

This man remembers wartime English beer as 'even more watery than it is today', a common criticism reflected in the story of the Yorkshireman who when the barmaid, handing him his pint of beer, remarked, 'It looks like rain', replied: 'Aye, I thought it wasn't beer.'

In the first world war excessive drinking had led to the imposition on Britain of the rigid licensing system which persists to this day, but in the second drunkenness was never a serious problem and the arch-prohibitionist, Lady Astor, M.P. for Plymouth, declared, with some exaggeration, that 'No government since the world began has ever cared less about temperance than this government'. Most M.P.s' questions were now about there being too little drink rather than too much and ministers were always being asked to provide more beer for miners or for those helping to get in the harvest. These requests rarely succeeded, any more than the suggestion made in 1943, when the beer shortage was at its height, that all alcoholic drink should be rationed. There would, a minister explained, be 'the difficulty of proper pointing as between champagne and mild and bitter'.

---

* The bottle shortage affected all drinks. Despite a national campaign to persuade people to return their milk bottles, many roundsmen had to deliver milk straight from the churn into the housewife's jug, and one might be asked for 'a shilling on the bottle', instead of the customary twopence, when buying a bottle of lemonade. The 'returning the empties' principle also applied to other goods, from toothpaste tubes to cotton reels, though this shortage was eventually overcome by using cardboard tubes instead of wooden spools.

# 23

# BEST FACE FORWARD

'With leisure and beauty-aids so scarce, it is very creditable to look our best. Let us face the future bravely and honour the subtle bond between good looks and good morale. Put your best face forward.'

Advertisement for Yardley cosmetics in *Housewife*, June 1943

One afternoon in 1943 the manager of a Ministry of Labour office in a small Berkshire town released his female staff from their duties one by one for a reason not covered by any Civil Service regulations: there were hair-grips in at a local shop, and each women or girl wanted the chance to buy some before they vanished. The government might class hairdressing and cosmetic manufacture as luxury trades, to be as far as possible closed down; the men on the spot, employing women, knew better. As beauty-writers in the women's magazines constantly reminded their readers: now more than ever it is our duty to look our best.

The war produced no great change in women's fashions. In the early months the fashionable thing was to wear uniform of some kind and two years later, when clothes rationing began, merely finding any smart clothes and time off to wear them became a sufficient problem without bothering about new styles, even if dress designers had not themselves been otherwise occupied. But there were some general trends. Particularly in the early days, women's suits and overcoats took on a military look, with severe lines, square-padded shoulders and fake epaulettes. Military influence was also obvious in the siren suit, later made even more popular by Winston Churchill, which consisted of a zipped or buttoned jacket, with ample pockets and large, draught-excluding hood, and matching trousers resembling ski-pants. Like the uniforms of ambulance-drivers, A.F.S. girls and wardens, the siren suit made trousers respectable. One women's magazine described 1940 as 'the only time in our history that women have worn trousers openly in the streets without derisive comment'. They went with the other items of 'blitz wear', 'sweater, wedge shoes and turban, all perfectly functional'.

If the skirt was the first casualty of the war the second was the hat. Before the war no well-dressed woman went out without a hat but within a few months to wear one became regarded almost as a sign of unpatriotic frivolity. The government gave a lead by treating hats as an unnecessary luxury and in 1942 even talked of moving the remains of the trade from Luton, the traditional hat-capital of Great Britain, to some area like the North East coast where labour was less in demand. This threat led to a town's meeting in a Luton cinema, a high-level deputation to the Board of Trade and a warning by the Town Council that 'The temper of the people is rising. Unless some concession is made we shall have to be very careful that things don't get beyond our control.' Fortunately the proposal was dropped before the angry hat-makers of Luton, armed with hat-pins and cutting-out scissors, had actually marched on Whitehall, but the civilian hat trade had a tough time for the remainder of the war. There were complaints in Parliament about the 'fantastic prices' being charged for hats—one woman in Edinburgh remembers being asked seven guineas for 'a rather dim affair trimmed with a scrap of fur'. Some women wore men's felt hats with the crown pushed out and a new ribbon or feather added, but Hugh Dalton at the Board of Trade refused to produce a utility hat, believing that women would not accept it. He did finally authorise two simple basic designs in wool felt, the 'one star' version selling at not more than a guinea and the 'two star' at not more than twenty-five shillings, but all other types of hat remained uncontrolled.* But most women solved the hat problem by wearing a head scarf, either tied loosely beneath the chin or in a turban style, which, like trousers, became accepted as both smart and socially acceptable.

But if headwear was sensible, hair-styles were not. 'History will record that we foolishly let our hair float loosely in the wind beneath the turban', acknowledged *Housewife* in 1945, looking back to 1940, though it blamed the style on 'the influence of the American film-stars'. It was in fact *one* film-star, Veronica Lake, whose hair fell attractively over her shoulders, who set this fashion which appealed to many women precisely because it was feminine and impractical. The style caused the Ministry of Labour much anxiety due to the risk of accidents if flowing hair was caught in factory machines and women were urged to adopt styles which could be tucked beneath a cap. The patriotic fashion became the 'Victory Roll', with hair rolled up tightly round the head, with an upswept curl on the top. A London nurse remembers that 'girls and women cut the top off a stocking and put it on their heads and curled up the hair and tucked it in. With curly hair and deft fingers it could look quite attractive.' A Bradford teenager noticed that as the war continued it became the custom to wind an old stocking or twisted scarf around the head, and

* The hat trade had suffered badly from loss of imported supplies. Its straw hoods had come from Italy, its velour from Austria and its braids from Switzerland. One Luton firm which in 1940 built bales of old braid into a blast wall was a few months later glad to demolish the wall to use the contents in its factory.

tuck the hair into this 'foundation', producing a semi-circular 'sausage' which removed the need for curlers. An Oxford undergraduate found that the fashionable styles there in 1943 were the page-boy, with the hair straight except for the curl at the end which was kept in place with kirbygrips, or the more sophisticated 'pompadour' where the hair was piled on top of the head, with the hair from the back being tucked underneath and held in place with the invaluable kirbygrips. One beauty-writer recommended in 1941, 'the easiest set in existence . . . the coronet of disc curls round the head. When this is dry, the curls can be combed over the fingers into big, loose, upward-moving curls or, alternatively, into a round-the-head roll. A modified page-boy is another good bet, the hair being rolled in curls and brushed sleekly under.'

But keeping one's hair in place, whatever the style, became increasingly difficult as the simple necessities so long taken for granted began to vanish from the shops. One of the earliest to go was the kirbygrip, made of high quality spring steel, and the substitutes which appeared were often made of soft steel which never regained their original shape and constantly fell out. This was a shortage that affected all age groups. A nurse in a Liverpool eye hospital remembers 'one old lady was absolutely heartbroken when her box of hairgrips fell on the floor. "You can't buy them anywhere", she wept, and had me down on my hands and knees retrieving them before she would let me do anything for her.' An eighteen-year-old Ilford waitress received one day a highly unusual tip from a male customer—a packet of hairclips 'for your lovely hair'. Substitute hairpins, made of plastic, were equally unsatisfactory. One young City office worker found them 'about as much good as a piece of stick'. Curlers, too, became hard to find and many women fastened their hair overnight in pipe-cleaners. An even more basic lack was of combs. A Birmingham housewife still possesses one curious souvenir of the war— a large comb made of aeroplane aluminium, and a twenty-year-old land girl once cycled several miles to Stratford-on-Avon to obtain her solitary comb, which was 'large and green, resembling a garden rake. . . . Even the German P.O.W.s'—those sad and sullen men—'laughed when they saw it.'

Although younger girls were largely called up, many hairdressers were exempt because they were running one-man businesses and these were on the whole boom years for the hairdressing trade. A Coventry girl, twenty in 1939, acquired early in the war her own hairdressing business near 'a small factory estate where more and more girls were taking over men's jobs . . . and they came to join the young matrons who had been my former clientele', until she was so busy she needed an assistant. Besides the normal hair-cut (then costing 1s.), shampoo and set (2s. 6d.), Marcel wave (3s.) and permanent wave (from 15s. to 30s.) she was now called on to provide a new type of hair treatment, in discreet private sessions, for 'women who realised with horror that they or their children had become infected with lice . . . in air-raid shelters'. She discovered, too, a new skill as a mechanic, for when 'an elderly man and a boy' were sent to repair one of her pedestal driers, they proved, after dismembering the machine, to be quite unable to repair it. 'Extremely cross,' she recalls, 'I undid screws, exposing the fault, and did the job myself', and when a bill arrived she sent it back, suggesting that she should be paid instead, 'as I had instructed the supposed mechanics in a new branch of their trade'. This business, although prosperous, eventually had to be sold after the blitz of November 1940 had interrupted its supplies of water and electricity, and the owner's assistant had had a nervous breakdown following the death of her pilot fiancé.

Regular work and high wages meant a rush on the hairdressers. 'A permanent wave is a necessity for women who are doing war work unless their hair is naturally curly', asserted one advertisement in December 1941. 'The demand for Eugene waves has, naturally, greatly increased this year.' Securing an appointment to have one's hair done became increasingly difficult. One young I.C.I. research chemist, working on penicillin development in Manchester, with only one day off a fortnight, was reduced to going to a men's hairdresser who gave her a 'very peculiar' cut. To cater for the shift-worker many hairdressers—unlike other shops —now opened longer than before the war. One who was twenty when the war began, and who ran a hairdressing salon at Goole in Yorkshire, found that many of her clientele did not arrive back in town until 7 p.m., so that she was often still finishing off a four-hour permanent wave at midnight. 'I even started appointments at seven o'clock in the morning to shampoo and set or Marcel wave before they went to work', she remembers, and the day was so full that 'my meals were brought in on a tray from next door'.

In the early days most hairdressers took shelter when the siren sounded and one working in Barking in the autumn of 1940 remembers that 'we would often take the clients down into the Anderson shelter in the yard backing on to the salon'. This provided too little room for even the simplest treatment, but in the spacious shelters of the big stores assistants could be seen completing the usual rituals interrupted by the Luftwaffe. In August 1940 the house magazine of the John Lewis group reported that 'At Chelsea and at Peckham several customers who were having their hair shampooed were able to have it set and dried in the shelters', while 'at Peter Jones the system of waving being used . . . was hurriedly changed over to one that needed no electricity . . . and was a great success'. In future, it was announced, hair-driers would be provided for use by customers in mid-treatment.

Later in the war the hairdressers' main problem became the lack of essential materials. Bleaches, hair-tinting dyes and hair-setting lotion were all scarce, but the most troublesome shortage was of shampoo. 'Good, perfumed shampoo was hard to obtain', a Dorset hairdresser remembers, 'but the customers always liked to think they had the best. . . . One trade secret was to make shampoo out of green soft soap, by adding water and bringing it to the boil. This made a thick liquid to which we added verbena essence and the customers thought they were getting a very expensive hard-to-get shampoo.' Another luxury was to have a towel provided. From October 1942, when they went on coupons, one was normally expected to take one's own, making it easy to pick out women on their way to keep a hair appointment.

Hairdressers were strictly forbidden by the manufacturers to sell for home use materials intended for their salons, and many ingenious concoctions were produced to take their place. One young Birmingham housewife made her own shampoo from Persil or Rinso, adding half a cup of vinegar to the final rinsing water, and a Somerset teenager sacrificed the family rations to make a sugar-and-water setting lotion, 'a sticky process' she admits. Those who could not afford to visit the hairdresser made do with 'home-perm' outfits. One Timber Corps member in Somerset invested 14s. 6d. plus tax in her first home perm, which was optimistically called 'Endura'. The curlers were made of wire which was covered with strips of brown paper and the waving liquid smelt like rotten eggs. It gave, she recalls, a good curl but even though she was working in the open air it took a week to get rid of the smell.

The rationing of the most basic cosmetic of all, soap, came into force in February 1942. Most men, unless they had a very dirty job, when they qualified for an extra allowance, a privilege they shared with small babies, found it possible to manage on the ration, for each four-week period, of three ounces of toilet soap—equal to one small tablet or rather over half a bath tablet. Young girls, for ever washing themselves or their 'smalls', and mothers, with the family laundry to do, found it more difficult to manage, though the ration could also be taken in the form of rather larger amounts of hard soap, soft soap or the wartime detergent, 'No. 2 soap powder'. Shaving soap remained unrationed and this proved many women's salvation. The concentration of production in a few firms meant that many familiar types of soap vanished, along with the elegant wrappers of peacetime. A tablet of pre-war soap became something to treasure. One Scotsman remembers that when he bought a large oval cake of Elizabeth Arden geranium-perfumed soap as a birthday present for a girl friend in London, the recipient was thrilled and vowed it should be kept, unsullied by hands or water, on her mantelpiece. A teenage girl in a Norfolk village reacted in the same way when some kindly Americans gave her a large cake of toilet soap when she was ill. 'I didn't open it for ages. I put it beside my bed and just looked at the wrapper and sniffed the beautiful scent.'

The rationing of soap produced the inevitable jokes about the shortage being welcomed by small boys, but the reality was not always very funny. An Islington teacher remembers questioning one pupil about his home circumstances and finding that his mother sold most of his coupons, including those for soap, the obvious lack of which had prompted her enquiry. Although, like so many firms, their problem was meeting the demand, not stimulating it, the soap manufacturers bravely kept their names before the readers of the women's magazines. 'Driving through blitzes won't spoil that schoolgirl complexion', one comfortingly assured them in 1942. 'You can be quite confident your skin will show no sign of strain if you keep Palmolive in your kit.' 'Here's good news, girls', asserted another manufacturer. 'Even if you are sometimes disappointed because your favourite shop is temporarily out of Lux Toilet Soap there's no need to worry. . . . With a little care, Lux Toilet Soap . . . can be made to go twice as far.' The same magazine carried soap-saving hints, like putting one's scraps of soap in a pan, pouring on boiling water, and leaving the mixture to harden into a usable size piece. Another method was to put these left-overs in a tin and punch holes in the lid. This, 'swished in a basin of hot water', to quote one housewife, 'washed greasy plates or stockings or our hair'. 'It is very little known that any material, but particularly woollens, can be most successfully washed with glue dissolved in hot water', began one women's magazine article in August 1942, going on to give detailed instructions. Some people claim to have made their own soap from paraffin, beeswax and animal fat. My own efforts, using a school chemistry textbook, produced only an unusable and repellent mess, resembling blackened dripping.

From 1941 onwards, cosmetics began to become scarce, partly because elaborate make-up was by now becoming accepted even in towns where hitherto anything more than a discreet touch of powder had been frowned on. (In the formerly staid streets of Harrogate it was said to be possible in 1939 to pick out the Air Ministry office workers and other evacuees by their more heavily made-up faces.) The shortage occurred just as many women began to have cash to spare for personal luxuries. 'For girls like me, earning good money for the first time in their lives,' a Bournemouth office worker, sixteen in 1939, admits, 'it was a constant vigilance of chemists' shops to snap up their small consignments of lipstick and other beauty aids. . . . We would pay anything at all on the black market for perfume, and how wonderful it was when we came by a bottle—a fragrant whiff of better times in a world gone mad with war.'

But scent was the scarcest item of all, for the ingredients or finished products had often been imported and the blitz had made things no easier. 'With two factories bombed and the limitation of supplies, these perfumes cannot, for a little time, always be obtained', advised Bourjois, the makers of *Evening in Paris*, and *Ashes of Roses* in 1941, in a notable understatement. The cosmetic shortage seemed to young girls just beginning to use make-up as cruel a blow as the lack of trouser turn-ups did to their brothers. A Bradford teenager was so worried by it that she bought scarce items at every opportunity: 'A hoarder, I once counted thirty-one boxes of face powder I had stored away in an old gramophone.' Another woman well prepared for the cosmetic famine was a Midlands housewife, whose 'hobby had to been send for any sample offers going in scent, cosmetics, etc. . . . I had all makes and hoards of vanishing cream, night cream, lipstick, perfume, toilet water, the lot . . . I treasured them more than gold.'

Yet in some quarters there was still a lingering feeling that to take trouble over one's appearance was unpatriotic. 'Christmas this year won't be quite like the Christmas of other years', admitted a *Housewife* article in December 1941. 'Some of us will be anxious, others lonely and tired. But isn't that just one more reason why you and I should include our faces in the scheme of decoration, and cheer up ourselves and others? . . . Many of the drab faces still to be seen belong to those who, though they may plead lack of time or money, just can't be bothered. Isn't it worth that extra five minutes in the morning to be a cheerful sight?' Most women evidently thought it was, for a queue invariably formed immediately the news spread that a supply of some well-known brand of cosmetics had been delivered. It was, a young girl from Battersea felt, 'a red letter day when the local chemist got his quota of Max Factor face powder'. A typist working at a Regional Food Office in the Midlands remembers similar excitement when 'word got round that Marshall and Snelgrove had Coty cosmetics. . . . All the girls, and some of the men, for their wives, got together' and ordered a bulk supply. 'It was a marvellous sight to see so much and for weeks afterwards the stationery stock-room at the office had a gorgeous smell.' Special allocations were sometimes made to factories, where the girls had less opportunity for shopping. A Hereford woman remembers that the monthly supply of face powder at her factory was welcome, but had one disadvantage: after exposure to the air it often turned orange.

Although perfume, being largely imported, almost completely vanished, and all types of cold cream became scarce, home-made, or shop-made, cosmetics became a minor wartime industry. A Barnes housewife, then aged twenty-five, feels some 'local chemists must have made a fortune from the weird and wonderful face creams they made up themselves and charged the earth for', but later she went into the same business herself 'in a West End store . . . after meeting up, during her work, with a woman who knew how to make mascara. It meant giving her some of my soap coupons and an air force friend made the partitioned dish to set the stuff. We sold quite a lot of this under the counter, but coupons ran out.' Some chemists even developed a 'jug and bottle trade'. One South Wales housewife remembers taking a jar along to her local chemist to have it filled with two shillings' worth of home-made vanishing cream.

The women's magazines urged their readers, confronted by this crisis in their lives, to remain calm and resourceful. 'Now we must be *really* beautiful', one writer told her readers in July 1941. 'Having faced the facts and shed a tear for the luxury bath salts, jewel-tinted eye-shadow, rainbow powder and exotic hair rinse, which have gone the way of brightly lit streets, cream-filled cakes and Continental holidays, let's dry our eyes and decide upon the policy we are going to adopt on the beauty question.' The policy, it appeared, was remembering that 'basic beauty depends upon health and intelligence rather than upon cosmetics', and 'eking out the cosmetic ration' by such devices as adding 'a few drops of warm almond oil' to melted down lipstick ends, to 'use as a cream rouge', or to cleansing creams to make them go farther and disguising unperfumed eau-de-Cologne by pouring it into an almost empty perfume bottle. In fact, as with so many shortages, conditions began to improve as manufacturers concentrated on a few lines in a standard size, and used simpler packaging. Shampoo, for example, now acquired a drab, wartime look in envelopes of coarse brown paper.

The worst shortage for most women was of good brands of lipstick—others, one teenager considered, were 'more like coloured candles'. As an Ipswich housewife explains: 'One could do without having one's hair permed, but one needed that lipstick to show that one's flag was still flying.' A North London woman remembers that in her district, a poor one, lipstick was rarely used for going to work but hoarded for special occasions. Each was used to the very tip and any tiny fragments left were melted together in a lipstick case, or in an eggcup standing in hot water.

Many substitutes for missing cosmetics were tried, though some recipes used rationed items. 'Shredded Castile soap' dissolved in water was, one woman remembers, a good shampoo, but adding an egg made it even better, while caster sugar—even scarcer—was said to ensure smooth skin when applied to damp hands. Glycerine on the lips was recommended in place of lipstick or a solution of cooked beetroot, sealed in place by vaseline. A Wiltshire housewife had an even simpler method: she used to rub her cheeks and bite her lips to make them red. Mutton fat, warmed and rubbed into the skin, was also good for roughened hands, according to a Liverpool housewife who also made her own face cream. 'When you broke an egg you just put a few drops of cream from the top of the milk and a couple of spots of olive oil in the shell, mixed it up and put it on your face', though as it would not keep you had to have your beauty treatment while you cooked the dinner. Other hints were using bicarbonate of soda, dusted under the arms, to counteract perspiration, margarine wrappers, or a mixture of olive oil and chopped beeswax, to soften the skin, shoe-polish or burned cork as eyelash mascara, and Reckitts Blue to lighten grey hair. One Tonbridge woman's whole make-up consisted of ordinary starch on her shiny nose and a teenage girl working in a Yeovil aircraft factory used the transparent 'dope' from the paint shop as clear nail varnish. The simplest method of all was that followed by one shop assistant seen by a surprised colleague rubbing her finger along a dusty shelf and then carefully drawing it along her eyebrows—a remarkably cheap alternative to eyebrow pencil.

One popular beauty treatment was a home-made face-pack, mixed from Fuller's earth. A Yorkshire woman, then a young girl, will never forget the first time she made one. 'It was dark green in colour . . . and when it dried, oh boy! Your face was held in a grip of steel. . . . You dare not look in the mirror because the sight was so side-splittingly funny. You just risked losing half your face if you did.' The wife of an A.F.S. man remembers the sad fate of a friend in a similar situation when two small boys came to the door selling manure at sixpence a bucket. She did not speak for fear of cracking her face pack, silently shaking her head and beginning to close the door, at which one of the boys, eager for a sale, remarked: 'But missus, it's hand picked!' This was too much for her; she burst out laughing—and ruined her beauty treatment.

With so many women working, days lost through 'time of the month' troubles became of national importance and the companies making the products involved tactfully responded to the challenge. 'Period pains mustn't hold up our war effort', the maker of one brand of tablets reminded potential customers. 'Young ladies in great-grandmother's day . . . could afford to have "off days" when domestic duties and polite pastimes were laid aside. Women today can't,' explained a manufacturer of sanitary towels. The fact that this necessity was never scarce sometimes caused confusion to children who had heard their mothers speak of the shortage of towels and some, trained to buy scarce goods on sight, proudly took packets home to their mothers. One Northampton woman, then a small girl of seven, remembers a similar incident at a family Christmas party in 1944. On a visit to Woolworths she had, amid the sparsely filled counters, been struck by the sight of the 'mountainous piles of sanitary towels', and later, playing 'I went to market', where each player had to include some new article on a list of items purchased, 'as my contribution I added, "And a packet of sanitary towels", to be greeted by a shocked silence. As I was stubborn I refused to change the item, as I thought I had been clever to pick such a hard-sounding name; and so the game was abandoned'—an example of the strange, roundabout ways in which the war could intrude into even the most innocent occasion.

# 24

# SAUCEPANS INTO SPITFIRES

'The war is driving Hitler back
But here's one way to win it.
Just give your salvage men the sack
And see there's plenty in it.'

Advertisement in *Picture Post*, 14th February 1942

While many wartime jobs were undertaken as a disagreeable duty preserving or collecting salvage was one task which many people thoroughly enjoyed. Those whose families had for years complained of them throwing nothing away, suddenly found their prudence vindicated. Their defence had always been 'it may come in useful sometime'. Now sometime had, perhaps to their own surprise, arrived.

The campaign to collect scrap metal was launched under the Chamberlain government but only, and almost literally, got off the ground under the impetus of Lord Beaverbrook and Lady Reading. The moment can be fixed precisely, 1 p.m. on Wednesday 10th July 1940, when Lady Reading, as head of the W.V.S., broadcast an appeal to housewives.

. . . The Minister of Aircraft Production is asking the women of Great Britain for everything made of aluminium, everything that they can possibly give to be made into aeroplanes—Spitfires, Hurricanes, Blenheims and Wellingtons. Now you're going to be able to have a chance of doing something positive that will be of direct and vital help to our airmen, and of doing it at once . . . I am asking for the things which you are using every day, anything and everything, new and old, sound and broken, everything that's made of aluminium. . . . Cooking utensils of all kinds; bodies and tubes of vacuum cleaners, coat hangers, shoe trees, bathroom fittings, soap boxes, ornaments and even thimbles may be of aluminium. If you are doubtful, give our aeroplanes the benefit of the doubt and be generous. . . . Very few of us can be heroines on the battle-front, but we can all have the tiny thrill of thinking as we hear the news of an epic battle in the air, 'Perhaps it was my saucepan that made a part of that Hurricane.'

Lady Reading had told her audience that 'whoever gives at once gives twice as much', and one W.V.S. official, leaving Broadcasting

House with her a few minutes later, was astonished to see women already hurrying to the collecting depots with saucepans in their hands. A near-frenzy to surrender their pots and pans seized the housewives of Britain and some arrived with them still warm from the stove. One housewife in Conway, North Wales, remembers 'my husband when he heard the appeal wouldn't let me have the tea already made, but rushed off with the teapot to the dump', collecting her other saucepans on the way and leaving her with only one. Some enthusiastic women bought brand-new sets of saucepans especially to hand in. The Royal Family contributed the miniature kettles and teapots given to the two Princesses by the people of Wales, though one mother who handed in her daughter's doll's tea set remembers wondering how far that would go towards an aircraft.

Articles of sentimental value went with the rest. One sailor's wife was only too pleased to take an aluminium hot water jug (a wedding present) to put on the heap at Folkestone. 'It was only a little thing, but helped towards another Spitfire. I have never regretted it.'

The reputation of this aircraft helps to explain the success of the appeal. One old lady handed in her frying pan with the request that it should be used towards a Spitfire, as she had decided that it had the edge on the Hurricane. A Rotherham girl, then aged fifteen, felt that, 'This exterminator of the Luftwaffe had only to have the slightest whim and it was catered for immediately, so . . . in my mother's absence I proudly presented two of her best big saucepans, all the lids I could lay hands on, our bath tub (zinc) and my dad's metal shovel. The caller went away extremely delighted, while I dreamed of seeing a Spitfire in our living room. When I was found out, oh dear! I was up-braided, down-braided, walloped soundly and was sent in disgrace to forage for the articles I had deprived the household of. . . . My mother completely "did her nut": "You'll get no ruddy dinner till you get some pans", etc.'

Press cartoons showed women looking proudly up as a fighter made of kitchen utensils flew overhead and claiming to identify their particular saucepans, while several W.V.S. members had tactfully to refuse the aluminium artificial limbs which one-legged patriots wished to present to the nation. One woman working at W.V.S. headquarters wrote to her mother on 11th July: 'These last two days have been hectic with aluminium. . . . Already we have sent lorry loads down to the aluminium works. . . . It poured in everywhere day and night and I have made my first war sacrifice and given up my lovely aluminium casserole that cost £1 in peace time.' Collections begun in W.V.S. offices and borrowed shops overflowed down the stairs and on to the pavements outside. A Putney warden, looking out of her Warden's Post at the heap of metal accumulating outside, felt she was living in the middle of a rubbish dump. An eighteen-year-old law student at Oxted, Surrey, found that his first duty as a newly-enrolled L.D.V. was to render unusable the aluminium articles which crammed a thirty-foot-long garage. It took him two days' hard work with a sledgehammer, and left him with blistered hands, but a vacuum cleaner defeated him; he could not bring himself to smash it. Meanwhile new donors constantly arrived, explaining self-consciously as they handed over their jelly-mould or hot water bottle that this was their private contribution to the war. Only a few people still thought first of their own needs. A Putney housewife saw one woman dutifully put an old saucepan into the huge collecting box, and then carefully select a better one to replace it.

By the time the great aluminium appeal ended, two months later, it had yielded a thousand tons of metal, enough for many squadrons of fighters, and its psychological effect was tremendous. Whether its practical results were as valuable may be questioned. As was soon pointed out, the scrap merchants' yards were already crammed with aluminium and the government could perfectly well have requisitioned all the aluminium goods still in the shops. The Ministry's reply, that only 'virgin aluminium' in articles of pre-war manufacture was needed, not the impure variety now in use, was not convincing, but by the time disillusionment set in the women of Britain had more important things to think about, like replacing their missing saucepans, which were to be remembered with increasing nostalgia. One South London warden was soon bemoaning the hours she had to waste on household dusting because she had given away her vacuum cleaner attachments, a Birmingham housewife lived to mourn her fish slice, a Wallington one her colander. Several years later when the local Guide company called on a salvage-collecting tour on a deaf old lady in Dorking she 'indignantly', one of them remembers, 'shooed us out of her garden shouting that we certainly could not have her saucepans'.

As the war situation worsened the need for salvage increased. At first the larger local authorities were legally compelled to organise salvage collections, then the smaller towns, and they had a strong incentive to obey as everything collected was sold to keep down the rates. Few, unfortunately, shared the proceeds with the dustmen who did the work and there were many complaints from housewives who had carefully separated their household waste into bones, paper, metal, rubber and pig food, only to see the whole lot pitched together into the same dust-cart. Few were satisfied with the explanation that there were separate compartments inside it or that everything would be re-sorted at the depot.

Reclaiming salvage was the responsibility of the Ministry of Supply, apart from metal, which belonged to the Ministry of Works, and soon their appeals were competing for space with those of other ministries.

'Is this your house?', demanded a typical advertisement in 1943. 'Paper, metal tins, bones, string and other materials go into it every week. But how much comes out again as salvage? Is your house slacking?' This basic campaign was reinforced by special appeals. 'Drivers!', urged the Ministry of Supply, in July 1942, 'all worn-out tyres and tubes—lying discarded in your garage, shed, garden, or elsewhere—are wanted at once. Take *yours* to a local garage for despatch to a government depot.' Housewives were the target in September 1943. 'Sufficient aluminium to build fifty Lancaster bombers is lost each year through aluminium milk bottle caps being thrown away. . . . Save your caps and hand them in a paper bag to your milkman.' Other national publicity reiterated such surprising facts as that 'One envelope makes fifty cartridge wads. . . . Goloshes . . . teapot spouts make . . . jumping boots for paratroopers', that a single chop bone could provide cordite for two cartridges and that a six-inch length of wool from every home would add up to 600 sets of battle-dress.

Large bins and boxes labelled 'metal', 'paper' and so on now began to appear in every residential road, and often housewives took it in turn to have them outside their front door, though one Birmingham housewife remembers how 'in the summer nobody wanted the bone bin outside their house and it got pushed around. It had to be kept inside the front gate as it was dangerous on the footpath because of the black-out.' The pigbin was equally unwelcome, particularly once the local animals discovered its existence. Another Birmingham housewife remembers how 'a horse which drew a baker's van always made for a particular pig bin down the road, pushed off the lid and started eating the bread inside'. Dogs preferred bone baskets though some councils thwarted all but the largest intruders by attaching the baskets to bus stop signs, a long way from the ground.

Many methods were tried to keep public interest in salvage alive. Bermondsey and Bethnal Green challenged each other in December 1941 to a paper-collecting competition; Paddington ran a 'Mile of Keys' campaign to collect a million keys. Salvage drives were often linked to war savings weeks, the need for thrift providing a common theme. One village in April 1943 ran a competition to see who could collect the most discarded ploughshares, a single team recovering forty. One can only hope there were no indignant farmers next day minus a plough. But by far the most successful technique was the house-to-house visit, yet another job for those matrons of all work the W.V.S., and in the first six months of 1940 alone volunteers paid more than half a million salvage calls on London homes. One W.V.S. member's boast is that, if ever asked what she did in the war, she can reply, 'I drove a rag and bone lorry'—a twice-weekly duty, undertaken in Yeovil, while her husband was at sea. The wife of an electrician working in Northern Ireland has an even better tale to tell. 'I persuaded the local major's wife to accompany me with her donkey called Tilly (short for Utility)', she remembers, 'and a small cart to collect jam jars and old iron, which we left in O'Hara's barn for the W.V.S. van from Coleraine to collect. This was great fun. It was amazing how much we collected.' In many places W.V.S. members rode beside the dustman, to preach the salvage gospel to each housewife as the dustman emptied her dustbin. Such efforts were sometimes too successful. One woman who asked her council to collect some metal proudly delivered to the large lorry which was sent five sardine and three corned beef tins, all carefully cleaned and polished.

This was a perpetual trouble: the public, constantly assured that even the smallest contribution was important, found it hard to accept that it might not be worth the trouble of collection. The problem never was overcome in many rural areas, and village dumps organised by W.V.S. members often degenerated into unsightly, evil-smelling heaps which remained uncollected for years unless the W.V.S. themselves toured them with a lorry. More successful were W.V.S. work parties which dismantled old electric light bulbs and batteries, W.V.S. canvasses of office waste paper baskets, and W.V.S. 'Bone Drives'—one member who called at a dogs' meat shop found herself presented with the skeleton of a whole horse, which she heroically dragged into her car. 'The need for scrap rubber', recorded the official W.V.S. history, 'sent W.V.S. members to fish for old tyres in ponds and streams and to have collecting-boxes for small oddments in all offices and depots.' Cajoled by the W.V.S., many women could be seen shyly dropping discarded corsets on their local salvage dumps and the W.V.S. also took on the job of locating scrap metal on farms throughout the whole of Wales. But despite all their efforts, much salvage remained uncollected. When, at my school in Sussex, groups of boys were sent to scour the countryside for scrap metal the results were impressive, for two boys discovered an enormous accumulation of rusty oddments piled up around the school incinerator. After lying uncollected for weeks the whole heap of broken bicycles, dented petrol cans, and the rest, was taken back to the same dump where, I suspect, it remains to this day.

Children were usually ideal collectors of salvage, naturally enthusiastic and hard to refuse. 'There are not many things that small boys can do,' a correspondent pointed out in *The Times* in 1941, 'but this is one.' Later in the war the government started the Cog Scheme, the 'Cogs', children formally enrolled as salvage collectors, being recruited through local schools. Some operated without adult help; in one group, at Honor Oak, the youngest 'cog' was three and the oldest fourteen, later replaced by a boy of eleven. There was a Cog Song, *There'll always be a Dustbin*, a Cog salvage-poster competition and Cog badges, and in some places the scheme doubled the amount of salvage collected.

Even in the salvage world there was a regular, military style hierarchy, with ranks and its own badge—a modest dark brown plastic affair, a capital 'S' in a circle, topped by a crown. Hull, for instance, was divided up into areas, each with its own Chief Salvage Steward. One remembers being responsible for a large area, covering 12,000 houses, with below her a Steward for each street, divided in turn into groups of eight houses. One housewife in each group was 'made a bit special by being . . . responsible for the tidiness and proper use of the bins'. The job could be exhausting. This woman wore herself out, but, even as she lay in bed, a casualty in the battle for salvage, a queue of children formed up stretching down the stairs into the street, junior members of the salvage army waiting to report to their commander.

The easiest salvage to collect was always waste paper, partly because it was also the easiest to sell. The press, too, had a personal interest in paper saving, and *Picture Post* in February 1942 reminded its readers:

> The war is driving Hitler back
> And here's one way to win it.
> Just give your salvage men the sack
> And see there's plenty in it.

The W.V.S. took selected members on tours of paper-mills, where they saw the disastrous effect that a single paper-clip or rubber band could have on a whole consignment of waste paper, and special arrangements were made for shredding confidential business papers, but more interesting to most salvage workers were the collections of beribboned love letters and private diaries that now came into their hands. A housewife living in the country near Aylesbury who remembers that 'there was no rush to do the salvage for the village. As we found space for it in an outhouse it became my very own unglamorous job', found her reward 'one bitterly cold Sunday afternoon. The remains of somebody's autograph album arrested my attention. On one page I read "Do your Duty, never mind if it is out in the cold, or by a nice warm fire". A flattish box revealed some love tokens, love letters; other letters concerned a family quarrel, which should no doubt have been retained after sorting out. Could I ask the suspected owner if she had made a mistake? I kept the box more or less in hiding for some time and eventually "made salvage" of it.'

Early in the war collecting boxes for 'Books for the Forces' had appeared in Post Offices and periodically there were attempts to obtain out-of-date books for salvage. The Ministry of Supply looked on private libraries as a large, if scattered, reserve of raw material and in 1943 it decided the time had come to call on it, particularly because by now wartime paper had become frail, rough and yellow after being repeatedly repulped, and good quality, pre-war paper was needed to improve its quality. The Book Drive, it was realised, had its dangers, but most local authorities wisely arranged for every load brought in to be checked by at least a junior library assistant. One librarian still remembers her anxiety that, with time for no more than a glance at the title page, she might have sentenced some valuable item to destruction as she and another girl sat at long trestle tables in the stone-floored decontamination centre in the small town of Dewsbury, near Leeds, sorting each volume into the appropriate pile, while heaps of books piled up remorselessly all-round them. The whole campaign yielded fifty-six million volumes in a few months, of which five million went to the Forces, a million to replace lost stock in bombed libraries and the rest to the mills for repulping. It was the greatest clear-out of bookshelves in British history.

The scrap metal drive had been launched in January 1940 and by July the new Minister of Supply, Herbert Morrison, was already having to assure the public that the material collected had not been forgotten, a statement repeated at frequent intervals, less and less convincingly, for the next five years. By August he was describing the rag-and-bone man as 'the saviour of the nation' and was having to restrain Falmouth Council from sending for scrap the guns of the famous *Bellerophon*, on board which Napoleon had surrendered. A frenzy for the destruction of irreplaceable historic relics seized both private citizens and local councils. One vandal in Keswick actually sent for scrap Nelson's minute gun from the *Victory*. Other philistines in Plymouth cheerfully pitched into the melting pot cannon captured from the Spanish Armada and a three-hundred-year-old ducking stool, and Southwold in Suffolk was only just prevented by some enlightened individuals from turning into scrap five two-hundred-year-old cannon captured at Culloden, the last battle fought on British soil. I well remember my sense of loss on coming home one school holidays to Newbury to find that the Crimean War cannon and the first world war field gun in a local park, on which as a small boy I had spent many happy hours mowing down imaginary enemy hordes, had simply vanished without trace. Other councils were equally ruthless, ignoring the value to morale of such memorials to earlier British victories—though the sending for scrap by the War Office of 10,000 cavalry swords was hailed as a sign that at last the Army was no longer fighting the Boer War. In August 1942 the last excuse for wanton destruction was removed when the government firmly stated that antiquarian objects were not sought as scrap.

But the scrap metal campaign continued to provide many citizens with an excuse for the agreeable task of urging sacrifices upon their neighbours. One *Times* reader in July 1940 calculated that 250,000 razor blades were being thrown away each day and that a monthly house-to-house collection would yield ninety tons of metal a year, though he did not volunteer to take on the job. Another razor blade user six months later was indignant that the Ministry of Aircraft Production, to which he had patriotically sent 200 old blades, had told him to add them instead to his local salvage dump. He was only silenced by a letter from the Controller of Salvage pointing out that as a million blades made only one ton of steel there were other items more worth collecting. The war also seemed to offer to many motorists a chance for revenge on an old enemy. 'Could not the Belisha beacons follow the park railings into the melting pot?', asked one embittered driver in May 1940. The campaign against the hated beacons, a monument to their namesake, a former Minister of Transport and only introduced in 1934, continued until 1942, when an official spokesman explained that to pull them down would not be worth the effort. Nor did a suggestion to root out bus stops, attaching the signs instead to the nearest telegraph pole, or to remove all lamp-posts, meet with government approval. But *Times* readers, ever ready to set others to rights, were not discouraged and continued to suggest the collection, compulsory or voluntary, of varied items like company seals, sash window weights, such 'Victorian flummeries as window box supports', garden rollers and worn-out golf clubs, with the slogan 'Scrap iron from scrapped irons'. The most fervent efforts of all were directed against slot-machines, which were vigorously defended by the British Automatic Company. Contrary to appearances, asserted the company in May 1942, the machines were not derelict although 'invariably emptied as soon as filled', and 4,500 surplus ones had already been sent for scrap. Instead of making, as one letter-writer had suggested, 'their first and final contribution' to victory by being melted down, the machines survived to fight, or at least infuriate the thwarted would-be customer, another day.

The tempo of the salvage drive accelerated steadily until by April 1943, the peak year, it was making a substantial contribution to keeping imports—and local rates—down. Since the start of the war, three million tons of paper had been recovered, so that half the paper and board manufactured in Britain was now 'home-grown'; 130,000 tons of rubber had been reclaimed, kitchen waste was coming in at the rate of 31,000 tons a month, sufficient to feed 210,000 pigs, and 110,000 tons of scrap metal were being collected every week. By the end of the war the total salvage collected amounted to nearly six million tons, about five million of them being scrap metal.

The greatest single source had been iron railings, and unfenced parks and squares and thousands of private garden walls with crumbling holes or substitute fencing remain to this day as reminders of the great railing drive. 'It seemed such a dreadful thing to help to kill other people with these', a Bedfordshire woman considered, but a Liverpool housewife remembers that she felt willing to give up anything to get the war over quickly. Digging one's garden for victory was at best a form of passive resistance; the railings round it could actually go off and fight.

The removal of the railings round public parks and gardens was generally popular. 'Dare one hope', wrote a resident of Montpelier Square to *The Times* in April 1940, 'that the exigencies of war will at last rid London and other places of one of their major disfigurements—iron railings ... Some believe that the removal of railings would mean an instant rush of undesirables—miscellaneous humans, rampageous cats, furtive dogs and the like ... So far as this square is concrned, the cats have always used the garden as their *lebensraum*. The most senile tabby, feeling the urge of spring, can vault the foolish fence with ease. If all useless railings in this country could be fired forthwith into the Greater Reich it would considerably enhance our amenities.' Soon the papers were full of praise of the joys of being railing-less. The heart of Exmouth, it was said, had been converted 'from a commonplace, ugly, town centre into one of distinctive attraction', and at Bournville, a garden city, one could now really enjoy the central greens and their daffodils. The desire to see the railings hurled down soon became a test of one's democratic spirit. It was a scandal, one man declared, that children should have to play in the streets while square gardens were locked up, their aristocratic owners having timorously fled to Scotland. 'Public authorities have in the past dearly loved railings. Was it a self-righteous sense of administering to "Bumbledom" morality and Puritan prohibitionism?' asked another reformer. On 10th May 1940, the day the Germans began their breakthrough in the West, a victory of a different kind was being foreshadowed in London: the Minister of Supply opened the *Railings for Scrap* exhibition. Despite opposition from such bodies as the Metropolitan Public Gardens Association, which apparently existed to prevent public gardens becoming too public, and suggestions that the disused London tramlines ought to be dug up first—later in the war they *were* removed—by October nearly 1,000 councils had removed their railings or surveyed them. 22,000 tons of railings had already reached the furnaces where, it was explained, they were 'good in themselves, easy to handle and yielding almost their own weight in first-rate metal'; imported scrap provided only half as much.

One obvious repository of railings was churchyards and many vicars gladly surrendered these to the common cause, particularly since, it was said, they had discouraged the public from taking an interest in churchyards and encouraged the growth of ivy. The chancellors of many dioceses made their distinctive contribution to the war effort by granting a general faculty, or permission, for church railings to be torn down, but those round private tombs presented a tougher problem. Some vicars, with doubtful legality, simply announced in their parish magazines that private railings which no one came forward to protect would be removed. One woman created for herself an unusual war job of trying to trace the owners so that the dead, too, could do their bit, but the results were disappointing since she merely found herself faced with a bill for making good the damage to the devastated monuments.

Many private citizens rather spoilt the gesture of volunteering to sacrifice their railings by demanding that their neighbours should be compelled by law to follow their example. Certainly, on aesthetic grounds, there was good reason for this, for few streets looked worse than those where a few houses exhibited railing-less walls or jagged metal roots and the rest retained their peacetime splendour. The response to the railings appeal also varied enormously between towns. In Birmingham and Liverpool railings became a rare sight, while in Chelsea, where the occupants of one square had in 1938 complained about their lawns being spoiled by air-raid shelters, the campaign was only saved from total failure by a public-spirited vicar who gave up his church railings. As one resident candidly explained, removing the railings might reduce the value of a property and 'The only just or reasonable solution is to make the removal of all such railings compulsory'.

And this at last was what the government did. In September 1941 orders went out to all local authorities to begin a survey of unnecessary railings and every landlord or tenant was warned he had only a fortnight to appeal against removal on artistic, historic or safety grounds. The new drive, designed to raise half a million tons of scrap, enough for 300 destroyers, was officially launched in October by the removal of some railings from Buckingham Palace. In February 1943 there was a ceremonial severing of the railings outside the Royal Exchange in the City and it was promised that such unfashionable defences of private property as window grills and anti-burglar spikes would also be torn down. The Russian ambassador, too, made his contribution to what, eighteen months earlier, had still been an unjust capitalist war; in October 1942, graciously waiving his railings' diplomatic privilege, he solemnly cut the first of those outside his embassy.

The official policy was to regard railings as a reserve and to have a thorough 'sweep' in one area after another, a word made fashionable by the large-scale raids which British fighters were then making over France. The descent of a Ministry of Works gang, armed with crowbars and oxy-acetylene torches, on some peaceful suburban street or village lane was in fact not unlike a military attack, and the raiding parties were often led by ruthless, masculine, women, impervious to all entreaties. In Devon the gangs had, like an invading army, left the hedges blazing behind them and stripped the gates from cottage gardens all along busy main roads, the domineering female in command retorting curtly, 'Children are the responsibility of the parents', when mothers protested at the danger from traffic. In the Malvern area another fearsome woman had torn down the fences which kept cattle in and rabbits and sheep out; in Warwickshire one gang had in a few frenzied minutes removed the sliding steel gates from the village hall, the gate across the school porch and, a local farmer publicly complained, 'the iron hurdles which fence off my corn ricks'. When he protested the official in charge 'informed me . . . that there was a war on', yet a whole lorry load of scrap on his farm had already lain uncollected for a year. At Gravesend light fencing protecting the edge of a seventy-foot-high cliff had been uprooted, yet here, too, hundreds of tons of scrap lay about in derelict factories. A schoolboy from a Welsh mining village near Swansea who saw the wrought-iron railings of the school and older houses 'sawn off at the base and carted away by council men' . . . can also 'remember huge iron gear wheels for lock gates lying rusting on the bank where my friends and I would perilously cross the canal on a narrow board behind the lock gates. There used to be a rail . . . but that was removed' by 'the railing sawyers'. From his Derbyshire estate the writer Osbert Sitwell wrote to *The Times* to protest against 'the various acts of vandalism and sabotage' committed in the name of the Ministry of Works, whose storm troops had burned off gates rather than lift them off their hinges, and left forty-seven acres of good grazing land open to the road, while old German guns, weighing far more than the removed railings, lay uncollected a few yards away.

All these protests were ignored as were those about the removal of the guard rails from a large London housing estate, which provided even less metal, but had prevented children running into a busy road. Meanwhile, despite the indignant efforts of the local council to secure them for scrap—they would have yielded forty-five tons—the railings round Salisbury racecourse car park were declared exempt, as vital to the war effort, though anything more obviously expendable it would surely have been hard to find.

But, despite such lunacies, if the weight of metal collected was any guide the railings campaign as a whole was a success. By May 1942 10,000 tons a week, from around 100,000 houses, were being collected, and by September 1944, when further removals ceased, the total weight of railings demolished had reached a million tons.

Whatever its beneficial effects on public parks and gardens, the massacre of the railings often had a disastrous effect on the appearance of private houses. A Dunfermline housewife loathed the unsightly chicken wire erected instead on top of her garden wall to prevent small children clambering into the street. A Walthamstow woman found that the removal of the iron fence dividing her house from her neighbour's actually meant a decline in neighbourliness. 'We used to use this to hang our carpets and mats over when cleaning the hall. After the railings went we had to hold carpets in mid-air to brush them.' More serious was the fact that such sacrifices were often wasted. 'Victorian Ryde', remembers one resident, 'had been rich in ornamental iron railings separating many Victorian villas from the public footpaths. We'd simply no choice . . . when the cry arose to hack them off for scrap. Borough workmen spent many busy weeks on this job—and . . . how sadly naked our poor house fronts looked. The saddest part of the story is that three quarters of the railings never left the island scrap piles. Doubtless, even now, piles of rusted ironwork could still be found under brambles, etc.' In Reading, an architectural draughtsman noted that, at the end of the war 'Most of the railings were still piled up in dumps in the local railway sidings unused'. He observed sadly the ruin achieved by the railing removers. 'We were cozened into believing that the aspect of our streets would be improved. But individuality asserted itself rapidly and every householder was soon competing with his neighbour in the originality of his fencing. Railings . . . had given some degree of planned homogeneity to streets which now broke down into competing units. People who did not re-fence soon found the bricks of their low curtain walls falling loose and disappearing one by one and their small gardens becoming mudponds. By the time paint and rust had been separated off the metal recovered from such railings as did reach the melting pot could hardly have been worth the trouble. Many solid Georgian and early Victorian railings were destroyed and the manner in which they were literally pulled down often ruined their fine moulded brick or stone bases.'

The final disillusionment came when the cheques for compensation arrived. One Reading family, who estimated their loss at £45, the cost of replacing the requisitioned railings, received seventeen shillings. But even this was generous compared to the payment made to a South Wales woman, who, for her gate and railings, was offered by a grateful nation the munificent sum of—one shilling.

# IS YOUR JOURNEY REALLY NECESSARY?

'The time has come for every person to search his conscience before making a railway journey. It is more than ever vital to ask yourself: "Is my journey really necessary?" '

Railway poster, 1943

'Imagine ten or a dozen people, and boxes, all standing in the vestibule at the end of a corridor for some ten hours from Birmingham to Darlington—some vomiting, others fainting'—that is one man's memory of one wartime railway journey. 'Train travel was a nightmare', he remembers, a description that many other people will heartily echo. By 1944 passenger trains were covering a third less mileage than before the war, but every one that did still run was squeezing in more than twice as many people as in 1938. The only consolation to the traveller—and not a very comforting one it must be admitted—was that crowded trains benefited him as a taxpayer. On the 1st September 1939 the government had taken over the four main-line railway companies and the London Passenger Transport Board, guaranteeing them in return a minimum annual income, any additional receipts being divided equally between the companies and the government. It proved an excellent bargain, for the railways during the war made a substantial profit.

Railway services have never been worse for the ordinary civilian traveller than during the war but never was the relationship between him and the railway worker more cordial. Cigarettes sometimes miraculously appeared from under the counter for customers in railway uniform and the most successful of all radio wartime documentaries did not deal with a great military operation but with *Junction X*, a vital railway centre.* 'Food, shells and fuel must come first', one railway placard reminded passengers. 'If your train is late or crowded—*do you mind?*' The astonishing truth was that the public, once convinced the sacrifice of its comfort was necessary, did *not*.

And necessary it was. Altogether 350,000 special trains were run for the Forces alone during the war and every military operation took its toll of engines, coaches and trucks. It took 260 special trains to carry the

---

* Some radio experts considered this the best programme ever broadcast, though no one now seems to remember it.

B.E.F. to Southampton in 1939, 200 trains to carry the ill-fated Norwegian expedition up to Scottish ports in 1940, another 1,100 to take men and material to embark for the campaign in North Africa. Between March and July 1944 up to 1,000 special trains a week were scraped up somehow during the great build-up before and after D Day. Every new war factory, every dispersal of food or timber or oil to safeguard reserves, meant more work for the railways. In six months 1,700 freight trains carried 750,000 tons of rubble from the bombed streets of London to the flat fields of East Anglia to build runways for Bomber Command, while the ruins of Birmingham were carried south to provide forward bases in Kent and Sussex for British and American fighters. Wartime slogans about 'the lines behind the lines' may have jarred on the weary traveller, as he fumbled to get out his dried egg sandwiches in the crowded corridor of some blacked-out train, but this did not alter the fact that they were true.

If overloading was the worst of their troubles, the railways had other problems. The black-out slowed every operation down, especially during air raid warnings, which meant that extra lights must be extinguished, the call-up of 100,000 railwaymen left the railways so dangerously undermanned that by 1943 the Ministry of Labour was actually directing men and women into railway work, and the shortage and poor quality of fuel greatly reduced the performance of steam locomotives. Maintenance work, too, was postponed and as the war went on carriages grew steadily older and shabbier. Eventually such a serious shortage of engines developed that, between 1942 and 1944, to the delight of train spotters, 400 American Army locomotives had to be lent to the railway companies to pull British trains. Some came complete with American crews. A schoolboy returning from his home at Godalming in Surrey to school at Wimborne in Dorset remembers the unusual sight that confronted him when he changed trains *en route*. 'In about 1943 I dismounted from my perch in the guard's van at Brockenhurst to find that the ancient, wheezy tank engine which normally ran along the branch line had disappeared. In its place was a full blown "Wild West" engine of vast proportions. It had a cow catcher, a bell, the traditional siren, U.S.A. in large letters along the tender and a negro crew complete with uniforms that I had only previously seen in films. The guard was another negro and the Southern Railway guard merely travelled in the van and did nothing. . . . The huge American engine travelled very slowly, it hooted at bridges and the bell was rung at stations and level crossings. For some reason it also ran with an enormous headlight at night, which must have upset the more busybody wardens.'

The opening weeks of the war were the worst so far as the black-out was concerned. In many carriages at first there was no lighting at all and one often sat inadvertently on another passenger's knees, while where lights were provided they were too dim to read by. This provoked so many complaints that in December a great improvement occurred. On suburban trains narrow shafts of light were now thrown on to each seat from a boxed-in central fitting, while long-distance corridor trains with blinds had black strips painted round the edges of the windows and almost normal lighting inside, though all lighting was turned off when the warning went. These rules remained unchanged until September 1944 when normal lighting returned in trains with curtains, and in mid-April 1945 it became permitted everywhere except on the coast.

Travel by train after dark was an eerie experience, especially when one's carriage was in total darkness. A Luton woman remembers hearing strange voices relate where they were going, and why, all through one pitch-black night, from 9 p.m. till 7 a.m., on a journey to Scotland, and only being able by the light of dawn to put faces to them. I can well remember waking up in a train to find a pretty W.A.A.F. asleep with her head on my shoulder. A Northampton woman endured six hours in pitch darkness, in a non-corridor train in a siding at Crewe, on a journey to Southport, spent in community singing led by soldiers going on leave. Servicemen were traditionally helpful and cheerful companions—though they could be troublesome in other ways. One woman travelling from Manchester to London remembers some who removed every light bulb in the compartment before trying to pass 'dud' tickets to the ticket collector, and another woman travelling from Glasgow to London encountered nine soldiers who, in an airless carriage, made themselves comfortable for the night by taking their boots off. The worst feature, however, was their equipment—kitbag, 'large pack', 'small pack', belt with pouches and even rifle—which made even the most sociable an uncomfortable travelling companion. Most civilians were none the less extremely helpful to travelling servicemen. I still feel grateful to the willing hands which pulled me aboard the already moving last train from Paddington, when, after six months in the Army, I went home for my first leave in 1944. A woman from Saxmundham, Suffolk, remembers changing trains at Rugby in 1940 when her connection was too crowded for her to board it. 'Just as the train was moving off, however, an English sailor came dashing on to the platform dragging his kit. The same hands which had almost pushed me off the train now opened doors from inside to pull the sailor in. . . . In peacetime I would have resented this, but I was as anxious as they that he should not miss his precious leave.'

Travel became markedly more difficult after June 1940 when all but the smallest station name signs were taken down. In the words of one woman, 'train journeys were practically a mystery tour' and even to be on the right train was an achievement. A sixteen-year-old girl, travelling from Bristol to Rotherham on a foggy night, was 'astonished to find that someone had removed all the station signs. . . . When I arrived I failed to recognise my own station . . . and was eventually deposited bag and baggage in Leeds, thirty miles from home. If it hadn't been for the fact that it's a dead end there the Lord knows where I should have finished up.' A City secretary, travelling to work daily from Potters Bar, felt 'we were absolutely snookered. . . . We became strangers in our own beloved London. . . . The porters, unused to any form of broadcasting, made a shocking job in the beginning. It was even more confusing than the dim lighting. Many a time we went on too far or hopped off too soon.' A Nottingham woman took only one railway journey during the war—and that was more than enough. 'It was in 1943 and we went on holiday to Buxton. It was a nightmare—we didn't know where we were and could only get off when the train had to stop for water. . . . We found ourselves near Blackpool.' A West Country woman travelling home to Somerset from Manchester remembers the exceptionally long train, designed to compensate for reduced services, 'I was assured', she remembers, 'that I was on the correct half for Bristol but I finished up in South Wales. It took me hours to get back to Yeovil.' One railway poster advised, 'If you can't see the name and can't hear the porter's voice —ask another traveller. . . . If you know where you are by local signs and sounds—please tell others in the carriage'. But in the darkness even the most familiar station looked strange and I can recall a woman confidently alighting one evening from my compartment at Newbury Racecourse station, then used only by army traffic, before anyone could stop her and being left behind as the train pulled out. The BBC organist, Sandy Macpherson, had the unnerving experience, while travelling on an unlighted non-corridor train from Manchester to Sheffield, of finding himself and the only other passenger, a woman, abandoned at a small station, with no lights and no staff, the engine having unaccountably been removed. It was only after a long wait that the two castaways were spotted and rescued by a guard from a passing train.

Although they caused lengthy delays, air raids proved less dangerous to the railway passenger than had been feared. The railways had made remarkably thorough preparations, especially against gas, and notices in every compartment warned passengers against touching the outside of the coach after a raid. Advice was also given on how to behave when the warning sounded:

If an air raid occurs while you are in the train
1 Do *not* attempt to leave the train if it stops away from a station, unless requested by the guard to do so. You are safer where you are.

2 Pull the blinds down, both by day and night, as a protection against flying glass.

3 If room is available, lie down on the floor.

These were sensible instructions, and one woman remembers 'being machine gunned in a train going to Brighton . . . and being the bottom layer on the train floor', and a woman travelling back to Hull with her mother remembers a similar attack at King's Cross, when 'We crouched on the carriage floor as the train pulled a little way out of the station'. Later in the war, when there ceased to be room even to stand in comfort, let alone lie down, these famous instructions became something of a joke, as did the announcement broadcast in the early days at main-line stations: 'The air raid warning has sounded. Passengers can go to the shelters or proceed by their trains; members of the Forces *must* take shelter.' To the peacetime notices about services being interrupted by breakdown or fog was now added a third, phrased with true English understatement;

In consequence of the line being obstructed by

MISHAP

passengers are warned that trains proceeding to . . .

will be delayed.

At first far more delay was caused by the rule that when the siren sounded trains must stop at the next station so that passengers could get out and take shelter if they wished, the train then proceeding at only fifteen miles an hour, raised in November 1940 to twenty-five and in February 1941 abolished altogether during daylight—at night the maximum speed during an alert was thirty miles an hour. Apart from the major disruption caused by the blitz, trains and stations were favourite targets for hit-and-run raids by single aircraft throughout the war and the railways also suffered a good deal from V.1 attacks, which caused nearly 1,600 incidents, out of the total of 9,200, 6,000 of them serious, which they suffered during the war. Altogether 900 people, 400 of them railwaymen, were killed on railway property due to enemy action and 4,500 injured.

For most travellers hunger was a more frequent annoyance than bombs. All restaurant cars had been withdrawn on the outbreak of war and though they were restored six weeks later, the number was steadily reduced until in May 1942 catering was provided on only seventy-two trains and these, too, finally lost their dining cars in April 1944. Their absence came as a bitter deprivation to better-off travellers. Freddie Grisewood, hurrying about the country to speak on behalf of the Kitchen Front, once stood all the way from London to Sunderland in a crowded train, addressed an audience of 5,000 people, was rewarded with a bun and a cup of tea and then had to stand again all the way back to London, a total of sixteen hours without a seat or a meal. The journalist J. L. Hodson, visiting war factories, recorded in June 1942 a foodless journey to the North, at the end of which he had to make do with potted meat sandwichesand coffee in a hotel. The following month, on a journey back from the West Country he prudently ignored assurances that there would be a luncheon car on the train and took cheese and lettuce sandwiches with him—very wisely, it turned out. To those not used to carrying their own food on journeys such meals had an amusing, picnic quality. The popular writer Charles Graves described the scene in a first-class compartment on a journey to Newcastle in November 1943. 'Round about midday it was amusing to watch one's fellow travellers thinking about the luncheon they had brought with them. . . . The first to feel the pangs of hunger was . . . a captain in the A.T.S. She munched a few spam sandwiches and produced a couple of apples. Then the man from Newcastle, on my left, brought out some dried egg sandwiches. I riposted with a flagon of beer and an actual tankard which I had brought with me. Then a naval officer produced two boiled eggs as his opening gambit. I retorted with some ham sandwiches and a couple of tomatoes. And so it went, until everyone was eating. It could really make quite a good revue sketch.'

Once arrived at a station there was no guarantee of getting a meal, for station buffets were for most of the war crowded out and often closed early due to lack of food or crockery. By August 1942 the shortage of cups in refreshment rooms was so acute that notices urged the public, 'Bring your own'. An army officer's wife travelling from London to Scotland remembers that at Crewe, where the train stopped, the queues were too long for her to obtain any refreshments. A Farnborough woman remembers an equally hungry journey to Lancashire, which involved six changes, instead of the usual one, but all the buffets refused to serve her family, their food being reserved for servicemen only.

Better-off travellers often complained of third-class passengers occupying first-class seats on crowded trains, but they received little sympathy, for first-class travel was widely regarded as contrary to the democratic spirit of the times, and many demands for its abolition were made, until in October 1941, as a compromise, all trains running only within the London Transport area became third-class only. Sleeping cars, on long-distance trains, continued to run throughout the war though most berths were reserved for official travellers.

Another restriction, which affected everyone, was the withdrawal of 'cheap day returns' and other excursion tickets, especially as rail fares were several times raised during the war. The only remaining cheap tickets now were for Civil Defence workers and Home Guards going on duty, shift workers, people going to farm camps, war workers transferred away from home and—to discourage them from bringing their children back—the parents of evacuees, who were limited to one cheap trip to see them every one or two months. At holiday times, instead of colourful posters enticing the public to visit the seaside, notices sternly tried to discourage travelling. 'Stay at home. You may be stranded if you travel', warned one at August Bank Holiday 1942. The public accepted all this, and many other regulations, like a limitation of passenger luggage to 100 lb., with exemplary patience but finally revolted in February 1943 over what seems the most trifling of issues, a total ban on the carriage of flowers by rail, even as personal luggage. Flowers, it suddenly appeared, were for many people a treasured reminder of more spacious times and the outcry involved even such unlikely rebels as Ursula Bloom, who proudly described boarding a train in April 1943 carrying a large bouquet and hoping to be challenged. She was not—and a few weeks later the ban was, surprisingly, dropped.

Nowhere were flowers more needed than on the average station. In peacetime the railways had prided themselves on the smart appearance of their property but now both buildings and rolling stock grew daily more stained and battered. All decorative painting had ceased, and woodwork was now often given a protective coat of tar instead of paint. Main line waiting rooms, depressing places at the best of times, were now filled with servicemen or other passengers bent dozing over a table or stretched out on it waiting for some belated train, and the cheerful pre-war posters advertising holiday resorts had been replaced by lists of seaside towns one was not allowed to visit—and by the ubiquitous slogan, 'Is your journey *really* necessary?' First coined in 1939 to discourage evacuated Civil Servants from going home for Christmas, from 1941 the question was constantly addressed to all civilians, for, after considering a scheme for rationing travel on the 'points' principle, or to ban all travel without a permit over more than fifty miles, the government had finally decided to rely on voluntary appeals and on making travel uncomfortable by reducing the number of trains. From Christmas 1941 no extra long-distance trains were run at holiday times; normal services throughout the year had already been heavily reduced. Conditions were at their very worst from April to October 1944, after which an improved timetable was introduced and the slow climb back to peacetime standards began. But most people, however patriotic or unwilling to travel they were, had to go by train sometime, and minute-by-minute accounts of slow and crowded rail journeys soon became as common as bomb stories. In these every 250-pounder tended in recollection to become a land-mine, but the tellers of travel stories had little temptation to exaggerate. No one who went by rail during the war is likely to have forgotten the experience. Conditions were hardest on long-distance services, and most intolerable of all between King's Cross and the North. Here is one woman's account of a journey from York to London on 9th August 1943.

At York station the King's Cross train comes in. A knot of pushing people gathers at each doorway. A thin stream of other people straggles out, servicemen hauling on kit bags and civilians dragging cases. Almost before the last one is out the first of the pushing crowd is climbing in. An enormously fat woman elbows her way purposefully through followed immediately in her wake by her meek little grey wisp of a husband. He manages to occupy the tiny space made behind her and is swept along by the crowd pushing behind. His hat is knocked off and he protests feebly. A soldier and myself stand on either side of the carriage door and smile tolerantly at each other . . . then we in turn squeeze our way in and halt at the first corridor window. The corridor is already full. There is no more room. A score of servicemen pile in behind us and the door is squeezed to. . . . The luggage is piled round us; five soldiers retire into the lavatory and shut the door. We can hear their grunts and sighs as they settle their packs on the floor and the heavy thud as one of them seats himself with his back to the door. We all smile and make ourselves as comfortable as possible. An aircraft mechanic sits on the floor and promptly goes to sleep with his head on his knees. The train lurches and sways. We sway with it and the long slow hours pass in a stifling dream. There is no food. An R.A.F. man unpacks some sandwiches and shares them with a pal; the others smoke and doze. I hand round pieces of a precious slab of chocolate. . . . Every now and then a child is passed over the heads of the crowd towards the lavatory. Someone bangs on the door and the soldiers inside open it cautiously. They admit the child and discreetly turn their backs. A naval officer helps with knicker buttons. The child is handed back over the heads of the crowd. The lavatory door shuts. The soldiers resume their interrupted sleep.

Others have similar recollections. A Roxburgh man visiting relations in Hounslow in autumn 1944 remembers how when his train stopped in Yorkshire it was immediately stormed by a crowd of servicemen, desperate to get on. One young woman in his compartment, finding her way out blocked by these new arrivals, turned and rushed back towards the door at the far end of the coach, only to be swept back by another stream of passengers. Utterly unnerved, she threw her hands above her head, shrieking hysterically—though, he believes, she got off eventually. 'You had to be active to travel by train at all', a Birmingham woman discovered. 'Those who were unable to climb through windows or push against those who were already standing in the corridors were likely to be left behind.' One acquaintance, lucky enough to find herself in front of a door when a train stopped, was 'pushed right through the compartment and out into the corridor' by the pressure of people from behind. Another Birmingham woman going home to Sussex for Christmas remembers how at Coventry, where the train was diverted, the munition workers who poured on board simply dismantled the tables and threw them out of the window to make room to stand. A woman from Gosforth, near Leeds, recalls a 'ghastly' journey home to Yorkshire from South Wales with her husband in August 1941, where, owing to an air raid on Birmingham, where they were to change trains, 'a bus took us some miles out to catch the connection. . . . When we got to this small station they literally pushed us into the train. There were soldiers and airmen everywhere, lying on luggage racks and on the floor. The corridors were packed to the doors. There was even somebody sitting on the lavatory seat. But we got there eventually and we survived. . . . We had to.' An Epsom woman remembers how she 'caused an officer some amusement by asking him, "Please keep my standing space while I go and get a newspaper"'.

On the whole, despite wartime friendliness, few people were willing to surrender their seat once they had secured it. A Southgate woman remembers an all-too-typical wartime journey to Bournemouth in 1944 with her two children, a girl of four and a baby a few months old. 'I left Waterloo in an air raid after queueing for a train; found no seats, so put the baby on the luggage rack. The corridor carriages were full of officers but nobody offered my little girl a seat.' A Worcester Park, Surrey, woman remembers a journey from North Wales with her children on which 'we had to stand all the way in the corridor while business men played cards in the adjoining carriage'. Even more annoying was the experience of a Wimbledon woman, during a holiday in Wales. 'My aunt and I had to change trains at Llandilo. The train was packed with soldiers. One kindly gave his seat to my aunt, whereupon his companion said that he would not have given up his seat, because we ladies probably did not know there was a war on. I did not tell him that my house had been blasted five times.'

A Twickenham woman, on another journey from Wales to London, remembers how 'each person who was seated in the compartment had someone else seated on their knee. The corridor was a solid mass of people. We sat waiting for the train to move, because the whistle had blown several times, but the guard came along and said it was too heavily loaded, and turfed some people off.' A young girl who travelled regularly between her home near London and her evacuated college in North Wales recollects 'travelling always in corridors, crowded up against soldiers who had sharp buttons or elbows or kitbags . . . people on floors, a child being sick non-stop and unable to move her or open a window because of the black-out'.

But not all crowded wartime journeys are remembered with repugnance. A Watford woman who travelled back to London from a holiday in Ross-on-Wye in 1942 or 1943 still feels that this was 'the happiest journey I have ever undertaken'. It had begun badly when a guard insisted 'No more on this train', but 'just as the train was pulling out, and the guard had his back to me . . . a corridor door swung open and a strong arm reached out and literally hauled me and my luggage into the train with a cheery "Come on, sisterr-r" in an American voice. . . . We stood packed close together—I was the only woman—and how those men ever visualised even one more person could have crushed in with them still amazes me. Standing thus all the way to London in a very slow train it was truly an impossibility to move one's arms or hands. With my small case between my feet, hefty army boots closed in . . . on . . . me time and again as I endeavoured to try and prevent cramp. . . . But, oh, wasn't it a happy journey? . . . How we talked—all of us, all the time. War was not once mentioned . . . As the hours passed we discussed books—religion—films—and pre-war holidays and hopes for future ones. Not one of us seemed to worry or think about the uncomfortable manner in which we were standing all those hours, like animals in a too-small pen . . . As we alighted on to the platform and laughingly rubbed stiff joints, we said our farewells rather as if we had known each other for years.'

With every corner of a compartment or corridor full, a place in the guard's van was a privilege. A Cheltenham woman, travelling from Glasgow to Yeovil, which involved three changes, found that her little Scottie dog, whom the guard obligingly took into his van, had a far more comfortable journey than his owner, being given drinks of water *and* having space to move in a pen made of suitcases. A Sompting, Sussex, man, was offered by a guard a space on the floor of his van, provided he did not mind sharing with two calves. 'Mind? I'd been brought up with calves, and I felt happier with them than some of the humans.' A Southsea woman, travelled to Yorkshire in a guard's van. 'We were sitting on kit bags belonging to troops who were moving up to Catterick', she remembers. 'My companion was an elderly titled lady, hatted, gloved, and with an umbrella, who sat rigidly upright all the way without a word of complaint, then shared her coffee flask and sandwiches with the guard and me.'

A Nottingham woman, travelling home to Manchester with her father after a family funeral, had an even stranger journey, for at Sheffield into the smell of burning wood from the recently bombed city intruded a more animal one. 'A lone billy goat, a pedigree one', was travelling on the same train to a farm in Cheshire. When the party changed trains at Retford 'I got landed with the goat . . . walked the beast up and down the platform, gave him a drink of tea and got a train to Manchester', though it turned out in fact to be going to Halifax. 'We had to change again, still with the billy goat, who was now quite friendly, but no less smelly. We reached Manchester eight hours late, very cold and hungry', and here she learned that her sister, a nurse in Sheffield, who had failed to meet them there as arranged, had 'been delivering babies by candlelight in the cellar, with her skirt blown off', but was unharmed.

Porters on most stations, although many women had replaced men, were non-existent. One army officer's wife, arriving in Scotland, after searching desperately for a porter had to throw her luggage out of the train as it was pulling out 'and then try to jump myself while it was gaining speed'. A Reigate woman remembers that 'There was many a time when I could not have done without the ready help of fellow travellers, who didn't even wince at the idea of carrying my trunk across the line to another platform'. The fear of assault felt by many women travelling alone in blacked-out trains was almost always unfounded. The wife of an R.A.F. pilot, in her early twenties, who travelled at night from Ipswich to Stroud 'was cared for the whole way by servicemen, each handed me on to another group or individual, all so nice. Five Gloucester Hussars sat on one seat so that I could sleep on the other. I got to Stroud at 6.30 a.m. in the dark, lay down in the reading-room to rest. A local bobby sat with me for protection, I thought, but he ran his hand up and down my thigh so obviously I was wrong.' A twenty-one-year-old woman research chemist was more fortunate when, at 2 a.m. one morning in 1943, she found herself, due to a diversion, deposited at Warrington by the London train, instead of her real destination, Manchester. A young airman offered to accompany her on her walk homewards via Weaste, though both, she recalls, were 'rather wary and walked very far apart'. From Weaste she got an all-night tram to a station where there was a solitary taxi full of young airmen going to Heaton Park, which was on her way home. There was 'no other taxis and the driver said I could come at my own risk', and she was not reassured by the cry that went up from the airmen, 'Oh good, a girl!', until someone explained that 'his cocker spaniel bitch had had four pups on the train and they couldn't keep her happy as they couldn't hold her and the pups. Bitch and pups were dumped in my lap and I had a large share of the taxi, while the boys crowded on each other and on the floor—and paid my fare.'

Travelling with a baby was enough to make even the bravest mother hesitate, but here too the almost universal helpfulness made the experience bearable. People became accustomed to looking the other way as mothers breast fed their babies in waiting rooms or carriages and a Dunbarton-shire woman had the rare experience of being complimented on her maternal skill by a bishop, with whom she was sharing a compartment. 'I had occasion to change the baby, using one of my precious disposable nappies, and being as discreet as possible; when I had finished His Grace leant over and said "You made a very neat little job of that my dear".' Many mothers had cause, too, to bless the immense capacity of the average pram. This is how one young mother prepared to transport herself and her small baby from bombed Coventry to join her husband in London. 'Into the hollow base I put pots and pans and foodstuffs. On the pram floor went the baby's mattress and blankets. Then a layer of baby's and my clothes, with a large sheet and blanket. Roped on top was a rolled up mattress covered over with black-out curtains. My single small suitcase held rations, candles, drawing pins, matches and our private papers.' All her efforts narrowly escaped being defeated by the ticket collector, who questioned whether a pram ticket was valid when the pram only contained luggage, but eventually, after studying the regulations, he let her through and mother, baby and baby-less pram had a comfortable journey in the guard's van.

In June 1940 an area up to twenty miles inland from the coast, from the Wash to Rye, was declared a Defence Area which no one could visit without good reason, and the area was later extended northwards to Berwick-on-Tweed and westwards to Dorset and parts of South Wales. Travel within the area was not affected and the strictness with which the rules were enforced varied considerably. In Dorchester, crammed with American troops before D Day, unauthorised arrivals were sometimes met off the train by a policeman, who saw them to the ticket office to buy a return ticket and then waited on the departure platform until they left. But a Glasgow woman, eager to see her recently-torpedoed son after two years' absence, found no difficulty about entering Portsmouth, though she was caught by a random check on identity cards while queueing for a sale of blitz-damaged goods. A policeman ordered her to leave Portsmouth at once, but 'no one bothered me and I stayed another two days'. One wartime schoolboy was delighted by the rumour of impending restrictions on visits to Bournemouth in the summer of 1942, which enabled him to leave school to spend his holiday there a fortnight early. Only in Protected Areas, with many military installations, where stricter control was imposed, were the regulations really troublesome. A young unmarried woman living in London found that she could still spend holidays at her mother's house at Sheringham on the Norfolk coast, as officially it remained her home, while her married sister required police permission, the only acceptable grounds being to visit ' "an aged parent or a sick relative". Mother', she recalls, 'said she would prefer to be an aged parent'—she was in fact a sprightly sixty-six. Owing to some curious quirk of the regulations she was allowed to take her two-year-old son with her but not her ten-year-old daughter, and during the visit 'a local policeman came to the cottage one morning to tell me that my time was up and I must go home', while her husband, coming to collect her, was questioned by police at a road block.

Londoners had always been proud of their Underground system and during the war it continued to carry millions of people to work, and to shelter hundreds of thousands more, with remarkably little disturbance. Flooding was the chief danger, and, after flood gates had been installed, one was liable to be turned off the Underground at the Strand or Waterloo and sent above ground, as during raids no trains ran under the river. Once the tube stations had been organised to cope with the influx of shelterers one became accustomed to stepping over sleeping figures when changing trains and to the sight of bunks and canvas-screened lavatories on the platforms, and the board reading 'Air Raid Warning' or 'All Clear' displayed by the ticket barrier. Women, too, soon became familiar as booking clerks and station porters—there were only 200 male porters, of 1,200, left by the end of the war. On the trains, lighting was at first almost as bad as on other suburban services with only three dim, blue lights to each coach, but after public protests small but adequate separate reading lamps were installed, while stations below ground were a cheerful blaze of illumination. Trains, unlike buses, still ran reasonably late—the last from Southgate into London was, I remember, not till 11.31—and the whole service was almost as comfortable and efficient as in peacetime.

To keep passengers informed of its work, the London Passenger Transport Board created one of the innumerable admonitory figures of wartime, Billy Brown of London Town, a typical suburban 'little man' dressed in striped trousers, dark jacket, bowler hat and stiff white collar and dutifully carrying both a gas mask and an umbrella. Billy Brown exuded an irritating smugness in such verses as:

> Down below the station's bright
> But here outside it's black as night.
> Billy Brown will wait a bit
> And let his eyes grow used to it.

Posters featuring him were often defaced, though in rather different ways from those suffered by an earlier L.P.T.B. character, 'Susan Sensible, or Black-out Sue'. One notice in particular, which pleaded with passengers not to pull off the heavy netting glued to the windows of Underground trains to stop flying glass, provided a constant challenge to graffiti-writers. Reminders that 'The fabric on the window is for your protection' produced little response, except from humorists who amended 'window' to 'widow', and a painted Billy Brown was called in to address a firm reproof to a thoughtless citizen shown pulling back the window netting:

> I trust you'll pardon my correction,
> That stuff is there for your protection.

This invited a famous unofficial reply, which sums up the heartfelt desire of many wartime travellers:

> We thank you for your information
> We want to see the bloody station.

# A GALLON OF POOL?

'The further restrictions on the private use of petrol will be warmly welcomed by public opinion.'

*The Times,* 13th March 1942

Petrol rationing began with a false alarm. After all-day queues at the garages on Tuesday 15th September, the day before it was due to start, there was a last-minute postponement until midnight on 22nd September, when it did finally begin. Though it was illegal to supply petrol to portable containers or to store it without a licence, people that day could be seen producing not merely petrol cans but barrels, wash-boilers, bottles and even buckets to be filled. The tennis court of an Ilford hotel-owner may still have two cans of petrol hidden beneath it; having buried them against the coming shortage, he could never remember exactly where. A physiotherapist working in Sheffield remembers how her father's hoarding of petrol 'in tins and glass containers in a queer place under his little workshop out in the stables where we had the garage' nearly had a far more serious result. Her brother, on leave from the R.A.F., was overcome by petrol fumes and had to be dragged out unconscious, the friend who carried him to safety and the doctor who treated him being both sworn to secrecy. The courts, too, were as tolerant of petrol hoarders as they were severe on black-out offenders. A Bolton baker who recklessly stored 260 gallons in wash tubs was merely fined £3.

Branded petrol was replaced on the outbreak of war by 'pool', a blend said to be superior to the peacetime 'No. 3' grade, though inferior to premium fuel. It cost 1s. 6d. a gallon, raised to 1s. 8d. and then to 2s. 1½d. Black market petrol, for which the cost was said to be 6s. 6d., was, at least in the early days, not hard to obtain, for though petrol for commercial use was dyed a distinctive red, it was a widely shared secret that the tell-tale dye could be removed by pouring the petrol through an ordinary gas mask filter. Every car-owner was entitled to a basic ration of petrol, the coupons being obtained by presenting the car log book at any Post Office, and a varying number of 'supplementary' petrol coupons were issued, for essential business or domestic purposes, to anyone who could prove that the basic ration was inadequate for his needs. The basic ration, based on the size of one's car, rose from four gallons a month for the tiny, box-like Austin Seven, to ten gallons for cars of twenty horse-power and over. A Ford Eight, a popular pre-war make costing around £100, received five gallons, a Vauxhall Ten, costing £182, six. The ration was sufficient only for 100 to 200 miles of motoring a month, and hints for petrol-saving soon filled the motoring magazines. The Royal Automobile Club advised drivers to keep their sparking plugs clean, to get into top gear quickly, and to maintain an economic speed of 20 to 30 m.p.h. 'Free running' or 'coasting', with the engine in neutral, and the driver keeping control only 'by gentle brake pressure', was also claimed to save as much as a third of one's normal consumption on a long journey. Another suggestion was for drivers to share the use of each other's cars, and under the government's *Help Your Neighbour* scheme, introduced in October 1940, 20,000 motorists who displayed a notice offering free lifts into and out of London received extra petrol.

The war years were a golden age for hitch-hikers. The official view was 'that a vacant place in a car travelling to or from . . . Central London . . . called for an explanation'. A young girl from Tooting working in a City insurance office remembers that she 'was often "picked up" by a stranger on the way to the station—a thing in these days it would . . . be unwise for a young girl to do'. One girl in the Timber Corps, working near Exeter, remembers lifts in an oxygen lorry and an empty hearse, and she did not despise the cross-bar of a bicycle when it was generously offered. A woman A.F.S. member, working in a North London factory, remembers that 'the buses were very erratic but in uniform I only had to raise my hand to get a lift. I rode on anything: coal lorries, railway delivery trucks and fire engines.' But, outside the city, vehicles were few. One A.F.S. man, hitch-hiking home from London to Coventry one weekend, needed thirteen lifts to do it.

The most popular, though illegal, means of making your petrol go further was to add paraffin to it, though one Barnes woman remembers a friend's car which ran on 'mothballs and paraffin, and made a terrible noise and smell as it went off like a shot'. Living in a hilly area had its advantages; a young Scotswoman remembers that 'we used to coast downhill . . . and, eventually . . . used pink paraffin instead of petrol and our car seemed to quite like it and performed very well, in spite of rather dark clouds of smoke which belched from the rear. Of course, before long we had to give up altogether and settle our dear old car up on wooden blocks in the garage.'

This was to be the fate of many much-loved vehicles, but some determined motorists did not give up without a struggle. During the first weeks of the war some cars appeared on the streets with what appeared to be a small barrage balloon tethered to the roof, usually housed in a wooden crate, for without this the gas bag, as it emptied, tended to sag rather frighteningly down over the front and sides of the car like a gradually deflating whale. To run one's car on unrationed town gas, while still receiving one's normal petrol ration, seemed highly attractive but before long most car-owners who had invested £30 in a gas bag and auxiliary carburetter began to regret their first enthusiasm. Not merely did the gas bag and crate—nine feet long, six feet wide and four feet high—make the vehicle harder to handle, but the whole 202 cubic feet of gas it contained only equalled a single gallon of petrol. Every twenty miles or, in a large car, every twelve, one had to stop for a refill, which took ten minutes, although the gas companies enterprisingly set up a network of supply points at ten-mile intervals throughout London. But in October 1942 further conversions were banned due to the growing fuel shortage, and existing gas-equipped vehicles had to be taken off the roads unless employed on essential work.

Gas propulsion for cars, using a gas bag on the roof or a heavy cylinder inside the vehicle, was a short-lived craze, but using producer-gas, generated as they went along, to power commercial vehicles, seemed at first a more practical proposition. The usual arrangement was for the vehicle to tow behind it on a trailer a burner resembling a large dustbin, and by early 1942 seventy-five firms, including many bus companies, were making use of this method. It proved, if not literally a non-starter, at least a frequent stopper. In theory a gas-powered vehicle had a range of 150 miles, but it was soon found that London buses needed stoking up again every eighty miles and got through a ton of anthracite each week. Gas-driven vehicles also needed constant maintenance and were troublesome to drive, for the burner had to be lit with a paraffin flare and coaxed into life with a blower, the engine had to be started on petrol before it could be switched over to gas and it then produced far less power and often gave up on any steep slope. The government was obviously wise to move cautiously, but gas propulsion for some reason made a great appeal to the House of Lords, and the peers' campaign for more energetic action by ministers reached a ludicrous climax in April 1942, when, to everyone's embarrassment and amusement, the coke-burners, led by a duke, actually defeated the government on a motion demanding that 50,000 vehicles be converted immediately, instead of the 10,000 proposed by the Ministry of Transport. Despite some good-humoured cheers nothing more was done and a few months later the growing shortage of all types of solid fuel, and of skilled mechanics to carry out the conversions, really settled the question. From 1943 onwards, aided by a slight improvement in petrol supplies, most bus companies, with great relief, converted their gas-burning vehicles back to using petrol.

By now, apart from army traffic, they almost had the roads to themselves. The beginning of the end for petrol-driven cars had come with a cut of a sixth in the basic petrol ration from October 1941, followed by a further cut in 1942. Then the final blow fell. On 13th March 1942, a black day for Britain's surviving motorists, it was announced that 'As from 1st July the basic ration will cease to exist', and even supplementary petrol would only be granted if really essential. 'These measures', it was announced, 'are designed to end pleasure motoring. . . . The government want all unessential cars taken off the road.' In this aim the government undoubtedly succeeded. In August 1939 there had been 2,000,000 private cars on the road, by October 1940, despite rationing, 1,400,000, but now the number fell sharply until by January 1944 only 700,000 private cars were in use over the whole country, and these were all growing steadily older and shabbier. In July 1940 it had become illegal to buy a new vehicle without a licence, which would not be granted to buy a private car, and by October no more cars for civilians were being made. It was not until June 1945 that it became possible even to apply for a new car and not until several years later that supply began to catch up with demand. The basic petrol ration was restored in the same month though rationing was not abolished altogether until 1950.

With no shining new cars in the showrooms, the price of secondhand cars inevitably soared. One Teignmouth family's Austin Twelve, bought for £180, was sold for £360 after 4,000 miles over bumpy country roads. A Flackwell Heath, Buckinghamshire, couple were equally fortunate. Their 1936 Ford cost fifteen pounds secondhand, was hard used by the air-crew who usually filled her, and after a respray was sold in 1947 for £200, which 'became the deposit for our house'.

Many people, as their cars wore out, or after the basic petrol ration was abolished, laid them up, a considerable, as well as a painful, undertaking. The R.A.C. recommended washing the exterior, reducing the tyres to half pressure and then removing them. To protect the engine one had to drain the radiator, remove the sparking plugs, pour a teaspoonful of engine oil into each cylinder, turn the engine by hand and then restore the plugs, finally mounting the car on blocks of wood beneath the axles, where it mutely awaited the defeat of Hitler.

For those motorists who kept their vehicles going, life was even harder. The black-out, hard for pedestrians, was a nightmare for motorists. The original rules had allowed only the use of heavily masked sidelights, with blackened reflectors and glass covered by two thicknesses of newspaper, but within a few days the use of the offside headlamp, heavily obscured, became permitted, and in January 1940 an official pattern mask became compulsory, resembling a black cocoa tin with three shielded slits cut in the end. Red rear lights—though not a number plate light—

were allowed and a narrow slit of light on direction indicators, though the use of lighting inside the car was forbidden. From 1st February 1940 a new speed limit of 20 m.p.h. after dark in built-up areas was introduced after a drastic increase in the number of road deaths, which in the last four months of 1939 was almost double that for the corresponding months of 1938. Although the motoring organisations misguidedly protested against the new limit, the House of Commons greeted it with cheers. Motorists also had, from September 1939, to paint the bumpers and running boards of their cars white, from May 1940 were forbidden to have a radio, even an unfixed one, in their car, and from June were compelled to immobilise the vehicle, if leaving it anywhere except in a locked garage, by removing 'part of the mechanism'—usually the rotor arm or the main ignition lead. Far more troublesome, however, was the removal of the signposts which occurred at the same time and led to a vast waste of time and petrol. A Chatham housewife remembers a typical car journey to her wartime home at Yeovil, a distance of about 150 miles, loaded with 'two Scotties, and a car-load of suitcases, bedding and various other things. It took me eight hours to complete the trip with no signposts (I didn't know the road) and only sketchy instructions from Chatham to Guildford.' Although the car had contained the month's petrol ration, plus two extra gallons, she arrived with only a cupful left in the tank. Not infrequently people ran out of petrol altogether. Sometimes cars had to be towed home by horses and one Yorkshirewoman remembers the macabre case of the funeral of her father's boss. Just before petrol rationing began her father had 'buried a two gallon can of petrol in his back garden, but was not able to use it as private motoring was forbidden'. Now came his chance, for 'halfway to the churchyard, a distance of three miles, as the cortège passed along our road, the hearse ran out of petrol and the undertaker's ration for the period was used up. My father returned home, retrieved the buried treasure and with great satisfaction and pride was able to help his old employer on his last journey.'

For the learner-driver, the war brought a new freedom. Driving tests were suspended on the outbreak of war and a wartime 'National Service Licence' issued to all applicants and though tests were resumed in January 1940, they were dropped again that summer. For the rest of the war learners could drive alone and without 'L' plates. The war brought, too, one change which benefited everyone: the general introduction of white lines down the middle of the road which had been the exception before the war. One Hampshire farmer feels that the person responsible deserved a medal; he found them invaluable when driving through the New Forest in the black-out.

In 1940 nine out of ten British families did not run a car and often regarded those who did as a privileged minority. Even *The Times*, no voice of the people, referred in June 1940 to 'concern and not a little public indignation . . . regarding the continued use of motor cars for what seems to be more or less selfish purposes'. The spectacle of crowded car parks at race meetings, to which the newsreels often drew attention, gave particular offence. One Newmarket man wrote to *The Times* in May 1941 to complain that 'thousands of gallons of petrol must have been consumed' by 'hundreds of motor omnibuses and cars converging on Newmarket from a wide area', and the general disgust at such scenes made the abolition of the basic petrol ration distinctly popular.* When Herbert Morrison admitted in the House of Commons that 'the large accumulation of cars at sports functions . . . has undoubtedly been offensive to public feeling', M.P.s cried 'Hear! Hear!' So did *The Times*. 'The further restrictions on the private use of petrol will be warmly welcomed by public opinion', it commented, referring to the widespread 'distaste at the sight of a large number of cars used for purposes which had not the remotest connection with the war'.

Indignant defenders of the basic ration did little except harm their cause. One middle-class woman publicly declared, to the surprise of her working-class neighbours, that 'a bus is not really much use for heavy shopping purposes'. One Yorkshireman threatened that if their petrol were cut further 'large numbers of people will leave the countryside and crowd into towns', provoking the very reasonable retort from an official spokesman that 'millions of people who live in the country have never owned a motor-car, yet they manage to exist'. Even an appeal to religion—it was said that, without cars, no one living in the country would go to church—failed to move the government. Apart from the aged or infirm, who would qualify for petrol, said a minister, churchgoers ought to walk. Fortunately for the reputation of motorists, many showed a commendable patriotism, like one Sussex woman who protested pointedly at 'the too prevalent attitude to the war: "It's all right for other people, but what about me?" . . . If we can only shop once a week and perhaps have to wait for buses and find standing room only when they come . . . we should do so cheerfully.'

After the ending of the basic petrol ration any driver could be stopped and required to prove that his journey was essential and that he was travelling by the shortest possible route. The law was rigorously enforced; in 1943 an engineer was prosecuted—unsuccessfully—for deviating from his authorised route by seventy-nine yards to visit a cinema, and in the following year a company director who went 1,240 yards out

---

* The public attitude was well reflected in a line in the popular film *San Demetrio, London*. A tanker captain, having, after desperate dangers, brought his vital cargo into harbour, comments bitterly: 'That ought to be enough to take quite a few racegoers to Newmarket'.

of his way to go home for lunch was actually convicted. The two most famous cases of misuse of petrol involved show business. In August 1943 the theatrical manager Jack Hylton was fined £155 for using petrol supplies for use on his farm to take himself and several actors from a theatre to the Savoy Hotel, though the gaol sentence passed on him was replaced on appeal by a further fine. The actor-composer Ivor Novello was less fortunate in the following year, in a case involving travel between the London theatre where *The Dancing Years* was being staged and his home in Berkshire. He took his four weeks in gaol badly, but a forgiving audience—rather inappropriately one may feel—cheered him on his first appearance on the stage after his release.

The regulations, though severe, were not unreasonably interpreted. The daughter-in-law of a vicar in a remote country parish in Yorkshire remembers that he had a small ration of petrol for parish duties and a little for shopping in the nearest town, seven miles away. An elderly, lame man living in a village in Cheshire was allowed three gallons a month, enough, as his 14 h.p. car was heavy on petrol, to go out about once a fortnight. The wife of a Sussex farmer found that their petrol allowance 'did permit the occasional trip to cinema or shops', but her 'retired parents were less fortunate. As well as a car, they had a motor mower for their large garden, and also made their own electricity. So it used to be "Shall we have some light, mow the lawn, or go for a ride?"' A Birmingham housewife evacuated to the country found her husband not wholly displeased when, during pregnancy, she developed varicose veins in her legs—it meant 'extra coupons to take me shopping'.

But not everyone was so conscientious. An office boy working for a firm of insurance brokers in the City found that 'there seemed to be no shortage of petrol for the directors' Rolls and Daimlers'. One of his jobs 'was getting the chief director's cigarettes. He only smoked Player's Passing Cloud and I had to scour the City for them. This sometimes took an afternoon and ran him up a taxi bill.' A Welsh farmer admits 'I was not short of petrol as our lorries and tractors used it, but I kept a permanent piece of work for the blacksmith in my car, his shop being situated next to the pub!'

Doctors, like farmers, were fortunate over petrol. As a Norfolk doctor remembers, 'Medical practice in a rural area with visits up to ten miles was a cast-iron reason for getting all I needed, though we had to be careful about "joy riding".' Night work, however, was, he found, very difficult using masked headlights, but country roads were then almost devoid of traffic. A Glasgow woman doctor remembers a boy remarking to her 'You're a doctor', in the street one day, explaining he had identified her 'Becus yer the only kin' o' wummun thet's got a car the noo!' A Northumberland G.P. found that his petrol requirements were invariably cut by about half, but most doctors, growing experienced, applied for twice as much as they really required and when he was desperately short a local farmer would rally round with tractor fuel. But even doctors had their problems. If a doctor went out for the evening for pleasure he was supposed to leave his car behind, which meant a serious delay if he were called to a case. One Kent doctor's daughter remembers another doctor being asked 'How many Emergency calls will you receive next month?' 'He received his coupons', she admits, 'in spite of the rude answer he gave.'

It was the difficulty of obtaining cars and keeping them serviced which troubled doctors more than lack of petrol. From November 1941 an official certificate from the Ministry of War Transport was needed to obtain any spare parts, except wheels or tyres, and from 1942 tyres were only replaced if an official inspector had confirmed that the existing ones were worn out. A Midlands doctor, who did his local calls on foot and reserved his car for longer distances, remembers how 'unless the inner tube was showing the advice was to come back after a few weeks'. Only the lucky chance that a local ambulance worker had a laid-up car and was willing to sell his tyres enabled him to keep his own car on the road, and with a reconditioned engine installed at 42,000 miles it carried him right through the war years, although by the end 'it had almost lost the rear compartment floor boards, the outside was shabby . . . often annoying other drivers because that odd-looking wreck could pass them with ease'.

This doctor, like many other people, regrets the loss of 'a camaraderie which has almost disappeared', and this was a great feature of wartime motoring. A Westmorland doctor found that 'Mostly people were enormously kind and considerate, and as for the garage hands—they turned out in the small hours in snow and ice and any weather without ever the smallest complaint if I was in bad trouble (which was seldom) and kept me on the road'. In Cheshire another doctor had a similar experience. 'One night,' he remembers, 'having gone to a confinement, I ran out of petrol. In the house of the patient a young soldier was on leave. He went out with an old petrol can and walked a long way to an all-night garage and returned with one gallon.'

In town it was not at all uncommon for the doctor to arrive by bicycle. One London woman doctor reluctantly abandoned hers in 1942 only when an unlucky skid brought it to a premature end. A Sheffield doctor remembesr that 'when my car went in for servicing I frequently had to do a round on a bicycle'. Sometimes he was lent a car by a patient but, as it was illegal to use petrol intended for his car in any other, this meant breaking the law. In some particularly remote areas, a familiar nineteenth-century sight, the country practitioner making his calls on horseback,

his bag slung from the saddle, was seen again for the first time for a generation. A Cambridgeshire doctor who rode his hunter had the great
satisfaction of persuading the Inland Revenue to agree an income tax
allowance of £90 a year for its keep.

At the start of the war there had been just under half a million motor
cycles on the road.* At first all types received the same ration, from the
most high powered to the humble auto-cycle which had so small a
tank that its owner was allowed to buy petrol for it by the half coupon.
In January 1940 the ration for motor cycles over 250 c.c. was raised to
three gallons a month—all others received only two. This made the
auto-cycle by far the most economical vehicle on the road, but it never
became really popular, though one architect, then living in Putney, still
remembers appreciatively how his faithful 'popper', despite its inbuilt
tendency to skid, carried him about Greater London through bombs
and bad weather, until the basic ration, for motor cycles as for cars,
was abolished in 1942.

Some people tried to solve their transport problem by the use of hired
cars, either self-drive or chauffeur-driven, though these too were governed
by strict regulations, especially as to the distance one could travel. The
law was most frequently broken by that most selfish, undeserving and
least patriotic of groups, the racing fraternity, to whom both government
and courts showed a ridiculous leniency throughout the war. A Lancaster
man who wasted eleven gallons of petrol in 1942 in transporting four
bookmakers to Newmarket races was merely fined £10, and one book-
maker who hired a car to take him to the St. Leger at Newmarket, as the
train was full, was actually held on appeal to have made an 'essential'
journey. Fortunately some other gamblers found that defying the
law was one bet that did not pay off. Three men from Burton-on-Trent
who hired a cab to attend Doncaster races were fined £1,200 and some
other patriots were fined £300 for similar offences in attending Ascot.
Taxis continued to ply for hire throughout the war, and in London at
least it was the arrival of the free-spending Americans, rather than petrol
rationing, which first made them really hard to find, though taxi queues,
then a novelty, at main line stations and, another novelty, sharing taxis,
went some way to relieve the worst effects of the shortage.

By 1944 expenditure per head of population on petrol for private
motoring was only one fiftieth of the pre-war figure. The basic reason
for the severity of rationing was less the need to save shipping space
than to provide fuel for the almost insatiable demands of the Forces,
especially the Strategic Bomber Offensive. A single Lancaster—the first
flew on a raid in 1942 and by 1946 7,000 had been produced—took
2,000 gallons of petrol to reach the Ruhr, and could use up to 3,540

* The number now is 1,152,000.

on a longer mission. In two major raids, on Wilhelmshaven and Düsseldorf, in November 1943 the R.A.F. and United States Air Force consumed between them 5,000,000 gallons of fuel in twenty-four hours. I can recall a master at my school calculating that a single Spitfire on a short flight used his car's basic ration for a year.* It was such arithmetic which made motorists accept cheerfully that great deprivation of 'doing without the car', despite the many well-documented stories which were circulated of waste of petrol by the Services, especially the R.A.F., where at least one pilot, refused seven gallons of petrol to drive himself home on leave, flew home instead, using 279 gallons.

For the ordinary, non car-owning, civilian, far more serious than the virtual abolition of private motoring were the sharp reductions in public bus services, already hard-pressed by the call-up of staff, and the lack of spares. Petrol and oil supplies to London Transport were cut by a quarter immediately war broke out and within four months more than 800 Central London buses had been withdrawn, some routes being closed down altogether and others operating only before 10 a.m. and after 4 p.m. The number of bus stops was also cut down to save petrol and a 'bus curfew' introduced. In London, from 1940 onwards, the last buses left the centre at 10.30 p.m., but in most provincial towns from 1942 none ran after 9 or at latest 9.30. Happily the belief that a car was almost a necessity of life was not yet accepted and most people took the new difficulties literally in their stride. If one went to a theatre and had to choose between leaving at the second interval or walking home most people preferred to walk. A Nottingham schoolteacher remembers a regular four-mile walk from the Theatre Royal, while a Yorkshire 'special' recalls that 'having to walk home . . . above three miles, carrying steel helmet, gas mask, handcuffs and truncheon caused me much weariness'. One Lancashire woman remembers that she and her friends, as young girls, when attending dances in Preston, several miles away, had to start queueing for the last bus at 9.30. People 'used to fight to get on' and 'lots of times we walked rather than face the crowds, yells, etc.'. Sometimes a cousin with a motor bike would, if he had some petrol, 'ferry' six or seven girls home one at a time on his pillion.

From 1942, the first buses on Sunday in most places did not run before 1 p.m., a blow to some church-goers but not universally regretted. One child living at Iffley, near Oxford, remembers that previously her mother, a strict nonconformist, had insisted on them all going to chapel. Now, as this meant a two-and-a-half-mile walk each way, chapel-going was greatly reduced and she was able to spend 'long, lazy mornings in bed reading'.

* The early Spitfire had a tank capacity of 85 gallons, a year's ration for a 15 h.p. car. Later versions carried 210 gallons.

Early in the war, Londoners became accustomed to the strange sight of the famous red London buses lined up at night under the trees in Hyde Park and other open spaces—partly to save taking them back to the depot, but also as a precaution against bombing. This proved very necessary. Within two months when the blitz began so many buses had been knocked out that London Transport had to appeal to other bus companies to lend it vehicles. Nearly 500 arrived within a week, from nearly every major city in the British Isles, and Londoners became accustomed to boarding vehicles in strange colours, bearing such inscriptions as 'Corporation of Manchester' and lists of highly improbable destinations. Later London Transport repaid its indebtedness with interest by sending 800 of its buses to such places as Coventry and Bristol. On Merseyside old red buses with outside staircases, lent by Manchester, were ungratefully known by all Liverpudlians as 'the red devils'. Later new buses everywhere were usually painted a drab grey.

Before the war, boarding a bus had involved a free-for-all, but in April 1942 it became compulsory, as services grew less frequent, to form a queue—one wartime regulation that has become permanent. The intolerable Billy Brown was ready as usual to exhibit his customary virtue.

> He never jostles in a queue,
> But waits and takes his turn. Do you?

Wartime buses were considerably less comfortable than those built before the war. To save materials and labour they had plain wooden-slatted seats, with no upholstery, like third class continental trains. More centre-facing bench seats were provided, to increase standing room, and soon single-deckers, which had once carried forty passengers, were managing to squeeze in sixty. In London and other cities windows were covered with anti-blast netting or strips of gummed paper, while everywhere after dark the only light came from heavily cowled, dim-blue bulbs, fitted into alternate sockets. The light was too faint to distinguish silver from copper and the bus companies, until many fitted a light to the conductor's uniform, were soon suffering from an unprecedented influx of foreign coins, some conductors genially calling out after dark 'Get out your bad tanners!' instead of the traditional 'Fares, please!'. Owing to the thinness of wartime ticket paper, it was, a Sheffield conductress discovered, easy to give two tickets in place of one. For drivers the black-out was a far greater nuisance than the bombs. The wife of a Rochdale bus-driver found that her husband's eyes became permanently bloodshot due to the constant strain of driving on dimmed lights. Country driving was little better than that in the town. A Mansfield woman was involved in one unexpectedly exciting journey which ended in the inexperienced driver landing the vehicle 'fairly and squarely in a ploughed field'. It was only extricated after half an hour of heaving across the furrows, not helped by the inevitable wit, who asked loudly, 'Have you been called up for the Tank Corps?'

Only a few women were recruited as bus-drivers, but by the end of the war a male conductor was a rare sight. The 'clippies' added a new interest to wartime travel, particularly in places where at first they had to wear their own clothes, and as one in Darlington remarks, 'It looked more like a fashion show than turning up for work.' It was the issue of trousers to conductresses, though not popular with male passengers, which helped to make slacks acceptable to women generally.

The good humour of bus-drivers and conductors, male and female, is for many people an outstanding memory of the war. A moment's wait to enable one to catch an early morning bus, a friendly word as one handed over one's fare at the end of a long day at a workbench, meant much, and many conductors, tired themselves, responded nobly. One twenty-one-year-old Post Office worker in the City, from which during the blitz an 'Express' bus ran to her home in Leyton, remembers, 'I had very little time to catch the last Express when I finished work at 5.30 p.m. . . . Many evenings I was helped on by conductors just as it was moving off.' A woman living in Street, Somerset, recalls 'the unfailing sweetness (love is not too strong a word) and humour of a bus conductress over the war years. Everyone loved her, and she gave everybody courage.' Many housewives, however, resented the priority often given to anyone in uniform or working clothes. A Cardiff housewife remembers a long wait in a queue which ended in her being 'the last permitted passenger. Just as I was about to get on, a woman from behind me pushed to the fore. "I've been working on cranes all day at the Dowlais. I want to get home. Housewives can wait!" The bus inspector pushed her on. I couldn't argue. I had to stand for another hour for the next bus, knowing that my children would be waiting on the doorstep, frightened, as I had never been away from home before when they returned from school.' In Rotherham even dirty overalls did not guarantee a seat, for only shift workers could use the buses after 9 p.m., and they had to produce a special badge. Sometimes conductors applied informal selection tests of their own. I can remember one at the bus station in Newbury appealing to anyone only going as far as council estate on the outskirts of town to alight and walk instead, to make room for people going to more distant stops.

Official regulations about standing passengers were relaxed during the war and even in London one conductress remembers coping with twelve people standing, while in country districts the only limit recognised was often that imposed by gravity. One woman returning to the

Oxfordshire village of Enstone from a shopping trip in Oxford remembers how 'the bus became so full that people had to sit on the stairs'. When Woodstock Hill proved too much for it, several passengers got off and walked to the top, like passengers on an eighteenth-century mail-coach. One Harwich woman, then a catering worker in her twenties, experienced some typical journeys in rural Essex.

> We had one particular private bus service, petrol driven, which made a point of never leaving anyone behind, however full the bus. Sometimes there were many more standing than sitting; or there would be four to a seat, girls sitting on laps, with plenty of good-natured chaff about what so-and-so's wife would say when she heard what her old man got up to on the bus. At stops there always seemed to be someone at the very back of the bus to get out. Amid groans from those already squeezed as tight as could be in the aisles, and squawks as others got the traveller's elbow or shopping basket in ribs or sometimes eyes, yells of dismay as toes were unavoidably trodden on and precious stockings possibly ruined, those nearer the exit piled out, sometimes into pouring rain, and in winter into pitch dark, to let this one person out. Then all piled in again with a careful check each time by the conductor, ensuring that no one was inadvertently left behind in error.

The war meant a reprieve in many cities for trams, and for trolley buses, though their silent approach made them a great menace in the black-out. For a few weeks during the blitz a riverboat service operated between Westminster and Woolwich, and one woman working on the Isle of Dogs remembers going to and from work in a small six-seater rowing boat. London lost its remaining Green Line coaches in September 1942, and at the same time all remaining long-distance coaches were withdrawn, although for a long time they had only served points not covered by other means of transport.

Despite all the difficulties of wartime travel, many people, motorists and non-motorists alike, have pleasant memories of that brief period when the roads were empty, as they had not been for thirty years. With no carrier's cart to the nearest town and fewer bus services, many villages now became more isolated than at any time in their history.

For cyclists these were golden years. I can recall long afternoons of cycling in the Berkshire and Hampshire countryside without seeing a single car off the main roads, and very few on them. A Suffolk school matron remembers cycling to a dance with her long evening dress draped over the handlebars; a London A.F.S. woman arrived for duty, complete with tin hat and gas mask, on the crossbar of her husband's bicycle, though, she admits, 'I was no lightweight'; an Oswestry housewife kept up the ritual of meeting her husband at the station, but with a bicycle to carry his bag home; a whole West Country concert party, complete with 'props', cycled eight miles to give a show at Avonmouth. At the start of the war bicycles had suddenly risen in the social scale, *The Times* reporting 'an exceptional demand by well-to-do people for machines', and a shortage of red rear lamps which had become compulsory when the black-out began. Front lamps had to be heavily masked, with a hood over the upper half, the bottom half covered by paint or card, and the reflector blacked out. Many families now went on cycling holidays and it was not thought out of the way to arrive by bicycle at a hotel or boarding house, though before long new machines became few. I can remember a long wait before obtaining my first bicycle in 1943, and it compared poorly with pre-war models, for every inch was painted black and there was no chromium, no three-speed and only a miserably 'tinny' bell. Bicycle pumps were almost as scarce as bicycles. Mine was a poor, frail, inefficient object, with a connection only half the normal length.

The horse now also came into its own for the last time. By 1942 a good plough horse was fetching £200, and one intended for riding £250 or more, while a pony and trap changed hands at 155 guineas and governess carts, unwanted pre-war, at £20 to £40. Even in towns the horse reappeared and in the same year Irish hunters were drawing Post Office vans in the City and West End. An Aberdeen women remembers the usual problem which confronted her husband, a coal-heaver, due to the shortage of horses. The team which pulled his lorry was reinforced by a Belgian one, which 'knew no English and my husband couldn't speak his language, so it was very difficult for man and beast'.

# FIVE INCHES IN THE BATH

'As part of your personal share in the Battle for Fuel you are asked
NOT to exceed five inches of water in this bath.'
  Notice issued by the Ministry of Fuel for display in hotel bathrooms,

October 1942.

If, one day in the middle of the war, the neighbours of a Hendon woman
had seen two small girls earnestly breaking up her garden path they
might have assumed that the children were 'digging for victory'—but
they would have been wrong. As one of the children, now a mother
herself, explains: 'My friend's mother had spent years making a cinder
path in her garden and when coal was short us children had the job of
digging it up and sifting the coke out of it.' This sacrifice is typical of
the lengths to which people went to combat an enemy perhaps even
worse than hunger: cold.

The fuel shortage took the country, used to an abundance of cheap
coal, by surprise. In May 1940 the gas companies were still urging
housewives to use more gas, and the government's problem was that
the country had too much coal, for the fall of France had led to a slump
in overseas sales. In the next few months, mining ceased to be a reserved
occupation for anyone under thirty, thousands of young miners were called
up and thousands more, disillusioned by pre-war unemployment, seized
their chance to escape from the pits by volunteering for the Army or
moving into the rapidly expanding war factories. By 1941, with factories
and power stations everywhere crying out for more coal, the government,
too late, issued an Essential Work Order, to prevent any more miners
leaving their jobs, and released 33,000 ex-miners from the Army. Already
there were 84,000 fewer men in the pits than in 1938 and, even more
worrying, each miner was on average producing less coal than before
the war, partly because so many young men had left the industry, but
also because many miners, now, for the first time in their lives, earning
good money and safe from the sack, took time off when they felt like it.
Since supplies to industry could not be cut, it was the domestic consumer
who suffered. The government, short of ten million tons of coal a year—
the industry's total output in 1941 had been 206 million, twenty million
fewer than in 1938—appealed in January 1942 to everyone to economise.

In April Hugh Dalton announced the decision to introduce a comprehensive fuel rationing scheme from the first of June, to be worked out by the famous economist Sir William Beveridge.

The public, impressed by the success of food and clothes rationing, welcomed the plan to put coal on coupons, as did Labour M.P.s, who hoped it might be the first step towards nationalisation of the mines, which alone, they believed, could raise the miners' morale and increase output. Right-wing Conservative M.P.s opposed it for the same reason, seeing in fuel-rationing the thin end of the wedge of public ownership. This, they argued, was contrary to the basic principle on which the Coalition Government rested, of 'everything for the war, whether controversial or not, and nothing controversial that is not needed for the war'. Others, on both sides, felt, as *The Times* parliamentary correspondent reported, that 'the proposed saving of less than 2,000 tons of coal a week seems disproportionate to all the cost and trouble involved'.

They were not persuaded by publication of Beveridge's scheme, which was both neat and ingenious. While clothes had at first been provided on margarine coupons, fuel was to be supplied on clothes coupons, until special ration books were ready. Coupons would be handed over when coal or paraffin was delivered or collected or the gas or electricity meter was read. People over sixty-five would be able to exchange clothing coupons for extra fuel and the chilly North would get a 30 per cent larger ration than the sunnier South.

The reaction of ordinary citizens to the plan was well expressed by one who pointed out in *The Times* that 'What the British public finds it hard to bear is an unfair distribution of an essential commodity in short supply. If even-handed justice is dealt out they will buckle to as one man and see that the scheme devised . . . is carried out.' But rank and file Conservative M.P.s had never been enthusiastic about even-handed justice and they particularly disliked the proposals to ration gas and electricity, which would affect their middle-class constituents more than working-class families, with smaller houses and fewer modern appliances. This was the Tory back-benchers' finest hour. They had failed to keep Chamberlain in, but at least they could keep fuel rationing out. In the end the government, dependent on Conservative support and led by a Prime Minister who distrusted all restrictions on principle, gave in.* It was decided to release 7,000 more miners from the Forces, and to give men called up in future a choice of going down the mines instead, and in June Churchill created a new Ministry of Fuel, Light and Power to run the mines, through their existing owners. As its first minister he appointed

* These M.P.s had, of course, been elected in 1935 on a peacetime programme. Harold Nicolson, a fellow M.P., wrote of them in his diary in December 1941: 'All the good Tories are either in office or serving in the forces and the dregs stink'.

Major Gwilym Lloyd George, who had been a successful second in command to Lord Woolton at the Ministry of Food. Local Fuel Offices were set up throughout the country and a full-scale publicity campaign was launched to persuade everyone to save fuel by rationing themselves.

It began on Sunday 24th June 1942 with a broadcast by Major Lloyd George, and with full- and half-page advertisements, which made a dramatic impact in the scanty newspapers of the time. They instructed the conscientious citizen to go round his house removing inessential electric light bulbs, to eat cold food instead of hot whenever he could and, if he lived in the country, to replace coal with logs. At the same time a new range of regulations banned shop window lighting and the manufacture of most electric appliances from coffee percolators to curling tongs, while even vacuum cleaners and electric blankets could in future only be made under licence. Every patriotic family was asked to work out its 'fuel target', the maximum amount of fuel it ought to use. Although one man remarked pointedly in *The Times* that 'Lord Woolton never suggests a tea target or a sugar target but says what we can have', most people conscientiously settled down to the complicated calculation involved, which resembled working out one's income tax allowances. One was entitled to a 'personal allowance' of fuel units for everyone in the family, a 'house allowance', according to the number of rooms in use, and a 'regional allowance' related to the part of the country in which you lived, the North and Midlands being allowed more units than the South. Finally the householder had to translate the total number of units to which he was entitled into the maximum amount of fuel he could, as a true patriot, consume in the next twelve months, each unit being 'worth' half a hundredweight of coal, a gallon of paraffin, fifty units of electricity or 500 cubic feet of gas. Including all types of fuel met complaints that it was unfair to ration coal while leaving families with electricity or gas unaffected, but the word 'target' caused some misunderstanding. Cartoons showed well-meaning but confused old ladies turning proudly round from the electricity meter to claim, 'We've nearly reached our fuel target already!'

Working out the family fuel target and ensuring that it was not exceeded provided many children with a new and agreeable wartime task. A Palmer's Green schoolboy enjoyed appointing himself 'fuel target overseer and checking the meter readings each week. I also made some cardboard rings to slip under the light switch cover in the shape of a face. The knob of the switch formed the nose and I wrote "please turn me off" round the edge.'

No one, in any case, could escape the constant barrage of exhortation which poured from the Ministry of Fuel and its able and ingenious

Director of Publicity, Commander Stephen King-Hall, a well-known political commentator. *Fuel Flashes* assailed the housewife's ears as she listened to *The Kitchen Front*, short films explaining the proper way to poke the fire confronted her at the cinema, and, week after week, military-sounding *Communiqués in the Battle for Fuel* and *Battle Orders* confronted her in the newspapers and magazines. 'In the Battle for Fuel we must not neglect our defences', instructed *Fuel Communiqué No. 3* in September 1942. 'LAG YOUR HOT WATER SYSTEM NOW!' *Fuel Communiqué No. 6* consoled shivering housewives, 'the infantry in the Battle for Fuel', with the news that 'an Order has been issued prohibiting the use of central heating in government offices, hotels and large blocks of flats until after October 31st. . . . It is hoped by this prohibition to save sufficient fuel to manufacture 1,000 Spitfires.'

'*Share your fires*', ordered *Communiqué No. 7*, in November. 'One well-warmed room in one house is more sensible (and much more comfortable) than two rather chilly rooms in separate houses. . . . So don't delay—get together with your friends and neighbours now and work out a scheme for sharing firesides this winter.'

So greatly had English reserve crumbled by this time that this advice was actually taken. A Kingston-on-Thames woman became used to 'fireside sharing' with neighbours on alternate evenings and one living at Thames Ditton, if friends were out when she called, would always try their neighbours' so see if it was their turn to provide the fire. A Beckenham woman recalls each neighbour arriving with a lump of coal as his or her contribution to the fire. The members of a play-reading group at Buckden in Huntingdonshire, which met at different houses in turn, always did the same and a Biddenden, Kent, schoolteacher who visited a friend without electricity 'lugged along' a typical wartime load: 'A bottle of milk, three eggs, tin hat and gas mask and a tin of paraffin.' But to use a sitting room at all seemed an indulgence to some experts. 'Have your meals in the kitchen', suggested one eminent scientist in a broadcast in July 1942, 'make it comfortable by bringing chairs from the parlour and having a screen, perhaps an old curtain on a clothes horse, to keep off draughts.'

The housewife was advised, to use the Ministry's own military jargon, to attack the waste of fuel on three fronts: lighting, which used about one twentieth of all domestic fuel, cooking, which accounted for about a sixth, and space and water heating, which took three-quarters. No patriotic husband, it appeared, ever plugged in any bulb brighter than sixty watts, while anyone who cleaned out the kitchen boiler must be sure to use the ashes again, for 'by putting them through a sieve about one million tons of coal could be saved'. A Yorkshire housewife noted how her attitude to 'the pyramids of pre-war ashes', left behind by the previous owner of her house, changed. Previously she had resented them. Now they suddenly became a valuable reserve of fuel, through which she sifted 'to keep the stove going for baths'. The Ministry of Food produced a spate of recipes for 'Food without Fuel', many involving cheese, which could be eaten raw. . . . 'Every inch of the oven,' housewives were reminded, 'ought always to be loaded with as much cooking as possible—your neighbours' as well as your own.' Above all, no well-run kitchen ought to be without a hay-box, which used no fuel at all. The ideal design, according to Mrs. Ethel Taylor of Sutton, who patriotically shared her experience with the readers of *The Times*, consisted of 'a strong wooden box . . . 23 inches by 17 inches by 17 inches, raised on feet, divided into two sections and tightly packed with 20 pounds of hay. Each section has a well in the hay to take a saucepan or casserole. . . . Anything which requires long, slow cooking cooks to perfection in the box after being brought to boiling point on the gas-ring and keeps hot for at least eight hours. We do porridge, potatoes, prunes, stews, etc. . . . On Friday we had one pound of leg of beef, price 10*d*., which was . . . cooked in the box all day . . . was beautifully tender and full of flavour and provided ample meat for five persons.'

Despite such champions, hay-boxes never came into general use, except among former Girl Guides, who had discovered their value at camp. The secretary to one Girl Guide commissioner, working in North Wales, put their hay-box, made of tin, to a use not envisaged by the Ministry of Food. On cold days in the office, when she found herself shivering in spite of 'a foot muff round my feet and a travelling rug all round my knees', the tin would be put in the fireplace and the hay set alight. 'I didn't much care for this', she admits, 'because sometimes the smoke used to bring tears to my eyes and my clothes used to stink of fire.'

As the hot-water boiler was usually the last fire to lose its fuel supply the kitchen now became more than ever a family centre, in the evenings as well as during the day. One Sunbury family, to lend a holiday touch, and a reminder of warmer days, to evenings spent listening to the radio among the saucepans and tea towels, used to sit round the boiler in deck chairs. But some families felt middle-class standards must be kept up at all costs and in one huge and freezing cold vicarage in Morecambe the family used, one member of it recalls, 'to sit in the drawing room, by the fire, enclosed by two large Victorian screens, with ice on the windows'. This girl's future mother-in-law used to cook the breakfast wearing a fur hat; it was, she felt, still not the done thing to eat breakfast in the kitchen, the only warm room in the house.

By 1942 British homes were already using four million tons of coal a year less than in 1938; in 1943 another four million tons were saved, and in 1944 consumption dropped by three million more to only 33 million tons, three-quarters of the pre-war amount. Coke, though also short, was a little more plentiful, and advertisements explained how best to burn it on an open fire. For many families the advice given by the Ministry of Fuel's answer to Dr. Carrot, the anonymous and faceless Fuel Watcher, in October 1943, 'Do not light a fire just for the sake of having a fire', was unnecessary; they had nothing to light one with. The wife of one commando officer remembers this as, for them, the most miserable period of the war, made worse by memories of their recent service in Egypt and India. She spent the winter of 1942 in an Essex farmhouse and, she wrote, 'I have never, I think, been so cold in my life. We had a large bomb hole in the ceiling and no other heating except a shaky oil heater. My husband and I would lie there inventing advertisements offering to exchange this attractive place for a field, etc. . . . We had, I think, the meanest landlady possible. She used to sell us her tractor coal at five shillings a bucket, but this really did not burn properly, and I was always frozen. She also shared her oil cooker with me and usually used the oil I had put in, leaving it empty for me—and we were a long way from the shops to get the oil.'

A Streatham housewife also feels that the fuel problem was 'the worst thing during the war. . . . When we first registered I had to wait from January to March . . . and as it was a bad winter we huddled over a gas fire at the top of the house. When the coal arrived in March, it was already turning warm and so it lay, mainly in the shape of dust, with one or two large lumps on top, in the coal box outdoors until September.' But even coal dust was not to be despised. The most popular recipe for making use of it involved mixing it with water, cement or earth and pressing the mixture into shapes in an egg box or flower-pot. A Walthamstow housewife found that when her son and herself had finished a coal-brick-making session they looked like chimney sweeps, but the results were no substitute for a good fire, and when the coal man did at last call they would have a cheerful blaze every night, until as their stocks began to shrink they would again start to count the lumps. Once they were reduced to chopping up two wooden chairs which her husband had made and putting them on the fire. Sugar bags full of coal dust were also widely used and old food cans, which glowed red hot for a long time and gave out a surprising amount of warmth. A Rayleigh housewife also tried vegetable peelings—tea-leaves were used in the same way— and made firelighters from rolled-up newspapers. Like many families, whenever hers went for a country walk they would take a bag to gather wood and fir-cones for the fire. Once they collected conkers instead, but they were not a success, as they exploded all over the room. Nor was the experiment of a Warwickshire housewife who emptied a feather bed in among the coal dust, and merely created an appalling, evil-smelling mess. A Redditch woman thought highly of old wallpaper, soaked in water and squeezed into balls. A Birmingham housewife was glad to burn old shoes, but she sympathised with her husband's remark one chilly night as they were climbing from a cold bedroom into a cold bed: 'They ought to send the soldiers here to harden them up before they go to Iceland.' One Luton family, who built their fire up at night with potato peelings, had in the kitchen a whole row of buckets, each playing a special role in keeping them warm. 'We had coal in one bucket, coke in another bucket, slack in another, small wood, big pieces of wood, a precious lump of coal; another of potato peelings, pieces of fat, gristle, paper bags all in boxes, old newspapers, all sorts of things to burn.' An Ilford woman got her 'best laugh' of the war from 'a substitute for fuel, supposed to be some sort of waste from munitions. It was the colour, shape and size of, and resembled exactly, elephants' droppings. When you poked the fire it became impaled on the poker, from which it refused to be parted. It didn't give much heat, but caused a load of laughs.'

To obtain fuel people walked long distances and waited for hours. Often coke could be obtained from a local gas works, if one fetched it oneself. An Ipswich factory worker remembers how 'one would see the women pushing old prams or boxes on wheels going down to collect their . . . coke—not that one got much heat from it, but it helped to keep the fire in overnight and with a shortage of paper and wood it was a job to light it once it went out.' A Sutton housewife remembers that even collecting one's own coke involved arriving 'before eight o'clock on Saturday morning. The allowance of 28 lb. per person wasn't much but if more than one person in the family went it could work out very well.' A housewife living in the country near Coventry made a three-mile journey with a wheelbarrow to fetch coal. A London housewife remem-·bers walking two miles to a shop offering logs for sale. 'It was bitterly cold, and only the thought of the lovely blaze I was going to have kept me going, as I staggered home with them, only to find that they wouldn't even smoulder, let alone blaze.' A Birmingham housewife's 'husband cycled off on my old bike some miles from here to an open-cast coal site and walked back with a sack full of little pieces he had sorted out in the snow'. A Surrey woman watched her parents 'sitting with hot water bottles on their laps. On walks I would collect any stray wood, fir-cones, and oh the triumph if a coal cart had dropped odd lumps of coal! Empty cotton reels were saved as lighters, and in the mornings ashes were carefully sifted.' An Exeter woman 'queued up for nearly one-and-a-half hours for just one sack of Coalite and we burnt it all up trying to thaw ourselves out—Oh happy days!' One Middlesbrough housewife kept herself going by constantly promising her daughter: 'When the coal does come I will set the chimney on fire.' And this was exactly what, celebrating its arrival with an enormous blaze, she did.

Not only private houses were affected by the fuel shortage. The customers in one Ilford pub constantly complained of cold bars, while the landlord's daughter was coping with the chill in the family's quarters by wearing slacks and sweaters with pyjamas underneath. A London University student watched the temperature in her hostel at Bangor drop to 45°, while the students worked in overcoats, swathed in eiderdowns and nursing hot water bottles. She was, she remembers, furious if anyone came to borrow a book when she had got herself nicely wrapped up for the evening. The junior nurses in a Northamptonshire children's home formerly occupied by the Army had one unusual duty—chopping up dozens of army lavatory seats to light the matron's fire. In the office of a New Cross food factory the girls sat with their feet in the waste paper baskets to keep them warm.

Like the food shortage, the coal shortage pressed least on those living in the country. A housewife living near Leicester bought a woodman's saw for ten shillings from the local blacksmith and would return from country walks with cut logs laid across her pram. She learned, too, to cut out pieces of turf to burn on the back of the fire. 'It was messy but slow burning, and gave out a good heat.' As with food, farmers rarely went short, and any who used a steam engine for threshing received a special supply of coal, some of which ended up on the farmhouse fire. But even they sometimes went cold and one living near Clitheroe in Lancashire shivers at the memory of cold nights sitting up without a fire during lambing time, or while waiting for a sow to farrow. Country districts, too, often suffered from delayed deliveries of coal. One Birmingham woman who moved into a remote country cottage dreaded wet weather, for she had to cook as well as heat the house, with solid fuel, and under muddy conditions the coal lorry could not reach her house. A housewife who made her wartime home in a seaside chalet in North Wales kept warm by gathering driftwood on the shore. Her coal allocation was tiny, for the bungalow had only been used in the summer in peacetime, and supplies were based on pre-war consumption. An Englishwoman who spent the war in a little fishing village in Northern Ireland with no gas or electricity found peat a good substitute for coal.

Sometimes sitting in an unheated house and, even worse, seeing one's children shivering with cold, proved too much for peacetime principles. A North Wales housewife was terrified that her husband and several neighbours would be caught when they cut down a dead tree on some waste land near their home one night and hastily cut it up and shared out the logs. An Ossett, Yorkshire, housewife recalls how 'one night we all had colds and not much left to put on the fire, so the men went out with a pram to get some coke which was in a heap outside the mill gate. They had just filled it when a policeman came along. They thought he would report them, but instead he helped them to fill the pram, and pushed it back to our house, came and joined us in our sing-song, had a drink with us and then went out to continue his duty.' The city-dweller had, too, one source of fuel denied to the countryman. One Walthamstow man recollects that with 1,500 houses destroyed by bombing in the district there was never any shortage of waste timber. And, as many families consoled themselves, going down to the shelter early in the evening did at least save fuel.

A constant anxiety in the country was running short of paraffin, a common source in smaller houses of both light and heat and often used in larger households to drive a private generator. One woman living in North Wales regularly walked four miles to fetch paraffin and the wartime housemistress of a girls' public school evacuated to Somerset described a scene worthy of reproduction on a Christmas card: 'One winter we were practically snowed up. There was no central heating in this mansion where about two hundred of us were housed, only open fires and oil stoves. The paraffin was exhausted and had to be got from the town four miles away. We found a sled in an outhouse, Mary [her son's pony] was harnessed to it, and a fatigue party of stalwart girls set out. They arrived back at dusk tired but triumphant with a large cask secured to the sled. The triumph was somewhat deflated when it was discovered that the cask had a leaking tap and had been leaving a trail of our precious ration all the way home.'

Although the steadily falling output of coal per man was the real cause of the fuel shortage, the government refused to cut the miners' traditional, and lavish, free allowance of coal. A London housewife evacuated to the Midlands remembers how 'We only managed by going on long walks and collecting wood from disused pit heads and making brickettes with cement and coal. Many times we had to collect our own meagre hundredweight. . . . Surrounded by miners with tons of coal in their garden, this was not exactly amusing.' A Barnsley housewife's 'coal ration just ran to one fire in the daytime but by supplementing it with logs I could light the kitchen fire twice a week for washing and baths. . . . The miners . . . could have fires burning day and night. My next-door neighbour had a cellar full of coal, yet this was one commodity they did not part with.' 'Free coal' was the less defensible in that, owing to Ernest Bevin's efforts, the miners were no longer badly paid; by June 1942 they had already risen from 54th to 23rd in the table of industrial earnings. But miners could go on strike, and not infrequently did; less privileged families had to shiver in silence.*

With electric blankets no longer manufactured, hot water bottles obtainable only on a doctor's prescription and ordinary blankets on priority dockets, even going to bed could be a chilly experience. A Barnsley housewife regularly 'ironed' the bedclothes before climbing between them. A Rotherham woman remembers how her father revived a nineteenth-century custom by using bricks, 'heated in the gas oven. They stayed hot through the night, wrapped in old towels'. A housewife living in the Cotswolds used to wrap up the oven plate in a piece of flannel material to serve as a bed warmer, and one in Leyland, Lancashire, lined her blankets with brown paper to keep the warmth in. In mid-winter merely to be warm became an end in itself. Some people went to the pictures, irrespective of the film, merely to save their coal. But a really warm cinema was unusual. A Luton woman used to take a hot water bottle with her in the one and nines and a Liverpool girl often carried a travelling rug to put round her legs and knees. A nurse living in Wembley remembers similar preparations for Saturday night concerts in the un-heated church hall. A Camberley schoolteacher was afraid she would gain an undeserved reputation as a drinker, for spending so much of her time in the lounge bar of the local hotel. She did not like drinking, but it was the only place in the district that was really warm.

The coal shortage also pressed hard on the mothers of young children, for nappies had to be washed, fuel or not. One Purley housewife still remembers the bitterly cold March when no coal had arrived, though it had been ordered for months, and 'The babies were only nineteen months and six months, so drying their washing was indeed a problem. It was not so bad for myself', she adds, in words many mothers would echo. 'I never had time to sit down and get cold.' But even the nappy problem was not insoluble. The wife of a Hertfordshire farm labourer remembers proudly that 'everyone but me had drying problems,' after she had taken on the job of cleaning the village school, for it had five combustion stoves and was always warm, so she used to take her weekly wash there to dry in bad weather. 'I often feared the headmaster would return and discover the smalls', she admits, 'but I felt very pleased with my "fringe benefits".'

If there was a black market in coal it was on a small scale. A Hayes factory worker remembers that a coal-man used occasionally to call on their estate with a lorry load, for which he demanded cash and minimum

---

* In 1942 the government was so exasperated by one particularly unreasonable strike that the ringleaders were sent to gaol and a thousand miners fined, though the sentences were never served or the fines paid. One wonders if a military unit which mutinied would have got off so lightly.

orders of half a ton. More important was being on good terms with your coal-man. This was a time when pre-war good deeds were often repaid with interest. A Coventry woman remembers, after moving house, a coal-man knocking at the door before she had even registered with a coal-merchant, explaining 'Your dad got me a job in the twenties, when work was hard to get and I had a young family to support. This load's a gift—a housewarming present. . . . Where d'you want it putting?'

One popular suggestion for saving fuel and keeping warm was to walk up or down stairs. One London firm reminded its employees in November 1942, 'When we have to use the lift, let us remember the well-worn slogan, "Is your journey really necessary?" ' Harold Nicolson, arriving at Broadcasting House that month for a meeting to discuss how the BBC should handle the Beveridge Report, dutifully walked up to the Board Room on the third floor, the use of the lift below that level being frowned on. Many people had more imaginative suggestions to advance. 'Is breakfast toast essential?', asked a Hampshire reader of *The Times*, while another, in Eastbourne, asserted that 'Cold water ensures a smoother shave, prevents stubble and is best for the skin in every way'. A titled lady confided to other readers, troubled by fuel-wasting deposits in their kettles, her domestic secret: 'A small piece of loofah keeps my kettle in perfect order.' One 'early to bed war worker' wanted the BBC to shut down earlier to force everyone else to adopt similar hours and other listeners praised listening in the dark. 'Last evening', one reported in October 1942, 'the switching off of the electric light enabled me to appreciate the more the welcome return of the Brains Trust to the air.' 'Might we not thus get a new insight into the works of the great masters?', asked a music-lover. A note of engaging individuality was struck by other correspondents. 'The Rev. Edward Thomson writes from Paddock Wood vicarage', it was reported, 'to recommend for personal warmth the Chinese hand-warmer. It is . . . a sort of flower-pot shaped like a pudding basin and encased in bamboo basket work.' One Scotsman advised an economical substitute for the vanished hot water bottle, 'a flannel bag well filled . . . with dried cherry stones heated in the oven'.

Ordinary people, who did not write to *The Times*, found less colourful methods of coping with the fuel shortage. A Rothesay, Bute, shopkeeper used to save hot water by doing the washing-up only once a day, and a young girl in Luton acquired a skill of which she is still proud in middle age: how to wash up using only half a kettle of hot water. But the most popular method of economising on water heating was to have an almost empty bath. Early in the 'fuel target' campaign the chairman of the Fuel Research Board had broadcast an appeal for yet one more war-winning sacrifice. 'A big saving could be made', he told the country, 'by cutting down the depth of the bath water to five inches, marking the five-inch level with a spot of enamel.' Taking too much hot water had long been a cause of domestic bickering and this suggestion was widely adopted. At my school anyone caught with his bath water above the official black 'Plimsoll line' was liable to be ordered out and beaten on the spot, and, though unable actually to thrash offending guests, hotels eagerly seized the opportunity to economise at their expense.* The Hotels and Restaurants Association willingly distributed a notice for posting in every hotel bathroom:

### THE BATTLE FOR FUEL
As part of your personal share in the Battle for Fuel you are asked NOT to exceed 5 inches of water in this bath . . . Make it a point of honour not to fill the bath above this level.

Bedrooms in even high-class hotels were now left unheated in the name of patriotism (though there was no patriotic reduction in the bill) and dining-room menus became even sparser. One schoolboy at a Somerset boarding school was bitterly disappointed, on arriving for a meal with his parents at a hotel in Weston-super-Mare, to find only the 'Fuel-Saving Breakfast' on the menu, consisting of nothing but toast and corn-flakes.

The battle of the bath water was fought in many homes. The members of one family at Huyton, Lancashire, agreed to a choice: either four inches of water clean and hot, or eight inches, less hot and less clean, incorporating the previous user's four. Many families used the same water in turn, but on a changing rota, so everyone got a decent bath, in clean water, occasionally, and a Paignton housewife 'used to wait a fortnight and then use ten inches'. In the privacy of the bathroom some citizens cheated. A woman living as East Coker near Yeovil remembers her husband, when caught using more than his ration, protesting humorously that five inches was inadequate 'to cover his whereabouts'. One young Central London office worker eked out the ration at home by visiting the public baths during her lunch hour, though here—as I also found, in 1944—the five-inch limit was rigorously enforced. One Scottish family, living at Stonehaven, achieved the ultimate in fuel saving: 'There was a line on the bath; one or two small children used the same water and then the soapy water was used . . . for putting on to the coal in the cellar to make it burn longer.' A South Benfleet housewife saved coal for the weekend, when her husband came home on leave, by living in the kitchen beside the Ideal boiler all the week. 'The boys were bathed each night either in the sink or in the large zinc bath in front of the kitchen fire,

* On the morning I left school in 1943 I celebrated by having a bath full to the brim.

except when Daddy came home. We then used the bathroom starting with the boys, then me and then Daddy, adding a small amount of hot water each time. We made great fun of this weekly event.'

Of all the civilians affected by the coal shortage—and it hardly seems to have touched some parts of the country—those with most cause to remember it were the unfortunate 'Bevin Boys'. From 1942 all young men called up could opt to go down the mines instead, but in four months only 1,100 did so. In November 1943 Ernest Bevin broadcast an appeal to sixth formers in grammar and public schools to volunteer for mining— the only schools broadcast ever taken by my school. We were deeply impressed by Bevin's earnest, if unpolished, manner, but none of us responded. The appeal had little more success elsewhere, and in the following month the government announced that in future a ballot would be held as each new intake of eighteen-year-olds was called up, and those with the unlucky registration numbers would be directed down the mines. The scheme was universally unpopular. Middle-class parents bitterly objected to their sons being forced into the toughest type of manual labour, while working-class boys in mining areas, fearing they would be singled out for the pits, hastily volunteered for the Army. (When I joined up in February 1944 my unit was largely composed of such recruits.) Some young men went to prison rather than become miners and many of the 45,000 'Bevin Boys'—the figure includes both volunteers and 'ballotees'—who did reach the pits were a constant source of trouble. One described, in a book about his experiences near Sheffield, how the first information given to new arrivals by ex-trainees was which local doctors were 'softest' about issuing medical certificates and 'information on the best ways of jiggery pokery was always passed around'. Another Bevin Boy, who served in Northumberland, found that he and other recruits 'were herded by Ministry of Labour and colliery officials from one depressing shed to another. Incredibly heavy boots were thrust at them from one side, invariably ill-fitting helmets from another.' Their first two weeks at work 'were in most cases spent in stone-shovelling on the top of a slag-heap. Fierce winds lashed the dust into the eyes, ears, noses and throats as they flung the stones down the heap. For eight hours they did this, taking only twenty minutes off to chew sandwiches between teeth caked with dirt.' The younger miners 'were inclined to treat the Bevin Boys as subjects for laughter'. They 'were not aware that Mr. Bevin had compelled them to work in the pits and considered they were either physically unfit to join the Forces, or lacked the courage to do so. . . . One lad, who reported for work on the first morning dressed in his oldest sports coat and flannels, was considerably embarrassed when a small boy of about fourteen remarked, "Is it Sunday?" '

The fuel shortage—which meant at bottom the coal shortage—was never really overcome. In 1942 the government had postponed rationing for political reasons. In 1943 it dared not introduce it because the ration could not have been met. That year various firms had temporarily to stop production on a hundred occasions because they had run out of coal, but most of the stoppages were brief. The Battle for Fuel had not been won by the country's 700,000 miners. Their output continued to fall, and their absences continued to rise, until they celebrated 1944, the year of D Day, with strikes which cost the country three million tons of coal and the lowest level of production on record, 184 million tons. It was the savings made by the ordinary family which enabled the country to scrape through without disaster. In one Lancashire household a lump of coal from those icy days is still treasured, as a reminder of the kindliness that made them bearable. It was given by a neighbour so that the married daughter of the family should not come home from hospital with her first baby to a cold house. 'Our ration arrived', the recipient remembers, 'so it was never used. But as a symbol it is worth a fortune.'

# WAR WORKERS WANTED

'Whatever your temperament and whatever your talents there is room for you and an urgent need for you. No woman need fear to volunteer for fear there will be no niche for her.'

CAROLINE HASLETT, *Munitions Girl. A Handbook for the Women of the Industrial Army*, 1942

One day in 1941 a twenty-nine-year-old Hull housewife was able to produce at the breakfast table a letter from the Ministry of Labour which ended a domestic wrangle that had been going on ever since, as a Civil Servant, she had been forced, several years before, to resign on her marriage. Her husband had steadily refused to let her take another job, but now, as a childless wife, she *had* to work whether her husband liked it or not. He did *not* like it, complaining 'They've played into your hands', apparently believing, she recalls, 'that the whole war had started just so that Mrs. B. could take a part-time job', and soon she was, as required by the Ministry, happily back at work again.

The war meant a similar change for the middle-aged wife of a Dagenham school-keeper. On their working-class council estate it was 'not done' for a wife to go out to work and in any case, the only vacancies were for charwomen. She, too, welcomed the Ministry of Labour's letter, going most willingly to make smoke-bombs in a local factory.

Most typical of all was the eighteen-year-old daughter of a building craftsman in Andover, who eagerly volunteered from sheer patriotism to leave her job as a draper's assistant to go into munitions, even though it meant leaving home, and within a few weeks she was living in 'digs' and making Sten guns and shell parts in a Royal Ordnance factory.

Of all the changes brought about by the war none was more striking than the transformation in the public attitude towards women going out to work. Before September 1939 a single girl who took a job she did not really need was regarded as having done so at the expense of someone less fortunate, while in all the white-collar occupations, including teaching and nursing, a woman was forced to resign on marriage. By September 1941 a woman without dependants who did *not* take a job could be sent to prison and by 1943 even grandmothers were being compelled to work.

Although it was the women war-workers who caught the public imagination, men continued to make up the bulk of the industrial army, and under the National Service Acts all males up to the age of sixty-four could be directed into essential employment. One case-history, that of an assistant in a department store at Welwyn Garden City, is typical of many. He registered with the twenty-four-year-olds in March 1940, was found medically unfit in May, due to an ulcer, and in July 1941 was called for an interview to the local Ministry of Labour office and found a new job in a local chemical works, manufacturing vitamins. 'Started new job at 2 p.m. today and *do not* like it', he confided to his diary in August. 'Came home at ten o'clock with clothes stinking of an assortment of . . . acids . . . and full of advice on what you must not do if you want to live, such as having a spot of water on my clothes when in the sodium room. . . . I'm in a huge place . . . rather like the boiler room of a ship, only far worse. I'm on F stage, known as the suicide squad, as the fumes are often dangerous and twice the sodium has flared up, burning the operator as he fed the lumps into the doings . . . I never was fond of "stinks', at school anyway.' Before long his health had been so badly affected that he was transferred to another department, 'a great improvement, but not exactly "class". I'm known as "Frank, mate" by the other three packers and we spend all day posting stuff to doctors, hospitals and chemists.' A month later he became store-keeper in the glass and rubber store—and spent a peaceful war, apart from long nights of Home Guard duty, and being bombed out.

Great Britain's mobilisation of its population went much further than in the first world war and far beyond anything achieved by any other combatant nation, except perhaps Russia. Every generation was involved in the Battle for Production. The Parliamentary Secretary to the Ministry of Labour told the House of Commons in September of a man who had permission from his firm to go to work at eight o'clock, an hour late. He could not arrive any earlier since his wife had to be at another factory at seven, and he had to take their child to its grandmother who 'did not come back from her night shift until seven o'clock'.

By 1943 more than a million people over sixty-five were in paid jobs— many more were doing voluntary work—and of 33 million people between fourteen and sixty-four nearly 23 million were in the Forces, Civil Defence or a full-time job. Of the 17 million women in this age group nearly eight million were in paid work and another million had voluntary jobs, the remainder being mainly mothers caring for young families which, as Bevin said, was 'a form of national service'. Fewer than one in ten single women aged from eighteen to forty was not working, usually because of illness, while four out of five childless married women of the same age had a paid job. It was from these sources, and from mothers who worked part-time, that the nation managed to expand the labour force in the munitions industries from the one-and-a-quarter million of 1939 to a peak of eight-and-a-half million in 1943. About one-and-a-quarter million of the new workers had come from the unemployed, about five million from other industry, and the remaining two-and-a-quarter million had not worked before or had had non-industrial jobs.

A high proportion of these new factory-workers were women. In the aircraft industry, the most insatiable claimant for wartime labour, by 1943 they made up 40 per cent of all employees. In engineering, also traditionally a man's job, they numbered 35 per cent, in chemicals and explosives, most dangerous of wartime jobs, 52 per cent. In the Royal Ordnance factories only 14 per cent of pre-war employees had been female; by 1943 it was 57 per cent and in some establishments actually reached 85 or 90 per cent. The speed with which women took to industrial work, and the dramatic increase in production which followed, far surpassed the rosiest forecasts. As Churchill's deputy, Clement Attlee, not the man to pay lavish compliments, said in September 1942: 'The work the women are performing in munition factories has to be seen to be believed. Precision engineering jobs which a few years ago would have made a skilled turner's hair stand on end are performed with dead accuracy by girls who had no industrial experience.' The patriotic keenness of girls in their late teens and early twenties was also striking. The great hero of the young munition worker living with my family was the American dance band-leader, Glenn Miller, and in 1943 she had, for the only time in her life, a chance to hear him in the flesh at a local concert. Alas, that week she was on 'nights' at the factory, and instead of being 'ill' for a night, or 'accidentally' missing the bus, she forced herself to catch it as usual. By such sacrifices the war was won.

At first the slowly-expanding munition factories had all the labour they could absorb but in March 1941 Ernest Bevin broadcast an appeal 'for a great response from our women to run the industrial machine'. So many women, especially in shops and offices, immediately gave notice in their existing jobs that the Ministry of Labour had to urge them to carry on until there was a vacancy in a war factory. One West End store reminded employees that 'National need does not require that young women should leave their present employer in the lurch in their haste to get into some form of more direct war work', and warned would be 'Bevin Beauties' that if they left without the firm's consent they might be refused a job after the war—an empty threat as it turned out.

Another major source of labour was domestic service. Increasingly desperate advertisements for staff appeared in *The Times*, but by December 1942 even millionaires were losing their servants. 'I mustn't grumble, as I have had three years and three months of comfort', commented 'Chips' Channon philosophically on the forthcoming direction of his butler and cook into war work. Many better-off families, however, seem to have felt they had a divine right to have their chores done for them and the comb-out of cook-generals and parlourmaids caused widespread grumbling, partly because many middle-class women now had jobs of their own and, for the first time, really needed help in the house. One successful journalist recorded in his published diary in January 1942 how he had gone down 'to the local Labour Exchange to raise hell' when threatened with the loss of his housemaid, leaving the family with only 'a sixty-year-old cook', but, to his great indignation, the interviewing officer 'said she did not care' and his maid duly went off to the war, as a land-girl. Bevin had little sympathy with such complaints —even as a Cabinet minister he cleaned his own shoes, to Churchill's great astonishment—and many women, once they had got over the first shock, even enjoyed their new freedom. One Surrey hairdresser remembers 'an elderly, aristocratic, well-groomed lady' showing her a parcel of cod's roe wrapped in newspaper, and asking 'Do you know how to cook it?' 'For thirty-four years she had been served by a butler and cook, who had now gone on war work. "For the first time in my life", she said, "I am allowed in my own kitchen—it is such fun." '

The systematic calling-up of women for war work was designed more to ensure a regular flow of recruits than for lack of volunteers and by October 1942 all women aged up to forty-five had been called for interview, though many older women were left in their existing work. No mother with children under fourteen was compelled to go out to work, and so many women now discovered hitherto hidden maternal instincts that pregnancy became known as 'the prevailing disease'. Unmarried women were not immune to it. One young mother, working as a Ministry of Labour clerk in Lincolnshire, noted cynically that though unemployed girls 'were immediately drafted to the Forces or munitions, . . . quite a few of them thwarted the war effort by discovering that they were pregnant by the time their call-up papers came through'. Childless women, without dependants, were classed as 'mobile', and unless married to servicemen, could be sent anywhere, but this produced remarkably few complaints and many girls secretly welcomed the chance to get away from parental supervision. Although some Scottish M.P.s, rather in- sultingly, predicted that clean-living Scottish lassies were bound to be corrupted if sent to the aircraft and vehicle factories of the alien English Midlands, if such cases occurred they attracted no publicity.

In December 1941, for the first time in British history, unmarried women and childless widows, aged nineteen to thirty, became liable to call-up to the Forces. About a third chose to enter a factory instead, and in fact comparatively few women were actually conscripted for the Forces, for the W.R.N.S. always had enough recruits and even the A.T.S. and W.A.A.F. only needed to call up women aged from nineteen to twenty-four to keep up to strength. After January 1944 this, too, became unnecessary and even voluntary recruitment had to be restricted to seventeen- or eighteen-year-olds. Many young women, in contrast with most men, were, a then seventeen-year-old Manchester girl remembers, 'mad keen to go into the women's Forces'. She herself, when she had persuaded her boss to release her from her own reserved job, was immediately called to the Employment Exchange, where 'I had a travel warrant pushed in my hand and was told to get the next train to South Wales to report to a munition factory. After bitter words had passed between the elderly female clerk and myself, I flatly refused to go' and 'was let off until I joined the A.T.S. in 1943'.

'Folks called for interviews . . . were often violent and the language they used was terrible', one Ministry clerk in Liverpool remembers. 'They shouted all over the place. Once our poor supervisor was hit over the head again and again before being rescued. Another time a woman asked for the head supervisor and then produced a hatchet from under her coat to threaten her with.' The same office regularly received crude and ill-spelt anonymous letters from women denouncing their neighbours. 'Why isn't Mary . . . working? She should be making bombs. She is living with a Chinaman.' 'Lil Ward don't do any war work or make "munitions" like she ought. She had a black man in her house all day. Call *her* up.'

Soured by their experiences in the bitter pre-war years, some officials had acquired a reputation for being ill-mannered and tyrannical. Ernest Bevin claimed in May 1941 to 'have tried to humanise the Labour Exchanges', insisting, for example, on staff saying 'Good morning' to callers, but as the Ministry's 44,000 staff had during the war to carry out some 32 million registrations and some eight million personal interviews, some lapses were, perhaps, inevitable. The clerk at Reading who handled my call-up was certainly the rudest official I ever encountered and one Sheffield housewife who, after years of trying to get a job, was in fact delighted to be called to register, found the sympathetic and sensible clerk who first interviewed her a great contrast to the more senior official, a 'young lady of the superior self-confident type . . . with a Girton accent', who pompously lectured her on her duty when she asked if, as she had a schoolboy son, she could work less than a full week. 'I called her a "whippersnapper",' she later wrote. 'I am not quite sure what a whippersnapper is but it sounds impressive.' A Cardiff housewife remembers how when women in her age-group registered, they were at first mustered, officiously and unnecessarily, by 'a big, buxom sergeant-

major type of woman' whose bellowed orders they finally defied. 'When
we left, there was no sign of the sergeant-major ma'am. It was the first
good laugh we had enjoyed for weeks.' But this same woman was,
she admits, 'quickly cut down to size' when, as the mother of three
small children, she was labelled 'Not gainfully employed'. It was, she
felt, 'humiliating . . . to realise that one was considered the lowest form
of human life, of no use to the government, to the war effort, or to the
A.R.P.'

The mobilisation of the whole population was achieved with astonish-
ingly little friction and Bevin's contribution to winning the war ranks
second only to Churchill's. Like Lord Woolton, he knew instinctively
what the public would accept, and it was said of him that 'He could neither
read, write nor speak—and did all three triumphantly'. Clement Attlee,
no mean judge of character, called him 'straight', and though few people
really liked Bevin everyone respected him. He resisted suggestions 'to
conscript everybody as though they were in the Forces', insisting that
'a citizen . . . will accept one thing when in uniform . . . but immediately
he is out, he is an entirely different person'. Bevin's instinct as a minister,
as it had been as a trade union leader, was always for negotiation, rather
than orders or threats. Although, from July 1940, all strikes became illegal,
Bevin allowed several highly damaging and irresponsible ones to go
unpunished, rather than endanger his good relations with the unions.
Their trust enabled him to persuade them to accept the loss of one cherished privilege after another, from the 'dilution' of skilled trades by
unskilled labour to the 'designated craftsmen' scheme, under which,
when necessary, skilled men agreed to work as labourers, at their former
rate of pay.* (The men concerned jocularly described themselves as
'desecrated craftsmen'.)

Bevin's one really unpopular decision was the 'grannies call-up',
the registration for war work, in July 1943, of women aged from forty-
six to fifty. Two hundred M.P.s signed a motion of protest and speakers
of both sexes and parties in the House attacked Bevin's plan as 'a blot
on his escutcheon . . . a reflection on his reputation', 'a disaster', the
cause of 'deep disgust . . . throughout the country' and 'the extra straw
that breaks the camel's back'. This was the first public sign of unwillingness to make more sacrifices and might have alarmed a lesser man but
Bevin was not easily budged. He promised publicly that no woman in
this age group would be forced to neglect her family and in September
organised at the Albert Hall a meeting of 8,000 women from all over

---

* Since millions of men in the Forces were already doing unskilled jobs at far below
their normal rate of pay, this is another example of the privileged position of the
civilian throughout the war. Once a man was in uniform, no union, much less a
Bevin, protected his interests.

the country, the largest such gathering of the whole war. They were addressed by the biggest assembly of ministers ever brought together on any public platform during the entire war, from the Prime Minister downwards. This obvious concern for women's opinion, rather than what was said, made a deep impression; one young W.V.S. worker wrote proudly that she had sat 'within spitting distance of the War Cabinet'.

The change in their way of life for young women who went from peaceful jobs and decent homes to work in the great war factories, especially if it meant leaving home, was at least as traumatic as that experienced by their brothers in the Forces. The eighteen-year-old Andover girl mentioned earlier, who volunteered to work in an Ordnance Factory near Reading in 1941 when several of her workmates, aged twenty, were directed there, remembers how she 'was *so* cheerful on the train. I was the only one who wanted to go. But after six weeks, when they had settled down, I was so miserable and homesick, I would have given anything to have gone home.' Fortunately, soon afterwards she met my elder sister, another volunteer in the same factory, and after coming to stay with us 'for two weeks' remained most happily for the rest of the war, becoming, as she still is, almost a member of the family.

These two girls undoubtedly worked far harder, and contributed far more to the war effort, than I did as a soldier. Even though service life was often unpleasant there were, too, usually some 'cushy' periods, but it was never 'cushy' on the factory floor. The two girls were up before 6 a.m., to leave home at 6.30, had a long walk to catch the special factory bus at 7.10 a.m. and, after working an eleven-hour day, were lucky to catch the 7.30 p.m. bus back from the town, arriving home with time only for a quick meal, wash and change before going out dancing or to the pictures. 'We were', the girl from Andover believes, 'selfish really, thinking only of having fun. Working in a factory was not fun, though. To be shut in for hours on end, with not even a window to see daylight, was grim. The noise was terrific and at night when you shut your eyes to sleep all the noise would start again in your head. Night shift was the worst of all though—that ghastly sensation of never feeling really awake and meals all different and the light summer evenings were the worst of all . . . The work was very monotonous, often on very tiny component parts . . . I think boredom was our worst enemy.'

Another enemy was physical discomfort. I can remember my sister's hands—in contrast with my own—pitted with sharp metal splinters and covered in oil sores. A Blackpool dress-shop worker directed in 1942 into the local Vickers Armstrong factory, where she helped to sew the fabric on to the wings of Wellington boba drs, remembers how when the output was stepped up to a wing amye, this meant sewing seventy feet of Irish linen, specially treated to make it hard, at eight painful stitches to the inch. 'Repair work', she remembers, 'was awful on our hands as it had been treated with dope, a sickly-smelling paint, smelling of pear drops and very inflammable.' Perhaps the most unpleasant, and certainly the most dangerous, work of all was in the bomb and shell filling factories. For safety reasons, plants handling explosives had to be isolated and the individual buildings dispersed, often meaning two or three hours a day spent in travelling and a long walk on the site. The chemicals, too, could have unpleasant side-effects, and one woman who worked in one of the largest plants, at Chorley in Lancashire, found that not merely her hands but the soles of her feet turned bright yellow.

Many private companies turned over, with remarkably little fuss or delay, to entirely new products. Littlewoods of Liverpool, the mail order and football pool firm, were soon turning out instead up to 500 barrage balloons a month. The friendliness of the balloon girls was famous. One new recruit, then aged twenty-two, experienced at her medical examination an unusual example of it. 'We had to give the nurse a sample of urine . . . I couldn't manage a drop. One of the other girls, a very rough and ready sort, said, "Don't worry love, here's some of mine". Evidently she was all right or I wouldn't have passed my medical.'

Factory work, particularly for women not used to it, was physically exhausting. The balloon-makers, for example, worked twelve-hour shifts, four days 'on', followed by two days 'off' and then four nights 'on', so that the body never really adjusted itself to a regular rhythm. Most women, however, soon discovered a toughness and resilience that surprised even themselves and even ceased to notice the incessant noise. One young Scotswoman, directed into a factory making Lancaster bombers and Sunderland flying-boats three miles from her home, 'had never heard anything like it. Two thousand people were employed there and all of them seemed to be beating aluminium sheets with a wooden hammer and those that were not were riveting. My head soon ached and the noise had the effect of making me feel exhausted.' Later, the factory changed over to making metal tracks for temporary airfields. 'They were riveted together on large frames and I had to climb up . . . and inspect the rivets with people riveting on all sides of me. The noise was . . . actually traumatic to the ears and this, together with the . . . heavy smell of paint, was really the last straw as far as I was concerned.'

Far more trying to many girls, from sheltered backgrounds, than either the hard work or the perpetual din, was finding themselves thrust into what seemed at first to be, in speech and behaviour, a different world. One eighteen-year-old shop assistant from a thoroughly respectable home was puzzled, on entering an ordnance factory in Berkshire, by one woman 'who was always coming to work with black eyes. She was always walking into lamp-posts—or that was her tale. I was so dim. I believed her.' Another of her workmates was known expressively as 'a Yank basher'. A nineteen-year-old Lancashire girl from a middle-class home, employed at a parachute factory near Burtonwood, 'to reject work which wasn't 100 per cent perfect and keep a sharp lookout for sabotage, stealing of silk, crossed or severed cords, etc.', found that 'the types of women employed there opened my naive young eyes. . . . Ye Gods—what a mixed bunch! Their language horrified me, their habits nauseated me, their casual talk of sex shocked me. The married women were sometimes worse than the single ones—one of my own A.I.D. colleagues used to wave her husband off to his night shift at the front door and open the back to her American "friends".* She possessed more nylons, etc., than anyone I knew. There were plenty of the good types of course—real down-to-earth, generous souls who hid hearts of gold beneath their rough exteriors and there was a strong feeling of comradeship that seems to be missing today.'

Life in a war factory included many hardships, of which those outside, dazzled by rumours of the high wages sometimes earned, were often unaware. In winter it was dark when the workers entered the factory and dark when they left it again, while in between they probably worked in artificial light. The title chosen by J. B. Priestley for his wartime novel about life in an aircraft factory, published in 1943, was *Daylight on Saturday*, but it was not always daylight even then. Although hours eventually settled down to about 60 for men and 55 for women, reduced after 1943 to 50 to 52, at peak times longer hours were worked, especially in 1940.

By the middle of the war women were everywhere accepted in jobs formerly the preserve of men, as illustrated by a contemporary joke: a burly workman asking 'Have you seen my mate, the one with the page-boy hair-style and the bright red fingernails?' Most men who did, reluctantly, accept women assistants before long grudgingly admitted that they were 'not too bad', while many women discovered that, for all the feminists' talk of equality, they were in fact less capable of doing many jobs than men. A London housewife who became a pipe-fitter's mate at an oil refinery found that she could not even lift her fitter's tool-bag off the floor, let alone carry it around the plant. A friendly foreman told her reassuringly; 'Not to worry as long as I knew what a hammer and stillsons were, I'd be all right. I felt very ashamed', she confesses, 'but had to ask "What *are* stillsons?"'† Being a fitter's mate proved hard work, with hours from 7.45 a.m. to 5 p.m. with only half-an-hour for

---

* Employees of the Aeronautical Inspection Department, who scrutinised the output of firms supplying the Ministry of Aircraft Production, tended to come from a higher solid background than most factory workers.

† A stillson is a type of pipe-wrench, with an adjustable jaw.

dinner, and the job was a filthy one. 'They must have expected Amazon women, as we were issued with blue overalls which wrapped round twice and nearly touched the floor. These didn't last long, as the men fitters refused to let us climb ladders until we were issued with trousers.'

As late as May 1941 the Ministry of Labour were still finding it necessary to publish press advertisements appealing to employers 'to employ more and more women. Look constantly to women for your new recruits. They are excellently suited to many types of work.' This was the year when industry finally acknowledged that there was a war on and women had soon penetrated into every type of factory. They were even accepted in the shipyards, which combined revolutionary politics with extreme conservatism in their working practice—Bevin himself had failed to persuade a group of Welsh shipyard workers to work with unskilled mates.* One Clydesider still marvels at this 'greatest novelty. . . . We had girls in giant cranes, driving mobile cranes and doing electric welding, painting and electrical wiring and . . . they fitted in as if they had always been there.'

Just as the public fancy had been tickled by the idea of women rat-catchers, so at first women in dirty or physically demanding jobs got a good deal of publicity. Louisa of Walthamstow, who took over her father's chimney-sweeping business, was a godsend to the newspapers. A female blacksmith, who formerly taught music in a boarding school at Broadstairs and now worked ten hours a day making chains for railway wagons, was interviewed in *In Town Tonight*, and another spinster in the same works, who had once worked for a wine merchant and now drove a steamhammer, also attracted attention. But the public still found it hard to get used to the idea of women carrying out jobs requiring mechanical skill and any entering people's homes were liable to be asked deflatingly if a *real* electrician or carpenter could not be sent instead. A woman telephone engineer in Brighton, arriving with her leather tool-bag, 'was frequently mistaken for a nurse', or 'welcomed with enthusiasm as the new cook. The disappointment on the faces of the two dear old ladies', as they realised the truth, 'was quite distressing'. She also remembers while 'doing a fitting job at a Hove mansion, where the military were just settling in . . . watching a hefty private washing out his "smalls" and another grappling with the washing up whilst I was up a ladder running cable on a wall that had to be plugged. All offers to exchange jobs were, however, ignored.' On another occasion, she 'happened to be working in a remote spot where a corporal and three men were in charge of a top secret installation. . . . They wanted a batter

* Another example of his 'soft' approach to the unions. A tank driver or machine-gunner who had behaved in the same way would speedily have been court-martialled and might have been shot.

pudding, but no one knew how to make it with the dried eggs. As dinnertime drew near, and we were preparing to pack up, the corporal asked me if I liked batter pudding. Saying "yes" was my mistake, for I was escorted to the inner recess of the Nissen hut where milk, flour and the carton of eggs were standing at the ready. It did not take long to knock up the batter and . . . we all dined off prime roast beef and Yorkshire pudding.'

After some local councils had begun to employ women rent collectors, others recruited female house-painters, and some even trained women as plumbers' mates, an innovation popular with housewives as they always cleaned up afterwards. Postwomen soon became a common sight, at first usually in skirts, then more commonly in slacks, though only able to carry a smaller load than a man. This job, too, many women discovered, was a good deal harder and more tiring that it seemed at first sight. A Luton postwoman recalls that though 'we had a lamp tied on to the front of the bag, or on our coat, in winter it was sometimes pitch-black going to work at 5.45 a.m. I remember one winter morning, just starting my "round". . . . The snow was a few inches deep, the daylight was breaking . . . but it was not sufficient to read the addresses on the envelopes. I took out my first packet of letters, and undid the string, holding the letters; then decided to turn on my lamp. Whoops! All the letters shot out of my hand, into the snow. I had to get down on my hands and knees, and fish out the letters, but the wet snow had melted and washed out some of the addresses on the envelopes—and blurred all the writing. It was a nightmare delivering *those* letters.'

For younger women the usual alternative to entering a factory was going into public transport. One Sheffield housewife of forty found herself considered too young for clerical work, but readily accepted by the Transport Department which earlier in the war had rejected women recruits as too old at thirty-one. 'At this period of the war', she believed, 'the Siamese twins would have got a job on the trams.' She encountered one fellow 'clippie' aged seventy-four—she had done the same job in the first world war—though two candidates were rejected as too fat for squeezing down the bus gangways. This woman thoroughly enjoyed her job. 'The trams . . . rejuvenated me . . .' she wrote, 'giving a chance to my face to lose its pallor and wrinkles', though she was not amused by the passenger who observed helpfully, 'Change of life' when she appeared flushed after hurrying up and down the stairs, nor by the well-dressed women who loudly informed their travelling companions that they did not normally travel on public transport. (It was, she found, too, frustrating to see such women, with ample time for shopping, carrying delicacies like oranges that she had not been able to buy for a year.) The drunks were also a problem, particularly on Saturday night,

made worse by magistrates who dealt with them with ridiculous leniency.*
She suffered, too, from the activities of another very different but equally
anti-social group. 'To many people', she complained, 'the sight of any
girl in any kind of uniform, even Salvation Army uniform, at once
suggests immorality', and many passengers apparently believed that the
driver and his conductress regularly rounded off their turn of duty by
having sexual intercourse. Up at 3.30 in the morning and on her feet all
day, she suffered, too, from perpetual tiredness, often feeling too worn-
out on getting home to cook, or even to have a bath, and her feet swelled
so alarmingly that she had to wear her teenage son's shoes. Yet she also
enjoyed the status which, despite the slanders, it gave a woman to be in
uniform, and when she was offered an 'inside' job she turned it down,
even though 'hardly a night passed when I did not dream of rushing up
and down stairs, tortured by ringing the bells as passengers were alighting
and dragging them miles along the road'.

On the railways, women booking-office clerks, porters and ticket-
collectors became an everyday sight, and though there were no women
engine drivers, a few women took on the responsible post of guard. One
twenty-two-year-old London woman was sent with three other women
in January 1945 'to different stations on the G.W.R. to learn the road
from the few remaining elderly male guards, who . . . hated the sight of
us'. She was, she found, expected to be able to know where the nearest
signal box was if the train stopped between stations, but 'How can anyone know where a train stops suddenly when everything looks the same?'
Having completed their training the 'lady guards' were issued with
'rough navy blue jackets with four pockets, navy blue slacks and a navy
peaked soft cap with GUARD on the front in yellow, and given a haversack containing journals, twelve detonators, Rule Book, red and green
flags, the guard lamp—we had to learn how to clean and change the wick
and fill the thing—and a whistle and carriage door key'. Thus equipped
there came the proud day when, unimpressively labelled 'Bottom Link',
she set out on her first journey in charge of a train, from Paddington to
Oxford.

I arrived looking, as I thought, very smart, with all the gear I have
mentioned, and my hair was then a long 'page boy' style. First I
had to find the right train and which platform it was on, then get
my things arranged in the guard's van. To my amazement there were
other occupants. Two big dogs, muzzled, newspapers, cases, hens,
rabbits, prams . . . and two small children—all these were in my care . . .

* This was true throughout the country. Why these pests, interfering with the
leisure and comfort of their fellow citizens, should have been treated with humorous
indulgence is a minor mystery of the war.

but I needed someone to look after me. The next job was to go and see the driver, and tell him how much weight there was on the train. I got very muddled so he, all of fifty years old and with thirty years' experience on the railway and his father before him, gave me a withering look and raised his eyes to the sky. Nevertheless he said to me 'Just wave your flag on time and keep the journal going!' The time came to give 'Right Away'. My knees shook so much I nearly missed getting in the train myself, but we were off. I left all the children and animals to themselves—I am scared of dogs anyway—and just hung out of the window, praying for the train to get to the next station, where I had to give out cases, etc., and receive various things into the van. After a nightmare of nerves on my part and blowing the whistle at the wrong time and the station staff joking and teasing all the way to Oxford I finally arrived. Then, horror! I heaved the bundles of newspapers out on to the platform and the dogs (I had ignored their existence all the way) had somehow chewed all the edges of the newspapers. I flung everything out and got my stuff away and vanished before anyone found out. The driver was happy when I saw him because the train was on time. He was frying eggs and bacon on the red hot shovel his fireman used for stoking the train—apparently the cleanest way of cooking, though how he got the food in war time was another mystery.

A twenty-four-year-old Hounslow woman bravely took over her reservist husband's milk round. 'I'd never driven a horse in my life', she remembers, 'but I was young and cocky then and rather than admit I was nervous out I went with the foreman.' No sooner had he left her on her own than the siren went and, following the official procedure, she had to take the horse out of the shafts, turn it round and re-tether it with its head between them to prevent it running away. 'What a performance!' she remembers. 'If it hadn't been for a couple of friendly "coppers" I don't know what I would have done.... After the All Clear, off I go again. . . . After doing a few calls I had to turn back and get to Staines Road, which was parallel to the one I was in, with Hounslow Heath in between. All of a sudden it didn't matter what I said or attempted to do, the horse, Blue Cop by name, wouldn't budge. The situation was saved by soldiers billeted on the Heath, who . . . although roaring with laughter, came to my rescue. Apparently the previous man used to take a short cut right across the Heath . . . stopping for a mug of tea and a wad and one for Blue Cop.' Another problem horse was 'Demon', who could not resist pig bins. He would 'drag along with the brakes on and lift the lid and help himself. He was no respecter of pigs or me so I used to keep going back to houses I hadn't served. One man used to hide the bin as soon as he knew it was time for me.' Another lady milkman had an even worse experience when she left her horse, 'Mischief', to have a cup of tea. 'When she came out, Mischief had vanished. Several customers had scoured round without result, when a lady on a bike came tearing up the road saying she'd spotted the blue and white cart from her bedroom window in the grounds of the Big House, which was surrounded by a tall wall. . . . How she got in there without guidance, I'll never know. We managed to get the horse out first, then the van without damage, except for a bit of grass.'

Many women who took over men's jobs during the war discovered for the first time, like war-workers in factories, 'how the other half lived'. A twenty-three-year-old Scots girl's only previous contact with poverty had been the arrival of tramps begging at the door, a frequent occurrence, since her mother was generous on the grounds that 'Beggars were often angels in disguise'. Now, as an investigator for the Public Assistance Board, her daughter found that the disguise was often impenetrable. Her introduction to her new job was a warning from a colleague only to sit on the edge of a chair on her calls, for fear of picking up vermin, and on one of her earliest official visits she sat through a "blow by blow" account of a miscarriage. . . . In my grandmother's household it had been taboo for me even to see my father in shirt sleeves.'

By the end of the war one insurance company alone employed 15,000 temporary collectors, mainly women, and their experiences, too, were often eye-openers. A housewife from Wellington in Shropshire 'rode many miles collecting insurance in all weather conditions, going into houses with conditions I never knew existed . . . houses without water (except one communal tap outside), light or sanitation, some indescribably filthy; children without "potties" being put to squat on newspapers in the corner of the living room. Babies newly born and only a week or so old with no clothes—just wrapped in bits of old cloth.' A Liverpool housewife who 'worked four days a week cycling round collecting premiums . . . was very surprised when one of my first death claims came along and the bereaved, without any invitation to me, took me in to view the deceased. I was very wary after that.'

Wives were not the only members of the family who tried to take the place of a missing male. In Welwyn Garden City a young salesman, directed into a factory job in 1941, was astonished two years later when his mother, in her sixties, went to work for his old employers. The John Lewis partnership was by January 1942 suggesting that employees should recruit relatives and friends to work part-time. A young woman living near Belfast, after all the men had gone to work in the shipyards, and the insurance office where she worked had been bombed out, made her war work, helping her father to keep up a local golf course, with great success, as described in a later chapter.*

By 1943 almost everyone who was not physically unfit or wholly taken up with household duties had a job of some kind. One Harrow woman was struck by how rapidly conditions changed. When at forty, early in the war, she tried to find work 'no one wanted you, but nine months later things were different. I met women of over eighty working.' She disliked her own first job, preparing vegetables in a canning factory, but thoroughly enjoyed her next one, as a full-time gardener, growing vegetables on the firm's sports ground. A Dorset housewife saw the steadily mounting shortage of labour reflected in the age of her family's gardener. The first to be called up was replaced by his uncle, who in turn gave way to other relatives, so 'they got increasingly older and older. The last one we got must have been his grandad. He finished up by having "turns" and the daily woman had to take him home. . . . I think she was his cousin.'

Many women, especially those with Red Cross training, took up nursing, either full- or part-time, as their war work, and this produced many startling experiences. A Sheffield housewife had been working as a nurse at the local hospital for only three days when she had to walk across the darkened grounds to help lay out a dead Chinaman. An ex-secretary, expecting to be sent by the Ministry of Labour back to work of the same kind, was astonished to be sent instead to Potters Bar hospital as a floor scrubber. On arriving at the hospital she was ordered to clean out the operating theatre and asked the way from 'an old boy wandering along the corridor with a long thing under his arm and a bucket', politely enquiring about his job. His reply made her wish she had held her tongue. He was, he told her, on his way to the incinerator, the object under his arm being 'a man's leg wot's just been amputated, and the bucket is full of bits and pieces from people's insides. . . . Satisfied?' Later, duly scrubbing the theatre floor, she discovered some other gruesome objects, but bravely stuck the job out until she 'graduated to assistant cook and only scrubbed on the maid's day off'.

Women who went to work in the wards also had to overcome their initial embarrassment. A then teenage girl from Lichfield, acquiring practical nursing experience for a Red Cross examination, has not forgotten the moment when, just after the sirens had sounded, a young male patient called for a nurse. 'Both my friend and I dashed to his bedside. To his enquiry "Is there a jerry about?", I replied soothingly, "No, of course there isn't", while my friend, to my amazement, said "Yes, I'll see to it". Her deduction proved correct, as she dutifully returned to the bedside with a "bottle", while I retired . . . giggling my

* See Chapter 37.

head off.' Another Red Cross worker, a secretary during the day, was, she remembers, torn during raids at her London hospital between one old lady crying for her rosary and her neighbour calling for a bedpan.

Yet, despite all their worry and weariness, the war years gave many women their first real chance of independence, and frequently, opportunities they would never have had in peacetime. A seventeen-year-old secretary in a newspaper office in Scotland found herself rapidly promoted to journalist simply because all the young men had been called up. The expansion of canteens, requiring catering specialists and managers, and welfare services of every kind meant a rapid growth in the type of job which educated women had often sought in vain. The opening of nursery schools for war workers' children enabled many women to enter child-care work, which was often the fulfilment of a life-long ambition. One former midwife who agreed to help set up a London day nursery recalls how 'set up' meant literally what it said, for 'the furniture came packed flat, and as there were no men to put it up we women had to put it together. The first cupboard I put up fell on top of me in pieces.' But before long she had mastered this new skill too, like millions of other women who, with no man about the place to do the job for them—or to mock their first, clumsy efforts—soon learned to replace tap washers, repair broken chairs, mend fuses and even—as some still proudly recall—to drive a nail in straight. By 1945 the legend that women were frail, helpless, impractical creatures was as dead as the crinoline and the bustle.

# UNDER THE COUNTER

'No person shall in connection with . . . any sale by retail, wrap or pack with paper any article which does not reasonably require such wrapping or packing for its protection.'

The Control of Paper Order, May 1940

So often was it said that 'The war will be won on the factory floor' that the country's office and shop workers, without whom no works or ministry could have stayed in action, nor any family been fed, became the forgotten army of the Home Front. In fact many white collar employees had as exhausting a routine as any in boiler-suits. The experiences of one Cheltenham woman who, after working for an author, in May 1939 became secretary to the controller of a rapidly expanding aircraft company were not wholly untypical. In 1940 this secretary, like everyone else in the factory, worked for months from eight in the morning to ten at night, or even later, seven days a week, but in 1941 when the manual workers' hours were almost back to normal, she continued to work at the Battle of Britain pace. The year, she wrote, consisted solely of 'work, work, work . . . no time to visit the doctor or dentist, let alone have hobbies or read'.

Girls in the works, protected by their unions, were allowed fifteen minutes' break in the morning for a hot drink. They had an hour for lunch and another break for tea. At 7 p.m. they finished promptly, and buses waiting in the car park to take them to their homes. I was not protected and did not have a break. Frequently at lunch times RHC would decide to 'work through'. How I dreaded those words. Sandwiches were sent over from the canteen and I would eat mine while I was taking down shorthand. Later RHC would eat his in peace, while I was typing. "Tea time" meant drinking a cup of tea while I typed. Many times I had just poured it out when RHC rang for me, and it would be stone cold when I got back. I tried asking for permission to drink it while it was hot but it made him so bad tempered I eventually preferred to let it get cold.

But such demanding jobs often had the compensation of making a direct contribution to the war effort. One young Morden girl who answered a press advertisement for shorthand-typists for a government department found herself, to her surprise, employed at a former school on Wandsworth Common, taken over by M.I.5. Her department was engaged in counter-espionage, interviewing people who had, or claimed to have, escaped from Europe. 'We worked very hard', she remembers, 'when a boatload of escapees arrived in this country, thinking nothing of taking down a whole bookful of shorthand at one sitting. . . . Here was one part of the Civil Service that didn't sit drinking tea all day long.'

In many offices unusual hours and A.R.P. and fire-watching duty totally altered the pre-war routine. At the War Office, where many staff slept at night, 'the presence of females', one young girl found, 'caused some disquiet. Duty officers would frequently sleep on camp beds in the corridors outside their rooms and sometimes when we were on our way out to breakfast we would round a corner and surprise one or two in their underwear.' When a bomb fell nearby she and other women 'rapidly donned slacks, jumpers and tin-hats and emerged from our sleeping quarters. The first sight that met our eyes was a revered member of the Administrative Class clad in pink silk pyjamas and a tin hat. . . . He was far more perturbed by our arrival than he had been by the bomb and scuttled for shelter at the double.'

In most places, air raid warnings caused far greater disturbance than bombs. An office boy working in a City firm of insurance brokers had orders to 'collect each department manager's and director's papers when the sirens sounded, put them in his special steel box, and convey the lot to the basement strong room. I soon worked this down to a five-minute limit—ten boxes from the fourth floor via the lift to the basement. Sometimes we had days when . . . no sooner had I got everything in the strong room than the All Clear sounded. As I pantingly gave everyone their boxes back the warning sounded again, and so on.'

Banks were at first even more cautious and at the start of the war they seemed never to be open, closing at 2 p.m., extended to 2.30 in the summer of 1941, and to 3 p.m. in 1942. In the early days, whenever the sirens sounded they shut altogether but in the autumn of 1940 they decided, like everyone else, to carry on working, with business being conducted if necessary in the basement or even under the counters. Often the volume of work had greatly increased; vaults were crammed with family treasures, there was a large increase in the use of night safe wallets to prevent cash being blitzed overnight, and all branches handled hundreds of thousands of clothing coupons as another unspectacular service to the public. The most dramatic change from peacetime was that managers were actually encouraged to lend money. 'We wish to impress upon you', the Midland Bank told its managers in May 1940, 'that no request for accommodation on the part of producers engaged . . . on armament or supply work is

Fleet Street, October 1940.

**Getting to work**

Coventry, November 1940.

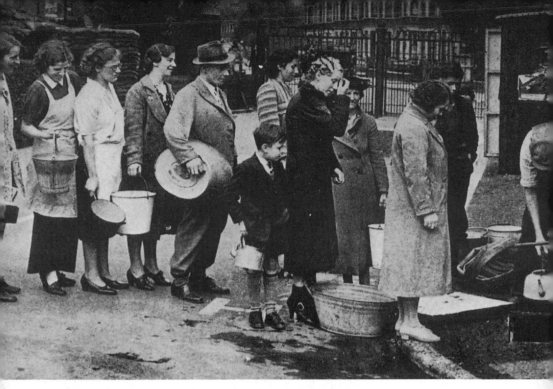

Citizens queuing for water from a standpipe.

**After the raid**

Cats waiting to be fed.

Domestic interior, 1941: A Morrison shelter.

**he fruits of experience**

Street scene, 1941: Static water tank in Grantham.

R.P.56
20,000 GALS:

**Wartime-travel**

On the London to Scotland express

'There's a boy coming home on leave.' London terminus, 1945.

North London railings being taken for scrap, April 1940.

**Salvage**

W.V.S. collecting aluminium in West London.

'Saucepans into Spitfires.' An aluminium dump, July 1940.

'New clothes for old.' W.V.S. clothing exchange in action.

Coupon-cutting in Woolworths: June 1941.

Make do and mend class. A proud mother display's her daughter's siren suit made from an old coat.

Jam. The Women's Institute in full production.

Pork. Pigs on bomb-site with A.F.S. pig-keepers.

to be turned down by you, however out of the ordinary, without reference to your district head office.'

Even more vital to the nation than its supply of cash was the safety of its food supplies and thousands of women found employment in local Food Offices. The Food Office where one young London girl worked was housed in the children's room of the local public library. 'We had no safe at the library so that all ration books and documents had to be locked up in a cell at the local police station about a hundred yards away. When my superior was off duty I had to go to the police station to do the necessary deposition of these documents and I came in for some ribbing from the men on duty there.' She had another unusual job. 'The bottles of orange juice for children under five years old were my pet hate. The bottles came in cases made of cardboard and invariably one bottle would be broken, spreading orange juice over the other thirty-five bottles. These all had to be washed before they were handed out and I loathed the smell of the orange juice.'

An Esher housewife has disagreeable memories of issuing ration books. She was sent by van to a remote village to sit, wrapped in a rug, and distribute them in a freezing, unheated hall. Conditions in army offices were often even less comfortable. A teenage shorthand-typist at an R.A.S.C. Command Supply Depot at Lichfield worked in 'offices . . . set up in dark, wooden store houses; we had trestle tables for desks and these were covered with brown, hairy army blankets. The floor was just mud.'

The office boy had been the subject of many pre-war anecdotes and he still existed, though now reinforced by office girls. A Walthamstow school-leaver lost his job in the office of an electrical factory for 'throwing stones into the nearby River Lea, thereby splashing the managing director's office windows, when I should have been taking the black-out frames off the roof lights'. A girl working in a Kent office remembers that 'at one point we had a very scruffy, not too clean, office boy, who occasionally proudly presented one with some rather dubious chocolate, which . . . he brought inside his gas mask case. As sweets were in very short supply one felt unable to refuse.'

As commercial premises enjoyed little priority in obtaining fuel, many women's chief memory of their wartime offices is of being perpetually cold. At a Friendly Society head office in Tunbridge Wells the older women clerks sat swathed in rugs and the younger ones huddled in overcoats, while the duplicator had to be moved into the boiler room, hours before it was needed, to thaw out the ink.

With a frequent lack of power after raids, and a shortened lunch hour to enable staff to get away earlier, before black-out, taking sandwiches to the office became more common. The working day, often 9 or 9.30

to 6 pre-war, now ended at 5.30, 5 or even earlier. The opening hours of a City Post Office were cut from 8 a.m. to 7 p.m. to 8.30 a.m. to 5.30 p.m. —still longer than they are now. Dress for both men and women became less formal. In banks and government offices clothes rationing dealt a death-blow to the traditional striped trousers and black jackets, and even stockbrokers ceased to wear top hats. A woman working in the office of a radio firm in East London remembers on the outbreak of war two characteristic announcements: both smoking and married women would in future be allowed in the office. But many peacetime customs survived. A secretary in one London firm contributed to a new form of office collection; when a colleague lost all her clothes in the blitz, every other girl gave one garment of her own to help her rebuild her wardrobe. Tickets continued to be sold for raffles, but with new prizes. In a Tunbridge Wells office, a lemon sent to a junior typist from overseas raised thirty-five shillings in sixpenny tickets.

In all offices except in the Forces, the war made itself felt through the constant reminder: 'Don't waste paper'. Good quality paper, as used in legal documents, was particularly hard to obtain, and one girl, starting work in a solicitor's office, remembers being terrified of wasting a sheet by making a mistake. A woman working as a clerical assistant in the supplies department of the Post Office headquarters recalls how 'savings were effected by using cheaper paper, printing both sides and closing up the text in order to reduce the size of a form'. As paper was pulped and re-pulped it acquired an appropriately khaki tint, and became grained with straw-like fragments. Single-spacing became the rule even for drafts, and typewriter ribbons, also scarce, were used until barely legible, then turned over. One girl student at a London commercial college remembers typing by mistake on top of an already completed page, for 'What I had thought was a pale impression showing through the reverse side . . . was in fact someone else's newly-typed exercise, done with a ribbon even more worn than my own.' New typewriters, a favourite target for thieves, could only be bought with a special permit. The Cambridge don, A. S. M. Gow, was refused one when his machine was stolen in November 1943. 'The detective told me', he wrote, 'that six or eight typewriters have been stolen here and this was no doubt a specialist, for though he went through my drawers, he left some gold studs and other valuable objects, taking only some chocolate.'

Private stationery did not become really scarce until 1944, but the use of 'economy labels' on envelopes became general early in the war, and the Post Office even produced a special envelope with no gum on the flap to prevent any miscreant from actually sealing it down. To use a new envelope became something of an occasion; one W.V.S. worker wrote to her mother in August 1944: 'I'm celebrating the fall of Paris by using . . . a new envelope . . . I was so sick of sticky labels!' In the closing months of the war stationery became even scarcer. 'I was simply delighted to get an envelope to post back to you', the same woman wrote in February 1945, 'because . . . I've been into five shops this morning and can't get an envelope at all. It was no good . . . getting any sticky labels because I had no old ones to stick them to.'

By 1941 only pencils of bare, unpainted wood were being made. To many people they seemed to sum up the drabness of wartime life and one London girl still remembers her 'special pleasure' at acquiring 'two Venus pencils with their characteristic green and gold pattern. . . . They were so precious that I didn't dare to use them for quite a while and kept them just to look at.' Some offices issued holders, to enable the last inch of pencil stub to be used up, and a pre-war Civil Servant, working for the Ministry of Labour in Newcastle, noticed other signs of Whitehall's commitment to total war. 'Drawing pins, which were always a disgrace, doubled up more than ever. . . . Sisal twine was more hairy. . . . Special carbons to take ten thin clear copies of documents now took only five, which was anathema to the typing staff.' Indelible pencils ceased to be issued for a different, more romantic, reason: 'Apparently some girl at H.Q., owing to a tragic love affair, had tried to dig one in the artery of her wrist in the endeavour to poison herself.'

By 1944, when it was raised in the House of Commons, one shortage which affected everyone was the lack of toilet rolls. In offices out-of-date files were raided to provide a substitute. 'We never went anywhere without something that could be used as toilet paper', a Luton woman remembers. 'That was a real luxury.' A Surrey housewife 'loathed the indignity of entering a public lavatory and being asked whether I needed paper. I always tried not to need it and so appear mutinous.' A W.V.S. volunteer, staying with friends near Cranbrook in August 1944, recorded a great triumph in a letter to her mother. 'May W. asked me to get some toilet paper if I could. I managed to get some thick stuff at a terrible price and commented on the price to the shopkeeper who agreed with me heartily and said . . . it was an awful price, "especially as it was only reconditioned".' A Croydon housewife would let her neighbour know that the vital article was on sale, by calling out 'Boots have stationery in'. A Liverpool woman attended a whist drive at which ' "the booby prize" was a toilet roll. I remember someone remarking, "I don't know about 'booby prize'. I'd have been *very* glad of it!" '

The children of a Dorking family, inspired by the victory rolls of triumphant fighter pilots which they could see from their windows, pinned up in the bathroom over the empty holder a verse setting out a simple war aim:

> When this cruel war is over
> And once more we live in clover
> We will have a Victory Roll—
> Meaning no death-taking toll,
> Merely that the Bowrings have
> Proper paper in the lav.

Despite constant reminders of the paper shortage peacetime extravagance persisted. 'Paper is being wasted in this House', employees of the John Lewis Partnership were admonished in May 1941. 'Don't throw obsolete forms into waste-paper baskets; treat them tenderly, turn them over and you will find they . . . can be used . . . to take the carbon copy of letters.' One employee, it was revealed, having examined the paper discarded by a colleague had reclaimed seventy-three re-usable sheets. In 1941, that miserable year of incessant defeats, rummaging through other people's waste-paper baskets was at least one way of hitting back at the all-conquering Germans.

But the chief influence of the paper shortage upon the retail trade was in the visible change it made in shopping habits. In May 1940 all shops had been ordered to cut their paper consumption to only 30 per cent of the pre-war level and the Control of Paper Order in that month laid down that 'No person shall in connection with . . . any sale by retail, wrap or pack with paper any article which does not reasonably require such wrapping or packing for its protection.' This meant the immediate end of the traditional shop assistant's question, 'Shall I wrap it for you, madam?' and most people speedily adapted themselves to taking their own wrapping paper with them, or doing without it.

A Mayfair shoe repairer's aristocratic clients obediently arrived with paper bags to carry their shoes away. An Essex housewife returning from a party was delighted to see kippers on sale. 'I joyfully bought the two allowed me and carried them home by their tails, held well away from my dress.' On another occasion, at the newsagent's, she overheard a typical wartime request, 'Haven't you got yesterday's evening paper? *The Times Educational Supplement* is much too expensive just for wrapping up fish.'

The paper shortage, troublesome though it was, was probably the least of the retail trader's wartime worries. It was he who bore the brunt of the citizen's grievances about rationing and austerity and the illusion was widespread that to be a grocer or butcher was to own a gold mine, with the chance to take free samples thrown in. It was rarely appreciated that rationing, which the customer found so irksome, was even more frustrating for the shopkeeper. On him, too, fell the brunt of carrying out the innumerable regulations which it was easy to infringe inadvertently, even if he did not succumb to a hard-luck story from someone who turned out to be a Ministry of Food enforcement officer. One housewife from North Ilford is still vexed at those who, because her husband 'was the manager of a large grocery and provisions store . . . imagined I lived well as a consequence. My husband was a very conscientious man and never allowed anyone, including me, to have more than they were entitled to. I queued in the shop with all the other customers.' A woman called to take charge of two grocery stores, in Morecambe, when her sister had a stroke, 'soon began to realise the . . . strain . . . was the cause of my sister's illness. . . . The work in connection with rationing was enormous.' She herself, due to an 'overspending' of 'points' by a former manager, was fined £25, a bitter humiliation, since 'my firm and family had for many years . . . had a reputation for fair dealing and honesty. . . . On my return home, I just had a good weep, feeling very stunned, but I had to carry on somehow.'

This woman soon discovered other pitfalls which at this time, June 1944, beset the retailer. There were suspiciously sweet-toothed customers who begged for 'tins of syrup . . . to make toffee to sell for a Comforts Fund', dishonest employees, like one whose rooms contained whole tea chests full of stolen 'packets of tea, . . . margarine, butter, any amount of sugar, jam, wines and spirits', people who ran up bad debts, harder than ever to collect due to the constant 'coming and going' of wartime and the frequent pilfering of goods on the railways, so that 'Scarcely any consignment of boxes or parcels was intact'. But the rationing regulations were the greatest headache and, to catch up with her stock-taking and paper-work, more than once she 'stayed up all night until the staff arrived the next day . . . I was most thankful when I had an offer from a company to buy the whole concern'.

For small shopkeepers, Sunday night was coupon-counting night. The son of one grocery shop manager remembers that it became a family chore to sit around the big kitchen table and sort out and count all the bits of paper. 'Many a night I was sent late to bed whilst the rest of the family carried on counting.' One Plymouth girl's first job on leaving school was worthy of Jack Warner. She became a 'coupon-counter-upper' in a grocer's shop for a wage of £1 a week. Another young girl acquired a similar job, that of 'part-time ration book filler-inner', in a relation's shop in a small village in County Derry. 'Most of my uncle's customers did not bother to fill in their names and addresses on the counterfoils', she remembers. 'It was no good asking them to, they would only have given the books to another shop. . . . We had not finished one three-month period of books when another started rolling in. It was a complete shambles.' Later books, fortunately, covered twelve months and soon, of course, it was the customers who were anxious not to offend the butcher. A young Central London shop assistant was amused at the way rationing changed her social life. 'When I worked in a shop in a fairly good quarter, all the posh women "made friends" of us girls and treated us quite handsomely for extras. . . . We even got invited to tea with people quite out of our station in life, and of course we always went with half a pound of butter, which they paid for. . . . When rationing ended, so did all these marvellous friendships.'

Sweet coupons were particularly disliked by shopkeepers. 'How fiddling those coupons were to count', remembers a Fulham sweet-shop owner, who used to collect them by threading them 'in hundreds like beads on cotton'. The total was entered on a special form in return for which the Food Office issued a voucher for future purchases. If you miscounted and claimed too few, you would not be able to buy your real entitlement from the wholesalers, while any mistake in the other direction might easily land you in court. The regulations were rigorously enforced. A Woodstock grocer still begrudges the ten shilling fine he had to pay for a minor oversight, when he forgot to mark off the bacon coupon on one ration book sent up to the Food Office to obtain an 'emergency card' for a holiday.

An equal nightmare was the fear of being too generous and running out of rations, and many were the indignant glances—few were brave enough to put their criticism into words—at butchers who included too much bone in one's shilling's worth of meat or grocers who included the rind in one's miserable two ounces of cheese. A fourteen-year-old girl who worked in a village shop in North Norfolk was instructed by her boss on no account, when she weighed the butter and margarine, to let the scales do more than just balance or she would not get the required amount out of each pack.* But however conscientiously shop assistants tried to be fair, some customers always believed that a favoured few were receiving preferential treatment. Whole suburbs acquired a reputation as 'under the counter' districts. One Streatham woman, whenever she saw anything handed privately to another customer, would automatically call out, 'I'll have one of those!' A Lancashire grocer's assistant confesses that when asked for the hundredth time ' "What have you got under the counter?", one day, in exasperation, I said "My feet!" '

Food shops always had at least rationed stock to sell, but in the ladies shoe trade from about 1942 the shelves were almost permanently empty. A woman in charge of the ladies department of a large, old established firm in Regent Street remembers that as the queue of would-be customers 'got larger and started earlier . . . sometimes when I arrived . . . I ventured

---

* Her pay for this exacting job was 7s 6d a week, plus free dinners, which were fortunately excellent; her boss kept his own pigs.

to tell the tail end that they might be unlucky, but they became abusive, so I gave up trying. . . . You can imagine how disgusted and badly treated they felt when told that our quota had been sold, after waiting an hour or two. From then on I spent the rest of the day trying to explain why they could not buy when we had shoes in the shop to sell. . . . This saying "No" took a lot out of me as customers always blamed me, especially when they knew me, and said "What difference does one pair make?", as if they were the only ones.'

Shoe repairers had an almost equally worrying time. The experiences of one forty-year-old businessman who had 'staked everything' on the high-class shoe repair business he had opened in Berkeley Square, shortly before the war began, are probably typical of many firms. At first his trade slumped, as his regular customers fled to the country, and he also suffered from over-strict price control, which was only relaxed after the Boot Trade Federation's president had deliberately defied the Order and had been acquitted. Then, in mid 1940, 'the customers returned. Young men-about-town whom we remembered as "all rolled umbrellas and bowler hats" turned up smartly clad in uniforms of every branch of the Services. . . . Elegant ladies, who formerly appeared almost too frail to hold a parasol, arrived in the uniform of Red Cross officers. . . . The monthly quota of leather never lasted out the period. We tried to induce one customer in three to have rubber instead of leather on their soles. Generally the substitute was declined. . . . Shoe polish and creams were at a premium and it was only by tempting approaches to warehouse packers that we were able to keep up any kind of stock. . . . Wrapping paper and shoe-bags vanished from trade-merchants stores.'

But clothes rationing also 'solved the age-long problem of what to do with uncollected work. Even well-to-do ladies would ask in a whisper if I had any good second-hand shoes to suit them.' And the blitz created a truly appalling problem: 'My shop and contents was blasted into the street and my wife and I spent the whole of a Sunday finding and pairing up 450 pairs of shoes from the pavements and gutters. It was heartbreaking work, followed by frustrating weeks of identifying the shoes with the owners, for all the work tickets had been scattered to the winds.'

Incidents of this kind were a constant worry in the service trades. The manageress of an Ipswich dry cleaners remembers that when the firm's works was bombed 'garments already in the shops had to be returned uncleaned . . . to give the people a chance to get them done elsewhere', though this was a slim one, as all dry cleaners were strictly rationed to so many orders a week. 'This meant a mad rush on a Monday morning and then the rest of the week explaining to the disappointed ones why their orders could not be accepted, or taken in and stored till next time.'

Before the war the retail trade had been notorious for its long hours.

One Fulham newsagent's had opened pre-war from 5 a.m. till 9 p.m., or 10 on Saturdays, and on Sundays from 6 a.m. till 8.30 p.m., with no break for lunch. The blitz brought its hard-worked owners some relief for the newspapers now never arrived before 7 a.m. and they closed as soon as the evening siren went. Later, 'the ever increasing shortage of goods' and the need to save electricity—the light had to be on all day as the windows had been blown out by a bomb and boarded up— justified lunch-time closing and shutting in the evening at 6.30 p.m., 'air raid or no air raid'.

Large shops and department stores, which pre-war had usually opened from 9 a.m. to 6 p.m., also shortened their hours. In October 1939, for no very good reason, the Home Secretary forbad shops, except tobacconists, to be open after 6 p.m., or 7.30 p.m. on one late night a week. In October 1941, with factory hours far longer than pre-war, shop hours were reduced still further, except for food shops and very small shops, and all large stores in Central London were forced to close at 4 p.m. Other shops were allowed to stay open till 6, but few did and 4 p.m. closing from November to January became the rule for the rest of the war. By now store closing hours were almost as confusing as those of public houses, with, in most cases, 6 p.m. closing until September followed by closing at 5.30, 5 and 4 for a few weeks each, and then, as the days lengthened, gradually back to 6 again. After 5, however, there were usually few customers. 'The public', complained the director of one famous store, 'don't appreciate the facilities offered to them', though the truth was probably that they were bewildered by the constant changes.

Despite complaints about arrogant or ill-mannered shop assistants, most shop staff remained remarkably polite, though the pre-war deference was often replaced by a democratic matiness and one was more often called 'dear' than 'sir' or 'madam'. Although one was expected to carry anything portable the large stores continued to deliver bulky goods, with several firms pooling their deliveries to the same area.

A greater wartime change was the reversal of the normal commercial roles. The customer now pleaded to be allowed to buy from the shopkeeper and the shopkeeper begged the wholesaler to do him the favour of accepting his order. Many resourceful shopkeepers also tried to develop new sources of supply. One newsagent in the Midlands, unable to obtain any toys from his usual wholesaler, bought a van-load of wooden horses on wheels from a local fish and chip shop, after his wife had seen a child pushing a new one in the street and had tracked it down to this source of supply. They immediately sold out, but his second order was never met; the mysterious toymaker proved to be a deserter from the Army. The owner of a Morecambe off-licence, who bought from a casual caller 'some highly-coloured stuff . . . frightfully expensive', to meet the shortage of liqueurs, discovered that no one, even at the height of the drink famine, ever bought a second bottle, and 'we were landed with dozens of bottles'. A wartime publicity film, *Black Market*, warned against just such transactions, and showed a man making lip-stick by the gallon in a dirty bucket in his backyard. (This was unfair to the black marketeers; their source of supply was usually plain theft.) Some shopkeepers also became their own manufacturers. One Essex publican eked out supplies of spirits by mixing them into a home-made punch, and a grocer in Woodstock one Christmas, when 'we could not obtain mincemeat . . . made it out of cut-up prunes, suet supplied with the meat allowed for sausage making and apples, which were plentiful. We mixed the whole lot in a large tray and then did it up in one pound jars and pleased our customers.'

One of the most striking adjustments to wartime conditions had to be made by the advertising business. The slump in trade in September 1939 hit the agencies hard but eventually most unemployed copywriters, artists and account executives found government jobs and this influx of able advertising men into government offices was responsible for the enormous improvement in official publicity which soon occurred. Many who stayed in their peacetime jobs were at full stretch with official work, like the 'Go to it' campaign run by one well-known firm, Bensons, and the 'Potato Pete' campaign created by Saward, Baker. But the bulk of the agency business was still with ordinary commercial clients and a careful reader of press advertisements could almost have deduced the course of the war from them. In the winter of 1939 the great themes were saving money, keeping fit and A.R.P. 'A wartime money-saver. Get a tube of Kolynos today', recommended a toothpaste firm. 'Wartime living affects your liver', warned the makers of Carters Little Liver Pills, while 'Bob Martin's fit and hysteria tablets' were, it appeared, 'an im-portant item of A.R.P.' to counteract that distressing wartime condition, 'hysteria in cats and dogs'. Already a high proportion of the smiling faces which appeared in the illustrations to advertisements were in uni-form. 'No artificial light in my sector', boasted a warden puffing away at Four Square tobacco, 'and no artificial flavouring in my pipe.'

The blitz brought other changes. 'Share the shelter but don't share the germs', the makers of Milton disinfectant advised. 'I am a draughts-man in a "hush hush" department', explained the narrator in a Horlicks advertisement. 'One night after working late I got back to my digs to find I wasn't allowed in—time bombs near. Dead tired, I dragged myself through the black-out to my brother Jack's.' But after taking Horlicks, 'I am a new man now. . . . The chief says if there were more like me, well, Hitler would throw in the towel.' The makers of Dubonnet even found inspiration in the threatened invasion: 'Les poissons attendant l'invasion.

Nous aussi, avec un grain de sel—et un Dubonnet.' ('The fishes wait for the invasion. So do we, with a grain of salt—and a Dubonnet.') The involvement of women in the war effort was reflected in the advertisements for 'Mrs. Peek' puddings. A woman warden, reproved by her husband for serving yet another cold dinner after being on duty all day, fears she will have to give up her A.R.P. work. Soon he is remarking 'Darling, what a fine hot pudding. I guess you've resigned your job', to which she replies, 'No, I haven't. I'm still helping my country and Mrs. Peek is looking after your dinner.'

Later in the war advertisers had the strange task of urging the customer to manage without their products. 'Take care of your Barling Pipe'. 'For the present, please go easy with the soda'. 'If you have any Vapex please make it last.' As 1944 dawned a more optimistic note was struck. 'Oldhams little black box will be yours to conspire with after the war is over, frustrated motorists were promised. 'Many men are beginning to think of the day when they put away their service cap for good', admitted the makers of Van Heusen shirts. But the spirit of wartime advertising was best caught by the makers of Roses Lime Juice, whose pre-war advertisements had featured an avuncular butler, Hawkins, and his wayward young master, Mr. Gerald. Mr. Gerald now proved to have the right stuff in him, for the war had hardly begun before he was appearing in subaltern's uniform. 1942 found Hawkins duly writing to Mr. Gerald about the evacuees and the potatoes on the clock golf lawn, and dreaming of the 'ample Roses Lime Juice after the war, when all headaches and hangovers will be where they belong, on the other side of the Rhine'. By the autumn the young master was home on leave, genially engaging in such exchanges as this:

' "Home Guarding and digging for victory have certainly wrought havoc with the perimeter of your bread basket, Hawkins."

"I viewed the matter, sir, with mixed feelings. As a butler I deplore the loss of poise. As sergeant in the Home Guard, however, I find it all to the good. May I carve you a little more Spam?" . . .'

# ASK THE W.V.S.

'We have learned that it is no good talking about things, we must do
them . . . We have done work we have never thought to approach and
we have carried burdens heavier than we knew existed.'

Seventh Birthday Message from the Chairman, W.V.S. Bulletin,<br>June 1945

All the national women's organisations made a contribution to the
war effort, but only one was wholly directed to winning the war, the
Women's Voluntary Service for Civil Defence—or W.V.S.* These
initials had been designed to be memorable while not lending themselves
to ribald amendment, though a few full-time W.V.S. workers did jocularly refer to themselves as 'Widows, Virgins and Spinsters'. The public
as a whole, however, never made the sort of jokes about the W.V.S.
that it did about the Land Army or A.T.S. and it attracted no nicknames,
except such respectful ones as 'the women in green' or 'the voluntary
ladies' and, perhaps fortunately, one suggested slogan, 'The women
who never say "No"', did not catch on.

The W.V.S. had been founded, as mentioned in an earlier chapter,
in May 1938 to attract women into Civil Defence and to teach them how
to protect their families.† The Dowager Marchioness of Reading, forty-
four-year-old widow of a famous Viceroy of India, became its first
chairman. She had begun a long career of public service as a Red Cross
V.A.D. in the first world war, and soon proved an excellent choice. 'When
she was in the Tothill Street building you became aware of her presence
in it; her energy vibrated through the building', remembers one young
woman who worked with her at W.V.S. headquarters. 'She was not
beautiful, though striking and with a soft and pleasant voice. . . . She
took us into her confidence and . . . worked untiringly and expected us to
do the same.' She was equally admired by those who met her during her
constant journeys throughout the country. One subordinate, busy in a
canteen, was highly impressed when Lady Reading rolled up her sleeves
and helped her to finish the job, before getting down to business. When

* The 'Royal' in its present title, W.R.V.S., is a post-war addition. *Now Royal V.S*
† There is some dispute about the actual date. The first public appeal for volunteers
was made on 16th June, not 18th June as stated in the official history of the W.V.S.

she visited a grimy Rest Centre, instead of criticising, she asked for a bucket and scrubbing brush and was soon on her knees, hard at work. Once W.V.S. headquarters in Westminster was damaged by a bomb, but Lady Reading refused to agree they were unusable, and every member of the staff on arrival was simply handed a broom until by 9.30 the offices were in action again.

Lady Reading always insisted that no one 'was to be deprived of doing their bit'. 'We had', one of her staff remembers, 'to find suitable work for everyone who volunteered, however difficult this was.' A former art student, having revealed a knowledge of human anatomy, became Salvage Officer, responsible for collecting bones. One former 'diplomatic wife' who joined the W.V.S. in York in 1942 found that 'my special knowledge of languages—Bulgarian and Russian—was quickly channelled to London. . . . Within days of asking if I could help them with classifying patterns for knitting I found myself in the War Office.' An elderly charwoman who offered her services to another W.V.S. centre agreed, after a shocked glance round the disordered office, to make keeping this clean her war job. A seventy-year-old Derby woman, stone deaf but eager to do some kind of war work, was found a place at a local sewing meeting. 'Once a week', her daughter remembers, 'I would see her on to a bus complete with her sewing machine, and she would be met at the other end and spend a useful and happy day.' An even more typical W.V.S. recruit was a mother who in 1939 had taken her children to Cornwall. 'I was so horrified at all the middle-class women . . . sitting about on the beaches doing nothing that I joined the W.V.S. and got some things going, like a canteen for the troops, who arrived to put barbed wire on the sand dunes. . . . In August I organised a big regatta—children's races and stalls and tea, etc., on the cliffs.'

The W.V.S. began with five members, recruited by Lady Reading from names in her address book. They in turn telephoned their friends. This method of growth led to suggestions, perhaps justified in the early days, that the W.V.S. was essentially a rich women's organisation, providing an interesting occupation for those who could afford maids and boarding schools to look after their homes and children. One M.P. accused the W.V.S. of consisting of 'society women' and 'young débutantes', whose unpaid activities undercut those who had to work for their living. Even Lady Reading's democratic refusal to create ranks led to the criticism that instead members would still be judged on their social status.

But such charges were soon answered by the simple test of success. Apart from acting as a recruiting agency for the other A.R.P. services, by August 1939 the W.V.S. had already 336,000 members of its own and by 1941 the total was almost a million. Only 200 of these were paid, though staff such as typists were sometimes supplied by local authorities. Many members did not even claim their expenses and some housed local head-quarters rent-free in their own homes. The W.V.S. was a triumph for patriotism and the voluntary principle; no other civilian organisation cost the country so little or gave it so much.

The character of the W.V.S. was expressed in its uniform, smart, hard-wearing and practical, being designed by the leading London dressmaker, Digby Morton. As other colours had been earmarked by the women's Services, the W.V.S. chose green, though, as some people thought it unlucky, grey was also woven into the fabric, and a beetroot red jumper and hat trimmings were added to provide a touch of colour. The emphasis was on saving work. The greatcoats could be slept in without looking too dishevelled in the morning, and did not show the dust; the pleatless skirts required no ironing; there was no collar or tie to slow one down when dressing in a hurry and the blouse had short sleeves which would not need to be rolled up. The hat, a 'schoolgirl felt', which could be worn at any angle or shape, was justified by Lady Reading as allowing the wearer to express her individuality. It was also typical of the W.V.S. that they bought their own uniforms and gave up coupons for them.

Evacuation, when 120,000 women acted as helpers and escorts, pro-vided the W.V.S. with its first great test and billeting and collecting clothes for evacuees remained one of its regular jobs throughout the war. One woman at W.V.S. headquarters found herself called on to write an authoritative guide on how to deal with bed-wetting. As she says, 'You discovered all sorts of unexpected talents.' Later W.V.S. members acted as escorts to the small parties, largely of under-fives, who left London throughout the war, coping with problems like that of a brother and sister who turned out, when their 'mother' visited them two months afterwards, to be unrelated; the little girl, aged three, asked, before they set out, to identify her still smaller brother, had pointed instead to another small boy she preferred. Such escorts often spent fifteen hours a day in trains; some travelled 100,000 miles in three years.

In May 1940 Lady Reading had addressed an Order of the Day to her County Organisers: 'Please do not hesitate to take such lead as is de-manded of you ... W.V.S. is looked upon as a strong, efficient machine which can carry an immense load.' The truth of this claim was proved in the next few weeks. W.V.S. members bore the brunt of caring for the troops as they arrived from Dunkirk, the 25,000 evacuees from the Channel Islands who disembarked at Weymouth, and the 12,000 women and children, compulsorily evacuated from Gibraltar, who descended on Liverpool. During the Battle of Britain W.V.S. teams fed the ground crews on bombed airfields, stitched together the first L.D.V. armlets and even, in Lincolnshire, made 2,000 Molotov cocktails in a weekend, in intervals of cooking the Sunday joint. One determined member in a Yorkshire village sent to headquarters a classic report: 'General Position satisfactory. One German parachutist captured by me yesterday.' She had disarmed him with a pitchfork.

During the blitz pre-war training in emergency cooking in dustbins and home-made ovens came into its own, aided by mobile canteens and eventually by eighteen Queen's Messenger Convoys, of twelve vehicles each, manned by fifty W.V.S. During these perilous months respectable middle-aged ladies in W.V.S. uniform could be seen asleep in the street on bomb-damaged doors resting on milk churns. As the girl in charge of the canteen from Worcester reported, 'she had never expected to be cooking stew in the main street of Coventry but she suddenly found herself doing something even more peculiar as she . . . brushed her teeth in the main square'.

The relatively few women who owned their own cars were constantly in demand, the standard, off-putting, question asked of volunteers being 'Do you mind driving children who will probably be sick in your car?' After the abolition of the basic petrol ration in 1942 the W.V.S. was made responsible for running local Volunteer Car Pools to provide a reserve of transport for use in emergency. The 20,000 drivers under the scheme—about half were W.V.S. members—were among the few civilians able to keep their cars on the road, but they paid a heavy price for the privilege. One, in a typical week, carried salvage, clothing, orange juice, cod liver oil, rosehips, chestnuts and several passengers, including a nurse and a Ministry of Food official, and in a typical month all the cars in the scheme clocked up 3,600,000 miles. Every journey had to be accounted for in great detail and many W.V.S. drivers still remember the form concerned with particular loathing. Accidents were remarkably few, though one volunteer achieved an all-time record of seven in eleven days, writing in on the twelfth to say that she had 'nothing to report except that an island hit me'. In a countryside almost bereft of both private cars and buses appeals for W.V.S. help were never-ending. As one woman in charge of a Transport Department complained in a letter home, 'Lunch time . . . just means that one answers the telephone with one's mouth full instead of empty.'

The ordinary citizen probably did not realise how closely the W.V.S. was enmeshed in the whole structure of wartime administration. At headquarters in London experts on every subject, from 'under fives' to 'salvage', were constantly in touch with government departments. Similar liaison occurred at every lower level, from the Civil Defence Region, covering several counties, to the local Centre in every sizeable town. If other women's organisations sometimes felt that the W.V.S. got more than its fair share of the publicity and the credit, the explanation was simple: for the W.V.S., war work was not just a temporary activity, but the whole reason for its existence. Thus whenever some new problem affecting the civilian population arose it was natural that the cry should go up from hard-pressed army commander or harassed Town Clerk 'Ask the W.V.S.' The W.V.S. were called for in the Highlands in 1942, when the whole population had to be moved, complete with their property, from an area required for battle training and another 800 families, many with large herds of cattle, had to be evacuated for the same reasons from the Slapton area of Devon. In the following year, scores of middle-aged and elderly W.V.S. members turned out uncomplainingly in fog and dark day after day, to serve hot food, often in pouring rain, to the thousands of men, scattered over the Thames-side marshes near Tilbury, who were working day and night to build the concrete breakwaters and caissons of the 'Mulberry' harbour.

Also in 1943 the W.V.S. took on the heart-rending task of setting up Incident Enquiry Points near to any major 'incident'. A woman who helped in such work can still remember the kindly way in which one member of the team, who had proved especially good at breaking bad news, took a soldier aside to tell him that all his family were dead. The system had only been operating for a month when a single bomb on the Cinderella Dancing Club in Putney High Street killed eighty-one people outright and injured 200 more. This was the sort of incident that everyone dreaded most, for no one knew who, or even how many, people were present, and for the W.V.S. team, installed in the public library a hundred yards away, it was a nightmare few days. The heavy dust on the faces of the victims made it hard even for close relations to identify them and one man had to be told on successive visits that two of his sons had been killed and the third crippled for life. Often W.V.S. workers went with the bereaved families to the mortuary. As Lady Reading had said in a broadcast, their work 'was not nice but necessary'.

Many people have cause to feel grateful for similar help in wartime emergencies. A Bath schoolteacher has not forgotten the cups of tea provided by the 'women in green' at a mass funeral she attended for victims of the Baedeker raids. A bride at Willesden, when no choir could be found for her wedding, was delighted when the W.V.S. staff of a nearby Rest Centre obligingly put down the blankets they were shaking and went into church to deputise for the missing choristers. A forty-five-year-old widow with five children twice had cause to bless the W.V.S. when travelling. 'Once, on arrival at Holyhead, a worker came and said "Shall I mind the children, or cope with your tickets and luggage for you?" She took the children off to have tea and buns while I got through Customs, etc. Secondly, on York Station . . . tired and nervy after the journey from Dublin and wondering what to do with the children, a very fashionable young woman with a car found us . . . took us the W.V.S. Headquarters and found a nursery school for the younger ones and lodgings for me, all in about one hour.'

Women with little time to spare from caring for their families could join the W.V.S. Housewives Service, which aimed to ensure that in every street there was at least one sensible woman to act as a steadying influence and to give simple first aid. My mother, well known to her neighbours as the voluntary collector for the Hospital Savings Scheme, and the automatic confidante of any woman in trouble, was typical of those recruited. She was proud of her badges of office—the 'Housewives Service' card in the window, the W.V.S. armband—and of her satchel of first aid supplies and the bottle of cold tea, recommended for burns, she kept in the larder. An Ipswich woman with a similar satchel which contained a bottle of Lysol antiseptic was very worried when her son used it as a hairwash, for it proved irreplaceable. Only victory brought relief for she was told her first aid equipment need not be returned.

The motto of the Housewives Service, attributed to Saint Augustine, was 'A little thing is but a little thing but faithfulness in little things is a very great thing'. It was a text which applied to all those women who did unspectacular work behind the scenes. Darning soldiers' socks was one of the commonest such jobs. One Scottish burgh alone had thirteen working parties constantly busy with their needles and in another area W.V.S. instructors visited military camps to run classes for the soldier in this domestic art. A highly disagreeable task undertaken almost everywhere was making camouflage nets. Net-making frames were set up in village halls and even large private houses; a Portsmouth naval wife recalls spending two days a week for years 'netting' in the garden of an admiral's house. Any woman would drop in whenever she had a few hours to spare. The W.V.S.'s historian has described how 'The dust and fluff from the scrim half choked the women knotting it on to the nets and the dye left their hands and clothes deeply stained. Crawling about . . . with bruised knees and aching backs, elderly women drove themselves on for that extra hour which meant so many square feet of cover for the British Army.' A Ranger who regularly 'went netting' at the W.V.S. Centre at Tunbridge Wells remembers this as 'the filthiest job I have ever known. We used to wear overalls, a scarf round our hair, a mask something like a surgical mask. It was such a dusty job we drank as many cups of tea as the ration would allow.'

Throughout the long years of the war Lady Reading rallied her troops with visits, personal letters and messages in the W.V.S. monthly *Bulletin*, which always began with an appropriate quotation, like Nelson's plea before Trafalgar for 'a great and glorious victory' and Drake's famous prayer before Cadiz on carrying through 'any great matter . . . until it be thoroughly finished'. Lady Reading's own message, in June 1945, was almost worthy to rank with these. She referred to the 'seven years since W.V.S. was started—which to most of us seemed like seven centuries. . . . We have learned that it is no good talking about things, we must do them, and . . . to do that we must take pains, dislocate our lives and our comfort. . . . We have done work we have never thought to approach and we have carried burdens heavier than we knew existed. . . . We now know that in life no obstacle can block, it can only impede; that tiredness is an incident not a finality.'

Before the appearance of the W.V.S. the best-known women's organisation had been the Women's Institutes, and with a W.I. in almost every village, they were ideally placed to help the war effort, but the movement, 'out of respect for the beliefs of its Quaker members', according to its historian, instead closely restricted 'the participation of Institutes in war work'. This misguided capitulation to an insignificant and unrepresentative minority 'evoked considerable criticism . . . within the movement' and led to a 'heavy fall in membership' from 332,000 in 1939 to 288,000 in 1942.* But happily there was nothing half-hearted about the patriotism of many individual W.I. members, among them Lady Gertrude Denman, the fifty-five-year-old wife of a former Governor-General of Australia. 'Trudie' Denman was a tough, colourful and somewhat mannish character, a keen rider to hounds, a heavy smoker and an early pioneer of short hair and riding breeches for women. She had little interest in her husband or in domestic life, but had many excellent qualities, forthrightly speaking out against snobbery, 'yes women' and mealy-mouthed euphemisms.† Lady Denman was no Lady Reading and inspired respect rather than devotion, and as in 1939 she had become head of the Women's Land Army, she had little time left for Women's Institute affairs. But she appeared at their Annual General Meeting in 1943, declaring that 'There is no doubt that to our dying day the words salvage, war savings, herbs, hips and haws and meat pies will bring back poignant memories to all of us, but they will also remind us of practical work well done.'‡ This is not a bad summary of what many W.I. members did during the war, and though the original evacuation plan they prepared was replaced by one drawn up by the W.V.S., W.I. members took a leading part in billeting and welfare work, which even the Quakers' sensitive consciences would allow. A

* The comparable organisation in urban areas, the Townswomen's Guilds, gave whole-hearted support to the war and its members took part in all the activities, from running canteens to collecting salvage, described elsewhere in this book.
† She strongly criticised the Family Planning Association for example, for referring to the 'act of mating' in a publication instead of 'sexual intercourse'.
‡ Lady Denman died in 1954.

housewife from Twyford in Berkshire remembers her local Women's Institute as 'a hive of industry' with 'knitting circles, make do and mend, jamming, economy cooking, etc.' 'We had a household Jobs Mending School', a housewife living near Hitchin remembers, 'teaching us how to mend a fuse, put a washer in a tap, sharpen scissors—all sorts of jobs that the man of the home usually does. . . . A "School" was usually held in a hall in a town . . . for women to come in by bus . . . and then they could go back and carry their knowledge to their own Institutes. . . . We were instructed from national headquarters . . . to make as much as possible of the Social Half-Hour', which had always ended W.I. meetings, 'as it was important for women to relax from the troubles of the war. I went to a "school" in London to learn all sorts of silly games and entertainments so that women could really "let their hair down"—and then I went round the other Institutes in the country to teach them how to make their amusements.'

It would, however, have needed more than a social half-hour to raise spirits if Hitler had won and by far the most important contribution the Women's Institutes made to the war effort was in increasing food production, the same need which had led to the foundation of the first Institute in 1915. More than a hundred thousand fruit bushes and packets of vegetable seeds were supplied to members and many housewives also had cause to feel grateful to the W.I. co-operative markets which had been well established even before the war. The aim was to cut out the middleman and sell fresh produce direct to the housewife, the grower paying a small commission on sales. Fresh vegetables, fruit and rabbits were the staple items, but some organisers developed such sidelines as honey, goat's-milk cheese and butter, joints of young goat—not very popular—and ducks' eggs. The markets had mainly been in towns, but now many village markets were opened, one organiser remembers, 'in the W.I. Hall, on the green or in someone's porch. It was easier to staff these. One could rush home and put the stew in the oven and snatch a few more lettuce from the garden to sell.'

The war also gave a great impetus to other rural arts and crafts, which in peacetime had been no more than an interesting hobby. With clothes rationed, home-weaving enjoyed a new vogue and some members conscientiously gathered the wool left by sheep on hedges and barbed wire, the real enthusiasts even weaving the resulting thread on their own looms. The hedges round Gayton-le-Marsh in Lincolnshire alone yielded sixty-five pounds of wool, which were knitted into comforts for the Russians, and the daughter of a Kent vicar recalls parishioners carrying small bobbins and spinning wool into thread as they walked along. She attended one Women's Institute exhibition at which all the women manning the stalls wore suits made from wool they had gathered themselves and then dyed with home-made vegetable dyes—onion skins for yellow and nettles for green. One Dorset handicraft enthusiast, having obtained a permit to buy fleece, spun it into yarn on her Manx spinning wheel and then organised a class of knitters to make sea boot stockings for the Merchant Navy. Another Women's Institute member is even on record as collecting the combings from her Pekinese dogs, which were made into gloves for her husband.

The W.I. had always resented the gibe that it was based on 'jam and *Jerusalem*', the hymn which always ended its meetings, but with imported fruit and sugar at a premium, jam-making suddenly became a patriotic duty. At the government's request, to prevent fruit going to waste now that few housewives had sugar to spare, the Women's Institutes set up a network of 5,800 Preservation Centres. The government provided most of the equipment, 500 canning machines were presented by the women of the United States, and members of the Women's Institutes gave their skill and labour free. In the summer of 1941, 1,300 tons of fruit were saved by the jam centres from being wasted and turned into 2,000 tons of jam. The gardens of houses abandoned by their owners provided a particularly rich harvest, and the five remaining W.I. members in the Kent coastal village of Hawkinge alone produced between them the astonishing total of fourteen hundredweight. There were no perquisites. The government supplied the sugar and, where necessary, paid for the fruit, but the women who did the work were not allowed to buy a single jar of their produce and each one had to be full to the very brim as it would be sold as part of someone's ration. The quality of the jam was also strictly laid down. One leading W.I. member, who became a travelling Jam Inspector, another job reminiscent of *Garrison Theatre*, remembers 'tasting' visits, with a Ministry of Agriculture official, to private kitchens, school rooms and village halls, to check that all the jam contained the specified amount of sugar. 'The result', she considered, 'was a stiffer and sweeter jam than most countrywomen liked but the Centre jam had to stand up to pretty varied transport conditions.' Obtaining empty jars was a great problem, but 'graveyards were very good hunting grounds'. Many villages were still without electricity, so that much of the jam had to be boiled up on oil stoves. Once the process had started the rule was, whatever happened, to 'Keep on stirring!' 'It was nothing unusual during a raid', one eye-witness remembers, 'to take one's primus and jam with one under the table, so that the jam didn't go off the boil. Sometimes a near miss rocked and dislodged the rows of jars waiting for collection. Sometimes when bringing in the fruit one had to take to the ditch.' But, as all jam-makers agree, bombs were a minor annoyance. 'What everyone hated most were the wasps.' In the Dorset village of Henwood the jam centre was, the local Institute's 'war diary' records, 'popularly known as the Wasps Paradise' and a drawing shows it instantly identifiable by the swarms of wasps barring the entrance. One housewife from Buckland in Gloucestershire recalls that after one year in which only these fruits were available she never wants to see another pot of rhubarb and gooseberry jam again, and the archivist of the Spetisbury W.I., near Blandford, while proud that their Centre made 1,100 pounds of jam, has also recorded that it gave some members 'a deadly hatred of sieved blackberries, sugar percentages and other trials of the W.I. preservers'. A Suffolk schoolteacher remembers one small perquisite her mother, who was the local W.I. president, gained from the 'pounds and pounds' of plum jam she made. 'The recipe said all stones were to be removed after the sugar was added. Instead of throwing these stones away they were taken home by the members and used again to boil up with their own fruit at home, thus saving their own sugar ration.'

Country writers had often talked romantically of 'the harvest of the hedgerows' and in September 1941 the Ministry of Health, announcing that rose-hips were twenty times as rich in Vitamin C as oranges, appealed for support for national rose-hip collection week. 'The hips', it was announced, 'can be gathered from wild or cultivated bushes, but they should be free of bits of stems and leaves.' Collecting hips was a job which everyone could tackle and for small children the payment involved—threepence a pound, from a greengrocer or a W.V.S. or W.I. collecting centre—was an added attraction. A Surrey girl, then aged six, remembers picking a whole pound and a Merseyside schoolgirl and her friend used to make special trips into the country for the purpose. A NAAFI worker at Richmond, Yorkshire, spent her off-duty time that Autumn stripping the hedges near the camp where she worked. By December 200 tons had been obtained and a year later rose-hip syrup was actually on sale, this sticky, apple-flavoured liquid often being supplied instead of welfare orange juice.

Although the Ministry warned that 'haws, the red berries of the May, are not wanted', they were in fact useful for feeding pigs and one teacher evacuated to East Anglia still remembers her surprise on enquiring for one of her small pupils to be told 'He's gone a-hawing, miss', which in the local dialect sounded like 'a-whoring'. Conkers were gathered for the same purpose, and nettles and other wild plants, to replace the imported raw materials for many common drugs. One prison governor remembers collecting large coltsfoot leaves which were dried in the prison laundry. A housewife living in a remote part of Wales gathered foxgloves. A woman living in a large country house near Petersfield collected sacks and sacks full of nettles ... We got large amounts of belladonna in the surrounding woods. For Culpeper [a famous pharmaceutical firm] we dried hawthorn leaves, marigold flowers, shepherd's purse, wild geranium and so on.'

Wild herbs were also used to enliven wartime diet. Drying them was a problem. An ordinary airing cupboard would do at a pinch, but at Penrith, in Cumberland, the W.V.S. used a room over the ovens in a local bakery and stretched old net curtains between trestles to serve as drying racks until permits arrived to buy timber and wire netting. A woman living near Mansfield, who organised a P.O.W. Relatives Association to send quarterly parcels to prisoners, remembers that one speaker at their monthly meeting voiced 'a cry for herbs to add to their stews and soups. . . . My house was the centre for seventy-five pounds of herbs as I had excellent hot cupboards for drying mint, sage, thyme and even crushed onions, and the Red Cross included these in small containers in the food parcels.'

Although the Red Cross, unlike the W.V.S., was limited by its rules as to the help it could give civilians, it took the lead in many good causes, especially those connected with the Services. A London woman who organised Red Cross Sewing afternoons, held in her house and other houses in turn twice a week, remembers making pyjamas and shirts for the wounded. About twelve housewives attended each session from 2 p.m. to 4 p.m., taking it in turns to provide the tea. 'Most of them I had to watch', she remembers, 'as they would put sleeves in the wrong way round and collars on for cuffs, etc.' A Forest Hill woman organised Bridge Drives and Bring and Buy and Coffee Mornings to raise money for the Red Cross. One elderly lady who attended, an excellent bridge player, was known as 'Arsenic and Old Lace', because the bottles of home-made mayonnaise which she proudly presented as a prize 'as if they were gold' were notoriously uneatable. To the great relief of the other women, when one unfortunate male did carry off the prize, he prudently left it on someone's doorstep on the way home.

Perhaps the best known Red Cross activity was its 'Penny a Week Fund', to raise which an army of volunteer helpers collected a penny a week from people in their road or office. The Fund, used to buy comforts for the Forces, was eventually bringing in £50,000 a week, a third of the Red Cross's total income. A typical collector was the wife of a sailor in the submarine service. 'Sometimes on my rounds', she remembers, 'people would say "It can't be a week since you came last", and I got upset and said to my dad, "Do they think I want the money for myself? I shall pack it in", and my dad would say "Do you do this for public acclamation or for the boys' parcels?" and I would be ashamed and still carry on. When, in August 1945, . . . I met New Zealand soldiers in hospital and heard their glowing tributes to the woman who collected the money for the parcels that showed them they weren't forgotten, I was so very thankful I had stuck it out.' One Guildford woman, who made her collection only once a month, found that her visits were welcomed because they occurred in the last week of a rationing period and so reminded her subscribers to use up any surviving 'points'.

Of all the ways in which the nation's housewives helped their absent menfolk the most universal was knitting. Small girls, busy mothers, even —a Kidderminster woman remembers—gallant grannies with arthritic fingers, all knitted. The clicking of needles could be heard constantly in many a shelter and in the semi-darkness of wartime trains. People knitted in the cinema, on buses, in queues, in the dinner hour at work, especially during the first long winter of the war, when few were actively contributing to the war effort. A Civil Service office worker remembers struggling with her needles in crowded rush-hour trains in October 1939 and 'one felt very guilty if one was knitting in any other colour than navy, khaki or Air Force blue. When one of my brothers returned through Dunkirk, I knitted myself into a frenzy and completed a pair of socks in a week, setting my alarm for 5 a.m. for the purpose.' '1940 and 1941', a then fifteen-year-old Girl Guide at High Broome, in Kent, remembers, 'saw us knitting garments for the Services. A W.V.S. Knitting Centre in Tunbridge Wells provided the wool and patterns and this was sorted out into our ages and how well we could knit. . . . Seaboot stockings and polo sweaters for the Navy were the worst for they were big and chunky and made of oiled wool. The prettiest were the dark red pullovers for the Indian Army.' A Leicestershire girl living on a farm detested having to knit navy and army socks at school, while her mother went to the rectory one afternoon a week to knit more. One woman recalls a curate friend learning 'to knit his own socks, as he could not visit parish knitting meetings without something to do', and a Conway woman remembers that at the local knitting circle her own husband learned to turn a heel as well as anyone, but she spent hours pulling out and rewinding other knitters' inadequate work.

This was the thankless task of many women, although to cater for unskilled knitters a special ribbed pattern for socks was provided to fit any size of foot. 'Gloves and socks were knitted on two needles', a King's Lynn woman remembers, and the socks had no heels, 'just straight', so that 'they gradually worked under the feet when marching and were most uncomfortable'.

It is hard to know whom one sympathises with most, the unfortunate wearers of such garments or the reluctant knitters bullied into taking on a job they knew was beyond them. One Northolt first aid worker remembers the choice of occupations on duty: cleaning cupboards and sterilising instruments, helping a dentist with his children's clinic or knitting 'Dover Patrol Pullovers'. She was no knitter and could not turn corners, but was told it was her duty to knit what parts of the garment she could, and the sister would 'increase' and 'decrease' for her. As the knitters laboured they also had to answer questions on first aid.

The first enthusiasm for knitting had already begun to ebb when clothes rationing, in June 1941, struck it a further blow. After complaints, the government agreed to supply twenty-four ounces of coupon free wool a year to anyone wishing to knit for the Forces, but a year later the scheme was wound up and thereafter coupon free wool was supplied only to recognised 'knitting parties'. Many women were no doubt secretly glad to see the last of the heavy wools of the past few years—especially the stiff oiled wool used for naval garments, which left the hands raw—and there was a boom in the thinner, two-ply wools which went further, an important consideration when every two ounces of wool 'cost' a clothing coupon. The decline in the popularity of knitting was helped by rumours like that which caused one young Cardiff mother to leave her afternoon knitting party—that the socks they were making were piling up unwanted and the class was merely to give middle-aged women a feeling of helping the war effort. A young Central London office worker, who knitted constantly herself and contributed sixpence a week to the office 'wool fund', heard an even more disheartening story: that the troops were using the lovingly knitted, but unwanted, garments to clean their guns.

# HIT BACK WITH NATIONAL SAVINGS

'Achtung!'
　Mine goot freund Herr Gobbles has this morning to me told that
Watford are a War Weapons Week having . . . I demand you not to
save your money. . . . It will be to me a great blow if you your half
a million get.

Adolf.'

Mock message from Hitler, Watford War Weapons Week, April 1941

The one commodity that was not scarce during the war was money.
Some groups, like servicemen's families, remained badly off throughout
the war and the pay of most white-collar workers, like teachers, was
slow to catch up with the rising cost of living. For the upper middle-
class, too, their maids called up and their clothes growing threadbare,
the war meant a drastic drop in their pre-war standards. But, for the working
class as a whole it was a time of unprecedented prosperity, the beginning
of the climb from pre-war insecurity to post-war affluence. Many families
now had two or three incomes instead of one, while most war jobs, if
disagreeable, were correspondingly well paid. A Welwyn Garden City
fabric salesman who had earned 35s. a week, plus a little commission, in
1939 and was 'very hard-up indeed', was by July 1941 earning £3 10s.
and on taking a thoroughly unpleasant job in a chemical factory had
an immediate rise to £4 10s., while in 1943 his mother began to bring
another pay packet into the home. A twenty-year-old Newbury shoe-
shop assistant who had earned 35s. a week at the beginning of 1941 was
soon taking home £4 2s. 6d., which included a bonus for reaching her
production target, from her new job making torpedo components in a
war factory. In a ship repair yard, visited by a London journalist in
1942, average earnings were £5 14s. 8d., though a few highly skilled
men, working very long hours, earned £11 or even £15. In a tank
factory at the same time the men averaged £5 7s. 10d., but some reached
more than £10. Even though some badly-paid occupations, like farm
work, brought the figure down, by the end of 1943 the average wage
for a man was £3 18s. 6d. and for a woman £2 15s., but many individuals
earned far more and 'white collar' earnings were now beginning to slip
behind those of manual workers.

Another great change was that, for the first time, ordinary working-class families now began to pay income tax. The first wartime budgets sharply increased the standard rate of income tax from the pre-war 5s. 6d. in the pound to 7s. 6d. in September 1939, 8s. 6d. in July 1940 and 10s. in April 1941, where it remained, but it was the reduction in personal and earned income allowances, along with steadily rising wages, which for the first time brought most industrial workers within the income tax net.

Before the war there had been only 3,800,000 income tax payers in the whole country and even by 1941 the total was only 6,000,000. Then, following the cuts in allowances, the number almost doubled to 10,200,000—by 1945 it was 12,500,000. The Welwyn shop assistant turned chemical worker mentioned earlier noted with astonishment in his diary in September 1941 that in future he would be paying income tax, though it would be deducted from his pay in weekly instalments. This was another wartime innovation, first introduced in 1940 for the benefit of weekly wage-earners—pre-war a whole year's tax had had to be paid in a lump sum—though at first the tax due was calculated on a man's earnings several months before. The new method proved so popular, however, that it became the basis of a full-scale Pay As You Earn system, applied to all tax-payers and based on current earnings. The credit for PAYE, one of the most useful legacies of the war, really belongs to 'colourful Kingsley Wood', an enthusiastic innovator, and an experienced politician with a remarkable instinct for survival. In May 1940 he skilfully transferred his allegiance from Chamberlain to Churchill at just the right moment, being rewarded in October with the post of Chancellor of the Exchequer. He died, unexpectedly, in September 1943 on the day he was to introduce the Bill setting up the PAYE system, but it was taken over by his successor, Sir John Anderson, and, as a result of public pressure, extended to cover not merely wage-earners, or lower-paid salary-earners, but all employees, coming into effect on 6th April 1944.

Kingsley Wood was also responsible for another, far less successful, innovation, Post-War Credits, which were also introduced in the great Budget of April 1941 which really put the country's finances on a war footing.

As already mentioned, this Budget sharply reduced personal allowances and to make these cuts more palatable it was promised that the money involved would be repaid after the war. By then, however, it amounted to £765 million, and successive Chancellors could not bear to part with it, as had always been expected, in one splendid flourish. Post-war credits were instead repaid slowly and grudgingly, and the final round of repayments only began in 1972, thirty years after the state had compulsorily borrowed the money.

Another wartime tax measure has become permanent, purchase tax, introduced in the summer of 1940. Although the Labour Party at first opposed it, as non-selective, so that it would press hardest on the worst-off people, the public as a whole readily accepted it, though shopkeepers who had to collect the new tax were less enthusiastic. The aim of these and other taxes—like the inevitable increases in drink and tobacco duties—was not so much to raise revenue as to 'mop up' purchasing power, and prevent inflation, and in this, though money had never been more plentiful or goods more scarce, they undoubtedly succeeded. During the first eighteen months of the war prices had risen sharply, but in April 1941 Kingsley Wood announced that the government meant to hold the cost of living steady at its new level of 25 to 30 per cent above pre-war, a figure raised in 1944 to 30 to 35 per cent. Wage rates, which up to 1941 had begun to fall behind prices, now more than caught up; and by the end of the war average earnings were up by nearly 50 per cent on 1939, although nearly 30 per cent of the average income was now going in taxation compared with only 21 per cent in 1938.

A strange feature of taxation in wartime was that the public constantly urged the government to spend more and the Chamberlain government's last Budget, in April 1940, was strongly attacked for being too small. By December 1940 the war was costing £10 million a day, double what it had done in May, and by December 1944 £13 million. Taxation provided only from 39 per cent to 55 per cent of the money needed. The rest, from nearly two-thirds to nearly a half, had to be borrowed from the public and, in lending their money, it was hoped, they would also help to keep prices down.

The National Savings movement, begun in 1916 to cope with similar problems during the first world war, had left behind a strong organisation of local and regional committees. On 22nd November 1939 a new campaign was launched by the Chancellor of the Exchequer with the slogan 'Lend to Defend the Right to be Free', later largely replaced with the more aggressive message: 'Hit back with National Savings'. Patriotism was already a bigger stimulus to saving than the prospect of profit, but the new seventh issue of National Savings Certificates also offered slightly more generous terms to savers with each 15s. certificate rising to 20s 6d. in ten years, another 20s. certificate, worth 23s. after ten years, being added in January 1943. There were also four issues of Defence Bonds, of which anyone could hold up to £1,000 worth. These offered a return of 3 per cent and a small tax-free bonus on maturity and, for the larger investor, various types of government stock. Deposits in the Post Office Savings Bank, founded by Mr. Gladstone in 1861, also helped to swell the total raised, but for most citizens National Savings meant savings certificates. It was to obtain these that many people bought a weekly sixpenny savings stamp and it was savings certificates which conscientious uncles and aunts posted to small nephews and nieces at Christmas in special Christmas cards and which patriotic schools awarded as prizes instead of books. My school, perhaps fearing that certificates might be cashed, went one better and instead issued a printed note merely promising to pay up when peace came. I can still remember the deep disgust and disappointment with which, instead of the expected volumes, I received these miserable slips of paper as a reward for success in English and history, although, more honourable than the nation, the school did at least redeem these 'post-war credits' after the war.

The War Savings drive combined a network of savings groups, which made it easy to save regularly, with a series of special campaigns to keep enthusiasm alive and raise large lump sums. Running a Savings Group appealed to many people unable to take a more active part in the war, and group secretaries included people in their seventies and at least one blind woman, but most were housewives, often those same 'willing horses' who were the backbone of every form of service, from A.R.P. to collecting salvage. By the end of the war nearly every school had its savings group, and there were almost 80,000 in shops, offices and factories, seven times as many as in 1939. Many people authorised regular deductions direct from their pay and some employers added an extra certificate for every five or ten bought in this way. Certificates were also sometimes given as prizes for ideas which saved the firm money or fuel—almost as important after 1942. Street or village savings groups had been almost unknown in 1939 but by 1945 numbered 120,000. In the peak month, June 1943, nearly a quarter of the population belonged to one of the country's 300,000 savings groups and posters and advertisements everywhere urged one to 'Back them up with war savings' or to 'Fight in the Streets. Belong to your Savings Group'.

Collecting money is never very agreeable, but many group secretaries are still glad that they faced the weekly, wearisome trudge from door to door, often in cold and rain. An Enfield woman is still sometimes stopped in the street by grateful savers eager to tell her how they have spent the savings she encouraged them to make. A Colchester housewife used to be 'hours taking the stamps round as I was invited into all the houses I called at and had a little gossip at each one. I got to know quite a lot of people through this.' A young mother living in a Sussex village found that running a Savings Group 'was something I could do with a small baby. I used to take her in the pram, with my large dog tied to it. It was quite a poor village but I still remember how kind people were, insisting on giving me sweets for the baby, and flowers and fruit from their gardens, even making her toys at Christmas, and saving scraps and bones for the dog.' A ten-year-old schoolboy from Palmers Green enjoyed doing his mother's round for her; one woman, after buying her regular shilling stamp, always gave him a penny for himself. The wife of the manager of a Sunderland chemist's shop did her weekly collecting every Friday evening dressed in her Civil Defence tin hat and rubber boots. This struck an appropriately martial note—and made it easy to go on duty if bombs started to fall.

Many attempts were made to vary the unexciting routine of saving money. The National Savings movement ran a poster competition for schools, with, of course, savings certificates as prizes, and the best 400 entries were sent on tour in the United States. Slogans were also invited for a new poster on the 'nest egg' theme, suggestions ranging from 'Send Hitler the shells' to 'Only one egg this month—THESE [i.e. savings certificates] can be purchased every week'. National efforts of this kind were supplemented by local ingenuity. In the Cotswolds village of Buckland auctions were organised at which all the goods were a free gift and the successful bidder bought National Savings Certificates to the value of the purchase price, so got the article for nothing. Schools frequently had a chart displayed in the hall recording the amount saved by each class in the preceding week and a publican's daughter from Ilford remembers that her contribution was always popular, for her family saved all the threepenny pieces taken over the bars and gave them to her to invest; often the total reached £2. A nine-year-old school girl living with relations at Mansfield, Nottinghamshire, had another incentive to try to buy a savings certificate, for 'my uncle said that if I agreed to save a shilling a week towards this goal he would make up the difference if my pocket money had sunk to less than a shilling on savings day. Each week . . . he would ask how much I had left and add to the amount if necessary. Some weeks I had sufficient to meet the deposit, but I often hadn't and I remember the day when his part of the bargain cost him 11½d. towards the 1s.'

The National Savings movement contributed to the gallery of wartime cartoon characters a new and sinister figure, the Squander Bug, an evil-looking insect, more likely to frighten anyone away from extravagance than, as he was alleged to do, to tempt him into spending his money. To some children he became a bogey man, haunting their nightmares with his plump body, thin feelers, pointed, slightly Satanic, ears and long, rat-like tail. 'The "Squander-bug"', warned one leaflet, 'causes that fatal itch to buy for buying's sake—the symptom of shopper's disease.'

The proper cure was also shown—a large boot descending on the hastily-fleeing insect with the caption: 'Squash him!'

From 1940 onwards local Savings Weeks became a regular feature of everyday life. The week usually began on a Saturday with a parade through streets crowded with shoppers, pride of place being given to whichever service the week was in aid of. As, naturally enough, the local units were rarely willing to release their best men for the job, the detachment concerned often had a somewhat unmilitary look and many parades were enlivened by such mishaps as the civilian Red Cross women having to break ranks to assist their fainting weaker sisters in the A.T.S. or W.A.A.F. (The land girls, made of sterner stuff, took standing about in some chilly market place during interminable speeches far more calmly.) Any well-organised Week usually included an outdoor religious service, a fancy dress parade, sports events and fire-fighting or anti-gas demonstrations and a large barometer would stand outside the town hall, recording the community's progress towards some improbably high target. The competitive element was strongly in vogue here, too. When Luton was challenged by Watford to raise more money for Warships Week, the challenge was delivered at the Town Hall by a knight in shining armour on horseback, but alas—the days of chivalry were dead and Luton won, collecting £1,400,000, £200,000 more than Watford. Competition was particularly effective when two towns had traditionally been rivals. Huddersfield, for example, had always been his home town's rival 'in cricket, football, music and everything else', wrote one Halifax man. 'Having ascertained their chosen date, we fixed ours for a week later.' When it was learned that Huddersfield's target was sufficient money to buy three destroyers 'someone sugested that we should go all out for three submarines so that we could torpedo Huddersfield's destroyers, but this was regarded as perhaps not quite the right spirit'. Halifax in the end also set its sights on three destroyers and easily achieved its target, although the Royal Engineers who were to have been the centre-piece of its parade never turned up—they were all busy in Sheffield clearing up the damage after a heavy raid the night before.

The success of the Halifax week made the name in the savings world of its chief organiser, Sir Harold—later Lord—Mackintosh, a keen Methodist and a firm believer in the nineteenth-century virtues of thrift and hard work, which had carried his own family from a tiny back-street shop to ownership of the most famous toffee-making concern in the country, and which he combined with a great interest in twentieth-century methods of publicity. In 1941 he joined the National Savings Committee and, after taking charge of its publicity, became its chairman, and thus head of the whole War Savings drive, two years later. Like many similar wartime appointments, this proved an excellent one, for Mackintosh not merely encouraged people to save, but did so in a colourful, and even exciting, way which helped to relieve the tedium of wartime existence. One of his brainwaves was to borrow the elephants from Bertram Mills's Circus to take part in War Savings parades, with posters hanging from their sides, and at the end a ceremonial tableau where they held huge replicas of a National Savings Certificate aloft in their trunks. For 'Warships Week' the bridge of a battleship was erected in Trafalgar Square, from which bands played martial music, and for 'Wings for Victory' Week the Square was turned into an airfield with a four-engined Lancaster parked in the middle. His most famous stunt was releasing 1,500 pigeons on the opening day of the Week, each one supposedly bearing a good luck message to the chairman of a local savings committee. 'The sky was thick with them', he later wrote. 'The press and newsreel cameras clicked like machine guns and the pigeons all flew back to the R.A.F. Communications Centre where they had come from, less than a mile away.' For 'Salute the Soldier' Week a special march was commissioned from Eric Coates, and Sir Bernard Montgomery, victor of Alamein, was invited to make a propaganda film and, it need hardly be said, accepted while a special 'Salute the Soldier' revue, not however, featuring the Field Marshal, also toured the country.

Similar ingenuity was often shown at the local level. In Warships Week in 1942, for example, Tottenham announced that it proposed to raise £700,000 to 'buy' H.M.S. *Hotspur*, which bore the same name as its famous football team. At Watford in April 1941 a leaflet appeared in support of its War Weapons Week which purported to come from 'Old Nasty' himself. 'Achtung! Mine goot freund Herr Gobbles has this morning to me told that Watford are a War Weapons Week having. My patients is exhausted. I demand you not to save your money. If you another destroyer buy, it will sink my U Boats which are guarding the seas. . . . It will be to me a great blow if you your half a million get. ADOLF.' In a less good-humoured vein another leaflet showed bombed houses, and urged 'Get Your Own Back. Your blood boils when you hear of the fierce deeds that Hitler and his murderous gang commit. For every blow they strike at civilisation you must hit back. . . . Lend to attack.'

Often peacetime amusements, like fancy dress parades and beauty queen competitions, were revived under the guise of patriotism. A London plastics factory, one secretary who worked there remembers, 'always elected a beauty queen to preside over the affairs and . . . held dances, competitions and raffles. . . . Tea was a great treasure to many people, but we never used our allowance and I was able to take a packet or two to be raffled. Some people would spend quite fantastic amounts trying to win a quarter.' A hairdresser living in a small village near Goole in Yorkshire remembers her daughter winning a fancy dress competition in the village hall, in a costume made from bunting left over from the Coronation. The prize was the first savings certificate to be issued during the town's Salute the Soldier Week.

For children as a whole the excitements of War Savings Weeks perhaps went some way to make up for other wartime deprivations. A teenage girl from Bath shared in her brother's pride when his model aircraft were borrowed for exhibition in a local Wings for Victory Week display. In North Wales a horse box belonging to the Girl Guides and converted into a mobile canteen made a regular appearance in such parades, with Guides seated on the roof semaphoring patriotic messages with flags. A then schoolboy in Twickenham remembers 'a friend and I would mount our own displays of toys . . . in sandboxes in front of our houses to catch our unwary neighbours and make them contribute. I only hope that all the money we collected went into the tins.' This boy also remembers that when the Army provided Bren-gun carriers with caterpillar tracks to take the public for rides, starting outside the Town Hall, there was such enthusiastic response that 'In no time the tracks had completely torn up the surface of the council's private road'.

A regular feature of all the Weeks, as of the whole savings campaign, was the issue of 'price lists' for various items of equipment. A large firm might set out to raise £20,000 for a Wellington bomber or £40,000 for a Lancaster, and smaller savers would aim at £138 for a 2,000 pound bomb, or even a modest hand-grenade, costing 4s. Before a Savings Week the employees of an office might be found solemnly discussing whether to aspire to £50 for a Lewis gun or to content themselves with a sub-machine gun, at £30. The result of all this effort was that quite small places often raised surprisingly substantial amounts. The vicar's wife in one Northumberland village remembers an anxious few hours when during one Week she acquired more than £500 to keep overnight; she could not decide whether it would be safer hidden under her bed or in the cellar.

The first special savings drives, War Weapons Weeks, were held between September 1940 and October 1941 when the nation's thoughts were on re-equipping its Forces, and they were followed by Warship Weeks, from October 1941 to March 1942, when rationing was making the country realise its debt to the Navy, and Wings for Victory Weeks in the spring and summer of 1943, when the R.A.F. was hitting back at the Germans. This was the climax of the campaign and even the smallest towns managed to squeeze a Spitfire or Hurricane into their main streets and to display large bombs on which the public were invited to stick and sign savings stamps which, it was promised, would be faithfully delivered by the R.A.F. Mild old ladies would be heard remarking, as they stuck on their stamp, that they hoped it would help to smash some German town, and mothers watched proudly as small children signed their names on a bomb destined to kill or maim German families.

The sum raised by small savings—Savings Certificates and Post Office deposits—in Wings for Victory Week, £160 million, was the largest of any wartime campaign and never were ordinary citizens so personally involved in reaching their target. A factory worker from Liverpool, staying in York for a weekend, remembers what happened when she decided to draw some money out of the Post Office. 'I joined a long queue . . . got to the counter and asked for a withdrawal form for £3. The woman behind the counter said very loudly, "What did you ask for?". I repeated it and every eye turned toward me, while the woman picked up the book, found my address and almost spat: "From Liverpool and you come here to take our money out! Are you aware that this is our Wings for Victory Week!" I grabbed the book and shot out of the door like a Spitfire—easily my most embarrassing moment.'

By 1944 the prevailing war weariness was beginning to affect even the most resolute saver and Salute the Soldier Weeks, held between March and July, aroused less interest. Many places found difficulty in reaching their target, which was often achieved only after last-minute appeals to local businessmen, and though more money was raised than in previous Weeks—£628 million—it came from large savings, for small savings were heavily down. The same trend was even more marked in the Thanksgiving Weeks, planned for June and July 1945 but not held until the autumn, and which swelled the total sum raised by all the great campaigns to £2,777 million. But more important than helping to finance the war was the lift the campaigns gave to morale. 'In these Weeks', Mackintosh later claimed, 'we did more than raise money; we raised hearts too. The bands played, the flags flew, the men marched, and . . . the people at home felt they were taking part in the war.'

Several million pounds saved during the war will never be repaid and lie in a special 'unclaimed assets' account of the Treasury's Consolidated Fund. This was made up, for instance, of money received from the sale of savings stamps stuck on bombs, or the War Savings fair at my school where the boys cheerfully spent their money without receiving—or indeed expecting—savings stamps in exchange. We felt ourselves well rewarded by the break in school routine and by such side-shows as releasing a 'bomb' on a target from an electro-magnet rigged up by the science department, or identifying various masters in a 'Rogues' Gallery' from pictures of them as babies. There were many similar private efforts. One London woman for ' "Warships Week" made needle-books from circles or heart-shaped pieces of cardboard, lightly padded with wadding and covered with scraps of silks and velvets. . . . I sold these little books for a shilling a piece and made twenty-five shillings.' A Hampstead girl started a private library, lending her books at a penny a time, also holding a jumble sale in the kitchen of a friend's house. A Colwyn Bay housewife remembers a minor adventure collecting jumble for sale for war purposes. 'Near where a friend lived in a very nice group of houses, lived a prostitute, much to the horror of the people living near. This friend dared me to call—which I did. We called this person Piccadilly Lil! Lil was charming and most helpful. She called me in while she sorted through her clothes, but I declined and said I would arrange to have them collected, which I did. She sent a wonderful pile and a cheque.'

The usual destination for such free gifts to the nation was the local Spitfire Fund, raised to buy an aircraft outright. A Ministry of Information official, present when a shot-down British pilot landed in a tree in a vicarage garden in Kent, helped to pass round a steel helmet among the bystanders which raised £8 towards a new fighter. In at least one London office everyone contributed a penny after each raid in 1940 and forecast the time of the next. If someone guessed right, she won the whole kitty, but if all were wrong the money went to the fund. A then twelve-year-old schoolgirl from Merseyside remembers her mother giving a valuable silver tea pot and hot water jug to the Spitfire Fund in gratitude for their having survived the blitz. Later a rival to the Spitfire Fund was developed in the 'Buy a Bomber' scheme. A commercial school teacher in Dorchester remembers donating a pair of nylons to be auctioned for this good cause, which realised the remarkable sum of £18.

But it was the Spitfire, its very name seeming to recapture the grand, defiant days of 1940, which remained the real idol of the nation, and none of its successors—the Tempests, Typhoons, Mustangs—ever replaced it in popular affection. Curiously enough, the most famous Spitfire Fund of all did not exist. Week after week, in the popular radio series *The Old Town Hall*, in 1942, the band was asked to guess the title of some popular tune from a clue sent in by listeners, the penalty for failure being 'A penny on the drum for the Old Town Hall Spitfire Fund'. In fact every misguided guess had been scripted beforehand; and the noise of the pennies raining on the drum was produced, not by the generous musicians, but by the BBC Sound Effects Department.

# EIGHT COUPONS FOR A CASSOCK

'It is greatly to be hoped that the clergy generally will set aside the not unnatural impulse to reproach . . . those members of their swollen congregation who are making their rare appearance at a service.'

*The Church Times* on the National Day of Prayer, 5th September 1941

To many people it seemed entirely right that when the war began they should be in church. If there was not a wholesale turning towards religion at the start of the war, there was in many places an increase in congregations. The perils of 1940 increased this tendency, and never was prayer more fervently said than 'Lighten our darkness . . . and protect us from all the perils and dangers of this night', during the black-out and the long ordeal of the blitz. Later in the war, the situation changed and if there was little overt hostility to religion there was more polite indifference. The wife of a Cambridgeshire clergyman dates the change from 1942. From 1939 in her parish there had been a noticeable increase in congregations; from 1942 they began sharply to decline. Those who had become Christians 'for the duration' had, it appeared, failed to last the course, although many people did still turn to religion for support. 'More often than not', a young Rotherham woman remembers, 'the women would leave in tears. . . . The church became a sort of sanctuary for those who had received the dreaded telegram.' A schoolgirl living in Kent remembers how 'one always looked round at the beginning of the service to note absentees and hoped it wasn't a sign of bereavement. An announcement was always made of local service victims at the commencement of the Notices.' Many churches prayed regularly for all local servicemen by name and often kept a book where parishioners could enter the names of loved ones in danger, replaced at the end of the war by a Book of Remembrance listing the fallen.

In peacetime the parish magazine had not, perhaps, been the favourite reading of many young men but during the war it was often a welcome link with home and conscientious vicars regularly posted copies to parishioners in the Forces. St. Matthews Memorial Methodist Church, Walthamstow, one women, then aged twenty, remembers, 'tried to keep in touch with the boys away from home by having open Omnibus Letters in the vestibule so that members could add a few lines'. In Nottingham a former captain of the local cricket club 'sent a monthly bulletin to anyone from the Parish in the Forces, telling them all the news of the Parish, Cricket Club, etc.'. Helping with addressing and folding such letters, or contributing to the cost, became yet another of the small ways in which church-goers helped the war effort.

Parish magazines at this time often gave a remarkably illuminating picture of conditions at home—so much so, indeed, that the Ministry of Information sent out a special circular warning their editors against boasting that the congregation had gone up due to the erection of an aircraft factory or that the church canteen had served 10,500 buns to men embarking for overseas from a local port. A regular reader of the parish magazine of Holy Innocents Church, Fallowfields, Manchester, for instance, could deduce a good deal about daily life in Britain from the fact that for its early-morning communion services on Christmas morning 1940 'we shall have a few small night-lights in church so that people can just see their way about'. Two years later, in June 1942, the same church, celebrating its seventieth anniversary, was warning that 'Owing to the rationing difficulties it is impossible to arrange for a tea, so people are asked to have an early tea at home and to assemble in the school at 5.30 p.m. . . . We shall move into the Lancaster Road Room for light refreshments. . . . You are asked to bring your own sugar, of course.'

Although the clergy were exempt from call-up it had been agreed before the war that in the Church of England both vicars and curates would accept guidance from their bishops, though some suspicious Anglo-Catholics had warned against any attempt by Low Church bishops to seize this opportunity to rid their dioceses of High Churchmen. Many younger clergy joined up, as chaplains to the Forces, leaving their less military-minded colleagues to carry on. A clergyman from Lancaster, asked by his bishop to 'hold the fort' while a colleague went into uniform, found himself running single-handed a parish which had formerly employed a staff of three. 'Life', his wife recalls, 'was hectic, with often six services on a Sunday, in six different places. At one time he was responsible for burying all the dead in Lancaster, which meant going to three different cemeteries with only a push bike for travelling.' Many clergy, especially in the East End, gave heroic service during the blitz, though a few could be seen, according to contemporary observers, 'wandering aimlessly about' the Rest Centres. One in Chelsea provoked the wrath of a first aid worker, who heard him console a woman widowed in an air raid by telling her she should feel grateful not to have been killed with her husband.

Churches in the early days were often used as unofficial shelters, because of their solid walls and the vague feeling that they should enjoy some supernatural immunity from being hit. (This hope was not well founded; probably more churches were destroyed than any other type of public building.) A City of London secretary who attended a Roman Catholic church in Willesden Green, a district known as 'Little Ireland', has described a typical scene there:

> The Church was left open all night and the Priest stayed there, with a camp bed in the Vestry. A couple of Sisters of Charity also stayed in the Church. Many people who were frightened to stay in their own beds hurried around to the Church and stayed there lying on the floor or on the pews. When bombs came too near, the Priest would emerge from behind his curtain and we would all say our Rosary and invoke the assistance of the Holy Virgin . . . I remember once remarking to the Priest that it was a sad sight to see so many Irishmen there Sunday mornings still not sober from the night before and he remarked drily, 'Well, it may not be a good sight but the fact that they never miss, means that we can always put our hands on them when we want them, especially if a Colleen discovers she is having a baby.'

Oddly enough, when a church was bombed the result was often a larger and more dedicated congregation. When the church I attended, St. John's, Newbury, was totally destroyed in 1943, the congregation joined in the hymns and prayers at services in the nearby infants school far more heartily than in the old building. When the elderly priest celebrated mass in a classroom decorated with children's drawings and multiplication tables, he seemed spiritually, as well as physically, far closer to his flock than he had ever done in the vast Victorian chancel of his church. St. John's had too, in its temporary home, for the first time in its history, a midnight mass on Christmas Eve, a custom continued ever since.

Even when a church escaped damage, the war intruded in other ways. A schoolgirl in a Kent village noticed how, when the preliminary 'yellow' warning was received during a service, 'a messenger would slip in the door and the word would go round the A.R.P. members, etc., and quietly they would leave'. A housewife living near Birmingham remembers a mid-week service the afternoon after the raid of Coventry. 'The minister was late. When he did arrive he was unshaven, had no tie on and looked dreadful. He sank down on his knees in front of the altar, put his head on his hands and wept. He had been out all night administering to the injured and the dying.' Nor could that traditionally remote figure, the country rector, remain in ignorance of the ordeal of his brethren in the cities. Readers of *The Church Times* were told during the summer of 1941, for example, that in Devon alone fifty-six churches had been damaged by enemy action and fourteen destroyed. One parish on the Kent coast, 'the church nearest the enemy', had included in its records such novel entries as 'Evensong: shelling during service', and on Easter Day, 'Heavy machine gunning during morning service.'

Many church-goers only began to appreciate what their church had meant in their lives when it was destroyed, and standing among the ruins at a patronal festival they sang such hymns as

> We love the place, O God,
> Wherein thy honour dwells . . .

Some vicars greeted even such destruction with Christian resignation. An Ashford mother, worshipping in a church with no roof, was highly impressed when the vicar thanked God for leaving the walls standing, to which her small son added loudly, to her embarrassment, 'and the chairs and door'. A Hastings woman witnessed an equally unusual incident 'when a friend lost her hat in church. A large hole had been made in the church roof overnight by shrapnel and a sudden gust of wind sent the hat gaily hopping over several pews.'

Although some clergy led their congregation to shelter in the crypt, most, as in this church, simply carried on and this same housewife spent more than one 'morning service with my family, listening to the planes overhead and mentally deciding which stout wall would be most likely to provide some protection if the bombs began to fall'. She was struck, too, at her son's confirmation, by 'the calm dignity of the "laying on of hands" while the planes and guns fought noisily overhead'. A housewife in a Lincolnshire village remembers evensong one Sunday when 'the bombs were falling . . . the old parson shouting to make himself heard. Some people slid out quietly but my family and I thought if the parson could stick it, we could.' A Westcliff-on-Sea housewife was attending her Congregational church one Sunday evening when 'it got very noisy . . . the minister, as he was praying, said "Even now the angel of death is hovering over us" '. She did not, she admits, find this a particularly comforting thought. This church, like many, suffered due to evacuation a drastic decline in congregation, from 600 to a scanty twenty-five. There were corresponding increases in congregations in reception areas where hitherto almost empty churches were suddenly crowded out. In one peaceful Thames-side village, to which a girls' boarding school moved from Kent, the elderly rector, on the point of retirement, suddenly found 'he had a church packed to overflowing with girls, and confirmation classes to arrange'—a situation to which he 'responded nobly'.

The requisitioning of church halls and crypts as A.F.S. stations, rest centres, and canteens, affected far more churches than the bombing.

In one Watford parish even 'the schoolroom and vestries were converted into first aid departments' so that 'all meetings, whether Sunday or weekday, had to be conducted in the church, often with great inconvenience'. A Denbighshire Sunday School teacher sympathised with the older members of the congregation at her church who were deeply shocked when their church hall became a 'wet' canteen, serving beer. But many churches started their own canteens and individual Christians often faithfully carried out the Biblical injunction to entertain strangers. I have the happiest memories of supper at the Church of England vicarage at Lanark in Scotland, after attending Evensong, a brief reminder of civilised living after the squalid barbarities of the barrack room. Nor do I feel any ill will towards the evangelical sect which enticed a friend and myself into their chapel in the same town under the pretence that it was a canteen, and compelled us, before we were entertained, to sit through a splendidly traditional revivalist meeting, with many a cry of 'Hallelujah'. A Southampton woman, then a young girl, remembers how her church, Above Bar in the main street, 'was always packed and . . . after the first evening service all the young people and servicemen and women used to go to the hall at the back of the church for a good sing-song with cups of tea and biscuits. How we enjoyed those days! Later at night teams of young people from the church would visit air raid shelters for the public and hold services there. Then we would walk home through what seemed like showers of shrapnel.'

The most persistent of all the wartime problems that afflicted clergy was the black-out. Most churches moved the time of their Sunday evening service, either permanently or during the darker months, to 3 or 3.30 p.m., though a few preferred to keep to the traditional time and hold the service elsewhere. A young office worker from Birmingham remembers attending services in the blacked-out schoolroom where 'If black-out time came during the duration of the service the caretaker (who had very big feet) proceeded to put up the shutters whatever solemn prayers or moving sermon was taking place'. At early-morning services in the winter the congregation usually sat in darkness and only the priest had a pale light to read by, though, as one parish magazine put it, 'anyone is at liberty to use a torch if they want to read their books as long as they keep it pointing downwards'. A Gloucestershire woman recalls carrying a torch as she went up to receive communion in the dark, and at Braintree the congregation at Christmas, one man remembers, would sing the whole of the mass at midnight from memory. At the parish church of St. Edward the Confessor, Romford, the only light provided at the 7 a.m. weekday service was at the altar from 'two candlesticks about nine inches high with shades about two inches wide at the top . . . and at the people's communion it was necessary to carry a small screened lantern and focus the light on the chin of each communicant and hold the paten under his chin. . . .'

Darkness, and the nearness of danger, lent a deeper significance and devotional quality to many such services. One St. Albans girl found very moving Saturday evening compline in a small chapel in the Abbey, which had formerly been the Lady Chapel. Only the faint glimmer of light from the lamp burning before the reserved sacrament pierced the blackness and the eight to ten worshippers who regularly attended recited by heart words that had never seemed more full of meaning: 'Preserve us, O Lord, while waking, and guard us while sleeping, that awake we may watch the Christ, and asleep we may rest in peace.'

Really determined and ingenious laymen—the clergy rarely seemed to possess the necessary practical bent—did sometimes succeed even in the difficult task of blacking out a church. A popular solution was hat boxes round each suspended bulb. but some more elaborate systems were devised. The parish clerk of St. John the Baptist, Pinner, had persuaded the Parochial Church Council to have the windows measured for shutters even before the war began so that 'we could have services any time, day or night, including midnight communion at Christmas, with about 400 communicants, many from other parishes. . . . There was a very deep blue electric bulb in the porch and inside were two small lights in tubes, which gave sufficient light for the people to find their seats. When the service was about to begin, the doors were locked and the lights turned on full. . . . Most of the lights were switched off just before the end of the service so that the people would get used to the darkness outside.' At St. Mary's Deanery Church, at Bocking near Braintree, the general disappointment 'that our very popular midnight mass on Christmas Eve might have to be cancelled started me thinking', the vicar's warden remembers. The result was two strings of pale blue lights down each side of the church made from fairy lights left over from the annual Deanery Fête, shaded by jelly moulds from Woolworths covered with cellophane dyed red or blue. 'Two heavily shaded candles on the High Altar and a small voltage reading lamp for the priest completed the wiring and the whole effect was of very subdued moonlight. We at St. Mary's were probably one of the few churches where not a single evening service was cancelled during the whole of the war.'

But there were advantages in not having a blacked-out church. 'My welcome for three o'clock evensong', wrote one clergyman in *The Church Times* in September 1941, 'has nothing to do with lighting or heating. It is simply that it is very pleasant indeed to come home to a tea-table set beside a fire of logs and to be contentedly aware that the whole long evening is one's own, and likely to be free from any interruption save that of the anti-aircraft barrage and an occasional bomb.' It was, however, afternoon evensong, another cleric believes, which paved the way for the post-war decline in Sunday evening congregations.

The black-out led to some other memorable experiences. A BBC production secretary, evacuated to Bristol, found that when the BBC Staff Choir gave a candle-lit performance of Brahms's *Songs of Mary* at Christmas 1940 in the beautiful church of St. Mary Redcliffe, 'due to lack of black-out' this provided 'exactly the right mysterious atmosphere'. The wife of a Methodist minister had not forgotten a dark and cold January night when, after taking an evening service in the village chapel at Shillington near Luton, she arranged for a soldier preaching at another chapel to escort her home. He promised to sing to identify himself and she still remembers hearing the tramp of army boots through the winter darkness and a beautiful baritone voice raised in the famous Methodist hymn, *How happy are they who the Saviour obey*. A South Wales miner realised for the first time in the black years the beauty of the sky and the true significance of the words of the psalm, 'The heavens declare the glory of God and the firmament showeth His handiwork'. One newly ordained clergyman was highly amused when, during a raid, his train was halted outside Derby with all the lights off and the other occupants of the compartment, all railway men, 'were saying what they thought in definite terms, until one happened to strike a match for a cigarette and noticed my clerical collar. There was an awed hush thereafter.'

The war meant a considerable shifting of loyalties, both between individual churches and between different denominations. An Iver housewife remembers that when her church Sunday School was shut down most children were sent to one run by the Free Churches, and never returned to their old allegiance. A woman then living in the West End of London noticed how one by one the nearby churches were bombed—the vicar of her own church, St. Peter's Eaton Square, being killed standing on its steps—until only one was holding regular services. But some churches even managed to hold extra services. One Roman Catholic woman recalls how her church in Camden Town added a ten o'clock mass each morning and a daily afternoon service of intercession, with a special hymn for those in the Forces.

Many services took place held in unusual surroundings. A Hither Green Congregational church held services during the blitz in the church hall, 'as nearer the shelter', and at its height, the congregation assembled in the shelter itself, where 'the seating capacity was just over sixty—with a shoe horn. Those who managed to attend in the morning stayed away in the afternoon to make room for the others.' *The Church Times* in 1941 recommended open air services. 'Now that there is no spare petrol the parish priest must go to his people. Many evensongs have been said this summer on village greens, or in the shadow of barns or beneath haystacks.' The most typical development of the war, however, was probably the 'cottage meeting' popular in the Methodist church, where a few people met for a short service in a private house once a week. The wife of a Methodist minister, who organised five such meetings among members of his church, enjoyed the weekly Wednesday evening meeting in her home. 'Often we had twenty-five people there. They sat on the Manse table to form the gallery. One night we were singing so well we didn't hear the warning go and two elderly ladies, thinking the All Clear was the warning, when they arrived home sat under the stairs all night. But they were not dismayed, they told my husband—they read many of the hymns in the Methodist hymn book.'

One service could not be held in private houses, the wedding ceremony, though it frequently had to be arranged at short notice. A Lancashire vicar's wife, just out of hospital after a serious operation, found her convalescence cut short by the approach of D Day, for she constantly had to rise from her bed to obtain from soldiers on embarkation leave the details needed for calling the banns. The cosy peace of Christmas afternoon in a country vicarage in Northumberland in 1942 was, the vicar's wife remembers, shattered by a similar request. 'At about 3.30 p.m. two young American soldiers and two young women rang the door bell and said they wanted to be married. My husband said "When?", and they said "Right now". It was explained we did not do things quite like that and they were advised to see their commanding officer. The young men seemed so very young and nice—the young women were awful. . . . I had managed to make a Christmas cake. We gave them tea and they ate all the cake'—surely a stern test of anyone's Christian charity.

Rather disappointingly, the war produced no new hymns or prayers that gained general acceptance; even the *Gate of the Year* verse quoted by George VI had been written years before. One of the few new prayers of literary merit was found by an East London vicar in his church during the blitz.

Almighty and most merciful God, who dwellest not in temples made with hands; be thou the guardian, we beseech thee, of our churches and our homes; keep this thy house in peace and safety; and grant that all who worship here may find their refuge under the shadow of thy wings and serve thee with a quiet mind, through Jesus Christ our Lord.

Most special wartime prayers tended to remind the worshipper of the needs of those who were defending him and I can remember, attending a weekly evening service in the school chapel one Lent, how the list grew longer and longer as anti-aircraft gunners, searchlight crews and barrage balloon men were added to it. *The Church Times*, pointing out the need for similar prayers for forgotten groups on the Home Front, produced a rather odd selection: land girls working in hot greenhouses, 'washers-up in steam-laden canteens, the bus girls who feel the vibrations of the bus for hours after leaving the rear platform, old retired taxi-drivers nervous of the muffled blindness of the black-out', and, most surprising of all, since most G.P.s' trouble was not the empty surgery but the overfull one, 'panel doctors whose practices have vanished in the blitzed areas'. If these and other deserving categories were ever prayed for, it was not while I was in church; nor did I ever hear sung the most widely advertised of wartime hymns, *A Hymn for Today* by the Rev. Thomas Tiplady, said to have sold 146,000 copies by mid-1941:

> On the railroad be as light
> To the engine driver's sight.
> May each motor driver feel
> Thine own hand upon the wheel.
>
> In the workshops guide the hands
> Arming this and kindred lands;
> Firemen, wardens and police,
> Grant Thy strength and inward peace.

One lasting legacy of the war was increased co-operation between the different denominations, for at open-air services in support of War Savings Weeks, Anglicans and nonconformist clergy regularly appeared on the same platforms, and some places held special weeks of Christian unity, in which all the Protestant churches took part. A Congregationalist living in South East London remembers a typical development. 'The Anglicans, Baptists, Congregationalists and Methodists took it in turns to hold a united mid-week service at their church, conducted by their minister, the address being given by a minister or priest of one of the others.' The bombing of a church often broke down old suspicions. When one very 'high' Newbury church was bombed, Baptists, Methodists and Congregationalists all held collections towards its rebuilding fund. A deacon in a Congregational church in Hull was impressed that when the local Unitarian Church was destroyed his church immediately invited the Unitarians to share their building and for months 'the Congregational minister took one service and the Unitarian minister the other, and members of both churches attended as suited them best'.

On the whole, the most remarkable feature of church life during the war was the extent to which difficulties were overcome. The Congregationalist deacon just quoted admits that on the outbreak of war his 'first feeling was one of immense shock and some doubt as to whether one's beliefs could be right or, if they were, could prevail. Later a sense of balance was arrived at, and the departure of so many young folk to the Services seemed to arouse a determination in those who were left to keep things going.' The vicar of Christ Church, Oakworth, near Keighley in Yorkshire, where a Parish Breakfast in the nearby school after the 8.30 a.m. Parish Mass was a well-established institution, remembers that early in the war one of the helpers declared that the meal would have to stop for the duration—but it never did. Butter was a great problem, so every Saturday half a pound of margarine was beaten up with half a pint of milk and this produced a good pound of 'butter', to feed the three dozen parishioners who came to the breakfast.

The call-up, and competing Sunday morning activities like A.T.C. parades, thinned the ranks of most choirs, and, when they did keep going, choir practice was often held directly after the Sunday morning service. Many choirs even managed to wear robes, though often patched and ragged. A Coventry woman remembers a typical compromise: in her church the boys wore only their cassocks on normal Sundays, surplices being reserved for Easter, Christmas and other major festivals. Sunday Schools suffered more, especially in the cities, though some places had a form of 'cottage' Sunday School. 'In 1940', a woman Sunday School teacher in Coventry remembers, 'we closed the Sunday School proper and held it in our houses, each teacher in her own home. . . . We used to meet in the vestry after morning service to discuss the lesson with the superintendent and sometimes at her house on Sunday afternoons to plan the following week's lesson.' In the country, Sunday Schools were often strengthened by evacuees, and even that hallowed institution the Sunday School treat continued. One former Sunday School scholar still remembers a treat at Lower Heyford, Northamptonshire; instead of travelling by motor-coach to some distant picnic-spot, the children were taken to a large local garden by horse and cart. Other wartime difficulties both clergy and laity also took in their stride. At Ruthin, in Denbighshire, when the church verger and cleaner were called up the congregation took over their duties on a rota basis. But for a missing congregation, perhaps discouraged by the black-out, there was no substitute. One vicar's wife in Northumberland admired the honesty of a visiting preacher who, confronted by an almost empty church, told the three people it contained, 'You won't want to listen to a sermon, any more that I want to preach it, but there will be a collection—such as it is.'

One rival to even the most eloquent preacher was the radio. A Somerset church-goer remembers how 'our vicar found his congregation falling off at the time of the fall of France, so he installed a wireless and loudspeaker in the church, and everyone came before 6 p.m. and heard the news before evening service'. This routine worked well until the evening when the vicar, having announced a hymn at the end of his sermon, switched on the radio instead of turning off the pulpit light, and, while the choir and congregation attempted to sing *Rock of Ages*, the strains of Troise and his Mandoliers burst through the church.

Prudent parish officials had begun even before the war to build up a stock of wafers and communion wine. These did not become particularly scarce, though the parish magazine of Holy Innocents, Fallowfield, Manchester, was warning in April 1942, that 'white bread is being taken off the market shortly so that we shall have to use either brown or "standard" bread for the Holy Communion. . . . This may seem a little strange at first, but it will be quite within the law. The sort of white bread which we eat is a modern invention which the writers of the Prayer Book would never have seen.' Sanctuary wine was also obtainable after the Board of Trade had lifted an earlier ban on importing it. But there was no such concession over palm for crosses; one deacon, then in his first parish near Nottingham, found that Palm Sunday 1941 could only be properly celebrated by drawing on stocks left over from previous years, though some rural parishes raided the hedgerows for pussy willow. To the annoyance of low-churchmen incense, at 5s. a pound, charcoal to light it, at 9d. a packet, and candles at 3s. 1d. a pound could also be bought, but oil for sanctuary lamps was scarce and this, one clergyman believes, started the fashion for solid fuel lamps of the 'night-light' pattern.

The war, if it did not cause, also speeded up another change. With fewer and fewer women wearing hats sidesmen now began to turn a blind eye on bare female heads in the congregation. By June 1941 women were openly worshipping hatless in St. Paul's, and many lesser known churches, while not yet ready to go so far, would allow in bareheaded women as sight-seers. Women now began to take men's place even in church. One vicar proudly reported in *The Church Times* that he had replaced an absent sidesman by a sideswoman, who worked during the week as a bus conductor, so 'now she completes the full round of the week in collections', though churchgoers, she reported, were much more reluctant to part with their money than bus passengers.

At first the Board of Trade could not make up its mind whether clerical dress was covered by rationing or not. *The Church Times* commented that the 'order . . . which . . . greeted the Pentecostal Dawn* . . . is not enlightening about the number of coupons Mr. Wynn (the new Bishop-designate of Ely) will need before he can mingle without shame among his episcopal brethren. . . . The only item of chief pastoral raiment is gaiters (three coupons) if you exclude "apron or pinafore" (three

*Clothes rationing began on Whit Sunday, 1941.

coupons).' Future bishops, it suggested, anticipating the need for extra coupons, might have to prepare an 'episcopal bottom drawer'. Eventually it was ruled that vestments such as chasuble, stole or surplice, worn only in church, were coupon free but not clerical garments used for everyday wear. Clerical stocks and 'dog' collars would require one coupon each —though rationed by the leading clerical outfitters 'to three collars per order'—a cassock waistcoat cost five, and a clerical cloak or raincoat eighteen. What affected clergy most, however, was that eight coupons were demanded for a cassock, the full-length, black garment worn by almost all Anglican clergy in church, and by many, especially High Churchmen, outside it. Since this was their working dress many clergy contended that it should have been exempt, especially those who had just taken Orders. 'It was', one newly-ordained curate considered, 'plain unjust that a bricklayer could get extra coupons for his overalls but a priest could not for his, the cassock.' But the Board of Trade was unmoved by such complaints. A cassock, it pointed out, could be worn in place of a suit though it took only a third as many coupons. 'Here is an opportunity', suggested a correspondent in *The Church Times*, 'to restore the use of our dignified dress. Let us stick to our cassock and knickerbockers and go about in them always.' The families of the clergy had their own problems. The dean's daughter in one cathedral town caused consternation in the family when she announced that she was giving up genuflecting for the duration, to save wear and tear on her stockings—an excuse her father considered intolerably worldly.

Although no clergy defied clothes rationing, some firmly refused to allow a mere war to interfere with their duty in other directions. One Somerset vicar continued to ring the bells of his church despite the ban on doing so, 'on the grounds that the Canons of 1603 directed him to ring them for services, and no lay authority could absolve him from the obligation'. Lay authority, in the shape of a highly embarrassed policeman, did, however, finally persuade him to comply. Another clergyman complained that on attempting to make a telephone call on church business he had been told by the operator that only essential official calls were being accepted. On protesting that his call was on behalf of the Almighty, he was firmly informed that the latter's name did not appear on the approved priority list.

The ordinary problems of daily life also pressed hard on clerical families. That pillar of every parish, the vicar's wife, besides having to cope with blacking out and heating a vast vicarage, was expected to set a good example in such good works as taking in evacuees. She also had to undertake more frequent entertaining than the ordinary housewife. One resident in a Devon village remembers how providence came remarkably to the rescue when 'our vicar's wife, visiting my wife one morning, said the bishop was coming next day and she was at her wits' end what to give him for lunch. . . . At that moment our cat appeared from the wilds surrounding our garden with a rabbit in its mouth. This was duly served up for the bishop in a pie.'

The difficulties of daily living no doubt bulked larger in the minds of most Christians than the great moral issues of the war. All the Christian Churches, except the small pacifist sects, agreed that it was a just war and the clergy were soon being given an official role in National Days of Prayer. The most impressive of these occasions, on 26th May 1940, did express deep national feeling, but later Days of Prayer, in March and September 1941 and on each anniversary of the outbreak of war, produced more scepticism than faith, as the local mayor and corporation led detachments of Home Guards, A.R.P. workers and Girl Guides into church.* *The Church Times* counselled its readers against 'the not unnatural impulse to reproach directly or by implication those members of their swollen congregations who are making their rare appearance at a service. . . . Such a mode of attack seldom does any good.' By no means all clergy welcomed the Days of Prayer. One vicar of my acquaintance criticised them as being like 'calling on the old tribal gods for help' and a Devon vicar's wife thought they produced 'more show than sincerity'. Nor was the official form of service very inspiring. Congregations were required to 'ask forgiveness for all that has been amiss in our national life', not for strength to defeat the Germans, and many worshippers must have felt that it was carrying Christian forgiveness altogether too far not to ask God to punish the nation's foes but, only 'to turn their heart . . . that they may truly repent'.

The Church never really did sort out its attitude to the enemy. Some churches displayed posters declaring, 'I must have no hatred in my heart', though others played safe with, 'It all depends on me, and I depend on God'. At the start of the war a somewhat ludicrous dispute had occurred between the two archbishops as to whether a Christian could properly pray for victory, the Archbishop of Canterbury believing he could and his colleague at York believing he could not. Some conscientious clergy felt one must even pray for Hitler, who meanwhile was publicly thanking God for blessing his conquest of Poland. Roman Catholics had an especially confusing dilemma to face—not merely did the Pope not condemn Nazi atrocities but he actually congratulated Hitler when he survived an assassination attempt in November 1939. The Vatican continued throughout the war to consent, by its silence, to the butchery of millions of innocent people, but as the war went on, most people's early scruples about hating the Germans began to melt. Only on one

* Churchill wrote of his attendance at Westminster Abbey on 26th May 1940 that 'from my seat in the choir stall I could feel the pent-up, passionate emotions'.

major issue did Christian opinion in Britain ever disagree with government policy, the deliberate area bombing of German cities, which Bishop Bell of Chichester publicly denounced in the House of Lords in February 1944. Even here, however, the controversy never really caught alight, for the public as a whole simply did not believe the Bishop's charges, wholly true though they were, and the government maintained to the end of the war, with a persistence that Goebbels himself must have envied, the bare-faced lie that only military objectives were being attacked.* Even had the truth been known, however, the general reaction would probably have been one of grim satisfaction that at last the Germans were being given a dose of their own medicine.

On lesser questions of ethics thrown up by the war, the bishops tended to adopt a distinctly tolerant, man-of-the-world attitude. They refused to become alarmed over the alleged moral danger to young girls working in war factories or to service women who went into public houses, and one bishop jocularly replied to complaints that dances went on after midnight on Saturday, that he doubted if the Lord acknowledged the existence of Double Summer Time. If He did not, the Sabbath did not begin until 2 a.m.

* Air Chief Marshal 'Bomber' Harris, the head of Bomber Command, wanted the public to be told the truth. But the government, understandably ashamed of its policy, refused, the only occasion on which it deliberately deceived the public throughout the war.

# FULL SUPPORTING PROGRAMME

'Unless the war ends first it may in a year or so be difficult for film-goers to distinguish between rural England and Eden before the Fall.'

*Punch*, 11th November 1942

'More people packed into the cinemas than ever before, to escape. Flashes would come on or the manager would appear on stage and inform us that the sirens were going and those who wished to leave would have their money refunded. . . . Few moved, I can tell you. We could hear nothing, see nothing and with a lover's arm around your shoulder, whispering sweet nothings in your ear, and watching Clark Gable or Bing Crosby doing likewise in a more abandoned manner, who cared if a bomb did drop. One would go out happy!' That is how one middle-aged woman, then a secretary in the City of London in her twenties, remembers 'going to the pictures' in wartime, and it is a portrait that millions of others will instantly recognise.

The war had begun disastrously for the cinema industry with the closing of all cinemas by government order. In Grantham, groups of would-be cinema-goers, one observer noted, could be seen standing about on Monday 4th September, 'looking for all the world as though they had lost something'. At the Rialto, Leytonstone, the letters which had spelt out *Love Affair* and *Ask a Policeman* now read pathetically 'Watch for our reopening'. This came on 9th September and the stampede which occurred at some cinemas as the doors were flung back was a happy augury for the future. By December cinemas were open almost as normal, except that all performances now finished at latest by 11 p.m., although it was not until 1942 that the pre-war habit of weekly, or even twice-weekly, cinema-going—programmes still often changed on Thursday—was really restored.

The chief outward signs of change were the long queues, to which the manager now came and chatted with wartime friendliness, and the near-disappearance of posters, now limited to ten per programme—pre-war 300 had not been exceptional—and cut to a quarter the pre-war size. A more lasting change was that most cinemas now began to open on Sunday, to cater for soldiers and war workers away from home, though the films shown were usually both old and poor. Cinema foyers became popular sites for displays in aid of Wings for Victory Week or a war workers' recruiting drive; one enterprising manager even advertised *The Good Earth*, about peasant life in China, by mounting a Dig for Victory exhibition.

The government was understandably alarmed about the danger to morale if a bomb hit a crowded cinema and at first managers were supposed to warn every house of the procedure to be followed if a warning occurred, but this procedure was soon dropped, and an announcement was only made when the siren sounded. In 1940 and 1941 this happened so often that some unfortunate managers lost their voices, but helpful members of the audience could by now prompt any who stumbled over their familiar set speech or would call out 'O.K., we heard you!' as soon as they climbed on the stage. Eventually the warning was given merely by a red light beside the screen or a slide which read: 'An air raid warning has just been sounded. If you wish to leave the cinema please do so as quietly as possible. Those who wish to remain may do so at their own risk. The film now continues.'

A then teenager in Rotherham noticed how reaction to these announcements changed. 'At first the majority of people would file out and go home, but we soon tired of seeing only half the film . . . and eventually, more often than not, you would not hear one seat fall back. Hardly any bombs fell on our town, but when I was in Bristol . . . I found no difference, the patrons glued their eyes on to their favourite film star and to Hell with Hitler! . . . And they would stay to see the national anthem played to the end, too.' Towns unused to bombs were sometimes less courageous. A girl student from University College, London, who was in a cinema at Bangor when, for the only time, bombs fell there, remembers how, at 'the crash of glass as all the shop windows fell out and the cinema doors blew to and fro about thirty times with a great draught most people rushed out. But there were five students with me and . . . we stayed put, seeing the film to the end in a deserted house.' Far more typical was what happened at Chepstow, in Monmouthshire, when a nearby bomb shook the building. Several people got up to go—only sheepishly to resume their seats when a voice from the back shouted rudely, 'Sit down you silly b——s and watch the film.'

A Godalming housewife, at the cinema when the siren sounded, remembers how 'my son and I clasped each other's hands and "played brave". Soon there were loud bangs and we set our chins in determination to face whatever might happen.' Then it struck her that each 'terrific bang' only came after someone had got up to leave by the back door. The 'bombs' were caused by the slamming of the heavy exit doors and 'the

All Clear had gone immediately after the warning'. A North Country woman, then living in Barnet, remembers how 'One night we had just settled down to see *One Hundred Men and a Girl*—Deanna Durbin and Leopold Stokowski—when the manager asked us to leave and we found the next door building blazing, an oil bomb having dropped on it. As we had not seen the film and the cinema was intact we went back the next day and asked to see it free. (Our Yorkshire meanness I guess.) We were allowed in, but shortly after a notice was put up . . . that people would not be readmitted.'

If bombs were still falling at the end of the performance managers at first allowed the audience to stay put, sometimes showing the whole programme again. The Granada, Clapham, once put on five films in a night, though by 4 a.m. most of the audience were fast asleep in their seats. Sometimes the cinema organist played, to give the projectionists a break, or the usherettes led the audience in a sing-song. One manager, when the film was finally stopped after the electricity supply had failed, offered a £1 prize to the best amateur singer from the audience. He lived to regret it; nine out of ten chose the same song, *The White Cliffs of Dover*.

So popular were such late-night shows that before long managers in the East End were having to cope with queues of families, armed with blankets and fish and chips, seeking admission *after* the last performance, and soon, with cinema staff becoming worn out through lack of sleep, customers began to be turned out at the normal time, bombs or not. In fact cinemas were often surprisingly good shelters. Many were modern buildings which stood up well to blast and during noisy patches the audience would obtain added protection by moving under the circle balcony. Some cinemas survived quite serious damage. At Walthamstow, for instance, as no permit for repairs was forthcoming, the staff dragged tarpaulins over the shattered roof and set up buckets in the auditorium to catch any elusive drips. One film, with the ominous title *Opened by Mistake*, acquired in the film circuits the sort of bad luck reputation that *Macbeth* had in the theatre; three cinemas showing it were bombed. Even more hazardous was employing an usherette from Woolwich known as 'Land-mine Minnie'. She had been blown up no fewer than four times and at last, very appropriately, married a bomb disposal man. The worst enemy of most cinemas was incendiaries; the large, flat roofs seemed to attract them and a large cinema needed fourteen fire-watchers to protect it.

Even in peaceful areas a cinema manager was hedged round by innumerable troubles, from a ban on giving away monthly programmes— they could be sold for a nominal sum, like a penny—to a slump in income from sales of cigarettes and sweets, where rationing cut receipts by two-thirds. To young cinema-goers the hardest blow was the banning of ice-cream manufacture in September 1942—it returned in March 1945. One Birmingham schoolgirl, twelve when the war began, used 'to go to the cinema regardless of what film was on, as it was just possible they might have ice cream in the interval and I can remember my mother trying to save hers to bring home for my sister'. Various substitutes were tried. The Granada group employed a travelling chef to advise on making 'jellied sweets' and a then teenage girl journalist in Scotland sampled 'weird concoctions' of dates and figs when acting as her paper's film critic. Despite the cinema's importance to morale, no employees, except the chief projectionist, were even considered for deferment. By 1945 most cinema staff were under sixteen or over sixty, while at least one commissionaire was aged eighty-five. Fortunately their lot was far easier than in peacetime. People now queued without question and the manager was regarded as a friend, doing a useful job, rather than as the butt of every humorist sitting safely in the dark. Even the traditional game of trying to get in free through the exit lost its attraction; when the exit doors were blown off one cinema, at Clapham Junction, by a V.1 no one even tried to take advantage of the fact. Crowded conditions, too, perhaps helped to create a spirit of togetherness for, at least after 1942, almost any film could fill almost any cinema. Standing was not uncommon and a woman then living near Belfast remembers that one crowded Saturday night she heard 'a North Country voice shouting out in the middle of the big picture, "This is the first time I've ever paid to sit on t'floor!" '.

During the war, programmes became longer than ever, for to the traditional pattern of main feature, a supporting 'B' film and newsreel was added at least one official film, the much-criticised Ministry of Information producing a weekly 'short' and a longer film nearly every month, on subjects like salvage and careless talk. *Food Flashes* preached the virtues of eating potatoes, Board of Trade fashion films demonstrated how to convert an old jacket into a smart new skirt, and humorous films attempted to boost morale. The standard was often high. One classic specimen showed two men gloomily reflecting on the miseries of wartime life, and deciding to end it all by leaping overboard from a rowing boat off Southend. They do so—only to land in shallow water, so that they have to splash ignominiously back to shore resolving to make the best of things. Such propaganda was not really necessary, as the response to newsreels showed. These were so popular that they were often shown again at the end of the 'big picture' and 'films showing the destruction of the enemy', a then teenager in Rotherham remembers, 'were cheered with almighty roars. When the Italians were shown to be captured hoots of laughter would attack the masses, and when the Spitfires and Hurricanes sent the enemy crashing to earth in flames there was almost a standing ovation.' Another teenager, from Leyland in Lancashire, witnessed a typical reaction to newsreel shots of German soldiers standing stiffly to attention, for 'One bright lad shouted out, "Take t'coat hanger out then".'

Newsreels of British troops were watched closely in the hope one might see a relative and helpful managers sometimes arranged for a few frames of a newsreel to be copied and enlarged. One Ipswich woman came back from the cinema to tell a neighbour, ' "I saw your Johnnie in the News." Off she went to the next performance and there sure enough was Johnnie, among several other soldiers, preparing their evening meal at a camp "somewhere in England". She went to every performance that week. . . . No one thought it in the least bit odd of her, even though he was not on screen for more than ten seconds.'

Emotions during the war were often near the surface and, after 'a good cry' at the pictures, one could go home in the black-out without anyone noticing your red eyes. A young housewife from Leytonstone was so upset by *Adam had Four Sons*—all four were killed—that she ignored the raid in progress as she made her way home, and was still in tears when she arrived. The wife of an army officer remembers a miserable visit to a Lancaster cinema. 'My husband was going over to Europe in about two days' time and he had just . . . told me . . . It was one of the *Road to* . . . films, with Bob Hope, Dorothy Lamour, but . . . I did not take in any of the film at all.' She recalls another melancholy experience 'in Camberley sometime after he left. Feeling gloomy I decided to go to the cinema . . . and it was the most awful Russian film. The name escapes me, all I remember was the heroic defenders of somewhere and the Russian heroine driving a tank and squashing a German officer on the hill at the side of the road. . . . This made me feel very much worse and I left hurriedly.' A Birmingham nurse, doing Sunday duty at a New Street cinema, has memories of an equally grim afternoon watching *The Grapes of Wrath*, about the American depression. The audience, bored to tears, walked out, but she had to sit through to the bitter end.

To enable propaganda films to be shown even in the depths of the countryside, temporary cinemas were set up in local halls, or mobile cinema vans, mainly used at election times, toured the villages. One officer's wife, whose husband was posted to many remote spots, found that 'any films we saw in the country were usually interrupted by the film breaking several times to the loud shouts of soldiers, who usually had a good many comments to make'. For a young woman teacher living in the village of Buckland near Huntingdon any visit to a normal cinema meant a long and tiring bus journey, or a five-mile walk. She thoroughly enjoyed the films hired by the Methodist Guild and shown in the village Rifle Range, despite 'uncomfortable seats, spotty screen, a temperamental projector, but an enthusiastic audience of schoolboys and villagers'. A young Bath girl, evacuated to Somerton, attended in the village hall each week one of the last regular performances of a silent serial, in cliff-hanging instalments, *The Indians are Coming*.

But for most people going to the pictures meant a long, cold wait in a queue followed by three hours or so of blissful escapism in what one cinema-goer remembers as 'packed houses, thick with smoke, stifling'. Only the pre-war cinema-organ interlude was now sadly diminished; the coloured lights, changing to match the mood of the music, had often been extinguished to save fuel and the organist was probably female. Any male organist who returned on leave, especially in uniform, was sure of a tremendous ovation and personal appearances by local war heroes were also popular. But it was prudent to check their credentials. One 'survivor from Dunkirk', with sand in his boots to 'prove' his story, who offered to appear on stage at one cinema, was arrested shortly before he walked on as a deserter from the Pioneer Corps.

Under the influence of war, not merely were cinemas crowded but the British film industry at last attained maturity, and began to turn out films that were a great success all over the world. The first documentary to catch public attention in August 1940 was *Men of the Lightship*, due partly to the first use in a film of such words as 'bastards' as the sailors swore at attacking enemy planes. The real breakthrough came with *Target for Tonight*, released in 1941, which told the story of a raid on Germany by Wellington F for Freddie. Its actors were real airmen— later in the war they were killed on operations. The Crown Film Unit's *Coastal Command*, in the following year, was an even better film, justly praised by the critics for its 'astonishing realism'. The Army's turn came with *Desert Victory* in March 1943, notable for its dignified, restrained commentary—another innovation. Another successful documentary, *Western Approaches*, released in January 1945, told the story of the ordeal of the merchant seamen on the Atlantic convoys.

The realistic approach of these propaganda productions, made by the Crown Film Unit, strongly influenced for the better many commercially financed feature films. The outstanding example was *In Which We Serve*, generally released in January 1943 and inspired by the adventures of 'the happy and efficient ship' H.M.S. *Kelly* and its famous captain, Lord Louis Mountbatten, played by Noël Coward. *The First of the Few*, going the rounds from September 1942, was equally widely enjoyed, with Leslie Howard in the role of the designer of the Spitfire. His death the following year, when his unarmed air-liner was shot down, produced a wave of national grief. It was not until 1944 that a really successful fictional film about the Army was produced, *The Way Ahead*, starring David Niven, which described how a group of men from many walks of life were welded together into a fighting unit.

The A.T.S. had already been the subject of a popular film, *The Gentle Sex*, in May 1943. A then teenage girl from Blackburn still recalls how 'The sight of all those A.T.S. walking down that long road singing "She'll be wearing khaki bloomers when she comes" really got me. I was too young to join, but oh how I loved that picture.' The same impressionable film-goer was also impressed by *Millions Like Us*, about factory life. Its mere title indicates one of the great changes which came over British films during the war, for before 1939 working people had usually been depicted as either lovable idiots or as loyal, forelock-touching, and no doubt underpaid, servants. Now people with uneducated voices and ordinary jobs were portrayed sympathetically, though the male heroes still tended to be commissioned and the heroines to come from wealthy but gracious landed families. There were surprisingly few films about Civil Defence, the exceptions being the documentary *Fires Were Started*, in April 1943, and *The Bells Go Down*, a fictionalised story about the A.F.S., in the following month.* *The Lamp Still Burns*, about nursing, later that year, is still remembered by many women, but few people seem to have been impressed by the many films in praise of 'Englishness' that belong to the latter half of the war. A typical specimen was *Tawny Pipit* (July 1944), about a rare bird endangered by army manœuvres which, it need hardly be said, were postponed to allow it to breed in peace. To the same year belongs *This Happy Breed*, about a 'typical', cheerful working-class family's reaction to the war. The pro-Russian atmosphere of 1943 was commemorated in *The Demi-Paradise*, in which a visiting Russian was introduced to the English sense of humour and attended a village pageant, involving those same lovable villagers and vague vicar who had been the mainstay of so many pre-war comedies. Such films remained unaffected by the new realism, and fully merited the comment made by *Punch* in 1942, when reviewing *Went the Day Well*, which described an imaginary German landing in the English countryside. 'Branley Green is even more golden-hearted than Mrs. Miniver's village and unless the war ends first it may in a year or so be difficult for film-goers to distinguish between rural England and Eden before the Fall.' Far more inspiring were films based on British history, like *The Young Mr. Pitt*, played by Robert Donat, *The Prime Minister*, with John Gielgud as Disraeli, and *Lady Hamilton*, released in 1941, with Vivien Leigh in the title part. Churchill wept when he saw it and in many cinemas there was hardly a dry eye as Nelson, played by

* The book, of the same title, on which it was based was, however, autobiographical.

Laurence Olivier, died at Trafalgar saving his country from invasion.*
Another influential film, of a very different kind, was *Thunder Rock*,
released in 1943, starring Michael Redgrave, and based on a successful
stage play about the aspirations of a group of (as it turns out) drowned
travellers towards a better world. 'Its cracker-barrel idealism' moved
one young Bradford girl to apply, the day after she saw it, for release
from her job as a telephonist to join the A.T.S.

Other British films which did good business were *The Foreman Went to
France*, in June 1942, about a British workman and a couple of soldiers
successfully rescuing a party of children and some vital machinery during
the collapse of France, and, in the same year, *Next of Kin*, preaching the
need for security, and *One of Our Aircraft is Missing*, which described
the adventures of a shot-down aircrew escaping from occupied Europe
although films about resistance movements were normally not popular.
*We Dive at Dawn*, in 1943, gave a realistic picture of life in a submarine,
but was not such a success as *Pimpernel Smith*, starring Leslie Howard
as a quiet English traveller saving people from the Germans. Wartime
box-office records were also set up by *49th Parallel*, a long, and in my
opinion wearisome, film about Germans in Canada trying to escape
to the United States, and *The Life and Death of Colonel Blimp*, in which
a typical diehard of the 'old school' is duly discredited by a bright young
officer, though not till each has discovered a respect for the other.

No one British film stands out as *the* picture of the war years. My
own favourite, not released until June 1945, was *The Way to the Stars*,
outstanding for the accuracy of its picture of wartime England near an
R.A.F. station and the impact made by the Americans. It also contained a
charming, catchy song which admirably captures the atmosphere of the
period, *Let him go, Let him tarry*, and the one war poem to achieve
popular success, John Pudney's *Johnny Head in Air*.

Many other, non-war, films released between 1939 and 1945 also gave
a great many people much pleasure. They included (in order of release)
*Jamaica Inn, Goodbye Mr. Chips, The Stars Look Down, French Without
Tears* and *Tilly of Bloomsbury* in the first year of the war alone. Later
came *Kipps, Major Barbara, Hatter's Castle, The Man in Grey, Fanny by
Gaslight* and a series of films based on stage successes, including *Quiet
Wedding, Dear Octopus* and *Blithe Spirit*. Radio programmes were the
source of several undistinguished films, including *Band Waggon, ITMA,
Happidrome* and a whole series of adventures involving Inspector
Hornleigh, of *Monday Night at Eight*. Most wartime comedies are
also best forgotten, like the appalling *Mother Riley* series, featuring a
female impersonator, and some unfunny Crazy Gang performances. I

* *Lady Hamilton* was made in America but with a British cast and seemed in all
respects a British film.

enjoyed *The Ghost Train*, however, with Arthur Askey and even his *Backroom Boy*, in which he broke away from an obscure BBC job—his sole duty was to sound the Greenwich time 'pips'—into a series of adventures which ended with him luring the German fleet to destruction. Will Hay had also been established before the war, usually in the company of the 'fat boy', Graham Moffat, and the 'old man', Moore Marriott, and one of his best comedies, *Where's that Fire?*, enlivened the first Winter of the war. It was followed by several less successful, like *The Ghost of St. Michael's*, *The Black Sheep of Whitehall* and *The Goose Steps Out*, which involved Will Hay, in his favourite role of incompetent schoolteacher, becoming an instructor at a Nazi spy school. *The* film comedian of the war, however, was probably George Formby. At least one George Formby film with a title like *Come on George*, and full of songs, notorious for double meanings, and simple slapstick comedy, was released every year and together they must have made a significant contribution to morale.

Most really bad wartime films have long since been forgotten but two are still remembered. *Dangerous Moonlight*, about a pianist driven from his Polish homeland by German bombs, released in September 1941, became a tremendous box-office draw, despite its silly story and feeble production, because of its theme music, *The Warsaw Concerto*, which became world famous, and still, as one wartime teenager admits, 'conjures up the war atmosphere for me more than any old newsreel'. An American film which enjoyed even greater success about the same time was *Mrs. Miniver*, a typical Hollywood view of Britain in 1940 and of the trials of an upper-middle class family, complete with servants and American accents. Most British cinema-goers now look back on its sham heroics and phoney characters with irritation and embarrassment.

During the war British films, not merely overseas but at home, began for the first time to compete effectively with their American rivals. This was partly because, until December 1941, American films had virtually ignored the war and when Hollywood did begin to produce war films they seemed crude and simple stuff to British cinema-goers with first-hand experience of war and with their taste educated by films like *Target for Tonight*. Even my generation—my sixteenth birthday was a few days after Pearl Harbour—laughed aloud at the boastful heroics of American films, and speculated why, if the Japanese were so stupid and contemptible, in real life they always seemed to win. We particularly delighted, too, in the regular appearances of 'the Hollywood Jap', a stock shot of an enemy fighter pilot who at some point in every American war film was sure to be seen slumping forward as the bullets from some fearless American struck home. Only one American war film was a real success in British cinemas, *A Yank in the R.A.F.*, the attraction clearly being the R.A.F. rather than the Yank.* Only after the war did the Americans cease to under-estimate both the enemy and the public and begin to produce first-class war films, like *Twelve O'clock High*.

But in one field Hollywood remained supreme throughout the war, the musical, and if it was British films which showed what war was like, it was American ones which demonstrated how to escape from it. Most such films were, by their nature, unmemorable, but some are still remembered with gratitude for the light and cheerfulness they brought to a drab world. One London housewife felt that two Ginger Rogers films of 1940 (probably *Fifth Avenue Girl* and *Primrose Path*) made up for having to stand 'for about an hour on the cold pavement, in the black-out', and the 'lovely music and dancing' of Rita Hayworth's *Sally* compensated for 'aching feet after standing hours waiting to get into the crowded cinemas'. A Nottingham teacher found the four-mile walk home through the black-out well worth while after any Nelson Eddy and Jeanette Macdonald film, especially *Maytime*. A former land girl, then aged twenty, remembers her first visit to an Evesham cinema. 'We went after a frightfully bleak day on sprout picking and mainly because the cinema was warm and there was no fire in our "digs". Carmen Miranda cavorted around in a fruit-and-flowers hat, against a background of exotic scenery and tropical heat. We sang about

> "Having a heatwave,
> A tropical heatwave".

Sunshine, cheerfulness, good nature—these were the ingredients for which the British cinema-goer looked in American films during the war, and he was rarely disappointed, for this was the time of 'good clean fun' with a happy ending guaranteed. Mickey Rooney in *The Courtship of Andy Hardy*, Judy Garland in *The Wizard of Oz*, Deanna Durbin in *Spring Parade* and *It's a Date*, Betty Grable in *Down Argentina Way*, cartoons like *Pinocchio*, *Fantasia* and *Dumbo*, and 'crazy' films, like *Hellzapoppin*—all these helped British women to forget ration books and clothes coupons for a few hours. Above all, Bing Crosby, Bob Hope and Dorothy Lamour, together or singly, provided gaiety and glamour in light-hearted song-and-dance and comedy films like *Pardon My Sarong*, *Beyond the Blue Horizon* and their famous series of "Road" films, from *The Road to Singapore* (released before 1942, it need hardly be said) to *The Road to Zanzibar*, *The Road to Morocco* and many more. A few 'straight' films from Hollywood also did well in Britain. 1943, according to one cinema group, 'was the year of *Random Harvest* and *For Whom the Bell Tolls*', both based on famous books, and one of the

* I cannot remember hearing of this film, nor have any of my informants mentioned it, but it broke box-office records in 1942.

few successful U.S. war films, *The Sullivans*, perhaps because its theme was universal—a family smitten by the loss of all its sons.

Without any doubt, the outstanding film of the war, from either side of the Atlantic, was *Gone With the Wind*, or 'G.W.T.W.', as it soon became known. This was one Hollywood epic which really merited those favourite adjectives of the trailers, Gigantic, Colossal and Terrific, and it was also, a great draw in those black and white days, in Glorious Technicolor. Besides its spectacular battles and torrid love scenes, what really caught the public imagination was what then seemed its unbelievable length of 3 hours 48 minutes. Jokes about *Gone With the Wind* were common even before the film reached this country. It was said that people leaving the cinema had aged so much they had not been recognised by their friends and that those British actors who had discovered pressing engagements in the United States in 1939 had 'gone with the wind up'. In April 1940 *Punch* suggested that people would soon be tired of the mere title and its review in May was simply headlined 'You know what'. After this build-up *Gone With the Wind* ought perhaps to have turned out a disappointment, especially as it opened during the depressing Norwegian campaign. Instead it proved a smash hit, running continuously in the West End until D Day, and going the rounds of the circuits for years afterwards.* It caused no surprise when, at the height of the blitz, with thirty fire engines rushing round Leicester Square, not a soul moved from the queue outside the Empire Cinema. Seeing *Gone With the Wind* is an experience which stands out in everyone's memory. A London nurse remembers several warnings during the performance she attended but, of course, no one left. For a South Benfleet housewife, who saw it in 1942, it is her only recollection of going to the pictures during the entire war. A BBC secretary who went to see it one Saturday afternoon in September 1940 was astonished on leaving the cinema to find the sky flaming red over the docks and to hear the bombs and guns. She had been so enthralled by the film that she had not noticed the start of the blitz. A Scottish journalist who saw the film in Edinburgh early in 1941 felt the climax, during the great Fire of Atlanta of 1864, seemed 'very small beer' after the recent newsreels of the fire raid on the City. A group of Worcestershire land girls, struck by the scene 'where Scarlett tore up radishes and swore "As God is my witness I'll never be hungry again" ', constantly recalled it 'when we were radish-pulling or nibbling raw vegetables to allay our hunger'. A farmer living near Canterbury will never forget the afternoon he took his wife to see it: 'As we came out of the cinema planes started dropping bombs. We all lay down and ... a machine gun bullet ripped a bit out of my ankle. . . . When things

*In 1969 the same film, in a larger screen version, was again drawing the crowds in London.

quietened down we proceeded to Rose Lane to get our car . . . but there was no garage, nor Rose Lane! So we started to walk the four miles back to the farm . . . Next day . . . I searched the ruins of the garage and looking at the ruins of the walls I saw my car perched on top and in it were my riding breeches, for which I had given quite a number of coupons. The car was a total wreck. So much for *Gone With the Wind*.'

The live theatre produced during the war nothing comparable to *Gone With the Wind*, which was described as the *Chu Chin Chow* of the second world war. The West End theatres were slower to recover from their enforced closure in 1939 than the cinemas. *The Dancing Years*, perhaps the outstanding stage success of the war, had gone on tour and only returned to London in 1942, while other box-office hits, like Emlyn Williams's *The Corn is Green*, also disappeared into the provinces. When the theatres did reopen the great demand was for undemanding comedy and as the stalls filled with subalterns on leave from France 'doing a show', most theatres took on a distinctly Great War look. The first great wartime success was *Black Velvet*, and other revues followed in rapid succession, their simple format, lending itself to topical sketches and requiring only simple sets, being ideally suited to wartime conditions. *Sweet and Low* in 1943 and *Sweeter and Lower* in 1944 with, according to *Punch*, Hermione Gingold as 'the queen of all stirrup-pumpers', are still remembered, but few now recall many items from such shows as *All Clear, Lights Up, Come Out to Play*, or, in October 1940 when time-bombs had given the word a double meaning, *Diversion*. Officious wardens, the Home Guard, the removal of the railings, women 'clippies', these were the staple subjects at first, though later the war intruded less. 'What people want', wrote *Punch* in February 1940, commenting on a sketch about evacuated children in a country vicarage, 'is a show which will make them laugh.' But laughter had to be of a suitably decorous kind and *Punch* was very severe on the wartime coarseness already creeping into entertainments like *Funny Side Up*.

The blitz made a far greater mark upon the theatre than on the cinema, since people were reluctant to go far from home. With their audiences gone, many London theatres simply closed down and transferred their productions to the provinces. Only the ladies of the Windmill, a great wartime institution, faithfully undressed throughout the blitz, the theatre's proud motto, 'We never closed', being amended by the wits to 'We never clothed'. New plays were launched outside London, moving to the West End after May 1941 when the London theatre got gradually back to normal, though last performances still started at six in the evening so that one was out again by nine. Until well on in the war, when there was a vogue for serious, 'talk' plays about the brave new world after the war, like Priestley's *Desert Highway*, most successful plays were either of the very lightest kind or revivals of established classics. Shakespeare, Shaw, Ibsen, Congreve, Sheridan, Wilde, Barrie, Maugham—rarely was there a time when the work of one or more of these was not to be seen somewhere on the London stage. Two new productions reviewed in the same week in February 1943 neatly reflect the taste of the period: a farce called *A Little Bit of Fluff* and Bernard Shaw's *Androcles and the Lion*. The chief 'middlebrow' entertainment consisted of thrillers and comedy-thrillers. Several Agatha Christie crime plays had long runs, notably *Ten Little Niggers*, and people also flocked to see *Arsenic and Old Lace* in December 1942, *Pink String and Sealing Wax* in September 1943, and *Uncle Harry* in April 1944. Other plays which people still remember were *Acacia Avenue*, the musical *The Lisbon Story*, which opened in 1943, and revivals of such undemanding pre-war successes as *The Merry Widow*, *The Quaker Girl* and *Lilac Time*. The Players Theatre, which re-created a Victorian after-supper cabaret in a basement in the West End under the title *Late Joys*, had a great vogue. Although the theatre warned members to 'Bring rug and cushion if you wish to stay the night', all mention of current events was forbidden. Any reference to 'the war' was swiftly followed by the explanation that the speaker must mean 'that little affair with Bismarck' or the 'fight against the scourge of mankind . . . Cetewayo, King of the Zulus'.

The most successful new comedy, later made into an even better film, was Noël Coward's *Blithe Spirit*, about the embarrassments of a handsome young author whose first wife inconsiderately returned from the dead to threaten his second marriage, a theme considered slightly shocking in 1941. *Blithe Spirit* ignored the war but the other great comedy hit of the period, *While the Sun Shines*, by Terence Rattigan, first produced in December 1943, was set in wartime London. It dealt, with a now distasteful blend of snobbery and improbability, with the complications which occur in the flat of a millionaire earl, serving as an ordinary seaman in the Navy, when the night before his wedding to the daughter of a hard-up duke, a U.S. Air Force officer, a Free French lieutenant, and the earl's former mistress, now working as a typist in the Air Ministry, arrive in rapid succession. Although in every way lightweight and conventional, the play still has a certain period interest in its references to Spam, the Beveridge Report and the razor blade shortage. A year later Rattigan followed this success with *Love in Idleness*, an even more snobbish comedy, given a poor reception by the critics. It ran for only six months, a sad come-down after the 1,000 performances of *While the Sun Shines*.

The real atmosphere of the middle of the war is well captured in Rattigan's only serious play, *Flarepath*, first produced in August 1942 and set in the lounge of a Lincolnshire hotel where the wives of a bomber

crew wait for their husbands to return from operations. References to
the shortage of whisky and phrases like 'pukka gen' set the play firmly
in its period; when one character tears up a vital love letter, the hotel
proprietor admonishes him sternly: 'There's such a thing as salvage.'
What gave the play its theatrical force was the constant nearness of
disaster, with a splendid dramatic climax when a bomber is heard to
crash on take-off off-stage. This incident led to controversy as to whether
the play might not be harmful to the morale of 'sweethearts, wives and
mothers whom the mere indications of such happenings may fill with
alarm and despondency', but the play soon attracted crowded houses
and ran for eighteen months. Equally successful, though now less
remembered, was Esther McCracken's *No Medals*, in praise of the
wartime housewife, which opened in October 1944 and ran well into
peacetime.

The dispersal of so many companies made the war years for provincial
theatre-lovers the richest period of their lives, and not merely large
cities but remote districts like North Wales and the Lake District
also benefited. One woman living in Newcastle-on-Tyne found on
reaching London in January 1945 that she had already seen every new
play in the West End. A young mother in Nottingham noted in her
diary about a matinée of *No Time For Comedy*, with Rex Harrison and
Lilli Palmer, in February 1941: 'Excellent play, beautiful acting. War
had provided us with at least this luxury.' In July at a far smaller place,
Kendal in Westmorland, it also provided her with the chance to see
*Thunder Rock* acted by the Old Vic Theatre company, and in the following
month, back in Nottingham, she saw *Dear Brutus* with an all-star cast,
headed by John Gielgud and Roger Livesey, 'the chance of a theatre-
going lifetime'.

Not all wartime theatre-going memories are on this plane. A Portsmouth district nurse's chief recollection of visiting the King's Theatre at
Southsea, which had a high reputation, is of sitting in the ninepenny
upstairs seats, eating crisps, in the absence of sweets, ready to run down
eighty steps to the shelter. And for one woman, then newly married
and in her early twenties, *The Gondoliers*, which she saw the D'Oyly
Carte Opera company perform one day in 1942, will always have a
particular poignancy: 'It was only about two months after my husband
had gone overseas', she remembers, 'and one song was so appropriate
I sat and cried:

> "And O my darling, O my pet,
> Whatever else you may forget
> In yonder isle beyond the sea,
> Do not forget you've married me." '

# MUSIC WHILE YOU WORK

'This coming week there will be, twice every day, half an hour's music meant especially for factory workers to listen to as they work.'

*Radio Times*, 26th June 1940

Nothing can more rapidly recall the whole atmosphere of the war than the popular songs of that time. *MacNamara's Band* carries me instantly back to a stuffy Scottish barrack room, smelling of boot polish and blanco, in February 1944, and a then teenager in Central Scotland feels the same about *Jealousy*. 'I have only to hear this . . . and the whole atmosphere of the war floods over me, with memories of some of the partners with whom I danced this tango.' For a former land girl in Worcestershire, '*Moonlight Becomes You* recalls when three of us were sent to move the mounds of rubble and chippings which had been left on the roadside. We were armed with pickaxes and huge shovels, and were aching from head to foot by about lunchtime. The girl driving the tractor with the loads sang *Moonlight Becomes You* all that dreary day. People hung out of passing cars to gape at us; one man yelled at us that we would have done credit to the Kremlin.' The girls also sang *Whispering Grass*, wryly quoting the sentimental words about 'the wind and rain upon your face' on wet and cold days and *You are my Sunshine* on brighter ones, 'the words often changed to *You are my Woodbine*, thus illustrating the cigarette shortage'.* Another woman, then working in a village shop in Norfolk, is back again, an excited teenager, at the weekly dance in a barn, full of Americans, whenever she hears *Who's Taking you Home Tonight?*, always played as the last waltz. A Nottingham schoolteacher has equally happy memories of Scout dances, at one of which she met her husband. Their usual 'last waltz' together was *I'll See You Again*. The Dunkirk period was irremovably fixed in the mind of one young Scottish male student by the tune *East of the Sun*,

* This unofficial version was widely sung. The text current in a Hull school at this time was as follows:

'You are my sunshine,
My double woodbine
My box of matches
My Craven A.'

sung by Frank Sinatra, and tunes *Tuxedo Junction* and *In the Mood*, both associated with Glenn Miller, recall to a woman then living in Northern Ireland 'the flying feet' of visiting troops jitterbugging in Irish dance halls. Another Glenn Miller admirer, now a housewife in Andover, remembers his versions of *Little Brown Jug, Moonlight Serenade* and *Pennsylvania Six, Five, Thousand*, while *A Sleepy Lagoon* brings back concerts in her munitions factory near Reading, where one young man known as 'the Theale Bing Crosby' regularly sang this as his favourite number. A woman then aged eighteen, and living in Palmers Green, has similar memories of *Apple Blossom Time* at the 'Royal' dance-hall, Tottenham, and the 'Paramount' in Tottenham Court Road. A Sidcup woman then in her late thirties, with two young children, remembers that each morning as they emerged from the shelter to find their house still standing, though often a little more scarred, her family would sing, like many more, *There'll Always be an England*. To a Glasgow factory worker *When They Sound the Last All Clear* recalls 'the blitz on March 13th 1941 when our firm fairly got it. Seventy to eighty of our mates were wiped out; we dug them out for a fortnight afterwards.'

For most civilians Vera Lynn singing *Yours* can equally turn back the years. Is it, one wonders, only nostalgia that makes the music of the popular songs of that time seem more tuneful, the words more comprehensible, the feeling behind them more genuine than of any since? Certainly the dance music of the war years was enjoyed by all age groups, and respectable middle-aged citizens were not ashamed to be caught humming the hit tunes of the moment in those years when 'popular' music was truly popular.

To each period of the war belongs its own tune. In the last uneasy months of peace the cinema organists, those great barometers of popular taste, were entertaining their audiences with *Two Sleepy People, Begin the Beguine, Three Little Fishes* and *Little Sir Echo*. In May *The Beer Barrel Polka*, better known as *Roll Out the Barrel*, began its remarkable career. It was soon being sung by drunks blundering home in the blackout, by frightened shelterers as the bombs fell, by shipwrecked sailors adrift on rafts—even by Winston Churchill in high spirits. To the first winter of the war belong patriotic songs like the disastrous *We're Gonna Hang Out the Washing on the Siegfried Line, Lords of the Air* and songs on the theme of separation, like *Wish Me Luck as You Wave Me Goodbye, We'll Meet Again* and *There's a Boy Coming Home on Leave*. The cinema was a source of many cheerful numbers: *Pinocchio* had everyone singing *When You Wish Upon a Star* and *Give a Little Whistle, Gulliver's Travels* made popular *It's a Hap-Hap-Happy Day* and *The Wizard of Oz, Over the Rainbow*. As the blitz began, in September 1940, the tunes one heard everywhere were *A Nightingale Sang in Berkeley Square* and *The Last*

*Time I Saw Paris.* 1941, a gloomy year, was on the whole a period of jolly tunes—*I've Got Sixpence, Amapola, I Yi-Yi-Yi-Yi-I Like You Very Much* and *Kiss the Boys Goodbye.* This was considered faintly shocking, as the singer was bidding farewell to her boy friends on marrying her 'sugar daddy', but *Room Five Hundred and Four,* where the couple concerned had spent a blissful, married, weekend, restored the respectability balance. The same could hardly be said of the most enduring tune of 1941, *Bless 'Em All,* often heard in a bawdier version, but the song of the year was *Yours,* its supremacy in the record shops only being challenged by *The White Cliffs of Dover.* 1942 was the year of *That Lovely Weekend, I Know Why, Some Sunny Day* (when, audiences were assured, 'I know we'll meet again'), and the still popular *White Christmas.* Other successful American tunes were *Chattanooga Choo Choo, Deep in the Heart of Texas,* and one of those 'crazy' songs that suddenly caught the public fancy, *Elmer's Tune.* My own favourite wartime tune also belongs to this year, *Don't Sit Under the Apple Tree,* and there was one of those ambiguous titles which caused the BBC so much heart-searching, *Why Don't We Do This More Often?* The ever vigilant Corporation, sensing sin, were said to have amended the second line from 'just what we're doing tonight' to 'just what we're doing today'. 1943 brought other problems with *It Can't be Wrong,* and *Ev'ry Night About this Time,* but most hits of that year were safely sentimental: *You Were Never Lovelier, My Heart and I,* and *Don't Get Around Much Any More.* The stage success, *The Lisbon Story,* popularised *Pedro, the Fisherman* and an American film contributed the strident number '*Murder', he says, every time we kiss.* This year, too, people began to look forward to the end of the black-out with *I'm Gonna Get Lit Up When the Lights Go Up in London* and two years later the singer who had made it famous was duly broadcast singing it, champagne glass in hand, from a balcony above a lighted Piccadilly Circus.

A more surprising success was the English version of *Lili Marlene,* taken over by British troops from the Germans in the desert after the Ministry of Information had tried and failed to commission a suitable British rival to it. While the V.1s clattered over London in 1944 the crooners were, rather prematurely, singing *Shine on Victory Moon,* and troops in Normandy, tuning in to the Forces Programme, were being treated to some of the silliest songs of the war, *Mairzy Doats and Dozy Doats* and *Is You Is or Is You Ain't My Baby?* 1945 was, musically speaking, even less distinguished. In June, the month after victory in Europe, the best selling records were *Don't Fence Me In* and *We'll Gather Lilacs,* joined in July by *I'm Beginning to See the Light.* After that, at least so far as the songwriters were concerned, it was peace.

Although there was a spate of songs based directly on the war in the first

**'Your duty now is war work'**

Painting aircraft interior.

Fastening fabric on aircraft wing.

Factory-outing, wartime style. A party of munition workers watching a demonstration of mortars they helped to build.

Tank factory in North East England.

Land girls: Propaganda.

Land girls: Reality.

Women coal-heavers.

Careless talk.

War Work.

**Some wartime advertisements**

Save money.

Save coal.

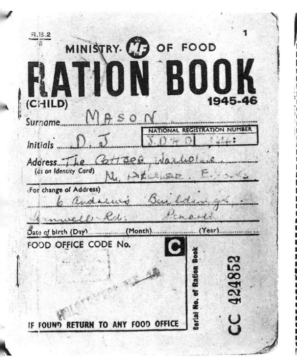

Ration book.

Clothing coupons.

**Some wartime documents**

Meat coupons.

Identity card.

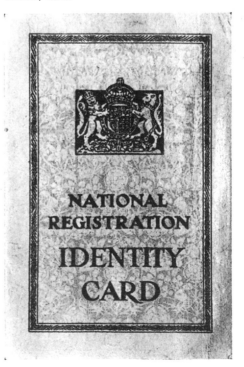

**Some wartime sights**

'No cigarettes' sign in Bristol.

Cardboard wedding cake cover in confectioner's window.

The 'V' sign on a pub door. (A plentiful supply of beer was a rarity, worth advertising.)

### Time-off

Dancing on Plymouth Hoe, July 1941. (Note uniformed musicians, and barrage balloon.)

Visiting a shot-down Messerschmitt. (The usual charge for a close inspection was 6d for the local Spitfire Fund.)

V.E. Day procession in Whitehall. (The young men in civilian clothes, an unusual sight, were university students.)

**Victory**

The end of the civilians' war. A bonfire in a Croydon Street, V.E. night.

few months—twenty-five had appeared by the end of November 1939—few really caught on. Who now remembers such black-out-prompted numbers as *Crash! Bang! I Want to Go Home*; *Till the Lights of London Shine Again*; *Follow the White Line*; and *They Can't Black-out the Moon?* *Even Hitler Had a Mother*, banned by the Lord Chamberlain before the war, and *Will Santa Claus Wear a Tin Helmet?* were other titles typical of the early part of the war and some mothers were moved to tears by *Goodnight, Children Everywhere*, written 'with a tender thought to all evacuated children'. The services inspired many short-lived songs, like *Oh, ain't it grand to be in the Navy*—written by a civilian, one suspects—*Reckless Jeff of the R.A.F.*, *Somewhere in France with You* and —only too prophetic as it turned out—*We Won't be Long out There*.

But songs tied to some topical event rarely, to use a post-war term, 'made the charts'. The BBC's list of the most popular records during the blitz months, for example, does not include *Billy Brown of London Town*, about how that heroic citizen 'stood up and saved the Town when London Bridge was falling down', or *The King is Still in London*—'cos it's where he wants to be'. The only anti-German song of merit was Noël Coward's classic *Don't Let's Be Beastly to the Germans*, though *Der Führer's Face* had a brief vogue in January 1943, a vulgar novelty number which ended with a promise to 'heil'—accompanied by the blowing of a 'raspberry'—'right in the Führer's face'. The Italians, being generally despised, were considered safer game. When Mussolini's troops were driven back by the Greeks, the Decca company were quick off the mark with the record *Oh! What a Surprise for the Duce* (*they do say, he's had no spaghetti for weeks*) and later in the war another songwriter ingeniously commemorated a British advance with the remarkable lyric: *Where do we go from here? Now that We've Captured Bardia*. (The answer, judging from past British form in the desert in those pre-Montgomery days, was probably 'Backwards'.) Several successful songs were based on a phrase that caught the public imagination, like *Coming in on a Wing and a Prayer*, in 1943, credited to a pilot landing a badly damaged aircraft, and *Praise the Lord and Pass the Ammunition* about a 'sky-pilot' or ship's chaplain who had broken off a service to feed the guns.

Almost as effective in recapturing the past are the names of the bands that played these wartime tunes. Several times a day, live or on records, the BBC broadcast programmes of dance music by orchestras led by Jack Payne, Harry Roy, Geraldo, Joe Loss, Victor Silvester, Billy Cotton, Mantovani, Jack Jackson and, perhaps most popular of all, Henry Hall. On one famous occasion in Bristol at a concert for war charities Henry Hall and Sir Adrian Boult changed places and conducted each other's orchestra, with great success.

Formal dances were not popular during the war. One Birmingham girl found that 'Dances were pale ghosts of their pre-war selves. No evening dresses and a shortage of partners. It became quite usual for two girls to partner each other. Have you ever imagined doing the tango with your sister?' But the local 'hop' had never been fuller or gayer. The entry which one Gloucestershire office worker made in her diary for 25th October 1939 could have been written at any time during the next six years by thousands of other girls of her age: 'Dance at Town Hall, Cheltenham. Packed out with servicemen. . . . I had a jolly good time, made some dates which I shan't keep and was jolly glad we had managed between us village girls to have a taxi home.' Getting home became even more of a problem as the war went on, with late-night buses withdrawn and no private cars on the road, while servicemen often had to be back in camp by '23.59 hours' and civilian males tended to be despised as escorts. A Hampshire farmer remembers bitterly: 'The girls had eyes only for the boys in uniform.' A then teenage girl from Leyland recalls how 'We knew some civvy farm workers. . . . We always went into Preston Saturday and Sunday. They did too and when we'd left our boy friends, R.A.F. men, we'd look for them. They'd set off and walk just to annoy us, saying "Oh, you've got R.A.F. men—walk by yourselves". Scared, we were, of the dark too.'

The great London dance halls were full throughout the war. For one London girl, seventeen when the war began, 'my fairyland and escape route to relaxation were my almost weekly trips to the Hammersmith Palais. Here I unwound in an atmosphere of gaiety, bright lights, friendliness, humour, all embalmed in the colourful drapes, décor and scintillating music which Lou Preager provided. For the young it was a paradise shut away from the stark reality of the bitter world outside. How I loved those evenings. I travelled twenty-nine stations on the Underground to get there and twenty-nine to get home again. The girls always managed to look colourful and attractive, and the servicemen of all nationalities appeared suave and handsome in their varied uniforms. We danced the night away jiving, jitter-bugging, waltzing, with a rumba and a tango thrown in. . . . It was wonderful, wholesome fun. I met some of the nicest lads I have ever known there.' 'The Lyceum, London, became a focal point for teenagers to meet servicemen of every nationality', remembers an Ilford girl. 'I . . . knew three girls who met their respective future English, Norwegian and Dutch husbands there. It was terribly crowded, smoky and dimly lighted.' But at local dances, they 'invariably had to make do with records and there were hardly any refreshments'. Invariably, too, there was either a shortage of partners or an embarrassing surplus, for while there were military units stationed in the district the dance halls overflowed with men in uniform only to empty overnight during the long months when they went overseas, so that, as one twenty-year-old girl Food Office clerk found, 'you often had to dance with boys of sixteen and seventeen or else your girl friend'.

Yet, for girls who loved dancing, the war was a happy time. A then teenage girl living near Tunbridge Wells observed how 'Dances altered according to the latest troops. The London Irish were good at reels. The Newfoundlanders brought a few Canadian ideas with barn dances—similar to our country dances, but oh the bumps we suffered in learning the jive when the Yanks arrived.' An endless variety of young soldiers passed in procession through our lives, a woman of the same age living near Glasgow remembers. 'Polish troops were stationed in our village and with their dark good looks and gallant manners wrought a certain amount of havoc with the sentiments of the local girls. . . . One evening at our local Palais de Danse, I was invited to dance by a handsome Pole. The dance, as it turned out was a Highland Schottische and I was not completely sure of its intricacies myself. To explain it to somebody with only a limited knowledge of English was just too much. However, my dancing partner solved the problem by making rather wild and exuberant charges from one end of the dance hall to the other, and as he was wearing army boots, most of the dancers gave way before this performance'.

Meanwhile in East Anglia one girl in her early twenties, living near Ipswich, was often cycling to as many as four dances a week. 'All the villages ran at least one a week and frequently more', she remembers, 'endeavouring to stagger them from neighbourhood to neighbourhood... I danced with Czechs (oh, those marathon Viennese-style waltzes), Dutchmen, Scots, Americans, Poles, French and, of course, men from all over England, Wales and Ireland—and even a New Zealander—an international initiation into all styles of dancing. It was truly the time of my life from that point of view as I adored dancing.' A London girl discovered that merely to venture into another part of London might produce an entirely different type of partner. 'You never knew with whom you were going to dance . . . I remember a dance at Putney that was attended by a number of New Zealand Air Force officers, whereas at Wimbledon our partners were American soldiers. During the raids on London I went to a dance where there were a number of Canadian Fire Service men who had volunteered to come to England to help the London A.F.S. men.'

One of the strange results of the war was that the most quiet and decorous resorts suddenly took on the character of garrison towns. The older residents, who had retired there for peace, might grumble, but the younger generation were delighted at the change. A Bournemouth girl, sixteen when the war began, found that her social life was totally transformed, by the arrival of 'thousands of Australian, Canadian, New Zealand and Rhodesian troops'.

They filled those stuffy hotels to the brim . . . with their youth and gaiety . . . and I loved it. So did many other girls of my age. Gone were the dreary evenings spent at dances when there were never enough partners to go round. Now one was besieged with partners in their dark and light blue air force uniforms, one would only get half way round the floor before being partnered by someone else. This "excuse me" system seemed the only way to share the girls around. But this, although delightful, brought another problem. Our shoes wore out too quickly, and ate up our clothing coupons with alarming speed. After the dance was over, one could be fought over by two or even three admirers, so taking our pick from the young man of our choice, we would be wined and dined in a first class hotel or restaurant which had been formerly out of bounds for ordinary girls like us. If this is war, I thought, why am I enjoying it so much? These brief friendships and love affairs were sweet and fleeting. I must have seen hundreds of snapshots of loved ones treasured and warm from a battledress pocket, to be shown with pride from many remote places overseas . . . I was always genuinely interested because I wanted to travel myself. They came and went without tiresome farewells, and we did not wonder or worry too much about being stood up on a date. There was always a fresh face to take over, another whirl of gaiety before they, too, moved on.

Later the life of the young women of Bournemouth became even more exciting with the arrival of the Americans. 'Almost every night found me dancing on an excellent but crowded floor to one or another of America's top line orchestras. Coca Cola flowed as champagne, there was plenty to eat, it was like finding an oasis after a long trek through a burning desert.'

A land girl, working near Evesham, and her friends 'cycled to a village dance, one evening a week, whatever the weather, about four miles away. There was a nearby Air Force station, so partners were plentiful. Later on, we were invited to sergeants' mess dances and American dances . . . The Americans fetched and delivered us home again in a large truck, and regaled us with lashings of beer, ice cream and cake. Jive was all the rage, and boogie-woogie. There was generally a scuffle at the end of the dance, rounding up missing members. On a Saturday there was a dance in the village, and our farmer used to tour the buildings round the hostel afterwards, tapping the couples with his walking stick and generally breaking up any romantic association.'

Most single girls probably had an equally gay time during the war, even those with boy friends in the Forces, the general feeling being that no admirer could reasonably object to a little harmless flirtation, particularly if he did not know about it. Nor, considering their dull and lonely lives, was it surprising that some servicemen's wives helped to swell the crowds on the dance floors. A shorthand typist living near Cheltenham who attended a dance where a wedding ring was found on the floor was amazed at the number of 'single girls' who immediately looked to see if it had fallen from its hiding place in handbag or handkerchief. Servicemen were even less inclined to be troubled by moral scruples. A young girl in Suffolk attended one Christmas dance where the 'lads' from a local unit had taken bets beforehand to see who could produce most pairs of panties next morning, the trophies being hung over the breakfast table like a line of washing.

But the prevailing atmosphere of wartime dances was one of innocent enjoyment and good fun. To make oneself look attractive before a dance, with everything from dancing shoes to lipstick hard to find, was to score another of those minor victories over Hitler that added up to high morale. Girls working long hours at unaccustomed manual labour still managed to find the energy to go dancing night after night; one wartime bus conductress from Billingham, County Durham, never used to miss a dance even when she had to be up at 5 a.m. next morning. The office of a Hereford filling factory, where a coach used to call after work to take the girls straight to local dances, took on the appearance of a beauty parlour. 'As it was a government department, discipline was rather lax', one employee remembers. 'Summer dresses were taken to work. . . . We washed our hair at lunchtime, set it in steel clips, then all afternoon in the office we covered our heads with scarves made into the turban style and several people went to have their eyebrows plucked by their colleagues or painted their nails.'

Wartime dances were held in some strange places. One evening, this woman remembers, they might be dancing in the huge ballrooms of old manor houses, taken over as American officers' messes, the next in Nissen huts on an R.A.F. station. A then nineteen-year-old clerk in a grocer's shop in Stonehaven attended a dance in the granary at a local distillery, which left them all with sore throats next day because of the dust from the grain. A Portsmouth district nurse remembers dancing beneath dim lights along the aisles between the counters, in an unblacked-out Marks and Spencers. A Dulwich woman recalls how 'My sister and I frequently went to dances held in the fire station; the engines were put into the back yard. If an Alert were sounded during the dance, one was suddenly left standing whilst all the men on duty rushed off to put on their jackets. The dancers were moved to the walls, the doors both ends rolled back and out roared the engines taking our partners with them. Mostly that was the last we saw of them.'

At the start of the war dance halls, like cinemas, had been closed by law, but soon they were allowed to reopen until 10 p.m., and then till 11 p.m., though the war intruded in such notices as: 'Gentlemen, your gas masks cannot be accepted in the cloakroom'. By December 1939 dance-floors were crowded everywhere, from expensive night-spots like the Dorchester and the Café de Paris to the Streatham Locarno and the Paramount, Tottenham Court Road, popular even during the blitz as it was below ground level.* The current desire to be cheerful was reflected in the demand for livelier dances. Quicksteps became more popular than waltzes, 'excuse me' dances became frequent, and noisy, novelty dances were accepted everywhere, like the *Palais Glide* and the *Lambeth Walk*, popularised by the Lupino Lane show, *Me and My Girl*, a pre-war hit revived in 1944. Wartime togetherness was epitomised by *Boomps-a-Daisy*, a jolly, vulgar dance—its climax involved the partners banging their bottoms together. For the first time in the more staid dance halls one also heard *Knees Up, Mother Brown*, banned by the BBC before the war, and by many managers, but as the music company concerned explained, 'Now we can get away with it. It's wartime.'

The black-out caused at first a general dislike of lowered lights during dances, but also inspired *The Black-out Stroll*, which consisted of walking steps, followed by 'the romp' of three short steps and a hop, and culminated in the lights going out, after which you found yourself dancing with someone else. The *Black-out Stroll*, unlike the black-out, was short lived, as was a dance invented during the first desert campaigns, the *Tuscana*, 'supposedly based on the Italians' way of fighting, i.e. one step forward, two steps back.' The *Hokey-Cokey* also gained general acceptance and the *Conga*, but the greatest innovation was 'jitter-bugging', which spread like wildfire with the arrival of the first Americans in 1942. Jitter-bugging, or jiving, really meant making up one's own dance from a few basic steps, and as demonstrated by the G.I.s, never noted for their bashfulness, involved violent gymnastics which sometimes ended up with swinging one's partner around with her feet off the floor. Other dancers often gathered round to watch a really skilled couple of jitter-bugs in action, and before long managements everywhere were forced to take down their 'No Jitter-bugging' notices.

In June 1940 the BBC introduced two special daily half-hour programmes for factory workers at 10.30 a.m. and 3 p.m., when production normally began to flag. *Music While You Work* was before long a national institution—it ran until 1967. Almost every famous band played for the programme at some time, and at first 'vocal numbers' were popular, only to be dropped when it was realised that many girls stopped work to write down the words. At other times of the day, factory workers provided their own amusement and a Rotherham girl remembers up to

* The Café de Paris was bombed in March 1941 with the loss of thirty-four lives.

twenty different tunes being sung at once in her factory, usually including *If I had my Way, This is a Lovely Way to Spend an Evening* and *Tonight*.

Ernest Bevin was a strong supporter of music in factories, and it was partly due to his encouragement that ENSA began to provide entertainments for civilian workers as well as for servicemen. ENSA—the letters stood for Entertainments National Service Association—had been set up on the outbreak of war by the West End theatrical producer, Basil Dean, and its earliest concert party gave its first performance to the troops only one week later. Its first dinner-hour show for factory workers was at Woolwich Arsenal in July 1940 and was attended by Ernest Bevin and broadcast. (The loud 'ping pong' noises, heard on the air as Bevin shifted his considerable weight on the metal table on which he stood, were at the time one of the minor mysteries of the war.)

Basil Dean was 'anxious that ENSA should not be regarded as a giant foxhole' and the Ministry of Labour were certainly no less anxious. In 1942 it even proposed to call-up all chorus girls aged between twenty-one and twenty-four, the very years when their charms were greatest, though after protests the girls were saved. But deferment for ENSA performers was by no means guaranteed, and many of the criticisms of ENSA which were heard simply reflected the fact that there was not enough talent to go round. Many top-class stars did in fact work for ENSA, like George Formby, who gave a lead by performing at the enormous ordnance factory at Chorley at both midday and midnight, and the average show, if undistinguished, was at least adequate. I can still remember two I saw in the Army early in 1944. One, with Sybil Thorndike, was undoubtedly too good for its audience; the other was a typical 'end of the pier' show, which was talked about for days afterwards. Other people have agreeable memories of ENSA productions like *Night Must Fall* and *Nine till Six*, a popular choice because it had no men in the cast. But some shows were clearly abysmal. After one in Manchester one man jumped on the stage and shouted, 'Three cheers for the audience.' A woman then working in a radar components factory in Surrey remarks, 'About ENSA, we had to endure them about once a month and endure it was.' A factory scientist in a tank factory in Lancaster told one journalist in 1942: 'There have been so many bad ones that the name ENSA kills them.' Whoever was to blame for the poor reputation of ENSA it was not Basil Dean, who was highly critical of the sort of group which consisted of 'the raucous comedian perfunctorily snapping up his "feed" lines from the vamping pianist . . . the faded soprano with over-large dentures . . . the baritone with an air of Blackpool about him'. After seeing for himself a company arriving 'five minutes late, the women in untidy slacks . . . and the men in mufflers and caps', he issued an order that every ENSA party must wear evening dress or costume. It was also, he suggested, hardly tactful to begin by telling your hard-working audience what a sacrifice you were making in condescending to appear at all.

An almost worse problem was the comedians, constantly accused of being 'blue'. Dean himself dismissed on the spot one particularly blatant offender and the BBC was sufficiently troubled by similar complaints about vulgarity on the air to commission a special enquiry on the subject, which revealed that most people thought the present standards were 'about right'. But in army camps and factory canteens, many comedians did tend to assume that in wartime anything was acceptable. A then teenage girl remembers an ENSA concert in Andover which 'was pretty good but slightly blue—and we were sitting right next to an ex-school teacher of ours and her husband so even if we did get the point we didn't dare to laugh'.

Appearing in a factory canteen was far from easy, with one's best lines liable to be ruined by 'the incessant clatter of plates and dishes, knives and forks alternating with tramping feet and the sharp ping of the accurate check-takers', so that the £8 to £10 a week most ENSA performers earned was hardly lavish. The critics of ENSA were answered, too, by the steadily rising demand; by March 1941 a hundred parties were touring the factories and many more giving one-night stands in local halls, tickets being sold for as little as threepence or sixpence, to local servicemen or war workers. Even the poorer concerts probably did some good. One factory superintendent reported that output went up 5 per cent after each concert and a factory doctor at Chorley made the curious discovery that food consumption also rose during performances.

As the war went on there was a general increase in the nation's seriousness of purpose. 'The simplest entertainments', Basil Dean considered, 'were failing to meet the spiritual challenge of the hour' and in October 1940 ENSA also began to provide 'good music parties' in factories. These were rarely popular, the minds of the audience, Basil Dean decided, being conditioned to some more energetic response than mere listening, and many people have embarrassing memories of some string quartet playing gallantly away while their unappreciative listeners walked out or barracked the unfortunate performers. Evening concerts in a large hall or cathedral, catering for all the factories in the district, with tickets at a shilling a head, proved far more successful. For the first major concert, Sir John Barbirolli took the Hallé Orchestra to Wigan, and that month Basil Cameron conducted the London Symphony Orchestra in a performance in Stepney. As many of the audience had never heard good music before, it was soon realised that one must capture their interest at once with a really lively work, like the Overture to *Prince Igor*, the *Carnival Romain* and the *Hungarian March* from *The Damnation of*

*Faust.* Later works could safely be more demanding and an impromptu poll taken by Sir John Barbirolli showed that most factory workers particularly enjoyed Debussy, whose peaceful, harmonious music offered the greatest contrast to the usual factory noise. All the leading British orchestras played for ENSA at some time—the famous Boyd Neel Orchestra actually gave 300 ENSA concerts in a single year—and between October 1943 and May 1946 ENSA provided nearly 400 full-scale symphony concerts for war workers, a remarkable total by any test.

While providing serious music and drama was for ENSA something of a sideline, it was the main activity of CEMA, the Council for the Encouragement of Music and the Arts. Begun as a private venture in January 1940, CEMA was soon being backed by the Treasury, by 1942/43 to the tune of £100,000 a year, despite the scepticism of Ernest Bevin, who sturdily dismissed its output as 'too 'ighbrow'. Inevitably CEMA and ENSA became to some extent rivals, but there was room for both. In two years CEMA provided 2,500 concerts in villages and small towns, some with audiences of only twenty people, as well as 4,500 thirty-minute concerts in factory lunch hours or midnight dinner-breaks, with audiences of up to 7,000. The usual group consisted of a singer, violinist and pianist, though a few solo musicians bravely faced audiences alone. CEMA also helped to finance many larger national orchestras. In 1943 alone it backed nearly 300 symphony concerts by top class orchestras, attended by 350,000 people, providing a guarantee against loss, which, most encouragingly, was frequently not required.*

CEMA also bravely set out to take opera and ballet to audiences which had never seen either before, re-forming such famous companies as the Ballet Joost and the Ballet Rambert. For many people such performances are among their outstanding memories of the war. A wartime land girl remembers how 'in 1941, on a miserable November day, we saw the Anglo-Polish ballet in Cheltenham, with Alexis Racine dancing *The Spectre of the Rose*. It was my first visit to a ballet, and was the highlight of our lives for months to come.' A Bradford housewife was equally excited when the Carl Rosa Opera visited the town. To overcome black-out difficulties many concerts were held on Sunday afternoons. One young London girl, like many other music-lovers, particularly enjoyed those at the Cambridge Theatre run by Jay Pomeroy. 'It was here', she remembers, 'that I first heard Tchaikovsky's overture *Romeo and Juliet* and have loved the music ever since.' A Birmingham woman, then in her twenties, has another memory of Sunday afternoon concerts in the Town Hall. During quiet passages in the second half of the programme the starlings could be heard screeching and squawking as they settled down for the night on the roof.

* CEMA was succeeded after the war by the Arts Council.

The best known of all wartime concerts were those held at the National Gallery and Royal Exchange at lunch-time on weekdays. One typist in a City office still regrets the long queue for one in June 1942 which prevented her getting into the Royal Exchange to hear Myra Hess, but she did manage to hear Isobel Baillie, and a Jewish woman pianist, who it 'seemed . . . was expressing violently on the piano all her pent-up feelings, remembering the Jewish sufferings in Germany. The W.V.S. supplied us with a good cup of coffee, with synthetic cream, for sixpence after the concerts. It was a glamorous break for us during the bleak war.'

Much of CEMA's work, like ENSA's, consisted of providing, or encouraging, straight drama, through subsidies to provincial theatres or touring companies or through sponsoring groups of its own, especially for factory hostels, the aim being to provide each one with a play a month. 'Many members of these audiences have never seen a living actor on the stage before', CEMA claimed, and it was a common practice to explain the plot beforehand to enable them to follow it. Even with admission charges of 1s. or 2s., many plays 'broke even'; some, to general astonishment, even made a profit. Significantly, plays about the war were not wanted, for if the cinema's strength lay in its realism, the appeal of the theatre was its artificiality and remoteness from daily life. It was classics like *Arms and the Man, Twelfth Night* and *She Stoops to Conquer* to which audiences responded, while the greatest success of all was remote in every way from wartime Britain, *Hedda Gabler.*

The war was also a boom time for amateur entertainers, in spite of shortages which ranged from grease-paint to leading men. CEMA encouraged amateur talent with grants to local music societies and drama groups. ENSA was less enthusiastic, and Basil Dean knew of amateur casts of which the audience had expressed their opinion by walking out. It gave little help to amateur companies, but most in any case were only too happy to pay their own way, like a wartime bus conductress from Ilford who 'used to play in a small band composed of transport workers and we would visit gun sites Sunday evenings. If there was an Alert the hall would empty, the soldiers to their sites and we would take our tin hats and sit in the shelter or trench until the danger had passed and then resume.' A then newspaper reporter from Weymouth would go out 'almost each night doing troop shows...It used to be my invariable habit, being a typical greedy young teenager, to gravitate toward the nearest kitchen on arrival at the searchlight post, or whatever it was. Later, when I did more U.S. Army shows, I ate food that I had never seen or heard of before.' This girl's costume included a 'real Hawaiian grass skirt outfit,' and one of her wartime sacrifices was responding politely to 'all those corny jokes about lawn mowers at so many hundreds of shows'.

Amateur theatricals for civilians also flourished during the war. I can remember at Newbury a succession of wartime Christmas pantomimes produced by a local dancing school, which filled the largest hall in the town for a full week. The girls' costumes might be mainly unrationed curtain netting, the orchestra elderly, the comedians sixteen- or seventeen-year-old boys from the local Grammar School, but no one was disposed to be over-critical. When the male lead singer, awaiting call-up, sang *The Convoy Must Go Through* every heart responded when the comedians emerged from under the bed to point skywards and announce *Jerry's over!* the joke received a hearty laugh as did references to the villains who had broken into the royal palace and stolen a box of matches and the queen's margarine coupons.* I remember even better the colourful scenes of dancers whirling round to the music of *The Skaters' Waltz* or the *Rosamunde* overture, the very antithesis of the drab everyday life outside.

Many other people have similar memories. A Saxmundham, Suffolk, woman who organised village concerts with a local youth club nailed ten hob-nails under the toes of the dancers' tap-shoes as the usual metal plates were not available. A Liverpool housewife appeared, as a bride in an amateur play, in a white nightdress with a lace curtain for a veil. One resident of the Somerset village of Wanstrow, who took part in a Christmas pantomime there can still see, 'the rather pretty V.A.D.s we had dressed up as fairies in the net supplied for making plaster casts; and myself as the poor, deserted "widder woman" complete with orphan baby'—an appropriate role, since she was the local Billeting Officer. A Surrey housewife attended a typical wartime version of *Dick Whittington*. 'All went well until the fairy, one of the land girls, came out on cue, not airy-fairy but horsey-noisy. She had been standing waiting for her cue in her land army shoes as she was cold. It brought the house down.'

---

* Civilians almost always referred to the enemy as 'Jerry', despite attempts to popularise the grimmer-sounding name 'the Hun'. Noël Coward's *Don't Let's Be Beastly to the Germans* mentioned 'the Hun', as did an embarrassing mock-dialogue between *The Londoner and the Hun* performed by two comedians during the blitz, while martial-minded Home Guard commanders also favoured the term. One argued that it was wrong to call a German a Jerry 'since a Jerry was a useful object'.

# CAN I DO YOU NOW, SIR?

'Radio has become part of all our lives ... The BBC has to try to please everybody without offending anybody.'

*Radio Times*, 21st June 1940

When at nine o'clock every evening throughout the war the chimes of Big Ben introduced the news, they commanded instant silence. Many wartime children were puzzled because their normally indulgent parents insisted on absolute quiet at these times and in the home of one North-amptonshire girl, then aged ten, the chimes were removed from the family clock for the duration, to prevent their noise competing with Big Ben. The wireless day—the term 'radio' was then little used—built up towards this moment; members of the families separated by the war promised to remember each other as the chimes sounded; and a Big Ben Minute Association was founded, whose members promised to say a special prayer as each stroke rang out. In some homes an equal ritual surrounded the six o'clock news. A Manchester housewife remembers how her children automatically fell silent at it—they knew the bulletin might, indirectly, have news about their absent 'daddy'. For this was the first war in which everyone was able to learn of British victories—or, at first—defeats within minutes of the news being released, and to have 'heard it on the news' was always accepted as proof of an item's authenticity.

Pre-war BBC news bulletins had often seemed needlessly dull and, by agreement with the newspapers, the 'first news' had not been until 6 p.m. Now the content became far more interesting and there were frequent bulletins from 7 a.m. till midnight, with special 'news flashes' during other programmes for important items. From May 1940, when they began to give their names, the newsreaders became almost family friends. Crowds gathered whenever they appeared in public, and they were pursued by eager autograph-hunters, Alvar Lidell's signature, due to his unusual Christian name, being particularly in demand. Freddie Grisewood, affectionately known as 'Ricepud' to listeners to *The Kitchen Front*, John Snagge, who announced major events like the Fall of France or the D Day landings, and Bruce Belfrage, who carried on reading the nine o'clock news in October 1940, despite a bomb on Broadcasting

House, plainly heard by millions of listeners, all became national celebrities, as did war correspondents, like Richard Dimbleby, Frank Gillard and Wynford Vaughan Thomas, who sent back despatches from the battle fronts for *War Report* and *Into Battle*. The BBC also brought the war home to its listeners through broadcasts by eyewitnesses, both servicemen and civilians, about events like the attack on Coventry or the first thousand bomber raid on Cologne. As usual, the technical achievement involved was rarely appreciated though recording was still in its infancy and reporters had to take with them heavy and cumbrous disc-recording equipment or even a whole recording car. Apart from such inserts almost all programmes went out 'live' so that unfortunate speakers on the overseas service, broadcasting to countries with different times, often had to attend at the studio in the middle of the night.

The war gave a great stimulus to the semi-dramatised feature, based on real life. Some of these now have a distinctly dated sound, like *East Coast Convoy*, in January 1941; 'He's diving. And I'll bet ten quid against the dirty end of a deck mop it's a Jerry!' In *Women Hitting Back*, another typical feature, 'the Guide, or the Summoner ... or the Voice of Urgency, or Britannia' delivered himself of such sentiments as 'Nell Smith, what will you do? . . . Over your husband's prison camp, perhaps, British bombers fly deep into Germany. You can help to make that roar louder and longer.' But at their best such programmes, blending fiction, music and actuality, were immensely popular, like the still remembered *The Battle of Britain* transmitted in May 1941, which was full of frightened German voices shouting 'Achtung Schpitfeur' as a counterpoint to calm R.A.F. accents declaiming, 'Tally Ho' or 'Good Show'.

One of the most successful innovations was the five minutes of *The Kitchen Front*, broadcast at 8.15 every morning from June 1940. Introduced by the pleasant, friendly voice of Freddie Grisewood, the programme was an immediate success; the first week alone brought in 1,000 letters, plus many parcels of cake and other gifts from housewives who had tried out the broadcast recipes. *The Kitchen Front* made the name, too, of an even more famous wartime voice, the rich, reassuring, fruity tones, exuding good humour and commonsense, of the Radio Doctor, a British Medical Association official, Dr. Charles Hill, who had never, in fact, been in general practice, but soon became the G.P. everyone would have liked to have had.* The Radio Doctor caused Freddie Grisewood, a BBC man of pre-war vintage, many a headache. Often, Grisewood has admitted, he would look at the Radio Doctor's script and say, 'But Charles, you can't possibly say that over the air', only to be given the reply, 'Oh, can't I? Just you listen to me.' One of the

* Charles Hill—Lord Hill as he now is—later achieved the remarkable 'double' of becoming both Postmaster General and Chairman of the BBC.

Radio Doctor's favourite themes was the need for regularity in bodily habits and imitations of him talking about the bowels were a frequent turn at wartime concerts. At least one listener, then a young City typist, still remembers his praise of 'that humble black-coated worker, the prune'. 'Another of Boxing Day's little troubles is constipation', the Radio Doctor told listeners just after Christmas 1940. 'Too much food and too much arm-chair and the body's reply is "What I have I hold". . . . Visit the throne at the same time each day, whether you feel like it or not.' It was this direct, simple style, in striking contrast with the pomposity of many pre-war broadcasters, which captivated listeners—that and the Radio Doctor's obvious humanity, revealed in June 1943, for instance, in this tribute to babies. 'I am old-fashioned enough to believe that no home is really complete without one. . . . It's upon those round, gurgling, dribbling articles, upon the food and fresh air and care we give 'em, that the future of this old country of ours will depend. Up the babies.'

Another popular aid to good health was *Up in the Morning Early*, later renamed *The Daily Dozen*, and broadcast after the 7 a.m. news every morning. A Chingford woman, then a young office worker, remembers her daily ritual as soon as she heard that lively signature tune, *Up in the Morning Bright and Gay*. 'A brisk male voice would ask me to fetch a chair and be ready to begin. I would rush to put the kettle on and then grab the back of a chair and swing my legs (one at a time of course) backwards and forwards trying to keep my back upright. I had to keep away from the wardrobe mirror so as not to kick it and I used to stay near the bed so that if the siren went I could dive under it. Usually whilst I was performing these keep fit antics the kettle would be boiling dry, but I think they helped to get me going in the mornings, especially if I woke muzzy-headed after a noisy night.'

Comic sketches, in which an over-exuberant, keep fit enthusiast became inextricably trapped in some strange bodily contortion, were a frequent feature of amateur entertainments, but the programme which attracted most imitations, both serious and light-hearted, was *The Brains Trust*, at first known as *Any Questions? The Brains Trust* was the first serious programme ever to attract a vast, mass audience like *ITMA* or *Music Hall*. After a modest beginning in January 1941 as a programme for serious-minded members of the Forces, it was soon being repeated on the Home Service and, as its producer proudly described, 'rose from the early obscurity of Wednesday afternoon half-hours to peak time broadcasts of forty-five minutes each on the two best days of the week'. At first it attracted fifteen letters a week; by the end of 1943 it was receiving 4,400—more than *Sandy's Half Hour*—and being listened to by nearly one in three of the adult population. As its most famous member, Professor Joad, declared, it became 'a nine day wonder that lasted into a tenth day'.

The programme's format was simple, with ten or a dozen questions being asked each week of the three resident members, with one visitor, the subjects ranging from, 'Who made God?' or 'What is beauty?' to 'What is a sneeze?' or 'Why is there no blue food?'. But, whatever the topics, millions of people accepted what the speakers told them. *The Brains Trust* had only to mention a book for it to go out of print, as happened to *War and Peace*. When *The Brains Trust* denounced advertising or over-protective parents, they provoked splendid public storms that boosted the listening figures still further. When Joad declared succinctly 'astrology is nonsense' the astrologers hit back by giving him remarkably gloomy horoscopes in the following Sunday papers. Joad, an academic philosopher, with a thin squeaky voice, was the lynch-pin of the programme. When he spoke at public meetings mounted police had to escort him through the crowds. A 'Professor Woad' appeared in a West End revue; and the Ministry of Food launched a dish known as 'Joad-in-the-hole'. The second member of the team, Professor Julian Huxley, a serious-minded scientist and secretary of the London Zoo, was, the programme's producer considered, 'an unwilling passenger to the headlines' but the third resident 'brain', Commander Campbell, a retired naval officer who specialised in tall stories, revelled in his sudden fame and Campbell's catchphrase, 'When I was in Patagonia', became almost as famous as Joad's 'It depends what you mean by . . .' The Brains Trust formula became popular everywhere—in schools, churches, prisoner-of-war camps, as part of Dig for Victory campaigns or holidays at home programmes—while political brains trusts provided a legitimate way of evading the party truce. The programme which had inspired them all retained its popularity until after the war and even had a final lease of life on television in the nineteen-fifties.[*]

If Sunday afternoon was *The Brains Trust* time, Saturday evening belonged to *Saturday Night Theatre*, begun in 1943 and still running. Its first play was adapted from a story by Dorothy L. Sayers, who also unintentionally provoked the greatest broadcasting controversy of the war with her religious series *The Man Born to be King*, which began in December 1941, and which, for the first time, included an actor playing the role of Christ. Extreme evangelical organisations thundered, not for the last time, about the BBC's wickedness, the Lord's Day Observance Society denounced Broadcasting House as 'a temple of blasphemy'

---

[*] Joad, however, had destroyed his public reputation in 1948, when he was convicted of travelling without a railway ticket. This did not surprise Commander Campbell, who had remarked on his meanness, which always led Joad to try to evade standing his round of drinks.

likely to annoy the deity just when 'the favour of Almighty God is of supreme importance', but the only result was to publicise the series, which was an immense success. Another outcry greeted the start of the American-style thriller series, *Appointment with Fear*, which it was said would frighten children. In fact, children were soon pleading to be allowed to stay up to hear it, *Appointment with Fear* became a national catch-phrase, and the sinister voice of Valentine Dyall, as the Man in Black, was added to the repertoire of amateur mimics.

Although many people seemed to regard attacking the BBC as their special form of war work, there seem, curiously enough, to have been few complaints about one broadcast which was both vulgar and untrue, a *Postscript* by the American journalist, Quentin Reynolds, in August 1941. Reynolds addressed Hitler as 'My dear Mr. Schicklgruber' and sneered at Goebbels— 'your little Gabby man'—for his club foot. Such abuse was ill-conceived and unnecessary; Goebbels, despite his disability, had consistently run rings round the Ministry of Information, while Hitler never had been called Schicklgruber, a perfectly respectable name in any case. The fact that this talk was wildly popular is a reminder of how a war can debase standards, though happily the BBC did not descend to such muck-raking again.*

One programme which was an unexpected hit was *The National Anthems of the Allies*, broadcast on Sunday evenings. A Rotherham girl 'loved this tribute paid to the fallen countries and ... would soundly scold anyone who dared to make a noise while it was being broadcast. On the following day I could always be heard chanting the *Marsellaise* till I was told in no uncertain terms to pack it up.' A Dorchester woman felt that as the 'bombers came roaring over on Sunday evenings the sound of the national anthem was like a prayer for the safety of the people living in Bristol'. The Dutch national anthem, sober and dignified, was generally considered the most tuneful, but the national anthem of one ally was never heard. On Sunday 22nd June 1941, after Russia had been invaded, many people listened eagerly to see if the BBC would add the *Internationale* to the existing list. It did not and rather than broadcast this hymn to revolution the whole programme was soon afterwards dropped.

One reason, perhaps, why wartime broadcasting was so successful was that the BBC's two channels, the Home Service with its news, features and plays, for information and 'middle-brow' entertainment, the Forces Programme, for background listening and relaxation, matched very well the two great needs of wartime. But the 'Forces', which became from February 1940 a second national network, was by no means all trivial and many of its programmes suddenly 'caught on' with civilian

---

* Quentin Reynolds did also, very helpfully, stress American support for Britain. But it was not this but the abuse of Hitler which attracted attention at the time.

listeners, like *Ack Ack, Beer Beer,* a light-hearted magazine programme intended for men on anti-aircraft and balloon barrage sites. A BBC production secretary who worked on the series found that the need for improvisation and the prevailing sense of urgency often produced far livelier broadcasting than in the leisurely days of peace, and on the whole the BBC was remarkably successful in catering for the nation's diverse and fluctuating tastes. As *Radio Times* pointed out in June 1940, 'Radio had become part of all our lives and even those who were not radio enthusiasts before the war now find themselves compelled to listen to the news. Some listeners think it is wrong to have anything frivolous on the air at all until the war is over. . . . On the other hand, some say that they are giving long hours to war-work and they look to the radio for amusement and diversion to refresh them and help them to carry on. The BBC has to try to please everybody without offending anybody. . . . Changes are constantly being made in general programme planning . . . to bring broadcasting into line with the prevailing mood of the nation.'

One of the changes was the launching of a series of half-hour shows for war workers, staged in a factory but broadcast live. The first series *To Brighten the Break* was followed by *Workers Playtime,* broadcast three times a week in the dinner-hour, which led Ernest Bevin to pay the BBC the highest compliment he knew, when he called it 'a factory for entertainment and education'. General Pile, the famous head of Anti-Aircraft Command, had said of *Ack-Ack, Beer Beer* that it had 'dug up talent in the most unlikely places' and an attempt was made to do the same in *Works Wonders.* A typical edition, from a factory in Wales in March 1943, included Miss Jones from Costs Department, singing *My Hero,* Mr. Pugh the Personnel, giving his rendering of *The Mountains of Mourne,* Mr. Davies the Inspection, whistling *When the Blue of the Night* to his own guitar accompaniment, and the whole works choir joining in *Men of Harlech.* The Forces were also regaled in the same year with *Fireaway,* an off-duty entertainment given by the N.F.S. in the Birmingham Region, which included such topical and professional jokes as:

'You know that static water tank just down the road? Well go and put your head in it three times and only take in out twice.'
'Why does Hitler sleep with a net over his bed? He's afraid of our Mosquitoes.'*

Everyone tended to be indulgent during the war to amateur performers, but one amateur talent contest during the war was a success by any standards, the competition to 'Write a Tune for £1,000'. One listener,

* The Mosquito, a very fast light bomber, was one of the outstanding aircraft of the war.

then a schoolboy in Walthamstow, found the competition highly frustrating, for the weekly playing of the entries always seemed to coincide with an air raid, which either meant his leaving on A.R.P. duty or the BBC going off the air. He can hardly, however, have failed to hear the winner, the still-popular tune *Cruising Down the River*.

Audience participation programmes of every type were popular during the war, especially record request programmes linking servicemen and their families, like *Sandy's Half Hour*, mentioned in an earlier chapter, and quiz programmes. One wartime schoolboy, living near Bushey Park in a typical middle-class home, remembers his surprise at 'hearing other ranks being informed and intelligent. Members of my family used to remark on this, "Bright chap for a gunner/ordinary seaman/lance corporal" and it was difficult for them to realise how comments like this illustrated one of the worst of British faults . . . the snobbish awareness of class and rank.' Other wartime children, and their parents, have warm memories of *Children's Hour*. A Swansea schoolboy found that all the grown-ups used to listen to *Toytown*; a Sheffield schoolgirl felt that Romany's 'talks of the country gave us the sensation of security and peace'. And everyone, adults and children, loved 'Uncle Mac', who conducted the programme, and his final words, 'Good night children, everywhere'.

Before the war not every family could afford a wireless set, and they later became unobtainable, but by 1945 there were 9,700,000 radio licences, nearly a million more than in 1939. The new sets made, from 1944, resembled a plain wooden box, with a tuning scale of tin-plate and the 'on/off' switch awkwardly placed at the back. Another obstacle to listening for homes not 'on the mains' was the shortage of high tension batteries, which were sometimes lacking for weeks at a time; one also needed to get one's low tension accumulator re-charged every three or four days, but this, which cost in 1939 about fourpence a time, was in my experience never very difficult. Portable radios were still a rarity so that wartime listening was a family occasion and a favourite programme was looked forward to for days beforehand. Pre-war the BBC had not employed a resident group of repertory actors but now the same voices were heard in play after play and, like those of the announcers, the voices of Gladys Young, Carleton Hobbes, Norman Shelley and other familiar names became a reassuringly permanent feature of life.

But it was the variety artistes and comedians who were the real idols. The early months of the war had belonged, as already described, to *Band Waggon*, followed in 1940 by *Garrison Theatre*, but 1941 saw the start of *The Old Town Hall*, presided over by a strident American personality, Clay Keyes, and including 'the night watchman, Old Ebenezer', whose dramatised stories invariably began 'One night as I was sitting round my old fire bucket'. The high spot of the programme has been mentioned in an earlier chapter, 'the radio sensation, the one and only "Can you beat the band?" ' in which the band had to guess the title of a tune from clues sent in by listeners. The correct answer to 'How close is Hitler to Old Nick?', for example, was not *Time alone will tell* or *Arm in Arm Together*, but *Cheek to Cheek*. Even connoisseurs of bad puns winced at the catch questions, like this one heard in 1942: 'What did the shopkeeper reply when the customers said, 'Can you let me have four oranges?' 'Can I? Four? Gertcha', i.e. *Can I forget you?*

Appealing to an even less sophisticated audience was *Happidrome*, which also ran from 1941 well into peacetime, a variety show linked together by the comedian Harry Korris as 'Mr. Lovejoy', who struggled to instil a little sense into his two foils, 'Enoch', a dim-witted youth whose usual response was 'Eh, I don't know', and his escort 'Ramsbottom', regularly urged to 'Take him away, Ramsbottom'. The trio became so famous that one Somerset farmer called three of his cows 'Ramsbottom, Enoch and Me'.

Some successful pre-war series also managed to adapt themselves to wartime conditions. 'The roar of London's traffic' continued to be stopped for *In Town Tonight* every Saturday right through the war and listeners still heard the chimes telling them 'to take an easy chair, for *Monday Night at Eight* is on the air', complete with *Puzzle Corner, Inspector Hornleigh Investigates*, and 'your old pal, Syd Walker, as that lovable character, the wandering junk-man philosopher', confronting listeners with some homely dilemma and the question, 'What would you do, chums?'

The war also made a new reputation for several established comedians, like Robb Wilton, who had been delighting audiences for years as Mr. Muddlecombe, J.P. Mr. Muddlecombe was soon even more entangled than ever in cases in which legally non-existent defendants were claiming ration books, or unsuitable applicants were applying for A.R.P. posts, but the war also created for Robb Wilton a brand new role, as a patriotic citizen, constantly frustrated by his own stupidity and his wife's lack of co-operation. His monologues always began, 'The day war broke out' and recounted his unhappy adventures as a would-be sailor, firewatcher or special constable and—his classic turn, constantly repeated—as a Home Guard. Having boasted to his wife, 'I'm supposed to stop Hitler's army landing', he is greeted with the deflating retort, 'What, *you*? . . . I think we'd stand a better chance if you were on the other side.' When he goes to visit a relation in hospital, 'When I got home the missus had taken all my clothing coupons. I said to her, "What have you taken all my clothing coupons for," She said, "Well, how was I to know you'd be coming out again?" ' To get away from it all, 'me and the missus went to the seaside for the day. . . . We booked first class for comfort and there were only 137 of us in the guard's van.' Personally I cannot remember a single one of these characterisations, but for many people Robb Wilton was the outstanding comedian of the war and the Rotherham woman who 'used to be in stitches over him' was clearly not untypical. His melancholy, faintly-aggrieved voice expressed in some strange way, like the very different manner of other successful wartime comedians—'Mrs. Feather', constantly in a muddle on the telephone, or 'Gert and Daisy', a pair of good-natured charwomen—the frustrations and bewilderment of the ordinary citizen at large in an increasingly complicated world, willing to be a patriot but far from eager to be a hero.

After *Band Waggon* ended its run late in 1939 Arthur Askey turned up in many variety programmes, often singing his classic *Bee Song*, but did not star in any other series of his own. His former partner, Richard Murdoch, was by 1944 making a new reputation in *Much Binding in the Marsh*, 'the most notorious R.A.F. station in the country today'. A typical sketch in *Music Hall* one Saturday evening in 1944—*Much Binding* had not yet been promoted to its own series—involved Murdoch as the station commander in preparations for a forthcoming station entertainment:

'Well the show must go on or, as we used to say at Cambridge, Per Ardua ad ENSA. . . . Any response to the notice you put up this morning?'
'A long queue outside sick quarters.'

The noise of an aircraft landing is followed by the arrival of Kenneth Horne, as a senior officer:

'That's the A.O.C. all right. I keep on telling him our tennis court is no place to land a Sunderland . . .'
'Rather a ropy landing, I'm afraid. I was eating some crisps and I swallowed the bag of salt.'
'Oh bad show, sir.'
'I should say it *is* a bad show. They're in very short supply.'

Both Robb Wilton and *Much Binding in the Marsh* were essentially English in their humour, but one of the most successful comedy shows of the war—*Hi Gang!*—was basically American. While some British stars had found pressing engagements in America on the outbreak of war, Ben Lyon and his wife, Bebe Daniels, both American citizens, had chosen instead to face the rigours of life in wartime Britain—and the British public honoured them for it. The spirit of the programme, from the moment that Ben Lyon called out, 'Hi Gang!' and the audience yelled back, 'Hi Ben!', was friendly and cheerful. As a Carshalton housewife remembers: 'Radio was a lifeline and *Hi Gang!* was ours, raid or not. We all sat indoors under the stairs or table while our friends Ben and Bebe made us laugh and forget briefly Jerry and his hate.' Apart from musical items, and some remarkably phoney-sounding messages of support frcm stars safe in Hollywood, the programme consisted of quick-fire cross-talk, usually with Ben Lyon as the butt, as in this dialogue in January 1942:

Ben Lyon:    Oh well, as the unexploded incendiary bomb said, 'I don't want to set the world on fire'.

Vic Oliver:    Now Listen, Lyon. I warn you. If you're going to continue with those awful jokes I'm going to kick your teeth in. Both of them.

Another victim, who never actually appeared, was 'Momma':

Ben Lyon:    That handbag was made from a genuine old walrus. Not you, momma. Sit down.

Bebe Daniels: I wish you'd stop being so rude to her, Ben. After all, everything I am I owe to Momma.

Ben Lyon:    Why don't you send her the shilling and square the account? Ha ha ha Boy! Am I registering tonight?

Bebe Daniels: I didn't know the sixty-fives had registered yet.

By general consent, although a few independent-minded stalwarts refused to find it funny, *the* comedy programme of the war was *ITMA*. It had, in fact, begun its run just before the war and the original title, *It's That Man Again*, had referred not to Tommy Handley but Hitler. Soon, however, it became so much a part of the wartime scene that its mere name seems to evoke the memory of a blacked-out sitting room at 8.30 on a Thursday evening with, perhaps, a siren wailing in the distance. Somehow in *ITMA* star, supporting actors, script-writers and producer combined to produce a comic masterpiece. Tommy Handley was in 1939 already an established comedian, though far from being a household name, and this was the first show of his own. The whole performance revolved round him, for it consisted of a series of encounters between him and a succession of weird characters. At first he was Minister of Aggravation and Mysteries, working in the Office of Twerps, and coping with the persistent disapproval of the hidebound Civil Servant, Fusspot, whose constant lament was 'It's most irregular'. After Dunkirk, jokes at the expense of government departments became less popular and Tommy Handley became instead a factory manager, farmer, hotel keeper, mayor and prospective M.P., but his nominal position was unimportant for he was endlessly interrupted by visitors or the telephone. One of the first and most famous callers was the German, Funf, whose sepulchral voice—produced by Jack Train speaking into an empty tumbler—was heard in September 1939 announcing himself on the telephone as 'Funf, your favourite spy', to which Handley retorted: 'It may be Funf for you, but it's not much funf for me . . .' Funf, like so many *ITMA* characters, rapidly became a wartime craze. When people collided in the black-out, they would reply 'Funf' when asked 'Who's that?'. A cartoon in *Radio Times* showed a puzzled staff officer holding out the telephone to his general and explaining 'It's a Mr. Funf, sir', and a London housewife who had moved a great deal and never even heard of *ITMA* remembers her husband, who had answered the telephone, telling her quite seriously, 'It's a foreigner—says his name is "Phumph".'

By February 1940, when the first series ended, another *ITMA* ritual had also become established. Jack Train would say, 'It happened on a Friday', to which Tommy Handley would reply, 'Friday?', both then echoing the same word or a similar phrase like 'dry day'. A second series in 1941, with Tommy Handley as mayor of 'Foaming-at-the-Mouth', a run-down seaside resort, introduced 'Ali Oop', the saucy post-card vendor, asking, 'You give me licence to peddle on the pier?', Sam Scram, an American, who invariably burst in crying 'Boss, boss, sumpin' terrible's happened', Lefty, an ex-gangster troubled by his 'noives', and the Commercial Traveller, who greeted everyone with 'Good morning, *nice* day'. Politeness was also the hallmark of Claude and Cecil, who constantly deferred to each other in a famous dialogue: 'After you, Claude', 'No, after you, Cecil', which one soon heard whenever people stood aside for each other and was said to have been used by bomber pilots circling over Berlin. Lifts were the happy hunting ground of admirers of the diver, who was always ushered in by gurgling noises and the phrase 'Don't forget the diver, sir', followed by 'I'm going down now, sir', often heard as a lift began to descend. A London office worker, when given ether in hospital after being injured by blast, remembers absent-mindedly murmuring, '"I'm going down now", to the surprised surgeon'. 1941 also saw the first appearance of Signor So-So—'Ah Meestair Hand-Pump. I am diluted. To me, you are indescribable'—and another catch-phrase, 'Notting at all'. But an even more famous newcomer was the charwoman, Mrs. Mopp, with her soon immortal question, 'Can I do you now, sir?', and two other much-copied phrases, 'I brought this for you, sir', and 'Ta ta, for now', often abbreviated to 'T.T.F.N.' This became a popular way of saying goodbye while 'Mrs. Mopp' has passed into the language as a synonym for charwoman.

Later series introduced a whole new galaxy of personalities: Miss Hotchkiss, the hard-boiled elderly secretary, Peter Geekie, who was blamed for everything, but never actually appeared, and 'ancient Mark

Time', whose invariable reply was 'I'll have to ask me dad'. A real Miss Hotchkiss wrote to the producer to say that for the first time she was proud of her name, while any schoolteacher asking who was responsible for some classroom misdemeanour was likely to be met with a cry of 'Peter Geekie'. But the most famous creation of all was probably Colonel Chinstrap, played by Jack Train. The Colonel, if not a raving alcoholic, was certainly an exceedingly heavy drinker, and from his first appearance in the autumn of 1942, any reference to 'a double', any word that could be misheard as 'gin', 'sherry' or 'whisky', would be followed by the Colonel's voice agreeing enthusiastically, 'I don't mind if I do', soon a popular method of accepting any invitation. In a typical programme, in June 1943, a remark about the carpet being sandy led to this exchange:

Jack:     Did I hear you say brandy, sir?
Tommy: No Colonel. . . . Get back to bed and I'll squirt your breakfast through the keyhole.
Jack:     I say, Handley, is my nose red?
Tommy: Well, soak it and see.

Victory itself would hardly have been complete without a special edition of *ITMA*. In it Colonel Chinstrap, thirsty to the last, boasted as he drained his glass: 'Sir, I have celebrated every victory since Mafeking.'

What was the secret of *ITMA*'s almost universal appeal? Francis Worsley, its producer, believed that one source was its topicality—the ITMA team listened to the six o'clock news on transmission days for last-minute ideas—and his firm ban on suggestive jokes. Another reason was Tommy Handley's good nature, as a result of which producer, scriptwriter, star and supporting actors worked together 'in . . . harmonious association . . . unfailing good humour and good fellowship'. The conditions of wartime broadcasting also helped to foster these qualities. The early broadcasts went out live from Clifton Parish Hall, with the artistes sitting on the floor or on the grand piano when not at the microphone, and later broadcasts, until *ITMA* returned to London late in 1943, went out in equally cosy discomfort from a chapel hall in Penrhyn, near Bangor. Whatever the real reason for *ITMA*'s popularity, the public gave the credit to 'Mrs. Handley's boy', and when he died suddenly at the age of fifty-five, in 1949, vast crowds lined the streets for his funeral and St. Paul's was packed for his memorial service—the first ever held there for a comedian.

# OUT OF PRINT

'This book is produced in complete conformity with the authorised economy standards.'

Text of an announcement in wartime books, agreed by the
Publishers Association 1st January 1942

One of the minor consequences of the war was that books written by candlelight were once again read by it. A woman living in a village near Frome in Somerset found the easiest way to transport herself back to Jane Austen's peaceful days was to read her by candlelight, as the German planes passed overhead on their way to Bristol. A young Wimbledon woman working in a Food Office, who still remembers her sense of triumph when she at last found a copy of *Emma* to complete her collection, also 'read Jane's books by the light of a candle in the Anderson shelter and when I was on Civil Defence duty at the municipal building during Alerts'. The critics had often held it against Jane that, though writing during the Napoleonic wars, she had never mentioned them. Now this very absence of war gave her work its greatest appeal. A Honiton housewife 'read . . . old friends, who kept a note of sanity in life, Jane Austen, Thomas Hardy, Dickens, giving us glimpses of what seemed another world'. A Buckhurst Hill housewife enjoyed 'the quiet books' most: *Pride and Prejudice*, *Cranford* and—a little less tranquil perhaps—*Jane Eyre*. A scientific Civil Servant found his escape fron his daily work at the Ministry of Aircraft Production in Dickens. '*Pickwick*', he claims, 'stands up to every test.'

Some readers found they could best forget the war by immersing themselves in long and solid family histories like Sir Hugh Walpole's *Rogue Herries* series, John Galsworthy's *Forsyte Saga* and its sequels and Mazo de la Roche's *Whiteoaks* books. One Bradford housewife became addicted to Proust after receiving *Swann's Way* for her birthday and the successive volumes of *Remembrance of Things Past* saw her through the whole war. A Clydeside shipyard worker took on an equally formidable task, reading the whole of Gibbon's *Decline and Fall of the Roman Empire* and, perhaps by way of light relief, Tolstoy's *War and Peace*, which became *the* foreign classic of the war, after the Brains Trust had recommended it, the BBC had serialised it and all things

Russian had become fashionable. To obtain a copy of this interminable novel became a triumph equal to securing an extra egg; I remember being delighted at being finally lent the three volume Everyman edition in 1944.

Some people found security by returning to childhood books. A Birmingham housewife's favourite shelter reading was Kipling's *Puck of Pook's Hill* and *The Just So Stories*, and Kenneth Graham's *Wind in the Willows*. A London bus conductress admits, a little shamefacedly, 'the book I used to keep near ... was the omnibus edition of *What Katy Did* ... I found the three books of *Katy* very refreshing and as far removed from those awful days as it was possible to get'.* Other readers turned back to the Arthur Ransome stories. *The Big Six*, published in 1940, did not mention the war but *Punch* noticed in Christmas 1941 that 'The Schoolboys Annuals are ablaze with enemy machines in a thick cloud of black smoke'. Mary Treadgold's *We Couldn't Leave Dinah*, the reviewer reported, 'begins in a Pony Club and ends with an attempt to invade England', though the German children, as every true horse-lover would have expected, spared their intended victims at the sight of their Pony Club badge. Even into books for infants the war intruded and many a stocking that Christmas included *The Adventures of John Balloon*, a runaway barrage balloon. Other children's books still remembered are the *Pollyanna* series and *The Blitz Kids*, both unknown to me.

The past offered another obvious way of escape from the disagreeable present and many women discovered a passion for 'costume' romances by authors like Jane Lane, Georgette Heyer and Margaret Irwin. More solid books in a period setting, like Phyllis Bentley's long saga of life among the Yorkshire mill-owners, were also popular and two historical novels, Clemence Dane's *He Brings Great News* and Thomas Armstrong's *Dover Harbour*. H. E. Bates *Fair Stood the Wind for France*, about an escaping air crew, was also much praised, though his best work is generally agreed to have been the short stories about the R.A.F. which he published under the pseudonym of 'Flying Officer X'. Daphne du Maurier, already famous for *Rebecca*, which was made into an excellent film, consolidated her reputation in 1941 with *Frenchman's Creek*, made into a very poor one, and *Hungry Hill* in 1943. The following year saw the appearance of Elizabeth Goudge's much-loved *Green Dolphin Country*. Several of C. S. Forester's excellent novels appeared between 1939 and 1945, including one of the best Hornblower stories, *The Commodore*, but the two historical novels which made the greatest stir in those six years were both by Americans. Margaret Mitchell's *Gone With the Wind*, published just before the war, made as deep an impression as the film. A South Benfleet housewife remembers struggling to read this heavy volume while propped up in bed during an air raid, awaiting the arrival of her second baby, and a Croydon housewife, reading the book while

* *What Katy Did*, by Susan Coolidge, was first published in 1872.

knitting a Merchant Navy sweater, found her needles moving faster and faster the more exciting the story became. At the end of the war *Forever Amber*, by Kathleen Winsor, was for a time even more eagerly sought after, being considered highly scandalous. *The Annual Register*, looking back on the reception given to it, commented with notable understatement that 'some of the critics thought that Kathleen Winsor's picture of the court of Charles II did not deserve the 800 pages of paper which it occupied'.

Several 'straight' histories published during the war also achieved something of the popularity usually confined to best-selling novels, notably Arthur Bryant's *English Saga* and his series of books on Britain's struggle against Napoleon, leading up appropriately to *The Years of Victory* in 1944, the theme also of Carola Oman's highly successful *Britain against Napoleon*. Another best-seller was G. M. Trevelyan's *English Social History*, published in 1944, a 'cosy', sunlit picture of the past bearing little relationship to reality, but perhaps all the more popular for that reason. Also widely read was *The Long Weekend*, by Alan Hodge and Charles Graves, a history of daily life between the wars which, besides being entertaining, had the merit of being true. Other widely read non-fiction included the first volume of Sir Osbert Sitwell's classic autobiography, *Left Hand Right Hand* and, more surprisingly, an alleged correspondence between two devils, C. S. Lewis's *The Screwtape Letters*. Also of lasting importance were two books published in 1945 expressing disillusionment with Communism and marking the end of the popular infatuation with Russia, George Orwell's satire *Animal Farm* and Arthur Koestler's book of essays *The Yogi and the Commissar*.

The war was not a good time for war books and most of the best war memoirs and novels were not published till several years later. The one personal narrative published during the war which seems likely to survive is *The Last Enemy* by Richard Hillary, an Oxford undergraduate turned fighter pilot who was killed shortly after his book appeared in 1941. Another popular book on the R.A.F., now out of print, was *The Thin Blue Line* by Charles Graves. The best wartime book on civilian life during the first year of the war was Margery Allingham's *The Oaken Heart*, published in 1941, and on the blitz the two most talked-of books were John Strachey's *Post D* and the anonymous *The Bells Go Down, the Diary of a London A.F.S. Man*. A series of humorous articles by D. W. Stonier, published under the title *Shaving Through the Blitz*, were widely praised and later re-issued as a book. Eclipsing any successes by ordinary publishers, however, were the fantastic sales of official publications produced by His Majesty's Stationery Office. Its shabbily printed threepenny pamphlet, *The Battle of Britain*, and the illustrated sixpenny version which followed, sold five million copies, making it easily *the* best-selling title of the war, and its only rivals were other government publications like *Front Line*, about the blitz, *Bomber Command*, *Coastal Command* and *Battle of Egypt*.

Besides the hunger for escapist reading, there was also a demand for books on politics and international affairs and many very bad ones were published. Of lasting importance in helping to shape opinion was Lord Vansittart's *Black Record*, published in 1941, which catalogued Germany's successive attempts to enslave her neighbours, and which involved me in a bitter argument with a progressive-minded master at my school who denounced it as unhistorical nonsense. A contemporary at another school was equally influenced, in the opposite direction, by Victor Gollancz's reply to Vansittart, *Shall Our Children Live or Die?* We both, however, eagerly read another series of Gollancz books which, in their bright yellow jackets, could be seen not merely heaped high in the bookshop counters but piled on temporary bookstalls in the street. *Guilty Men*, blaming the Chamberlain government for the country's plight, was published in July 1940 and reprinted nine times within the month. *The Trial of Mussolini*, in 1943, on similar lines, created an almost equal sensation, but probably the most effective of the whole series was *Your M.P.* in April 1944, which reviewed the voting records of every Conservative back-bencher, and is generally credited with contributing to the crushing Labour Party victory in 1945.

More obviously helpful to the war effort was the stream of books on rural life which poured from the presses—agriculture and the art of war were the only subjects on which more books were published than in peacetime. The Ministry of Agriculture had declared that 'Books can help you to dig for victory' and any farmer with a glimmering of literary talent could sell his manuscript as easily as his pigs—more easily, as no permit was needed. Titles like *England is a Village* or *We Like the Country* appeared every month, only rivalled by instructional manuals like *A Book of Farmcraft*. 'Can you handle a shovel, a pitch-fork, a hoe, a hay-knife, a bagging hook?' one of its reviewers asked his readers accusingly in 1942. Of all the books of rural reminiscence published during the war one at least, though dealing with an earlier era, is sure to survive, Flora Thompson's *Over to Candleford*, a sequel to her *Lark Rise* published before the war.

Most novels written during the war and given a contemporary setting have a distinctly 'pot-boiling' feel, like Graham Greene's spy story, *The Ministry of Fear*, and, even worse, J. B. Priestley's now forgotten *Blackout in Gretley*, also about spies, or *Three Men in New Suits*, about the problems of demobilisation. His *Daylight on Saturday*, published in 1943, about an aircraft factory is, however, still of interest and has recently been reprinted in paperback. Evelyn Waugh's *Put Out More*

*Flags* reveals, like many other wartime novels, the traumatic effect evacuation had on the countryside and at the very end of the war he published what many critics consider his best book, *Brideshead Revisited*, about an old Roman Catholic family. Several Somerset Maugham novels were published during the war, including *Christmas Holiday*, and a large volume of short stories, *The Mixture as Before*, though the war was not mentioned in them, but it was books set it wartime England which first began to make the name of another novelist, Nevil Shute. *Landfall*, *Pastoral* and *Most Secret* provide an accurate picture of the period, though such post-war books as *Requiem for a Wren* and *The Chequer-Board* do so even more effectively. Two A. J. Cronin books, *The Keys of the Kingdom* and *The Green Years*, came out during the war and Howard Spring's immensely successful *Fame is the Spur*, in 1940, was followed four years later by the first of a long series, *Hard Facts*. To the same category of a 'good read' belonged Norman Collins's *London Belongs to Me*, published in 1945 and partly set in the early years of the war. Another picture of the blitz can be found in Henry Green's *Caught* (1943), a hard-to-read, intellectual's book about the A.F.S. Ernest Raymond's *The Last to Rest*, published in 1941, describes, for a wider audience, the growing involvement in the war of an ordinary middle-class family and I also greatly enjoyed Nigel Balchin's *The Small Back Room*, published in 1943. This vividly illustrates both life in the Civil Service in wartime and the anxiety under which parents lived then, as the climax of the plot is the dismantling of a 'butterfly' bomb after a similar bomb has killed a child.

One famous critic, Lord David Cecil, had complained in 1940 that 'Literature in every form has stayed where it was in 1939. No new vein has been discovered and the old veins seem to be producing less and less.' Another academic authority, Professor Ivor Evans, had complained that 'The war has produced no new literature. Not a scrap.' Neither can have drawn much consolation from Eric Knight's *This Above All*, selected by *The Annual Register* in 1941 as 'the first significant novel brought forth by the war'. The plot concerned a soldier evacuated from Dunkirk who met and speedily seduced 'Prudence (whose name belied her), a member of the W.A.A.F. of good family. Love under a haystack and . . . in a deserted hotel . . . was all that wartime conditions permitted. They talked for days and nights at cross purposes, he attacking our social system and she valiantly defending what is good in it.' Eventually the hero is killed in an air raid leaving Prudence pregnant. 'Mr. Knight', commented the reviewer, 'has written a bold, outspoken novel. That he was permitted to publish his discouraging opinions . . . proves that we do possess liberty that is worth defending to the last ditch.' *This Above All* was later filmed and now seems very tame but at the time was considered very shocking and its surly, rebellious 'anti-hero' was perhaps the predecessor of the post-war 'angry young men'.

Except during the blitz, most public libraries stayed open long hours during the war and every sizeable town also had a branch of Boots Booklovers Library and the Chain Library, the latter consisting, one Luton woman remembers, of 'half a shop, shelves of old books, and an elderly lady behind a little counter'. I have equally grateful memories of Boots where a 'B' class book cost only threepence a week. The backbone of most branches was light fiction by writers like Angela Thirkell, whose novels about country life among the well connected came out remorselessly every few months throughout the war. As the *Punch* reviewer commented on *Marling Hall* in 1942: 'She had made out of dull events something even duller. . . . The atmosphere of snobbishness is quite withering.' Another popular woman writer, of far greater merit, was Monica Dickens, whose highly coloured account of her experiences as a wartime nurse, *One Pair of Feet*, published in 1942, was one of the most widely enjoyed humorous books of the war. *The Fancy*, in 1943, gave an excellent picture of everyday civilian life, including a surely unique description of how rabbit-breeders, 'the fancy' of the title, managed to keep up their hobby. Other women writers whose wartime books are still reprinted or remembered with pleasure include Frances Parkinson Keyes, Cornelia Otis Skinner, for *Our Hearts Were Young and Gay*, and Dorothy Evelyn Smith, for *Oh the Brave Music*, which one family living near Hendon aerodrome took it in turns to read aloud while in the shelter. A Southampton girl, living under similar conditions, became equally attached to the books of Jeffrey Farnol. E. M. Delafield, whose pre-war *Diary of a Provincial Lady* had been a great success, published in 1940 *The Provincial Lady in Wartime*, covering the first three months of the war. But already jokes about large-size gas masks and 'little evacuments' seemed sadly dated. Like so many wartime characters the provincial lady had been overtaken by events and this proved to be her last appearance for the duration. Richmal Crompton's William, however, continued to flourish right through the war, under titles like *William Does Hit Bit* and *William Carries On*, whether he was collecting salvage and depositing it in the wrong house or planting with vegetables the cherished rose garden of some local resident who had un-patriotically refused to dig for victory.

Despite so much real violence in the world, crime stories were as popular as ever and established writers soon adjusted themselves to wartime conditions, with books like G. D. H. and M. Cole's *Murder at the Munition Works*, Carter Dickson's *Murder in the Submarine Zone* and Freeman Wills Crofts's *Death of a Train*, about a precious consignment of valves threatened by traitors, and *Enemy Unseen* about a murder involving the use of Home Guard grenades. A new Dorothy L. Sayers book and several by Agatha Christie were also published and Edmund Crispin made his début with *The Case of the Gilded Fly*. Adventure story writers rapidly put their characters into uniform and Hammond Innes's heroes were soon capturing a secret U-Boat base on the Cornish coast in *Wreckers Must Breathe* and thwarting an airborne invasion in *Attack Alarm*.

In 1942 *The Annual Register* had complained that 'three years of war seem to have left English novelists rather debilitated and some have ceased writing "for the duration" ', but American novelists were still working with their usual full-blooded vigour. Ernest Hemingway's classic *For Whom the Bell Tolls* had been published in England in 1941 and John Steinbeck's *The Moon is Down*, about occupied Norway, also made a deep impression in England. Oddly enough it was an American writer, Alice Duer Miller, who wrote the best known poem about wartime England, *The White Cliffs*, which ended with a famous line about not wishing to live in a world in which England was dead. The war produced no Rupert Brooke. The reluctant, realistic conscripts of 1939 were a very different breed from the starry-eyed volunteers of 1914 and the pre-war poets had cultivated a deliberately obscure style, comprehensible only to a privileged minority. When, during the first months of the war, the press asked, 'Where are the war poets?', the cynics replied, 'In America'. It was true. To their eternal discredit, several writers who had been prominent before the war in urging resistance to Fascism discovered pressing engagements abroad when the war they had predicted actually arrived. The missing writers, whatever their reasons for being away, were, understandably, criticised in the press and House of Commons and even Harold Nicolson, no enemy of literature, wrote in his diary in April 1940: 'We all regret bitterly that people like Aldous Huxley, Auden and Isherwood should have absented themselves'. Film stars, another notably non-heroic group, had at least the excuse of being in Hollywood to carry on their profession. Most of the missing writers later returned to Britain and even the young Dylan Thomas, who had not fled but proved unfit for military service, found a congenial form of war work, drunkenly writing scripts for propaganda films which were never made, in the intervals when the pubs were closed. So far as the ordinary public was concerned, however, the poets might as well have stayed away. Although the death in action of two soldier poets, Sidney Keyes and Alun Lewis, was deeply mourned by poetry-lovers, the ordinary reader had probably never heard of either and only John Pudney's poems about the R.A.F. came near to gaining a popular audience. The Home Front inspired even less poetry than the Forces. Wilfred Gibson wrote two books of verse, *The Alert*, published in 1942, and *The Outpost*, in 1944, on such homely themes as the black-out and the nine o'clock news, but I cannot recall ever hearing them mentioned, much less quoted, at that time.* A long, patriotic poem by the novelist, Francis Brett Young, *The Island*, was well reviewed but not much read. W. H. Auden, Louis Macneice and Stephen Spender all published new volumes and T. S. Eliot produced his *Four Quartets*, but he could hardly be called a popular poet. Yet there was a vast public eager to buy intelligible poetry, as the great success of Field-Marshal Wavell's *Other Men's Flowers*, published in 1944, made plain—but this was a collection of straightforward, memorable poetry, the very antithesis of the fashionable intellectual verse of the nineteen-thirties. Two excellent anthologies containing both prose and poetry, compiled by Walter de la Mare, were also published during the war and must have given many readers, as they have me, endless pleasure since, *Behold this Dreamer* (1939) and *Love* (1943).

In peacetime publishers feared the critics; in wartime they dreaded the government. In 1940 they had persuaded the Chancellor of the Exchequer to drop the proposed purchase tax on books, but at the end of the year the book trade suffered an appalling blow in the great fire raid on the City, when five million books were destroyed. Early in 1941 the Chairman of the Publishers Association warned that the next great battle publishers and writers would have to fight would be for adequate supplies of raw materials and on New Year's Day 1942 an almost unprecedented line-up of eighteen famous writers, including Bernard Shaw, H. G. Wells and J. B. Priestley, protested in *The Times* that to save the book trade only a trifling number of key-workers need to be reserved and only a tiny amount of paper be provided—less than 1¼ per cent of the total national consumption. 'Unless action is taken . . . soon', they warned, 'to arrest the disintegration of the book trade, the public, which is turning more and more to books for the help they give, will ask and get nothing.'

But irreplaceable compositors and book-binders continued to be called up, and 25,000 tons of paper a year were to be delivered to the War Office alone, against the 20,000 tons allocated to the whole publishing trade. In 1943 the trade received only 25 per cent of its pre-war supplies, grudgingly raised after protests to 42 per cent. The resulting book famine affected every section of the reading public, especially children and students. Of what use was it for the Board of Education to urge that children should be taught the history of our great allies, one headmaster asked in 1943, if the recommended books were unobtainable? Even the moral education of his pupils was being endangered, another headmaster

* When I advertised in *The New Statesman* for books about civilian life during the war, *The Alert* was the only one offered.

complained; he had been waiting two years for a supply of Bibles. The L.C.C. was able, with the best will in the world, to spend on books only a third of the pre-war figure and many textbooks were, it reported in 1945, now 'shabby and dirty' and 'unless more paper is made available the efficiency of schools will be increasingly impaired'. The Royal College of Nursing warned in 1943 that the training of nurses was being held up, as half their textbooks were out of print, and a Cambridge bookseller complained that medical and science students were being handicapped in the same way. The 'serious shortage of books ... means a real impediment on the war effort', an M.P. for the universities protested in October 1943.

Those who wanted to read books for pleasure or reference came off even worse. 'D. H. Lawrence and the Brontës have apparently disappeared for the duration', reported a Brighton bookseller in 1943. 'Some might be tempted to sell Jane Austen, English dictionaries and the *Oxford Book of English Verse* only underneath the counter as they are so scarce.' One M.P. told the Commons in 1945 of a bookshop which had received only sixty copies of Trevelyan's *English Social History*, although it had orders for 1,000. Scarcest of all were cheap reprints of the classics. By the end of 1941 500 of the 970 titles in *Everyman's Library* were already out of print, and by 1945 one bookseller found he could obtain only one-twelfth of the number of copies in this series he required.

That matters were not even worse was due to the initiative and good sense of the Publishers Association, which voluntarily negotiated among its members a *Book Production War Economy Agreement* designed to save paper while doing as little harm as possible to book design. The results of the agreement, which came into force in January 1942, were soon evident to every reader in thinner books, narrower margins, smaller type and the note which appeared at the front of almost every volume: 'This book is produced in complete conformity with the authorised economy standards.' Even these changes, which included running-on Forewords, Introductions and chapters until it became difficult to know where one ended and another began, did not go far enough for some readers and there was a vigorous campaign in the press against dust jackets, which were only saved after it had been pointed out that they protected the binding. A few firms took advantage of wartime conditions to sell sloppily-produced volumes, badly bound and laden with misprints. Occasionally reviewers protested. *Punch* wrote of *The Saturday Book*, a popular annual anthology, in 1942, that 'No paper shortage can excuse the villainous layout of the book. The print looks

* Even more infuriating was the frequent omission of the date of publication, a slovenly practice that saved no paper at all and wasted everyone's time.

like an advertisement for patent medicines.' But on the whole most publishers succeeded in turning out books that were legible, if rarely handsome, though in spite of the economy measures, the number of new books published went remorselessly down, from 15,000 in 1939 to 6,700 in 1943, where it remained till after the war.

One result of the book boom was the growth of new publishers, who could use any paper they could find—they often advertised for 'free' supplies—and were not rationed to a fraction of their pre-war consumption. Lacking 'back lists' they specialised in new books and the public found it bewildering that new titles should constantly be published while textbooks and classics remained unobtainable. Suggestions for a test of quality to ensure that worthwhile books received a higher priority than ephemeral trash were always resisted by the trade on the grounds that any test was bound to be subjective. One right-wing M.P., pilloried in *Your M.P.*, actually asked in the House, 'Why is paper available for political lunatics who produce political pamphlets which . . . are detrimental to those who read them?' It hardly needed Hugh Dalton's reply, 'We do not exercise a censorship upon lunatics', to remind the public that that way lay Hitlerism and the denial of everything for which the war had been fought. But it is still hard not to feel that publishers themselves might have been more discriminating about the way in which they used their precious stocks of paper.

The paper shortage pressed almost as hard on the newspapers. As soon as the war began, most newspapers became thinner simply because trade was bad and advertising scarce, but by the summer of 1940 Norway had been overrun and newsprint had become strictly rationed. The *Daily Express*, sixteen, twenty or even twenty-four pages before the war, had by July 1940 fallen to six and by 1941 to four—i.e. one double sheet. Smaller size papers, like The *Daily Mirror* and The *Evening Standard*, were normally eight, and *The Times*, by restricting its sales, managed to provide its readers with eight closely-packed pages, occasionally increased to ten or twelve. Most Sunday papers were eight pages long. Although these heavy cuts came just when news—and government advertising—was plentiful, the papers, thanks to skilful sub-editing, managed remarkably well with their limited space and little of importance seems to have been omitted.

Apart from the *Daily Mirror*, at one time threatened with suppression for publishing a cartoon which infuriated Churchill, who misunderstood it, and the Communist *Daily Worker*, which was for a time shut down for opposing the war effort, the press largely abdicated during the war from its traditional role of criticising the government. Fortunately it still found room to expose occasional lunacies by the military, like that of the C.O. who ordered his men to shout 'Hi-de-hi!' whenever they met an officer, a phrase which rapidly became a national joke and gave its name to a West End revue. The popular newspapers also conducted a foolish, and unsuccessful, campaign in the summer of 1941 against the employment of Italian prisoners-of-war on British farms, harmless and amiable men who soon proved both useful and popular. Despite all the claims on its space, the popular press still found room for comic strips, like The *Daily Mirror's* Jane, who was constantly losing her clothes in a variety of embarrassing situations, and for animal stories. The papers took up so enthusiastically a modest appeal by the Ministry of Agriculture for hedgehogs for research on foot and mouth disease, that packages containing these innocuous, if prickly, creatures were soon flooding the Post Offices and an appreciable number, who had escaped in transit, made a dash for freedom before being rounded up by sorting office cats. No reporter became as well known as the BBC war correspondents, but one humorous feature-writer did become a national institution, Nathaniel Gubbins, with his *Sitting on the Fence* column in the *Sunday Express*, which regularly caught the wartime atmosphere. In May 1940 a favourite Gubbins character, 'Sally the Cat', is declaring, 'I will have, nothing to do with foreign cats who might belong to the Fifth Column', only to be reproved by her owner: 'If refugee cats come here I expect to see them eating and drinking out of the same saucer.' Nathaniel Gubbins also provided his own guide on 'What to do when the invader comes. . . . The first instinct of any sane person is to run like hell. This, however, is not only un-British but would congest the roads. Moreover most people . . . can't run like hell for more than a hundred yards.' In July 1941 an entry in the 'Diary of a worm' records the latter's unsuccessful appearance in a Home Guard musketry competition. 'On way home, wife says if worm had taken her advice . . . and joined wardens instead of showing off in khaki wife would at least have been spared shame of seeing worm make fool of himself.' The austerity Christmas of 1942 found 'Uncle Nat' dialling T.U.M.—'I suppose even a stomach can have his memories'—and other Gubbins characters included 'Margaret's father', a forerunner of Colonel Chinstrap, 'waiting for Stalin to broadcast so he can give a vodka party', the Dog and the Cat, now eating better than their owners and wondering whether 'as we can't get enough for them to eat . . . it would be a kindness to have them destroyed', and the invariably pessimistic cousin Florrie. 'Letter from an aunt' reported in February 1945: 'Florrie came round to tea (last of the grapefruit marmalade) and told us that Hitler's last throw will be incendiary rockets as big as St. Paul's Cathedral.'

As newsagents could no longer return unsold copies, newspapers were sometimes rapidly sold out and a housewife living on the island of Bute, off the Scottish coast, 'often had to queue for about an hour before the steamer came in to Rothesay, to make sure of getting a copy' of her evening newspaper. Printed newspaper contents bills appeared for the last time in April 1940, being replaced by scrawled home-made bills or chalked messages on boards, another wartime change which became permanent.

As magazines were unable to take on new subscribers, readers were often asked to pass on their copy to someone in the Forces from a list of names kept by the magazine and I still feel grateful to the reader of *John o' London's Weekly* who sent his copy on to me each week until I was demobilised, though this book-lover's magazine has, like so many wartime publications, since vanished.

My favourite boyhood reading, *The Magnet*, was a minor victim of the war. This twopenny schoolboys' magazine had survived the first world war and seemed at first to be coping well with the second. Already during the first winter of the war at blacked-out Greyfriars, Mr. Quelch and the boys of the Remove had successfully tracked down a German spy, and a suitcase full of tinned food hoarded by Fisher T. Fish had been discovered by Billy Bunter who, in a typical Greyfriars' phrase, had 'scoffed the lot'. The sudden closing down of *The Magnet* in July 1940 still seems to me an act of vandalism and it was soon clear that the paper's readers were more loyal to it than its owners. When I sold several years' accumulations of *Magnets* to a local newsagent crowds of eager customers besieged his shop and he had to ration each to a single copy. We both showed poor business sense; *The Magnet* has now become a collectors' item.

The most famous magazine to be founded during the war was *Horizon*, an intellectual monthly, costing a shilling, and designed by its editors, the critic Cyril Connolly and the poet Stephen Spender, to preserve civilised values in a world at war preoccupied with lesser matters. 'We view over the waters the summit of an Ararat that is for ever bracing and reassuring', ran the publicity for the first number in December 1939. Curiously enough one of the earliest issues of *Horizon* contained an attack on *The Magnet* for allegedly inculcating snobbish values in boys, by the Old Etonian Socialist, George Orwell. Frank Richards, *The Magnet*'s sole author and then in his seventies, made a highly effective reply, revealing in turn that he did not think much of *Horizon*. According to Mr. E. S. Turner, 'He saw that it contained a picture which did not resemble a picture, a poem which did not resemble a poem and a story which did not resemble a story. From this he deduced with some accuracy that it must be "a very high-browed paper indeed".' The other influential literary magazine of the war was John Lehmann's *Penguin New Writing*, founded in 1936 but achieving far wider popularity from 1940 onwards. This, less self-consciously intellectual and *avant-garde* than *Horizon*, I found far more to my taste, and though my sole attempt to contribute to it was unsuccessful, many young writers did make their literary début in its pages.*

The growing demand for good music and serious literature was accompanied by a new interest in the visual arts. Some of the crowds which flocked to the National Gallery to hear the lunch-time concerts returned to look at the few pictures on show. Most of the Gallery's treasures were now stacked in safety deep below the Welsh hills, but a single masterpiece was exhibited in the vestibule each month, and there were several well-attended exhibitions, including one on nineteenth-century French painting, which had the queues stretching down the steps into Trafalgar Square. The Tate Gallery had also sent its collection to safety—very wisely as the building was badly damaged by bombs—but regular exhibitions were held of recent acquisitions.

Painting became a popular recreation for Civil Defence workers and firemen with time on their hands, and an exhibition of their work was held in a Bond Street gallery. CEMA, the Council for the Encouragement of Music and Arts, did its best to foster the rising interest in painting. In the early part of the war it financed the sending of exhibitions all over the country under the title of *Art for the People*, and from 1942 it began to send on tour national exhibitions like the Tate Gallery's Wartime Acquisitions. It also commissioned work from living artists, but soon discovered that oil or water colour paintings hung in canteens could be ruined by steam. Lithographs were supplied instead, from original designs by artists of such standing as Barnett Freedman and L. S. Lowry, and CEMA reproductions of colourful works by such artists as Renoir and Degas, which must have brightened the lives of many a weary war-worker.

Although some artists worked on camouflage or poster design many painters were selected as official War Artists by a committee set up by the government in December 1939 and their unmilitary figures were soon appearing in the desert and in shelters, steel foundries and fire stations. Few, if any, ever painted that great war heroine, the housewife at *her* battle station in the kitchen, though one War Artist's painting of a fish queue now hangs in the Imperial War Museum. Regular exhibitions of the War Artists' work helped to demonstrate to ordinary people that contemporary painting was not something to be puzzled over, but to be enjoyed.

It was claimed, too, that many painters profited from being forced to seek out new subjects and that, for example, the landscape painter Paul Nash added a new depth to his work in paintings like *Totes Meer*— *Dead Sea*—which showed a beach littered with wrecked German aircraft,

* I still feel grateful for the kindly letter of rejection I received—a great contrast to most editors' reaction to unsolicited work.

and that Stanley Spencer matured as a painter by getting out of the graveyards which had hitherto obsessed him into the shipyards, full of living
riveters and boiler-makers. Certainly Graham Sutherland's and John
Piper's haunting pictures of bomb damage seem likely to live, while
Henry Moore's paintings of the London Underground during the blitz
seem to evoke the discomfort and degradation not merely of the shelters
but of war itself.

# OFF DUTY

'Thousands of Londoners are finding that holidays at home can be enjoyable and interesting.'

London Transport advertisement, August 1944

One day during the middle of the war a young mother and her small daughter might have been seen crossing London between railway stations, obviously going on holiday. The small girl lovingly clutched her favourite toy, a nightdress case in the shape of a panda. But zipped inside his cuddly body was not a nightdress but a week's butter and margarine rations. Many other people have equally vivid recollections of wartime holidays, for every moment was precious and they were surrounded, too, by an aura of conscious defiance, for once, of the government which from 1941 urged every patriotic citizen to take his holidays at home. Local councils organised special attractions to encourage him to do so. The *Programme of Events for Holidays at Home* put out by the borough of Barnes in South West London in 1942, for instance, included a band concert, a Punch and Judy Show, a display of physical training, an Old World Fayre and Comic Cricket Match, another cricket match, presumably not comic, between the A.R.P. and the police and, a real sign of the times, a Saturday concert in aid of the Barnes Anglo-Soviet Friendship Committee. The only trouble about this imaginative venture was that one might never discover its existence, for in a frenzy of paper-saving the borough distributed its publicity leaflet only to alternate houses, asking readers, 'When you have perused the contents will you kindly pass it next door at one number higher than your own'.

The L.C.C. also tried that summer 'to make Stay-at-home holidays Play-at-home'. Before the war the idea of British people enjoying themselves in the open air had always seemed particularly shocking to puritans, but now to dance in the parks on a summer evening became not merely respectable but actually patriotic. In London, weather permitting, one could do the quickstep or the *Lambeth Walk* out of doors at thirteen different places every evening that summer, or take one's choice between thirteen different open-air entertainments, though with all the comedians, one suspects, telling much the same jokes. (The popular subjects in mid-

1942 were land girls, women in trousers, dried egg and the match short-age.) The capital had never presented a gayer appearance. Every swimming pool offered its swimming gala, every open space, from Victoria Park to Clapham Common, its fair or play—CEMA devoted a special effort to drama suitable for open-air theatres. The only trouble was, as usual, the queues, which on August Bank Holiday formed up every-where, especially for the boats at Richmond, where the tow-paths were jammed with dutiful holiday-at-homers. 30,000 people, that blazing hot day, crammed into the Zoo to see, besides its usual inmates, a typical if rather depressing wartime addition: an 'Off the ration' exhibition featur-ing model pig-sties and hen houses made from asbestos and cement instead of the usual materials. By 1944 London Transport was having to tackle the difficult task of encouraging people to stay at home, while discouraging them from even making day trips. 'Thousands of Londoners are finding that holidays at home can be enjoyable and interesting', one advertisement that August declared. 'But in seeking the pleasures of London and its countryside remember that, in this fifth year of war, London Transport's resources are limited. Be considerate in your trans-port demands.' Presumably the most considerate citizen of all stayed within his own four walls.

Cardiff was another place with a full programme of events. A local Boy Scout recalls how 'on Saturday afternoons at one of the local parks we staged theatrical type incidents like "Scout foils bandit armed with knife" and "Scouts show how to tackle German parachutists"'. A young housewife in the same city remembers that 'Holidays, for us, were trips to the city park where the children could paddle in the lake or have a little paddle boat out. Sometimes we picnicked in the fields beyond the golf course, or enjoyed a Field Day in the village, organised by the Townswomen's Guild, with hoop-las, lucky numbers, etc., races for the children and the most popular stall of all, a new version of Aunt Sally, throwing hard balls at jam jars to see how many one could break. There were no prizes, but oh! what a relief it was to hit out at something, if only a jam jar!'

I can remember a very different holiday-at-home entertainment—a conducted tour of the site of the first Battle of Newbury. One clergy-man's family in Somerset tried sleeping in the spare room for their week's holiday and going on day trips to Yeovil, Bristol and Bath. A Palmers Green girl, then aged eighteen, booked for a different West End show every night for a week and spent her days at the local swimming pool, becoming so tanned that her friends insisted she must have been away. It is not, in fact, only in retrospect that wartime Summers seem all sunshine and wartime winters all snow. There *were* several outstand-ingly good summers, particularly 1940, and at least two bitterly cold winters, 1939 and 1941. A North Ilford housewife has memories of two contrasting days out with her husband, then on leave, during the summer of 1944. One day, at the half-empty zoo, where the bored animals, missing their usual attention and titbits, greeted them with delight, was a great success. The next day 'We travelled for two hours to get to Richmond Park to find we couldn't get in as it had been taken over by the Army. It poured with rain and V.1s were dropping everywhere. As a day out it was a disaster.' At its best, a wartime day off could provide a break that one never forgot. This is the outstanding holiday memory of one Scotswoman, then aged twenty-three:

Apart from staying a week with an aunt in Edinburgh, I had no holiday during the war. One day stands out in my memory as so perfect that perhaps it was better than a mediocre week or fortnight. At risk of appearing before the absentee committee at the factory, I took a day off work in beautiful weather in the early summer of 1944. With my Polish fiancé and by devious routes, we managed to make our way to the shore of Loch Lomond. The weather was perfect and the Loch looked still and sleeping, with only the reflections of the great Ben darkening the waters. The wild gorse was out and the sight of its yellow blossoms went straight to my heart after the dark days spent in a factory. We hired a rowing boat and rowed our way up the Loch, quite impervious to the Loch's rather evil reputation for dangerous currents, and spent a wonderful day on one of the islands. Returning at evening, now very hungry, we went to a hotel for an evening meal. The day's enchantment lasted and we were served the most delightful meal of salmon with salad. In the darkening evening we started to make our way homeward, when suddenly we heard the sounds of men's voices singing. It was a company of Polish soldiers, singing *Loch Lomond* as they marched along, so far from their own land. (Many Poles sang this song so well that they were frequently asked to do so at concerts and I believe it was recorded before they eventually returned to their homeland.) As a postscript to this day, I must say that the old superstition that it is unlucky for lovers to visit the Loch proved to be—in our case—quite unfounded.

Most truly peaceful holidays where 'you wouldn't have known there was a war on', the highest compliment any resort could be paid, were inland. The Lake District is remembered with particular pleasure. 'It was another world it was so peaceful', felt a Nottingham housewife who stayed with friends in Kendal. 'This part of England seemed to be quite untouched by the war', a young girl working for the Air Ministry who spent two wonderful holidays there discovered. The Derbyshire dales, too, were a haven of tranquillity. It was, one woman Civil Defence worker from

Sheffield decided, when hiking there during her husband's leave, well worth getting stranded there in out-of-the-way places with no buses, for 'It was heaven to get away from it all for a while'. A Hornsey house-wife, whose husband and herself only left London for one week to stay with cousins in Bedfordshire, still vividly recalls 'the blessed relief, the peace and quiet'. But nearer the coast these were often missing. A housewife from Sunbury, in Middlesex, remembers a fortnight with relatives at Hassocks in Sussex in early October 1940: 'The weather was absolutely beautiful and we thoroughly enjoyed the change. The only drawback was the occasional "dogfights" one could see in the distance.'

One of the most successful wartime schemes provided free or assisted holidays for tired Civil Defence workers and the owners of several stately homes generously offered them for this purpose. One North London couple, both wardens, enjoyed a marvellous week as the guests of a titled couple in Dorset, where they spent 'many happy hours wan-dering round the estate as well as doing small tasks such as collecting the eggs and helping in the vegetable garden'. A Birmingham housewife, married to an auxiliary fireman, benefited from the free railway ticket issued to him 'to take a rest from the blitz. We decided to go to Blackpool. . . . We loaded the pram with spare tins of food, in among baby clothes, then covered the pram with sacking and lashed it down. It was a pleasure to sleep in a bed and not be woken up with sirens. But there were no amusements on the front and half the beach was taken up by the R.A.F.'

Late in the war the government provided holiday hostels for exhausted war workers who had worn themselves out in the Battle for Production. One was managed by a London man who had run a rest-centre during the blitz, and now arrived, in September 1943, to take charge of a large empty house standing in twenty acres near Shrewsbury. 'Coming as I had from the rubble-strewn streets of London the grounds seemed out of this world', he later wrote. 'The very grass on the lawn, neglected though it was, felt like velvet under my feet. And in the woods the yell-owy-gold and brown leaves of autumn were already falling from great oaks and tulip and chestnut trees.' Inside, the building offered a striking contrast to the average war factory, with its 'light and spacious rooms with floor-to-ceiling windows . . . walls panelled in rich dark oak and fireplaces with wide open hearths—one actually had steps built in', for the climbing boys who had once cleaned it. But he was brought swiftly back to the present day by the host of forms he had to complete to re-equip it. One shortage was of toilet accommodation, 'but when I indented for a dozen chamber-pots . . . I received a form on which to state for what purpose the utensils were needed'. He apparently filled it in con-vincingly; the missing articles arrived in a large crate labelled URGENT.

Later came the intended residents whose appearance spoke for itself. 'One chap, looked like death warmed up when he came to Radbrook Hall', the hall's manager observed. 'He used to fall asleep during meals.... We nicknamed him "Sleepy". Before he left he was as fit as a fiddle.'

Except in the largest hotels one was expected, if staying more than a night or two, to take one's own sheets, towels and soap, plus emergency ration cards, or one's ration book, for any stay longer than three days. Many holiday-makers also took extra food with them. A Huddersfield housewife and a friend carelessly hoarded up their points for a large tin of salmon to ensure at least one solid and festive meal during their holiday, but halfway to Blackpool realised they had left it at home. A seventeen-year-old girl from Barking, who went to Colchester for a week with a girl friend—they chose it because it was not too far from their home—had an opposite experience. Halfway through the week the friend discovered a mouldy pork pie in her suitcase, thoughtfully put there by her mother. Disposing secretly of this pie became the great problem of the holiday, for throwing food away was a criminal offence. 'We carried the wretched pie around for two days', one of the girls remembers, 'attempting to rid ourselves of it. Each time we tried to hurl it over a hedge someone would come into view or a farm tractor would start up somewhere and we'd almost drop the thing in fright. Attempts at leaving it under the seat of a bus always failed, too, as someone would seem to be observing us. . . . Our guilty conscience enhanced our fears.' Eventually fate provided the answer, for having decided to treat themselves to a good meal in an expensive café 'with wicker tables and chairs, potted palms and expensive carpeting . . . and to blazes with the expense', they found that 'the one waitress . . . seemed to regard us as intruders and completely ignored our presence. . . . After at least twenty-five minutes . . . we decided to leave, but before we indignantly did so our eyes met. . . . The pork pie was retrieved from the bag and placed under the chair. Leaving our memento behind, we sailed out and flew down the road feeling as guilty as if it had been a bomb we'd planted.'

The way in which these two obviously jolly girls had found their accommodation was in itself not untypical of wartime. On arrival at the station they asked the advice of the nearest milkman, who immediately gave them a note to 'Darling', his wife, 'a short insignificant little woman with curlers and buck teeth', who readily agreed to put them up for a week and finally invited them to accompany her to a dance at the local barracks. 'She giggled, simpered and twittered as she explained that "Hubby" went to Home Guard duty on Fridays', and her way of preparing for this occasion had her two guests 'in silent convulsions. . . . Her hair rolled into tight corkscrews, frills, buttons and bows abounded and she must have been adorned with every trinket she possessed. Bangles by the tier, brooches, necklaces, ear-rings and flowers in her hair.' But she had a partner for every dance and even captured an exceptionally handsome sergeant who responded to the girls' welcoming glances by coming towards the little party and then to 'our utter consternation smilingly by-passed us both and invited our companion to dance'.

Most of their holiday was spent 'exploring the countryside, drinking in the loveliness of it all . . . in the evenings we would go to a dance, ending up in *Alf's Cafe* for a mug of tea and a wad one evening with our escorts, if they were English, or supper at *The Duke's Head* if our escorts were American or Canadian soldiers'. The climax of their holiday was a bus trip to Clacton with two American airmen. 'The beach was cordoned off with barbed wire, but we were able to sun ourselves in deck chairs along part of the promenade. To actually see the sea again was a refreshing experience and we all shed our coats and soaked up the sun and told each other about ourselves. . . . They were with the American Air Force stationed at Earls Colne near Colchester and the tension which built up resulting from the many missions they flew over Germany was very apparent. . . . We had a wonderful day, ending with a chicken dinner in the evening. . . . We had arranged to meet them the following evening, but only one came. . . . Several of the planes had been shot down and the boy we'd spent the previous day with had been killed. . . . We returned to work feeling much sadder, older and wiser.'

Sometimes, as in the guest house in the West Country where a Surrey girl stayed, visitors were expected to make their own beds every morning and to help with the washing-up on Sundays. Almost everywhere such luxuries as early-morning tea and breakfast in bed disappeared, though some hotels compromised by providing tea-trays for guests to collect from downstairs. But what really decided the success of a wartime holiday was the food and many people's chief memory is of being permanently hungry. Among main courses still remembered with horror are a single sardine and a small piece of lettuce, and baked potatoes served with margarine. There was also some outrageous profiteering. One Civil Servant from Newcastle-on-Tyne still begrudges the 7s. 6d. she was charged for one new-laid egg and some stale 'bread and scrape' on a farm near Edinburgh; a reasonable price would have been 1s. 6d.

Plentiful eggs could easily make a holiday by themselves. A Birmingham couple were delighted to encounter in Uttoxeter a landlady who apologised for having nothing to offer them except eggs. They chose to stay at the same guest house on the return journey and were offered two dozen to take home, the holiday souvenir of a lifetime. The young wife of a maintenance fitter at Boots in Nottingham remembers how, after buying a tandem in 1941 and cycling to a farm in the Hope Valley in Derbyshire, they 'lived like lords' for a week on home produce.

Their next holiday was less successful; after going by train to Buxton, they spent a whole week feeling hungry. A thirty-year-old nurse from Willesden managed to forgive the fleas and dirt in the bedrooms of the farm she stayed at near Bodmin, for the food was 'fabulous'.

Second only to food in importance was the absence of air raids. A young girl working at a factory in Staines found that her greatest joy during a long weekend at Weymouth was simply to go to bed and sleep through until the morning without being wakened by sirens. A secretary working in London remembers 'going for a week's holiday to Babbacombe with a friend during the blitz and arriving at our lovely hotel on the cliffs complete with tin hat and gas mask and feeling so stupid because there it was all peace and beauty. . . . It was another world. . . . Never have I appreciated the birds and the peace and calm of the trees and flowers as much anywhere since.' A woman who rented holiday apartments on the Island of Bute off the Scottish coast found that her visitors always 'wanted to come *before* their time, and were reluctant to leave until the last boat on the last day . . . I always felt sorry for them. . . . If it hadn't been for the supply depot ship and the submarines in the Bay, we would hardly have known that there was a war on.'

Bute was clearly an exception. Most seaside holiday resorts provided only too many reminders of the war. A Scoutmaster from Stafford who visited Margate on New Year's Day 1945 felt that it resembled a ghost town. The beach was deserted; coils of barbed wire barred the promenade; the parish church had been burned out and only about five shops in the main street were still in business. A housewife from Hayes, Middlesex, who spent a day in the same town felt she had 'never seen such desolation, with weeds growing through shops and hotels. But as we and two other people got out of the station the smell of lavender was marvellous.' Today she has only to smell lavender to be carried back again to that hot wartime day. A twenty-three-year-old schoolteacher from Nottingham, who visited Mablethorpe in Lincolnshire with a friend, was glad to leave it again, for although the sun shone, the town was deserted and the beach mined and covered with barbed wire. Holiday-making in wartime was symbolised for a London housewife by a day spent on the beach at Exmouth sitting between the barbed wire fences, until the guns started up across the water and she decided that it was time to go home. In many seaside towns a section of the barbed wire was moved at low tide to enable residents to reach the sea and one Plymouth woman who bathed from her house in the early morning was furious at being asked for her identity card on her way back. With no pockets in her swimsuit, she had left it at home. But some determined bathers were not to be deterred even by barbed wire. One woman cycled twenty miles to Hayling Island with some of her workmates, who managed to crawl through the barricades to picnic and bathe on the beach. (One can only hope the Germans, had they landed, would have been more easily deterred.)

Apart from the wired-off sea, few resorts could offer much by way of entertainment for they were supposed to discourage visitors rather than attract them. But the war provided some sights of its own. A Birmingham housewife has this memory of wartime Weston-super-Mare. 'Every day sections of R.A.F. recruits were "square bashing" on the front and each year that we went we would find that the age of the men had gone up by about five years ranging from nineteen years in the early days to thirty-fives and forties in 1944. It saddened me almost more than anything. I kept wondering what had happened to all the lads of the earlier years.' Later in the war coach trips became a forgotten luxury but a London nurse on holiday near Plymouth in July 1940 remembers one when 'there was an air raid with reports of parachute landings. Our coach and all the vehicles on the road were ordered into a large inn yard by a valiant and determined clergyman, his grey hair streaming in the breeze as he brandished a weapon that looked to us to be a relic of the Crimea.'

Even mothers willing to sacrifice their own usual week at the seaside found it hard that their children should also be deprived of this irreplaceable childhood pleasure and in the summer of 1945, with victory in Europe won, many families refused to wait any longer. That year many women were moved to tears by hearing childish voices asking at railway stations, 'What are those things for, Mummy?', as they saw other children carrying buckets and spades, saved from earlier years. None of the other seaside treats—the 'windmills', the sand-moulds, the kites and paper flags—was yet to be seen in the shops. A Huddersfield housewife who spent four days at Blackpool discovered that though buckets and spades could not be bought anywhere they could be hired, for 4s. 6d. a set, of which 2s. 6d. was a returnable deposit, prices fixed in her mind because two of the precious spades were lost, 'so it was an expensive holiday'.

The very phrase 'working holiday' had a wartime ring about it, and on the whole such experiences were not a success. The falling-off of support for agricultural camps has already been mentioned; one member of the Women's Land Army, reversing the usual movement, decided to spend her holiday working as a domestic in the local hospital, but she soon regretted it as it merely provided another form of hard work. More happily remembered are cycling and camping holidays. Cycling, with the roads empty, had seldom been more enjoyable, though accommodation was often difficult to find due to spare rooms being filled with evacuees. An Ealing family on a cycling holiday at Whitsun 1941 found every room in Leighton Buzzard taken and had to spend the night in a wood near Woburn Abbey, plagued by cold, discomfort and the noise of the guns in the distance. They gave up trying to sleep at 5 a.m. and, too tired to ride, walked their machines several miles to Aylesbury for breakfast. When they did find a bed, in guest houses or private homes recommended by the Cyclist Touring Club, prices were not unreasonable: from 4s. to 6s. 6d. for bed and breakfast, rising in small hotels to 9s. or 10s. For some reason adults arriving alone by cycle were often objects of suspicion. One London woman booking clerk who knocked at the door of one house near Newbury in her cycling cape on a wet, dark night, had it slammed in her face amid screams from the woman inside who had mistaken her for a German parachutist. Later, a local hotel also viewed her with distrust, offering her companions a bed, 'but', pointing at her, 'not him'. Finally she secured a room, without food, at the local pub. 'Wringing wet, I trudged upstairs. In the morning I struggled into my wet shirt, pants and everything else and made my way to the hotel.' The miniscule breakfast offered there did little to revive her spirits: 'Porridge (one spoonful and it was gone) followed by two chipolata sausages three inches long, half a slice of bread and "That's your lot!" . . . I had some good times cycling during the war', she sums up, 'but I learnt my lesson, to take my own food and a change of clothing.'

Self-catering holidays, with food and service in hotels so poor, had obvious attractions. The parents of a Sheffield schoolgirl, with a sister, 'In 1941 when we were ten and fourteen . . . rented a house for a month ten miles away on the edge of the Derbyshire moors. It was near enough for my father to be able to keep an eye on the family firm and . . . for us to take our own transport, bikes, horse and ponies. Also we decided to take our own independent milk supply in the form of one of our goats . . . My sister and I . . . had to do the milking. The goat to be given a holiday was noted for its temperament and we had omitted to practise on her beforehand. At every attempt to milk her, she sat down. After two days the farm man was brought over to milk her, and after another two days she was sent home!' A Northampton couple went to even greater trouble, buying a large poultry hut to serve as a holiday home, and hiring a coal cart, complete with horse and driver, to move it to a country site five miles away. The holiday began in fine style. 'The horse was fixed up with a gay rosette beside each ear and a bright coloured ribbon bow decorated its tail', the father of the family recalls. 'We loaded the cart with hut, camping beds, kitchen and cooking kit, blankets and a bell tent for our two evacuees to sleep in. I cycled in front and my wife, daughter and the two boys cycled at the rear of the cart. A policeman I knew called out as we passed him, "What's that you have on the cart? Our new secret weapon?"' Erecting the hut in the blazing hot July sunshine proved no joke; nor did the giant hail-stones which pounded the roof that night or the storm which first rocked the hut on its foundations and then flooded it out, along with the tent. 'We . . . borrowed spades . . . and dug trenches round the tents and hut. For a time I thought I was back in Flanders. But next day the sun shone again and we never saw another cloud in the sky for a whole week. I shall always remember that wartime holiday. . . . Voted by my family as the best we ever experienced. After all, there was a war on, and our troubles were chicken feed by comparison.'

Organised sport suffered even more than ordinary holiday-making. When the first football matches were held after the outbreak of war, even the sarcastic remarks made to the referee had changed. 'Take your gas mask off!', he was loudly advised when he missed a suspected foul, and 'Blow the siren and let's take cover!', when play was slow. But a far greater change was the smallness of the crowds. At first they were limited to 15,000 in 'safe' areas and 8,000 elsewhere, but in fact only 5,000 people turned up to the first wartime 'friendly' at Fulham at the end of September. A system of district competitions, with eight leagues in England and Wales and two in Scotland, was hastily improvised, involving eighty-two of the eighty-eight leading clubs, but they attracted only a third to a tenth of the 1938 'gates' and the spectators seemed listless and bored.

For later seasons a War Cup competition was introduced; the cup itself stayed in the cellar of a pub in Portsmouth, home-town of its pre-war holders, and was periodically put on display, becoming regarded as a form of talisman for the city's survival. The playing season was extended to June but other innovations pleased the fans less. Matches often began up to two hours late due to raids and some had to be abandoned altogether, the score at the time being counted as the final one. Many grounds were badly damaged by bombing and more by neglect; at Old Trafford, Manchester, by the end of the war there were trees six feet high on the terraces. Even worse for the soccer enthusiast was the unpredictable behaviour of his favourite team. The places of called-up players were filled by anyone available, including spectators. This produced such strange results as 'Brighton and Hove Albion 0—Norwich City 18'. The Brighton team consisted of five of its own players, the two Norwich reserves and five soldiers recruited from the crowd.

With results so unpredictable, interest in the football pools, too, slumped during the war, aided perhaps, by the feeling that it was tempting providence to try to win a fortune in such times. I remember this providing the plot of a short story written by a classmate; the hero, having declared that the danger of his house being hit is as remote as his chance of winning the pools, dies in the bombed ruins just as the congratulatory telegram arrives.

To save the Post Office work, the pools had been banned at the start of the war, and when they returned in November 1939 the promoters did everything they could to forestall public criticisms. They formed a single organisation Unity Pools, to which almost all belonged, and printed their entry coupons in the newspapers, which the investor had to cut out and post to the nearest of some forty towns, from Aberdeen to York. But the enemies of gambling were not satisfied, complaining that 'the pools created an unreal demand for newspapers', and were 'an undesirable factor of life in wartime'. Other critics wanted to see part of the pool given to war charities or the prizes paid out in savings certificates. In fact the number of people 'doing the pools' slumped to only ten per cent of the pre-war figure and even a first dividend often brought in no more than £1,500. It was not until the season of 1946/7 that football and the pools were restored to their pre-war glory.

Cricket-lovers are likely to look back to the war with even less pleasure. From 1940 to 1944 there was no county championship and no real-first-class cricket, so that keen cricketers had to content themselves with friendly one-day matches between scratch sides, drawing on local amateurs and professionals and on any first-class players in the district. One Northampton man still recalls his feeling of horror at seeing 'Cricket pitches bulldozed to make way for air-raid shelters. To me, a cricketer, it seemed at the time to be a gigantic act of vandalism.' The Ministry of Agriculture promised that 'there would be no interference, except under grave emergency, with private cricket grounds', but the Germans showed less consideration. On 27th August 1940 *The Times* cricket correspondent reported 'For the first time probably in the history of cricket "raid stopped play" at Lord's on Saturday.' But somehow the game survived and a trickle of bats, balls and stumps continued to be made. I cannot, alas, recall a single game at my school ever being cancelled due to lack of equipment and, though a few rugger pitches were ploughed up, the cricket pitches remained sacrosanct.

Professional lawn tennis tournaments ceased for the duration. Wimbledon itself was taken over as a decontamination centre, and local tennis courts often provided useful sites for Ack Ack batteries, while members of clubs which did manage to keep going sometimes felt rather embarrassed at enjoying themselves. A twenty-six-year-old shop assistant at Welwyn noted in his diary for Tuesday 21st May 1940: 'Everything here is perfectly peaceful, the weather is lovely.... Playing tennis nearly every night seems a bit caddish with such an awful war raging, but it seems better than moping to me.' This was a reasonable conclusion and, later, such qualms troubled most players less. By then a greater problem was the shortage of partners—and of balls and rackets. One young tennis player still recalls his embarrassment at having to queue up among the expectant mothers at a West End store to buy a single nappy, to tear into strips to bind the handle of his racket.

Many sports clubs became casualties of the war. An eighteen-year-old girl working at the G.P.O. headquarters at Mount Pleasant remembers that the staff struggled to keep the office hockey team going, but the pleasant 'after the match' party ceased, and after two seasons the club had to be disbanded. Another Civil Servant, working in Ipswich, 'continued to play hockey, badminton and table tennis. All players got a few balls or shuttles by any possible means and added them to the club stocks. Hockey club uniform was a problem. We did not want to look too "rag-time" but could not ask members to spend coupons on sports uniform. Eventually we heard of surplus W.R.N.S. blouses on the market; bought a supply and had them dyed club colour. These were worn with navy shorts—everyone had navy shorts or shorts which could by dyed navy. The purchase of white paint for balls was permitted. . . . A number of forms had to be completed but we got the paint, far more than needed. The surplus was sold at cost price to a friend who had a boat . . . for which he could get no paint. Matches were all, of course, with local teams but we kept the club going.'

Golf, for some reason, had always seemed to many non-golfers to symbolise time-wasting, and some golfers themselves had not, perhaps, forgotten the pre-1914 rhyme about the dedicated golfer who had been

> Playing golf when the Germans landed
> And the thought of England's shame,
> Almost put me off my game.

In the summer of 1940 it became a rare sight to see a man carrying golf clubs; one leading club found itself one Saturday with only four foursomes and four pairs playing. The founding of the L.D.V., besides providing another counter-attraction, also gave a number of golf clubs some much-needed support. 'Four ball cliques joined up together, did their guard together and often finished up with a round of golf before going to business', the commander of one Leeds platoon reported. The club tea-room became the unit guard room, the drying room its armoury and 'we had the assistance of the green keeper and his staff in the making of a bomb-practice range and bayonet fighting assault course'. Some of these members, their C.O. admitted, 'find it difficult to forget golf. . . . At first their reports had a smack of golf in them, e.g. "Flares seen over the thirteenth green".' Often during these weeks, as during the flying bomb summer of 1944, players took shelter in the rough or the bunkers before continuing their round. A set of emergency rules issued by the secretary of Richmond golf club in 1940 admirably illustrate the determined golfer's refusal to be put off his game by a mere war.

Players are asked to collect bomb and shell splinters to save these causing damage to the mowers. . . .

A ball moved by enemy action may be replaced as near as possible where it lay or if lost or destroyed a ball may be dropped not nearer the hole without penalty.

A player whose stroke is affected by the simultaneous explosion of a bomb or shell or by machine gun fire may play another ball from the same place. Penalty one stroke.

Many golf courses were taken over, wholly or partly, by balloons, searchlights, anti-aircraft guns or whole military camps and all were covered with anti-landing barricades, an extra stroke being allowed if a ball struck one. *Golf Monthly* for April 1943 recorded with shocked horror the fate of one seaside course taken over as a Royal Artillery training ground. When asked by his men what targets they were to fire at, 'the officer, who incidentally could not be a golfer, said, "What better do you want than the eight greens that are here?" And so this championship course . . . was blown to pieces. . . . There will never again be eighteen greens that will be playable upon.' But *Golf Monthly* was not wholly pessimistic about the future. 'Notwithstanding persistent efforts . . . to get all golf courses put under the plough and take every golf clubhouse for military service, we believe that in 1943, for any club that faces the situation in a sane and sensible manner, the prospects are all right.' Indeed it was every golfer's duty to keep up his game as 'the best insurance against cracking under the stress and strain of war work and tightening war economy. Get into the fresh air . . . and take full measure of the light chatter and the happiness at the nineteenth hole.' Keen golfers also justified the time they spent on the golf course by taking part in competitions for war charities. But even helping the war effort could not excuse dangerous ventures into professionalism and the 'Royal and Ancient' Club at St. Andrews solemnly warned that 'The offer of War Savings Certificates in any form of golf competition is to be deprecated and anyone competing for such a prize would be held to be "playing for a money prize" '.

Many non-golfers still cast envious eyes on the land given up to the game and official visitors sometimes, to the horror of club secretaries, suggested such compromises as ploughing up half an eighteen hole course or reducing a nine hole course to six holes. The best protection against having your finest fairways ploughed up was to turn them into grassland. One golf course near Belfast constructed just before the war was only saved from the plough on this condition. 'The golf course', the daughter of the man who made it recalls, 'was a first-class one.

All greens were completely weed free under the vigilant supervision of my father. . . . When war started all fairways were promptly fenced off and cattle grazed on the rough while sheep roamed on the immaculate fairways.' The course's condition was soon threatened even more by lack of labour. 'Gradually the staff of ten men dwindled to two . . . Father and I maintained the golf course between us for four long years. We had to overhaul a forty-year-old mower and . . . bought a good strong cob for £15. We very soon trained Mick to pull the mower . . . I mowed the precious greens by hand.' The same family even managed to overcome the shortage of golf balls. 'Fortunately for us our local grocer was also an extremely keen golfer. Golf balls were as gold to him and occasionally a little extra ration of this or that was sent along to the green keeper's house where [he hinted] we might find a few balls for him, old or cut or in any condition even.'

For while clubs could usually be obtained somehow, though steel-shafted ones ceased to be made, there was no substitute for the golf ball and the price rose sharply, reaching 5s. apiece, although the official price for the top quality 'Silver Ring' type was 2s. or 3s. In Dundee, late in 1943, two enterprising men dragged a pond on a golf course and retrieved 473 lost balls for re-sale, but were arrested and fined, less for stealing than for indecency: one man had been naked and the other had worn nothing but his pants. A year earlier the Controller of Rubber had, *Golf Monthly* reported, caused 'consternation in the whole golf ball business' by banning the remould of old golf balls but, as a result of protests, 'wiser counsels prevailed and the order was rescinded'. *Golf Monthly* also warned against buying balls from unknown firms. One golfer, it reported, had managed to sink his putt, but as it dropped into the hole 'a bit of the ball fell off'.

Racing was the subject of bitter controversy throughout the war, though greyhound racing produced less ill-feeling than horse racing, for meetings were shorter and most of those attending them were clearly working men who had travelled on public transport. The black-out at first almost killed 'the dogs', but soon meetings were being held in the afternoons and shift workers, it was claimed, made up most of the crowds. Later in the war, to save petrol and manpower, Herbert Morrison was put under pressure to abolish the sport, but he refused, arguing that 'within reason public entertainments act as a lubricant, rather than a brake, on the war effort'. To mollify public opinion, however, greyhound racing was further restricted to one day a week per track, which had to be either a Saturday or a public holiday. Other sports, he pointed out to the House of Commons, had made comparable sacrifices, like professional boxing, which now had only ten per cent as many big fights as before the war.

But it was horse racing which caused the real indignation. At the start of the war many young thoroughbred horses were put to sleep, but by mid-October racing had been resumed, at Newmarket, and a month later the tote re-opened, at Newbury, a course later put to better use as an army camp and as an assembly site for gliders. Other sections of the sport also made their contribution to the war effort. A Newmarket woman recalls how 'the horse-boxes designed by my father to carry the world's finest race horses were requisitioned for transporting delicate radar equipment—a few being left to carry mares and foals and horses still in training to the remaining few race courses'. 'Few' was the word. By 1942 only a fifth as many race meetings were being held as before the war and in October Herbert Morrison announced further cuts, explaining that future events would be confined to courses chosen 'with a view to economies in the use of public transport'. But, against all the odds, racing survived. Had Sir John Anderson, a Presbyterian, remained Home Secretary it probably would have been banned. That it escaped was due to a strange alliance of aristocratic Conservatives, who regarded racing as a recreation for gentlemen, Ernest Bevin who argued bluntly that 'when a chap's thinking about who's going to win the 2.30 he isn't thinking about me', and, above all, Herbert Morrison, whose inclination was always towards both 'fun' and freedom. This was certainly a far from unworthy motive. Whether the result was a matter for pride is perhaps debatable.

Though racing was suspect, other country sports were regarded as both patriotic and respectable, as helping to keep down vermin and thus save food. There was no shortage of sporting cartridges and one twelve-year-old girl, living in the country near Sheffield, acquired the curious accomplishment of learning to shoot at rabbits through the open bathroom window with a twelve bore sporting rifle. Later in the war she often supplemented her sweet ration by winning bars of chocolate at fairground rifle ranges. Several packs of foxhounds managed to carry on right through the war, though, one keen horsewoman living in Buckinghamshire remembers, 'mounted followers were necessarily few and their horses often unclipped and less fit than in normal times'. This had its advantages. Her pack, the Old Berkeley, 'hunted on Saturdays, which it had not done before, and the small fields and the slower pace of the hunting made it an admirable school for novices and children'. The season did, however, finish early, at the end of February instead of May, to avoid the risk of harming growing crops. This countrywoman, like many others, took to using a pony and trap, or paying calls on horseback. This method of travel she found 'quickly gave a feeling of mutual interest with the farmers', when she visited them as a part-time W.V.S. welfare officer for their land girls. To get herself and her family to distant meets of the hunt she relied on 'a wonderful fifteen hands Irish hunter, Paddy. This horse I used to harness to the trap, drive as far as Holyport, with two or three children, hire ponies for the children, hunt Paddy myself with the Garth hunt, and at the end of the day he brought us all home again. Not a bad performance on war-time feeding.'

# ANY GUM, CHUM?

'If Britons sit in trains or buses without striking up conversation with you, it doesn't mean they are being haughty and unfriendly. Probably they are paying more attention to you than you think.'

*Britain* A booklet of advice *For all Members of American Expeditionary Forces in Great Britain* c. 1942

One evening towards the end of the war an Ayrshire girl, then in her twenties, found herself forcibly drawn away 'by a boy with a broad Scots accent' from the Polish soldier with whom she had been dancing at a church hall social. 'Have nothing to do with thae fellahs', he told her firmly. 'They go to bed with hair nets on.' This rumour, true as it happens, as a Dunfermline housewife confirms, was only one of the successive shocks that the people of the British Isles sustained between 1939 and 1945. Towns which had barely seen a foreigner before the war, villages where a visitor from another county was considered a stranger, became accustomed to hearing in their streets, and even in their own homes, strange tongues they could not even identify. The Scottish girl already mentioned also met Norwegians, Canadians, 'brash and quarrelsome', French Canadians who played ice-hockey but 'would fight at the drop of a hockey stick and threw the puck at the spectators'; Indians; Dutchmen; 'a full-blooded American Indian with a scar over one eyebrow'; the burly G.I. who, during 'an old Scottish singing-game . . . despite my 5 ft. 8½ in., lifted me off my feet and gave me a darn great kiss to accompanying yells of encouragement'. This was nearly her last encounter with an ally, for her mouth had been full of chewing gum, which 'went half-way down my gullet and stuck. Much back-slapping prevailed before it was recovered.'

But in most places, especially in Scotland, it was the Poles who came first and, until the Americans arrived, made the greatest impact. Another Scots girl, at Broughty Ferry in Angus, remembers the arrival in 1941 of 'hordes of Polish Army officers . . . many of them cavalry, in uniforms which looked like something out of an opera. . . . As an eighteen-year-old . . . the year the Poles were stationed here was one of the most exciting I have known . . . we must have been mesmerised by the glamorous uniform, broken English and lavish generosity.' Another young woman at Hawick, not far away, found they seemed little handicapped by lack of English, as 'they were able to get anything they wanted, from soap to laxatives, by using pantomime'. A Midlands clergyman liked the Polish airmen he met in Nottingham, despite the local story that they knew only two words of English, 'girl' and 'bed' and always used them together.

Later visitors also obligingly conformed to the expected national stereotypes. The Norwegians really did have a blond and open-air look, the French actually were gallant towards women, the Americans were, just as one expected from the films, self-confident, gum-chewing and generous. Least popular on the whole were some notoriously rowdy Scots regiments and several ill-disciplined and boastful Commonwealth units. An Ipswich woman remembers an Australian entering her family sweet shop with the observation, ' "The war will soon be over now that we are here. Limeys never were fighters." My reply was that we had managed very well so far, thank you.' Men from the occupied countries, were, by contrast, grateful to Great Britain. The commander of a force of 'specials' in a rural district of Cumberland remembers 'one night when . . . I had about twenty six-foot Norwegians dancing a sort of "ring-a-ring-of roses" round me in the middle of the village square—very undignified for a 5 ft, 7¾ in. Special Police Commander. . . . All very friendly, however, with a chant they sang of "You ally. You ally!" '

Foreign civilian refugees, excluding pre-war arrivals, were less popular. A teenage girl from Balham's chief memory of the French refugees billeted on them is that they used 'to run like rabbits every time there was a raid, taking our best eiderdowns and pillows with them'. The Chelsea artist, Frances Faviell, struggling to teach a party of refugees from the low countries English, found much of her time was spent in trying to prevent the men fighting each other. A Potters Bar housewife who had lived in Belgium and spoke the Walloon language, found serving on a committee to welcome Belgian refugees disillusioning. 'Every morning the Belgians in our house went out around the town. They visited every sweetshop and tobacconist and pleaded for "chocolat" for their families, and . . . would arrive home around mid-day with sacks—yes, sacks—absolutely chock full of sweets and cigarettes and would flaunt them around the house.' Later, after escorting male Belgians to Bristol and finding them a hotel, she woke 'in the early hours to find one of the trio getting into bed with me. He had a penknife near my arm and was going to kill me, he said, if I said "no". I said "no" and I jolly well meant it but he had locked the door and pocketed the key.' After a prolonged resistance, she was able to escape, unharmed, when the maid brought her morning tea.

Opinion was far more divided about 'The Yanks', who, with their smart new uniforms, bulging wallets and obvious eagerness to please, brought a breath of fresh air to the grey, bomb-damaged streets of war-time Britain, from early in 1942. In the next three years several million Americans passed through the British Isles *en route* for other battlefields or manned the airfields and supply bases of East Anglia and Southern England; three-quarters of a million arrived in the five months from January 1944 to D Day. The West End of London seemed to have been taken over by these newcomers and comedians told the story of how they had actually seen an Englishman in Grosvenor Square, heart of the 'American occupied' area. Outside London the sight of gum-chewing G.I.s was almost equally common with, as one Scottish girl remembers, 'peroxide blondes draped over their arms', wearing 'cameras like strings of beads'. In Devon, during the great build-up for D Day, the narrow lanes became one way for miles to accommodate their large staff cars and quickly-moving Jeeps; no American ever seemed to walk anywhere. Near Newbury I spent long afternoons one holiday watching as the wide stretches of common which had been my childhood playground were submerged beneath the concrete of runways for a fleet of American Dakotas, which, on the night before D Day, were to carry thousands of airborne troops into Normandy.

Other foreign troops, despite the language barrier, had largely been left to find their own feet, but great trouble was taken by the American authorities to enable their men to fit into wartime Britain. Every newly-arrived G.I.—the term derived from the phrase 'government issue' and meant any ordinary soldier—was issued with a booklet warning of the pitfalls surrounding him. 'The British are often more reserved in conduct than we. . . . So if Britons sit in trains or buses without striking up conversation with you, it doesn't mean they are being haughty and unfriendly. Don't be misled by the British tendency to be soft-spoken and polite. If they need to be they can be plenty tough.' The pamphlet warned against using expressions like 'I look like a bum', which might be offensive to British ears, but misunderstandings did still occur. A woman who worked in an American Army Post Office at Sutton Coldfield found herself hastily shushed into silence when she asked for a rubber—American for a contraceptive. Another Englishwoman in Ipswich remembers raised eyebrows when an American visitor explained that he was 'piddling in the garden', the American equivalent of 'pottering about'. The official pamphlet cautioned its readers that 'You can rub a Britisher the wrong way by telling him "we came over and won the last one" ', and many Americans discovered with pained surprise that the first reaction to their presence was usually 'About time, too!' On the whole most Americans conquered their natural self-assertiveness remarkably well; the widely-heard story of one who asked for a beer 'As quick as the British got out of Dunkirk' was almost certainly an invention of Lord Haw-Haw. Another popular joke was, however, home grown: that the Americans were all right except for four things, they were over-paid, over-fed, over-sexed—and over here. Despite such pleasantries most British civilians liked the Americans. The tremendous zest and thoroughness with which they did whatever they set their hands, feet or minds to, whether it was unloading a ship, jitter-bugging in a dance hall or trying to get off with a girl, particularly impressed everyone. The Americans went at every job as if they meant to win the war if not this week then certainly next. In Newbury they caused much amusement by their flamboyant method of collecting their troops' pay from a local bank. British units would send a single officer with a briefcase; the 'Yanks' employed a convoy of jeeps, which would scream dramatically to a halt in the peaceful market place, and a posse of tough-looking, American military police would leap out with tommy guns at the ready. When a local community had been inconvenienced by the Americans, they immediately went to enormous pains to set matters right. 'The American Army had a fine reputation among the civilian population which was not shared by other forces', a then schoolboy living in Dorset believes. When the ancient gateway to his house was damaged by an American army vehicle 'it was repaired to the original colour within two days'. After a farm belonging to a friend's father was damaged by American tanks on manœuvres, 'within a week the "Yanks" . . . repaired all the hedges and harvested the crop, with jeeps towing old-fashioned binders'.

For the first time, baseball was played in many parts of the British Isles, often as a novelty at fund-raising open-air events. 'One Saturday I helped at the First Aid Post of a park baseball match', a Birmingham Red Cross worker recalls. 'Despite warnings, people would *not* keep their distance. We were kept constantly busy treating bruises.' But the greatest impact the Americans made on the younger part of the population was as providers of 'candy', their sickly, and singularly tasteless, chocolate bars and chewing gum. Crowds of small boys gathered outside American clubs to pester them for gifts, or called out as American lorries passed: 'Any gum, chum?' which rapidly became a national catchphrase. The wife of a farm worker living near Dorchester, who forbad her small son to ask directly for sweets, found that he managed to come home loaded up with them simply by saying 'Hello!' as American soldiers marched past. At Christmas here, as in many places, the Americans gave a party for the local children, collecting them by jeep—a great thrill. A London housewife still remembers the G.I. who gave her son and daughter a banana each at Lime Street station, Liverpool. 'We were quite overcome at this "manna from heaven".' A Glasgow housewife recalls that her one-year-old baby had never tasted an orange until some passing American soldiers threw her some from their lorry, with a shout of 'Oranges for the baby'. The cinema, unexpectedly, was one area where differences between the two countries were marked. Many Americans extinguished their cigarettes on entering, believing there to be a no-smoking rule. Some hard-drinkers took bottles of whisky into the back rows with them, leaving the empty bottle under the seat, while the common American habit of lodging discarded chewing gum under the arms of the seats was a constant irritation to the cinemas' depleted staffs. G.I.s as a whole, however, had the reputation among cinema managers of being extremely polite, and few resented their courteous enquiries as to whether 'the blonde usher' had gone home yet. A Northampton woman admits that at the pictures she used to think they had eyes in the backs of their heads. 'If you happened to adjust a stocking they would all swivel round as if it had been an order.'

The Americans' capacity to make themselves unselfconsciously at home amused many British people. A Northampton woman's most vivid memory is of seeing American soldiers 'propped against a wall in the sunshine reading and eating cherries out of a paper bag'. Other people remember whole rows of them seated on the edge of the pavement with their feet in the gutter. But most people's outstanding memory of the Americans is of their astonishing good nature and open-handedness. They were particularly lavish with their cigarettes and their long cartons of *Lucky Strike* and *Camels* became a familiar sight in many homes. Everyone was also astonished by the fantastic lavishness with which they were equipped and fed. Every G.I. had been warned before his arrival that Britain was short of food, but few of them had realised what this really meant. An Ipswich girl recalls that the six American guests her family invited to tea were 'a bit glum' when offered 'bread and butter-marge mixture, lettuce from the garden, home-made jam and fatless, sugarless "cake". . . . I have often wondered . . . if any of them ever realised that that was our last meal of the day.' The same young woman attended a dance at an American base where 'We were regaled during the intervals with fresh coffee, gorgeous American style doughnuts . . . a great dish of "wizard" ice-cream . . . and best of all real, huge, fresh oranges. I took mine home, as did some of the others, and we also scrounged some of the peel from those who ate theirs and this went into our pockets or handbags and was taken home to be stewed with golden syrup and kept in a jar for flavouring cakes and puddings.' I can remember my father, who frequently visited American camps on business, being astounded at the bowls of sugar on the mess tables and at hearing one G.I. grumble because there was chicken for 'chow' again. It was hardly surprising that we found it hard to persuade an American we entertained to accept even a single slice of unrationed cake. We put this down to his reluctance to eat British rations, but I now suspect he was simply not hungry.

One American habit that caused general astonishment, as a then teenage girl from Barking remembers, was that 'Americans had a way of taking something from each dish and plate on the table, and placing the lot on one plate. . . . One tea-time I remember an American staff-sergeant piling his plate with apple tart, pilchards, cheese, tomatoes, watercress, bread and butter, custard tart, and fairy cakes. Mother and I tried to appear unconcerned, but before our eyes he managed to consume the lot quite tidily, eating pieces of each at the same time. He must have enjoyed it for he repeated the process twice more. His hostesses ate very little I'm afraid. They were riveted with fascination!' Such hospitality was usually lavishly repaid. Another Ipswich family found that when their regular visitor, an American corporal, was on 'K.P.'—Kitchen Patrol— 'he would slip something into his rucksack . . . a few pats of butter, coffee. . . . One day he appeared with a seven pound tin of corned beef. We had not seen such luxury for years.'

A wartime schoolgirl remembers a glimpse she caught of an American storeroom in the local rectory. 'It was like looking into Aladdin's cave! There were things there that I had forgotten ever existed. Corned beef, dried apples, prunes, etc., butter by the barrel, sugar by the sack, tinned goods of every description, cakes and biscuits and *scented* soap with pretty wrappers. One of the nicest things about looking at this treasure trove was all the coloured labels. We just got things handed to us as they were.' A Richmond, Surrey woman who helped at an American Red Cross Club found 'It was agony to see the waste that went on there. I have seen "boys" help themselves liberally to what would have been a week's ration for me; then eat a few mouthfuls; and then (horror of horrors) stub out a half-smoked cigarette in the middle of the plate. Tomato and orange juice flowed like water—all brought over by our Merchant Navy.'

This last was a legitimately sore point; and had the U.S. Forces in Britain been put on the same ration scales as their hosts this might have done more to convince them of Britain's sacrifices than any amount of cautionary pamphlets. But, despite such potential sources of friction— and such minor irritants as that in London it seemed from 1942 onwards impossible to hire a taxi as they were all monopolised by G.I.s—most people still have pleasurable memories of their first contact with the Americans. A London 'clippie', whose No. 23 bus called at a London station as a detachment of American sailors arrived, is typical. 'They stormed the bus, they could not have cared less the destination, they held out their hands full of change and it was left to me to take the required fare. I finished the journey with sufficient gum and candy to last the war. They were friendly and full of good spirits and I found they made that particular day.' A thirty-year-old Mansfield, Nottinghamshire, housewife formed an equally favourable first impression. Previously Polish troops had been stationed in the town, 'grim, sad men who tramped with downcast eyes and wild or empty faces, to attend each Sunday the Catholic church nearby'. Now came 'the first Americans, a complete contrast, young, gay. There had been a violent thunderstorm, in which we were caught, I wore the first mini-skirt, involuntarily, a crêpe dress which soaked, shrank and shrank. The Americans, boots off, were paddling across the flooded road carrying those who wished to cross over, pretty girls mainly, and enjoying themselves hugely in the process. They certainly brought life and vigour to the town.' A Somerset housewife, then eight months pregnant, remembers a very tedious train journey from Stranraer to Euston. 'We stopped at Crewe in the early hours of the morning and as the railway buffet was locked and barred a whole crowd of American soldiers with a mobile canteen crowded along the platform and insisted on providing me, and the rest of the carriage . . . with hot coffee, rolls, cakes, sweets and chocolate—and would not take any payment at all.' A young North London girl remembers how in an Underground train in 1944 two Americans thrust into her hand a box of chocolates they had only just opened, ' "You take these, honey!" the soldier yelled as he dashed from the compartment. "I guess you kids don't get half enough candies over here!".' She also witnessed another act of kindness when a G.I., after seeing a girl who was waiting at a bus stop admiring a floral buttonhole in a nearby florist's window, went in and bought it, handing it to her with the words, ' "I'd like you to have this because this is a great country, and you English are such nice folks". A bus drew up and she didn't even have time to thank him before he disappeared.'

It was such experiences, constantly repeated, that caused the first mutual suspicions to be replaced by a bond of understanding against which all Goebbels's lies beat in vain. In time the Americans even became sure enough of their place in the affections of the average Briton to dare to tease him. An Ipswich woman who worked at an American camp found that the sound of *There'll Always be an England* on the radio would always produce 'much good-natured chaff from any G.I. within hearing range. "Of course, while we keep it for you", they'd say.' The Americans were natural, unabashed, unselfconscious and friendly and silence in a train or shop or queue—which they insisted on calling 'the bread-line'—they seemed to regard as a form of bad manners. I can remember two incidents which delighted my mother, then in her fifties. When she was hurrying to join a queue one morning a cheerful

American, applauding her brisk stride, called out cheerfully to his companions: 'Say, grandma's joined the Ats!' On another occasion, when she was waiting on a railway platform, an American beckoned her over and begged her to talk to him as she reminded him of his 'mom'. A Somerset vicar's wife remembers a similar meeting, when her husband, a very short man, who rode his pony round the parish, encountered a huge U.S. army lorry head on in a narrow West Country lane. 'Out jumped the officer and said, "Say, now, fancy a little man, on a little horse, in a little country".'

It was often alleged that the Americans were sex-mad, but the truth seems to be that they merely possessed the obvious advantages of money, novelty and being on the spot. There were girls who went blonde over-night because the G.I.s preferred fair hair, and a disreputable minority did hang around U.S. army camps, but most girls managed to have American boy friends, just as they had British or French or Polish ones, without becoming promiscuous. And if, as often did happen, friendship led to sex and sex to unwanted babies, the real cause was not American lust or British 'easiness' but war itself. Most people took a practical, down-to-earth attitude to this problem. A widow then in her forties, living in Sussex, agrees that 'It is no use disguising the fact that more than ordinary relations blossomed under the strain of war loneliness on both sides. . . . The Americans and Canadians were generous and courteous and supplied the place of lovers, husbands and brothers to many women.' The warden of a Land Army hostel in Bedfordshire found it difficult to get all the girls in at night, as there was a big American camp nearby. 'She managed remarkably well', her daughter remembers. 'All the weddings took place from the Hostel with American goodies provided. No babies arrived indecently soon but there *were* one or two near misses.' A young boy living in a Welsh mining village near Swansea observed that the American Army 'brought gum, cubes of sugar . . . and babies. I remember the grown-ups talking, but for all the stigma which was sup-posed to be attached to illegitimate birth thirty years ago, my impression is that people realistically put it down to "the war". . . . They were the result of a little Welsh hospitality to someone from far across the sea who had come to risk death alongside our own men.'

Whatever happened off the camp, the Americans were punctilious about the proprieties at any function where they were the hosts. A shorthand typist at a Cheltenham printing works found her escorts 'very nice and most courteous. . . . They knew how to be attentive and made one feel like a million dollars, with their "Hello, my honey-bunch", etc.' 'Most of the girls did like the Americans', acknowledges a wartime factory worker from Andover. 'At first we decided that we would have nothing to do with them, but they had charm—and most of them were lonely, ordinary boys, who were so glad to go into a home again and be treated as one of the family. When one very big batch of them came from Iceland, where they had been stationed for two years, the rumour went round Andover that it would not be safe for any woman to be out, but they were very quiet and well behaved.'

Inevitably it was not the innumerable innocent relationships which were publicised, but the few less typical scandals. The newspapers were fond of sending reporters to Piccadilly Circus on Saturday nights to describe the scenes near the Americans' largest London club, Rainbow Corner, where blatant prostitution—girls were said to have been seen turning down five pounds as inadequate—gave a new currency to an old wartime joke that all London harlots now claimed to belong to the Free French, though they were neither French nor free. Nor were all the stories of respectable young mothers wheeling prams being stopped by G.I.s brandishing pound notes exaggerated. A young preparatory school matron, nineteen when the war began and married to an officer serving in Burma, often found herself greeted on arrival at the station after journeys between Suffolk and Gloucestershire by Negroes, jingling money in their pockets. A young woman travelling to London from Birmingham, with her two small sons, had an even more embarrassing experience after she had chatted to a young American going on leave.

> Suddenly he became very quiet and serious. He explained that he'd saved up for this visit and had a full month's pay, which he showed me. . . . Some of the money was earmarked for his basic living expenses; some for travelling between his various planned highlights, while the rest (and he peeled off a wad of notes) he'd intended to spend on the holiday. Holding the money towards me he asked shyly, 'Is it enough? . . . Of course I'll pay for the cab to take the children home, and I'd only expect one night. . . . I don't know the rates down here, ma'am, and I realise a lady must cost more, but if you'd just tell me how much.'
> 'Is this how you behave at home?', I asked.
> Shocked, he said 'Oh, no, ma'am! Not in the States. Our girls aren't like you over here.'
> . . . At the camp girls came from miles around, offering themselves, and he'd thought it normal custom in Britain.

In 1942, when the first coloured Americans arrived, Britain had very few coloured citizens of her own and a Negro was regarded as an interesting curiosity. A then teenage girl from County Derry in Northern Ireland, looking back today, finds that 'Out of the hundreds of Americans stationed in our village the one I remember most was the only coloured American in the company. He was known affectionately to everyone as "Smokey".

Talk about the Pied Piper, no matter where you saw Smokey he was surrounded by a gang of children. We all loved him. He was killed in France soon after D Day, and we all felt we had lost someone very special to us.' This was the general attitude and licensees who banned coloured G.I.s from their premises were unpopular. A Warwick office worker remembers that 'in some pub bars the Negroes were not served. . . . Our soldiers didn't like this and in one case there was a free-for-all fight because of it.' Relations between the coloured G.I.s and British civilians were always excellent, but some serious disorders occurred between white and coloured Americans. One Bristol woman remembers 'a real set-to with a machine gun and everything' and the wife of a Dorset farm worker recalls a near-battle in her village, where, after an argument at a local pub, rival parties of whites and blacks blocked the roads with their jeeps and held each other off with poles and branches, until the Military Police arrived and dispersed them. At Kingsclere, near Newbury, there was a tragic end to a similar incident when a number of coloured G.I.s, shut out of a pub by white ones, fetched their rifles and bombarded the premises, killing several people, including the licensee's wife. It is a sad and ironic commentary on the great war to save democracy that the only battles on British soil were between white and coloured Americans, supposed to be on the same side.

It took the coloured G.I.s a little time to realise that in Britain they were not regarded as an inferior order of beings. An Ipswich W.V.S. member who helped in the local Y.M.C.A. found that she actually had to persuade them that 'they were allowed to walk on the pavement when white people were on there too, that they could use the trolley-buses, go into restaurants, shops, etc'. But this did not prevent them being beaten up by their white comrades for daring to make use of their new-found equality. For this woman the final disillusionment came after attending a New Year's Dance at a coloured American base.

We were collected and driven to Eye in Suffolk. It was a very cold drive with thick snow, but the welcome made up for the discomfort. No alcohol was allowed, so we had soft drinks and coffee, but there was plenty of food. You talked and danced, but were not allowed to leave the hall unless you were accompanied by another of the guests. All round the wall the white M.P.s stood watching. . . . There was a jazz band which played all the time. When it was time to leave at twelve we were packed back into the lorries. Of course our companions of the evening wanted to see us go and that was the start of the trouble. The M.P.s . . . beat the boys who came out unmercifully, so that any pleasure we may have had at the party was spoilt for us all. The guards in the lorry were just as cold as we were, but because we were white

they dare not come too close. This was the last straw and in no uncertain terms we told them that we did not feel the same way at all.
We shared the blankets provided for our warmth and finished the
journey sitting back to back. The coloured boys had the last word:
'Thank you for treating us like humans, missie.' I never went to another
party run by or for Americans.*

The British people, it was often said, were not good at hating others
and this was confirmed by the reaction to the hundreds of thousands
of Italians and Germans who arrived in this country as prisoners of
war. When the first Italians were sent to work on British farms there
was a ridiculous public outcry, based, apparently, on the insulting belief
that no British woman could ever say 'no' to a foreigner, but before
long the Italians were not merely tolerated but positively popular. In
Berkshire, as I saw myself, people thought it a great joke when the lorry
loads of Italians going off to work in the fields cheerfully shouted 'Musso
win!' at them and made suitable, if more colloquial, replies. In Hertfordshire, a schoolteacher living in a small village between Potters Bar and
Hatfield discovered that the Italians had no wish to escape and 'Their
only anxiety was lest they should be left behind when the lorry collected
them at the end of the day. One phlegmatic corporal would be in charge
of some thirty to forty Italians. They sang snatches of opera all day, did
as little work as possible and adored the children. I used to hear "bam-
bino" often and find them enticing the children through the hedge. One
season when Italians and land girls were put to work together on harvesting
and threshing the result was . . . like scenes from a comic opera.' A
group of land girls in Worcestershire, one remembers, soon found that
it was not their virtue that was endangered by the Italians—only their
bicycles, for the prisoners, if short of spare parts for their own machines,
would help themselves to screws or nuts from the girls' cycles. So little
were they to be feared, this girl recalls, that one foggy November night
when she returned by train from a weekend at home a party of Italians
met her with a torch and shared with her their Red Cross biscuits.
A young Dulwich housewife, living near a large prisoner-of-war
camp, often saw parties of them employed on road mending 'in their
distinctive suits, navy blue with large green patches on the leg front
and back. They . . . seemed very cheerful and usually gave the girls a
whistle. A few used to stand outside the local pub hoping that someone
would . . . bring them out a drink; they were nearly always lucky.'
The Germans were much less popular. A Hertfordshire woman, who

---

* An interesting fictional account of the British public's reaction to American
maltreatment of coloured troops is given in Nevil Shute's novel *The Chequer Board*
(1947).

liked the Italians, found that 'The German P.O.W.s were very different … They never smiled or spoke but glared sullenly at us as we hurried past. I was thankful when they moved on.' But they impressed everyone with their capacity for hard work. A Cornish farmer still remembers how efficiently a gang of them drained a marshy bit of ground on his farm and a Suffolk farmer's wife admits that their prisoners worked so well— far better than a detachment of 8th Army men who also helped on the farm—that she gave them extra food at mid-day. However much one loathed Germany as a nation it was hard to dislike all its members as individuals. The NAAFI manageress at a camp near Richmond, York-shire, remembers one who 'was always at hand if he saw me trying to lift anything. Another from the German Navy only wanted to be back with his family, whose photograph he carried and was always showing me.' Sympathy for the Germans sometimes indeed went beyond all reasonable bounds. One nurse in Surrey found that the ward sister was actually stealing the staff sugar to give more to her enemy patients. That strange mixture of loyalty and ruthlessness which makes up the German character was best revealed perhaps by the wife of a farmer living near Portsmouth who casually mentioned one day to a prisoner working for them, who was devoted to the family, that a certain cat in the village was a general nuisance. The prisoner went away without a word and returned a little later to say that the cat would trouble her no more. He was right; it was never seen again.

# SECOND FRONT NOW

'When the engine of the pilotless aircraft stops and the light at the end of the machine is seen to go out it may mean that explosion will soon follow.'

Statement issued by the Ministry of Home Security,
16th June 1944

Between the Fall of France in June 1940 and D Day four years later, the military side of the war was for most people only in the background. It was not that they had ceased to be interested; it was rather that, having chosen a leader, they were content to put their trust in him. The House of Commons grew during these years increasingly out of touch with public opinion as a whole but its massive votes of confidence in the Prime Minister reflected the national sentiment very accurately. Churchill's speeches never lost their power to rally the country behind him. As one Devon housewife puts it: 'Winston seemed to us to be our only anchor in a swirling, uncertain world. Just to hear the sound of his voice gave us reassurance and hope.'

The military events which caught the imagination of the ordinary citizen, and became for a few days subjects of general conversation in queues or pubs, were not always decisive or even important. The first, on the night of the last great blitz on London in May 1941, was the flight of Rudolf Hess, Hitler's deputy, to this country. This had not the slightest effect on the course of the war but at the time raised everyone's spirits, though its propaganda possibilities were hopelessly mishandled. As one Harrow woman, fresh from seeing the arrival 'of a convoy of . . . last night's air raid victims' at her local hospital wrote in her diary: 'Many people somewhat annoyed to hear that Hess is being fed on chicken, fish and eggs, when our ration of meat is a shilling per week per head', while the Minister of Information later caused further offence by referring to Hess as 'an overgrown Boy Scout'.*

Also in May 1941, the long pursuit of the German pocket-battleship *Bismarck* aroused great public excitement. 'At one o'clock a great cheer went up in the whole store as the radio announced "The *Bismarck*

* The reasons for Hess's flight remain mysterious. He is still, in 1970, in gaol as a war criminal.

is sunk" ', a Welwyn Garden City salesman recorded. 'Men dashed up-stairs to lunch shouting the news to each other and it was a very thrilling few minutes. Some *good* news was almost too much for many people after what we have been through.' Jubilation over the *Bismarck* was overshadowed by the simultaneous loss of H.M.S. *Hood* and the news of yet another 'glorious evacuation' by British troops, this time of the Mediterranean island of Crete, where Hitler's combined airborne and seaborne assault was widely expected to serve as a dress rehearsal for the invasion of England. Already that year the British public had had to swallow the German conquest of Jugoslavia and had seen the British Army sent to save another ally, Greece, humiliatingly driven out, with the loss of all their equipment. Nor did the news from Egypt bring much consolation. A brilliant offensive by General Wavell, between December 1940 and February 1941, had carried British Forces into Libya and captured 100,000 Italians. In March the Germans counter-attacked under a general whose name was soon far better known—and respected—in Britain than any British commander's, Rommel, and caused the whole British front to collapse. Although the lost ground was partly regained in November, by January 1942 the British troops in the desert were once again in retreat. No wonder people began to say in the pubs that what the British Army needed was a German general—and any transfer fee would be justified to get one.

Meanwhile on 22nd June 1941 Germany had invaded Russia. Even my school felt this was important enough to allow us to hear a radio and I remember sitting in the school library on that sunny Sunday evening listening to Churchill's speech welcoming this new ally. Six months later, on 6th December, Pearl Harbour, when Japan attacked the United States and Britain, caused less surprise and even some grim satisfaction. The sinking off Malaya two days later of the *Prince of Wales* and *Repulse* produced a far greater shock. To lose a battleship, much less two, seemed almost worse than to lose an empire. The fall of Hong Kong on Christ-mas Day 1941 also deeply stirred British opinion, and anti-Japanese feeling became so violent that there was an outcry against the release a few months later of thirty interned Japanese chick-sexers whose services the country badly needed. To 1941 belongs, too, the 'V' cam-paign, launched in July to encourage people in the occupied countries to defy the Germans by making the 'V for Victory' sign at every oppor-tunity. Beethoven's Fifth Symphony, the opening bars of which resem-bled 'V' in Morse code, was greatly in demand at patriotic concerts and there was also a rash of 'V's in Britain, chalked on walls, or traced in the dust on unwashed cars.

1942, which Churchill later called 'the Hinge of Fate', began with a run of disasters. In mid-February Singapore fell and 85,000 British soldiers surrendered to far fewer Japanese, the worst British military defeat on record. The public, however, was far more indignant over the escape down-channel three days earlier of the German battleships *Scharnhorst* and *Gneisenau*, described by *The Times* as 'the most mortifying episode in our naval history since the Dutch got into the Thames in the seventeenth century'.* Public confidence was almost as shaken when, in June, the 33,000 strong garrison of Tobruk surrendered to a force barely half its strength—by July the enemy was at the gates of Cairo. The ill-fated raid on Dieppe in mid-August did little to raise spirits. Hailed at first as a victory, the realisation that it had been a costly failure, with more than half the 6,000 Canadians taking part killed or captured, was all the more bitter.

But, against all the evidence, the tide was about to turn. On 30th May 1942 the first Thousand Bomber raid on Cologne had proved that in the air at least Britain was no longer on the defensive, and in the autumn at last came the longed-for success on land. On the night of 23rd October British forces attacked at El Alamein. Ten days later people were warned not to switch off their radios and go to bed, 'as at midnight we are giving the best news we have heard for years'. Then the jubilant voice of Bruce Belfrage announced: 'The Germans are in full retreat.' In one Berkshire war factory that midnight the news was re-broadcast over the loudspeaker system. A cheer went up and every girl on the night-shift, one of them still remembers, bent back over her machine with new enthusiasm. The landing of the Americans in North Africa six days later was for the British public an anticlimax, as was the ringing of the church bells to celebrate Britain's first real victory. But at last the civilians had found a hero to admire—a British general who actually won. Thereafter General Montgomery, the victor of Alamein, became a public idol; 'Monty', who with his ebullient self-confidence and unconventional uniforms, could do no wrong.

1942 ended with the start of the great Russian offensive at Stalingrad, and the announcement on 26th January 1943 that resistance had ceased, with 350,000 of the once invincible *Wehrmacht* dead or captured, was the beginning of a year of victories. On the shores of the Mediterranean the British, advancing from Egypt, and the Americans advancing from French North Africa, joined hands. In July Allied Forces landed in Sicily and two weeks later Mussolini was overthrown. Harold Nicolson, attending a village fête in Kent in August, watched the customers at a side-show throwing darts at pictures of Hitler and the Emperor of Japan. Few aimed at the Italian dictator for 'people do not want to throw darts at Mussolini as they say he is "down and out"'. (He was indeed; two

---

* An enquiry into the affair showed that a combination of circumstances had favoured the Germans, but also that they had quite plainly outwitted the British commanders.

years later he was shot by his own countrymen.) In September 1943 the Allies landed on the mainland of Europe near Taranto and on the 8th Stuart Hibberd announced at 6 p.m.: 'The best news of the war so far', the surrender of Italy. That night the BBC broadcast a special celebration concert, and in the streets a few people cheered and waved flags, but the rejoicing was premature. A long, bloody and, it is hard not to feel, pointless campaign followed, and when, in June 1944, Rome finally fell the news was overshadowed by events nearer home. Of far greater importance, it is now clear, were the facts that in July 1943 shipping losses were cut to less than a third of the previous level and thirty-seven U-Boats were sunk—the turning point in the Battle of the Atlantic.

The title of the BBC's annual Christmas programme traces the changing course of the war. In 1940 it had been *Christmas Under Fire*; in 1941 *To Absent Friends*; in 1942 *The Fourth Christmas*. Now, in 1943, the theme was *We are Advancing*, the BBC adding, 'towards victory, towards understanding'. It was not, one suspects, understanding with the Americans that was meant; that had been achieved already, as those who had heard the year being ushered in by 'distant shouts of *Auld Lang Syne* sung with an American accent' could testify. It was the Soviet Union to which the British public was now anxious to bind itself. A few British citizens had a bad conscience about Britain's past treatment of the Soviet Union; but most merely admired the valour and endurance of the ordinary Russian, who, they felt, had ever since 1941 been fighting their battle for them. (Russia's alliance with Germany in 1939, which had made war inevitable, was conveniently forgotten.) Exploiting these emotions were those same British Communists who, until June 1941, had denounced the war as a capitalist plot. Now, for the only time in British history, Communism became respectable. Membership of the Communist Party trebled and in the shipyards and factories Communist shop stewards, usually the chief troublemakers, became overnight dedicated to increasing production. All the talk was of Russia's achievements; America's far greater, and far less selfish, contribution to the common war effort was taken for granted. As one American told a journalist friend in mid-1942 when people in Lancashire spoke of 'our great ally', they invariably meant Russia not the United States. The same journalist visited factories where any man taking it easy was urged: 'Come on, give Joe a break', 'Joe' being Stalin, and one factory manager reported that his men admitted they were glad to be producing tanks for Russia rather than for their own country. In the London fire brigade, the poet Stephen Spender discovered, 'They worship the very thought of Stalin. Russia is their only religion.' It was firemen on night duty who were responsible for many of the 'Second Front Now' and 'Strike Now in the West' slogans which were painted on walls during 1942 and 1943.

But by no means all those who clamoured for an immediate invasion of Europe were Communists. The public as a whole was undoubtedly disappointed that D Day did not come in 1942.*

People took what comfort they could from an appeal for anyone possessing photographs of foreign scenes to send them to the Admiralty for the use of British intelligence, and many still treasure the official note of thanks which described their souvenir postcards or snapshots as 'a valuable contribution to the national war effort'. But when 1943, too, passed without the hoped-for assault, though the newspapers and newsreels were full of the vast battles in Russia, there were renewed suspicions, at least on the left, that the Churchill government still regarded Russia as the real enemy and were glad to see her weakened. The government, meanwhile, could hardly reveal the callous, ungrateful manner in which the Russians treated the British sailors who, under appalling conditions and at fearful cost, sailed convoys of supplies which Britain could ill afford to spare through the northern seas to Russia, or the real reason why D Day was delayed—the shortage of landing craft. Frustrated in its desire for an invasion of France, the public became even more frenzied in its admiration of all things Russian. The BBC, which in June 1941 had refused to broadcast *The Internationale*, was by December mounting a special concert in honour of Stalin's birthday, attended by the Russian ambassador, with a Guard of Honour provided by the BBC Home Guard, and later there were frequent programmes about Russian history and a highly successful serialisation of *War and Peace*. But the public mania was insatiable. Harold Nicolson described in *The Spectator* in May 1942 how his references at public meetings to China or the United States produced only perfunctory applause, 'yet one has only to mention Russia and . . . one feels upon one's cheek the wind of the wings of passion'.

The government, unable to restrain the national hysteria, wisely took advantage of it. In September 1941 production was boosted by Tanks for Russia Week when, it was promised, every tank produced would be sent to 'our gallant Russian ally'. Mrs. Churchill launched an Aid to Russia fund; the King presented a special Sword of Honour to Stalingrad; everywhere Anglo-Soviet Youth Friendship Alliances and Salute to Stalingrad funds sprang up. In Croydon Russian droshkys toured the streets collecting donations, in Bodmin the proceeds of selling for salvage two Russian guns captured at Sebastopol a century before were given to the same cause, in London one borough, in a frenzy of pro-Russian sentiment, painted its dustbins bright red. The climax came with a week of celebrations in honour of the twenty-fifth anniversary of the Red

* D Day was the American term for the first day of any operation but was always understood at this time to mean the invasion of Western Europe.

Army in February 1943. In a dozen cities throughout the country leading politicians, from left-wingers like Sir Stafford Cripps to millionaire Conservatives like Lord Beaverbrook, spoke to vast and enthusiastic demonstrations, and Basil Dean, head of ENSA, staged at the Albert Hall the largest production ever held there, *Salute to the Red Army*, which was also broadcast. Laurence Olivier declaimed a speech by a Russian hero; John Gielgud, as the voice of Moscow Radio, intoned such un-English sentiments as 'Over to you, Red Army . . . and death to our enemies'; the Royal Choral Society sang *The Volga Boat Song* and massed bands wound up the proceedings with *The Internationale*. No one was tactless enough to recall that the Red Army's first heroic victory had been over Poland, to defend whom Britain had gone to war, nor its second over Finland, over which Britain had contemplated war with Russia herself. Nowadays, as one journalist noted in his diary that summer, all Russians were, according to their sex, either virgins or saints.

But still there was no Second Front and by the beginning of 1944 there hung over the British Isles a feeling of expectancy. People hummed *Paper Doll* or *A Lovely Way to Spend an Evening*, and went to see George Formby in *Bell-Bottom George*, or a new star, James Mason, in *Fanny by Gaslight*. J. B. Priestley's comedy, *How Are They At Home?*, had just opened. So had the Royal Academy Exhibition, which contained few war scenes, though painters complained of a shortage of turpentine and brushes. Cigarettes were, for once, plentiful, but matches were almost unobtainable, the government had lost another by-election to the new party, Common Wealth, Princess Elizabeth had celebrated her eighteenth birthday and everyone was reading *Your M.P.* In *Punch* the jokes were about the black-out, clothes rationing, bus queues, G.I.s, queues, fire-watching and Holidays at Home. Everyone now had a new excuse for putting off a job. 'I'll do it', they would say, 'after the invasion', or, as one young woman at W.V.S. headquarters wrote to her mother on 23rd January, 'I feel I must see the dentist before the second front starts.'

The desire for the final act in the long-drawn-out drama to begin was made more acute by a sudden renewal, in January 1944, of German night raids on London. The 'little Blitz', as it was known, of the next three months was only a pale shadow of the attacks of 1940 and 1941, but after nearly three years of relative tranquillity people had lost the sheltering habit and were highly indignant at having to regain it. 'Here we go again—9.20 sirens went', noted a Putney woman in her diary, in February 1944, before going on to recount the all-too-familiar facts of an incendiary bomb in the chimney and windows shattered by blast. Another reminder of 1940 was a sudden increase in the popularity of Civil Defence workers, whose stock had slumped during the long lull. A woman ambulance driver who, in early January, had been insulted in the street with shouts of 'Doing your knitting?' and 'Money for nothing' was, a few weeks later, offered nine oranges, instead of her ration of two, merely because she was in A.R.P. uniform.

As winter gave way to spring and spring to summer the skies were seldom silent, and the once empty roads of Kent, Sussex, Hampshire, Dorset and Devon were crowded with seemingly endless convoys of lorries, tanks and bulldozers, all heading south or west towards the invasion ports. At Wimborne, in Dorset, one boy found that 'As D Day approached even the school buses had a G.I. as assistant conductor. These guys actually did the stopping and starting, leaving the regular conductor (female) to collect tickets.' A Somerset vicar's wife, whose home lay near the railway, enjoyed 'the beautiful sound of the trucks on the line' as trainloads of supplies poured into local dumps. Near Newbury a large hill was sealed off as airborne troops endlessly practised assaulting it, in rehearsals for an attack on a battery covering the Normandy beaches. In Conway, North Wales, there was equal speculation about the mysterious concrete constructions along the River Morfa, at a site known locally as 'the jam factory'; they were in fact piers for the 'Mulberry' Harbour. A Women's Institute Market Organiser, travelling all over West Sussex, kept silent about the dukws (amphibious landing craft) and lorries massed around Beaulieu and Chichester Harbour. In Dorchester the principal of one commercial school gave up trying to dictate to her pupils while Sherman tanks struggled up the steep hill outside, and 'arranged with the pupils that they should study their notes while we endured the deafening sound outside. 'So many streets of the town became one-way that employers gave their workers an extra fifteen minutes to cycle home for lunch, past the pistol-hung 'snowdrops' on duty at every street corner.* 'Whenever we took a country walk', this resident remembers, 'we saw G.I.s in camps and a notice hung up on a pole which said "Do not speak to the troops".' As the day approached, a smoke screen was laid over the town and finally 'It was very quiet outside and hardly any traffic on the roads. The whole atmosphere was one of tension... Everyone appeared geared up and ready.'

People in southern England woke early on Tuesday 6th June 1944, after a night broken by the roar of an apparently endless stream of aircraft making for the coast, some with gliders swooping behind them like great, silent birds. At Westcliff-on-Sea one young mother had stood for what seemed hours in her garden with her two sons watching the aerial procession pass overhead down the Thames Estuary. Near Portsmouth one farmer was struck by the contrast between the noise in the

---

* American military police were nicknamed 'snowdrops' because of their white helmets.

sky above and the sudden silence of the roads. In Central London Stuart Hibberd, who had been sleeping at Broadcasting House for several days past, ready to announce the great news, was 'awakened soon after 5.30 by the noise of hundreds of planes' and found the preliminary warning had now come in. Here, as in most parts of the British Isles, the morning was sunny and dry. Later there were cloud and showers in the North which spread to the Home Counties.

A sub-editor on duty at Bush House, headquarters of the BBC overseas service, in the early hours of D Day 'first began to suspect that something was up when top BBC brass in immaculate lounge suits began to look in. When at 4 a.m. the Assistant Controller . . . appeared with a large steaming jug and ordered coffee all round for the staff, we *knew* it was the day. Around 6 a.m. Goebbel's news agency announced the news of the landings. . . . Our own announcement was not till ten o'clock by General Eisenhower. . . . After breakfast, though I was now off duty, I came up again to the newsroom. Most unusually, they had a monitor loudspeaker on and it was "trailing" Eisenhower's speech in all the North Sea languages in countdown fashion. "En quarante-cinq minutes, le General Eisenhower . . .", "In drei-und-vierzig minuten . . ." "In 40 minutes . . . In 30 minutes . . ." It built up the tension beautifully and . . . for me, the rest of D Day was a bit of an anticlimax.'

Listeners at home first learned what was happening from the eight o'clock news, which merely quoted the German reports. Official confirmation did not come until 9.32 a.m., when the calm, authoritative voice of John Snagge announced that 'D Day has come. Early this morning the Allies began the assault on the north-western face of Hitler's European fortress'. The moment when they heard the news, like the time four years before when they learned of the fall of France, is still vivid in many people's memory. A Dumbarton woman proudly told the postman. In Huby, near York, one soldier's wife went down on her knees and thanked God—an act completely out of character. In my army training centre in Islington our instructor, with a singular lack of perception, urged us on to new efforts with the reminder that this was the quickest way to join our comrades on the beaches. In one household in Marylebone the maid was told by the milkman, and its owner celebrated with a festive lunch: the first new potatoes of the year, sliced eggs, and a large glass of sherry. All over Britain that evening eager diarists excitedly recorded the stirring news. 'D Day at last! Invasion! Hurrah! God save the King!', wrote one fifteen-year-old Cheshire schoolgirl, in a frenzy of patriotism. In Welwyn a factory worker, enjoying the last day of his holiday, could not wait to make the usual end-of-the-week entry and allowed himself the luxury of a special page, jubilantly headed '9.45 a.m. INVASION OF EUROPE BEGINS'. That evening the whole nation listened to a broadcast by the King, whose restrained, desperately sincere style, as so often, matched the country's mood:

> Four years ago our nation and Empire stood alone against an over-whelming enemy and with our backs to the wall. Tested as never before in our history, in God's providence we survived that test. . . . After nearly five years of toil and suffering we must renew that cru-sading impulse on which we entered the war and met its darkest hours. At this historic moment, surely none of us is too busy, too young or too old, to play a part in the nation-wide vigil of prayer as the great crusade sets forth.

D Day was not followed by a sudden victory; instead came the V.1s. Of all the bombs that descended upon the British Isles between 1939 and 1945 none is remembered with more bitter loathing. This first unmanned aircraft, with its harsh-sounding engine, scuttling remorselessly across the sky like some science-fiction monster, seemed even more sinister than the bombers which preceded it and the rockets which followed, while to have one's house wrecked or one's family killed just when this seemingly interminable war was drawing to a close seemed not merely tragic but pointless.

The first four flying bombs clattered across the Channel in the early hours of 13th June 1944. Although the government had long been expecting the new attack, it came as a complete surprise to the general public, and when the first V.1s, flame spurting from their tails, crashed to earth, eye witnesses were jubilant, believing a raider had been shot down. But on Friday 16th June Herbert Morrison put an end to the rumours by announcing that pilotless aircraft were now being used against the British Isles, and warning that 'When the engine of the pilotless air-craft stops and the light at the end of the machine is seen to go out it may mean that explosion will soon follow, perhaps in five to fifteen seconds.'

The new missiles were at first known as 'flying bombs', 'buzz bombs' or 'pilotless aircraft', and later by their German name of 'V.1', short for the German for 'Revenge Weapon'. Within a few days, however, the most popular description was 'doodle-bugs', an inappropriate term, since the bombs were both fast and purposeful. 'We call these things by pet names to help take the sting out of them, but there's no doubt they are becoming a real nuisance', one Welwyn man wrote in his diary on 3rd July. 'One flew over here at 5.30 a.m. . . . I lay as though glued to the bed muttering to myself "For God's sake keep going" interspersed with "For Christ's sake don't stop".'

As soon as the attack began, the capital's anti-aircraft defences were moved to the coast; squadrons of fighters patrolled above the fields of Sussex and Kent, now renamed 'flying bomb alley'; and, as the last line of defence, 2,000 barrage balloons were massed on the southern outskirts of London, being, as their commander said, in 'very much the same position as the goalkeeper'. Most were massed along the twenty-mile ridge between Cobham and Limpsfield near the centre of which lay the village of Eynsford. Stuart Hibberd, fresh from clearing up the broken glass at his own home at Bickley in Kent, wrote of Eynsford in his diary: 'Everywhere one looked one saw large, fat barrage balloons tethered . . . every few hundred yards or so. It was as though a convoy of prehistoric baggage-animals of gigantic size had halted to be fed and watered for the night.' A housewife and Civil Defence worker living near Sidcup also remembers 'with joy the summer Saturdays when . . . we would pack our lunch, get out our bikes and cycle out into the country towards . . . Eynsford. We would stop at the edge of a barley field and have our picnic. There was a splendid view as we were on rising ground. We could see the little hamlets nestling in the valleys . . . we could hear the larks singing . . . and we could look up and see the massive balloon barrage. If the sirens sounded, we could watch with a feeling of detachment as the "buzz bombs" roared over, seeming to thread their way between the balloons. Later on, we would cycle home, often to find the house blown inside out again, and fresh holes in the roof.'

Although only 2,400 of the 10,500 V.1s launched before the attack ended on 29th March 1945 got through to the capital, these were more than enough to make life in southern England exciting, if no worse. At one time during the height of the attack, in July and August, more than seventy flying bombs a day were raining down on the capital, and one Croydon dentist counted thirty-seven passing over his house in a single day. A few stray bombs, some launched from aircraft, landed as far afield as Portsmouth, Gloucester and Manchester or, due to steering faults, came down in Berkshire, Bedfordshire and Norfolk, but, once again, it was really London's battle. The worst-hit boroughs were all in South London. 140 flying bombs came down on Croydon, 126 on Wandsworth, 117 on Lewisham, while such badly blitzed districts as West Ham, with 58, and Bermondsey and Deptford, with 30, also suffered heavily. All told the flying bombs killed nearly 6,200 people and seriously injured 18,000 more, nine-tenths of the casualties being in London. They also did an enormous amount of damage, for though they caused no crater and rarely interrupted power or water supplies, the blast spread over a wide area, and during the V.1 and V.2 attacks nearly a million-and-a-half houses were destroyed or damaged.

The casualty rate was often high because the bombs came down at all hours of the day while people were going about their everyday lives and often in the open. The summer of 1944 was, therefore, many Londoners felt almost worse than the blitz and during July and August the alert was so often in force that one simply forgot about it, though warning of imminent danger was often given by sounding a hooter in short, sharp blasts, or hoisting a small red barrel on the top of flagstaffs and tall buildings. By far the best guide was one's own ears. That grating roar, resembling a badly-tuned motor cycle engine and growing steadily louder as the bomb approached, could break through every conversation, and when the engine, after a final cough, suddenly cut out, that was one's cue to take cover. Deaf people, who could not hear the bombs coming, had a frustrating few months. I spent the worst of the flying bomb period on an army training course in Islington and it was a common sight to see the civilian instructor, who was hard of hearing, still blithely holding forth in front of the blackboard, while all his soldier pupils had 'gone to ground' beneath their desks.

Although during June and July 1944 the bunks and platforms in the Underground filled up again with the same unimpressive shelterers who had patronised them in 1940 and about a million, largely mothers and children, old people and the homeless, were evacuated to safer areas, it was not hard after a time to become remarkably casual about the V.1s. I remember spending the lunch hour standing on the roof of my army training centre in Islington, idly watching the bombs coming in our direction, and merely ducking behind the parapet if any seemed dangerously close. Such indifference to them was not uncommon. I recall sitting in Hyde Park on a sunny Sunday morning at the height of the raids when everyone barely looked up at the bombs passing over.* After helping at one incident at the Royal Free Hospital on the evening of Wednesday 5th July, my diary records, I returned to my billet, 'swept up the plaster, found the back windows mostly shattered and a few with frames gone, and retired to the basement to sleep', where I was kept awake by an interminable argument between two other soldiers 'about whether they had seen one corpse or four'.

Stuart Hibberd, on his way home at Charing Cross after reading the one o'clock news on 1st July, noticed how the taxis blew their horns in warning at the noise of an approaching V.1 and how in his compartment 'more and more eyes were glued to newspapers in a vain pretence that buzz-bombs were a mere bagatelle'. Many other people have similar memories. One woman recalls 'having lunch one day in a small restaurant in Baker Street when the ominous sound of a doodle-bug was heard and it got nearer and louder. Everyone in the restaurant gradually stopped talking and eating and froze, with knives and forks poised in mid-air, until we all looked like statues. Then the usual bang was heard as the doodle-bug landed somewhere nearby, and it was wonderful to see every-

* One came down that morning on the Guards' Chapel at Wellington Barracks, killing 121 people and seriously injuring 68.

one just carry on eating and taking up their conversation without even referring to what had happened.'

People in cinemas and theatres became equally blasé. A twenty-three-year-old Palmers Green girl was watching Arthur Askey at the Princes Theatre when a V.1 'fell on the Holborn Swimming Baths opposite, the theatre shook and dust from the ornate carvings on the walls and ceilings of the theatre floated down on to the audience. . . . The show went on.'

Large firms placed their trust that summer in roof spotters, who sometimes gave a running commentary as each V.1 approached, and some citizens set up private spotting systems of their own. A Biddenden woman whose friend dreaded that a doodle-bug would fall while she was in the bath regularly stood in the garden at such times ready to shout a warning. A Harley Street doctor arranged for his wife to act as the family V.1 spotter and when she shouted 'Here comes a doodle-bug', the whole family would rush into the hall, which contained the least glass, and lie flat on their stomachs. A Purley housewife recalls how, 'If I was in the kitchen I could not have the tap running or the gas stove on because I had to listen for outside noises, so that I could collect the children from the garden and Edmund from his cot.'

It was a strange experience to see a V.1 or, even odder, several, clattering across the night sky, with a short jet of flame spouting from the tail, so that to one observer they seemed to be 'illuminated like little launches at a regatta'. Many people were struck, too, by the autumnal look of the streets in the vicinity of a flying bomb incident that summer, for the blast would strip the branches bare and heap the leaves an inch deep on the ground. One could, too, smell for long after the pungent odour of sap in the London parks when a V.1 had torn the bark from the trunks of the trees, and it was reported that no rabbits were to be seen there for the bunnies had prudently gone to ground and refused to emerge from their burrows. The Savoy Hotel, in a dangerous position only just across the river, became suddenly less popular as a spot for dining out. Estate agents discovered that flats on the south side of any large block were harder to let than those on the north. There was a shortage of bottled beer because the girls employed in the bottling plant refused to work surrounded by glass. The V.1s produced, too, the usual crop of jokes. One newspaper cartoon showed a parrot telling the cat lying beneath its perch: 'Purr if you must, but for heaven's sake don't cut out suddenly'.

On 7th September 1944 Mr. Duncan Sandys, chairman of the government's Counter Measures Committee against the German secret weapons, confidently told a press conference: 'Except possibly for a few last shots the Battle of London is over.' Seldom can any politician's prediction have been more rapidly or dramatically proved wrong. The following evening the first V.2 rocket landed at Chiswick, with a roar heard all over

London; the last was not to arrive, at Orpington in Kent, until 6 months later. Altogether 1,115 rockets landed on British soil, killing 2,800 people and seriously injuring 6,500 more, nine-tenths of them in London and its outskirts, though nearly 400 rockets landed in Essex and others were scattered as far afield as Berkshire and Norfolk. The V.2 was preceded by no warning, so that the first one knew of its arrival was a bright flash in the sky, accompanied by a supersonic bang and the roar of an explosion. The ton of explosive in the rocket's warhead produced a deep crater and total destruction nearby, though the damage covered a far smaller area than that produced by a V.1.

At first the government maintained strict silence about the cause of the loud explosions which echoed across London several times a day. 'This has been a week of bangs again', wrote one Putney woman in her diary in mid-October. 'On Friday night I awoke to a hideous explosion, followed by a smaller one, the house shook and I lay waiting and wondering, but it was just another "flying gas main" as we call these mystery explosions that . . . are still non-existent officially. Their noise is terrific, a flat enormous crack and then echoing rumbles.' It was not till 10th November that the Prime Minister at last admitted in the House of Commons that 'for the last few weeks the enemy has been using his new weapon . . . the long range rocket'. The scale of the attack never reached that of the V.1s, though at their peak about eight rockets a day landed, each causing on average twice as many casualties as a flying bomb. A few produced appalling death rolls, like the one which destroyed a Woolworths crowded with Saturday morning shoppers in Deptford in November 1944, killed 160 people, largely housewives with young children, and seriously injured 100 more. People talked very little about the V.2s. They attracted no nicknames and inspired no jokes. Amazingly to me—I hated and feared the V.2s—many people preferred them to the V.1s. 'I found the flying bombs when I was fifteen to sixteen more nerve-racking than rockets when I was sixteen to seventeen', an Essex woman remembers. 'There was no anticipation with rockets so that when the explosion was heard that was the first one knew and one was then either alive or dead.'

In 1914 the Germans had indulged their sentimental impulses with a Christmas truce. They did not do so thirty years later. An Ilford housewife has good cause to remember Christmas Eve 1944. 'I had reached the top of the stairs carrying a pile of books and toys to put in my little boy's stocking. I leapt with fright when the rocket fell and the toys and books cascaded from the top to the bottom of the stairs, and I was showered in dust that fell from the loft. "That's their idea of a joke", I thought. "A present from Santa Claus. Rotten bastards", I muttered. "Shooting rockets at little kids on a Christmas Eve".'

# WHEN THE LIGHTS WENT UP

'Until the end of May you may buy cotton bunting without coupons, as long as it is red, white or blue and does not cost more than one and three a square yard.'

Announcement by the Board of Trade, 7th May 1945

The war had been slow in starting. It seemed even slower in finishing. After the break-out from the Normandy beachhead in July 1944, hopes had been high that the war would end that autumn, but they faded with the failure of the airborne landing at Arnhem in September, and vanished completely in December with the Germans' breakthrough in the Ardennes. An entry in the diary of one London woman that month catches the authentic atmosphere of that last, miserable winter of the war: 'Absolutely nothing of note this week; fog, which made me lose my way coming home and fall all over the pavements to be rescued by a kindly soldier, ice and frost . . . the usual accompaniment of bangs from rockets . . . sirens one evening early and two doodles . . . droning over the house—a hateful boil on my neck. . . . People in the office have colds, pains and aches in limbs and crawl about with overcoats on and shawls draped about them. . . . With only cardboard and mica windows and no doors or walls to keep out the draughts it is pretty freezing and it seems our legs will never be felt again.'

The BBC's Christmas Day feature that year was called *Journey Home* but to civilians as well as soldiers it seemed a long, slow journey. The eager patriotism of 1940, the high excitement of D Day, were long past. Everyone was utterly sick and weary of the war. Rationing and shortages of every kind were more severe than ever. The Lord Mayor's banquet in November, one disappointed diner noted, took under half-an-hour to eat, and a West End hotel on Boxing Day could offer nothing more festive than dried egg omelette and cold apple tart.

The slow progress back to normality was symbolised by the dim-out. For years people had dreamed of the ending of the black-out, but when it came it proved a sad anticlimax. 'Half-lighting', as it was officially called, became legal at dusk on Sunday 17th September 1944. Henceforward, except on the coast, the government announced, 'windows, other than skylights, need be curtained only sufficiently to prevent objects inside the building from being distinguishable from outside. . . . This will make it possible to use curtains and blinds of the kind . . . normally fitted before the war.' But direct lights were still forbidden and 'dim-out' had to become black-out again if the siren sounded. The regulations were also slightly relaxed on car and cycle lamps, and better street-lighting was allowed provided it could be turned off during raids. The dim-out, *The Times* reporter found, 'made very little difference to the West End . . . though public houses and cinemas . . . had dispensed with black-out screens round their doors and a subdued light fell on the pavement'. Few private citizens bothered to make any changes but gradually the streets, especially outside London, became a little more cheerful. By December lighting on buses and trains was almost back to normal, and churches with stained glass windows could have their pre-war lights on. From the 9th December the dim-out continued even during an Alert, from the 27th head-lamp masks were abolished, and from the 30th one could light up one's number plate again. But it was not till 20th April that Herbert Morrison announced in the House of Commons to loud cheers the total abolition of the black-out from dusk on Monday 24th April 1945, except for a belt five miles inland from the coast, and this last restriction was not removed until midnight on 10th May.

The turning on of the lights produced little enthusiasm. 'Because of the shabbiness of what was behind the black-out curtains', remembers one woman living in Kent, 'I don't think there was the elation which one might have expected at their removal, with casement curtains faded and lace curtains rotted away.' A Civil Servant living at Branscombe in Devon found, like many other people, that tearing down the black-out in his bungalow was a very dirty process, for the dust and dead insects which had accumulated behind the shutters for six years now descended in a sudden avalanche. The need for economy robbed, too, the removal of the black-out of much of the expected joy. As a Birmingham woman remarks, 'we did not go mad and burn the materials. They came in useful for years.' Many young children, taken out by their parents to see the lights, were utterly bewildered by them and wept in terror. A Buckhurst Hill mother remembers her five-year-old daughter, who had never been allowed out after dark before or seen the moon, asking 'what that lamp was doing in the sky'. The young daughter of a Rochdale bus driver was taken out at dusk each evening for a nightly treat, to see, as she put it, in the words of a wartime song, 'the lights come on again all over the world'. A Barnsley housewife took her children to the local bus station to see the lights switched on again. 'A lot more mothers did the same', she remembers, 'and as the lights came on you never heard anything like it. Every child seemed to be saying "Ah!" at the same time.' But on the whole it was the adults who were more excited and old habits died hard. Many families for years afterwards spoke of 'doing the black-out' when they drew the curtains and hardly had the neon signs and illuminated shop fronts been turned on when they had to be switched off again. Two weeks after the final abolition of the black-out came an order banning floodlighting and decorative lights on seaside piers and bandstands, to save fuel—the first grim warning of post-war austerity.

During these last months of the war the public's slow progress back to peacetime freedom had begun. Between September and April it again became legal to buy a large-scale map, have a radio in your car, to sleep in an uncamouflaged tent, release a racing pigeon without police per-mission and sound a factory hooter. And now, at last, the war was really coming to an end. On 23rd March 1945 Montgomery's forces crossed the Rhine; on 25th April the Americans, advancing from the west, and the Russians, from the east, joined hands and cut Germany in two. For ten days now Union Jacks had been on sale in the streets of London and a secretary in a large plastics firm remembers that the Buying Department had been given a new duty: to have the bunting ready, though rolled up and covered, ready to unveil. For a shorthand typist in a solicitor's office in Denbigh the approach of peace meant being sent up into the dusty attic to disinter the stock of flags and wash them ready to hang out. For years the public had sung of that joyous day

> When that man is dead and gone . . .
> Some fine day the news will flash,
> Satan with a small moustache
> Is asleep beneath the tomb.

But when, on 1st May, the news finally did flash that Hitler had killed himself it was overshadowed by other events. The war which had begun so neatly ended untidily. At seven o'clock on the evening of 2nd May the BBC interrupted its programmes to report the surrender of all the Germans in Italy. At 10.30 programmes were interrupted again as Stuart Hibberd announced the fall of Berlin. On 4th May at 6 p.m. he gave his own name for the last time; the BBC was already hurrying its news-readers back into peacetime anonymity. At 8.40 p.m. John Snagge an-nounced the surrender of all German troops in Denmark and that evening I saw people leaning from taxis in Trafalgar Square, waving flags and cheering. But it was still not the end. By Monday 7th May the tension was almost unendurable. All day crowds thronged the West End, or gathered outside Buckingham Palace shouting 'We want the King'. Little work was done anywhere that afternoon. In the office of an insur-ance firm in Moorgate in the City one much-bombed-out woman sat and typed her diary. 'Still we wait. . . . Everyone is convinced peace will be . . . declared at 3 o'clock . . . Now it's nearing 4 o'clock and everyone says it will be 4, and so on. Everyone is tensed up and waiting . . . and almost in the same state of nervous anticipation as during the bombing. . . . No, not 4 o'clock though a crowd has gathered outside the Mansion House and press photographers are all over the place.' In the stores of a Hertfordshire chemical factory the storekeeper, whose home, too, had been damaged by bombs, also recorded an hour by hour description of events: 'This looks like being the long-awaited V Day', he wrote at 3 p.m. 'Rumours are flying about the factory. Every hour a crowd gathers round the little portable radio in our engineer's shop . . . A few minutes ago they said the German radio had already announced that Doenitz had signed the surrender terms . . . A stream of flags draped across the main factory roof will shoot up any hour now. I'm expecting a rush for my stock of beakers when the beer-drinking orgy commences.'

Also waiting for news that day was a young mother working on the barges carrying cargo from the Midlands to London. She had that winter had her eyes blacked and her hair covered with glass dust when her boat had been wrecked by a rocket, and been frozen up in locks during the bitter weather of February 1945. Now, like millions of others, she awaited the sole reward she expected—victory. Waiting for a train at Euston that Monday, on her way back to her boat, she heard the announcer say, 'Here is an important announcement'. The station fell silent, but when he went on: 'The 4.9 for Northampton will leave from Platform 7 and not as stated on the indicator', a howl of indignation went up from the whole crowd. A little later, back on board, she turned on her portable radio but 'the wireless battery had practically run down, which lent a nightmare quality to everything. We only dared to turn it on for a second at a time, judge by the tone of the voice what the news was, and hastily switch it off again.'

While the nation longed for news, the BBC was eager to give it but was forbidden to do so. Learning nothing from past mistakes the British government had, with barely credible stupidity, promised to keep the news of victory dark until a time which suited the Russians and the Americans, and just as on D Day, the BBC was only allowed to report what its defeated enemies said. By now, as expectation turned into frustrated annoyance, people everywhere were getting out flags. One W.V.S. headquarters worker, living in Fulham, that evening helped a friend who 'hung a huge nine-foot Union Jack across our road from her balcony to the balcony of two women who used to come into No. 25 for the doodles. . . . From my office window, on the top of St. James's station, flies a great Union Jack, where they used to run up the red flag for imminent danger.'

At 6 p.m. came the deflating announcement that Winston Churchill would not be broadcasting that night. Then, confusingly, and far too late, it was at last announced at 7.40 p.m. that the following day would be celebrated as Victory in Europe day and, like Wednesday 9th, would be a national holiday. The text of the statement that ended six years of war was miserably uninspired:

It is understood that, in accordance with arrangements between the three great powers, an official announcement will be broadcast by the Prime Minister at three o'clock tomorrow.

Frank Gillard, broadcasting from headquarters in France, could only talk of awaiting 'further developments'; the most exciting item in that night's news came from the Board of Trade, making its own distinctive contribution to the nation's gaiety: 'Until the end of May you may buy cotton bunting without coupons, as long as it is red, white or blue and does not cost more than one and three a square yard.'

The last night of peace had been marked by a tremendous thunderstorm. As if nature were determined to round the war off tidily, there was also a torrential downpour during the early hours of V.E. Day, Tuesday 8th May 1945, but this time people woken by the noise went peacefully to sleep again, free at last from the fear of bombs. The morning brought other reminders of September 1939. There was a cinema-organ on the radio, though the tunes, including *Victory Parade* and *Keep Your Sunny Side Up*, were very different and the hymns sung during the three services broadcast that day also had a cheerful sound, *Let Us with a Gladsome Mind*, *All People that on Earth do Dwell* and *Now Thank We All Our God*, the V.E. Day equivalent of *O God Our Help*. The climax of the day, at 3 p.m., was Churchill's broadcast from the room at No. 10 Downing Street from which Chamberlain had announced the declaration of war. 'Yesterday at 2.41 a.m.', Churchill told the nation, 'the representative of the German High Command . . . signed the act of unconditional surrender of all German land, sea and air forces in Europe . . . Hostilities will end officially at one minute after midnight tonight . . . but in the interests of saving lives the "Cease Fire" began yesterday to be sounded all along the front. . . . The German war is therefore at an end. . . . Long live the cause of freedom. God save the King!'

After the national anthem 'everyone drifted away', noted one woman who had listened to the broadcast in the W.V.S. shop in Westminster, 'but I sat on, alone with Mrs. G. We heard the short service which followed. Mrs. G.'s eyes were fixed miles away—on her two dead sons'. One soldier's wife, travelling to meet her husband, heard the official announcement in the station buffet at Peterborough. 'An old lady beside me burst out crying', she remembers, 'I did the same, a soldier whom I did not know picked me up and swung me around, the spare engine standing in the station just blew and blew on its hooter for a full five minutes, every-

one spoke to everyone else, we were all so happy.' Later, having joined
her husband in Huntingdon, they danced until four in the morning and
later still had a private bonfire—of all the letters they had exchanged
during their years of separation.

After his broadcast, Churchill drove to the House of Commons,
where he was loudly cheered, though less loudly, one M.P. observed,
than Chamberlain had been before flying to Munich. He was cheered
again, far more boisterously, when at six o'clock that night he appeared
on the balcony of the Ministry of Health overlooking Whitehall. The
crowd went wild with delight and Churchill, most unusually, delivered
an extempore speech: 'This is your victory', he told the civilians jammed
below him. 'It is the victory of the cause of freedom in every land. In
all our long history we have never seen a greater day than this. Everyone,
man or woman, has done their best. Everyone has tried . . . God bless
you all.' Afterwards Ernest Bevin beat time as the crowd sang *For He's
a Jolly Good Fellow* and then called for three cheers for victory. It was,
all in all, a most un-British scene.

So, too, were the celebrations which this day were taking place all over
the British Isles. In most places, after Churchill's speech had been heard
over the loudspeakers, the mayor spoke from the balcony of the local
Town Hall and there was a religious service, often relayed from a
crowded church to people outside. In most parts of England and Wales
the sun shone; temperatures reached the seventies, though in the afternoon there were some thunderstorms and heavy showers, and in Scotland it was a generally wet, dull day. But no rain could damp people's
spirits. Everywhere there were fancy dress parades and street parties,
and quiet residential streets echoed to the sounds of *Land of Hope and
Glory*, *There'll Always be an England* and, rather incongruously, *Knees
up, Mother Brown*. Although there was some drinking, the fun remained
remarkably good-natured and orderly. Weaving lines of housewives,
more used to queueing than dancing, wobbled their noisy way along
quiet suburban streets, elderly gentlemen who had rarely spoken to
their neighbours in their lives gravely put their right foot in and shook it
all about and 'did the Hokey Cokey'. Everyone wanted to add something
to the general din. That night in the West End I saw a man of about
thirty carefully dragging an empty petrol can behind him on a string,
so that it clanged on every paving stone. A Plymouth woman saw 'the
man next door walking across the road and feverishly banging the lid
of a dust-bin again and again with a sickly grin on his face'. A Birmingham woman remembers two pianos being dragged into the street where
she, a sober Civil Servant at the Food Office, sat down and 'played duets
with my former music-teacher'. A Harleston, Norfolk, woman remembers
'a jolly Scotsman who paraded our streets with his bagpipes playing the

conga, and we all followed on behind like the children followed the Pied Piper of Hamelin'. That day a fourteen-year-old Birmingham girl received her first proposal, and in a street in Chorlton-cum-Hardy, Manchester, the residents, having dusted the fairy lights and strung them on the trees as a final sign the black-out was over, 'got our air raid wardens helplessly drunk'.

The afternoon was the children's time, for everyone was determined to give them one ecstatically happy day to blot out the darker memories of the previous six years. Fancy-dress parades were held everywhere. A young girl living near Tunbridge Wells went as 'Freedom', 'dressed in my mother's white nightdress, sandals made from a pair of shoe "socks" and tape, and to my wrists attached two chains to look as if they had been broken'. An Ipswich housewife equipped her son as 'Rationing', in a suit made from old curtains, covered with out-of-date coupons. The food that day was such as many children had never seen before in their short lives. At Portobello, in Scotland, there was even ice-cream. At Colchester one small boy ate thirteen jam tarts. A small boy in Plymouth—no doubt like many more elsewhere—paid the party fare the highest compliment in his power; he tucked in so heartily he was sick.

This is how a Cardiff housewife remembers V.E. Day:

What a day. We gathered together on our bombed site and planned the finest party the children ever remembered. Neighbours pooled their sweet rations, and collected money, a few shillings from each family . . . and our grocer gave his entire stock of sweets, fruit, jellies, etc. All the men in the neighbourhood spent the day clearing the site. The church lent the tables, the milkman lent a cart for a platform, and we lent our radiogram and records for the music. We all took our garden chairs for the elderly to sit on. Someone collected all our spare jam jars. Black-out curtains came down to make fancy dresses for the children. Everyone rummaged in ragbags and offered bits to anyone who wanted them. That evening, ninety-four children paraded round the streets, carrying lighted candles in jam jars, wearing all manner of weird and fancy dress, singing lustily, *We'll Be Coming Round the Mountain When We Come,* and led by my small son wearing white cricket flannels, a scarlet cummerbund and a Scout's hat, beating a drum. In the dusk, it was a brave sight never to be forgotten.

All those whose stories have been told earlier in this book have equally vivid memories of the great day for which they had worked so long. In Welwyn the chemical factory worker often quoted in earlier chapters attended a monster bonfire, 'built and stage managed by the N.F.S. chaps. Very lights and rockets were fired off while merry gangs of youths and girls danced round the blaze singing and shouting. . . . I've never seen Garden City-ites go crazy before. Almost every other house had flags out and some made an effective display with coloured lights making a V over their doors, sometimes four feet high.' A young girl war worker returned from her lodgings to her home-town of Andover. 'We were most annoyed because we had a torch-light procession in Andover, and one of the officials would not let us have a flaming torch to carry— perhaps he thought we did not look responsible people! We had a great deal of fun dancing round groups of people singing *Happy V Day to You*.' A young woman working in an army records office in Bournemouth remembers how 'my sailor husband took Mother and I for a tour of the Hampshire villages, joining in their bonfires, singsongs, dancing in the streets, drinking our way through dozens of country pubs, swopping our personal stories of how we won the war. We even hugged and kissed complete strangers in the streets, to have those dreadful years behind us was so incredibly wonderful.'

Most people preferred to be with their own families, but some people felt that on this night they must be in Central London. Personally, I had no choice, for my army unit was going overseas next day, and while all around us the civilians were celebrating the end of their war we were hard at work carrying on with ours. I walked all through the West End that night and saw no drunkenness or rowdyism, only cheerful high spirits. A few girls plucked at the arm of any passing man in uniform, a few couples kissed long and publicly, often cheered by those nearby, a bearded naval officer conducted the crowds' singing outside Buckingham Palace with his telescope, two children, unable to climb on the roof of a car, perched themselves on the back of an invalid chair being wheeled through the crowd—these were the most disorderly events I could find to record in my diary. A woman working at W.V.S. headquarters, who made the same tour that night, reached a similar conclusion, as she described in a letter to a friend, written next day.

We all walked to Buckingham Palace. As we got in front of it the flood-lighting flicked on. It was wonderful . . . magnificent and inspiring and it seemed we had never seen so beautiful a building. The crowd was everywhere and yet one could walk through it. We edged our way to a good view of the balcony, which was draped with crimson, with a yellow and gold fringe. The crowd was such as I have never seen—I was never so proud of England and our people. It was a crowd of separate individuals. There was never any mass feeling. Everybody spoke quietly or was silent—everybody looked just relieved and glad. We waited. Coloured rockets went up behind us. Then the King and the Queen and the two Princesses came on to the balcony. We yelled and yelled and yelled and waved and cheered. They waved back to us. It was wonderful. . . . Then we began to walk. We went to a huge bonfire in the Park. People had joined hands and were circling round it. We walked by the lake—there were coloured lights in the trees and bushes reflected in the water. We came out of the Park by the Middlesex Guild Hall. It was floodlit in a warm yellowish light and looked medieval with flags from what looked like the battlements. We went to Big Ben. It was floodlit and looked magnificent. I heard myself say, 'Dear Big Ben! Dear Big Ben!' The Houses were floodlit from the river and all the lights alight along the Terrace. What moved us all beyond anything else was the great Union Jack on the Lords. It, alone, was floodlit by lights going straight upwards. It was just a great, lovely, Union Jack, flying grandly in the sky by itself. . . . We walked to the middle of Westminster Bridge and stood there. Searchlights were all rotating and making a kaleidoscope pattern all over the sky. County Hall was lit in two colours and the training ships in the river strung with coloured lights. . . . We walked back to Parliament Square and turned to face Big Ben. It was a few minutes to midnight. . . . At one minute past, all fighting was to cease. There was an empty plinth and H. climbed on it. She looked so straight and slim and elegant and someone said 'Statue of W.V.S.' But it seemed true and right to me. A. and I sat on the coping and S. and Mrs. H. stood behind us. The crowd all faced Big Ben. It was absolutely silent. Big Ben struck. Just before the last stroke it had reached one minute past. A great cry went up and people clapped their hands. Something went off with a bang. . . . The tugs in the river gave the V sign. It was unforgettable.

Many people have other, more private, memories of V.E. Day. A then teenage girl from Rotherham remembers a loss irreplaceable at the time: her uncle's garden bench was stolen to feed a bonfire. A Burton-on-Trent woman, who lived on a hill on one side of the Trent Valley, recalls 'walking down the lane late at night and seeing all the bonfires on the hills all around'. A Croydon woman remembers, when her young son asked for something for the street bonfire, she gave him an old strawberry basket she had been saving specially for the purpose. To her surprise, he went off whistling cheerfully. She discovered the reason when she went to the lavatory; he had also helped himself to her precious toilet roll only bought, after a great search, the day before.

One middle-aged widow, living in a Sussex village and struggling to bring up five children single-handed, having sent her fourteen-year-old son up to London—where he 'had a riotous time with a Brighton schoolgirl whom he met'—went out late at night with a broomstick to try to hit a rabbit in the fields, as we had nothing to eat for supper but cocoa and dried milk. I sat for hours in the twilight watching the bunnies play round their burrows but I could not hit one!'* Many other people have equally personal memories, not always happy ones. A Bristol housewife still shudders at the recollected taste of the huge bowl of custard served at the street party and made with dried milk and saccharine. 'It was awful.' An Ilford woman, joining in the celebrations in the High Street at East Ham, had to explain she had just had a wisdom tooth out and could not eat the food provided. 'Someone, I do not know who to this day, put a basin of bread and milk in my hand, and that was my victory celebration feast.' One housewife in Belgravia ceremonially burned her siren suit. A Biddenden woman had a long, lazy bath, luxuriating in the knowledge she would not be disturbed by V.1s. A London bus conductress, working all day, got home at 2 a.m., found a half-bottle of rum belonging to her sailor husband and sat on the step of her house drinking it with a girl friend. A woman living near Ashford has an embarrassing memory of taking her three-year-old son to church for the victory service, where he was asked to take the collection. He did so beautifully, but then spoiled the whole performance by helping himself to some money from the plate. The home of a dentist's wife from Woking still bears the scars of victory. She was so excited at hearing the news of the end of the war that she dashed into the street, forgetting to turn off her electric iron which, when she returned two hours later, had burnt its way right through to the carpet. Some housewives spent much of V.E. Day in an only too familiar occupation, queueing. The Ministry of Food, faithful in its trust to the end, had asked food traders to remain 'open on V.E. Day for at least one hour after the victory announcement', but the government's muddled way of releasing the news had thrown out everyone's plans. A young woman from Streatham remembers 'V.E. Day too well. A day off from the office and two hours of it spent queueing for bread, and a Canadian soldier just behind me telling me how he missed his beer at pub opening time through having to wait for the bread at the baker's shop.' A soldier's wife in Clapham, very pregnant and lonely, switched on all the lights in her flat and went out to see, for the first time, what it looked like from outside with the lights on. 'I . . . staggered down to the drive and round the front and side of the block . . . then feeling and looking like a fat bolster on legs . . . strolled out to see the jubilant population celebrating victory locally. Pianos and chairs in the gardens and on the paths, bonfires in every little street, cheering and singing all night—and me longing for someone nice to rejoice with.'

* This mother's earlier and more successful efforts to obtain food for the family are described in Chapter 13.

A Sheffield woman, already in hospital, felt the doctors and nurses were hardly giving her their full attention, for as her son arrived they were 'busy discussing how they were going to celebrate'. A Barnet housewife had the probably unique experience of spending both victory days in maternity wards. V.E. Day she spent consoling a girl whose baby was due and whose 'husband was overseas and she was in a dreadful state, so we stayed with her that evening'. By V.J. Day she was in hospital herself, 'with a very premature baby in an incubator', and 'It was most galling to see a bonfire in the hospital grounds and hear all the noise of the students and nurses celebrating. However, my lovely baby did live, which was celebration enough really.' A woman doctor in Westmorland was delivering a baby on V.E. Day. 'As it slid into the world triumphantly, after a long and difficult labour, *Praise my soul* resounded from the room below. We nearly joined in. I told the mother the babe should be called Victoria but she wouldn't.' A Leytonstone wife has never forgotten her home-coming with her husband from the local V.E. celebrations. As they entered the house he said simply, 'Now we can go in for a baby.'

For the ordinary British civilian V.E. Day was really the end of the story. Only those with relations serving in the Far East could summon up much interest in the campaign against the Japanese, and the country was soon preoccupied with its first General Election for ten years. On 23rd May, what Churchill called 'that famous coalition' had resigned and a Conservative 'caretaker' government took office.

The campaign which followed is, for anyone who had admired Churchill, best forgotten, particularly his notorious 'Gestapo' broadcast, said to have been inspired by his evil genius Lord Beaverbrook, which provoked incredulous disgust and wiped out overnight much of the goodwill and respect which even Labour supporters felt for the Prime Minister. The slogan *Send him back to finish the job* also backfired, when taken over by the very men who had tried to keep Chamberlain in power in 1940. (The counter-gibe, 'You can't vote for Mr. Churchill unless you live in Woodford', inspired a famous cartoon by Vicky showing top-hatted Tory candidates hoisting signs reading 'Woodford' all over the British Isles.) Personally I was never in doubt of the result of the election. The evidence of all the by-elections since 1942, the bitter anti-government feeling in the Forces, the leftward movement of opinion shown in numerous ways, like the vast success of Priestley's *Postscripts*, and the growth of the Common Wealth party, were plain for all to see. My own family was probably not exceptional. My parents had always voted Conservative, but in 1945 my mother voted Labour, while this was now not far Left enough for my father—he voted Common Wealth. My sister, voting for the first time, and already a staunch Labour supporter, brought the house down at the Tory candidate's meeting—housing was the great, serious, issue of the election as distinct from Beaverbrook's infantile stunts—with the cry of 'What do you expect us to live in? Glider boxes?', a reference to the discarded crates now littering the local race-course. Similar scenes were occurring all over Britain and the inept and unscrupulous Conservative campaign merely converted inevitable defeat into discreditable rout. Polling took place on 5th July, and the results, delayed to enable the Forces' vote to arrive, were declared on 26th July. They showed an overwhelming Labour victory with 393 Labour seats against 213 Conservative, and a Labour majority of 146 over all other parties combined. Many Tory ministers had lost their seats and had the Labour Party put up a candidate against him, Churchill might well have been among them.* To some civilians, his dramatic fall from office came as a shock. In my army unit however, and I expect in many more, the news of the election results produced considerably more jubilation than V.E. Day.

These months after the end of the European war had, for many civilians, a strangely unreal quality. Some were reluctant to abandon their wartime duties, and though Civil Defence began to be disbanded on 1st May, and the few remaining full-time A.R.P. workers were given a month's notice, some volunteers continued to visit their old Wardens Post or First Aid Post until it was actually closed down, and many Civil Defence clubs survived for years. Private citizens, too, often experienced a feeling of loss of purpose. A young Battersea girl, eleven when the war began, seventeen in 1945, felt that 'There was a great feeling of anti-climax. . . . Everything seemed dull and flat after the excitement and friendliness.' A Guildford housewife believes that 'Perhaps that grand comedian Robb Wilton put his finger on the spot when he said that "the day peace broke out" he chided his wife for not looking very cheerful, and she replied, "Well, there's nothing to look forward to now. There was always the All Clear." '

What the British public now had to look forward to, it was already clear, was the continuation of shortages and rationing for at least months to come. The basic petrol ration was restored in June, but petrol rationing continued until 1950, clothes rationing until 1949 and food rationing did not finally end till 1954. There were warnings of shortages of foreign currency and a financial crisis. The only bright spot was the unexpectedly rapid ending of the war against Japan, though it caused little of the excitement experienced in May. The dropping of the first atomic bomb

* He was opposed only by an eccentric and unknown Independent, who caused a sensation by gaining 10,000 votes, against Churchill's 27,000.

on 6th August, causing 70,000 deaths, closely followed by the second, on 9th August, produced a greater shock than the announcement, in the one o'clock news on Thursday 9th August, that Japan had asked for an armistice. Stuart Hibberd, walking from Broadcasting House to Oxford Circus immediately afterwards, 'thought everyone had gone mad. A.T.S. and W.R.N.S. were standing on the top of Peter Robinson's building showering down paper on people's heads below, and holding long paper streamers, which billowed out into the wind.' A Surrey woman, in the cinema that day, remembers that the lights went up, the manager walked on the stage and said simply, 'Japs surrender!' The audience began to sing *There'll Always be an England* and *Land of Hope and Glory* and everyone poured into the street.

But such celebrations were premature. Once again the final news was delayed and mishandled and it was not until 11.45 p.m. on Tuesday 14th August that the BBC warned listeners to stand by for a special announcement and not till midnight that the voice of the country's new Prime Minister, Clement Attlee, at last gave the tidings of victory:

> Japan has today surrendered. The last of our enemies is laid low. . . . Here at home you have earned respite from the unceasing exertions which you have all borne without flinching or complaint for so many dark years. . . . For the moment let all relax and enjoy themselves in the knowledge of work well done. Peace has once again come to the world. . . . Long live the King!

It was not an inspiring speech. It failed to stir even the audience I listened with, of soldiers in a billet overseas, though it meant that we could now begin to count the day to 'demob'. (It was fortunate we did not know how many: 764 in my case.) In the British Isles most people were already in bed and only in a few places were there any immediate celebrations. In the Somerset village of Holton, where my mother was on holiday, the rector roused his parishioners by ringing the church bell and gathered a small but jubilant congregation, who lustily sang the *Te Deum* while their neighbours still slept. In an army camp in Yorkshire the civilian canteen manageress, hearing the cheerful soldiers thundering at midnight on the door of her hut, assumed they had been drinking and called to them to go away. A young married woman in Rugby, hearing voices shouting in the street that the war was over, got out of bed, collected her friend from next door, and went to the town centre, where the two heavily pregnant women danced together round the clock tower.

Most British citizens only discovered that their country was at peace at 7 a.m. next morning, when a recording of Attlee's speech was broadcast, and a large number who had not turned on the radio went to work as usual only to find that they had to trail home again. It was a muddled, unsatisfactory beginning to the two-day holiday. The weather, too, was not kind: rain fell in many places about midday, though there were sunny periods, especially in the West of England. The speeches, the fancy dress parades, the bonfires, all had the jaded feeling of being a repeat performance and the crowds were generally smaller and quieter. One dean, horrified at the use of the atomic bomb, even refused to let his cathedral be used for a thanksgiving service. A South Benfleet house-wife found that her neighbours were also 'just too horrified' to celebrate very heartily and in few places was there much excitement. 'Europe was so much closer to us than the war with Japan', explains an Ipswich woman, 'and the same man who had carried us through the war was no longer at our head.' Many people's memories of V.J. Day are far from cheerful. A Teddington schoolboy, on holiday in Wales, witnessed a family row, because his seventeen year old sister 'had stayed out too late (midnight) and been seen with some soldiers'. A Reading family, going on holiday in Devon, who had prudently loaded up their car with petrol in case the garages were closed, found themselves stuck on Porlock Hill. A housewife living at Wellington, Somerset, was disappointed in the office celebration dinner: 'We were all hoping for a good square meal and all we got was fish and chips and a jam tart.' The owner of a Mayfair shoe repairing business experienced his first taste of peacetime service. When on V.J. Day, after an eighteen-month wait, a vital finishing machine was at last delivered he 'thanked the mechanic and asked him how long it would take to install. "What do you take me for?", he exploded. "This is V.J. Day. I'm going on the oil. Might come and connect it up next week."' A shorthand typist at a publishers' printing works in Cheltenham received a telephone message from the head of the firm just as she was leaving, telling her to give everyone an extra week's pay, which meant hours of extra work making up new pay-packets and re-calculating P.A.Y.E. For a 'special' police commander in Gosforth, V.J. Day was marked by the arrival of a constable in a car to collect his official Wellington boots, already being called in by a grateful government.

Just as V.E. Day, with its guarantee of the end of bombing and black-out, meant most to the civilians, so V.J. Day was far more important to those in the Forces, with the danger of being sent to the Far East removed and the end of their poverty-stricken servitude at last in sight.

A NAAFI manageress at an army camp in Yorkshire remembers the high spirits there. She won four prizes in the local sports, including a second prize in the three-legged race though he was 'six feet odd and I am five foot one. . . . Every time I had to go for my prize the boys yelled "Up the NAAFI".' One soldier's wife on her way home to New Cross on V.J. Day boarded a train at Manchester. 'Then the fun started. Our baby was only three months old and we put her up on the luggage rack to keep her out of the way of the celebrating troops. . . . One soldier had a huge kit bag and as soon as the train started he opened the kit bag and it was filled with bottles of beer which he willingly shared with everyone.' And at least one civilian thoroughly enjoyed himself. A Carshalton family tried, and failed, to restrain jolly 'Uncle Alf' from performing his party piece in the street: unscrewing his wooden leg and balancing a glass of beer on the sole of his 'foot'.

At 9 p.m. on V.J. Day the King broadcast to his people.

The war is over. You know, I think, that those four words have for the Queen and myself the same significance, simple yet immense, that they have for you. . . . There is not one of us who has experienced this terrible war who does not realise that we shall feel its inevitable consequences long after we have all forgotten our rejoicings of today . . . The British people here at home have added lustre to the fame of our islands and we stand today, with our Empire, in the forefront of the victorious United Nations. . . . From the bottom of my heart, I thank my peoples for all they have done, not only for themselves, but for mankind.

And so it was ended at last. In many residential streets the home-made signs were already hanging to greet the returning servicemen: 'Welcome Home'. Many a local newspaper carried news of the 'get you home service' run by volunteer motorists to meet demobilised soldiers at the local terminus, many a council wrote official letters of thanks to those who had served and organised parties in their honour.

There were no parties or letters of thanks for the housewife, whose burden had perhaps been the hardest of all, though she did have her place in the Victory Parade a year later. Clutching her still essential ration books, studying her sadly depleted wardrobe, contemplating the shabby furnishings of her home, the bomb-blasted windows, the crumbling plaster, and the wreck of the garden where the Anderson had stood, she must perhaps have wondered whether it had all been worthwhile—and known in her heart of hearts that the answer was a resounding 'Yes'. In the housewife's long battle there had been many Dunkirks and few El Alameins, many Pearl Harbours and few V.J. Days, but it was in the kitchen of the ordinary family, in the queue and at the Food Office, at the coal merchant's and at the Make Do and Mend Party, as well as in the workshops and on the battlefields, that the war had been fought and won.

For many women the real reward for all their endurance and sacrifice was still to come. This is how the war ended for a Glasgow housewife, who had not seen her sailor husband for three years, and whose second child had been born after he had gone abroad.

I was not sure, of course, just when my husband would arrive home but he turned up at 11.30 one night and I had to get out of bed to let him in, trying desperately to get the curlers out of my hair. The children did not wake up, however, and I'll never forget Bill's face as he stood looking down at his small daughter, whom he was seeing for the first time, and at his son, who had grown quite different from the baby he had left behind.

# POSTSCRIPT

For me, the war had begun with Chamberlain's broadcast. It did not end until more than eight years later, early in the morning of Friday 19th September 1947 when I at last got home and took off my uniform after being demobbed hundreds of miles away and spending the night in a station waiting room. The 'get you home' service for the demobilised of which the local newspaper had boasted had long since ceased to run. The Welcome Home parties were over and the last official 'thank you' letter written. For me to be home, and unharmed, after four wasted years, was enough. But I could not help reflecting wryly that to be in the Army had always been to be under-privileged and under-paid. Now, with the war won, it had become unfashionable as well.

# APPENDIX 1

# OUR DEAR CHANNEL ISLANDS

'Our dear Channel Islands are also to be freed today.'

WINSTON CHURCHILL, 8th May 1945

'We often hear about the food situation and envy the fortunate people in England.' This was the entry written in one Guernsey farmer's diary in mid-October 1941, for while no German soldier ever set foot on the mainland of the British Isles except as a prisoner, one British possession, the Channel Islands, suffered the full rigours of enemy occupation. Their experiences show what might have happened had the Germans disembarked at Plymouth and Dover instead of St. Helier and St. Peter Port.

When the war began the Islands were assumed to be so safe that children were actually evacuated there from Southampton and as late as March 1940 advertisements were describing Jersey as 'the ideal resort for wartime holidays in Summer'. The press also made much of the news that half the male population of Herm—one man—had joined up, and that the defence of Brecqhou rested on a seventy-year-old man riding a donkey called Clarabelle. The Islands' awakening was harsh and sudden. On Wednesday 19th June it was announced they were being demilitarised and that everyone wishing to leave must register at once.

The evacuation, planned in panic and haste, ended in muddle. No clear lead was given to a public desperate for guidance, and though priority was promised to women with small children and to men of military age, who might otherwise be deported to Germany, it was neither necessary—since there was ample shipping space for everyone—nor in fact provided. Some people, dismayed by the long queues and lack of information, gave up and went home again, while the men were given no chance to tidy up their affairs, and families were needlessly split up. There were agonising scenes as children pleaded with their parents to come with them, though one small girl bravely tried to comfort hers, when they tried to prepare her for years of separation, by assuring them she would do her best to forget all about them. Confusion was so complete that while practically no-one went from Sark, where the famous Dame, Mrs. Hathaway, advised those with land to till to stay, almost everyone left Alderney where the leading citizen, an Englishman, gave the opposite advice. On Jersey, meanwhile, people planning to leave were publicly denounced as 'rats and rabbits', so about four-fifths stayed, and on Guernsey an equally misguided poster campaign urged the public 'Don't be yellow', so that half remained, to provide cheap, if unwilling, labour for their country's enemies. In retrospect it is perfectly clear that the Channel Islands should have been wholly evacuated. The total numbers involved were only 93,000, far fewer than the contingents of evacuees easily handled by many individual British cities in September 1939. As it was, those left behind soon had the feeling of having been not merely abandoned but forgotten and apart from a few Red Cross messages, limited to twenty-five words, and delivered months late, received no news of their absent families and relations until after the war.

After the departure of the last ships, far sooner than was really necessary, an uneasy calm settled on the Channel Islands broken by air raids on both Guernsey and Jersey, where lorries loaded with tomatoes were mistaken for military vehicles and nearly 40 people were killed. But 'The Battle of the Tomatoes' was not repeated and for the rest of the war the few civilians killed on the Channel Islands were the victims of British bombs aimed at German shipping and fortifications. The demilitarising of the Islands was now, too late, announced to the world and two days later, on Sunday 30th June, the first Germans landed on Guernsey. Their commander obligingly agreed to enter the house of the Attorney General by the side door to avoid waking his children, who were sleeping in the hall, and on Jersey the immaculately dressed and monocled German officers formally accepted the surrender of the Island from the governor even though he was dressed in his oldest gardening clothes. Later encounters between the Islands' authorities and the Germans were marked by much military saluting and civilian hand-shaking. One leading member of the States, the Guernsey parliament, insisted 'there must be no thought of any kind of resistance' and the Attorney General appealed to its members to make 'this occupation . . . a model to the world', with 'the strictest conformity with orders and regulations issued by the German commandant and the civil authorities'.

Remembering that the Channel Islands had been abandoned to their fate by the British government and that people there were, like those in the other occupied countries, still stunned by the speed of the German victory, it is not hard to understand the reason for this policy. But the line between non-resistance and active co-operation was clearly hard to draw and it is hardly a matter for pride that the Channel Islands should have been the only enslaved country without a resistance movement, though one can feel grateful that as a result they were spared the murders, massacres and atrocities which marked German rule elsewhere. The price that had to be—or at any rate was—paid was that in the Channel Islands British civilians, however unwillingly, raised food to feed German troops, built emplacements for German guns, and oiled ammunition for use in invading the British Isles.

As a result of their decision to co-operate with the Germans, the Islands' authorities soon found themselves compelled to pass laws punishing their fellow citizens for remaining loyal. On Guernsey, for example, to forestall a German reprisal against a man who had abused a shop assistant for serving a German before other customers, an Act was passed in 1940 making criticism of any German punishable by up to a year's imprisonment, but only this one offender was ever tried under it and he was acquitted. The authorities also announced, on German instructions, that anyone found in possession of a leaflet dropped by British aircraft, *News from Britain—Distributed by the RAF*, could receive up to fifteen years' imprisonment, but no one ever did. (One woman, aged over eighty, who bravely wrote to the Germans declaring that she meant to keep her leaflet, as it contained a message from her legal sovereign, escaped with a reprimand.) Far more widely criticised was the offer by the Bailiff of Guernsey, under German pressure, in July 1941, of a £25 reward to anyone who would betray any fellow citizen he saw chalking up a 'V' sign. It was said publicly that the appropriate amount would have been thirty pieces of silver, but in any case it was never claimed. Nor were any British airmen handed over to the Germans, though sheltering them was punishable by death. It is noteworthy, however, that while hundreds of British airmen escaped from occupied Europe. all who landed on Guernsey were in fact captured or surrendered voluntarily.

Most people contented themselves with minor acts of defiance, like wearing 'V' badges made from British coins inside their lapels. One Guernsey woman, asked the name of her dog by three German airmen, snapped 'Spitfire!', but the gesture misfired as they stood up and saluted it. The whole island shared in the joke when official German news was printed in the fifth column of a local newspaper and a local dance band adopted as its signature tune *The World is Waiting for the Sunrise*. On the same island a clergyman was seen on his knees praying hard as the German bombers passed over that they would suffer heavy losses and prayers for the royal family, which the Germans allowed, were always said with hearty gusto. Throughout the occupation no serious public clash occurred, like the general strikes in some other occupied countries. A farewell dance held for one man being deported to Germany ended with the band, with more patriotism than tact, playing *We're Going to Hang out the Washing on The Siegfried Line*, sung so loudly that the Germans arrived and several guests ended the night in gaol. There were no general strikes or comparable demonstrations, but on Guernsey in November 1943 5,000 people, half the remaining population, turned out for the funeral of twenty British sailors, whose bodies had been washed ashore. The Germans behaved with great propriety and even fired a salute over the dead men's grave, though banning attendance at such funerals for the future. A near-riot also occurred on Jersey in September 1942, when mainland-born residents were deported to Germany, for crowds lined the streets shouting 'Churchill', and some boys played football with a German helmet, but fortunately no one was hurt.

The commonest form of resistance was to hide whatever one could from the Germans and to steal from them whenever one got the chance. When a large part of the Guernsey police force was found to have spent their nights on duty breaking into German stores they became highly popular, but others surely deserve greater admiration, like the two teenage sisters on Jersey sent to gaol for nine months for making the 'V' sign with their fingers and the Guernsey man who got twelve months for chalking a 'V' sign on the saddle of a German soldier's bicycle, to imprint it on the seat of his trousers. Another hero was a journalist on the *Guernsey Star* sent to prison in France, under appalling conditions, for sixteen months, for producing an underground newspaper, which was based on BBC news bulletins, taken down by the fastest shorthand writers on the island and typed on thin, tomato-packing paper. One feels respect, too, for the patriotic drunk who, armed with a bottle of brandy, swayed down the High Street of St. Peter Port one night in October 1943 shouting 'Balls to Hitler!'

until arrested, and, most of all perhaps, for the young Guernsey mother, whose children had been evacuated, and who was working as a waitress in a hotel and was one day refused her portion of rice pudding at lunchtime unless she would say 'Heil Hitler!'. Her reply had the ring of nobility about it: 'To hell with Hitler for a rice pudding—and made of skim milk at that!' For this trivial offence she was court martialled and sentenced to six months in gaol, after which she was always known by the inaccurate but honourable title of 'Mrs. Churchill'.

Not all Channel Islanders were as loyal. One who had imprudently said 'Heil Hitler' at a Christmas Eve party in 1940 was later found badly beaten-up and many local girls earned the contemptuous name of 'Jerrybags'. Towards the end of the war many 'Jerrybags' received threatening letters signed by the 'Guernsey Underground Barbers', reminding them that the punishment for girl collaborators was to have their hair cut off, and a basketful of scissors were ostentatiously taken for sharpening to a local shop. In fact many girls punished themselves by becoming pregnant; the exact number of illegitimate babies with German fathers is unknown, but was certainly several hundred. The imprisoned journalist previously mentioned, estimated, however, that 98 per cent of the population of Guernsey remained loyal to Great Britain, and at the end of the war the Home Secretary announced that only twelve cases of collaboration in the Channel Islands merited prosecution and even in those the evidence was insufficient for a conviction. Thus if few Channel Islanders were heroes, fewer still proved to be traitors and it proved possible to combine reasonably friendly relations with the Germans with a wholehearted desire to see them defeated. One Guernsey baker in his thirties confided to his diary in March 1941 that 'life has been quite tolerable owing to the general courtesy and inoffensiveness of the German officers and soldiers', but this did not prevent him commenting 'I rather fancy this job', when warned to be ready to drive a lorry to collect the loads of German corpses likely to be washed ashore when the invasion of England began. Three and a half years later, just out of gaol for illegal possession of a radio, his patriotism remained unimpaired: 'We had two nice air raids on the harbour this morning', he recorded cheerfully.

Although the Germans committed no atrocities against the native population of the Channel Islands, many slave workers brought from Europe were starved or worked to death, the Germans openly admitting that they regarded them as inferior, sub-human beings. The average Channel Islander was in fact a good deal more frightened of these often strange-looking and savagely repressed and hungry newcomers than of the Germans, whose discipline remained excellent, and who heavily punished any crimes committed by their own soldiers. The Germans did, however, commit one characteristic offence, no doubt on orders from above: the deportation of the Islands' tiny Jewish population, numbering about twenty. Nothing seems to have been done to save them and their fate is uncertain. In addition two thousand people, a 'tidy' total laid down in Berlin, consisting of all men not born on the Channel Islands, aged from sixteen to seventy, with their families, and including many elderly people who had retired there from England, were sent for internment in Germany. One man killed himself rather than go, and many tragic cases occurred where husbands or wives, who had volunteered to go with their spouses, found themselves separated as the sexes were sent to separate camps. Conditions in the camps were, however, satisfactory and many internees sent food parcels, saved from Red Cross supplies, back to their far hungrier friends on the Islands. People sentenced to more than a few weeks' imprisonment for occupation offences were usually sent to gaol in France. Eleven died in captivity. These, another dozen or so shot or drowned while trying to escape to Britain, and a few air raid victims were the Channel Islands' only fatal casualties. To stay there during the war was, in other words, far less dangerous than to be in Britain.

But it was also far more disagreeable. From the moment they arrived the Germans poured out a never-ceasing stream of orders, edicts and instructions, all enforced with typical humourless inflexibility. Some of the most annoying to loyal Britons were the adoption of German customs, such as driving on the right and of Central European time, then an hour ahead of British, though later in the war British Double Summer Time brought them into line. Less easily explained was the ban on cyclists' riding two abreast, though once the population had seen the reckless speed at which German drivers travelled and the trail of smashed gate posts and walls they left behind them, few cyclists felt disposed to argue about it.

The more serious restriction was the nightly curfew, after which no one was allowed out without a permit. The hours varied but were usually from 9 p.m. to 6.30 a.m., and during those hours a family was not even allowed to sit in the garden or a farmer to work on his own land. After several escapes to England, fishermen were not allowed to go more than a short distance out to sea and then only with an armed German escort. Supplies of fish dropped so sharply that long queues formed at 6 a.m. for dogfish or the normally unsaleable spider crabs. As the Germans became alarmed about an allied landing, they banned access to more and more cliffs and beaches, or covered them with mines, so that the inhabitants had the frustrating experience of being unable to go for a swim.

One of the greatest trials for the population was the feeling of being cut off from the rest of the world. The local press was strictly censored, and eventually the Guernsey papers were only appearing on alternate days and had shrunk to a single sheet, containing only improbable German communiqués and new orders to the civil population. The population thus relied wholly on their wireless sets for reliable news, as well as for entertainment, and when, in November 1940, all sets were ordered to be surrendered, the Guernsey man who described it in his diary as 'the worst blow so far' was speaking for the whole island. The order was believed, he noted, to be 'due to local people telling English-speaking Germans our news, who pass it on to their pals'. The sets were returned on Christmas Eve, this being regarded as 'the pleasantest Christmas gift' the Germans could have given the population, but were seized again, this time for good, in June 1942, on orders from Berlin. The Germans treated any breach of this law with great severity. The author of a leaflet urging the population of Jersey to keep their sets got five years in gaol; he had bravely given himself up after the Germans had seized ten hostages. Even to be caught in possession of a set meant several months in prison, but hundreds of home-made crystal sets were soon in operation. From a single large piece of crystal in the museum of the Jesuit College in Jersey one priest made sixty-three sets; in Guernsey a jeweller cut up an old meteorite for the same purpose, while soon every public telephone on both islands was out of action as the receivers had been stolen to make headphones.

Nowhere did the delay in starting the Second Front cause more despondency than in the Channel Islands. 'We are . . . beginning to wonder if it will ever take place at all', wrote one Guernsey farmer sadly in his diary in September 1932. By July 1943 he was even more depressed: 'We begin to think . . . that we shall end our days in bondage.' So many illicit sets were in use that any important news was all over the larger islands within an hour but owning a set was dangerous, for one shameful feature of the occupation was the number of anonymous letter-writers, who gave their neighbours away out of pure malice. At one time the police were receiving forty such letters a day until they began to take action only on those that were signed. This rash of anonymous letters, and a second epidemic of betrayals of those suspected of having hidden food from the Germans, remains a lasting blot on the Channel Islands' war record—and a reminder of the squalid depths to which British citizens could sink under enemy occupation.

Few people risked listening to the radio merely for entertainment but fortunately there were other diversions. The cinemas mainly showed German films but these often had English sub-titles, and the newsreels, though blatantly biased, were often excellently made. As a result of much derisive laughter in the wrong places the Germans eventually forbad any noise at all during films, including applause. This did not deter all the humorists, however, and one Guernsey audience, suffering the effects of inferior bread, were delighted by the wit who called out during a scene showing two German soldiers standing by the grave of a comrade, 'The poor b—— probably died of indigestion.' The few English films already on the Islands in 1940, which included *Keep Fit*, with George Formby, and *Top Hat*, with Fred Astaire, were shown repeatedly, until they broke down several times during each performance. The national anthem was banned, though sometimes played at private performances on 16 mm projectors, until these too were betrayed by some anonymous traitor. The one valuable German innovation—though unpopular—was a ban on smoking in cinemas. One Guernsey man, present at a performance of *Bill of Divorcement* in 1943, noted how 'a German police . . . caught two or three chaps, took their cigarettes away from them and ground them under his heel'. The occupation proved, too, to be a blessing in disguise for amateur theatrical companies, though performances had to finish by curfew. Anything offering music or laughter was particularly popular, like *No No Nanette*, and another Guernsey man was highly impressed when his maid got up to queue at 6 a.m. for seats for *Charley's Aunt*—the box office did not open till 10.

The first feeling of relief that the Germans had not proved worse was soon swallowed up in irritation at their perpetual requisitioning of goods badly needed by the Islanders themselves. The quality of the occupying troops also rapidly declined as the first, handsome conquerors of France, who had marched proudly along the lanes singing marching songs, went off to invade Russia and were replaced by men who seemed to the eyes of one Guernsey farmer, in April 1941, to be 'very fat, rough and unintelligent. They slouch along with a shuffling gait and compare very badly with our boys.' They behaved, he complained, like 'fat and vulgar locusts. . . . My car, lorry and row of trees are now gone and coal is to follow. I wonder if they'll want my wife? . . . Had we been left alone we could have done a Robinson Crusoe turn very well as our shops were very well stocked ready for a good visitor season or a siege.'

The earliest troops to arrive stripped the shops of every article on sale, from silk stockings to tinned foods, and their purchases were followed by wholesale official commandeering. Many hotels, schools and private houses were requisitioned and later some houses overlooking German batteries were pulled down. Transport went next. Private cars, lorries, and even motor buses had to be handed in, although at first some compensation was paid, an irreplaceable van costing £300 new being, for instance, valued at £165. Later, for no good reason, the Germans called in almost all the remaining vehicles and simply wrecked them, paying only the scrap metal value, so that the owner of a £1,000 bus received £5 for it, and a private-car owner was lucky to get 15s. As the public bus service on both Jersey and Guernsey virtually ceased, everyone got about by foot or on bicycles, often grossly overloaded. To move house, a frequent occurrence with the Germans seizing so much property, one had to find a horse and cart. Most shop deliveries ceased so that one could see, as one man did in 1943, an old woman in her seventies trudging painfully along for miles lugging a heavy can of tar for her fire, choked by the dust thrown up by passing cars stolen from her countrymen and driven by healthy young Germans. At weddings the bride and groom often arrived by cart and the guests came into church removing their cycle clips, while the dead went to their last resting place, like their forbears, on farm wagons. In the fields, with no petrol to be had and horses constantly commandeered by the Germans, women and children were harnessed to roller or harrow like wild beasts—for on one's land one's life depended.

A bicycle became precious and thefts so common that even the Germans carried the handlebars into shops with them. One Guernsey cycle dealer described in a letter to a friend after the liberation how in place of unobtainable valve rubber he used the insulation from electric cable, with fixing solution made from 'dissolving crêpe shoe soles in . . . carbon-bi-sulphide . . . and brake blocks . . . made from wood or old motor tyres'. When the last cycle tyres disappeared, they were replaced by lengths of garden hose lined with rope. The headmaster of one of the temporary schools set up to serve the few children left became a well-known figure at auction sales, buying up these articles for his pupils, but 'The children', the headmaster himself recalls, 'were remarkably keen on their school work and they attended very regularly and punctually.'

With no more coal being imported from England, people who had relied on solid fuel turned to gas and electricity, but the production of these had also been severely cut and the use of electricity, except for lighting, was largely banned. Families huddled together in one room with the weakest bulb they could find, though the power was sometimes inadequate even to read, and in school on a dark day the children could sometimes not begin work until 11.30 a.m. Social activities, like church services, were adjusted to fit the times the gas was on, which on Guernsey in 1944 was from 11 a.m.–12.30 p.m. and 6 p.m.—7.30 p.m.

Electricity was available at that time from 7 a.m.–1.15 p.m. and 7 p.m.–11 p.m. 'Candles are like sovereigns and can't be procured at all', one man noted in his diary. He milked his cows early in the morning by the light of a home-made lantern, which burned a mixture of paraffin and vinegar through a wick made from a bootlace, and gave a mere glimmer of light. The great treat for this family was the weekly fire. 'After dinner', he recorded one Sunday in October 1944, 'all the family gathers in the sitting room to watch mother strike the match which lights the weekly ruddy glow. The ancient and honourable company of fire worshippers gather round and express their enjoyment and gratitude. . . . Wood is nearly unprocurable for most people, coal has been gone for years and so we have to make a very special ceremony of our Sunday treat.' The Germans had forbidden the cutting down of trees, but in that last fearful winter of occupation there was much illicit felling and many empty houses were stripped of everything burnable. And not only empty houses: one might come home from a weary round of the empty shops to find one's front door missing. People sat permanently in their overcoats and went to bed at 7 p.m. Candles and paraffin were even scarcer than wood; as early as 1940 the candle ration on Guernsey was only two a week per family.

Every shortage experienced on the mainland of the British Isles, except for tomatoes and paper, came earlier in the Channel Islands, became more acute and lasted longer. Far more items were rationed, but rations could not always be honoured. Clothes rationing, for example, began on Guernsey in August 1940, nearly a year sooner than in England, but new clothes soon became virtually unobtainable or hopelessly expensive. A pair of men's underpants imported from France was priced at £3, more than the average family's weekly wage, a mackintosh at £17 10s., a pair of socks at 16s. The people of the Channel Islands were soon among the shabbiest in Europe and in the fields one saw men working in shirts made from patterned curtain material. A minor, but vital, shortage was of matches. The allowance was thirty, to last for an indefinite period. Tobacco was rationed, every male over eighteen being entitled to forty cigarettes a week, later reduced to twenty, though many people began to grow their own tobacco. Sweets and chocolate also disappeared early on. A few ounces of home-made Guernsey sweets were on sale occasionally and, as a Christmas treat, there was sometimes a bar of chocolate, for women and children only. English soap became precious, for the rationed variety from France merely stained the hands yellow and made the water muddy. Some ingenious substitutes were developed. Powdered cuttlefish was recommended in place of toothpaste, wreath wire used by undertakers was converted into hairpins, jellies were made from seaweed. One advertisement for policemen contained an unusual qualification: candidates must possess a bicycle with a dynamo, since batteries were unobtainable. One States agricultural inspector on Guernsey has not forgotten having four teeth out when the dentist only had 'very little cocaine left and that had been diluted to stretch it as far as it would go'. Afterwards, apologising for hurting his patient, the dentist refused a fee but was 'emotionally grateful' to be offered instead 'a few pounds of potatoes'. To one diarist conditions were summed up by an advertisement in March 1942, in which a titled woman appealed for some soap. Another Guernsey man was deeply impressed at seeing in the otherwise empty window of the most expensive cake-shop on the island the sole article it now had for sale: a bowl of wood-ash for cleaning saucepans, sold in twopenny packets. It was widely said that only two articles never became scarce on Guernsey, air and toilet paper, for the island had vast stocks of coloured paper for packing tomatoes.

But it was food which dominated everyone's thoughts, as imports from England ceased. There was no tea ration because there was no tea, no points scheme because there were no tinned goods to share out, no coffee, no cocoa, no dried fruit, no spices, and far smaller rations of butter, cooking fats, meat, jam, cheese and sugar than in England. Eggs and fish became even scarcer than in England and so much milk was seized by the Germans, and so many cows slaughtered, that the milk ration was rarely more than half a pint of 'separated', i.e. skimmed, milk a day and at one point sank to a quarter of a pint *a week*. Even salt was short, for to distil it from the sea required fuel and sea water was often used to mix dough for bread. The only article which, at least for several months each year, was plentiful was tomatoes and, with the export trade dead, at one time these were being given away free and fed to cows, which thrived on them. But the most alarming shortages of all, which England largely escaped, were of both Lord Woolton's famous 'fillers', bread and potatoes, which were strictly rationed, the amount varying according to sex and type of work. Heavy workers, this classification including, to the cynical amusement of the Islanders, the girls in the German soldiers' brothels, got more than sedentary ones. The usual bread ration was about 4 lb. a week, equal to two large sandwich loaves, but the bread was coarse, hard and grey and kept badly, and included a large proportion of oats and potato flour. The potato ration sometimes ceased for months at a time, when people raided the fields to root up the growing tubers. Some restaurants bravely stayed open, offering a choice between blackberry leaf tea and carrot coffee, though before long customers were expected to bring their own food or to give up coupons for restaurant meals. The only cakes, eagerly snapped up, were made largely of potato with dried grapes as raisins. For rissoles made from swedes and turnips, one eye-witness noticed in April 1942, 'there is a wild rush as soon as the shop opens each morning'. Often restaurants merely provided a place to sit down and by the end of the occupation many people would have starved but for the public soup kitchens which were opened, serving vegetable soup and rationed bread, and burning furze for fuel. In general, the farming population was better off than people in the towns, often managing to keep some eggs, milk and vegetables for themselves, and with access to substitutes like shredded sugar beet, used as a breakfast cereal. But even on the land life was far from luxurious. One farmer noted in his diary as early as November 1941 the anxious debates in his household over who was entitled to the last crust, while the potato ration, although he grew potatoes himself, was down to only 1 lb. a head, and for cooking the family were using linseed oil. His reaction to *The Kitchen Front* recipes heard on the radio in 1942, which encouraged people to eat more potatoes, was that England must be a land of luxury; the only ingredient mentioned in most recipes which was still available in Guernsey was water. It was a great event, worth recording in his diary, that it was his turn to lick the jam spoon. A typical meal, on Good Friday 1942, consisted of 'blackberry leaf tea with half a saccharine, sticky, sludgy brown bread, and a home-made bun of barley flour'. Animals came off even worse. Dogs, by an early German order, had to be kept on a lead and could no longer forage for themselves, while cats lived largely on limpets, scraped from the rocks by devoted owners. Some pets became food in their turn. One family, when their cat disappeared, reluctantly posted her as 'missing, presumed eaten'.

Food became the universal currency and frequent auctions were held at which scarce items fetched enormous prices: tea went for £25 a lb., butter for 25s., sugar for 16s., salt for 16s. A 4 oz. bar of Cadbury's fruit and nut chocolate changed hands in 1942 for 47s., a tin of peaches for 30s., one of Bird's custard powder for £4 2s. 6d., a bottle of H.P. sauce for 12s. Even a cake of soap on Jersey fetched 38s. 6d. Another Jersey man admits that 'after buying two pork chops for £7 I couldn't stand the pace'. His weight in June 1940 had been 13 stone. By the time he reached England after the liberation in 1945 he had visibly shrunk to 6 stone 10 lb. Often, due to the effects of near-starvation, people failed to recognise neighbours they had known all their lives and the wife of the Bailiff of Jersey hardly exaggerated when she remarked that she could now serve as a skeleton in an anatomy lesson.

From the summer of 1944 the situation deteriorated sharply, for with the Allies occupying the French coast the German besiegers were now the besieged. The German troops, longing for the war to end, began to say openly 'Hitler nix good', but the commander in chief of the Islands was a fanatical Nazi, prepared to ruin the Islands in a pointless last-ditch defence. By October 1944 no one, Islanders, occupying troops or their slave labourers, had enough to eat. Vegetables were rooted up from the fields in broad daylight, chickens stolen from their runs, cows milked secretly in the night. There was virtually no fuel and even the water supply was cut off for most of the day. Robberies became too common to be worth remarking on. Four, five, six attempts to break into one's house or grounds in a day were not uncommon. People lucky enough to own livestock brought them into their homes or garages at night, nailed boards over their windows, arranged home-made alarms of strings and buckets and sat up all night armed with pokers. Some desperate Germans tied the Islanders to their own tables or threatened them with their rifles as they ransacked their houses, but in general discipline among the occupying troops remained remarkably good.

Christmas 1944 on the Channel Islands was one of the most miserable anywhere in Europe. The only goods on sale in the chief market of Guernsey were eight turnips. The Christmas treat of the children of one family was a lump of sugar each, wrapped in Christmas paper left over from happier times. Another family celebrated with two slices of bread each. One farmer's family, more fortunate than most, sat down that day to potatoes cooked in linseed oil, followed by a shared apple, but many had their Christmas dinner at the public soup kitchens. By now many people were living for days at a time on cabbage soup and going to bed at midday as they were too weak to work. Potato peelings were a luxury, carefully retrieved from waste-buckets for baking in the communal bakehouses opened when private fuel supplies ran out.

But, two days later, the Channel Islands did receive a splendid present; on the

27th December the Red Cross ship *Vega* arrived laden with Red Cross parcels in response to a broadcast appeal for help. The parcels and the flour the *Vega* brought on this and later visits saved the Islanders' lives, and the Germans as a whole behaved with remarkable restraint and left the civilians to enjoy their treasure. By now the troops were far worse off than the population they were guarding, and one Guernsey man witnessed in March 1945 the depths to which 'proud members of the great and glorious German army had sunk', when he saw three junior officers eat their lunch of 'cabbage stalks pulled up from a nearby field'.

Everyone had dreaded that the commander of the Channel Islands would fight on, even after Germany had surrendered, but when Hitler's place was taken by Admiral Doenitz he decided to obey the orders of a fellow naval officer. On the 7th May the Germans on Jersey issued their last order, banning the display of Union Jacks until the war had officially finished, but the flags flew everywhere on the afternoon of the 8th, as crowds massed in the Royal Square of St. Helier to hear over the loudspeakers Churchill's end-of-the-war broadcast, which contained one all-important sentence: 'Our dear Channel Islands are also to be freed today.' Afterwards the Bailiff went down among the crowds, stood on a chair, and led them in *God Save the King*, which it had been illegal to sing for the past five years. On Guernsey the authorities discouraged all demonstrations until the liberating troops had actually landed. That night the only public rejoicings were held by the Germans, who marched about the grounds of one soldiers' club waving a blazing torch in one hand and a bottle of champagne in the other; the remnants of the mighty army which had terrorised all Europe was celebrating its final defeat. On Sark, fearful of British vengeance, the German troops locked themselves in their headquarters and, rather ignominiously, had to be dragged out by the liberating troops. On Alderney, used by the Germans as a prison for their slave labourers, there were no celebrations and only one bonfire, as the German garrison tried to conceal the evidence of their crimes by burning down the huts. But the barbed wire survived the flames, a grim reminder of what German rule had meant to Europe—and why the second world war had been the most just and most necessary in all recorded history.

# APPENDIX 2

# NETHERBURY'S CONTRIBUTION

Netherbury lies tucked away in the West Dorset hills and, like many another village in the length and breadth of England, it made its own special contribution to the war: had its own experiences, funny and sad; its own examples of courage and self-sacrifice. Its inhabitants worked together, helping each other and reflecting that calm and courage in the face of possible disaster which makes us all very proud to be English. . . .

The first warlike preparations must have been the giving out of gas masks and the early A.R.P. preparations. The old vicarage was chosen for the First Aid Post, the school for the Rest Centre. Everybody did a different job; wardens and special constables; fire service; first aid parties and rest centres; all were adequately manned. Noblest of all were the cottage mothers who opened their doors and their hearts to the evacuated children.

The first to arrive in September 1939 was a Roman Catholic school from Acton, which was evacuated to Slape Manor; the sisters living in the house, the priest being billeted at the inn and the children in various houses. In September, too, came a company of the Lancashire Regiment, to occupy the village hall, and the Women's Institute ran a canteen in the old New Inn premises for the soldiers. These were followed by the Sussex Regiment. In February 1940 a further batch of mothers and children came from Southampton. On this occasion there was trouble, as the mothers sounded as though they would rather have stayed to be bombed in Southampton than be buried alive in Netherbury. A vivid recollection is of one mother who refused to get out of the bus, or to be parted from her cat, which she had in a wooden box.

In May 1940 the Home Guard was formed. At first it was only about twenty strong, but finally comprised a force of eighty men, who were also drawn from the surrounding hamlets. The village had its own Defence Committee, presided over by the village leader, with heads of departments under him. Even if Netherbury was to be cut off from all the world, it would still carry on. There were weekly practices between the First Aid Post and the Rest Centre, with occasional exercises with the Home Guard and A.R.P. These were designed to be very realistic and generally ended with nurses and patients having a party at the Post with cups of tea all round. The stretcher party of four women practised with such zeal, that they could finally carry a sixteen stone man half a mile and over a narrow bridge, while wearing gas masks.

Soldiers from Dunkirk came to rest in the village and when the Battle of Britain started there was a good deal of aerial activity overhead. During the invasion alarm in September 1940 by some mistake the church bells were rung during the night, and the Home Guard turned out to their appointed stations, leaving the village to wait through the darkness for the battle to begin. Not until morning did they know that it was a false alarm.

Through the winter the W.I. gave weekly parties in the hall for their own children and the evacuees, in order to help the foster mothers. Two small evacuees in one home, who were helping to make a bed, said, 'What a big bed— there would be room in it for our mum and dad and you.'

A market stall was held in the square every week to sell surplus vegetables and the Scouts went round collecting green vegetables which were sent to Portland for the mine-sweeping flotillas.

Children with badges and armlets formed a most efficient salvage team, rushing round with trucks and barrows every Saturday morning. Some of the children can still remember a lone raider sweeping low over the roof tops. He did not drop any bombs, but the swastika on the wings, and the pilot, could be clearly seen by the boys and girls coming out of afternoon school.

Savings campaigns came one after another. For Warships Week, Netherbury had a model of a warship, on a wire across the square, and this moved on as the savings grew. For Salute the Soldier campaign, a life-size figure of a soldier, designed by a member of the W.I., stood guard over money bags, which increased as the week proceeded.

The year 1943 brought the Americans and three hundred of them were in camp at Farnham, half a mile away. They became very popular with everybody, especially the children, to whom they gave endless chewing gum and pennies. Weekly dances in the village hall were so well patronised by them, that £130 was raised for the Red Cross in one winter. By this time nearly all the young men had gone and people had almost forgotten what it was like not to be at war; many children could not remember the time without black-out and rations.

The days before D Day were anxious and exciting, for Nettherbury was in a prohibited area, where movement was controlled and no visitors allowed. A.R.P. precautions tightened in case of aerial activity during the invasion. It seemed as if it would never come, but it did come, and sooner han anyone had dreamed, came V.E. Day. Out went the flags and Mr. Stone fired his cannon.

Later the W.I. gave a dinner in the hall to members of the Home Guard and A.R.P., where about sixty men were entertained to cold meat, salad and a variety of puddings. A sing-song rounded off the evening. Netherbury's last war effort was to collect enough money to give every serving man and woman a wallet containing £2 on their home-coming. The war was over, the evacuees had returned, Netherbury and England were at peace; and some may think there was good in those days, when there was an atmosphere abroad which we have lost now. Like all our countrymen, we are at our best in a time of crisis.

*War History of the Women's Institute of Netherbury*

# SOURCES

I have used three sources of information in writing this book: books and other published material, including many official leaflets and advertisements; material provided, usually in writing but occasionally in interviews, by the numerous organisations and commercial concerns I approached, including such items as wartime house magazines and catalogues; and, by far the most important, hitherto unpublished contributions from individual civilians. In a few cases, mainly of personal acquaintances, I supplemented this material with interviews, often lasting several hours. Although I have made substantial use of the printed sources in providing factual information, I have wherever possible used unpublished material to provide description and illustrative anecdotes and have drawn on the reminiscences of ordinary people rather than on published diaries or memoirs. Wherever no printed source for a statement is indicated in the bibliography the quotation is from a hitherto unpublished contribution. As I promised contributors, no names are given in the text and in many cases, especially of doctors, the names are also omitted, at the informant's request, from the list of contributors which follows.

## I

## PRINTED MATERIAL

*Note: The place of publication is London, unless otherwise stated. Complete particulars are given only the first time a book is mentioned, but these references can be located in the index under the author's name or, where a book is anonymous, its title. Where, as was often the case, no date of publication was given, I have made the best estimate I can of the most likely year.*

## GENERAL ACCOUNTS

After I had finished my book, but before it had gone to the printers, Angus Calder, *The People's War* (Cape, 1969), was published. This would have greatly lightened my labours had it appeared earlier and is clearly indispensable for any serious student of the period. It differs radically, however, from the present book in drawing almost exclusively on published sources and in aiming to give a general history of social trends during the war rather than a descriptive account of daily life.

The official *United Kingdom History of the War, Civil Series* is indispensable
to the serious historian, but is not intended for the general reader and con-
centrates on government policy, rather than on its effects on the ordinary
citizen. One volume of the series, however, can be read for pleasure as well as
reference and this I have used extensively, i.e. Richard M. Titmuss, *Problems
of Social Policy* (H.M.S.O. and Longmans, 1950). It is supplemented by Sheila
Ferguson and Hilde Fitzgerald, *Studies in the Social Services* (H.M.S.O. and
Longmans, 1953). The best short factual summary of civilian life is *What Britain
has done 1939–45* (Ministry of Information, 1945), and I also constantly referred to the *Annual Abstract of Statistics 1939–47* (No. 48 H.M.S.O., 1948).
A popular 'picture book' with some useful information is Anon., *Ourselves in
Wartime* (Odhams Press, n.d. but c. 1944). A most thorough analysis of the
effect of the war on every aspect of daily life during its opening is provided
by Charles Madge and Tom Harrison (editors), *War Begins at Home* (Mass
Observation, n.d. but probably 1940), though, most unfortunately, it only
covers the period to December 1939.

Surprisingly few places felt moved to compile a history of their experiences
during the war and most of those that do exist tend to be a catalogue of air
raids and Civil Defence activities, with little if any reference to other aspects
of civilian life. Three notable exceptions are *Luton at War* (The *Luton News*,
Home Counties Newspapers Ltd., Luton, 1947), W. C. Berwick Sayers (editor),
*Croydon and the Second World War* (Croydon Corporation, 1949), and H. P.
Twyford, *It Came to our Door, Plymouth in the Second World War* (Underhill
Ltd. Plymouth, 1946). Shorter books of a similar kind are John G. O'Leary,
*Danger over Dagenham 1939–45* (Borough of Dagenham, 1947), Charles W.
Preston, *The Borough in Wartime, A Record of how the War of 1939–45
affected the Borough of Reigate* (Holmesdale Press Ltd. Redhill, n.d. but c.
1945), Anon., *Willingdon, The War History of a Bedfordshire Village* (Willing-
don Woman's Institute, 1946), and Bernard Drew, *Farningham against Hitler.
The Story of Six Years of War in a Kentish Village* (Kentish District Times,
Bromley, 1946). A unique source on village life, hitherto, I believe, unconsulted
by any historian, is the manuscript *War Record* of the Dorset Federation of
Women's Institutes, which contains contributions, of greatly varying quality,
from every village in the county and is now in the Dorset County Archives.

Personal accounts are more numerous. The best, which gives a unique
child's eye view of wartime life—the author was aged nine in 1939—is Derek
Lambert, *The Sheltered Days. Growing Up in the War* (André Deutsch. 1965).
A very thorough unpublished record of the daily life of a photographer and
warden in wartime Grantham is Walter Lee, *Day by Day* (5 volumes, n.d. but
c. 1945, in the Imperial War Museum). The best, and best-written, picture of
life in London just before and during the war is Frances Faviell, *A Chelsea
Concerto* (Cassell, 1959), while the outstanding book on the first year of the
war as seen in an Essex village (though, irritatingly, its real identity is not
stated) is Margery Allingham, *The Oaken Heart* (Michael Joseph, 1941, re-
published, Hutchinson, 1959). On the whole first year of the war E. S. Turner,
*The Phoney War on the Home Front* (Michael Joseph, 1961) is indispensable.
Two American visitors wrote rather 'thin' and 'cosy' descriptions of life in

Britain, Margaret Biddle, *The Women of England* (Houghton Mifflin, Boston, U.S.A., 1941) and Margaret Culkin Banning, *Letters from England, Summer 1942* (Harper, New York, n.d. but c. 1943). Most published wartime diaries are by journalists. A day by day account of comfortably-off middle-class life in London is provided by the successive diaries of Charles Graves, *Off The Record* (Hutchinson, n.d. but c. 1941), *Londoner's Life* (Hutchinson, n.d. but c. 1942), *Great Days* (Hutchinson, n.d. but c. 1944) and *Pride of the Morning* (Hutchinson, n.d. but c. 1945). A useful, though avowedly Left-wing, diary covering the period up to the end of 1942 of Hamilton Fyfe, *Britain's Wartime Revolution* (Gollancz, 1944). Also covering the same district, Marylebone, are the diaries of a BBC producer and Harley Street specialist Anthony Weymouth (a pseudonym), *Journal of the War Years and One Year Later* (Littlebury and Co. The Worcester Press, Worcester, 2 volumes, 1948), the diary for the period from March 1940 to February 1941 also being published separately as *Plague Year* (Harrap, 1942). A good account of experiences in 'Hell-fire Corner' in the early part of the war is given by a Ministry of Information official, Hubert S. Banner, *Kentish Fire* (Hurst and Blackett, n.d. but c. 1944), which would be more valuable, like so many books, if the date of publication had been included. James Lansdale Hodson, *Home Front* (Gollancz, 1944), gives some useful descriptions of conditions outside London, especially in factories. A deliberately light-hearted but often informative view of daily life is provided by Ursula Bloom, *The Log of No Lady* (Chapman and Hall, 1940) and *War Isn't Wonderful* (Hutchinson, 1961), which covers the whole period. On the first year of the war James Wedgwood Drawbell, *The Long Year* (Wingate, 1958), is also helpful and F. Tennyson Jesse and H. M. Harwood, *London Front, Letters written to America August 1939 to July 1940* (Constable, 1940). A short, deservedly little-known, diary by a wartime Civil Servant, who coyly but inadequately conceals his name, is Timoleon (i.e. Sir W. Y. Darling), *Kings Cross to Waverley* (William Hodge, 1944). A series of all-too literary accounts of various aspects of wartime life, which do contain a few useful facts amid the stylistic elegances, is provided by Stephan Schimanski and Henry Treece (editors), *Leaves in the Story. A Book of Diaries* (Lindsay Drummond, 1947). Autobiographies by BBC personalities are often useful on many matters besides broadcasting. The best are Stuart Hibberd, *'This—is London'* (Macdonald and Evans, 1950), Frederick Grisewood, *The World Goes By* (Secker and Warburg, 1952) and Bruce Belfrage, *One Man in His Time* (Hodder and Stoughton, 1951). I also consulted Vera Brittain, *England's Hour* (Macmillan, 1941).

Many politicians published diaries, autobiographies and biographies covering the wartime period, notably Harold Nicolson, *Diaries and Letters 1939–1945* (edited by Nigel Nicolson, Collins, 1967); *Chips: The Diaries of Sir Henry Channon* (Edited by Robert Rhodes James, Weidenfeld, 1967); Herbert Morrison, *An Autobiography by Lord Morrison of Lambeth* (Odhams, 1960); Hugh Dalton, *The Fateful Years, Memoirs 1931–1945* (Muller, 1957); Oliver Lyttleton, *The Memoirs of Lord Chandos* (Bodley Head, 1962); The Rt. Hon. Earl of Woolton, *Memoirs* (Cassell, 1959); John Wheeler-Bennett, *John Anderson Viscount Waverley* (Macmillan, 1962) and Allan Bullock, *The Life and Times of Ernest Bevin. Volume II. Minister of Labour 1940–45* (Heinemann, 1967).

For general reference on military events I mainly consulted Winston Churchill, *The Second World War* (6 volumes, Cassell, 1948–54) and Basil Collier, *A Short History of the Second World War* (Collins, 1967). A. J. P. Taylor, *English History 1914–1945* (O.U.P. 1965), was useful on military and general history. I referred constantly to those standbys of every historian, *Hansard's Parliamentary Debates*; *The Annual Register* and *The Times*. The other principal periodical publications I consulted were every issue of *Punch* and *Picture Post* for the whole wartime period; most issues of *Housewife*; occasional issues of other newspapers and magazines, national, trade and local, and, of the greatest value on commercial conditions, since contributions were received from shops in many different parts of the country, the weekly *Gazette* of the John Lewis Partnership. For the text of broadcast speeches I normally consulted *The Listener* and occasionally the original scripts.

CHAPTER I

On the early history of Civil Defence I used T. H. O'Brien (H.M.S.O. 1955), the local histories already mentioned and Stanley Tiquet, *It Happened Here. The Story of Civil Defence in Wanstead and Woodford 1939–45* (Wanstead and Woodford Borough Council, 1947), the source of the golf club story. The history of the A.F.S. and of fire-fighting throughout the war is admirably described by Sir Aylmer Firebrace, *Fire Service Memories* (Andrew Melrose Ltd. n.d., but c. 1949). On the Observer Corps and its relationship to Civil Defence, I consulted T. E. Winslow, *Forewarned is Forearmed. A History of the Royal Observer Corps* (William Hodge and Co, 1948). Charles Graves, *Women in Green, The Story of the W.V.S. in Wartime* (Heinemann, 1948), describes the recruitment and training of women for A.R.P. work and includes the incident of the bombs that went 'pop', and A.F.S. training is described by Henry W. Stedman, *Battle of the Flames. The Personal Story of the London Bombing as seen by one Auxiliary Fireman* (Jarrolds, n.d. but c. 1942). The 'old-established textile firm' was Hitchcock, Williams and Co. whose work is described by H. A. Walden, *Operation Textiles: A City Warehouse in Wartime* (no publisher stated, n.d. but c. 1947). The girl with her boots tied together is mentioned in the John Lewis *Gazette*. The government publications referred to, or consulted, were: *Air Raid Precautions: What You Can Do* (Home Office, March 1930); *National Service: A Guide to the Ways in Which the People of this Country May Give Service* (H.M.S.O., January 1939); *The Protection of Your Home Against Air Raids* (Home Office, n.d. but c. 1938) and the set of Public Information Leaflets, *No 1: Some Things you Should Know if War Should Come; No 2: Your Gas Mask. Masking your Windows; No 3: Evacuation, Why and How No; 4: Your Food in Wartime; No 5: Fire Precautions in Wartime,* (Lord Privy Seal's Office, Nos. 1–4 July 1939, No. 5 August 1939).

Other sources referred to include *Wills Cigarette Picture-Card Album: Air Raid Precautions Series* (n.d. but probably 1938); Richmal Crompton, *William and A.R.P.* (Newnes, May 1939); and Nevil Shute, *What Happened to the*

*Corbetts* (Heinemann, 1939, Pan Books, 1965). On the pre-war plans for evacuation I used Titmuss; Wheeler-Bennett; Dame Dorothy Brock, *An Unusual Happening*, reprinted in *The Story of the Mary Datchelor School 1877–1957* (Hodder and Stoughton, 1957): H. C. A. Gaunt, *Two Exiles, Being a Record of the Adventures of Malvern College During the War* (Sampson Low, n.d. but c. 1947); J. H. Leakey, *School Errant. The story of the war-time adventures of Dulwich College Preparatory School* (Dulwich College Preparatory School, 1951); and a printed letter from the Borough of Beckenham dated 29th September 1938. The reaction of East London to A.R.P. is described by the mayor of Stepney during the blitz, Frank R. Lewey, *Cockney Campaign* (Stanley Paul and Co., n.d., but c. 1944) and of Bethnal Green to Munich by George F. Vale, *Bethnal Green's Ordeal 1939–45* (Bethnal Green Council, n.d. but c. 1945). My source on *Bandwagon* was my own memory, supplemented by Robert Hirst, *Three Men and a Gimmick* (a biography of Arthur Askey and other comedians), (The World's Work, Kingswood, Surrey, 1957).

CHAPTER 2

In addition to the sources already referred to, I consulted, on office evacuation, G. L. Hosking, *Salute to Service. The Prudential in the Second World War* (Prudential Assurance Co., 1946) and John Wadsworth, *Counter Defensive, Being the Story of a Bank in Battle* (Hodder and Stoughton, 1946). The editor and journalist quoted is James Drawbell, the film technician was the anonymous author of *The Bells Go Down, The Diary of a London A.F.S. Man* (Methuen, 1942), the London woman writing to America was H. M. Harwood. The last day of pre-war television is described by Asa Briggs, *The History of British Broadcasting. Vol II The Golden Age of Wireless* (O.U.P., 1965); the rehearsal of *The Circle* by Val Gielgud, *British Radio Drama 1922–1956: A Survey* (Harrop, 1957); the exodus from Broadcasting House by Stuart Hibberd and his own adventures by Sandy Macpherson, *Sandy Presents* (Home and Van Thal, 1950). The quotations from BBC news bulletins, etc., are from records kept by BBC News Information and BBC Historical Records, especially 'P as B'—(Programme as Broadcast) details.

CHAPTER 3

Adrian Ball, *The Last Day of the Old World* (Muller, 1963) deals with the events of 3rd September 1939 all over the world. The barrage balloon nicknames are mentioned by Morrison and Frances Faviell and the lyrical description is by H. M. Harwood. On how the war affected the fish shops I used an article in the *Fish Friers Review*.

CHAPTER 4

The official publications I used included *Public Information Leaflet No. 2* and the following, all issued by the Ministry of Home Security: *Wartime Lighting Restrictions for Industrial and Commercial Premises* (May 1939),

*Wartime Lighting Restrictions: Lights Carried by Road Vehicles* (September 1939), *Wartime Lighting Restrictions* (December 1939) and *Ventilation in the Blackout* (1940). I also consulted G. W. Stonier, *Shaving through the Blitz* (Cape, 1943) and Evelyn August (editor), *The Black-Out Book* (Harrap, n.d. but probably 1939).

CHAPTER 5

Titmuss was the main authority and Dorothy Brock, Gaunt and Leakey were also useful. I also consulted B. S. Johnson (editor), *The Evacuees* (Gollancz, 1968); William Boyd (editor), *Evacuation in Scotland* (University of London Press, 1944); Anon., *London Children in Wartime Oxford* (Printed for O.U.P., 1947); *Town Children Through Country Eyes* (National Federation of Women's Institutes, 1940); *Water and Sewerage Survey* (N.F.W.I., 1944), *Report on Conditions in Reception Areas* (H.M.S.O., 1941) and various authors, *Children in Wartime* (A. Brown and Sons, Hull, n.d.). The 'sheep dip' story and quotation from *The Lancet* occur in Turner and 'the *Brighton Balloon Barrage*' in A.S.M. Gow, *Letters from Cambridge* (Cape, 1945). The dog with the friendly face is described by Graves, *Women in Green*. On the mechanics of evacuation, I used R. Bell, *History of the British Railways during the War* (Railway Gazette, 1946) and Charles Graves, *London Transport Carried On* (London Passenger Transport Board, 1947). A useful Ministry of Home Security leaflet is *To the Householder* (on one side) and *To the Person Evacuated* (on the other) (1942). I also consulted the following W.V.S. leaflets: *Information on Evacuation for Householders Taking Unaccompanied Children* (n.d.); *General Information on Evacuation for Reception Areas* (n.d.); *Information for Householders Taking Evacuees* (1944); *Information on Bed-Wetting for Householders Taking Unaccompanied Children* (1944); *The Cleansing and Care of Children's Heads* (n.d.) and *Evacuation: Instructions for W.V.S. Welfare Workers* (manuscript, 1944).

CHAPTER 6

On the evacuation of the BBC I used Antonia White, *The BBC at War* (BBC, n.d. but in fact 1941) and Gielgud. The visitor to the BBC at Evesham was Ursula Bloom, *No Lady*. On the evacuation of NALGO I used Alec Spoor, *White Collar Union* (NALGO, 1967), a model trade union history, on the Prudential, Hosking, and on schools *The Public and Preparatory Schools Yearbook, 1941* (H.F.W. Deane and Sons, 1941).

CHAPTER 7

The Mass Observation surveys are quoted in *War Begins at Home*.

CHAPTER 8

The main printed source on the call-up is *The Ministry of Labour and National Service, Report for the Years 1939–46* (H.M.S.O., 1947). The official history which reveals the poverty of soldiers' families and provided divorce statistics was Sheila Ferguson and Hilde Fitzgerald. On the council which dismissed its servicemen employees I used Alec Spoor and on the reactions of cinema audiences a manuscript Mass Observation Report, *The Content of Newsreels* (28th January 1940). Woking's attitude to evacuees is described by E. S. Turner, and a similar account, for High Wycombe, is given by B. S. Johnson. The attitude of an unnamed town in the Isle of Wight to soldiers about to go overseas is vividly described in Alexander Baron, *From the City, From the Plough* (Cape, 1948), a novel based on the author's experiences.

## CHAPTER 9

The best general sources on the period till May 1940 are *War Begins at Home* and E. S. Turner. The Londoner who wrote to a friend about the *Graf Spee* parade was H. M. Harwood. The misdeeds of the Ministry of Information are recounted by Norman Riley, *999 and All That* (Gollancz, 1940), the book referred to in the text. On the BBC in this period I used Sandy Macpherson, Val Gielgud and extracts from contemporary scripts in the BBC Archives. On Lord Haw Haw the outstanding source is J. A. Cole, *William, Joyce, Lord Haw Haw* (Faber, 1964), but I also consulted Charles J. Rolo, *Radio Goes to War* (Faber, 1943), which gives a contemporary assessment of his abilities, and Jonah Barrington, *Lord Haw Haw of Zeesen* (Hutchinson, n.d. but c. 1940), the facetious mock biography referred to. The rumour-bearing milkman is mentioned by Ursula Bloom, *No Lady*, the coffin wood by Margery Allingham, the rumour about Liverpool in the manuscript Mass Observation *Report on Liverpool* (22nd May 1941), and the rumour about Goering in Plymouth by André Savignon, *With Plymouth Through Fire* (Translated and published by Miss S. E. Ouston, Hayle, Cornwall, 1968). The little girl whose father thought firemen a waste of public money is mentioned by Firebrace, the insults to '£3 a week men' by Stedman, the 'windy Yids' story by the author of *The Bells Go Down*, who also describes morale among the firemen. Britain's attitude to the Finnish War is described by Douglas Clark, *Three Days to Catastrophe. Britain and the Russo-Finnish War* (Hammond Hammond, 1966). Reaction to Hore-Belisha's dismissal and to Lord Gort was described in the Mass Observation Report, *The Content of Newsreels*. The most convenient source of the *Gate of the Year* poem is Laurence Thompson, *1940. Year of Legend. Year of History* (Collins, 1966). The distinguished journalist was Sir Robert Bruce Lockhart, quoted by Turner, and the BBC producer who admired the spring, Weymouth.

## CHAPTER 10

The journalist impressed by the effect of the new government was Hamilton Fyfe. Alan Bullock describes the effect of the appointment of Bevin and Beaverbrook. On anti-invasion preparations I used David Lampe, *The Last Ditch* (Cassell, 1968), *If the Invader Comes* (Ministry of Information, 1940), *Enemy Invasion. What You Must Do* (City of Birmingham Invasion Committee, n.d.), *Invasion*

*Committees. Notes for the Guidance of Members* (Northampton County Council, 1942), and—the outstanding source—Peter Fleming, *Invasion 1940* (Hart-Davis, 1957). I also drew on Hibberd, Channon, Nicolson, Allingham, Wheeler-Bennett, Dalton and Drawbell. The text of a broadcast by Herbert Morrison on *Beating the Invader* appears in *The Listener* for 27th March 1941, of J. B. Priestley's *Postscripts* in *All England Listened. The Wartime Broadcasts of J. B. Priestley* (Chilmark Press, New York, 1967) and of Churchill's speeches in Charles Eade (editor), *The War Speeches of Winston Churchill* (3 volumes, Cassell 1951–2). On the Home Guard the main source is Charles Graves, *The Home Guard of Britain* (Hutchinson, n.d. but probably 1943), muddled and badly printed but containing many useful unit histories. A. G. Street, *From Dusk till Dawn* (Harrap, 1942), is the source of some lighter anecdotes and the text of Eden's speech can be found in *Freedom and Order. Selected Speeches of Sir Anthony Eden 1939–46* (Faber, 1947). Books on Home Guard training are John Brophy, *Home Guard Handbook* (Hodder and Stoughton, numerous editions from 1940), and Tom Wintringham, *New Ways of War* (Penguin Special, 1940). There is some factual information in John Brophy, *Britain's Home Guard* (Harrap, 1945) and I also used *The 8th (Burton) Battalion of the Staffordshire Home Guard: An Appreciation of their Record of Service to their King and Country* (no publisher, no date).

CHAPTER 11

My main source on the early stages of the Battle of Britain was Richard Collier, *Eagle Day* (Hodder & Stoughton, 1966), and on general conditions in Kent and Sussex at this time I used Banner. The meanness of Chelsea Council is mentioned by John Strachey, *Post D* (Gollancz, 1941), the flowers on Chelsea Andersons by Frances Faviell, and Anderson's reaction to such displays by Wheeler-Bennett. The warden who threw her tea on the ground was Barbara Nixon, *Raiders Overhead* (Lindsay Drummond, 1943), which is also useful on wardens' living conditions. On shelters I consulted the following Home Office publications: *The Protection of Your Home Against Air Raids* (1938); *Directions for the Erection and Sinking of the Galvanised Corrugated Steel Shelter* (1939); *Directions for the Erection of Domestic Surface Shelters* (1939); *Your Home as an Air Raid Shelter* (1940), *Make Your Own Air Raid Shelter* (1940).

CHAPTER 12

The main official sources I used were Basil Collier, *The Defence of the United Kingdom* (H.M.S.O., 1957); T. H. O'Brien, *Civil Defence* (H.M.S.O. and Longmans, 1955) and on the post-raid services Titmuss. I also consulted *The Care of the Homeless* (H.M.S.O., 1942), *Help for the Homeless* (no publisher but probably Ministry of Health, 1941), and *Care of the Homeless—Food Stocks in Rest Centres* (Ministry of Health circular, 1943). A more popular contemporary account was Anon., *Front Line* (H.M.S.O., 1941). On the London blitz the best general sources are Constantine Fitz Gibbon, *The Blitz* (Wingate, 1957),

Ritchie Calder, *The Lesson of London* (Secker and Warburg, 1941) and *Carry on London* (English University Press, 1941), which are particularly informative on some of the early mistakes. The experiences of particular areas or firms are described by Jerome Willis, *It Stopped at London* (Hurst and Blackett, 1944), a journalist living in Bayswater; H. A. Wilson, *Death over Haggerston* (A. R. Mowbray, 1941), the East End vicar referred to; Ben T. Tinton, *War Comes to the Docks* (Marshall, Morgan and Scott, n.d.), Lewey; Wadsworth, on bank conditions; Charles Graves, *London Transport*, on the use of the tubes; *The Swiss Cottager* (Dore Silverman, London, N.W.3., 1940); *The Warren Mag, Recording the Activities of Shelter 1940* (duplicated, 1940–41). The Home Office publication on making yourself comfortable in the shelter was *Your Brick Street Shelter this Winter* (1940), and I used two other Ministry publications *How to Put up Your Morrison Shelter* (1941) and *Shelter at Home* (1941). On the Morrison shelter I also consulted the script of the 'Horizon' programme about its inventor, Sir John Baker, on BBC television on 2nd January 1968. The African air raid warden was E. I. Ekpenyon, *Some Experiences of an African Air-Raid Warden* (Sheldon Press, n.d. but c. 1943). Details of pre-war estimates of likely casualties were given by O'Brien and by Raymond H. Fredette, *The First Battle of Britain 1917–18* (Cassell, 1966). The A.F.S. man who wrote about looting was the author of *The Bells Go Down*. Other sources I used on the London blitz were Nixon, Strachey, Berwick Sayers, Vale, Morrison and Wheeler Bennett; Anon., *Hampstead at War 1939–45* (Borough of Hampstead, n.d.); Anon., *From Dusk till Dawn. Letters by a Warden* (Constable, 1941), which is too vague and literary to be much use; Peter Conway, *Living Tapestry* (Staples Press, 1946), which contains an excellent account of life in various shelters; William Sansom, James Gordon and Stephen Spender, *Jim Brady, The Story of Britain's Firemen* (Lindsay Drummond, 1943); Negley Farson, *Bomber's Moon* (Gollancz, 1941); Elinor Mordaunt, *Here too is Valour* (Muller, 1941); Anon., *Middle Temple Ordeal* (Middle Temple, 1948); G. C. Curnock (editor), *Hospitals under Fire* (Allen and Unwin, 1941); John Ross and Leonard Dudeney (editor), *War Came to New Street Square. A Record of Wymans in the Great London Blitz* (n.d.); William Sansom, *Westminster at War* (Faber, 1947), which proves that a factually informative book can also be well written; Viola G. Garvin, *London's Glory* (Allen and Unwin, 1945), which consists largely of drawings; and A.S.G. Butler, *Recording Ruin* (Constable, 1942). On the Greater London area I also consulted A. H. Eyre, *Perpetual Target* (published by the author, Welling, Kent, 1946), which makes the legitimate point that people in other parts of the country often had no conception of what life in the South was like.

No comprehensive popular history of the blitz outside London exists, but I consulted the following local histories: Reece Winstone, *Bristol in the 1940s* (Reece Winstone, Bristol, 1961), which is mainly photographs; T. H. J. Underdown, *Bristol under Blitz* (H. W. Arrowsmith, Bristol, 1942); S. Paul Shipley, *Bristol Siren Nights: Diaries and Stories of the Blitz* (Rankins Brothers, Bristol 1943); Anon, *The Story of the Exeter Blitz* (A. Wheaton and Co., Exeter, n.d.); Anon, *Smitten City, the Story of Portsmouth in the Air Raids 1940–1944* (Evening News, Portsmouth, n.d.); Admiral Sir W. M. James, *The Portsmouth*

*Letters* (Macmillan, 1946); Anon., *Our Blitz: Red Sky Over Manchester* (Kemsley Newspapers, Manchester, n.d.); S. C. Leslie, *Bombers over Merseyside* (Liverpool Daily Post and Echo, 1943); T. Geraghty, *A North-East Coast Town. The Story of Kingston-upon-Hull in the 1939–45 Great War* (Hull Corporation n.d.); Claud Wimhurst, *The Bombardment of Bath* (Bath & Wilts Chronicle and Herald Bath, 1942); George Swain, *Norwich under Fire* (Jarrolds and Sons, Norwich, n.d.); George H. Ingles, *When the War came to Leicester* (C. Brooks and Co. Leicester, n.d.); Bernard Knowles, *Southampton. The English Gateway* (Hutchinson, 1951); and on Plymouth, Twyford and Savignon. Other, less informative, books I consulted were '*B*' *Group Harrogate: Civil Defence Wardens Service Souvenir*; H. J. Larcombe (editor), *City of Gloucester Civil Defence. A Record of Service* (Corporation of Gloucester, 1946); Dorothy Bingham-Hall, *The History of Civil Defence in No. 3* (*Weston-Super-Mare*) *Area* (1945). The most useful source on the fire-watching regulations was O'Brien and I also consulted a duplicated note *City of Birmingham: Revised Instructions Regarding the Method of Attacking Incendiary Bombs* (City of Birmingham, May 1944).

### CHAPTERS 13 AND 14

The main source is *How Britain Was Fed in Wartime: Food Control 1939–45* (H.M.S.O., 1946), and I also used *ABC of Rationing in the United Kingdom* (Ministry of Food, 1951 edition), numerous *Food Facts* and other Ministry of Food advertisements and, particularly valuable, *The Ministry of Food Bulletin*, a duplicated summary of news and instructions issued weekly to local Food Offices, which provided the text of the regulation banning iced cakes. I also consulted numerous wartime recipe books, including Susan Croft, *The Stork Wartime Cookery Book* (Stork Margarine Company, n.d.), *What to Give Them* (McDougalls Wartime Cookery Book, n.d.), both praised by many informants, Lettice M. Pither, *One Hundred Ways of Cooking Without Meat* (Pitman, 1952, but including some wartime recipes) and *Community Feeding in Wartime* (H.M.S.O., 1941). On Lord Woolton I used his own *Memoirs* and on his broadcasting technique Anthony Weymouth. 'Chips' Channon's remarks on the national loaf occur in his diary.

### CHAPTER 15

The main official sources were E. L. Hargreaves and M. M. Gowing, *Civil Industry and Trade* (H.M.S.O., 1952), which covers the whole field of civilian supplies, *Getting Ready for Baby. Make Do and Mend Leaflet No. 1*, (Board of Trade, n.d.) and *Welcome Little Stranger* and *Green to Start, Blue to Win* (Ministry of Food advertisements, n.d. but c. 1942). Woolton's concern for his 'preggies' is described in his *Memoirs*.

### CHAPTER 16

The main printed source was Ministry of Food advertisements.

CHAPTER 17

The main printed source was Titmuss, which provided the quotations from the
L.C.C. inspectors. On examination regulations I used information privately
supplied by the Oxford and Cambridge Schools Examination Board and
on children's out-of-school activities I relied heavily on information provided
by the Boy Scouts Association and on material in *Luton at War*.

CHAPTER 18

The outstanding source was Gow, and on the call-up of students I also used the
*Report of the Ministry of Labour and National Service* and Alan Bullock. I
also consulted Anon., *Report on the Evacuation of the College 1939–43* (King's
College, London, 1945).

CHAPTER 19

The main source was Arthur W. Moss and Elizabeth Kirby, *Animals were
There* (Hutchinson, n.d.). I also used the following publications by the
R.S.P.C.A.: *Animals and Air Raids* (1939); *Feeding Dogs and Cats in Wartime*
(n.d., but c. 1941) and *Feeding of Canaries, Budgerigars and Parrots* (n.d., but c.
1941). Charles Graves's securing of a tin of pet food is described in *Great Days*.
I also consulted the following published by N.A.R.P.A.C.: *Advice to Farmers*
(n.d.); *Wartime Aids for all Animal Owners*, (n.d.); and *Dogs, Cats and Birds
in Air Raids* (n.d.). On the Zoo I mainly used Edward Hindle, *Letter from the
London Zoo* in *Life* magazine (New York, 24th April 1944).

CHAPTER 20

The main official source is Keith A. H. Murray, *Agriculture* (H.M.S.O. &
Longmans, 1955), which I supplemented with leaflets published by the Ministry
of Food and Agriculture. The Ministry's wartime activities are described by
F. Howard Lancum, *Press Officer, Please!* (Crosby, Lockwood and Co, 1946);
on the Women's Land Army I used V. Sackville-West, *The Women's Land
Army* (Michael Joseph, 1944), which includes the accounts of difficult living
and travel conditions and the letter from the girl who loved life in rural Wales,
and W. E. Shewell-Cooper, *Land Girl. A Manual for Volunteers in the Women's
Land Army* (English University Press, n.d.), which contains the tests described.

CHAPTER 21

The main official source was Hargreaves and Gowing, supplemented by
Oliver Lyttleton, who describes Churchill's attitude to clothes rationing,
and Dalton. The effect of clothes rationing on a textile firm was described by
H. A. Walden and on the retail trade by the John Lewis *Gazette*, the source
of reactions to the first news of the scheme. Other publications I consulted

were H. E. Wadsworth, *The Utility Cloth and Clothing Scheme* (Manchester Statistical Society, 1948); Margaret Wray, *The Women's Outerwear Industry* (Duckworth, 1957); and the following Board of Trade Publications: *Clothing Coupon Quiz* (1941); *Rationing of Clothing, Footwear and Cloth: Notice to Traders* (1941); *Bank Accounts for Clothing Coupons: Trader's Instructions and Guide* (1942); *General Occupational Supplement for 1942–3* (n.d.); *An Iron Ration for Workers in Certain Very Heavy Industries* (1943); *Detailed List of Specifications* (i.e. for Utility Clothing) (n.d.); and numerous *Mrs Sew and Sew* leaflets.

CHAPTER 22

The main official source was Hargreaves and Gowing and I also drew heavily on contemporary complaints in *Hansard* and *The Times*. The following Board of Trade publications were also useful: *Explanatory Memorandum on the Limitation of Supplies (Miscellaneous) (No 5) Order, 1940* (1940); *General Merchandise Quotas* (1941); *Guide on the limitation of Supplies of Perfumery and Toilet Preparations* (1941); *Scheme for Ensuring Fair Shares for Supplies for Small Retailers of Hollow Ware* (1942); and for *Pottery* (1942); *Retail Services and Shortages, Report of Wartime Social Survey* (duplicated, Board of Trade, May 1942—January 1943); Kathleen Box, *Wartime Shortages of Consumer Goods* (Social Survey for the Board of Trade, April 1943—January 1945); and the separate report on *Bicycles* (1944). On utility furniture I used *Utility Furniture* (Board of Trade, 1945) and *Furniture: An Enquiry made for the Board of Trade* (1945). Lyttleton described his early efforts to save metal; the 'clippie' referred to was Zelma Katin, the BBC producer Weymouth, whose *Journal* is also informative on the drink shortage. The story of the tobacconists' trials was told by Bob Finlayson (pseudonym) in *Retail Newsagent* for 10th December 1966. Charles Graves's experiences of the drink shortage in 1942 and 1943 are given in *Great Days* and in 1944 in *Pride of the Morning*. The 'It looks like rain' anecdote comes from Hodson and other information on drink from *Hansard*.

CHAPTER 23

The indispensable source was *Housewife* and on hats I also used *Luton at War*.

CHAPTER 24

On railings I used *The Times*, on the W.V.S. Graves *Women in Green*, on salvage generally the W.V.S. *Bulletin*. The text of Lady Reading's appeal for saucepans came from the BBC Archives.

CHAPTER 25

My main source was Bell and Charles Graves, *London Transport*. I also used *Railway Posters and the War* (reprinted from *the Railway Gazette*, various dates) and, on access to the coast, a War Office leaflet, *Classes of Persons Permitted to Enter a Prohibited Area* (1944). Experiences of eating, or going hungry, on trains were related by Grisewood, Hodson and Charles Graves, *Pride of the Morning*, while Sandy Macpherson described being left in an abandoned train.

## CHAPTER 26

The main official source is *Wartime Transport Restrictions and Achievements in Britain* (duplicated, C.O.I., 1946). On London buses I used Charles Grêves, *London Transport*, on the early effects of petrol rationing and the black-out, Turner, on the black-out regulations for vehicles the sources quoted under Chapter 4 and on horse prices Charles Graves, *Great Days*. The fuel consumption of the Spitfire is given by Owen Thetford, *Aircraft of the Royal Air Force 1918–57* (Putnam, 1957), and of the Lancaster William Green, *Famous Bombers of the Second World War* (Macdonald, 1959).

## CHAPTER 27

On the coal industry I mainly used W. K. Hancock and M. M. Gowing, *British War Economy* (H.M.S.O., 1949), and Alan Bullock; on fuel saving I drew on Ministry of Fuel advertisements and on the Bevin Boys, Derek Agnew, *Bevin Boy* (Allen & Unwin, 1947).

## CHAPTER 28

The basic sources were the Ministry of Labour *Report* and Alan Bullock. On the recruitment of women I used the following official Ministry of Labour publications: *The Employment of Women. Suggestions to Employees* (1941); *On Your Way to Your New Job* (1941); *Going Away on War Work* (1941); and *Welcome to the War Worker* (1941). Unofficial publications on the same subject which I consulted were: Caroline Haslett, *Munitions Girl. A Handbook for the Woman of the Industrial Army* (English University Press, 1942); Vera Douie, *Daughters of Britain* (privately printed, 1959), a most useful and comprehensive survey of women's part in the war effort; Amabel Williams-Ellis, *Women in War Factories* (Gollancz, 1943), shorter but also useful, and two feminist tracts, of doubtful value to the war effort and less to the historian, Elaine Burton, *What of the Women* (Muller, 1941) and *And Your Verdict?* (Muller, 1942). Some histories of individual companies which I found useful were Anon. *From This Pool a Sword* (on Littlewoods of Liverpool) (Standard Art Co. n.d.), which describes barrage balloon manufacture, Anon., *Singer in World War II 1939–45* (Singer Manufacturing Co, Clydebank, 1948), Ernest Fairfax, *Calling All Arms* (on the Nuffield Organisation) (Hutchinson, n.d.), Anon., *Bournville Utilities: A War Record* (Bourneville Utilities, Birmingham, 1945) and Anon., *Roche in Wartime 1939–45* (Roche Products, Welwyn Garden City, n.d.). The West End store mentioned was John Lewis's, the millionaire 'Chips' Channon, the journalist who fought to keep his maid,

Charles Graves, *Londoner's Life*. The Sheffield bus-conductress quoted was Zelma Katin, *Clippie* (John Gifford Ltd. 1944). I also consulted on other types of war work Alison King, *Golden Wings* (Arthur Pearson Ltd. 1956), on the Air Transport Auxiliary, and on women on the canals Susan Woolfitt, *Idle Women* (Benn, 1947), and Emma Smith, *Maiden's Trip* (Macgibbon and Kee, 1948). On women's work in general I used Peggy Scott, *British Women in War* (Hutchinson, n.d. but c. 1941), and *They Made Invasion Possible* (Hutchinson, n.d. but c. 1944) and Margaret Goldsmith, *Women at War* (Lindsay Drummond, n.d.).

## CHAPTER 29

On office life in general I used Hosking and Wadsworth and, on conditions in Cable and Wireless Ltd., Charles Graves, *The Thin Red Lines* (Standard Art Book Co., n.d. but c. 1946). The intolerable R.H.C. is described in an unpublished memoir lent to me privately. On work in shops I made great use of the John Lewis *Gazette*, of the advertisement pages of *Picture Post* and *Punch*, of C. K. Shaw, *Industrial Publicity* (C. & J. Temple, n.d. but c. 1944), and of Grace Lovat and L. Fraser (editors), *Modern Publicity in War* (Studio Publications, 1941). The Midland newsagent was Bob Finlayson, whose experiences with the toy horses are described in *Retail Newsagent* for 28th January 1967.

## CHAPTER 30

Charles Graves, *Women in Green*, is the standard book on the work of the W.V.S. I also used Virginia Graham, *The Story of W.V.S.* (H.M.S.O., 1959), and the wartime copies of the monthly W.V.S. *Bulletin*. The W.V.S. also supplied much information from their archives and from the recollections of individual members. On the work of the Women's Institutes I used Inez Jenkins, *The History of the Women's Institute Movement* (O.U.P., 1953), and Gervas Huxley, *Lady Denman, 1884–1954* (Chatto and Windus, 1961), plus private information on the jam and market schemes.

## CHAPTER 31

On savings my main source was information from the National Savings Committee and various editions of *War Savings*, especially those for special events such as the Wings for Victory issue. I also used the Committee's souvenir history *50th Anniversary, 1916–1966* (National Savings Committee, 1966) and A. A. Thomson (editor), *By Faith and Work, The Autobiography of the Rt. Hon the first Viscount Mackintosh of Halifax* (Hutchinson, 1966). On taxation policy, I used mainly Hancock and Gowing, supplemented by Wheeler Bennett and Alan Bullock, who gives much information on wage rates, and on P.A.Y.E. I obtained information from the Inland Revenue.

CHAPTER 32

I used the *Church Times*, the official *Form of National Prayer and Dedication for use on the Third Anniversary of the Outbreak of War* and, on clothes rationing as it affected the clergy, information from Messrs. Vanheems. The aimless clergymen in Rest Centres are mentioned by Titmuss, and the indignant first aid worker in Chelsea was Frances Faviell. The Rev. Thomas Tiplady's verses appear in advertisements in *The Church Times* and an extract can be found in Turner.

CHAPTER 33

Although the early history of the cinema in wartime is mentioned in *War Begins at Home* the outstanding source, covering the whole war, is Guy Morgan, *Red Roses every night, An Account of London Cinemas Under Fire* (Quality Press, 1948), which includes a month by month diary of British films released. I used extensively Basil Dean, *The Theatre at War* (Harrap, 1956), and on the Players Theatre, Archie Harradine, *Late Joys and the Players Theatre* (Boardman, 1943). The text of *Flare Path*, *While the Sun Shines* and *Love in Idleness* is given in Terrence Rattigan, *Collected Plays. Volume I* (Hamish Hamilton, 1953). Most of the films mentioned I saw myself but for a contemporary 'middle-brow' opinion by a professional critic I largely relied on the *Punch* reviewer.

CHAPTER 34

The dances and popular music of the early months of the war are covered by *War Begins at Home*. On the popularity of tunes at other times I was guided by private recollections, by Guy Morgan, who mentions the titles most in demand in cinemas, and by an unpublished list of *Top Tunes*, prepared by the BBC.

CHAPTER 35

On the BBC, Antonia White, *The BBC at War* (BBC, n.d. but in fact 1941), is less helpful than its name suggests, being a slight and propagandist pamphlet. Far more useful are the reminiscences of individual broadcasters and producers, of whom Macpherson, Hibberd, Weymouth, Grisewood, Val Gielgud and Priestley have already been mentioned. Charles J. Rolo is also useful and Henning Krabbe (editor), *Voices from Britain, Broadcast History 1939–45* (Allen and Unwin 1947), an anthology of famous wartime broadcasts. I also consulted, on wartime features, Cecil McGivern, *Bomb Doors Open and other Radio War Features* (Allen and Unwin, 1941), Bill Maclurg (editor), *Ack Ack, Beer Beer* (Hutchinson, n.d. but probably 1943), Howard Thomas, *Britain's Brains Trust* (Chapman and Hall, 1944), and Commander A. B. Campbell, *When I was in Patagonia* (Christopher Johnson, 1943). On *ITMA* the sources include: Francis Worsley, *ITMA 1939–1948* (Vox Mundi Ltd., 1948), Jack

Train, *Up and Down the Line, Autobiography* (Odhams, 1956), Ted Kavanagh, *Tommy Handley* (Hodder and Stoughton, 1949), and on Tommy Handley's earlier career, Tommy Handley, *Handley's Pages* (Stanley Paul and Co., n.d.). Other information came from BBC Historical Records and scripts of the programmes concerned.

## CHAPTER 36

I made considerable use of *The Annual Register*, of contemporary reviews and of my own recollections. On book production I consulted *The Book Production War Economy Agreement* (Publishers Association, 1942), on the paper shortage *The Times*, on Nathaniel Gubbins *The Sunday Express*. John Lehmann, *I am my Brother* (Longmans, 1960), describes the origins of *Penguin New Writing* and wartime literary life generally. The history of CEMA is told in *The Arts in Wartime, A Report on the Work of CEMA 1942 and 1943* (CEMA, n.d.) and of wartime painting in Eric Newton, *Art for Everybody* (Longmans, 1943). On the press I also consulted P. Kimble, *Newspaper Reading in the Third Year of the War* (Allen and Unwin, 1942). The date of publication of books mentioned in the chapter is given in the text, but I also consulted the following post-war anthologies: Ronald Blythe (editor), *Components of the Scene: An Anthology of the Prose and Poetry of the Second World War* (Penguin Books, 1966); Brian Gardner (editor), *The Terrible Rain. The War Poets 1939–45* (Methuen, 1966); and Charles Hamblett (editor), *I·Burn for England. An Anthology of the Poetry of World War II* (Frewin, 1966).

## CHAPTER 37

If there is a comprehensive history of sport during the war I did not discover it. As it was I relied on Ivan Sharpe (editor), *The Football League Jubilee Book* (Stanley Paul, 1963), on *The Times* on Cricket, on *Golf Monthly* on golf and on private information.

## CHAPTER 38

The official guidebook for G.I.s was *Britain. For all members of American Expeditionary Forces in Great Britain* (no publisher or date). The figures of U.S. personnel passing through Britain were supplied by the Ministry of Defence. The colour problem is referred to in Dwight D. Eisenhower, *Crusade in Europe* (Heinemann, 1948). The agitation against Italian prisoners of war is mentioned by Lancum, and Frances Faviell described her experiences with foreign refugees.

## CHAPTER 39

Life in London during 1942 and 1943 is described by Robert Henrey, *The Incredible City* (J. M. Dent, 1944), and other diaries already referred to. The pro-Russian mania of the period is referred to by Nicolson, by Hodson, the journalist who encountered it during visits to factories, by Hibberd, who commanded the guard of honour for the Russian ambassador, and by Basil Dean, who described the Red Army pageant at the Albert Hall. The sceptic who doubted if all Russians were saintly and who also celebrated D Day with a special lunch was Charles Graves, mentioned respectively in *Great Days* and *Pride of the Morning*. Most books which deal with the V.1s and V.2s approach them mainly from the military point of view, rather than from that of the civilian at the receiving end, including Basil Collier, *The Defence of the United Kingdom* and *The Battle of the V. Weapons* (Hodder and Stoughton, 1964), and David Irving, *The Mare's Nest, The Nazi Development of Secret Reprisal Weapons* (Kimber, 1964), Ronald W. Clark, *The Rise of the Boffins* (Phoenix House, 1962), and Peter Wykeham, *Fighter Command* (Putnam, 1960). More detail about individual incidents is given in Frank Illingworth, *Flying Bomb* (Citizen Press, n.d.). Descriptions of life in Greater London during this time can be found in Robert Henrey, *The Siege of London* (J. M. Dent, 1946); Hibberd; Nicolson, who thought they looked like illuminated launches, and Charles Graves, *Pride of the Morning*, who refers to the decrease in popularity of the Savoy and of south-facing flats, and the timorous rabbits of Hyde Park.

### CHAPTER 40

No books deal specifically with this period. The disappointed diner at the Lord Mayor's banquet and at a West End Hotel was Weymouth. The mother working on the barges and waiting for the war to end was Susan Woolfitt. For events on V.E. Day I relied on private accounts, *The Times* and BBC historical records. I also quoted from Nicolson and Hibberd. On subsequent events I used A. J. P. Taylor, and R. B. Macullum, *The British General Election of 1945* (O.U.P., 1947).

### APPENDIX I

I mainly used Alan and Mary Wood, *Islands in Danger* (Evans, 1955), a model history of its kind, supplemented, on Guernsey, by Frank Falla, *The Silent War* (Frewin 1967), the journalist referred to, and by L. P. Sinel, *The German Occupation of Jersey* (*Evening Post*, Jersey, 1946). Most quotations, however, are from private diaries and other unpublished sources.

### APPENDIX II

The text is quoted direct from the manuscript *War Record* of the Dorset Federation of Women's Institutes.

2

## ACKNOWLEDGEMENTS TO ORGANISATIONS

The organisations listed below kindly answered my queries or lent me books or other material. Messrs. Saward Baker and Co., especially the Hon. Iain Erskine, gave me great assistance on wartime advertising and kindly made available to me their collection of Ministry of Food advertisements. The National Federation of Women's Institutes, especially Mrs. Molly Millard, answered many questions and traced for me some wartime experts on the jam and market schemes. The Women's Royal Voluntary Services, especially Mrs. Evelyn Dunbar and Miss Sheila Robertson, lived up to their wartime reputation for helpfulness by going to great trouble to provide me with information and also arranged for me to meet two other valuable informants, Miss A. C. Johnson and Mrs. M. Caroll Marx. The National Union of Townswomen's Guilds also supplied me with some information. The John Lewis Partnership, especially Mrs. Jean Harrison, kindly made available to me the files of the Partnership's *Gazette*. John Waddington Ltd. of Leeds answered my enquiries about wartime games. Mr. John Vanheems of the House of Vanheems, London, supplied me with information on the clothes rationing problems of the clergy, and Little-woods Pools, Liverpool, were helpful over wartime football pools. Mr. F. N. Pearce of the Midland Bank went to great trouble to answer some of my questions on wartime banking. Mr. H. D. N. Kyle of the Prudential Assurance Company kindly gave me a copy of *Salute to Service*, Mr. Hugh Williams of Hitchcock, Williams and Co. supplied one of *Operation Textiles*, and Mr. W. H. Pritchard of John Menzies (Southern) Ltd. obtained for me one of *War Came to New Street Square*, about Messrs. Wymans. Mr. Jack Olden of the Boy Scouts Association was most helpful on wartime scouting. The librarian of the Meteorological Office at Bracknell kindly searched out for me records of the weather on D Day and at other times and the information officers of the Ministry of Defence, the Ministry of Agriculture, the Ministry of Power, the Ministry of Transport and the Post Office also answered various enquiries. Mrs. J. Hooker of the National Savings Committee devoted much time to answering my questions on War Savings. Mr. R. C. Gowers of the Publishers Association was equally helpful about wartime publishing and obtained for me a copy of the Book Production War Economy agreement. The Royal Society for the Prevention of Cruelty to Animals and the Automobile Association both suggested sources of information. Mr. D. D. Lindsay, the headmaster of Malvern College, and the Rev. Canon H. C. A. Gaunt, a former headmaster, Mr. H. E. Woodcock, headmaster of Dulwich College Preparatory School and the secretary of the Datchelor Girls' School, Camberwell Grove, all kindly gave or lent me copies of the histories of their respective schools. Beaverbrook Newspapers Ltd. kindly gave me access to their library to study Nathaniel Gubbins, and Mr. Leonard England of Mass Observation Ltd, Dr. J. Marks of Roche Products Ltd., Welwyn Garden City, Home Counties Newspapers Ltd. of

Luton and the Press Officer of London Transport, all offered help which in the event I did not call on. I did, however, make extensive use of the Libraries of the Ministry of Agriculture, Fisheries and Food, of the Central Office of Information, and of the Board of Trade, where Mr. K. A. Mallaber located much invaluable material on wartime shortages. Like other writers of contemporary history, I am in the debt of the librarians and staff of many local authority libraries. Those of Luton, Redbridge, Croydon, Camden and Kingston-upon-Hull all saved me hours of labour by lending me elusive books, while Mr. W. Best Harris, City Librarian of Plymouth, and Dr. G. Chandler, City Librarian of Liverpool, also provided other information. I am also grateful to the Town Clerks of Croydon and of Gloucester, who lent or gave me material, and to the Chief Librarian of the Royal Borough of Kensington. Miss R. Coombes, Reference Librarian of the Imperial War Museum, and her staff, gave me great assistance, particularly in suggesting several valuable sources of the existence of which I was unaware. Finally I am in the debt of the BBC library and News Information Service, and of Miss Mary Hodgson, the BBC's Written Archives Officer, who went to great pains to trace for me details and scripts of many wartime broadcasts.

3

PRIVATE CONTRIBUTORS

The extent of my dependence on private contributions from individual citizens who kindly answered my appeal for reminiscences will be clear to everyone who has read the book. Under the various letters of the alphabet, names are listed in the order in which the contributions mentioned were received. The town is that where the informant is now living, not where he or she was residing during the war, and people whose names have changed (i.e. women who have married or re-married) since the war are listed under their present name, unless they have requested otherwise.

# LIST OF CONTRIBUTORS

Mrs. C. P. Agelasto, Amersham, Buckinghamshire; Matthew Anderson (Sen.), Walsall, Staffordshire; Mrs. Ethel M. Atkinson, Hull; Mrs. M. C. Avery, Old Marston, Oxfordshire; Mrs. K. L. Abbiss, Churchtown, Southport; Mrs. G. W. Ager, Exmouth, Devon; Mrs. Appleby, Hornchurch; Mrs. Adams, Aberdeen; Mrs. C. P. K. Anger, Portsmouth; Mrs. Alice Anderson, St. Paul's Cray, Orpington, Kent; Mrs. D. M. C. Andrews, Edinburgh, 4; R. C. Andreang, Hull; Mrs. D. Ardley, Buckhurst Hill, Essex; Mrs. E. Alford, Wootton Wawen, Warwickshire; Miss R. de M. Armstrong, Skipton-in-Craven, Yorkshire; Miss Helen Angus, Hawick, Roxburghshire; Miss V. Allcard, Llannon, Llanelli, Carmarthenshire; Mrs. E. Amory-Johnson, York; Mrs. Beryl Anderson, London, S.W.11; Miss C. Alder, Chichester, Sussex; Mrs. Winifred Atwell, Luton; Mrs. Abathell, Kidlington, Oxfordshire; Mrs. Violet A. E. Allen, Hyde, Cheshire; Mrs. Yvonne Alcock, Bearsted, Maidstone, Kent; Mrs. L. Andrews, Surbiton, Surrey; Mrs. B. Aston, Wingfield, Diss, Norfolk; Mrs. I. Ashton, Sheffield 8; Mrs. P. M. Adams, Headley, Bordon, Hampshire; Mrs. Joyce Armstrong, Kirkintilloch, Glasgow; Mrs. Gina Allen, London, N.2.; D. J. Archer, Cambridge; K. W. Allen, Newbury, Berkshire; Mrs. Rita Allen, Newbury, Berkshire; B. W. Ashurst, Leeds 11; Miss I. M. Brown, Beccles, Suffolk; Mrs G. Bennett, South Croydon, Surrey; R. J. K. Brooke, Hull; Mrs. H. Blowers, Ipswich, Suffolk; Barrington Bree, London, N.W.3.; Mr. & Mrs. Norman Booth, Bridlington, Yorkshire; Mrs. N. Baker, Piddletrenthide, Dorchester, Dorset; Mrs. Audrey Brasington, Consett, County Durham; Major R. O. Bridgeman, Beaminster, Dorset; Mrs. F. P. Baker, London S.W.1.; Mrs. Margaret Biggs, Rothesay, Bute; Mrs. N. Bunn, Middlesbrough; Mr. & Mrs. C. P. Brocklehurst, Wincle, Macclesfield; Mrs. Jean Brown, London, S.W.13; Mrs. D. M. Brewin, Attenborough, Nottinghamshire; Mrs. I. Barker, Leeds, 7; Mrs. E. Baker, East Hanney, Wantage, Berkshire; Mrs. H. Blunt, Marton, Blackpool; Mrs. Dorothy E. Bates, Westcliff-on-Sea, Essex; Mrs. B. Brookwood, Lovedean, Portsmouth; T. E. Browne, London, E.17; A. Badby, Great Bookham, Surrey; Mrs. Lyn Barnes, Purley Park, Reading; Miss Jenny Bellamy, Wilford, Nottinghamshire; Mrs. A. Burden, Little Massingham, King's Lynn, Norfolk; Mrs. Violet Buckingham, Leicester; Mrs. B. Balmer, Liverpool, 19; Mrs. M. Beeney, Tunbridge Wells, Kent; Miss June Ball, Kineton, Warwickshire; Mrs. Constance Booth, London, E.4.; Mrs. D. M. Brown, Brighton; Miss C. Budd, Weybridge, Surrey; Mrs. G. M. Bowring, Coldharbour, Dorking, Surrey; Mrs. D. Bryant, Tenterden, Kent; Mrs. C. Bosanquet, Fairfield, Stockton-on-Tees; W. R. Bray, Stratford St. Mary, Colchester, Essex; Mrs. J. A. F. Banham, Iffley, Oxfordshire; Mrs. C. Brown, Great Bealings, Woodbridge, Suffolk; John Bennett, Paignton, Devon;

Mrs. C. E. Breed, March, Cambridgeshire; Mrs. R. W. Bagnall, Bishops Stortford, Hertfordshire; Mrs. C. Booth, East Coker, Yeovil, Somerset; J. Boney, Rock, Wadebridge, Cornwall; Mrs. K. Beddoes, Birmingham, 32; Mrs. W. G. Britton, Sunbury-on-Thames, Middlesex; Leonard J. Barnes, Croydon, Surrey; C. H. A. Browne, Worthing, Sussex; Mrs. Ethel Beamer, Rhos-on-Sea, Merionethshire; Mrs. G. L. Binsley, Rubery, Birmingham; Mrs. M. Becker, Shenfield, Essex; Mr. & Mrs. A. G. Brown, Woodthorpe, Nottinghamshire; Mrs. D. E. Barnes, Houghton Conquest, Bedfordshire; Miss L. F. Borders, Swanley, Kent; Mrs. A Berry, Kirkheaton, Huddersfield; G. F. Bennett, Minehead, Somerset; Mrs. F. E. Bertrand, London, W.14; C. Brundrett, Prinsted, Emsworth, Hampshire; Mrs. E. Brownlee, Billingham, County Durham; Mrs. M. Beaumont, Ipswich, Suffolk; Mrs. D. Brindley, Hull; L. J. Bentley, Ewell, Surrey; Mrs. G. M. Burnie, Ashford, Middlesex; D. A. Butterworth, Kerridge, Macclesfield, Cheshire; Mrs. J. I. Baker, Billericay, Essex; Mrs. L. H. Blakeston, Cambridge; Mrs. G. Bell, Cuckfield, Sussex; J. B. Burgess, Liverpool, 14; Mrs. L. D. Bennett, Corringham, Essex; Mrs. E. Beaumont, Eastbourne; Mrs. R. Brown, London, N.14; Mrs. Sydney Bushby, Birmingham, 27; Mrs. Vera Barford, Romford, Essex; Mrs. R. W. Brown, Riston Grange, Hull; Mrs. Clare Breton-Smith, St. Leonards-on-Sea, Sussex; Mrs. Bingham-Hall, Weston-super-Mare; Dr. J. T. Baldwin, Edinburgh, 1; Bernard Bumpus, London, N.W.3; S. W. E. Bishop, Weybridge, Surrey; Maurice Barbanell, London, W.C.2; Mr. & Mrs. C. E. Crutchley, Northampton; Miss M. Carrington, Bognor Regis, Sussex; Mrs. Eileen Colman, Hull; John Cooper, London, W.C.1; W. D. Clemesha, Wivenhoe, Essex; Mrs. Lily Couch, St. Martins, Guernsey; Mrs. Patricia Cooper, Prestwood, Great Missenden, Buckinghamshire; A. R. Craddock, D.F.C., Malta; Mrs. P. M. Chenery, Cromer, Norfolk; C. A. Collins, Eastchurch, Sheerness, Kent; Mrs. Olive Cullingford, Hindhead, Surrey; Mrs. Evelyn A. Cureton, Birmingham, 9; Mrs. F. E. Corderoy, Enniskillen, County Fermanagh; Mrs. M. R. Clements, Barkingside, Ilford, Essex; The Rev. C. Skene Catling, Goudhurst, Cranbrook, Kent; Mrs. V. L. Carter, Ickenham, Uxbridge, Middlesex; Mrs. C. M. Coast, Helensburgh, Dunbartonshire; Mrs. D. Chapman, Horley, Surrey; Mrs. O. H. Clarke, London, N.W.10; Mrs. E. Cox, Swyre, Dorchester, Dorset; Mrs. Vera Carter, Rayleigh, Essex; Mrs. M. F. Calder, Hartley Wintney, Hampshire; G. A. Cushing, London, W.1; Mrs. J. B. Creaven, Hurst Green, Sussex; Mrs. E. Beatrice Cockett, London, S.E.4; R. C. Coates, Bimport, Shaftesbury, Dorset; Mrs. Violet Chesman, Folkestone; Mrs. T. Cause, Lelant, St. Ives, Cornwall; Mrs. K. Cormack, Reigate, Surrey; Mrs. E. Cooper, Sheffield; Mrs. V. L. Cooper, Birmingham, 19; Mrs. Sadie Crothall, Andover, Hampshire; Mrs. Cotton, Saxmundham, Suffolk; Mrs. L. Cooper, Sandringham, Victoria, Australia; Frank Collieson, Cambridge; Mrs. L. Corbett, Street, Somerset; Jack Cadogan, London, S.W.14; Miss V. Cox, Llanddewi Velfry, Narberth, Pembrokeshire; Gerald W. Drewitt, London, S.W.1; Miss Emma Dickinson, London, N.10; M. J. C. Dare, Caversham, Reading; T. H. Dean, Hull; Mrs. H. K. Dell, Ipswich, Suffolk; Miss E. O. Davies, Pembroke; Harry Davis, Harrogate; Miss Kathleen Dicker, Reading; Mrs. M. Drew, Sutton Coldfield; Mrs. J. Dunn, Teignmouth, Devon; Mrs. J. Dempsey, London, W.13; Angus A. Dalrymple, Toronto, 5,

Ontario, Canada; Mrs. K. C. Davey, London, S.W.19; Mrs. R. Dilly, Carshalton, Surrey; Mrs. Nellie Dyer, Flackwell Heath, Buckinghamshire; Mrs. E. Doherty, Huyton, Lancashire; Mrs. E. L. Dickinson, Newcastle-upon-Tyne, 3; Mrs. Irene Deakin, Penarth, Glamorganshire; Mrs. L. F. Donald, Dumbarton; Mrs. C. Dash, Wembley Park, Middlesex; Mrs. M. E. Dow, St. Ninians, Stirling; Charles Denyer, Sompting, Lancing; J. Downer, London, E.4; Mrs. I. M. Dubois, Purley, Surrey; Mrs. M. Dash, Deal, Kent; Mrs. D. Daddy, Folkestone; Mrs. B. Devereux, Bournemouth; Mrs. Joan Dumas, London, S.E.17; Miss J. Denholm, London, S.W.4; Mrs. E. Dunham, Ely, Cambridgeshire; Mrs. Dingwall, Merstham, Surrey; D. S. Dawson, London, E.C.4; Mrs. E. Elliott, Chesterfield, Derbyshire; Miss W. Eardley-Field, Bridgwater, Somerset; E. W. Eley, Lexden, Colchester; Mrs. L. M. Edwards, Combe Raleigh, Honiton, Devon; Mrs. E. Elbourne, Yeovil, Somerset; Mrs. M. Elliott, Rotherham; Mrs. G. Ellis, Cheltenham, Gloucestershire; Mrs. Eileen Evans, London, S.W.16; Mrs. Gwen Edge, Chapelfields, Coventry; Miss D. English, Guernsey; Mrs. E. Eagland, Stevenage; Mrs. D. E. Eggleden, Tenterden, Kent; R. H. Edmonds, Sompting, Lancing; Mrs. S. Elmore, Short Heath, Willenhall, Staffordshire; Mrs. E. Ewen, Gateshead; Mrs. S. M. Ellis, Nottingham; Mrs. Joan Ells, London, S.W.1; Miss M. Fancett, London, N.W.2; Mrs. H. Formon, Mansfield, Nottinghamshire; W. M. L. Francis, Oswestry; Mrs. K. Ford, London, S.E.21; F. S. Franklin, Thornham, King's Lynn, Norfolk; Mrs. M. Frost, Colchester; Reginald Ford, St. Mellons, Cardiff; Mrs. M. Forfar, Southampton; Mrs. E. M. Farrell, Woodford Green, Essex; Mrs. J. E. Forsyth, Broughty Ferry, Angus; Mrs. P. E. Favell, Crowborough, Sussex; Mrs. P. M. Flatman, Oakley, Basingstoke; Mrs. D. Fowell, Ruthin, Denbighshire; Mrs. Frank Forrest, Manchester, 10; Mrs. W. Froom, Liverpool 13; Mrs. A. Freeman, London, E.7; W. Fox, Hull; R. W. Ford, Earley, Reading; B. B. Fitzgerald, Stonehouse, Plymouth; Brian Franklin, Eastry, Sandwich, Kent; Mrs. J. E. Fold, Burgess Hill, Sussex; Mrs. E. Fletcher, Enfield; C. O. L. Finlow, Stafford; Mrs. Jean Fox, Eccleston, St. Helens, Lancashire; Mrs. Alyson Farrow, Paignton, Devon; Mrs. R. J. Flint, Kirby Bellars, Melton Mowbray, Leicestershire; L. Finkle, London, N. 13; Mrs. V. Forley, London, N.11; Mrs. S. Farnell, Halifax; Mrs. M. Fry, Croydon, Surrey; Mrs. E. P. Fennings-Mills, Hove; Mrs. M. Fuller, Liverpool 17; Dr. G. N. Fox, Worthing; S. F. Grant, St. Peter Port, Guernsey; Miss Beatrice Gethings, Saxmundham, Suffolk; A. J. Goddard, Fencott, Islip, Oxfordshire; Mrs. Ruth Gale, Hinkley, Leicestershire; Mrs. D. Gould, Southill, Weymouth, Dorset; Mrs. K. M. Green, Kingsthorpe, Northampton; P. J. Girard, Castel, Guernsey; C. M. Girdlestone, Saint-Cloud, France; Mrs. D. Graves, London, N.1; Miss E. H. Goscombe, Harrow, Middlesex; Mrs. J. Gambrill, Woking, Surrey; Mrs. K. Gale, Bristol, 3; Mrs. C. Greenstock, London, S.W.18; Mrs. Clare Gisicz, Blackburn; Miss R. Gunner, Gravesend, Kent; Miss M. L. Gurney, Boxmoor, Hemel Hempstead; Mrs. H. Gordon, Folkestone, Kent; Mrs. K. Glassman, London, N.W.10; Mrs. E. G. Gale, St. Leonards-on-Sea, Sussex; Mrs. Garlick, Tipton, Staffordshire; Mrs. N. Green, Wolverhampton; Miss Anne Greenleaves, Burnham-on-Sea, Somerset; David Grant, Felpham, Bognor Regis; Mrs. P. George, Westcliff-on-Sea, Essex; Mrs. K. Gosling, Bathwick, Bath; Mrs. G. M. Gifford,

Liverpool, 23; Miss M. Grigg, Ide Hill, Sevenoaks; Mrs. E. Gray, Kenilworth, Cape Town, South Africa; Miss H. M. Gibson, London, S.E.6; Mrs. W. Goolden, Oswestry; J. Guest, London, S.E.14; Mrs. F. I. Gooch, London, S.W.20; Mrs. M. George, Burntwood, Walsall, Staffordshire; Mrs. E. Gordon, Belfast, 5; Miss M. S. Garside, Eastbourne; Mr. & Mrs. R. Gundry, Alderney; Dr. Elizabeth Graham Kerr, London, S.W.3; Dr. S. Gibson, Liverpool, 19; The Rev. Frank Harwood, Minster Lovell, Oxfordshire; Mrs. M. E. Howson-Lewis, Great Billing, Northamptonshire; I. L. Humphrys, London, S.E.25; J. D. Hubert, Dall, Guernsey; Miss Vere Hodgson, Church Stretton, Shropshire; Miss M. Heeney, Manchester, 14; Mrs. F. M. Hooper, Exeter; Mrs. Meg Hyams, Elstead, Godalming, Surrey; Mrs. Grace Heggs, Village de Putron, Guernsey; G. K. Hughes, Farnham, Surrey; Arthur Higgs, St. Sampsons, Guernsey (deceased); Mrs. Joyce Hutton, London, W.3; Miss May Hickman, Cambridge; Miss Rose Harris, London, E.1; Miss Ella Horsey, Waytown, Bridport, Dorset; Mrs. Helen Heather, Loughton, Essex; Mrs. W. Halliday, Theydon Bois, Essex; Mrs. J. Hendrick, Lightwater, Surrey; Mrs. Poppy Hooper, Curdridge, Southampton; Mrs. D. M. Hitchcock, Wellington, Somerset; Mrs. A. D. Hooper, Wellington, Somerset; Mrs. Beryl Hood, Hurstpierpoint, Sussex; Mrs. G. Harman, Stubbington, Hampshire; Mrs. G. Hoare, Bognor Regis, Sussex; Mrs. A. G. Hughes, Kirkby, Lancashire; Mrs. M. R. Hall, Farnborough, Hampshire; H. J. Harris, Grafton Flyford, Worcester; Mrs. D. Huckell, Northampton; Mrs. L. Horwell, Sheffield; Mrs. P. M. Hillebrand, Lewes, Sussex; Mrs. A. L. Hickinbotham, Birmingham, 8; Mrs. E. A. Hall, Redditch, Worcestershire; Mrs. E. Hurst, Burgess Hill, Sussex; Mrs. M. Hughes, Liverpool, 10; Mrs. Irma Harman, London, S.W.11; Mrs. A. Hutchinson, Sunderland, County Durham; Mrs. S. A. Hughes, Redditch, Worcestershire; Miss Ruth Hayward, Halstead, Sevenoaks, Kent; Miss V. Hall, London, S.W.16; Mrs. S. Hayman, Rainham, Kent; Miss M. Hart, Ashford, Kent; Mrs. E. M. Hardy, Monkseaton, Whitley Bay, Northumberland; Mrs. I. Hammond, Kingston-upon-Hull, Yorkshire; Miss N. Hartley, Blackpool; Mrs. F. Harrison, Halifax, Yorkshire; Mrs. V. Harris, New Duston, Northamptonshire; Mrs. B. K. N. Hill, Leigh-on-Sea, Essex; Mrs. M. Heppenstall, Hook, Goole, Yorkshire; Mrs. V. Hyde, Hucclecote, Gloucestershire; Mrs. G. M. Harris, Hainault, Ilford; Miss E. Hewson, Bromley; Miss Olive E. Hallett, Birmingham, 30; Ian Hogg, Colchester, Essex; Mrs. D. M. Honey, West Wickham, Kent; Mrs. D. Humphrey, Grantham, Lincolnshire; Mrs. M. E. Hartley, Lower Slaughter, Cheltenham; Miss Kathleen Hanby, Sheffield, 5; Mrs. M. Harrison, Kelsale, Saxmundham, Suffolk; Miss E. Hooper, London, W.3; Miss D. R. Havery, Southsea, Hampshire; Mrs. M. K. Heath, Styvechale, Coventry; Mrs. V. M. Harling, Bilting, Ashford, Hertfordshire; Mrs. M. Hiley, Cambridge; Miss R. Hofberg, Cardiff; Mrs. M. Hallam, Barnet, Hertfordshire; John T. W. Hart, Kinoulton, Nottinghamshire; Mrs. N. M. Hill, Richmond, Surrey; Mrs. A. Hanson, Glasgow, C.4; Mrs. O. Hollands, Brenchley, Tonbridge, Kent; S. F. Hallgarten, London, E.C.3; Miss Susan Hare, Richmond, Surrey; R. S. C. Hall, Frithsden, Berkhamstead, Hertfordshire; Miss Janet Hoenig, London, S.W.15; Miss Mary Hodgson, London, W.9; Miss K. Ingram, Oxenholme, Kendal, Westmorland; Mrs. I. Ingham, Penwortham, Preston; Miss J. Ierston, Birmingham, 16; Mrs. Marta Jackson, Littlemore, Oxfordshire; Miss K. Judd, London, N.5; Mrs. H. Joynson, Birkenhead, Cheshire; Mrs. D. R. Jarvis, London, E.11; Miss Beatrice Jobbins, Watford; Mrs. Eileen Johnstone, Coulsdon, Surrey; Mrs. S. H. Jenneson, Staines; Miss F. A. Jaques, London, W.2; Mrs. Z. Jenyon, Cheadle, Cheshire; Mrs. E. Jeffryes, Harpenden, Hertfordshire; Joseph Joyce, San Francisco, 34, California, U.S.A. (deceased); Mrs. Edith M. Jones, Liverpool, 8; Miss F. E. Jackson, Prestbury, Cheltenham, Gloucestershire; Mrs. C. Johnson, Allenton, Derbyshire; John Joliffe, Wembley, Middlesex; Lieut.-Commander V. G. Jerram, Macedon, Victoria, Australia; Mrs. B. Jones, Woodbridge, Suffolk; Mrs. I. Johnson, London, S.W.11; Mrs. I. M. Kirby, Cheam, Surrey; Mrs. M. J. Keun, Ipswich, Suffolk; C. H. Kain, Stisted, Braintree, Essex; Mrs. E. L. Kempe, Osmington, Dorset; Mrs. I. M. Kiernan, Battle, Sussex; Mrs. Irene M. Knott, Derby; Mrs. D. I. Keys, Swanage, Dorset; Mr. & Mrs. S. Kay, St. Leonards-on-Sea, Sussex; W. J. Kerry, East Grinstead, Sussex; Mrs. P. Kellar, Bristol, 7; Mrs. A. Kent, Liverpool, 13; Mrs. E. L. Knief, London, E.6; Mrs. Lily, Messenger Lane, Hounslow, Middlesex; Miss Alison King, London, S.W.15; Mrs. R. M. Lawler, Trowbridge, Wiltshire; Mrs. M. Le Page, St. Peter Port, Guernsey; Mrs. E. M. Lynch, London, N.W.11; F. A. Lenoury, Forest, Guernsey; Mrs. M. Lemon, London, E.17; John Loughran, Greenock, Renfrewshire; Norman Levy, Hull; D. F. Lewis, Penarth, Glamorganshire; Mrs. H. Lawrence, Eccles, Manchester; Miss A. E. F. Fraser Lloyd, Westbourne, Bournemouth; Mrs. V. Lowery, Hayes, Middlesex; Mrs. Violet Lyons, London, S.E.24; Miss Linington, Biddenden, Kent; Mrs. B. J. Longley, Cranbrook, Kent; Mrs. I. Lord, London, S.W.12; Mrs. B. E. Lancaster, Rush Green, Romford, Essex; Mrs. E. C. Laird, Sandgate, Folkestone, Kent; Mrs. N. C. Leng, Leigh-on-Sea, Essex; Mrs. M. V. Lyne, Leamington Spa, Warwickshire; Mrs. E. Leadbetter, Maghull, Liverpool; S. V. F. Leleux, Northampton; Mrs. L. Longman, London, N.21; J. W. Lucas, Colehill, Wimborne, Dorset; Mrs. E. Lucas, Haslingden, Lancashire; Mrs. M. Lawrence, Andover, Hampshire; W. A. D. Lawson, Richmond, Yorkshire; Dr. H. A. Lake, Beaminster, Dorset; Ronald Lewin, West Byfleet, Surrey; John Lester, London, S.W.1; Mrs. F. E. Lipscomb, Woolton Hill, Newbury, Berkshire; Miss P. R. Longmate, Camelford, Cornwall; A. G. Longmate, Newbury, Berkshire; Miss Miriam Melbourne, L'Ancresse, Guernsey; Miss M. G. Mayer, Birmingham, 20; Mrs. D. Meech, Dorchester (deceased); David Merrick, Thornton Heath, Surrey; K. Morton Nance, Plymouth; Mrs. F. E. McCarthy, Whittlesey, Isle of Ely; Mrs. Daisy Middleton, Woods Green, Wadhurst, Sussex; Mrs. Rose Mather, Hounslow, Middlesex; John McKnight, Glasgow, W.4; C. H. Miller, Newport, Isle of Wight; Mrs. E. McDougall, Clarkston, Glasgow; Mrs. E. M. Metcalf, Darlington; Mrs. Marion McConkey, Uddingston, Lanarkshire; Mrs. M. Morris, Colwyn Bay; Mrs. Daphne Moakler, West Byfleet; Mrs. J. Mikkelsen, Broadway, Worcestershire; Mr. & Mrs. A. J. Mason, East Barnet, Hertfordshire; Mrs. E. Mogford, Laleham Village, Middlesex; Mrs. V. L. Mann, Birmingham, 34; Miss D. J. Muckleston, Harrow Weald, Middlesex; Mrs. Dora Mason, Burton-on-Trent, Staffordshire; The Rev. Rt. Hon. Countess of Mayo, Edinburgh; Mrs. P. McCafferty, Stopsley, Luton, Bedfordshire; Mrs. N. A.

Milgate, Rosemarkie, Ross-shire; Sydney Martin, York; Mrs. I. M. Macmillan, West Molesey, Surrey; Mrs. Muriel Miller, Southsea, Hampshire; Miss Doris Moore, Bourton, Gillingham, Dorset; Mrs. M. D. Morgan, London, N.9; Mrs. F. A. Musselwhite, Sutton; C. E. Murch, Whitstable, Kent; Mrs. D. E. McLintock, Lincoln; Mrs. E. Morris, Rainhill, Lancashire; Mrs. W. T. Morrison, British Forces Post Office, 40; Mrs. D. Morton, Sutton Coldfield; Mrs. N. Mercer, Tuffley, Gloucestershire; Mrs. B. M. Morris, Ryde, Isle of Wight; Mrs. E. Mars, Heaton Chapel, Stockport, Mrs. R. Martin, Barton Seagrave, Kettering; Harold A. Maple, Barking, Essex; Mrs. M. McDonald, Grappenhall, Warrington, Lancashire; Mrs. Olive Mann, Bridlington, Yorkshire; Mrs. M. G. Macdonald, Hailsham, Sussex; Mrs. Rosemary Moonen, West Huntspill, Highbridge, Somerset; Mrs. K. Murphy, Ruislip, Middlesex; Mrs. M. J. Martin, Littleover, Derbyshire; Mrs. C. Mackeprang, Kempsford, Fairford, Gloucester-shire; Miss F. Morris, London, S.W.16; Mrs. D. S. Mason, Coulsdon, Surrey; Mrs. H. McGrath, Manchester, 22; D. H. Macrae Taylor, Edinburgh, 10; Dr. I. Mostyn Williams, Beaumaris, Anglesey; Dr. Alan Marsh, Tunbridge Wells, Kent; Dr. Kenneth I. A. Macleod, Worcester, Massachusetts, U.S.A.; Dr. I. S. Mitcheson, Hythe, Kent; Miss Sally Marshall, London, W.11; Dennis Mann, Hampton Wick, Middlesex; A. G. Newman, Purley Surrey; Mrs. M. A. Newport, Hinton Charterhouse, Bath, Somerset; Mrs. G. Newman, London, E.5; Miss J. Nicholson, Gillingham, Dorset; Mrs. I. Northfield, Kidderminster; Mrs. V. Nock, Birmingham, 11; Miss E. D. Nixon, Northampton; Mrs. P. Newman, Biddenham, Bedfordshire; Kenneth Nicholson, Saffron Walden, Essex; Mrs. C. Newton, Bramhall, Cheshire; Mrs. S. Naylor, Clevedon, Somerset; Mrs. Beverley Norris, Exeter; Mrs. J. Oliver, North Queensferry, Fife; T. Okey (Senior), Titsey, Oxted, Surrey; Miss F. O'Neill, London, S.E.13; Mrs. Joyce Osment, Sherborne, Dorset; Mrs. D. V. Overton, Brixham, Devon; W. Oldroyd, Attenborough, Nottinghamshire; Dr. A. S. O'Brien, Altrincham, Cheshire; Mrs. Alfreda Pickles, Bradford, 8; Mrs. Muriel Perrett, Bryncethin, Bridgend, Glamorganshire; W. A. Philbrow, Birkenhead, Cheshire; Fred Perrett, Bourne, Lincolnshire; Mrs. M. Prickett, Watford; Miss Agnes Piggott, Sheffield, 8; Mrs. E. J. Pearce, Birmingham, 20; Mrs. E. Pringle, Rochdale; Mrs. G. Pimm, Bristol; Mrs. J. Plummer, Grayswood, Haslemere, Surrey; Mrs. Hugh Parker, London, S.W.1; The Rev. J. C. Parsons, Lowestoft, Suffolk; Mrs. B. Palmer, Colchester, Essex; G. Pibworth, London, E.17; Mrs. L. Pearce, Cheshunt, Hertfordshire; Ivan E. Phillips, Summerland, British Columbia, Canada; Mrs. D. J. Parks, Wallington, Surrey; Mrs. M. D. Pegler, Elstree, Hertfordshire; Mrs. W. E. Pym, Barnet, Hertfordshire; Mrs. Dorothy Percy, Liverpool, 13; Mrs. Joan Perry, Birmingham, 21; Mme Adrienne Parentani, Brussels, 16; Miss J. Park, London, N.21; Mrs. Pat Pitman, Shepper-ton, Middlesex; Mrs. C. Pryce, Brisbane, Queensland, Australia; Mrs. I. Phillips, Barnet, Hertfordshire; Miss Winifred Pringle, London, S.W.7; Mrs. M. J. Ryan, Charing, Ashford, Kent; Mrs. Freda Roberts, Taunton, Somerset; Theophilus Rowe, Pontyclun, Glamorganshire; Mrs. Beatrice Reynolds, Trimingham-on-Sea, Norfolk; Miss M. S. Roberts, Fittleworth, Pulborough, Sussex (deceased); P. B. Ricketts, Birmingham, 4; Mrs. P. G. Rust, Chippen-ham, Wiltshire; Miss J. C. O. Ray, Haslemere, Surrey; Mrs. P. Restall, Gillingham, Kent; Mrs. E. F. Rees, Liverpool, 6; Mrs. S. H. Read, Boarstall, Aylesbury, Buckinghamshire; Miss K. H. Robson, Tunbridge Wells, Kent; Mrs. I. E. Redman, Swindon, Wiltshire; G. B. Redmayne, Lymington, Hampshire; Mrs. Ivy Robinson, Ifield, Crawley, Sussex; Mrs. M. G. Rawes, London, S.E.23; Mrs. R. E. Rabson, Old Coulsdon, Surrey; Mrs. Vera Robson, Birmingham, 24; Mrs. Beatrice M. Robinson, Iver, Buckinghamshire; G. Ruscoe-Pond, Ash, Martock, Somerset; Mrs. E. Robinson, Litlington, Royston, Hertfordshire; Mrs. F. E. Ryan, London, E.6; Mrs. L. Rowe, Porthcawl; Mrs. G. E. Ross, London, N.14; Mrs. E. W. Ringham, Croydon, Surrey; Mrs. Olga Rickman, Harrogate; Miss S. Rushton, Bebington, Wirral, Cheshire; Mrs. A. A. Rowe, Kelsall, Saxmundham, Suffolk; Mrs. T. I. Rodd, Hastings; Miss V. M. Rowland, Winchester; Mrs. M. E. Read, Thames Ditton, Surrey; Mrs. N. Reed, Nottingham; Mrs. A. J. Rogers, Caxton, Cambridgeshire; Mrs. G. Robinson, Edgware, Middlesex; Miss L. Rathbone, Smarden, Kent; Sir Kelvin Spencer, c.b.e., m.c., Branscombe, Devonshire; Walter R. Spink, Hull; J. K. Sigournay, Brentwood, Essex; Mrs. A. D. Smith, Walton, Peterborough; Miss E. B. Sealy, Bath, Somerset; Mrs. A. Sutton, St. Clement, Jersey; Miss Elizabeth Smith, Greenock, Renfrewshire; Miss Dorothy Stucky, Enfield, Middlesex; N. Simpson, Skipton, Yorkshire; Alec Spoor, London, N.W.1; A. B. Smith, Ilford, Essex; Walter G. Syson, Hucknall, Nottinghamshire; Mrs. Joan Sims, Bracknell, Berkshire; Mrs. M. Shearer, Glasgow, S.1; Miss Marion Slader, Fishponds, Bristol; Mrs. Anne Short, Lincoln; Mrs. M. L. Shaw, Lansdown, Cheltenham, Gloucestershire; Mrs. Louise Shaw, Burnham-on-Sea, Somerset; Mrs. Hilda M. Starkey, Worcester Park, Surrey; Mrs. A. Stanyer, Clevelys, Lancashire; Mrs. E. Sanders, London, S.W.16; Mrs. H. F. Saunders, Benfleet, Essex; Mrs. D. L. M. Stone, Clacton-on-Sea, Essex; Mrs. J. Steen, Kenton, Middlesex; Mrs. D. Smith, Twickenham; Thomas W. Stevenson, Middlesbrough, Mrs. Ivy Stretton, Mitcham, Surrey; T. H. C. Squance, Knaresborough, Yorkshire; Miss Irene Stone, Bristol, 4; Mrs. Mary O. S. Smith, Llanerchymedd, Anglesey; Mrs. Joan Stonnill, Ovingdean, Brighton; Mrs. Muriel Stone, Chessington, Surrey; Mrs. M. Smith, Kingston-upon-Thames; Mrs. C. E. Sexton, Broadstairs, Kent (deceased); Mrs. R. Sligh, Brympton D'Everay, Yeovil, Somerset; Mrs. E. A. Stoakes, Holme Lacy, Herefordshire; V. Sherwen, Rushcombe, Stroud, Gloucestershire; Mrs. M. R. G. Shepherd, Berkhamsted, Hertfordshire; Mrs. S. J. Seury, Walton-on-Hill, Tadworth, Surrey; Mrs. D. Simmons, Peasmarsh, Rye, Sussex; Mrs. L. Sparling, Birstall, Leicester; R. W. Sidwell, Ashton-under-Hill, Evesham, Worcestershire; Mrs. P. Sharpe, Cherry Willingham, Lincolnshire; Mrs. B. M. Saillan, Lindfield, Haywards Heath, Sussex; Mrs. M. Stallard, East Newborough, Victoria, Australia; Mrs. E. Sanderson, Cleethorpes, Lincolnshire; Mrs. H. Sellars, Eastfield, Scarborough, Yorkshire; Mrs. M. A. Scott, Newcastle-upon-Tyne; Mrs. P. Sloane, Belper, Derbyshire; Mrs. J. E. Strickland, Eastrington, Goole, Yorkshire; Mrs. M. Stevenson, Cheadle, Cheshire; Mrs. Simmons, Enfield, Middlesex; Mrs. B. M. Sainsbury, Copnor, Portsmouth; Mrs. O. J. Stoker, Selly Oak, Birmingham 29; F. R. Sattely, Bath, Somerset; Mrs. Jane Stevenson, Grinshill, Shrewsbury; Miss Nesta Clive Smith, London, N.W.1; Mrs. M. Searle, West Coker, Yeovil, Somerset; Mrs. O. Silvester, Birmingham,

14; Dr. G. B. Stenhouse, Morpeth, Northumberland; Dr. J. Sapwell, Aylsham, Norfolk; Dr. Margaret Service, Glasgow, E.1; Dr. A. Spencer, Ravenshead, Nottingham; Peter Scroggs, Twickenham; Mrs. Sybil Scroggs, Twickenham; A. B. Smith, Ilford, Essex; Edward Thompson, Romford, Essex; Miss M. Tombs, West Harrington, Wells, Somerset; Mrs. Martha Tugwell, Hove; Bill Taylor, London, N.W.6; Miss June Taylor, London, N.W.8; F. R. Turrill, Woodstock, Oxfordshire; Edward Turner, M.B.E., Weston-super-Mare; Mrs. H. W. Taylor, Rickmansworth, Hertfordshire; Mrs. Helen Teal, Wath on Dearne, Rotherham; Mrs. P. J. Tapping, London, E.5; Mrs. Mary Truman, London, E.17; Mrs. Mabel Teer, Manchester, 21; Mrs. A. N. Taylor, Billericay, Essex; Miss B. Taggart, Douglas, Isle of Man; Mrs. M. E. Turner, Bideford, Devonshire; Mrs. V. J. Thomas, Kingskerswell, Devonshire; Miss P. Taylor, Cliftonville, Margate, Kent; Mrs. D. Tyler, Pontypridd, Glamorganshire; Mrs. M. B. Thompson, Goring, Sussex; The Rev. John Taylor, Irvine, Ayrshire; Mrs. J. D. Thain, British Forces Post Office, 34; Mrs. L. Town North Baddesley, Southampton; Mrs. M. Thomas, Winterborne Whitechurch, Blandford, Dorset; Mrs. N. M. Turner, St. Leonards-on-Sea, Sussex; Mrs. L. A. Taylor, London, E.17; J. E. C. Thomas, Rhyl; E. W. Turner, Basingstoke; Mrs. C. Taylor, Potton, Sandy, Bedfordshire; Mrs. L. C. Tope, Okehampton, Devonshire; Mrs. V. E. Turner, Hornchurch, Essex; Mrs. Amy Taylor, Munstone, Herefordshire; Mrs. D. P. Tucker, West Malling, Kent; Mrs. E. Tobin, Kingswood, Bristol; Mrs. M. Truscott, Appleton, Warrington, Lancashire; Mrs. W. Tarves, Calderwood, East Kilbride; Miss C. D. Thomas, M.B.E., Birmingham, 20; Miss I. E. Tabor, Harrow, Middlesex; Dr. Frances Taylor, Appleby, Westmorland; Miss Rhoda Thicknesse, London, W.1; B. Taylor, Rustington, Sussex; Mrs. Dora Terry, Reading, Berkshire; Mrs. A. K. Ufel, Twickenham; Mrs. Evelyn Vincent, South Croydon, Surrey; The Rev. Arthur W. Vallance, Chesterfield, Derbyshire; Mrs. M. F. Vickers, Staines; Mrs. Marjery Vidler, Woking, Surrey; Miss Phyllis Vaughan, Denbigh; Mrs. Arthur Watson, M.B.E., Lymington, Hampshire; Tudor Williams, Prestbury, Cheltenham, Gloucestershire; R. H. Wilkinson, Hornsea, Yorkshire: R. C. Wragg, Rochester, Kent; Reece Winstone, Bristol, 9; H. W. Watkins; Worcester; J. Williams, Cardiff; Miss A. Walke, Exeter; Mrs. N. Winter, Holywood, County Down; James Wiswall, Haydock, St. Helens, Lancashire; Miss D. M. White, Woodford Bridge, Essex; Mrs. F. M. Welch, Medstead, Hampshire; J. Wainwright, Skegness, Lincolnshire; E. M. Ware, Pinner, Middlesex; John G. Williams, New York, U.S.A.; Norman Williams, Denton, Manchester; Edgar Wells, Bexley, Kent; Miss Jean Wedderburn, Newcastle-on-Tyne, 6; Mrs. R. Woodbridge, Irchester, Wellingborough, Northamptonshire; Mrs. Lille Wharton, Manchester, 22; Mrs. R. V. Woodward, Rayleigh, Essex; Mrs. Dorothy S. Willis, Garforth, Leeds; Mrs. Arthur Watts, London, N.W.3; Mrs. J. I. Whitfield, Box, Stroud, Gloucestershire; Mrs. D. E. Way, Uckfield, Sussex; Mrs. E. White, Hull; Mrs. B. M. Williams, London, S.W.19; Mrs. N. Webster, Kelty, Fife; Mrs. Kathleen C. Wood, Romford, Essex; Mrs. Edith M. Wootton, Hayes, Bromley, Kent; Mrs. M. Wratten, Oxford; Mrs. Vera G. Woodhouse, Southend-on-Sea; Mrs. D. J. Walker, Yatton, Somerset; George J. C. Wolseley, Finmere, Buckingham; Mrs. P. J. Wood, Shrivenham, Berkshire

Miss P. Witherington, Southborough, Tunbridge Wells, Kent; Mrs. Hilda Weedon, Tonbridge, Kent; Miss M. Wightwick, Tunbridge Wells, Kent; Mrs. M. Wincott, Oldbury, Warley, Worcestershire; Miss W. E. Wake, Kenton, Harrow, Middlesex; Mrs. H. W. Wood, Bridlington, Yorkshire; Mrs. J. Whiteman, Dagenham, Essex; Mrs. L. A. Wilson, Harlow, Essex; Mrs. A. M. Weedon, Eastbourne; Mrs. H. Watton, Birmingham, 22; Mrs. O. N. Weston, Leicester; Mrs. J. Wicks, Tresillian, Truro, Cornwall; Mrs. I. Webber, Bispham, Blackpool; Mrs. U. M. Wilson, Hull; Mrs. Watson, Saxmundham, Suffolk; Mrs. M. Williams, Weston, Bath, Somerset; Mr. & Mrs. Whiteley, Nottingham; Mrs. J. M. Wilson, Cheadle Hulme, Cheshire; Mrs. K. Westey, Watford; Mrs. R. Wintle, Thornton Cleveleys, Fylde Coast, Lancashire; Mrs. R. Willis-Davis, Nairobi, Kenya; Mrs. P. Willmott, Offley, Hitchin, Hertfordshire; Miss M. Ward, Birmingham, 30; Mrs. Doreen Wilyeo, Port Talbot, Glamorganshire; Mr. Eric Wilkerson, London, W.11; Mrs. Margery Wilkerson (deceased); Keith Whetstone, Cambridge; Miss M. A. Waller, London, N.W. 5; The Rev. R. G. Young, Southampton; Mrs. Edna Young, Mannamead, Plymouth; Miss I. Yannarelli, Londonderry; E. Youell, London, E.10; Dr. J. D. Young.

# GENERAL INDEX

*Note:* The titles of books, films, plays, radio programmes and songs are not included in the index when they occur only in the main chapter dealing with those subjects. Where they are mentioned in other chapters they are indexed below. All place names except where they relate to political events, such as the invasion of Abyssinia, are listed in a separate index.

# INDEX OF PLACE NAMES